DAVID FONTANA (no relation to the publisher) has an
international reputation as an educationalist and psychologist. He is a Fellow of the British Psychological Society,
a chartered psychologist, and the father of a daughter
and a son. He has written many books and more than a
hundred articles and papers. He has been practising,
teaching and researching into child psychology for over
twenty-five years, working in addition with the wide
range of psychological and educational problems in
adults that have their origin in childhood experiences.
Throughout these years he has worked extensively with
parents and teachers on the delights, challenges and
frustrations(!) of raising children, and is widely experienced in both primary and secondary education. He is
currently Reader in Educational Psychology at the University of Wales, College of Cardiff.

Through all David Fontana's work runs the conviction
that we are formed as men and women largely through
what happens to us in childhood, and that in consequence the job of parenthood is one of the most important anyone can undertake. He is equally convinced that,
given the right guidance and encouragement, it is a job
at which all of us can succeed.

Amongst the books he has written are *The Education
of the Young Child* (1984), *Classroom Control* (1985), *Teaching and Personality* (1986), *Psychology for Teachers* (1988),
and *Managing Stress* (1989).

Your Growing Child

From Birth to Adolescence

DR DAVID FONTANA

FONTANA/Collins

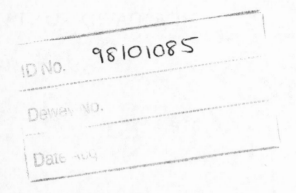
First published in 1990 by Fontana Paperbacks
8 Grafton Street, London W1X 3LA

Copyright © David Fontana 1990

Printed and bound in Great Britain by
William Collins Sons & Co. Ltd., Glasgow

with love to my children,
Helen and Julian,
the best of teachers.

Acknowledgements

I'd like to thank the many people who have helped, both directly and indirectly, with this book. My wife Elizabeth, for the love and care she devoted to the two children (young people now) to whom the book is dedicated. My mother, for the love and care she devoted to me in my own childhood. My brother Kenneth, for stimulating every conceivable aspect of my thinking for as long as I can remember. The tutors who guided my studies in my early years and helped me to love psychology and recognize its usefulness; in particular Charles Allen and the late Peggy Bradley of the Cambridge Institute of Education. The children and parents, the students and schoolteachers with whom I've worked over the years and from whom I've learnt so much. And last but not least, the staff at Collins/ Fontana, who have nursed the book along. Especially Helen Fraser and Robin Wood, for their enthusiasm and encouragement and for their wise guidance in helping identify the kinds of questions I should seek to answer. And Caroline Hartnell, for her superhuman editorial skills, and for the deft way in which she identified and persuaded me to abandon my prejudices. And Michael Fishwick and Juliet Van Oss, for their professionalism and kindness in seeing the project through to completion, and for their belief that books such as this should aim above all else to teach us how to be kinder to children.

Contents

Introduction

BEING A PARENT IS FUN. I know it doesn't feel that way when you're dragged from sleep in the middle of the night by a plaintive but determined little voice demanding you pay attention to *me*. But if it wasn't fun, people wouldn't be so keen to take on the job. Most couples want a child, and when they've got the first one they usually don't stop there. Speak to most parents, and in spite of the occasional grumble they admit they wouldn't have missed the experience for worlds. Being a parent opens up a whole new set of interests – interests that stem not just from having a brand new human being to care for and love, but from sharing his or her delight in exploring the world, and in discovering each day new wonders and excitements.

This is a book about having fun

So this is a book about having fun. It's a book written to help you enjoy your child, and to help her enjoy you as a parent. The more you give your child, the more she's able to give you in return. And 'giving' doesn't just mean giving her material things, important as, these are. It means giving time and encouragement and understanding, those priceless gifts that enrich a child's life and help her grow up happy and confident and able to tackle the many learning tasks that lie ahead. It means giving all you can to the parent – child relationship so that it grows into a bond of trust and affection strong enough to survive the storms and squalls that appear periodically even on the calmest of horizons.

For having fun doesn't mean enjoying a life full of good times. Being a parent isn't just a matter of sitting back and watching dutiful children doing as they're told and inviting the praise of all and sundry. Having fun means meeting the challenge of the difficult times as well as delighting in the good. It means sussing out what caused the difficult times and how they can be better handled in the future. It means learning from your child as well as helping her learn from you. Being a parent is watching another little human being, with a mind and will of her own, discovering what life is about and how she can live it creatively and happily. As a parent, you have to judge how to say 'no' to this human being without leaving her frustrated and angry, and how to say 'yes' without leaving her spoilt and over-indulged. You have to teach your child to strike a successful balance between her own wishes and the wishes of the rest of the world, so that she grows up knowing her own mind but respecting the minds of her fellows, independent and assured on the one hand, responsible and considerate on the other.

But there's more to parenthood even than this. Watching your child grow is also a way of reliving your own childhood. We each of us carry our childhood with us throughout life. We are each of us formed as adults very much by the experience we had then. By studying and understanding the world of the child we get to know more about our own lives. We get to see why we are the people we are, and we get to fathom out the origins of many of our own strengths and weaknesses. This helps us to cope with life, to develop our good points and to come to terms with the not so good. And it helps us to look at our children once more and to appreciate the effect that our actions as parents may be having upon their long-term development.

This is a book about parents too

Which brings me to another important point about parenthood. To make a success of the job you must accept that being a parent is going to change your life. During pregnancy, you'll already have found more and more of your talk and your thoughts turning towards the baby. Above all you'll have realized (if you're a two-parent family) that soon there'll be three of you. So far you've put all your love into the relationship with your partner, but soon there'll have to be some available for the newcomer. One phase of your life will soon be over and a new one beginning. Things will be different, and to make them work you'll have to adapt and change along with them. The responsibilities of parenthood are real enough, and unless you accept and welcome them you'll build upon resentments and dissatisfactions that will get in the way of your own enjoyment of the child.

If you're a single parent, your baby is going to bring about equally profound changes. There won't be readjustment with a partner to deal with, but there will be anxieties at having to bear the full weight of responsibility for the new life. The daily schedule, with only you to cope, will also be that much heavier, and there may also be a feeling of loneliness and isolation, without a partner to talk things over with and to listen to your excitements and your grumbles.

And whether you're a single or a partner parent there will be discoveries to be made about yourself. You may be awed by the sheer force of your love for your child, or dismayed by your possessiveness, or disappointed at your sudden spurts of anger or lack of patience, or delighted by the way you develop new interests along with your child. Or there may be envy of your partner for handling your child better than you do, or jealousy at their love for each other, or frustration because your partner seems to get it all wrong or won't agree with you on what to do for the best. Less easy to discuss, there may be resentments at your child for not living up to expectations, and maybe guilt for what you see as failings in the strength of your own love for her.

So this is a book about parents as well as about children. The two topics can't really be separated. In the relationship between you and your child, you're both of you adapting and changing and growing. You're both of you learning to see the other's point of view, learning how to give as well as take, how to compromise when necessary, how to understand what makes you both the way you are.

This book is about psychology

Since psychology is primarily about understanding what makes people the way they are, it follows that all parents have a little of the psychologist in them. This is a book to help you develop your knowledge of psychology further. It will look at all aspects of the psychological life of your child in the home and outside, drawing both upon the findings of psychological research and upon my own experiences as a psychologist working with children and adults. I can't promise it will cover every question you have about your child. All children and all parents are individuals. But it will say enough to enable you to reach your own decisions even on those matters not touched on specifically. Once you understand the way your child's mind and emotions work, you'll be in a position to decide for yourself why he or she acts as they do in a given instance, and what your own response to these actions should be.

Although this isn't a medical book, it does deal with physical development and the maintenance of good health. Mind and body are closely linked. If your child is to grow strong psychologically then his physical needs must be looked after as well. A child who isn't well psychologically often isn't well physically and vice versa.

This is a book about education

Just as every parent is a psychologist, so every parent is an educator. You are your child's first teacher, and throughout childhood you remain one of the best he has. He learns language from you, he learns about the world and what things are for and how they work. More subtly he also learns about right and wrong, how people should behave towards each other, what makes them happy and sad. He learns interests, opinions, attitudes. Psychologists call this 'informal' education, because much of the time it doesn't happen deliberately at all. It's part and parcel of family life, of being together under the same roof and talking and relating to each other. But the more you know about how your child learns, the more effective this informal eduacation will be.

As a parent, you'll also want to help with your child's **Formal and** 'formal' education. You'll want to help teach him to read, to **informal** write, to use numbers, to paint and draw and do craft work. **education** When he starts school, you'll want to know what's happening, and one day to help him with homework and projects. You'll

15

want to know how to help him with specific learning problems, and whether you can help him develop his intelligence
and his creative potential. When he's in his teens, you'll want
to know how to advise him on what school subjects to take
and how to plan and prepare for his future.

Education is about helping people learn how to cope with
life and with their own reactions to it, how to develop
necessary skills and interests, how to make the most of their
potential. In this book we'll look at both informal and formal
education, and discuss the ways in which you can best help
your child.

Making a route map for your child

Of course, however much you tell yourself that being a parent
is fun, there's no shortage of people wanting to warn you just
how difficult and challenging it can all be. We live in uncertain
times, with a breakdown in traditional standards and values,
and an upsurge of violence and lawlessness that leaves no
country and no stratum of society untouched. Some authorities tell us that the only way to raise children in such a troubled
environment is to go back to the firm discipline we imagine
(often quite wrongly) prevailed in the homes of fifty to a
hundred years ago. Others go to the opposite extreme and tell
us it's just no good trying to influence children these days and
we might as well give up on them. Mixed in somewhere
between the two is the currently fashionable argument that
the psychological approach to child-rearing has been tried and
failed. It's no good reasoning with children. It's no good trying
to understand them. Let's just accept they're little monsters
put there to make their parents' lives a disaster. Think of your
own convenience for a change, and if your children don't turn
out well don't start blaming yourself!

Trying to put the clock back   All three approaches are misguided and unfair both to the
children and to the great majority of parents. To take the first
approach, that we need to return to the discipline of our
grandparents. You can't put the clock back. The world is a vastly
different place from fifty or even twenty years ago. Modern
technology in the form of television, videos, computers, tape
recorders, means that a child today has access to vastly more

information and influences than we had as children. She knows more, judges more, and has more evidence on just how much of a mess the adult world is generally making of things. At an early age she's already looking outside the home, and her whole concept of who she is, of what life is for, and the function of the family cannot be other than very different from that of the child of even twenty or thirty years ago.

The second approach, that children are now beyond parental influence, is just as unrealistic. Children are still profoundly affected by their home life. And the challenges they meet outside means they need more guidance than ever. But it has to be guidance that accepts that children's horizons are immeasurably greater than they once were, and that the pace of change is ever increasing. Today's child needs the kind of guidance that will enable her to cope with things as they are now and not with things as they once were. Guidance of this kind demands more in the way of understanding, discussion, consensus. It comes best from parents who realize that their children live in a very different world from the one they themselves knew as children, and who are prepared to study their children and learn how this world affects them and how they see it.

'It's no good trying to influence children these days'

The third approach, that psychology doesn't work and you may as well do as you please with your children knowing that you're not going to influence the issue much either way, is by far the worst of the three. I hear it most from fashionable middle-class people who usually reveal on questioning that the haven't really 'tried' psychology at all. They've swung from extremes of over-permissiveness to extremes of strictness, so that no one really knows where they stand. Child-rearing for them has had far more to do with the latest fads and fancies than with any real attempt to understand children and give them the time and the love and the psychological help they need. Don't be deceived by this third 'approach'. It reflects no credit on those who preach it.

'Just suit your own convenience'

One good way of looking at child-rearing is to see your child as an explorer setting out to explore a strange country. If you wanted to help her by the first of the three approaches mentioned above you'd give her strict instructions based on how *you* would make the journey, showing her only the paths you know and insisting she keep rigidly to them. The problem will arise when she finds your map incomplete or inadequate or out of date. Since it does nothing to help her understand the countryside or find the best way over it, she's faced either with sticking to your map and missing the best paths and the best views, or throwing it away in disgust and striking out on her own with goodness alone knows what consequences. If you wanted to help her by the second approach, you'd give her no map at all and leave her to make silly mistakes, listen to the wrong kind of advice, and be open to exploitation by any number of unscrupulous fellow-travellers. If you used the third approach, you'd draw the map simply to suit yourself and take refuge in the notion that if she's going to go wrong she'll do it anyway regardless of the quality of your map-making.

Help your child understand the strange country she's exploring

Looked at in this way, each of these approaches is seen to be pretty unsuitable. So what should you do? The answer is to help her understand as much as possible about the countryside she's exploring, so that she knows how to 'read' it and follow the best path. By understanding the country, she can be helped to see where the pitfalls are, what routes to take and what routes to avoid, where to find the provisions and supplies she needs, how to familiarize herself with unfamiliar territory before committing herself to it, how to look for the best short-cuts, how to choose her fellow-travellers, how to help others who've got themselves lost.

But there's a second part to the answer. Not only can you help her understand the country she has to travel over, you can also help her understand her strengths and weaknesses as a traveller. Upon this self-knowledge depends her success in knowing how to develop her full potential and how to remedy or come to terms with her weaknesses – in short how to make best use of herself as a person.

This book is for parents who want to adopt this answer. Who want to equip their child for her journey through life. Who want to give their child guidance and direction, but at the same time want her to learn how to make proper decisions for herself. For parents who neither want their child to be a carbon copy of themselves nor to be lacking in suitable direction and purpose. For parents who want to have a loving and mutually rewarding relationship with their child and who want to take the time to get to know and understand her as an individual. Such a relationship isn't hard to come by. Our children repay us tenfold for everything we give them. Not through spoken words of thanks and gratitude (though these are nice when they come) but by growing into happy and useful and creative adults.

Why from birth to adolescence?

Many books on childhood concentrate on the early years or on adolescence only. This is a good approach, but it does take each group rather out of context. If we want to understand small children fully and why we should behave towards them in certain ways, then we need to know something about the adolescents they will one day become. Much of what we do with our small children lays down learning patterns that will only emerge to the full when they're much older. Similarly, if we want to understand the adolescent, we can only do so if we study the psychology of the small child and see the origins of later behaviour in what happened early on. To read only about early childhood is like reading a novel and finding it breaks off after the first few chapters, while to read only about adolescence is like starting a novel half-way through.

So although you can use this book for reference purposes, picking it up and reading different sections as you find you need them, the best way is initially to read it right through. In this way you'll get a picture of the whole child, and will come to understand the whys and wherefores of good parenting much more fully. You'll see, for example, why the child who isn't allowed to help in the home when he's small and messy may grow into the teenager who doesn't want to help however much you ask him. You'll see how the uncreative teenager or the teenager who has few interests in life may be traced back to the young child who was never allowed to show initiative, never encouraged to enquire and explore. You'll see how the rebellious teenager's fight for independence may stem from his parents refusal to give him sensible scope for this independence as he grows and matures through the years. Whether your child is a baby or a teenager when you first buy this book, do give yourself a chance to get the whole picture therefore. And take heart. Even though your teenager is in the

Get a picture of the whole child

midst of being unhelpful or uncreative or rebellious, once you see where these traits come from you can not only be that bit more patient and understanding towards him, you can also identify what to do in order to put things right.

A second reason for reading this book right through is that many of the topics with which I deal apply throughout the whole of childhood, but are dealt with only once. Thus although, for example, intelligence and creativity are of interest to parents of children of all ages, they are dealt with at length within the context of the primary school child, since it is at this age that such issues loom largest in parents' minds. On the other hand, topics which have a development theme, such as the child's sense of self-esteem and self-confidence, are touched on in several places. In either case, you need to read the book right through to grasp the full picture.

Childhood is a constant process of change and development

By going from birth to adolescence, the book emphasizes that childhood is a constant process of change and development. Having a child isn't just having a small baby. It's having a small baby who rapidly grows into a toddler and then into a schoolchild and then into a sprawling adolescent who fills the house with friends and noisy music. Childhood is a fleeting business. Talk to the parents of children who've grown up and are about to leave home and they nearly always say they can't believe the time has gone. Only five minutes ago it seems the children were starting their first day at school, and now just look at them. This book follows the whole process through. Read it and it will help you to see that your children really are just on loan to you. Make the most of them. Give them your time and your attention. Watch them grow. Study them and get to know them as people, as individuals in their own right. If times are bad, remind yourself it's only a phase and that your child will soon grow through it. If times are good, treasure them and cherish them. Like all things magical, childhood is there one minute and gone the next. Turn your head away for too long and you miss it. But watch and enjoy it and again, like all things magical, it will cast its spell of enchantment over you. And leave you saying, like the rest of us, that you wouldn't have missed parenthood for the world.

Who is this book for?

This book is for *all* those concerned with bringing up children. Though the nuclear family of husband, wife and children all living together under one roof may still be the norm, there are now many variants of this. Unmarried parents who choose to live together without a formal wedding. Single mothers who have no wish for permanent partners, or who prefer the friendship of other women. Separated parents who remain good friends and take an equal interest in their children. Separated parents who never communicate with each other. Grandparents, foster-parents, uncles and aunts who have sole responsibility for children. All these people are addressed directly or indirectly in this book, since what matters is the adult–child relationship rather than the formal context in which this relationship takes place.

And since what matters is the fact of childhood rather than the sex of the child (there are approximately as many girls around as boys, and they are every bit as important), the terms 'she' and 'he' are used interchangeably for the child throughout the book, except where I am talking specifically about one sex or the other. There is no acceptable neutral pronoun for the sexes in the English language ('it' is far too impersonal), so the use of both 'she' and 'he' is essential if the right balance is to be kept.

The use of 'he' and 'she'

The appendices

At the end of the book, detailed tables and information are given on all major aspects of children's growth, development and dietary needs. The appendices also cover teething, safety in the home and common childhood ailments and emergencies. References are given to the appendices at appropriate places in the book, but they can, of course, be studied at any point.

[1]

Preparing for Your Baby

SOME COUPLES COPE VERY EASILY with the prospect of parenthood. Both partners see the baby as the natural outcome of their love for each other. Having a baby extends and enriches the family, and they look forward to the event with complete confidence in themselves and in each other. Other couples, while feeling this confidence most of the time, yet have feelings of unease. There is nothing wrong with this. It is a natural outcome of facing the major change that is soon to take place. But where things can come a little unstuck is if either partner feels unable to discuss his or her unease with the other.

Talking your problems through

I'm not saying that whenever you have a problem of any kind you should rush at once to talk it over with someone else. People differ in their need to discuss their problems. Some people can never feel comfortable until they have got it all off their chest, while others prefer to puzzle the thing through for themselves. But when anxieties have to do with a major event like a new baby, then it makes sense to talk them through with your partner. Talking them through, calmly and sensibly, is a way of sharing every aspect of your emotions about the baby with each other. You'll be ready enough to share the feelings of excitement and longing, so share any misgivings too. Getting into the habit of discussing misgivings now will stand you in good stead in the years to come, when you're bound to have your moments of anxiety about other aspects of your child's life. So be open with each other. However silly your fears may seem to yourself. They may be to do with doubts as to how you'll shape up as a mother or father. They may be to do with a man's fears that he is going to be jealous now that he doesn't get all his partner's attention. They may be to do with a woman's fears that pregnancy has ruined her figure or that she'll be trapped in the house too often while her partner goes off with his friends, or that her partner will suddenly find her less attractive now she has a baby to cope with. Or maybe the man will feel anxious over his loss of freedom, particularly if most of his friends aren't yet fathers. If these examples look sexist, most of them work just as well the other way around. But behind them all lie very real worries about the effect the new baby will have on the parents' relationship with each other.

By talking things over, couples can reassure each other and avoid many of the possible pitfalls. At the same time they can face up to the fact that changes *are* going to happen. When we first marry or start living with someone, we often want things to remain the same for ever. But everything that's alive inevitably changes. Change only frightens us if we forget this basic fact. And if we forget that change also brings with it new experiences and new opportunities.

I know of course that some people don't make the best of listeners. Much as you may want to pour out your thoughts, your partner may be much less enthusiastic. This may be because he or she is the kind of person who never worries about anything, and who therefore finds it hard to understand why anyone else does. Or it may be because he or she is rather embarrassed about such issues, and prefers to go on as if they don't exist. I'm not proposing you try to change each other's nature. But I am proposing you each see matters of this kind as part of the give and take involved in your relationship. If your partner doesn't seem too ready to listen, then be careful not to overdo things, and don't choose moments when he or she is tired, or busy doing something else.

People who aren't good listeners

Similarly, if you are a person who rarely worries and finds it hard to listen to other people's problems, then remind yourself that everyone is different, and the gift of being a good listener is one of the most precious things that one person can give another. Try to see the situation from your partner's point of view, not only in terms of the changed circumstances with which he or she will have to cope once the baby has arrived,

25

but also in terms of the fact that for most people anxiety is a very real emotion, and one which they can best deal with in the presence of sympathy and support from those they love.

Dealing with negative attitudes

Things may be more difficult if the pregnancy happens to be unplanned and inconvenient, or if one parent wants it and the other does not. The one certain fact about an unwanted pregnancy, however, is that the baby had no say in the matter. If you feel at all resentful about the thought of the child who is on the way, you must bring yourself to see that the baby is the last person to blame. In fact blaming anyone, yourself included, will achieve nothing but unhappiness all round – in both the short and the long term. Babies soon sense whether they are loved and wanted. To respond to a new baby with feelings of resentment will ensure he or she quickly becomes confused and discontented, growing into an unhappy child who will in turn make life more difficult for you.

Feeling resentful will make things worse As with so many aspects of child-rearing, a negative attitude on your part will only lead to greater problems in the future. Relate well to your child from the start, and your child will relate well to you. Make mistakes in your relationship, and these mistakes will lead to worries that have to be put right later on. So if you do feel a little resentful about the thought of a child coming along, remind yourself that this attitude is only going to make things harder for everyone, perhaps most of all yourself. You do have the power to change your own attitudes, either by sitting down and thinking them through or better still by talking about them to your partner. To be stuck with the belief that we have no control over our own attitudes and feelings is bad psychology. Virtually the whole of the educational process, whether in the school or in the home, is based on the knowledge that we can change the way people think and feel about the world and about themselves. As a parent, you'll soon be expecting your child to change her behaviour when she comes up with something you consider undesirable. If she can change, so can you. Make a start now by working on your resentment or on any other negative feelings you may have about the coming birth.

The way to do this is firstly by facing up to the fact that **Face your** these feelings exist. Often we try to hide them from ourselves, **feelings** particularly if they make us feel guilty or inadequate. The result is that they go on lurking just below the surface, ready to break out when we are feeling particularly tired or upset or angry about something else. And by hiding these feelings from ourselves, we also make them appear a lot more frightening than they really are. Like the strange creatures we used to feel sure as children were lurking in the bedroom shadows. But once these feelings are faced, we often see they have no more substance than did these creatures of our childhood. They are merely born of an irritation that things haven't worked out more conveniently for us, or apprehension about the new demands soon to be made of us, or a feeling that we haven't been able to control things in the way that we might like.

None of these things amounts to very much, and as long as you don't allow yourself to make them too important they will evaporate once the baby arrives and you fall under her spell. The second step then, having faced these feelings, is to see them as a perfectly natural reaction, given the circumstances of your life, but as lacking in permanent substance. They're reactions to the abstract *idea* of a baby, rather than to the baby itself. Some people go in the opposite direction, as I shall discuss in a moment, and react with total enthusiasm to the prospect of a baby, forgetting that there will be broken nights and early mornings, and some sticky times mixed in with all the good. The truth is that when the baby comes, many of our preconceptions are swept away. Parents often confess that all their misgivings about the newcomer vanished the moment they first set eyes on the small new person, and realized it was now part of their lives.

Whatever your negative feelings about the baby now, **Don't become** they're not likely to last for long after it arrives. Particularly if **identified with** you don't parade them now and become identified with them. **your negative** Because although it's a good thing to talk your feelings over **feelings** frankly and sensibly with your partner or with close friends and relatives, if you go around telling all and sundry that you're not looking forward to being a parent it becomes something of a climbdown to admit after the birth that you were wrong. You risk having to hear people say 'I told you so', and none of us likes that very much. So there may be a temptation to stick to your guns, and to pretend even to yourself that you're still not happy with parenthood, even though it's no longer true. Some men brag to their friends that the idea of being a father leaves them cold, and because they allow this bragging to become identified with their masculine self-image find difficulty in dropping it even when they see how foolish it is. This is particularly so if they've boasted to their friends that no baby is going to keep *them* at home of an evening. They now have to risk hearing 'But I thought you said no baby was . . .' every time they want to spend time with wife and child.

The answer is not to become tied in to this kind of behaviour during the months of pregnancy. Go about the necessary domestic preparations for the coming of your baby, and recognize that when the day actually dawns you are probably going to enjoy it just as much as everyone else.

If you're a single parent

Single parents are in a different position in that they don't have the feelings of a partner to consider, and they don't have worries over the possible effect of the new baby upon their relationship with this partner. On the other hand, they don't have the support that a partner can bring, or the feeling of looking forward to a shared experience. In addition, they may have special worries over coping with a baby, in both practical and emotional terms (points to which I return in more detail in Chapter 3), and over the effect the baby may have upon present or future close relationships.

The way a single parent handles these matters will depend in part upon the reasons why they're embarking on single parenthood. If it's from choice, they will probably have thought things through carefully before conception took place. If it's from unexpected circumstances, like the sudden loss of a partner, they may have planned for the pregnancy but certainly not for the emotional traumas and practical difficulties that this loss will bring. And if it's from a casual affair, they probably won't have thought much about anything, and will now be faced with rapidly reorientating their whole future. But no matter what the reasons, the first advice to almost all single parents is that, unless you've already had a baby and know what's involved, you're going to need more support than you think. Even if your child is co-operative as a little saint, and you're able to stay with her 24 hours a day, there are going to be times when you're called away to minister to other relatives, times when you're unwell yourself and can't cope, and times when you need just a little social life of your own.

The second piece of advice is don't be reluctant to ask for this support. Some single parents feel, out of pride, they can't turn to their own parents for help. Not so. You've a right to expect help from your parents just as one day your child will have a right to expect help from you. It isn't a case of swallowing your pride unless *you* choose to see it that way. It's a matter of sound good sense. And unless your relationship with your parents is so unsatisfactory it's going to sour the atmosphere, your child will benefit from their help just as much as you will. **Ask for the support you need**

But parents or not, try and organize a general support group. The larger it is, the less call you have to make upon any individual member of it. Single-parent organizations exist which will help, but generally most people are ready to lend a hand *provided* they know in advance what will be expected of them, and *provided* they feel these expectations aren't too much. If there are things you can do in return, offer them, so that you'll be able to benefit others and keep your sense of independence into the bargain. If you don't organize your support in this way, isolation is going to be one of your biggest worries, prompting you either to blame your baby for the major changes she's brought about in your life, or to rely on her too much emotionally, which will make it hard for her once she's a little older and starts wanting her independence.

These points are returned to later, and don't need further elaboration now. But the third piece of advice is that all the other things that apply to prospective parents, such as the need for good domestic organization, apply particularly to you. People are much more ready to support those they see help themselves. A helpless attitude on your part when your baby arrives will soon remind people of all the other pressing **Be well organized yourself** things that just happen to be clamouring for their attention each time you feel the need to turn to them.

Finally, if you're a single parent because tragically you've lost your partner, don't look upon your baby as emotionally taking his or her place. This is hard, but your baby has to be loved for herself, not as a replacement, however precious, for someone else. (The same applies, incidentally, to all parents if this new baby follows upon the sad loss of an older child; the new baby has to be seen as a unique human being, with a right to expect its own unique relationship with you.) Children who are seen as replacing partners, either now or in the future, have emotional demands made upon them which are unfair and confusing to both of you. To the child because she doesn't know how to meet these demands, and to you because you forfeit the chance of satisfying these emotional demands where they belong, in a relationship with another adult or other adults.

If you're going to adopt

If you're going to adopt your child, you won't have the actual birth to plan for, but understandably you may have other things on your mind. As your child won't inherit his genes from you, you may wonder how he'll turn out, and whether the bonds of love between you will be as strong as if he did. Let's take the second of these two issues first. Emotional bonds between parents and children are not biological (except in the sense that nature has given us the capacity to love one another). They are the result of the relationships which parents and children create with each other. In the case of adoptive parents, who have probably hoped for a child for very much longer than usual, this relationship is likely to be an especially close and precious one. And in the case of the child, if you adopt him from babyhood he'll accept you right from the start without question, and will feel just as strongly towards you as any child does towards his parents. Later, when he learns of his adoption, this will in no sense alter his love for you. He'll accept adoption as perfectly natural (as indeed it is), and one of the most wonderful things that can happen in relationships between people.

Some parents wonder, if they move house soon after adoption and go and live amongst strangers, whether they should tell everyone their child is adopted. This is a purely personal thing, and there are no clinching arguments either way. My own view is that there is no need to tell everyone unless you want to, not because you have anything to hide but because occasionally adopted children can be teased by unthinking classmates, who like to pick on anyone who is remotely different in no matter how unimportant a way from everyone else. If you share my view, explain to your child when he first understands the facts of adoption that this is no business of anyone else's, so we don't bother telling them. If he asks why, explain that there are lots of things that happen within the family that are personal things, just as there are in every family. As he grows a little older and gets to see how other children tease each other over the least thing, he'll come naturally to take the same view for himself.

Do you need to tell everyone?

The best opportunity to tell your child he's adopted usually comes during the pre-school years. An adopted child has a right to know the fact of his adoption, and if this is explained to him early on he'll grow up with the knowledge and be untroubled by it. In fact, by the time he's around seven or eight years old he'll rarely even refer to it. A happy, loving home is of far more importance to a child than whether his parents are adopted or natural.

Telling him he's adopted

Go over the facts of conception and birth with your child, and then explain to him that some mothers can't keep their children, so they're given to other mothers and fathers who have a special love for children and want a child of their own more than anything in the world. Stress that these mothers and fathers are just as much real mothers and fathers as any other, and the children are just as much their children and are loved every bit as much as in any other family. Stress what a lovely idea adoption is, and how precious adopted children are and how much happiness they bring, and that it's not unlike the way grown-ups 'adopt' each other when they get married.

Because children of this age have short memories, you'll need to refer to his adoption, casually and lovingly, from time to time, until you're sure it's established fully in his mind.

31

After that, the subject need only come up again if *he* wants to raise it.

Sometimes, when a child is further up the school and taking biology lessons, he may feel rather different from his class-mates when he realizes he didn't come out of his adoptive mother's womb. When he mentions this to you, reassure him that everyone is different in *some* way from everyone else. The only important difference is the one experienced by children unfortunate enough to come from homes where their parents don't love and cherish them as they should. All that really matters is the relationship parents and children have with each other, not the biological details of whose womb you happened to be conceived in.

Adolescent identity crises

Another anxiety that some parents have is whether an adopted child will go through a particular identity crisis in adolescence, when he begins to wonder who he is and perhaps to ask questions about his biological parents. All children do have to find their emerging adult identity in adolescence (more about this in Chapter 8), but there is no evidence that adopted children find this any harder than do their peers. In fact, since adoptive parents are carefully chosen as likely to give their children the right family background, adopted children are often more secure and mature at adolescence than their contemporaries, and likely to take things much more in their stride. If they do have questions about their biological parents these should always be answered honestly, but it goes without saying that you should never, under any circumstances, go in for criticism of these parents in any way.

An older child or a child from a different ethnic background

If you're adopting an older child, or a child from a different ethnic background, the fact of his adoption is going to be more evident to himself and others than is the case with the child I've been talking about so far. Again, however, it's your total and unqualified acceptance of the child as *yours* that counts. Never use his adoption as an excuse if he has learning problems at school or gets into trouble of any kind ('Well you see, he's an adopted child'). Give him the security of knowing that he's yours and you take full responsibility for him. In an older child, he may take a while before he can fully accept you as his parents, but don't hold that against him. He's had far less say in the whole business than you have. Don't get it into your head that he's 'rejecting' you. Don't force yourself on

32

him, or expect a special kind of gratitude. Be patient and assure him of your understanding and support right from the start, and that you're on his side in life whatever happens. And in the context of this special relationship, allow his feelings for you to grow in their own good time.

If you're adopting a child with a handicap, you and the social workers responsible for him will have thought things through carefully, and will be convinced that you have the domestic facilities and the emotional resources needed to help you succeed. Also that your relatives and friends are behind you in your undertaking, as their support will be vital in the years ahead. It's sometimes said that a child with a handicap should not be adopted as the first child in a family, but should go to a home that already has experience of child-rearing under more normal circumstances. There is much truth in this, provided the older child or children have been fully consulted over the adoption, understand in detail what it will entail, and have agreed that it should happen. But individual circumstances do vary, and many parents are ready to go straight for a child with a handicap, and to give him the very home that he needs. The only general advice that can be usefully offered is that you must be quite sure you know what is involved in taking your child, and are as sure as you can be that you're going to be able to cope.

Adopting a handicapped child

Lastly, let's turn briefly to the first of the issues raised at the start of this section, namely how your adopted child will turn out. Let me assure you that adopted children tend to do better in most areas of achievement than peers of equal ability. This is because they have homes where parents are especially interested and involved in them. This environment is of crucial importance in determining your child's progress at school and the development of interests, goals and ambitions. The more you enrich your child's environment in the ways discussed throughout this book, the more opportunity he'll have to make full use of his potential.

How will your child turn out?

The same is true of your child's general behaviour. Very occasionally, adoptive parents will worry, for example, that their child may, in the case of a girl, be 'promiscuous', as perhaps her biological mother was assumed to be. These worries are unfounded. Our behaviour in life is very much shaped by our environment and the experiences it contains.

Your child's behaviour will be a reflection of this environment, not some programming in the genes labelled 'promiscuity' or 'anti-social behaviour' or whatever. If your child should ever express fears of this kind himself, reassure him that it's what he and those who love him make of his life that counts. The more confident and self-assured he is, the more readily he'll see the truth of this. And of course never accuse him (unfairly and quite wrongly) of 'taking after' his biological parents, or say you wish you hadn't adopted him or threaten to send him away. Parents can say some terrible things to children in the heat of the moment, things they don't mean and which they bitterly regret afterwards. But surely these are among the very worst. *Should* your child fall short of the expectations you have of him (which happens just as readily with non-adopted children), don't let yourself be disappointed and don't pass any disappointment on to your child. Love and accept him the way he is, not the way you hoped he might be.

Will I be able to cope?

It is a strange fact that although parenthood is probably the most important job in our lives, we receive little or no proper training for it. We don't allow people to become teachers until they've been trained. Nurses and doctors who deal with children all receive guidance on how to go about it. So do social workers and probation officers and everyone else who comes into professional contact with the young. Yet parents, who have the most vital task of all, are just left to pick up the necessary skills somehow, as if by accident. Many have little to go on except memories of how their own parents brought them up. Or they may rely on the advice of neighbours, or that of busy people like their family doctor or the health visitor. Unfortunately, competent as such professional people are, they have little time to give more than the most simple and straightforward advice.

A bit of worry is natural So it's not surprising that some parents-to-be have worries about their ability to bring up their child successfully, worries that are added to by watching the struggles of some other parents, and by hearing stories of how unmanageable children often are these days. But these worries are a lot healthier than

34

bursting with confidence and imagining that you're going to get everything right and be just perfect. Reading books about child-rearing can also be a little daunting, because it seems as if there is so much to remember, and so much that can go wrong if you aren't extra careful. But given a basic understanding of your child, a great deal depends simply upon common sense and upon your ability to keep calm and keep your sense of humour. Certainly there will be squalls ahead sometimes, but most parenting skills can be learnt easily and quickly. Given love and goodwill and a genuine interest in your child as a person, with needs and rights of her own, you're not going to go very far wrong.

How will the older child react?

If this isn't your first child, you will probably also have misgivings as to how older brothers and sisters are going to react. Will they take to the new baby? Will they be jealous? Will you have enough time and energy left over after caring for the baby to give them the love and attention they need? All this is dealt with later in the book, together with how best to prepare older children for the new arrival. But some parents do confess to sudden feelings of disloyalty towards an existing child or children at the thought of a new baby. The newcomer will not only change the lives of her parents, she will also change the lives of other members of the family. Watching an older child playing on the floor, blissfully unaware of the real impact of the changes that are soon to occur, it's natural to feel the odd qualm for her. So far the older child has had full attention from both parents, but soon that attention will have to be shared, which is bound to lead to a few problems at first.

But remind yourself that few children, given the choice later in life, would prefer to be an only child. Don't misunderstand me. There's nothing wrong with being an only child. It's simply that most children benefit from having a brother or sister around, to share things with and to argue with. So the new baby is a gift for your other child or children as well as a gift for yourselves; although they will miss out a little in some ways when the gift actually arrives, they will gain far more than they will lose, particularly if you are able to share out your time and attention properly and show them that they still have their own very special place in your heart.

Will the baby be all right?

Perhaps the biggest natural misgiving of all, however, is that your baby may be less than perfect physically or mentally. Luckily modern medicine can do much to reassure you that your pregnancy is a perfectly normal one, and that you will be one of the overwhelming majority who can look forward with confidence to a totally healthy baby. But should there be some doubt about the health of your baby, listen carefully to the advice of your doctors. Often something that sounds alarming when you first hear of it can be handled satisfactorily with the help of modern medical techniques and with parents who accept that come what may this is going to be *their* child, and they are going to give it the love and care it needs and to which it has a right. This is not to minimize the problems involved – and I shall talk about these problems and some of the things that can be done to cope with them in Chapter 4 – but it is to stress how important to success is your own frame of mind. Handicap in a child is not your fault nor is it the child's. No one need feel guilty. The way forward is to set about making both your life and the child's as happy and normal as possible.

Pregnancy should be a happy time

But let's not over-emphasize these misgivings. For most parents pregnancy is a happy period spent looking forward to the miracle of a new life. Don't wish this time away too fervently. Look upon it as a delightful curtain-raiser to the main event itself. Once any early problems of morning sickness have come and gone, most pregnancies are trouble-free. In fact many mothers say that apart from bouts of tiredness they have never felt better either physically or psychologically in their lives. Make the most of it. Enjoy the fuss that other people make of you, and the interest they show. Particularly for the mother-to-be, this is often a time of maximum attention. Relatives and friends are usually extra solicitous and helpful. Let them enjoy the pregnancy too, and feel a part of all that's going on. And when they tell you to take it easy, do as they say, no matter how active you usually are. A bit of spoiling doesn't do anybody any harm, and there'll be plenty of running around to do before many weeks have passed!

A realistic view of what to expect

Naturally you don't want to spend too much of your time thinking about the running around that is to come, but it's important to have a clear picture of what you're taking on. You're right to look forward to your child and the fun you're going to have together, but this mustn't stop you from being realistic. A baby is hard work at times. He isn't just a happy little creature who takes his feeds like clockwork and sleeps through the allotted hours without a murmur, waking with a contented chuckle and only too pleased to fit in with your routine. There are other sides to the story, equally inseparable from the business of being a parent.

These are best thought of under two headings, *servicing* and *crying*. There's no doubt that babies require a lot of servicing. They need bathing, changing, feeding and entertaining; they need someone to do their laundry, to mix their feeds (if bottle-fed), to clean the chairs and carpets and wherever else they casually choose to be sick, to dress and undress them. They need someone to shop for them, to clean and tidy their room, to get them in and out of the pram and their cot, to carry them around, and not to mind when best clothes are dribbled on or worse. They need someone to put their interests and needs first, who can keep going twenty-four hours a day if necessary, and who can miraculously still be on their feet at the end of it, ideally with a smile clamped firmly in place.

Servicing your baby

If there's no doubt that babies require a great deal of servicing, there's also no doubt that they go in for a great deal of crying. They explore with great interest all the various registers and frequencies of the art of crying, and all the various situations in which this art can be employed for maximum effect. They expect those around them to be experts at interpreting precisely what each cry means, and at coming up smartly with the antidote. And they expect you to stay patient and good-humoured throughout, no matter what hour of the day or night they choose to exercise their skills.

Coping with crying

Be under no illusions, babies require hard work and patience. In the early months, your life will literally revolve around your child, and there will probably be times when your physical and emotional resources are tried to the limit. But if you are prepared for this, and if you are able to think of it as a small price to pay for the happiness your baby will bring you, you will be able to cope when the time comes. And to cope without feelings of disappointment that your baby hasn't turned out to be the little angel you expected, or disappointment at yourself that you can feel tired and irritable and impatient at times. You will be ready to take the rough with the smooth, reminding yourself that babies can't always be perfect, and that however wearying a particular episode is, it won't last long. One of the best bits of advice for an overwrought parent trying to get a fretful baby to settle and to retain his or her own sanity is that children are babies for such a very short time. We are talking about months rather than years, and about a stage in life that once gone can't be wished back.

So be aware of the work that lies ahead as well as of the pleasure, and know that although neither you nor your baby will be perfect *all* the time, you'll both manage it *some* of the time!

Your baby's bedroom

This is going to be one of the most important rooms in the house from now on. Your first concern will obviously be that it should be physically safe for your child, warm, and within easy earshot. You must be able to hear your baby if she cries by day or by night. I shall have plenty to say about crying and the reasons for it in due course (see Chapters 3 and 4), but any crying is potentially a sign of distress, and you must be able to hear it.

Pleasant, interesting surroundings for your baby

Such essentially practical considerations out of the way, you can think about decorating your baby's room. Choosing wallpaper and colour schemes is great fun, and of more importance than you may think. Psychologists now know that babies are much more aware of their surroundings than was once thought. Long before they are capable of talking and expressing their thoughts, babies are influenced by all they see around them. So give *your* baby as pleasant and interesting an environment as possible. Sunny colours like soft yellows and pinks, and restful blues and greens, are all good. Put bright children's pictures on the wall, showing the nursery rhyme and woodland scenes that will soon be featuring in the stories you read to her. These pictures can be changed to suit her developing tastes as she grows older, and act as a pleasant stimulus to her imagination. If you have plenty of pictures, you can use wallpaper which is bright and cheerful but not so babyish that it will soon look out of place for a growing child. Far easier to replace pictures in the future than to replace wallpaper.

Don't neglect the space above the cot. In the early months, your baby will spend a lot of time lying on her back. Hang a mobile from the ceiling where she can see it, and she'll watch it with intense concentration during wakeful periods. But make sure it's well out of her reach, and securely fastened and not likely to collapse in a heap on her head.

Resist the temptation to overdo things though. A room with pictures crammed on every spare bit of wall and mobiles swinging from all over the ceiling will be too distracting. There'll be so much to look at that your baby won't take any of it in properly. Go for a nice balance of well-chosen visual material, avoiding anything which is likely to frighten (pictures of witches or wizards or of certain animals, though innocent enough to adults, may be terrifying to a small child), and including both a restful, peaceful element and something more lively and exciting. Something, in other words, to satisfy the different moods of childhood.

It is often helpful to think back to your own childhood when deciding what to include. Try to recall your own bedroom, and the kind of things that you liked. Probably your parents thought you didn't take much notice of them, for small children often don't communicate their feelings about such things, mainly because they are always there, and are in a sense taken for granted. But looking back now you can see them as part of the essential fabric of childhood, as experiences which define in memory what it was like to be small and impressionable and to look out on a world full of wonder and strangeness. A pleasant welcoming room, prepared with imagination and love, is one of the precious gifts you can give

Think back to your own childhood

your child. And in this preparation it is less a matter of how much money you have to spare than of your ability to see things once more through the eyes of a child, and to know how to feed her imagination in a happy and creative way.

[2]

Your Baby at Birth

PEOPLE BROUGHT UP ON BABY adverts in the glossy magazines are sometimes taken aback at the scruffy little creature who shows up on delivery day. This isn't the smiling, dimpled, hygienic object they'd been expecting. But if you think about it, the surprising thing is that your baby looks as well as he does. After all, he's been immersed in fluid and kept in darkness for nine months, hardly the best of beauty treatments. His eyes have been tight shut for most of this time, his legs and arms drawn up around him to fit into his cramped quarters, his body suspended upside down. To cap it all, he has just been squeezed down a narrow birth canal, and ejected into a strange outside world where his body has suddenly to take responsibility for its own life-support functions. Small wonder he isn't quite looking his best.

Viewed in this light, his skinned rabbit appearance is forgivable and of no importance when set against the miracle of new life. Many parents confess to an incredible feeling of wonder and ecstasy at this miracle. They're unsure whether to laugh or cry, and the best advice is to do both if you feel like it, and hug everyone within range. An extra strong bond of love often unites a couple at this moment, an unforgettable experience which no hospital, by excluding the father from the birth, has the right to deny. This love is often mixed with profound gratitude: towards each other for making this magic moment possible, towards the medical staff for their devoted help, towards nature or God for the precious gift now placed in their trust. Enjoy this experience. Don't be embarrassed to show your feelings in front of the midwife and the doctor or nurses. Far from wondering what all the fuss is about, medical personnel say that the unrestrained delight of happy parents adds immeasurably to their own pleasure at bringing a child safely into the world.

This isn't the place to discuss the pros and cons of the various childbirth methods, since this raises medical matters that are beyond the scope of this book. During the months of pregnancy all the necessary decisions will have been taken over whether to have your baby at home or in hospital, and over whether to use natural methods or not. The only point to stress here is that, if there aren't compelling medical reasons to the contrary, you should have been fully involved in these decisions. The birth of your baby is *your* event. You've a right to your say as to how it should be done, and many doctors and midwives are coming increasingly to accept this fact. You've also a right to your say as to how your child should be treated during and after the birth. At one time it was thought that babies had very little awareness of their surroundings and very little feeling at birth. We now know differently. So whatever methods of childbirth are being used, you've a right to expect that your baby will be handled gently and lovingly from the start, that the atmosphere around him will be subdued and peaceful, and that he'll be put immediately against the soft warmth of his mother's body. We're not quite sure what long-term psychological harm a baby may suffer from the shock of being brought abruptly into a world of harsh lights, loud noises and brisk impersonal handling, but some experts consider the trauma may go very deep and remain with him for life. Whether this is correct or not, there's no need to take the risk. The natural instinct of parents is to want to show their love for their child from the moment he makes his appearance in the world, and this natural instinct is probably a sure guide to the best way to proceed.

Particularly if the atmosphere is harmonious and relaxed in this way, many parents say one of the biggest thrills of the moment after the birth is to see their baby move. Movement is life, and as they watch him puckering up his face, turning his head from side to side, jerking his legs and arms, it dawns on them that he is a real person, a new human being come to take his place in the world. His first cry, whether induced by others or allowed to come naturally, is another moving experience, another sign that here is the latest addition to the human race.

Choosing what method of childbirth should be used

What will your baby look like?

As these feelings sweep over you, you will be feasting your eyes on your baby, taking in every detail. You will notice that the skin is usually covered with a greasy white substance known medically as *vernix caseosa*. This is produced by the glands within the baby's own skin from the sixth month of pregnancy onwards, as a protection against the effects of the watery environment of the womb. Usually this is allowed to flake off naturally in the first few days after birth, but it is sometimes washed off gently from the folds around neck and arms. You will also notice her mop of hair (present in about 70 per cent of babies, a surprise to those who think of babies as bald), quite luxuriant in some cases and usually dark in colour. For an unknown reason this hair falls out in the days after birth, to be replaced in six to nine months (later in some cases) with hair that is usually much fairer. Sometimes there is hair on other parts of the body too, but this also falls out in the weeks after the birth.

Your baby's head There is no reliable research on which parts of their baby's body parents look at first, but the head and face are normally high on the list. The head always looks large in proportion to the rest of the body, because your baby's brain at birth is already more than one-third of its adult size, whereas her body is only about one-twentieth. This shows the importance that nature attaches to the brain. The top-heavy effect is heightened by the fact that at birth the neck is so short as to look virtually non-existent, a wise precaution since long necks would be a hazard during the journey down the birth canal. Don't be alarmed if the head looks a little out of shape. The skull is really five bones, not one, and during birth these bones can move slightly in relation to each other, allowing the head to be gently squeezed as it passes down the birth canal without any damage being done. This out-of-shape effect (or *moulding*, to give the medical term) is therefore perfectly normal, and will right itself during the first few days or weeks of life.

The fontanelle The gap between the five bones of the skull is widest at the top of the head, at the spot known as the *fontanelle*, and you can often see the gentle pulsing of the underlying tissue with each of your baby's heartbeats. Usually the fontanelle closes between the ninth and eighteenth month of life, and the next largest gap situated at the back of the head (and known as the *posterior fontanelle*), even earlier at two months. Some parents worry that there may be a risk of injury to the fontanelle, but with normal care this is unlikely, given the toughness of the protective membrane covering the spot. The usual medical advice is that the fontanelle area can be touched and washed, provided you do it gently.

You will notice that your baby's face looks rather puckered **Your baby's** and even puzzled and cross, as if she's not sure she approves **face** of the way things are shaping up. Some parents comment that it looks positively elderly as well, with its deep creases under the eyes and wrinkled folds of skin around the cheeks and jaw. Have no fear that nature is playing tricks on you. These signs of premature ageing disappear during the first days of life once the effects of immersion in the amniotic fluid of the womb wear off, and as more fat develops in the layer immediately under the skin. Sometimes there are white, pin-sized spots known as *melia* or milk spots around the nose, and if forceps have been used there could be marks on the face, but all these disappear with time. The same is true of the reddish-purple spots on the cheeks and sometimes even in the whites of the eyes, caused by the rupture of small blood vessels during the squeezing the head receives during birth.

Don't confuse these spots with the reddish patch frequently present at the bridge of the nose and at the back of the neck. These are simple birthmarks (*naevus simplex*), or more poetically 'stork bites' from the supposed pressure of the stork's bill as he brings you your baby. The one on the nose soon fades, and though the other may persist rather longer this is of no importance, as it is soon covered by hair.

After looking at the face and head, most parents glance at **The genitals** the genitals. The midwife or doctor will have announced the sex as soon as these important bits of apparatus come into view, but it is always nice to confirm things for yourself and make sure everything looks as it should. In fact you may be rather surprised at the exaggerated size of what your baby is sporting, but before you come too impressed I should warn you that this is perfectly normal. The parts concerned only look large in relation to the smallness of the legs and abdomen, and the effect is soon lost as the body and limbs grow rapidly in the first weeks of life and put things into more realistic perspective.

The rest of the body   Looking at the rest of the body, you may notice a rather fierce-looking rash with red blotches and raised yellow centres. Known as *urticaria neonatorum* (baby's urticaria) this is quite harmless, and can disappear and appear again with amazing rapidity, usually clearing up altogether quite soon to leave no trace. Don't worry about any small birthmarks you may notice on the body either, such as the *strawberry naevus* (a raised red patch that appears at birth or a few days after) or the *mongolian blue spot* (another colourful name) which appears as a bruise-like mark usually on the lower back. These are all relatively common, and usually fade to nothing during the first three years or so of life.

In both boys and girls the breasts sometimes appear quite large, and may even excrete a drop or two of milk. This is because they have been stimulated by the female hormones in the mother's bloodstream during pregnancy which enlarge her own breasts. No action is needed, and the condition disappears in the first few weeks after birth. Also as a result of sharing the hormones circulating in the mother's bloodstream during pregnancy, baby girls sometimes have the lining of their wombs stimulated and this lining will be shed as a light 'period' soon after birth. Like any other bleeding, if this happens when your baby is no longer under the watchful eye of your doctor, it must be reported at once just to make sure that everything is as it should be.

While you have been giving your baby all this attention, she will probably have got to the stage where she decides to open her eyes. Nearly always these are blue, because the colour hasn't yet been fully formed. In the months to come they may well change to brown. The process is usually apparent by the end of the first month but it can take up to a year, so you will have to be patient before you can be sure what the mature colouring is going to be. By the time the eyes are open, the midwife or doctor will probably have cut the umbilical cord, and clamped the end securely. You may think rather a lot is still left attached to the baby, but this soon dries and after a few days simply drops off. Beyond dusting it with antiseptic powder and handling it as little as possible, you will probably be advised that it requires no special attention.

Medical examination of your baby

Looking your baby over in this way is only part of the process of checking on him physically. Sometimes soon after the birth, but more usually a few days later, your doctor will give him a more thorough medical examination. Be present at this examination, not only because it is *your* baby and you want to be on hand in case he needs you, but also to learn more about him. It's also a help to the doctor to have you there. Usually he will ask you to undress the baby yourself, so that he can see how the latter reacts – how he moves and holds himself, whether he over- or under-responds. These things give clues to physical alertness and general well-being. Next the doctor will carry out a more detailed inspection of external features, checking the appearance of the skin and the eyes, the shape and proportions of the limbs and hands and feet, the condition of the genitals, the shape of the torso, the look of the nose, ears, fingers and toes.

This done, the doctor proceeds to examine the internal organs. He or she listens first to the heart, using a stethoscope and feels the pulse of the heartbeat at several key points such as the femoral artery in the groin. Parents are sometimes alarmed at this point to be told there is a heart murmur, and naturally ask anxiously if there's something wrong. The word 'murmur', however, simply means the heart doesn't sound quite like normal, and your doctor will probably reassure you that such murmurs are very common indeed in the newborn, and the great majority of them are perfectly innocent. Often they fade gradually during childhood, but you need to know if there is one since a doctor who detects it later won't then get the idea that it has suddenly appeared (when it could mean there's something needing investigation). If there is anything at all unusual about the murmur then rest assured your doctor will explain it to you, and the same goes for anything unusual in the pulse (which could indicate a blockage of some kind in one of the arteries). After listening to the heart the doctor will gently prod your baby's abdomen to check that the main organs located there are as they should be.

The internal organs

The next stage in the examination (though this will have to wait if the examination is carried out early, since it can't be done until after the sixth day of life) is to take a small prick of

The Guthrie test

47

blood from the heel. This is known as the Guthrie test, and is a way of screening your baby for the presence of several rare metabolic diseases (diseases which would prevent his body from dealing with natural substances present in the diet). Left undetected, these diseases can lead to a build-up of the substances concerned with possible risk of damage to the brain or other organs. Once diagnosed, they can usually be treated very successfully by the use of special diets. The blood used in the Guthrie test is also routinely checked for signs of deficiency in the thyroid gland (the important gland at the base of the neck which plays a part in bodily metabolism). Sometimes a baby's first stools are also screened, this time for the presence of cystic fibrosis, a metabolic disease inherited through recessive genes from both parents and leaving the baby prone to lung and digestive problems.

Checking reflexes The doctor will also check your baby's reflexes. These are the natural neuro-muscular responses with which a baby is born, and which he uses to help him survive in his new independent life. The sucking reflex is the most obviously important of these, though this will already have been tested if your baby has had his first feed. Next to be checked is the grasp (or gripping) reflex. This is done by gently touching the palms of your baby's hands, and watching to see if the fingers curl round and grip whatever is touching him. The more you try to pull free, the harder he will grip, so hard in fact that he can often be lifted into the air, suspending the whole of his weight from his tiny fingers. The strength in his little fists, in relation to his whole body weight, is in fact at its greatest in the early days of life; apparently the ancient Spartans, as a way of safeguarding the physical robustness of their race, used to abandon any baby who failed to pass this test. The gripping reflex is left over from very primitive times when a baby's life depended upon his ability to hang on tightly to his mother in the wild, but your doctor is interested in it for the more prosaic reason that it reassures him the neuro-muscular system is functioning properly.

Other reflexes present in the newborn, which may or may not be tested at this point, are the gripping reflex in the feet (the toes curl down when the soles of the feet are touched), the walking reflex (when supported upright a baby attempts to walk with jerky leg movements) and the Moro or startle reflex (when his head and torso are dropped back on to a pillow, giving him the impression he is falling, he throws out his arms and legs as if to break his fall). Some doctors also like to give a basic test of hearing at this point by looking for a distressed response to a loud noise, and a basic test of seeing by observing head movement and eye-closing in response to a bright light.

Finally, the doctor will usually test for any abnormality in bones and joints. He can do this simply by feeling for the bones and perhaps flexing the joints, but he will pay particular attention to the hips. Sometimes the hip bones aren't properly in the sockets, and the earlier this is discovered and put right the better. Usually all that is necessary is extra padding (such as two nappies) to keep the legs apart, but on a few occasions an operation is called for, though this is usually left until the baby is a little older. **Bones and joints**

While he or she is carrying out this examination, the doctor will be able to reassure you on anything that may be puzzling you about your baby. For example, most babies tend to lie in the foetal position, with legs drawn up and elbows bent, but you may have noticed your baby has his own preferences. If he was a breech delivery he may hold his legs in a different position from normal, while breech or not he may for reasons best known to himself prefer lying on his back with arms up above his head. Or he may hold himself in a rather tense position, making it difficult for you to straighten out his arms and legs (never use force to do this). All these variations are perfectly normal, and are of no known physical or psychological significance. Even a baby who is extra tense isn't necessarily going to grow up more nervy than the rest, though if this tenseness is coupled with other signs of hypersensitivity then it may mean your baby finds the world a rather daunting place at first, and will need extra sensitive and gentle handling at least in the early months. **Bring up any worries you have about your baby**

Where does she get it from?

Usually at this point parents, unless they're adopting a baby, start to wonder about inheritance. They see their small baby in front of them, and they want to know exactly what she's inherited from them. Does she get her physical shape from them? Is the person she'll develop into already decided by her genes? What about her intelligence and her abilities? Broadly speaking, the answer is that inheritance lays down *potential*, the wide limits within which your child's development will take place. Environment – your child's life experiences – then decides how much of this potential will actually be realized. For example, inheritance may decide that at maturity an individual's height will lie within a certain range. Environment, in the form of adequate nutrition, will then determine where within this range her adult height actually happens to be.

Physical characteristics Most physical characteristics are explained in this way, with a child standing an equal chance of inheriting the appropriate potential from either parent. Children can also inherit characteristics from us that we don't seem actually to possess ourselves. This is because we carry these characteristics in our *recessive* genes, that is in the genetic material in our bodies that doesn't influence our own appearance because it's overridden by *dominant* genes, but which is just as likely to be passed on to our children as these latter. Thus we may, for example, inherit the genes for fair hair from our father and the genes for dark hair from our mother. The genes for dark hair may prove dominant in our case, but when we conceive a child the odds as to whether we pass on our dark- or fair-haired genes are even. Thus two dark-haired parents, if they both carry recessive fair-haired genes and both pass these on to their child, may end up with a blond offspring. Through the mechanism of recessive genes it's perfectly possible for a child to inherit characteristics which have lain dormant in a family for generations, with the genes concerned being handed on each time but each time being forced into a recessive role in the face of more dominant genes inherited from the other parent (think of the head-shaking over paternity that would be saved if everyone understood this simple fact!).

Temperament When it comes to personality and abilities, the picture is less clear, since these characteristics are much more influenced by environment than are physical qualities. But it does seem to be the case that children inherit the raw material of their personalities – *temperament*, as the psychologist calls it. Research on children in the early weeks of life shows that even at this young age many of them belong to contrasting categories. Some children are adaptable, friendly, regular in their habits and sunny in their disposition, for example. Others are the opposite, and generally less outgoing and more suspicious and fretful. These differences often persist through childhood, though parental handling plays a major part in determining whether the behaviour concerned actually develops into a problem or not (I shall be returning later to the subject of temperament in Chapter 4).

Now what about abilities? Musical talent, in particular, often **Ability** flourishes at a very young age, which suggests it's a strongly inherited potential. The same may be true of many creative abilities (and perhaps intelligence, though intelligence is a slippery concept best left until we can discuss it fully later) and many skills, including sporting skills and perhaps mathematical and scientific ability. But as soon as we move into these areas, so much depends upon the amount of stimulation, encouragement and opportunity we offer to a child.

We must be clear about one point though. To the best of our **What we** knowledge no learning or training acquired by a person in his **cannot pass on** lifetime makes any difference to his genes, and therefore to **genetically** what he passes on genetically to his children. We may train hard to run a four-minute mile or study night and day to pass an exam, but our children won't be born better athletes or scholars because of it. If we inherit high potential, then there's a good chance we will hand this on genetically to our children, as we've just seen. But we won't hand on genetically what we've been able to *do with* this potential. Before you start regretting this, remember that it works the other way too. However much we *neglect* our talents, we aren't likely to spoil the chances our children have of inheriting them.

The inability to pass our own learning experiences on genetically to our children also includes such things as morals, beliefs, attitudes, values and opinions. Again this is not necessarily a bad thing. If the human race is to have free will, then clearly each generation must be born with scope to make up its own mind about such things. It would be a poor lookout if we were automatically born with the attitudes and values that gave rise to the tortures and burnings of the Spanish Inquisition, or to the medieval penal code that hanged a man for stealing a loaf of bread. No, we each bring a certain independence of mind with us into the world. In practice, this means two things. Firstly, that children have an innate capacity for forming their own views on things, (and for disagreeing with their parents!) Secondly, that the learning experiences which you offer to your child are vital if she's to have a fair chance of developing views that are sensible and well-balanced, and suited to the life that lies ahead.

[3]

The First Six Months

WHETHER YOUR BABY WAS BORN at home or in hospital, let's take up the story with mother and baby both back home and getting to know each other. Some hospitals like to keep you in for a week if it's a first pregnancy, others will let you go home as soon as they're sure all is well with you both. Some mothers say they enjoy the rest in hospital, and the company of nurses and other mothers, but for most the trip back home can't come too soon. They feel that the baby isn't really theirs until they have him in their own home and assume full responsibility for his care.

Relating to your baby

Spend time with your baby For all parents in these first weeks and months, the most important principle in your general relationship with your baby is to spend plenty of time with him. Show him you love him. Pick him up, cuddle him, talk to him, smile and laugh with him. Remember he has to get to know you, just as you have to get to know him. He depends upon you. In the early weeks and months of life you are his world. He comes to know the gentleness of your touch, the sound of your voice, the feel of your body – to know them, in fact, long before he becomes able to distinguish your face from the faces of other people. You, his mother and his father, are the ones he has to learn to trust, and the more he sees of you the more sure he is of your ability to look after him and keep him safe.

Because we adults rely so much on language as our means of communication, we sometimes forget that there are other ways of saying things. For a baby, who has no language as yet, these other ways are all important. His knowledge that he

54

is surrounded by loving care is communicated to him not by words but by the frequency with which you pick him up, the tenderness with which you handle him, the softness of the sounds you make to him, the speed with which you arrive when he really needs you, the patience you have with him, the willingness with which you play with him when he wants your company. In short he learns about you from what you *do with* him rather than from what you *say to* him.

The second principle in your relationship with your baby is to allow yourself to have fun with him. It's not just that you're good for him, he's good for you too. The more relaxed and unhurried you are with him, the more pleasure you'll find in the relationship. Looking after a baby only becomes one long labour if you get into the wrong frame of mind. There are people around who get no fun out of life because they don't allow themselves any fun. There can be a temptation to be like this with babies. Some parents find themselves rather resenting the baby's helplessness, or the insistence with which he makes his demands, or the large chunk of time he takes out of the day, or the inconvenient moments he chooses to be sick or dirty his nappy. This can be particularly so if the pregnancy was unplanned, but it can happen with any baby. If you let yourself get into the habit of seeing the jobs your baby creates as a drag, or if you always become irritable and impatient when you are doing them and try to rush them through as quickly as possible, you're hardly giving yourself a fair chance of learning how to enjoy the relationship with him.

Have fun with him

Worse still, you're not giving your baby a chance either. He senses your hurry and lack of patience, and this makes him insecure and unhappy. As a result, he becomes more and more fretful, makes more and more demands upon you, and you both end up locked into a vicious circle, with each of you making life increasingly difficult for the other. The only way out of this circle is for you, the parent, to relax, slow down, and start to get a little fun out of things. It's no use expecting him to be the one to change. In the early weeks and months he's very much at the mercy of his own insistent bodily needs. However much you may want him to control himself he just isn't old enough to have the means to do so. As yet, he quite simply hasn't begun to have any choice in the matter.

I know that you may be under all kinds of other domestic

Be patient with him and personal strains, and may feel you haven't that much choice in the matter either. But whenever a parent becomes impatient or angry with a small baby they are only, quite literally, making things worse for themselves. The more they insist their baby stops crying, lies quietly in his cot and goes to sleep, the more disturbed he becomes and the more lustily he cries. A child who will settle in ten minutes with a parent who nurses him gently will still be bawling the place down half an hour later with a parent who shows scant sympathy with his problems and insists he stay in his cot to tackle them on his own.

The dangers of spoiling Naturally enough, when faced with advice of this kind, parents often ask whether they may be going to the opposite extreme. They become very concerned, even in the first weeks of life, as to whether they may be 'spoiling' their child. If they pick him up every time he cries, won't he grow into a little monster who wants things all his own way and has no concern for the feelings or rights of others? If he has only to shout in order to have them running to give him attention, won't he learn to use crying as a means of getting his own way over the least little thing?

These parental fears are perfectly understandable. We all have a horror of the conventional picture of the spoilt child who tyrannizes over his parents and thinks the world owes him a living for now and the rest of his life. I deal with the question of spoiling at length later in this chapter (pages 102–6) and also in Chapter 4 (pages 167–8). Suffice it to say here that in the early weeks a child always cries for a reason. The danger of spoiling is something that only comes up much later. One thing you can be sure of is that far more children are harmed by too little parental attention than too much.

Post-natal depression

No matter how much you've been looking forward to the birth, there's sometimes a feeling of anti-climax. Mothers are more prone to this than fathers, so much so that the maternal 'post-natal depression' is a recognized medical and psychological condition. A woman may suddenly find herself crying for no apparent reason, or with a heaviness of spirit for which she can't somehow account. On occasions there's a slight feeling of unreality, as if everything that's happened and is happening belongs to someone else. If her baby is fretful, and if she has little help in the house, physical tiredness may make things worse. Most unexpectedly of all she may not feel the overwhelming love for her baby that she anticipated, and find herself looking on him almost as a stranger, or thinking only with rising panic of the work and responsibility which she has let herself in for.

Some doctors consider that a drug called *oxytocin*, which is often given as an injection to speed up the expulsion of the afterbirth during the third stage of labour, may play some part in this. As a mother, your body has undergone major chemical and other changes during the nine months of pregnancy, and after the birth you have abruptly to get back to normal again. Advocates of natural childbirth say that nature must whenever possible be allowed to do this in her own way and in her own time, and any attempt to speed up the third stage of labour (or even the earlier stages) may lead to unnecessary emotional upheaval and render post-natal depression more likely. They also claim that natural childbirth methods, with their warm and caring attitude and their emphasis upon the instinctive wishes of the mother and her right to play a full part in decision-making, in themselves lessen the likelihood of post-natal depression. Instead of a confused and helpless mother, with other people doing things to her, natural methods give a woman the confidence-building experience of having given birth *herself*, surrounded by loving and joyful people who regard her and her baby as the most important people around. Certainly the evidence shows that mothers who give birth by natural methods do tend to suffer less from subsequent depression.

Natural childbirth methods may help

But whenever post-natal depression does occur, it must be treated with understanding and sympathy by everyone concerned, starting with the mother herself. If you feel depressed, don't become impatient with yourself or imagine you are somehow at fault. Tell your doctor about it, just as you would if you were physically unwell. In a few cases he or she may judge that the depression is severe enough for you to need specialist help in order to get over it, but usually you will be told quite rightly that it is a short-term thing, and will

Need for sympathy

disappear of its own accord as your body readjusts. Talk it over with your husband or partner, and with parents and friends as well. What you need is a sympathetic listener or two, people who won't tell you you're imagining things or not to be so silly or that they had a couple of dozen children themselves as easy as shelling peas and never once had a dose of the blues. While you don't want to be treated as an invalid, it's nice if those around you make a little bit of a fuss of you. After all, they fussed you when you were pregnant, and although it's good to see them going into raptures over the baby, it's right and proper they should still spare a thought for your part in the proceedings!

Don't force your feelings   When it comes to your own feelings for your baby, don't try to force things. This applies equally to fathers. You've got to give yourselves time to recover from the tremendous experience of the birth itself, and to work through any feelings of anti-climax or remoteness which you may have. Your baby still may not seem a proper person to you. She's part of your life, but you often have to get to know her ways and to see her emerging as a definite personality in her own right before you can feel the full warmth of your love for her. Be patient. Don't keep telling yourself how you 'ought' to be feeling. This warmth will come in its own good time. With some people it happens immediately. With others it may take a day or two. With others, weeks or even months. Some parents say that although fond of their baby they couldn't feel a *personal* love for her until she got beyond the newborn stage. Some parents, particularly fathers (probably due to the mistaken cultural conditioning that babies are not men's work), find it hard to relate to small babies at all, and begin to feel the full joys of parenthood only at the toddler stage or even older.

Problems only arise if you begin to feel guilty or deeply disappointed about this gradual process. You end up feeling dissatisfied with yourself, and resentful towards your baby for not *making* you feel as you think you should. Concentrate instead upon a calm, relaxed and gentle attitude to your baby, caring for her as well as you can, and things will soon develop as they should.

DAILY CARE

The importance of routine

Once you have your baby home, you will quickly begin to settle into a routine. You will find out what suits him best, and how you yourself can plan things so that he can have the care and attention he needs without leaving you worn out each day and without a minute to yourself. Each baby has a natural rhythm, a bodily clock that tells him when he's hungry, when he's ready for sleep, when he wants to fill his nappy, and when he is feeling extra alert and wants to be with other people. In some babies this clock is a pretty regular timepiece, and this helps you because you usually know what a particular bout of crying at a particular time of day actually means. Other babies are less sure of themselves, and sometimes even seem to take a perverse delight in upsetting whatever plans you make for the day ahead. It's almost as if they know you're wanting to get something important finished in the kitchen during their afternoon sleep, or that you've planned to settle them quickly in their pram after the two o'clock feed so that you can take them to a friend's tea party. The more carefully you plan, the more unerringly they seem to disrupt things.

Of course they're not really being perverse, however much it seems that way at times. They're simply responding to the mysterious workings of their own body. Doubtless they would much prefer, if they had a choice, to fit in with your schedules and be like the little baby next door who always seems to come up smiling. But that isn't the way of it. And there is no remedy other than to be as patient as you can and just accept that your baby is as he is, and that you must work with him and not against him.

Naturally though, with any baby, you will try to nudge his schedule gently towards what is most convenient for you. Within careful limits, a feed can, for example, be put back a few minutes each day until he is ready for it half an hour or so later than at first. You do this not by letting him cry for the extra few minutes, but by picking him up and distracting him until you are ready to give him the breast or the bottle. Nine

Adjusting feeding times to suit your convenience

times out of ten he'll get the message and feel the pangs of hunger just that little bit later each day. If he doesn't, then let him be the best judge and abandon your attempt at adjustment. Similarly, a feed can often be brought forward by offering it to him a few minutes earlier. But don't keep tinkering around with things, or be inconsistent from day to day. Babies are creatures of habit, and thrive best on a settled routine as close as possible to their own biological clock.

Feeding

In the first weeks of life, a baby lives in a little world bounded by feeds, sleep, baths and nappies. To him, these things occupy the importance that international affairs do for a politician. In fact they go further, since he knows nothing else. Carefully programmed by nature for his own survival and thus for the survival of the species, a baby goes through the twenty-four hours of the day responding to the sensations that come from within and from outside his body, registering some as pleasant and responding to them with contented pleasure, registering others as unpleasant and protesting strongly about them until someone manages to put them right.

By far the most important of his sensations have to do with feeds. Hunger, quite clearly, is experienced by a baby with a totality and an intensity at which we mere adults can only marvel. Watching a baby responding to the insistent calls of his body it is as if he is experiencing hunger right down to his finger tips. And dull is he of soul who isn't prompted to plug an appropriate source of nourishment into the eager little mouth. But because of its insistent nature and its vital importance to their baby's well-being, parents often find that knowing how to deal with this hunger is one of their major quandaries.

Feeding schedules

Fixed feeding versus demand feeding

Their first worry is usually *when* to feed, and in few areas of child-rearing have fashions fluctuated more wildly than in this. First the experts advocate fixed feeding (feeding at set times during the day), then the pendulum swings to demand feeding (feeding when he's hungry), now it seems to vacillate between the two, with different experts advocating different things. Parents are torn between waiting for the hands of the clock to creep slowly round to the appointed hour (to the background of indignant protests from their baby) and rushing to offer the breast or bottle at the first sign of a whimper, however inconvenient this may be for their own planned programme during the day.

The reasons for the disagreements amongst the experts are grounded in psychology rather than in medicine. No child is likely to be harmed physically whether he is fixed fed or demand fed, assuming he is already in good health and assuming he takes the right amount of nourishment without forcing during the twenty-four hours. But dire *psychological* consequences are predicted by experts on both sides of the fence should you ignore their advice. If you fix feed, it is said, you risk leaving your child unhappy and confused while you wait for the clock, with the result that he will grow up anxious and disturbed, unable to trust others or to feel at peace with himself. On the other hand it is said that if you demand feed then your child will grow up believing he can have anything he wants just when he wants it, without thought for the wishes of others. Either way, it seems, you're going to bring up a psychologically damaged child.

When experts disagree to this extent amongst themselves the chances are there is no real right answer. In fact, but for the unwelcome spectre of 'spoiling', there would probably be no need to agonize over finding one. The natural reaction of any parent when faced by a hungry baby is to feed him, and not to bother how long it is since the last meal. If one studies animals, this seems to be nature's way of going about things. And there is not a scrap of psychological evidence that by following nature's practice you're going to end up with an undisciplined child. On the other hand, nor is there a scrap of evidence that by nudging a child gently towards a regular schedule in the way we indicated in the last section you're going to do any damage either. Clearly it *is* more convenient for parents if, within sensible limits, a baby does have a set feeding schedule, and this often fits in best with his own inner workings anyway.

So the simple rule is to find your baby's natural rhythm and work with it, compromising sensibly where possible with your

**Find your
baby's natural
rhythm**

own preferred schedule, but always prepared to vary things
when your baby shows the need. If he's hungry only two
hours after his last feed, then by all means bring the next one
forward. Maybe he's been extra active during these two hours
and used up a lot of energy. The chances are he'll now go five
or six hours before he's hungry again, so you'll soon be back
to routine.

Most babies settle into a four-hourly routine through the
twenty-four hours, staring at about 6 a.m., which probably fits
in with some basic inborn rhythm. It isn't usually advisable to
make determined efforts to change this natural rhythm even if
you're a late starter and would prefer to be up at eight rather
than six, or because a later start fits in better with a parent who
is on shift work. Stay with your baby's natural rhythm. It may
be inconvenient for you, but it's important for him. Of course,
even the most regular of babies may want to move these feeds
forward or back a little, or may want one or two of them
(usually the 6 a.m. and the 10 p.m.) earlier while leaving the
rest where they are. This is fine, and you and he will both be
much happier if you indulge him in these little idiosyncrasies.

In the first three or four days of life, a baby in fact takes very
little food. He sleeps most of the time. But at the end of this
short period, and just when a breast-feeding mother begins to
produce her supply of milk, he starts to wake more frequently
and may want to feed ten or twelve times during the twenty-
four hours. On each occasion he will take very little, and it
isn't a good idea to try and coax him to take more in order to
give yourself a longer break between feeds. Surprisingly
quickly, however (usually by about two weeks), he will settle
of his own accord into the standard routine of six feeds a day
at four-hourly intervals.

**Dispensing
with the night
feed**

By about six weeks your baby will probably start to dispense
with the 2 a.m. feed, and will sleep right through from 10
p.m. to 6 a.m. Dispensing with the night feed is a great boon
for tired parents, and seems to happen because at six weeks a
baby's bodily metabolism settles into a pattern closer to our
own, being at its lowest ebb at around 2 a.m. Thus she won't
really want to wake at this time, and you don't have to do
anything to try and 'train' her, beyond perhaps waiting to see
if she'll drop off to sleep again quickly should she start
whimpering a little at this time.

If she doesn't go back to sleep, decide that she still needs her 2 a.m. treat for another night or two, and get up to her. Trying to get a child to go through the night before she is ready can cause her to go on waking and fretting nightly much longer than is necessary. Waking at 2 a.m. feeling hungry and at a low ebb, and then finding you're left to cry it out on your own in the darkness, is hardly the best way to soothe the mind.

Of course, not content with waking up when you'd much rather she stayed asleep, a baby often falls asleep during feeds when you'd much rather she stayed awake. This pattern of nodding off can become a pretty predictable one. You and she both get comfortable in the nursing position, the nipple or teat is offered and duly accepted, a nice sucking rhythm is established, then lo and behold the eyes become unfocused, the eyelids start to droop, the sucking rhythm gets slower and slower until finally, but for the occasional token effort, it peters out altogether. Fine for her, you reflect in some disgust, but not so fine for you. If you let her sleep now, with less than half her feed inside her, she's bound to wake up again in an hour or so and in high indignation start demanding her rights to the other half. The only solution, you tell yourself, is to keep jigging and rousing her until she's done the decent thing and got rid of it all. So you and she proceed, alternatively sucking, jigging and sucking, until the last dregs are drained. Neither of you enjoys the performance very much, but it seems like a job that must be done. **Falling asleep during feeds**

Not so. The odd experimental little jiggle at the first sign of her expression glazing over, just to see whether the situation is retrievable, is quite in order. But if you keep her at it in the face of her obvious preference for sleep you'll waste far more time and energy that you would by putting her down and feeding her again in an hour when she's really hungry. The same applies if she sleeps through the appointed time for her feed. She's telling you that at the moment her need for sleep is greater even than her need for food thank you very much. So let her have her way. As she grows a little older she'll find less and less difficulty in staying awake, and the problem will cure itself without special effort on anyone's part.

Even if she doesn't fall asleep, you may find your baby doesn't take all her feed at one or other of her meals. She **Leaving half her feed** wants half of it, and cries just as energetically for it, but leaves the rest. This may happen occasionally, or become a habit. Fine. Don't try to force her, or worry that she'll be hungry half-way to the next feed. As long as she's taking sufficient over the twenty-four-hour period, that's all that matters. After all, we adults don't eat the same amount at every meal.

If you're breast-feeding, you won't notice these small variations much anyway. Even if your baby feeds for the same amount of time at each meal, she may actually be sucking more lustily and taking more at certain times than at others. It's only when we bottle-feed that we keep looking anxiously at how much is left and expecting her to take the same set ration every time, or worrying that she's polished off the whole bottle and still seems to want more.

Don't worry too much about your baby's feeding habits The best advice, both for now and for when your child is older, is not to agonize too much over her feeding habits. Most feeding problems at any age are caused by well-meaning parents rather than by children themselves. That is by parents fussing over what a child *ought* to be having at mealtimes, instead of taking a sensible matter-of-fact attitude to the whole business. As far as the small baby goes, this means you ask yourself if it's fair to let her cry from hunger when you have the means to feed her close at hand, and if it's fair to keep trying to force food on her when she clearly doesn't want it. Babies are far too sensible to feed for the sake of it. Stuffing food down unnecessarily is a vice that appears later in life. Babies will neither cry for a meal when they don't really want it nor refuse food when they've got space left. As long as your baby is fit and well and gaining weight satisfactorily, you can be pretty sure that she's got the business of feeding properly worked out. Have her weighed regularly, report any sudden changes in feeding habits to your doctor immediately, listen carefully to medical advice on how much she should be taking over the twenty-four hours, and you won't go far wrong.

But do remember that although we think of feeds primarily in terms of food, the liquid they contain is even more vital. Babies can very quickly become dangerously dehydrated if they don't drink enough. Your doctor must be told at once if your baby refuses two feeds in a row, even if there are no visible signs as yet that dehydration is becoming a problem.

Breast or bottle?

Another of the major fashions in feeding is whether to use the breast or the bottle. Again the pendulum has swung back and forth over the years, with the wishes of mothers themselves unfortunately often the last consideration to be taken into account. Experts who favour the bottle argue that it allows you to monitor the amount your baby takes at each feed, and to keep the quality of the milk constant. Those who favour the breast argue that breast-feeding increases the physical bond between mother and baby (with good psychological consequences), and that mother's milk is best suited to a baby's needs and may also help his resistance to common infections.

In some parts of the country, the advice you receive seems to depend upon your doctor and your hospital. One hospital wants mothers to give in to the convenience and controllability of bottle-feeding, while its neighbour in the next town argues it is unmotherly not to breast-feed. No wonder mothers end up confused, and with guilt feelings if they go against official policy.

Let's start by saying that there's no conclusive psychological evidence that babies are better off with either breast or bottle. Nor is there any evidence that mothers who breast-feed love their babies more or have a closer bond with them than mothers who bottle-feed. Both children and mothers can flourish psychologically whichever method is used, with the single proviso that bottle-fed babies should be held in the same close intimacy during feeding as breast-fed ones. No shoving the teat at arm's length into your baby's mouth while you carry on with your own meal or read a book!

Part of the current feeling against bottle-feeding has been sparked off by its introduction into developing countries, where sterilization procedures are more difficult, and where babies in consequence often pick up dangerous infections that can be avoided if the breast is used. There has also been doubt about the quality of some of the baby milk supplied to developing countries, and a fear that in certain cases there may have been commercial exploitation. Equally, there have been worries that since the antibodies present in mother's milk are of particular importance in the Third World, where standards of hygiene and baby care are not yet as high as in the

Bottle-feeding in developing countries

West, depriving a child of this milk might make him more vulnerable to local diseases.

These points are strong arguments in the Third World, but they don't apply to the same extent in the West. Provided parents are meticulous about sterilizing all equipment, and are careful to use the right formula baby milk, there should be no problems. In addition, manufacturers are working all the time to bring their products closer and closer to human milk, and although it may never be quite the same as the real thing, standards are improving with each year that passes.

Advantages of breast-feeding   Undeniably many mothers greatly enjoy breast-feeidng, and say that the experience is of value in itself whether or not it carries any long-term psychological benefit for them or their child. Equally, there is no denying that mother's milk is specially designed and attractively packaged by nature with small babies in mind. It thus contains all the nutrition they need in just the right quantities. It also contains antibodies from the mother's own blood which help protect babies from common infections during the early months of life. Because mother's milk is less fat than cow's milk, breast-fed babies are also less prone to obesity than those who are bottle-fed. So clearly breast-feeding is a good idea if you can manage it. It also has certain convenience advantages over bottle-feeding in that there are no feeds to be mixed or utensils to be sterilized. And the physical sensation as baby sucks away, described variously as ticklish or erotic, is universally held to be pleasant. Finally it prolongs the period of the baby's absolute physical dependence upon his mother, which many mothers quite naturally feel enhances the significance of their maternal role.

Advantages of bottle-feeding   However, if you are unhappy about breast-feeding, or if you find it too difficult or the milk supply inadequate, there's no need to feel you are letting your baby down. As I've said, there's no evidence that bottle-fed babies are less healthy in the long run than breast-fed, and bottle-feeding does have certain advantages. In the first place you can undertake it more easily in public (though anyone who is offended at the sight of a mother breast-feeding has no business to be). Secondly, the quality of bottle milk is independent of the mother's own health and diet. This is particularly important if the mother has to be prescribed drugs for any reason, or if she can't give up smoking or alcohol. Even foods which are actively good for a mother's own body, such as onions, grapes, garlic and certain other fruits and vegetables, can affect the composition of the milk and upset the baby's digestion.

Thirdly, bottle milk isn't affected by the contraceptive pill, which some mothers want to resume taking as quickly as possible. The influence of the contraceptive pill upon mother's milk isn't known for sure, and it should quite definitely be given a miss until a breast-fed baby is fully weaned. To set against this, we know that breast-feeding in itself seems to lower a mother's chances of conceiving before her baby is weaned, so you may find you can dispense with other forms of contraception in any case. But be warned. Plenty of women do conceive while they are still breast-feeding. So if it is very important to you not to start another pregnancy yet, then don't rely on your natural protection. And if in doubt, talk the matter over fully with your doctor.

But the fourth advantage – and one which I regard as of major impotance – is that using a bottle allows the father to do his share of the feeding. Not only is this helpful for the mother (particularly where night-time and early morning feeds are concerned), it allows the father to be more involved with his baby, and to play more part in creating the warm and caring atmosphere within which babies thrive. Strangely, some men confess to feeling awkward when feeding or even when just holding a small baby. There is no need for this. In the human race, as in many branches of the animal kingdom, nature plans for males to play an important part in child-rearing. The paternal instinct (about which I have more to say later) is very strong in the human male, as strong in many ways as the maternal instinct in the female. Fathers who feel awkward at holding their offspring aren't showing a 'natural' response to what is by rights 'women's work' therefore. They are simply responding to a rather dotty social conditioning which says there is something unmanly about a father loving his small son or daughter and wanting to express this love through physical care and affection. So let fathers follow their natural instincts and claim their rightful share of the parenting tasks.

The father's role in bottle-feeding

Older brothers and sisters, grandparents, aunts and uncles can also be roped in to give a bottle. This helps a baby become used to other people around him from an early age, and helps his social development.

Is breast-feeding more time-consuming?

It is sometimes said that breast-feeding is much more time-consuming than bottle feeding. Beware of this argument, not only because, apart from in the very early weeks, it is untrue, but because it implies that feeding is something that should be over and done with as quickly as possible. Your baby's feeds are the high spot of his day. Not only does he gain pleasure from the milk itself, he also enjoys the act of sucking. Nature has programmed him to suck, and he must spend a certain amount of time sucking every day if he is to fulfil a deep innate need. Sucking calms him and soothes him, and seems to contribute to his sense of psychological security. It is quite wrong to imagine that babies who are allowed plenty of sucking become 'addicted' to the habit, and carry it on well into childhood. The child who sucks long after he has been weaned is far more likely to be the child who was allowed *insufficient* sucking when a baby, or who has some other insecurity in his life which the comfort of sucking helps him to deal with.

Never rush your baby's feeds

Of equal importance, feeding time allows your baby to be with *you*, snuggled in a cosy intimacy from which you can both benefit enormously. Not only does your baby enjoy this pleasant experience for its own sake, he also comes to associate it with you, which helps the growth of his love for you. He gets the clear message that you're not only a person who feels good to the touch and who sounds good, you are also a person who brings him the most enjoyable experiences going. He links the joys of feeding with your presence, and will soon being to link them with your face too. Notice how as he grows a little older he gazes long and deep at you while he is feeding, with a serious appraising expression, as if he is taking in every part of your face and storing the image in a very special part of his memory. This is why, even if he is bottle-fed, *most* of the feeding should be done by his own parents, so that he can come to know them in this profound and intimate way. As mentioned earlier, one major advantage of bottle-feeding is that it allows the father to be a full part of this magical experience. No wide-scale research has been carried out in this area, but I am in no doubt that fathers who do involve themselves fully in these early feeding experiences are likely to have a closer bond with their children, both in babyhood and later.

So don't be tempted to rush the daily feeds. Allow your baby to enjoy them, and allow yourself to take an equal pleasure in the experience. Stop thinking about all the other jobs waiting to be done. For the duration of the feed, give your attention fully to your baby. Allow yourself to relax physically and mentally. Parents have been feeding babies for countless thousands of years. It is one of the fundamental realities upon which the human species is based. It links us with other women and men across the centuries and across races and cultures. When feeding your baby you are doing the most natural and the most peaceful thing in the world; don't start comparing it in importance with all the mundane chores awaiting your attention.

If you are to breast-feed successfully, both physical health and peace of mind are vital. I don't mean anything special by physical health, just a good balanced diet and sufficient rest if you can get it. By peace of mind I mean you should stay calm and relaxed. Some mothers become very upset if there are any problems at the start, and feel as if they are failing their child. This is an understandable sign of their love and concern for their child, and of their own natural insecurities about their role as a mother. They say things like 'If I can't feed her myself I've given her a pretty poor start in life' or 'How can I ever be confident as a mother when I think what a mess I made of things right at the beginning?'. But understandable as these thoughts are, they're counter-productive. They make you tense and tearful, and make it harder for your body to see to things for itself. Your baby senses your unease as well, and this makes her anxious in turn. They're also unfair. Your ability to breast-feed is emphatically *not* a test of your motherhood. If you can't manage it, your baby will thrive perfectly well on the bottle. The only real test of motherhood is the care you show for your baby. Keep a sense of humour. You'll have far more important things to do in the coming weeks and years than hark back to breast-feeding and hold a few early problems against yourself.

Stay relaxed while breast-feeding

Once you relax, breast-feeding will usually come easily enough. But if it doesn't, don't persevere until you and your baby become frustrated with the whole business and with each other. Switch sensibly to the bottle. Your baby is born with the ability to suck happily at whatever gives her nourishment. As long as you allow both of you (and the father too) full enjoyment from the experience, things will work out well.

Beware of other people's advice   While on the subject of relaxation, there's another possible cause of tension for which you must be prepared – namely other people trying to tell you what to do! Advice is welcome enough from your doctor or health visitor or from knowledgeable relatives or friends, but all too often young parents are surrounded by well-meaning but interfering folk who remember when *they* had small babies and imagine that if you or your baby are different then it's a sign something is wrong. Such people can make you feel pretty inadequate. Don't let them. It's your baby and as long as you are following sound medical advice and your own rapidly developing experience of what works and what doesn't, you must be the best judge.

For example, since we know (page 95) that crying at the end of a feed is not necessarily a sign of insufficient milk flow, you will be guided by your doctor's advice on whether your baby is having enough food and not by the neighbour who shakes her head disapprovingly every time your baby fusses at feeding time and tells you that somebody with breasts your shape will never be able to produce enough milk.

Changing from breast to bottle   Some mothers who start off by breast-feeding decide after a while they want to change to the bottle, or perhaps to give the bottle as well as the breast. This could be to give the father a turn with the feeding, or because they are returning to employment outside the home, or because there are genuine fears that their milk is insufficient (though this is comparatively rare). If you are breast-feeding successfully, it's a good idea to continue until your baby is eight or nine months old, but if you can't for any reason, or want to give a bottle at some feeds, you need have no fears that the switch from breast to bottle, if done correctly, will do your baby any physical or psychological harm.

Usually a child who is accustomed to the nipple will change to the teat very readily. More readily, in fact, than a bottle-fed baby will get used to the breast. Make sure, however, that your baby experiences the same close intimacy when taking the bottle as she did when on the breast, and that you don't try to hurry her. This is particularly important if you are changing to the bottle on grounds of convenience. Perhaps you are taking up your job once more after finishing maternity leave, and inevitably this will mean some changes in your baby's routine. Few babies enjoy such changes, simply because they are in the process of learning how the world works, and find it very confusing if the things they've learnt are suddenly superseded by new routines. Your baby thought she knew what was going on around her, and now abruptly she discovers she doesn't. If to add to it all she is expected to forgo the leisurely, happy times she had with you when feeding, it's small wonder that she takes marked exception to the way her household is being run.

Weaning

Much as your baby enjoys his milk, there comes a time in life when he begins to hanker after more solid fare. The age at which this happens varies, but soon after six months a baby's supplies of the essential minerals such as iron stored in his body during the months in the womb begin to run out. This prompts him naturally to want solid food, since milk alone cannot replace these minerals. You can try him with solids before six months if you like, though never earlier than four months. When you do introduce solids, do so at the midday feed when he is likely to be at this hungriest. Try him with a very little on the end of a small spoon, and reduce it first to a semi-liquid consistency with a little sterilized milk. Since you will be giving him solids in addition to and not instead of his milk, it's a good idea to allow him to take the edge off his appetite with the breast or the bottle before you offer him the spoon. Make sure the spoon and the food it contains are of the same temperature as his milk, so that they don't come as an unpleasant shock. Scald the spoon in boiling water to sterilize it before use, then allow it to cool to just the right heat. Some babies will be quite happy with the spoon at first acquaintance, while others will leave you in no doubt that they think it a very poor sort of idea. Either way, a trial mouthful or two is all that is needed before returning him to the breast or the bottle. If he refuses or spits out the offering, then let him. As we will see, he's only acting in self-defence.

How and when to start

If things have gone well, repeat the trial mouthful next day at the same time. Don't be tempted to rush things. One or two spoonfuls at one meal a day are quite enough to begin with.

71

And remember that by 'spoonfuls' I mean just a little on the end of the spoon. Any attempt to cram in more will make your baby fear he is about to choke. Only prepare a small amount of solid food each time, and always keep up your strict standards of hygiene.

Introducing a feeding cup   Once the weaning process is well under way and your baby is cutting down on his milk, remember that he will now need plenty of drinks to compensate for the liquid he is losing. Introduce him to a special feeding cup, with a lid and a flat spout that reduces the risk of spilling. He'll need help with it at first, but as soon as he shows signs of wanting to hold it for himself let him have a try. You'll have to keep picking it up for him at first, but all these signs of growing independence on his part should be encouraged. Nevertheless, however competent he becomes with it, he may still prefer the breast or the bottle for a while at certain times in the day. Most babies drop the midday bottle or breast-feed first, then the morning and afternoon ones, keeping the evening bottle or breast-feed until last.

What about spoiling and feeding problems?   Just as parents agonize over whether they may be 'spoiling' their baby by their feeding methods in the early weeks, so they agonize all over again when it comes to weaning and solids. If they are too lax and allow their child to take or leave food as he likes, won't this produce not only a feeding problem in the short term but a spoilt little monster in the long? Once again, many of these fears are misplaced, and based upon a misunderstanding of exactly what is happening when a child is taking his food.

Certainly, some children do cause more parental headaches than others. With one child, for example, you only have to bring the spoon within range for him to open his mouth as dramatically wide as a baby sparrow. As he gets older, he takes to new tastes and textures with equal alacrity, and mealtimes become a pleasure all round. With another child, the appearance of the spoon produces a look of disgust and a mouth clamped tight against what he clearly sees as your attempts to poison him. Should you persevere in these attempts, tempers become increasingly frayed on both sides. You are determined that he will open his mouth and take the food that you know is good for him, while he's equally determined he won't.

Pleasant as it is to have a child like our first example, a child like the second is emphatically *not* a feeding problem. We all need food to live, and babies are sensible folk and have no wish to starve. Besides, as we've already seen, mealtimes are the highlights of their day. So no baby is born a feeding problem, in spite of natural differences in the readiness with which each child takes to new gourmet experiences. When feeding problems develop, the cause, as I said earlier, is therefore much more likely to rest with us than with him.

What goes wrong? To answer this question, let's go back to the child who tries one mouthful of solids and then clamps his mouth tight against a repeat performance. Up to now, he's taken all his food in the form of warm liquid, and very acceptable it was too. And suddenly here you are trying to poke a hard object into his mouth and deposit some strange lumpy material for him to swallow. Probably the miracle is not that he refuses to do it but that some babies are quite happy about it. After all, their undeveloped taste buds get very little out of the experience, and they haven't yet got the idea that it's all going to do them good. Rugged, adventurous little souls decide to give it a try, and find it helps to satisfy their hunger pangs. But others act just as sensibly, and out of a natural instinct for self-preservation spit it out and put up the shutters against the next spoonful.

How feeding problems start

If you try at this stage to force the spoon between your baby's lips he naturally becomes frightened and struggles even harder to keep his mouth closed. You see this as defiance, and decide to show him who's boss, and things begin to get very fraught indeed. Even if you manage to slide a spoonful in at the side of his mouth in an unguarded moment, the unappetizing concoction is promptly oozed out again at the other side. The pair of you skirmish away until in the end either his wails or your own impatience convince you it's time to give up and turn to other things.

But though we can laugh about it, think for a moment what this kind of scene is actually teaching your baby. Up to now you've been a provider of happy feeding times, a person he can trust and with whom he feels perfectly safe. Suddenly, everything changes; feeding times are no longer happy and you are no longer someone with whom he feels safe. This frightens and confuses him. What sort of person are you really, and what sort of a world is this to live in? The loving relationship that was developing between the two of you comes under threat. Moreover, the very sight and feel of the spoon now make him nervous. Being a quick learner, he starts buttoning down his mouth the moment you produce it. So you can see that what seems like a straightforward battle of wills is in fact nothing of the kind. He isn't trying to defy you for the sake of it, or to score a victory over you; he's trying to protect himself against something that threatens and worries him.

How to avoid feeding problems How can you avoid this sort of situation developing? The answer is not to force solids on him. Take your time over weaning. If he refuses the spoon the first time you offer it, leave it for a day or two before you try again. If you've started early, leave it altogether until he's six months, even a little older if he shows no signs of being dissatisfied with just milk. And when weaning does start, let it take several weeks if that's the way he wants it. You're not in a race. No matter that all your friends have babies who were weaned ages ago. There's no evidence that a child who weans late is any slower in other ways. The important thing is not to upset your baby or yourself, or to store up trouble for you both in the future. Babies who learn to associate feeding times with strife and tension don't only feel generally less happy about life now; they often develop negative attitudes towards food that lead to the very long-term feeding problems their parents are so anxious to avoid.

Naturally you feel irritated when your small offspring stubbornly refuses to open his mouth when you ask him nicely, but your irritation is caused because you are treating him *as if* he understands what is happening and has come to a deliberate decision to defy you. Treat his actions instead as an inborn reflex, put there by nature to protect the very young from harm. Given time he'll learn that this reflex isn't necessary, but this learning will take much longer if you become angry and try to force him. Instead, be philosophical and throw the unwanted food away, congratulating yourself on how sensible you are instead of seeing it as a defeat. Needless to say, your child's 'victory' at this stage isn't going to make him grow up self-willed and wanting his own way. It will simply leave him more reassured that you are there to protect and care for him.

74

Even children who take to solids happily from the first can become problems if they have too much forced on them too quickly. Initially, they will want only very small amounts, and should never be made to finish up what you've prepared for them simply because it's there. Initially, they will also still want their full quota of milk, but over the weeks they will take more and more from the spoon, and show less interest in the breast or bottle. Once they start pushing the nipple or the teat out of their mouths with their tongue early in the feed it shows that they are coming to the end of their need for it. Reduce the amount of milk offered accordingly, until they dispense with it all together. But let your baby be the best judge of the timetable involved. There's no harm at all if a child still enjoys a few minutes at the breast or bottle weeks or even months after his contemporaries have turned to sterner stuff. Such a child still needs to suck, and should be allowed to go at his own pace. Thumb-sucking or any kind of dry sucking in a child is far more likely if he has been deprived of sufficient sucking in babyhood than if he has been allowed to 'over-indulge' (see Chapter 5 for more on thumb-sucking). **Let your child set the pace**

A relaxed attitude on your part will keep feeding difficulties at the weaning stage to a minimum. Nevertheless there are minor problems that can arise, and you need to know how to deal with them. Mostly they stem from the fact that your baby is an individual, with his own likes and dislikes. Get to know what they are. Don't be over influenced (to stress the point again) by what other parents tell you about their children. Allow your child the right to be a bit different if he chooses. Listen to what other people tell you, discuss it with them, but if it doesn't seem suitable don't act on it. Even your doctor won't pretend to have all the answers. Doctors go on learning throughout their professional lives, and he or she will be interested to hear what you have to say about your baby's reactions.

One of the most common problems to arise around this time is the child who is a slow eater. Usually she was also slow with her milk, but the habit becomes more noticeable now. You put her in her chair and give her her food, only to find that despite initial enthusiasm she loses interest after the first mouthfuls and pushes it around her plate and allows it to go cold. Often such children seem to need surprisingly little food, **The slow feeder** sometimes for two or three days together, and then make up for it with (for them) quite a blow-out. Discuss the problem with your doctor, but if your baby is gaining weight satisfactorily he or she will reassure you that there is nothing to worry about. Your child is simply a small eater, and will probably remain that way throughout childhood.

From your point of view, patience is essential. Prepare only a little food at mealtimes, giving her a second helping if she wants it rather than overfacing her from the word go. Leave the food in front of her for a decent interval, but if it's clear she's lost all interest, take it away and lift her down. Resolve from the start *never to make mealtimes into a battle of wills*. I know it's frustrating to sit and watch a child playing with her food when you've gone to the trouble of preparing it. And I know it's worrying if you think she isn't having all the nourishment she needs. But the old adage of taking a horse to water but not being able to make it drink applies equally to babies. Provided your doctor reassures you that your baby is in good health, then she is receiving sufficient nourishment whether it looks like it or not. If she goes short one day, then clearly she makes up for it the next.

Never be tempted, by the way, to put a spoonful in your baby's mouth and then pinch her nose, which produces an automatic swallowing reflex on her part. You may not be doing much physical damage, but psychologically you're giving her the idea that mealtimes aren't fun, and that food is something that has to be stuffed down against one's will. The problems you are creating for her and for yourself will come home to roost in the years ahead. Remember that far more harm is done by people over-eating than under-eating, and by bolting food down than by taking it slowly. Your child is already showing that she has a sensible attitude towards food, eating only when she feels hungry and at a speed that suits her. Resolve to stay philosophical about it, and to let her go at her own pace.

The fast feeder Some babies of course go to the other extreme. They seem to be perpetually hungry, and only have to see food to go at it like folk possessed. The temptation here is to try to slow them down, as you feel convinced that all this bolting can't be good for their insides. While they're still on the bottle it's certainly a good idea to try them with a teat with a smaller hole, but if this leads to frustration then switch back to the previous size. Don't keep pulling the teat out of your baby's mouth when she's in mid-suck. The comic look of distress that crosses her face the moment the full import of this action dawns on her is quite enough to tell us how she feels about it. Not only are you upsetting her, you may also find that she feeds even more quickly in future out of sheer anxiety. You're teaching her that she can never be sure she'll be allowed the next mouthful, so she naturally feels she must try to get it while the going is good.

No, if your baby is a fast feeder that is her nature, and there's little you can do about it. In spite of the virtues of slow eating and when she's older of chewing each mouthful before swallowing it, naturally quick eaters don't seem to have more digestive upsets than naturally slow ones. Problems arise mostly in people who are made to eat more quickly than is comfortable for them. Provided a baby is allowed to find her own preferred rhythm and stick to it, she isn't likely to go far wrong.

This is more a problem associated with the slightly older child, and I will be returning to it later. But even at the earliest stage of weaning, your child will show definite preferences for one food over another. Now that she's on solids, she's being offered a variety of different tastes and textures, and naturally she likes some more than others. Again, let her be the best judge. Just because something seems appetizing to you it doesn't automatically mean it does to her. If you try her with something she doesn't fancy, take it away and don't bother her with it until she's a little older. Her tastes in food are developing and changing rapidly at this age, and something she dislikes today may be quite acceptable a few weeks later. Similarly she may suddenly go off a food that she's enjoyed up to now. Don't force it on her. Accept that for the moment she's stopped enjoying it, but she may change again in the future.

The faddy eater

Some experts believe that these fads and fancies fit in with what a baby actually needs for good health at the time. In their view, she will take what her body requires, and refuse those things which at the moment may not be suitable. Whether this is entirely accurate or not, cases of babies in good health voluntarily starving themselves of essential foods are virtually unknown. And whether she knows best every time or not, a baby certainly knows best the great majority of the time. In any case, if your doctor thinks she is going short of something essential, this can usually be given to her in a different form, such as drops which can be added to her favourite dish. (Though be warned; babies are remarkably and infuriatingly adept at sussing out additives of this kind and scornfully rejecting the resulting concoction!)

Don't be disheartened by your child's faddiness

Some parents confess to feeling very disheartened by a child's faddiness. Each mealtime they try to give her something nice, only to find she turns up her nose in disgust. Sometimes this seems to happen every time she is faced with anything new, although she may take to it later. If you do find yourself downhearted, reason it out with yourself. Sure you only want 'what is best' for your baby. You look forward to preparing a varied and tasty diet, and your baby finishing each mouthful with a delighted gurgle. She ends up happy, and you end up with a warm feeling at what a successful parent you are.

Unfortunately life isn't quite like that. 'What is best' in reality means allowing her to experiment a bit with flavours and textures. Simply because she isn't bolting everything down doesn't mean you're not being a successful parent. Success lies in respecting your child's needs and wishes. Children who are shown this respect are much less likely to be faddy later in childhood than children who have food forced on them now and who build up bad attitudes to it. Besides, you can't win a battle of wills with a baby over food, short of disastrously and dangerously trying to hold his mouth shut after every mouthful. So if you choose to join battle you'll end up losing, which could teach her the habit of holding out against you in other things too.

Mothers who are reluctant to give up breast-feeding

One final problem, this time stemming from mother rather than baby. Some mothers don't want to give up breast-feeding. They feel it brings them closer to their child, and they enjoy the experience. The result is a temptation to keep at it, even after their babies show clear signs of losing interest. The best procedure from the mother's point of view is to drop breast-feeding as soon as it becomes clear it has fulfilled its purpose. Try not to feel too much regret. It would often be nice if we could keep our children from growing up, but

78

constant change is the basic characteristic of all life. To have a child dependent upon your body for her basic nutritional needs is a good feeling, but your child has a right to her independence, just as we had a right when we were small. Be thankful for all you have been able to give your child during the months of nursing, and enjoy watching her grow daily more confident and assured, and more aware of all the other exciting things that surround her in the world.

PHYSICAL AND PSYCHOLOGICAL DEVELOPMENT

Naturally you want to feel that your baby is making good progress in all aspects of development. This means not just physical development but mental development too. Your baby is a brand-new human being, with life in front of him, and you want some idea of how he will turn out. Is he destined to be one of the brightest children in his class? Is he going to be a scientist or an engineer one day? Or perhaps a musician or a writer? Is he going to take after his mother or his father, or one of his grandparents? In short, how successful is he going to be at coping with life, and what particular abilities and interests is he going to have?

How forward is your baby?

Understandable as these questions are they carry a certain danger: if you build too clear a picture of what you want your baby to become, you may well be disappointed if he doesn't live up to it. So don't think too much about the future. Concentrate instead upon the present, and relate to your baby as he *is* rather than as some day he will be. One of the first things you will notice is what a miracle of adaptation and ingenuity he is. Remember, a baby comes into the world knowing practically nothing about anything. You could say he is like a visitor from another planet who has no guide to the way we do things here. Except that he's far worse off than a visitor from another planet. A visitor from another planet would at least know that the strange sounds we make are some sort of language, and have a definite meaning. He would also know that there are differences between living things and inanimate things, that some experiences are likely to be

Don't have too many expectations

79

dangerous, that different objects have different qualities. Above all he would be able to *think*, even if only in his own language, and thus to reason things out, to make choices, to commit things to memory and so on.

Your baby has none of these advantages. The learning tasks that face him as he sets out on life are therefore truly daunting, and the miracle is that he tackles them with such a will and to such amazingly good effect. Of course, some babies seem to make quicker progress than others, but don't read too much into this. Development in many physical and psychological areas tends to go in spurts rather than at an even pace, and a child who seems to be falling behind a little may suddenly race ahead and pass everyone else. Whatever you may have heard to the contrary, we can't really measure such things as intelligence with much accuracy before a child is four or five years old, and a child who may seem rather slow in the early years may be more than holding his own by the time he starts school.

A lot depends on you In any case, a great deal depends upon you. The more time you spend with your baby, the more you play with him and talk to him, the more you find suitable things for him to handle and look at, the more you are likely to stimulate his rate of progress. After all, if he is going to learn about the world and how it works, then he must be given the right opportunities. No matter how good his brain, he won't learn much if he's just left to lie in his cot or his pram most of his waking life. He wants to be up and doing, to be where he can see what's going on in the house and what his family are about. He wants to be somewhere where people can notice him and start communicating with him. He wants, in other words, to join in the fun of living.

Physical development in the first six months

Height and weight Naturally you are interested to know whether your baby is making the right sort of physical progress during the first six months, and many parents like to keep a record of weight and height gain. Your clinic will be doing this in any case, but there's no reason why you shouldn't keep your own charts if you wish.

Weight and height (length) charts are given at the back of the book (Appendix 1), with separate ones for girls and boys, and you can use them to plot your baby's progress against the average for his age. The curves marked on the charts show the wide variations that exist in weight and height gain in normal children, and you've no need to worry if your child is smaller or larger than average provided he or she falls within the limits shown. The important thing is that weight and height gain follow the general direction of the curves, and do not show sudden sharp increases or decreases. Discuss any such with your doctor, who will in any case be keeping a close watch on such things.

Like growth, other aspects of physical development take place in a more or less predictable sequence during the first six months, though with individual variations. Watching for these advances is a fascinating business, and most parents greet each one with pride and delight, as if their child was the first baby ever to be this clever. Quite right too. Babies are amazingly clever, and however often you study them it's always miraculous to see how quickly they begin to master their own bodies and their environment. Each time you see your baby acquire a new skill it's also a reassurance to you that development is perfectly normal. **General physical development**

Five of the major developmental landmarks in the first six months are the ability to lift up head and chin when lying on his tummy (four weeks), to lift up the chest in the same position (eight weeks), to reach out for an object though missing it (twelve weeks) to sit with support (sixteen weeks) and to sit on a lap without support and grasp an object (twenty weeks). By six months, some babies can even sit in a high chair and grasp a dangling object, though on average these two skills are acquired a few weeks later.

Always give your baby plenty of chance for physical movement. Let him have a long kick every time his nappy is off. Lay him on his tummy and hold his toys in front of his face so that he's encouraged to lift his head and chest. Let him hold your fingers and pull himself into a sitting position. Gently stretch his arms up above his head and straighten out his legs. Let him experience the joy of physical movement, and at the same time give himself plenty of necessary exercise.

The world as your baby sees it

What your baby sees in the first few weeks

Your baby can take in far more of what goes on around her than you may think. In fact some of her abilities, as we shall see shortly, verge on the incredible. But to take more basic matters first. What does a baby see when she *first* opens her eyes on the world? At one time, it was thought the answer was very little, since it was believed she couldn't focus her eyes properly. It was also thought that she was colour-blind, so that the world looked like a fuzzy, monochrome confusion. We now know this is quite wrong. Far from being a single-minded little creature aware only of internal problems such as hunger and thirst and discomfort, a baby is from the very first mentally alert, able to take things in, and very interested in what is going on around her. From the early days of life she can focus her eyes very well on objects 20 centimetres (8 in.) or so away. Objects nearer or farther than this are blurred, but this is good since it stops her being overwhelmed by what she sees and allows her to concentrate on one thing at a time. We don't know for sure whether she can see in colour or not this early, but it is a fair guess that she can, or at least that she quickly develops this ability.

A natural liking for the human face

So when your baby looks out at the world, even in the first weeks of life, she is already seeing the sort of things you see. Of course, she has as yet no idea what these things *are*. That is something she has to learn. But even so she shows from the very beginning definite preferences for certain shapes and objects over others. She will look longer at complex than at simple things for example, and at moving objects rather than stationary ones. This is one reason why she finds your face so fascinating (if you'll forgive the description of it as a complex moving object!), and the eye-to-eye contact she establishes with you during these early days is very important in helping her social development. She is already programmed, if we can put it that way, to like the human face, and the more she sees your face and comes to associate it with pleasant things such as feeding, bathing and playing, the stronger this liking becomes. And the stronger this liking, the more interest she takes in the rest of the human race. Until about the third month of life she can't usually recognize the difference between individual faces, so if she responds to one with

82

pleasure she responds similarly to most others. She is learning that people are good to have around, and this early lesson in socialization helps her become friendly and outgoing.

Since babies quite clearly get interest and benefit from looking at things, it is both kindness and common sense to give them as much opportunity to do so as you can. It's no good her powers of vision and hearing developing rapidly if there's very little for her to see and hear. Throughout childhood, children who are denied learning opportunities when their faculties have matured to the point where they can profit from them may be held back in their later learning. So it makes good sense to give your child an interesting environment, with plenty to see and hear and play with. I mentioned this when discussing your baby's bedroom in Chapter 1, but it can't be emphasized too strongly. I suggested a brightly coloured mobile hung securely above the cot, soft toys and any other safe objects with which you can capture and hold her attention.

Importance of visual stimulation

It is important to remember now and in the years ahead that your child learns most effectively when having fun. We adults have the odd idea that learning is a serious business, involving hard work and dedication, whereas in fact learning comes most easily if we are enjoying what we are doing. For your baby, the whole idea of separating work and play, learning and enjoyment, would seem strange (and rather silly) if we were able to explain it to her. For her, it is simply a matter of something capturing her interest, with learning taking place naturally and easily as a consequence. Nor can I emphasize too strongly that you should allow *yourself* to get fun out of all this too. Let me repeat, give yourself time to be with your baby. Don't rush feeding and changing and bathing in an effort to get her back in her cot as soon as possible. Make her a top priority. Lie her down on the floor or on the bed and sit with her, talking to her, singing with her, clapping and making movements that she can copy. Play with her toys and dangle them near her so she can follow them with her eyes and reach out for them. Tickle her tummy and have a good laugh with her. Surround her with happiness and show her that the world is a good place and that other people are fun.

Learning should be fun

By about six weeks of age, your baby's depth of focus will have increased to 45 centimetres (18 in.) or so, and will go on

What your baby sees at six weeks

increasing rapidly. This means that things that are farther away are now capable of capturing his attention, and your scope for playing with him greatly increases. Dangle a bright object in front of him and he will focus on it and turn his eyes to keep it in view if you move it from side to side. He'll be relatively easily distracted though – and it isn't until three to four months that he comes to gaze steadily at an object. He will notice you much more readily when you come near, and turn his head to watch you as you move from one side of his cot to the other. Many parents say that it is at around six weeks that they felt their baby started to emerge as a real little person, and this is because he now seems to be getting the hang of things. In six weeks he has come a very long way. Such a long way, in fact, that many of the things he can now do seem miraculous if we think about them.

Learning through copying

Try, for example, putting your tongue out at your baby and see what he does. The chances are that at six weeks (or shortly after) he will return the compliment. Great fun, you may say, but surely hardly miraculous. Think again. Not only has your baby noticed the subtle change that comes over your face when you part your lips and put out your tongue, he has somehow cottoned on to the fact that he has a tongue of his own and can stick it out in reply. How does he do it? How does he know that the object inside his own mouth corresponds to the object inside yours? And how does he know how to control this object sufficiently to get it to stick out? We just don't know. And rather than make wild guesses, it's better to wonder at it and at what a lot your baby can already do.

When you're tired of poking out your tongue, try opening your mouth wide and see if he copies that too. Then try pulling faces, the more bizarre the better. The odds are he'll promptly try and produce his own version. What he's showing you, in addition to the extraordinary powers of his young mind, is that he's got a natural instinct for copying. He doesn't have to get anything out of it, like an extra big hug (though this helps). He simply enjoys copying for its own sake, and the lesson we learn from this is that the more opportunity we give him for watching and imitating others, the better are his chances of learning. A great deal of early learning comes simply through copying, and though we may think that the ability to pull faces isn't going to get him very far in life, the important thing is that right from the start you are giving him the chance to watch your behaviour and have a go at it for himself. And by showing him that you approve of his attempts, you're making him all the readier to try again in the future.

At around six weeks or so, your baby usually gives his first **Smiling** smile. This is quite a landmark. Usually it happens when you are playing with him, or when he's lying on the bed looking up at you. Suddenly, without any special reason, his face opens into a smile that looks for all the world like pure delight, and a new and very special bond is formed between you. Don't be deceived into thinking his smile is simply a copy of yours, in the way that he's been copying the other faces you've been pulling. A smile is a spontaneous reflex, set off by some deep-seated happy feeling. Some people will try and tell you that at six weeks what we take to be a smile is simply a grimace caused by wind or discomfort. Don't believe it. *You* know the difference between his smile and his grimaces. He's smiling, and he's smiling because he's happy to be with you.

Of course, we must not expect too much of him as yet. He may not distinguish your face from other people's until about the third month of life, as I said earlier. After all, everyone has two eyes, a nose and a mouth, and the differences between the way in which these are arranged are quite subtle. As a result, once he starts smiling at you he generally favours other people in the same way, provided they handle him as you do and he feels safe with them. But from six weeks or so onwards (and sometimes even as early as two weeks) your baby *begins* the process of discriminating between the various faces that he sees, and by the time he reaches three months or so he will frequently turn and smile directly at you when there are several people looking at him, as if to tell you that although these other people are all very well in their way, they're not as special as you.

The more you smile back at him, the more he's likely to smile at you. Which brings us to another important point, namely that not only is it important for your baby to copy you, it is also important *for you to copy him*. Any action of his which he sees you copying is far more likely to be repeated. It's a two-way process. The more he copies you the more you copy him the more he copies you. And he's learning new things all the time, not only gestures and actions but also the pleasant give and take that is the basis of communication and of social relationships.

Eye-hand co-ordination

By about four months, a baby's vision has developed to the stage where her depth of focus is very similar to that of the adult. That is, she can focus on objects in much the way that we do, and you will often notice her staring fixedly at something in the room, as if pondering what on earth it can be. At about this time she is even able to perceive depth, and may show a certain fear of heights if she is not securely held.

Somewhere between three and four months she will reach the stage of staring intently at an object before reaching out to it, as if debating whether it is worth the effort or not. This shows not only her powers of focus and co-ordination but also the first signs of the ability to concentrate her attention, a very necessary skill if more complex learning is to take place.

This co-ordination between the visual impression of an object and the movement of arm and hand is an important step forward. It seems to depend in part upon what we call the *asymmetric tonic reflex*, which is a bit of a mouthful but which means the inborn tendency to stretch out an arm in the direction in which the eyes are looking. Such stretching inevitably leads to a baby touching things, and once her eyes can focus on them she soon gets the idea that she can deliberately reach out for them if she wishes. The asymmetric tonic reflex is only apparent in very small babies, and usually disappears soon after six months, but by this time it is no longer needed as a baby has learnt the skills of focusing and co-ordinating, and can now make an apparently conscious decision to reach out, using both hands if necessary.

Watch how your baby learns

Try a few playful experiments from time to time and notice how quickly your baby gains control over what she is doing. Hold or prop her up so that she has full use of her hands, then dangle something 20 centimetres (8 in.) or so away from her face. Does she reach out for it? What happens if you move it slowly from side to side? What happens if you dangle two objects instead of one? Does she seem to prefer one to the other? When she's reaching out to one or both of them, what happens if you give her a third? And so on. Watch her, too, when she is lying in her cot and is not aware that you are

86

near. Notice the things that attract her attention and the way she reaches for them and plays with them. Often you'll see her lying on her side gazing at her hands, as if fascinated by their complexity, and making graceful little gestures such as turning them this way and that by moving the wrists. It all adds up to the impression that your baby likes the look of her hands and indeed of most of the things around her. The world strikes her as a pretty interesting and exciting place, and this helps prompt her to be up and doing as soon as she can, so that she can find out more about it.

The world as your baby hears it

Just as your baby's powers of vision advance rapidly, so do his powers of hearing. So important is our eyesight to us that we often forget how much we rely upon hearing as well. A great deal of our learning throughout life is done through hearing and, sadly, to be born deaf (as we shall see when we discuss language on pages 154 and 247–255) is in many ways as great a problem for a baby as to be born blind.

Something of the importance that nature attaches to hearing is shown by the fact that a baby can hear long before he is born, usually between the eight and twelfth week of pregnancy. At this stage he moves in response to sounds, and lies in the womb listening to his mother's heartbeats, the sound of her voice (conducted by vibrations through the body), the swish of the blood through the placenta, and even the gurglings and rumblings of her digestive system. Don't worry that your over-active tummy may have given him a noisy and disturbed pregnancy. A baby actually seems to *like* these body sounds, because when recordings of them are played to him after birth they help to soothe him.

Coming from the familiar, muffled sounds inside the womb to the sharp sounds of the outside world is quite a shock for a baby at birth. Hence the emphasis in natural childbirth upon keeping noise levels down. In fact throughout the early months of life a baby has a dislike of loud noises and shows a characteristic response towards them known as *stilling* – that is, momentarily stopping his movements and opening his eyes wide, as if apprehensive of what may happen next. This reflex

Dislike of loud noises

87

action may correspond to that of animals who freeze when danger is near, but we're not sure. When you see your baby stilling, it shows you that his hearing is normal, at least for sounds at this level. It also tells you that he may have received something of a fright.

Since loud sudden noises cause a baby distress, often leading to crying as well as stilling, it is best to avoid them whenever possible in these early months. Babies are very adaptable, and if they have to live in a household where the noise levels approach those of a brass band in full cry they seem somehow to make the best of it. And there are wide variations from one baby to another in the degree to which loud noises are upsetting. But for the most part a baby's immature nervous system is happiest in an environment where sounds are kept to a conversational level, and in particular where *sudden* shouts and bangs and the like are avoided. (Though it must be admitted he's not averse to a little shouting and banging of his own at times, with a fine disregard for the nervous susceptibilities of others.)

Communicative synchrony We're not sure whether a baby can hear the full range of sounds registered by the rest of us when she is very small. Nevertheless from the early days of life she is sensitive to marked variations in volume and pitch. Watch her while you are talking to her very softly, or making low noises of one kind or another. You will see that she moves her limbs, often apparently in time to the sounds. This shows she can hear them, and also gives us evidence of what we call *communicative synchrony*. This daunting term refers to the small movements (nods, raising of the eyebrows, smiles, etc.) that we all make, often unconsciously, when listening to each other. These movements transmit no precise message, but indicate a social relationship between us, and play a vital part in easing and deepening this relationship (imagine how difficult it would be to hold a conversation with someone who simply stared at you without moving a facial muscle the whole time). There is no evidence of communicative synchrony in animals, and since it appears at such an early age in humans it seems to show we have an inborn desire to communicate with each other. So whether you remember the term communicative synchrony or not, watch your baby's movements when you talk to her and see them as a kind of 'talking back'. Her own way, if you like, of keeping up her end of the conversation.

Just as she can turn her eyes to keep an object in view at six weeks, so she will turn them towards the source of a sound. By four months, she will have reached the stage of turning her whole head, and will also show signs of distinguishing one sound from another. She'll have done this from the early weeks with your voice, but now she can recognize other domestic sounds. For example, watch her when you tap the spoon against her feeding bowl at mealtimes, or when you swish the water before putting her into her bath. By six months, she'll even be responding to relatively quiet sounds, particularly if they're high-pitched (like a small bell, for example).

Recognizing sounds

As far as pitch is concerned, most babies seem to have a preference for musical, higher notes over gruff, lower ones. If both parents speak to their baby in their normal tones, she tends to pay more attention to her mother than to her father, particularly if the latter is blessed with a rich bass. But of course most of us don't talk to babies in our normal voices. We tend to effect a rather artificial falsetto, which however much it may embarrass the bystander seems to be based upon an instinctive awareness of the sounds a baby prefers. Anyway, she seems to respond well to our theatrical efforts, and this further strengthens the growing social relationship we have with her.

Perhaps because of pitch, perhaps because it is often she who spends most time with her, the first voice a baby recognizes tends to be that of her mother. This recognition is obvious at about two months, but even as early as two weeks many babies tend to look in the direction of their mother's voice more frequently than towards other voices. Obviously the more often she hears her mother (or father) talk, the quicker she gets to know how they sound, so don't neglect holding long 'conversations' with her just because she doesn't understand the words. Get into the habit of chatting to her whenever you're near, as if you know she's taking every-thing in.

Wherever possible, take her around the house with you so that she can watch what you're doing. Talk to her and keep up a running commentary. Explain to her what you're doing when you dress and change and bath her, ask her if she's enjoying her feed, tell her the names of her toys and who is coming to visit and where you're taking her that afternoon. Chat to her when you're out together, describing the things you can see and the prices in the shops and whether it looks like rain. She'll enjoy the sound of your voice and come to associate it with you. Play her music and watch how sometimes she'll move her limbs as if in time. Repeat the sounds she makes and copy her movements so that she'll be stimulated into repeating them. Work as a partnership, you and your baby, exploring life together and getting no end of enjoyment out of it. In no time at all you'll be telling whoever cares to listen what a good little companion she is, for all the world as if she was able to talk back to you.

Copying sounds
And don't forget the rule that your baby's little tricks of behaviour will become more frequent if you copy them. So when she makes sounds, repeat them after her, and she'll reward you by becoming more and more vocal. Soon you'll be holding enchanting little dialogues of pure sound together, each of you mimicking the other and thoroughly enjoying it. A baby particularly enjoys the *combination of sound and sight*, so keep eye contact with her while all this goes on, letting her see the expression on your face and how your eyes and lips move. Play games too, like bringing your face near her and making a soft 'boo' sound each time. Her chortles and chuckles will tell you how much she enjoys it (would we could always get such pleasure from innocent things), and naturally it also helps her identify your face with the sound of your voice. This brings the relationship between you even closer, while your free use of sounds teaches her that the voice is a good way of relating to people. It also helps lay the foundations for the development of her language skills, as we shall see in due course (see Chapter 5).

Using his hands and mouth

The rapid strides a baby makes in the use of his eyes and ears during this first six months of life are matched by the progress he makes in using his hands – and in the co-ordination between hands and eyes which we have already talked about.

You have an advantage here because although you can often only guess at how well he sees or hears things you can actually watch what he does with his hands.

Usually you will find that the strong gripping reflex with which your baby is born (see Chapter 2) is starting to disappear at about three months. Before it does, he will grip thin objects tightly, but will have no success with fat ones because he can't open his hand wide enough. From three months or so onwards, however, he will still grip an object if you put it into his hand, but will only hold it briefly before opening his fingers and dropping it as if by accident.

Obviously advances of this kind depend to a great extent upon maturation, that is upon the natural development of a baby's muscular and nervous systems as he grows older. But you can encourage this development by giving him plenty of practice in looking at and grasping objects (though don't persist with any activity once he becomes bored with it). As with feeding and other activities, never see the time spent playing with him as a chore. It only becomes a chore if you're constantly thinking of all the other things you 'ought' to be doing around the house instead of being with him. If your mind is on something else, you deprive yourself of the pleasure you should get from his company. You also miss the subtle developments that are taking place in him daily. Whatever else has to be neglected, always give yourself sufficient opportunity to be with him, to relax with him, and to offer him your full attention.

Using his mouth

As your baby gains more and more control over his hands, so he adds another trick to his repertoire, namely putting anything and everything in his mouth. Watch him when he picks up an object, and see how he brings it in front of his face, looks at it carefully, then makes an apparently weighty decision and conveys it purposefully mouthwards. Parents naturally become concerned about this. They visualize the germs their baby must be swallowing, and wonder whether all this licking and dribbling may be a prelude to thumb-sucking. The short answer is take sensible precautions, then don't worry. All objects a baby plays with must be kept clean, and it is vital to avoid small objects on which he might choke or toys with eyes or fur that could come loose in his mouth. But he is bound to pick up some germs from every-thing he touches, however clean, and this helps him gradually build up resistance to some of the more common infections.

There is no connection between thumb-sucking (see Chapter 5) and the kind of behaviour we're talking about. Putting things in the mouth (usually called 'mouthing') at this early age is a natural reaction. All babies do it, and it provides them with learning experiences and pleasure. A baby's mouth is more sensitive than his hands, so by exploring an object with his lips and tongue he finds out more about it than just with fingers. In any case, he still uses his fingers as a single unit rather than separately, curling them round an object instead of using them to manipulate and investigate it as would an adult. What a baby can't investigate with his fingers he does with his mouth. And if you keep stopping him you will end up not only with a never-ending task but by interfering with his opportunities for learning. Worse, you may teach him that it's wrong to be curious about things and want to explore them. He's too young to realize that you're not against exploration, simply against exploration with the mouth. You can hardly expect him to understand that he must simply postpone this exploration until his fingers are well enough developed to do the job.

ISSUES AND PROBLEMS IN THE FIRST SIX MONTHS

No parent, however successful, avoids problems in child-rearing. What makes a parent succesful is the way these problems are tackled. One parent finds problems take him or her by surprise. He has no idea why they occur, and even less idea what to do about them. Each time problems crop up they throw him off-course, and he spends much of his time just wishing he lived in an ideal world where these things didn't happen. Another parent accepts that problems are simply a part of everyday life. Where possible he anticipates them and works out ways of avoiding them. When they do occur he thinks about what caused them and takes steps to put things right. Generally speaking, he's in control of his life rather than being controlled by it.

A successful parent realizes that many of the problems of child-rearing are primarily problems of adjustment. He knows his baby isn't a piece of putty, to be moulded to whatever shape suits his convenience, but a separate individual little human being, with her own ways and her own likes and dislikes. Part of his job, therefore, is to get to know her as a person, to organize the home in a way which takes her fully into account, to find how she can best learn the necessary lessons of early life, and to find out how he can foster and develop the necessary parenting skills in himself.

Dealing with crying

As a successful parent, therefore, you'll be aware that what suits one baby won't necessarily suit another. It's no good expecting your baby to stick to a particular routine just because most babies do. Her routine is governed by her own internal mechanisms, and though she will learn to fit in with you where she can, quite often she just doesn't find this possible. You'll also be well aware that your baby can't tell you in words when something doesn't suit her or when she's in difficulties of one kind or another. The only way she has of letting you know that things aren't as they should be is by crying and generally raising her voice. She doesn't do it just to make life difficult for you. In fact, she's no idea she *is* making life difficult. Many is the parent who could swear his baby waits for the precise moment he sinks into a chair before summoning him imperiously upstairs to attend to her needs, but the truth is your baby is a guileless little soul who has no idea of the strain she is imposing upon your feet (to say nothing of your nerves!). So bear with her. Time, after all, is on your side. However interminable a restless, difficult phase in a baby may seem when you are experiencing it, most of these phases are over very quickly, and soon fade from the memory to be replaced by happier things.

Why do babies cry?
I've just said babies cry when they want something. But sometimes it is hard to know just *what* it is they want. You're

93

sure your baby isn't ill. You know she isn't hungry, so what is it she's trying to tell us by crying? Does it mean that she has an awkward side to her nature and is going to grow up into a problem child? Does it mean you're doing something wrong in the care you're giving her? What exactly *is* the cause of it all, and what can be done to put it right?

When grown-ups cry, it's usually because things have become pretty bad, so we tend to think of crying as a sign that strong feelings are involved. But for a baby, crying is often more of a substitute for language. That's why no matter how much din she's been kicking up, the moment we go to her she has a knack of stopping in mid-breath and breaking out into a happy grin, as if to let us know that whoever was responsible for all that noise it certainly wasn't *her*! So when she starts crying, she's usually not all that upset. It's simply her way of calling out that it's dinnertime or that her nappy won't hold any more or that a favourite toy is out of reach or that she just doesn't feel too good about life. She only becomes *really* upset if her crying brings no response. After all, she's helpless to do anything about her problem herself, and if nobody comes to see to it for her she gets more and more agitated, more and more worried at your non-appearance, more and more cross, hot and uncomfortable.

Some parents find very early on that they can tell what it is their baby wants just by listening to the tone of her cries. They can distinguish the lusty yelling that tells of hunger from the irritable crying that tells of boredom or physical discomfort, and these are different again from the sharp, fretful cries that accompany pain or sickness. If your baby isn't as clear-cut as this about things, work carefully through the list of possible causes for her displeasure. A bit of detective work helps too, as does a measure of calmness and common sense. Let's look at the various possibilities in turn.

Is he hungry or thirsty? Thirst is an important cause of discomfort and potential danger in small babies. If the weather is hot, if your baby has started solids and has cut down on the amount he takes from the breast or the bottle, or if he is suffering from a stomach upset with loose bowel movements or vomiting, then he may need a long drink urgently. Always keep some boiled water in a sealed container in the fridge for this purpose, and take the chill off it by placing the container briefly in a saucepan or kettle of hot water. If he appears anxious for it, but starts fussing again after a few sips, then try him with milk as he may be hungry instead.

Frequently a baby cries after a feed, and you may think he is still hungry. He sounds as if he is in great distress, cramming his fists into his mouth as if desperately seeking food. You may hurry to get him another bottle, or offer him the breast again, only to find he sucks eagerly for a moment then pushes out teat or nipple and returns to his restless crying. For a mother who is breast-feeding, and who has no idea how much milk is still left in store, this can be a worrying performance, and may add to her fears that she has insufficient to satisfy her child. However, the truth of the matter is that crying after a feed is very common, often more common than crying before. It usually has to do with the fact that your baby just isn't yet used to the sensation of a full stomach. While in the womb, he took his nourishment in a steady flow through the umbilical cord, and had no experience of what a stomach feels like. Thus both hunger and fullness are new to him, and both may seem a bit distressing. To complicate matters, he may not even be able to distinguish between the two. When you offer him more food, he thinks this is the answer to his problems, and sucks away for a moment before discovering he's only making things worse. **Crying after feeds**

Remember that when we talk about fullness I don't mean your baby has been gorging himself. As I said earlier, babies are much more sensible than grown-ups, and stop feeding as soon as they have taken enough for their actual needs. Obesity in an otherwise healthy baby is far more likely to be caused by over-richness in cow's milk than by greedy feeding. Breast-fed babies very rarely put on too much weight, because their tipple is suited exactly to their needs.

One standard practice is to interpret this post-feed crying as a sign of wind, but this can be something of a fallacy. To hear some parents talk, you'd imagine their babies were born martyrs to this mysterious complaint called wind. At the first signs of crying the hapless infant is hoisted on to the parental shoulder like a small sack of potatoes, and his back vigorously rubbed and pummelled in an attempt to give him some relief. All too often the only result is a smart regurgitation of lunch or breakfast. In fact, babies suffer from wind less often than **Has he got wind?**

we think, though as we have seen they can take exception to a general feeling of fullness – sometimes made worse by a bubble of air in the stomach. By all means lift your baby to your shoulder and *very gently* rub his back if you think he is in discomfort, but as often as not what calms him is the pleasant feeling of having his back rubbed rather than the actual release of wind. Irrespective of any tangible results, this upright position also often brings relief, because his body is not so cramped. After all, a heavy meal in a doubled-up position wouldn't do us much good either. But he may insist that you get upright too, and walk him around the room, allowing the gentle movement and the changes of scenery to distract him from his internal misery. Should he still be a little uncomfortable when you put him down to sleep, lie him on his stomach so that he can bring up anything needful without the risk of choking.

Has she a pain of some kind? Other things can cause discomfort besides a feeling of fullness of course. Your baby may have a cold, which makes her feel stuffy and uncomfortable, and which can also upset her stomach. Or she may be teething (pages 111–12). Or she may have an infection of some kind, perhaps in one of her ears. Usually pains of this kind lead to sharp, sudden crying, and if there's an ear infection a baby often cries if the flap covering the opening to the ear is gently touched (page 110). If you think there is pain of some kind, or if your baby seems to have a temperature or is generally off-colour, contact your doctor at once. The crying that tells you your baby is in pain is a warning signal. Don't neglect it.

Does her nappy need changing? Does your baby's nappy need changing? Or is it perhaps too tight? Babies put up with an awful lot from nappies and plastic pants, but there comes a time when even the most hardened little warriors have had enough, and are driven to telling us so. Watch the lusty, happy way your baby kicks when you get her out of the wretched things if you want to know how much she prefers being free of them. Let her have a good kick every time you change her.

Is she too hot or cold? I'm often surprised at how insensitive otherwise loving parents are when it comes to dressing their babies for the heat or cold. I've spoken to parents who have the idea babies are insensitive to near-zero temperatures, and that their little blue hands or feet are no indication of how they are feeling, and

I've seen parents in light, crisp cotton on summer days letting their baby sweat it out in her bulky nappy and thick cardigan. No wonder babies cry. Remember that your baby is far more vulnerable to extremes of temperature than you are, and just as likely to feel uncomfortable and cross when she isn't properly equipped to deal with them. Some parents still have the misguided notion they must put their baby outside in her pram for a period each day whatever the weather if she is to grow up healthy. Certainly fresh air is excellent, but in the winter months she's better off in a warm, airy room rather than outside. No matter how well you cover her up, she'll soon have her top half exposed to the elements. Put the pram outside in warmer weather by all means, but make sure it's in the shade (the sun moves round very quickly when you're busy in the house), and beware of cats and dogs and bees and wasps.

After the first few days of life, a baby tends to settle into a **Is she tired?** routine of about fourteen hours sleep in every twenty-four hours, reducing to about twelve hours by the time she's a year old. With all this sleep it's hard to imagine that she feels tired during waking hours. In any case, if she's tired why doesn't she have the good sense to go to sleep, instead of lying in her cot and fussing? Nevertheless, odd as it seems, tiredness is a major cause of crying in small babies. Usually your baby wants to go to sleep, but something stops her. Maybe she's hot or her room is too bright, or a loud noise startled her just when she was drifting off, or she has a pain of some kind or she's feeling tense and unsettled because you've put her down too abruptly. Whatever the reason, she can't manage to drift off as she'd like, and the more she fusses and frets the less likely sleep becomes. Some babies, in any case, find it much harder to get to sleep than others, and often develop into children and adults who need rather less sleep than the rest of us. They're lucky of course, since the less sleep we need the more time we have to do other things, but they can make life very awkward for their parents.

If you think your baby often cries through over-tiredness, or if you suspect she just finds it difficult to get to sleep, buy a sling and carry her around with you in the house. Many parents enjoy having their baby close to them in this way, and the gentle movement and the warmth and comfort of your body soon lull her off. In some countries, mothers have traditionally wrapped their babies in a shawl, and carried them around most of the day, while in other cultures the baby is strapped to her mother's back. Either way, both mother and baby enjoy the warm contact, and the evidence suggests that children raised in this way tend to have few of the restless problems of early life.

Is he bored? People who themselves get fed up with their own company if they have nothing to do for five minutes nevertheless express great surprise at the notion that their small baby might be bored. They seem to have the idea that he's far too young for anything so sophisticated and world-weary. But the truth is small babies thrive on stimulation. They're programmed to learn about the world as quickly as possible, and spending hour after hour gazing at a blank wall or ceiling naturally leaves them frustrated and restless. They're also programmed to be sociable. Your baby wants to be with his family. He wants to be where he can see what's going on and where he can hear your voice and generally keep an eye on how you run things. As a general rule, don't leave your baby on his own when he's awake. As soon as he starts calling for company, bring him downstairs and put him where he can be with you.

Restless crying Many babies go in for what we call restless (or irritable) crying. For no apparent reason they start fretting, often at certain set times of the day or night, and quickly work themselves into a distressed state which nothing short of nursing them and walking them interminably up and down the room seems to ease. There seems to be an inborn factor at work here, so restless crying is usually no reflection upon your skills as a parent. It's simply that some children are extra-sensitive to physical and nervous sensations. When your baby cries for no obvious reason it's because he doesn't *feel* right. He hasn't yet adapted to the business of his own independent existence outside the warm comfort of the womb. The feel of his clothes against his skin, the sensations in his tummy and in his limbs, the sounds and the bright lights around him, all have a disturbing effect. Perhaps above all the stillness of everything, after the gentle movement he experienced during his nine months in the womb. His immature nervous system just can't cope. He needs the comfort of your body against his, the movement as you rock him or walk him up and down, the soothing sound of your voice.

Some psychologists and doctors think that restless crying is far more likely to develop in children who haven't experienced the loving care of natural childbirth methods. If the child is sensitive by nature, a brisk clinical introduction into the outside world is likely to leave him far more nervy during these early weeks and months than a gentle, supportive birth. Be this as it may, restless crying tends to be most noticeable from about the sixth to the twelfth weeks of life, and is often associated with so-called three-month colic, which is discussed shortly.

Of all forms of crying, that during the night is most calculated to wear down parents' patience. The shock of being woken up consistently in the small hours of the morning, when your own bodily metabolism is at a low ebb, together with the cumulative effects of tiredness, can place a heavy strain on the nervous system. Add to this the unhappy knack some babies have of waking you then crying intermittently, pausing just long enough each time to allow you to slide back to the brink of sleep before wrenching you into wakefulness again, and small wonder that parents feel themselves driven to distraction. **Persistent night-time crying**

Night-time crying of this kind, mercifully, doesn't last for ever. Like all other phases, in the end it stops of its own accord as your baby becomes more mature and better able to conduct her own affairs. We all hear stories of people whose babies have them up every night until the age of three or four, but this is rare, and usually indicates that something is going wrong during the day to make the child anxious and fretful at night. She may be receiving too little daytime attention. Or the parent who usually looks after her may have started work again, leaving her with a child-minder. Or there may have been other major changes in her daily routine. Or perhaps her parents, through tiredness, have been scolding her unduly during the day. Whatever the reason, a vicious circle can result, with the baby's night-time crying making the parents irritable during the day which makes them snap at their baby which makes their baby cry at night. The only solution is to recognize what's happening, and to realize that if you have other problems in your life it's no good expecting your baby to understand these and be extra co-operative. At the moment, she's unable to appreciate anyone's feelings other than her own.

How to deal with night-time crying

But thankfully most night-time crying is simply a phase, and doesn't indicate there's anything really amiss. So what should you do while this phase lasts? By all means let her cry for a few minutes to see if she drops off again of her own accord, but if the crying persists or sounds distressed you'll need to go to her. Remind yourself that she has no more wish to be awake than you have, and that she's no idea you were asleep. This helps put you in the right frame of mind. Speak to her soothingly, but don't let her see you and don't put on an extra light. If this doesn't do the trick, lift her out and walk around with her, still in semi-darkness. A rocking chair is very useful, since if you sit and rock while you're holding her the movement soothes you both. When you put her back in her cot, stay with her for a few minutes; she may half wake during these minutes, and the soothing sound of your voice will reassure her and often settle her without your having to lift her out again. Obviously both parents should take their turns at getting up in the night, so that neither becomes too tired or cross.

Some experts recommend that after a while you should make a stand and allow your baby to cry it out. After a few nights of this, the theory goes, she will learn that you're not going to respond, and she'll get used to the idea that she just has to go back to sleep on her own. Quite apart from the fact that ignoring her in this way requires nerves of steel (and a detached house miles from anywhere), it often doesn't work. Your baby wakes, finds herself confused and disorientated, and cries for help. If no one comes, she gets more confused and disorientated, and feels anxious and afraid. Such feelings won't help her sleep, either tonight or on subsequent nights. No wonder that night-time crying of this kind is thought to lead to fears of the dark as the child grows older.

Practical things that may help

Nevertheless, there *are* things you can do to help avoid night-time crying. First – it often helps if your baby is allowed a longer period of wakefulness after her last feed. Don't rush to put her to bed. Often waking in the night indicates that she isn't as tired as she might be. Or you can cut down a little on her daytime sleep periods. Maybe she's a baby who needs less sleep than the average. Second, you can put a small light in her room. Your baby is used to waking up when it's light, and can't understand about night-time (especially if she's a spring or summer baby). Don't worry that she may 'get used' to having a light in her room, and refuse to sleep in the dark. No matter if she does, but it's pretty unlikely. Extreme fears of the dark usually indicate some emotional insecurity (see pages 282–5), and the majority of children are quite happy to dispense with their baby light as they grow older. Third, you can bring her cot into your bedroom. This makes it much easier for you to soothe her, or to stretch out a hand and rock her cot. But if this makes no difference move the cot out again. There's no reason why both parents should have to be disturbed by her crying every night. If she still cries, try going to her and making soothing noises but refusing to lift her out. Assuming there's nothing really wrong, this sometimes reconciles her to the fact that once she's in her cot that's where she belongs.

One thing I don't recommend is bringing your baby into your own bed. Some experts claim this works wonders, but there are obvious physical dangers, even if slight. And she has to learn one day to go into her own bed, so you're only postponing the problem.

Next to night-time crying, the major problem of restlessness in babies is so-called *three-month colic*. First appearing at around six weeks, and persisting until three months or so, three-month colic is a daily period of irritable crying during which a baby appears to suffer from severe pains. He cries heartbreakingly, draws up his knees, and sometimes stuffs his fists into his mouth as if to obtain relief. Usually this period occurs at the same time every day, often lasting roughly from 8 to 10 p.m. You give your baby his 6 p.m. feed, change him, play with him, then put him to bed. He appears tired, drops quickly to sleep, but the moment you get downstairs he starts his agonized crying. You try leaving him for a few minutes but with each breath he becomes more desperate and there is nothing for it but to go and pick him up. Once this is done he quietens, but resolutely resists any attempt to put him back down again, and the whole evening is spent nursing him and walking him to and fro. Small wonder that some parents get the idea that he simply resents the fact that they want to have the evening to themselves!

Three-month colic

Three-month colic affects about 40 per cent of children to varying degrees, and we're not sure of the reason. In spite of the name, there's no guarantee that it *is* colic, or anything to do with digestion. True some babies bring up wind, but this doesn't ease matters much, and the wind may in any case have been swallowed after the crying started rather than before. A more likely explanation is that the baby's nervous system is particularly sensitive at this time of the day. I have already mentioned that restless crying seems to be associated with a baby's sensitivity to the novel sensations of his independent existence, and probably for this one period daily he feels these sensations extra keenly.

How to deal with three-month colic There's no simple solution to three-month colic. Try your baby with a bottle to check whether he's hungry or thirsty, but often he'll take a few sucks greedily and then give up. He thought the bottle was the answer to his problems, but he quickly discovers it doesn't help. Mainly what he wants is to be nursed, and rocked gently while you do it. Since rocking him or walking him up and down the room are tiring, a rocking chair is an invaluable ally. Sit in it and keep up a gentle movement, and often he'll fall into a fitful sleep. Brush up on your repertoire of songs too, since he seems to appreciate your singing voice (he'll learn to be more discriminating in the years to come). Don't rush to put him in his cot as soon as he's quiet, because the chances are he'll rouse again at once. Accept the fact that for six weeks or so you're going to devote two hours at this time of day to pacifying him. However much they drag at the time, the weeks soon pass. And suddenly one evening there will only be brief token fretful sounds from upstairs. Your baby will have gone to sleep after his 6 p.m. feed, and will slumber peacefully through until 10 p.m.. If this doesn't happen, the crying may now be 'attention only' crying (see page 104).

Is there a danger of spoiling?

I've mentioned spoiling several times in this chapter, but it's an issue that won't go away. Many parents have the idea that the way they respond to their baby in the early months of life determines very largely the kind of person she grows up to be. So if they pick her up every time she cries, she'll become a person who expects her own way all the time. They see the whole thing as a battle of wills. Their baby wants to be boss, and if they give in to her she'll take over the house and no one else will have a life of their own.

I'm not saying that parents who think this way don't love their child or want what's best for her. It's just that they're genuinely puzzled how to give their baby what she wants without turning her into a selfish little monster who doesn't care a fig for the rights of others. As proof of their anxieties, they point out that their baby will cry and cry until the moment she's picked up. Then she stops. If there was anything wrong with her apart from wanting to be picked up, then she'd keep on crying. Worse still, although she's happy enough when being carried around, she cries again the instant she feels herself being lowered back into her cot. Surely this proves she's well on the way to becoming the spoilt person no one is going to like?

Parental fears of this kind are understandable but groundless. As I said earlier, far more babies are harmed by too little attention than by too much. If you are going to make a mistake, be glad to err on the side of a little over-indulgence. If your baby cries, there's something the matter, and she relies upon you to put it right. Contrary to what you may think, she doesn't actually get much fun out of crying. You've only to look at her puffy eyes and running nose and pitiful expression after she's been at it for any length of time to know that. The fact that she stops crying when you pick her up simply shows she needed to be picked up.

Babies cry for a reason

I've said already that in the first weeks of life, crying is your baby's only way of showing you something is wrong. Maybe she's hungry, or too hot or cold or uncomfortable, or maybe she has a pain of some kind. Or maybe she's just finding it a little difficult to adapt to the business of being a separate human being. After all, a mother has to readapt physically to being independent of her baby, and it's not surprising that a baby should find it hard to adapt as well. In many ways it's worse for the baby, since she has no real idea of what is going on, and simply registers the confused sensations coming from her own body.

Looked at another way, her crying is also a compliment to you. She needs you, and often no one else will quite do. She is already used to your special way with her, and feels unhappy and even perhaps alarmed when handled by someone she recognizes isn't you. Feel pleased that your relationship with her is already the most important one in her life, and that it is through you she finds comfort and happiness.

Learning to interpret crying Around the sixth week of your baby's life you'll come to know, by the time of day, the nature of the crying, the state of her health and so on just how urgent her demands really are. Some babies have a habit of fretting a little before they drop off to sleep, probably because being tired makes them uncomfortable and they haven't yet learnt the answer is simply to relax and go to sleep. Such babies are often particularly interested in their environment, and never really enjoy being put down for a nap. Routine fussing of this kind needn't concern you, and after token protests your baby will usually drop off. The same applies when your baby wakes up in the night and cries for a few minutes until she goes back to sleep. Here the problem is simply that she doesn't want to be awake, and unless she cries persistently enough to wake herself properly she's best left to go back to sleep undisturbed. The simple rule is to listen carefully to her crying, and if she's getting worked up go to her; otherwise wait until she quietens down and then just peep to make sure everything is in order. If she doesn't settle, making soothing noises at her or rocking her cot gently is often enough to send her back to sleep, particularly if she doesn't catch sight of you and decide that while you're there you might as well earn your keep and lift her out.

'Attention only' crying If it becomes obvious after a while that your baby has fallen into the habit of crying each time she wants a little attention then you can if you wish be slightly firmer with her. There is usually a pattern about this 'attention only' crying. Your baby has just had her feed, so she can't be hungry, nor does she seem to be in discomfort. Her nappy is clean and dry, she is neither too hot nor too cold. She isn't teething yet and she isn't ill, and you know from experience that the moment you pick her up she'll stop crying and beam all over her damp little face. If you can resist the thought of this smile – and remember it's *not* a smile of triumph; she's genuinely pleased to see you – then you can leave her just that minute or two longer each time before you go and pick her up. The chances are she'll become bored and stop crying, or else drop off to sleep mid-wail.

Building up in this way, you can leave her for a full ten minutes (minutes that will go much slower for you than for her), but do creep up and look at her during this time, without letting her see you, just to make sure everything is all right. At the end of ten minnutes, if she's still at it with undiminished energy then go and pick her up. You can leave her a little longer if need be when she's older, but a small baby should never be left to bemoan her fate for longer than ten minutes at the very most. Unless she's grown tired of it all by this time, the chances are she will have become frightened at her own distress and at your non-appearance, and will have filled her nappy into the bargain. And in all cases where your baby has been crying and suddenly stops, look in on her secretly to make sure there's no cause for alarm. The chances of her choking or doing something disastrous are small, but they are chances you can't afford to take.

However, with most small babies firmness of this kind is rarely necessary. Of course your baby has to learn that she can't monopolize your attention. But it's easier for her to learn this when she's a little older, and can understand something of what goes on in the rest of the house during the day. At the moment, she's no idea you have a life of your own apart from her. As far as she's concerned, you cease to exist when you go out of her sight, and re-materialize miraculously when you come back into it again. It's also easier for her to learn she can't monopolize you when she's old enough to acquire language, and you can explain to her in simple words that you have other things to do and will see to her just as soon as you can.

The risk of spoiling comes later

So as a general rule, always give a small baby the benefit of the doubt, and go to her when it sounds like she needs you. The story that a small baby needs to cry 'in order to exercise her lungs' has scant truth in it, and was probably invented by distraught parents to make them feel better at leaving their baby to get on with it. It's a sad lesson for a baby to learn that crying when she wants your company leads only to loneliness and unhappiness. Far better she should learn it leads to the comforting sound of footsteps and gentle hands lifting her out and holding her against a nice warm body. Don't forget as

105

well that while she's lying on her own in her cot she has no opportunity for the stimulation and learning that come from being with others, and which is so important for her developing mind.

On balance, therefore, you don't have to worry about spoiling a very small baby with too much attention. You're not storing up trouble for yourself by picking her up when she cries. Risks of spoiling come later, when the child is old enough to understand more about the world yet is still given her own way in everything. That's how she fails to learn that other people have feelings and rights in addition to her own. As for early attention-seeking crying, the child will grow out of it as she becomes able to amuse herself more and to express her needs to you in other ways.

Dealing with your own feelings

The theme of this book is that having children is fun. However, we have to face the fact that a crying baby can be a strain on the nerves of even the most placid parent, while the more emotional ones can be driven to near distraction. Certainly there is something particularly insistent about the crying of a young baby. It seems after a time to catch us on the raw, and scientists consider that nature has programmed us to find it almost impossible to ignore. Parents often confess that after sleepless nights and dealing with endless fretting during the day they can all too easily understand the sad reasons why some parents abuse their offspring. Baby battering is a subject we'd all much rather avoid, but parents are driven near the limits sometimes by incessant crying, and we need to know how to deal with these powerful feelings in ourselves.

Try not to express anger to a baby It's much easier to advise patience than to put patience into practice, but no useful end is ever served by expressing anger to a baby. Your anger only makes him frightened and upset, and likely to cry all the longer and harder. Many parents say they could cope if they only knew what their baby was crying *for*. They've considered all the possibilities we've discussed in this chapter. They know he isn't ill, they know he isn't hungry, they know he isn't cold or wet or uncomfortable, and yet he still goes on crying. And they've tried all the remedies. They've rocked him in his cradle, they've walked him up and down the room, they've sung to him, but to no avail. If he

106

nods off, they know that however gently they lay him in his cot he'll wake up the moment his head touches the pillow and start raising the roof again. He seems to be keeping himself awake by a deliberate effort, and driven to distraction they yell at him why hasn't he got the *sense* to just shut up and let himself get to sleep (and everyone else too).

But I can't repeat too often that allowing yourself to express anger to your baby will only make things worse for everyone. If you feel your nerves have reached breaking point, lay your baby very carefully down in his cot, and then go out of the room and indulge yourself in a tantrum of your own. Pummel a cushion, beat the carpet, roll around the floor. Many parents say it is only by reverting to childish behaviour themselves that they can release their pent-up frustrations. Jump up and down if you like and pretend you are being very naughty and defiant with your own parents. Don't worry about feeling foolish. Some parents find it helpful to keep shouting 'I won't I won't I WON'T' as if to their own parents. It may sound funny but it works. It's as if the crying of our own baby has brought out the cross little child in ourselves, and we need to get him or her out of our system.

Release your own frustrations

There's no substitute for this physical release. Your frustration at your baby's crying gears you up for physical action, and since you mustn't take this out on him you need to use up the energy harmlessly elsewhere. If you bottle it up, you reach screaming pitch, which is no help to anyone.

After a few minutes of this delicious by-play you're usually calmer and able to face your baby again. Often the fact that you're now more relaxed with him does the trick, and he drops into a sound sleep. But if he doesn't, you're able to settle in for another shift in a better frame of mind. And when your baby does finally quieten, don't forget to congratulate yourself. Surprisingly few parents ever give themselves credit for being patient. As soon as their baby is sound asleep they try to forget the whole incident, or start blaming themselves for not having been more patient than they were. Instead, spend a moment or two thinking well of yourself. Certainly you could have done better, but then so could we all. The thing is you handled your own impatience, and this is grounds for satisfaction. It isn't a matter of conceit, simply of feeling pleased with yourself for a job well done. This short act of

Congratulate yourself for coping

self-congratulation helps build your confidence. Instead of dreading the next time your baby has a restless period, you know you'll be able to cope. Many parents find that this simple act of thinking well of themselves after a trying time with their baby also makes them feel much better about him too. Instead of blaming him for being difficult, they see the whole episode as something they and their baby tackled and came through together. And as an added bonus, it often helps them see the funny side of things, and have a good laugh over it all.

Accept your angry feelings This is essential first aid for your nerves, but there are longer-term things you can do as well. A vital step is to accept that both your baby's crying and your own reactions to it are perfectly natural. He's crying because that is how he tells you he's unhappy, and you're exasperated because whatever you do you can't pacify him. Neither of you is being unreasonable. You may be surprised at how aggravating he is and surprised at the strength of your own aggravation, but these things shouldn't overwhelm you. Babies have cried since time immemorial (we all did it ourselves once upon a time) and parents have been reacting much as you're reacting now. But somehow or other parents have coped, and so will you. Babies grow up, and this restless phase will soon be behind you both.

So accept your angry feelings. See them as perfectly natural. Work them off somewhere well away from your baby, and have a good laugh about them. They're human nature. They don't mean you've stopped loving your baby, or that you're no good as a parent. Your patience isn't inexhaustible, and instead of wishing it was (or worse still pretending it is) find practical strategies for venting your frustration harmlessly, and then return to your baby in a better frame of mind.

Practical things you can do There are other things you can do to help your baby and yourself. I've mentioned buying a baby-sling and carrying him around with you. If the fretful crying takes place during the day, wrap him up warmly, put him in his pram and take him for a walk. If you have a car, strap his carry-cot on the back seat and take him for a ride. Getting out of the house and giving you both some fresh air and a change of scenery will help him and you. The stimulation of new sights and sounds will also stimulate his learning abilities. If you have a tape-recorder, use that too. Make a tape of your own voice and play it to him, or experiment until you find a particular style of music he enjoys. Most small babies respond well to classical music, particularly something soothing like Bach or Mozart. Some commercially available tapes made especially for babies, with rhythmic sounds like a heartbeat, can also be very effective, or you can try recording domestic sounds of your own until you find a combination he likes.

If he's an active baby, put him in a play-pen where he can move about in safety, or use a baby-bouncer, but do set up these devices where he can see you, and let him out of them as soon as he's had enough. If you habitually leave him in them too long, he'll associate them with boredom, and won't want to go in them at all. Incidentally, this sort of hostility can also set in against his cot if you leave him in it unreasonably long. Many children who fret as soon as you put them down do so because they're sick and tired of the very sight of the thing.

At one time, another suggestion would have been to offer your child a dummy or pacifier, but such things are largely frowned on these days. This is partly on grounds of hygiene (they spend a great deal of their time on the floor) and partly because no baby looks his best with an unlovely piece of rubber and plastic clamped stolidly between his lips. Some experts also think they encourage thumb-sucking later, and certainly if your child needs a dummy to suck this usually indicates he isn't getting enough sucking at feed times. Ask yourself whether you've been rushing his feeds. Let him spend more time over them in future, and the chances are he won't want a dummy even if you offer him one.

What about a dummy?

When to call the doctor
Since crying can often be a sign that there's something wrong, this is a convenient point to discuss when you should seek medical advice. Should you consult the doctor every time your baby cries more than usual? Or when she seems to be off her food? Or when she's snuffly and generally out of sorts? Minor symptoms of this kind often cause the most heart-searching. We know to call the doctor at the first sign of anything serious, but we're unsure what to do about these lesser problems. We're anxious about our baby, but we don't want to bother the doctor unnecessarily.

Don't agonize too much. If you're worried, consult the

Better safe than sorry

doctor. If it's your first baby, you'll probably end up contacting him or her more often than you really need, but no matter. No doctor should mind being asked to look at a sick baby. He or she knows that small babies can be down one minute and up the next, and won't be in the least surprised when the baby you reported as quite poorly is bright as a button and beaming cheerfully at everyone by the time medical opinion arrives. Even if you feel a little foolish and fancy your doctor is rather impatient with you, think how much less patient he or she would have been had you delayed seeking help over something that turned out to be really serious.

An old and well-tried rule is that you should call your doctor whenever your baby looks different from usual (e.g. pallid or flushed) or behaves differently (listless, difficult to rouse, cries excessively, and so on). Loss of appetite, unusual bowel movements, raised temperature (the doctor should always be called if it's over 101°F – 38.5°C), indications of pain, excessive vomiting, rashes and difficulties in breathing should all be reported immediately. You should also contact your doctor if your baby has taken a nasty knock of any kind, particularly to the head. Your own common sense will tell you if the knock is a nasty one, but an additional guideline is that if your baby isn't back to normal within ten minutes of receiving the knock then your doctor needs to know. This applies also to burns and scalds; in fact *any* burn or scald is potentially serious, particularly if it raises a blister, and the wisest course is to tell your doctor anyway. You don't want to keep running to him or her, but better safe than sorry is the watchword with any childhood ailment.

Ear infections

This is particularly true of infections of the mucous passages (eyes, ears, mouth, genitals). Such infections are usually accompanied by a discharge, but with the ear this often doesn't develop until things have become quite serious. So treat any signs of pain in or around ears as a matter requiring prompt medical attention. Often ear troubles develop in conjunction with a cold. Your baby has been snuffly for a day or two, and suddenly you notice he gives a sharp distressed cry if you touch one of his ears or if he lies on that side when you put him in his cot. The remedy is an immediate visit to the doctor's surgery, taking care to protect your baby from the elements on

110

the way. Usually your doctor will prescribe antibiotics, which clear up the problem often as if by magic.

Particular difficulties arise if your baby is taken ill during the night. You're naturally reluctant to wake your doctor, and you wonder whether it will be all right to wait until morning. The best way of dealing with this kind of situation is prevention. It's quite rare for a child to become seriously ill in the night if he hasn't been showing symptoms during the day. So whenever your baby is unwell, ask yourself what's going to happen if he becomes worse at night. If there's a real possibility he may, take him along to the evening surgery to be on the safe side. And remember that if you do have to disturb your doctor during the night he or she is bound to ask whether your baby was poorly in the day, and if so why didn't you come along to the surgery. **If your baby is ill in the night**

Of course, it *can* happen that a baby who has been fit and well all day falls sick at night, and the dilemma of whether to call your dcoctor or not has to be faced. The rule is that should your baby turn out to be seriously ill no one is going to thank you for your thoughtfulness in *not* getting your doctor out of bed. Remember that until your doctor has been informed, the full responsibility for your baby's welfare rests with you. Should you phone him or her, there's a good chance they'll be able to make a diagnosis there and then, and will tell you not to worry and to bring your baby along to the surgery in the morning. Your mind will be put at rest, and if your doctor thinks you phoned unnecessarily, then when you come into the surgery guidance can be given you on what to do next time.

All this assumes you have a telephone, a great boon when there are small children in the house. If you aren't on the phone and don't have a friendly neighbour who is, make a habit of checking regularly that the nearest public telephone is working, and of reporting the matter if it isn't. An ounce of foresight is worth any amount of lamentations later.

Mother Nature is wonderful, but parents often question why she didn't arrange things better when it comes to cutting teeth. Many babies are martyrs to the whole business, struggling manfully for weeks with snuffles and with the fiery patches on their cheeks which bear vivid testimony to what's happening. There's a danger though that we put lots of **Is he teething?**

problems down to teething which in fact have nothing to do with it. This could mean we neglect things that ought by rights to be reported to the doctor.

If your baby does seem snuffly and in distress you can suspect teething as a cause even as early as three months. Occasionally, a baby is *born* with a tooth through the gums. But usually the first teeth make their appearance at around six months, and since these are almost invariably the middle two lower incisors, they cause little trouble. It is only when the double teeth start coming through that the real problems start (see Appendix 5 for more on teething).

Older brothers' and sisters' reactions

Most of what's been said in the book so far applies whether your baby is your first or subsequent child. But birth order does make a difference in a number of ways. Many parents admit to being more relaxed with second babies than with their first, worrying less over small problems and often making fewer demands for perfect behaviour. And generally, every-one seems to make that little bit less fuss when the new arrival isn't your first, which helps both you and him take things in your stride.

The main difference, however, is that with your second baby you have the feelings of an older child to take into account. Often these feelings can be very intense. So far, the older child has had you all to herself, but now she suddenly finds she has to share you with the newcomer; indeed the newcomer often seems to take precedence over her when it comes to claiming your attention. Naturally enough she feels jealous about this, and often seems to develop a positive hatred for her sibling, so much so that you're afraid to leave them alone in the room together. Don't worry that this shows an evil streak in your older child, or that the two children won't be friends as they grow older. Your first child is simply trying to protect her own interests, and her animosity towards the small baby is of an impersonal kind. She simply wants the baby out of the way sometimes so that she can have you all to herself again.

Jealousy is far worse in a two- or three-year-old child than in one of five or six. The five- or six-year-old is mature enough **The child of** to understand fully what's going on, and to realize that the **five or six** small baby is a human being like herself who needs care and protection. She's also mature enough to be more independent of you, and to feel happier about sharing you with someone else. Provided you draw her fully into the experience of looking after the small baby, and assure her how helpful she is to you and how you couldn't manage without her, she'll take a real pride in her new brother or sister, and will show herself competent and protective towards him. Don't forget, though, that your five-year-old is still only a five-year-old, with all the needs of a five-year-old. Particularly if she's just started school (Chapter 7) she may be going through a difficult time of her own, and in her more grown-up way she's still going to need plenty of your time and attention.

With a two- or three-year-old child things are more prob- **The child of** lematic, and you must accept from the start that unless the **two or three** older child is of an unusually placid (perhaps I ought to say angelic!) disposition, she's going to suffer the pangs of jealousy from time to time. So how do you cope with her? Let's emphasize again that her feelings are normal enough, and punishing her is neither fair nor helpful. Explain to her that the baby takes up a lot of your time at the moment because he's small and helpless and can't do anything for himself. So he has to be looked after, just as she herself was looked after before she grew big and strong. Sometimes your older child will try to hit the baby, half playfully half in anger, when you're nursing him, and when the older child feels most left out of things. Shield the baby from her attack, and don't take the matter too seriously. If need be, stand up with the baby so that he's out of reach, then take your older child's hand and walk over to the window or to somewhere else where you can distract her attention. Handled in this low-key fashion, the physical attack phase soon passes (though never leave the two children alone together until it does), and without the older child feeling you're taking sides against her.

You'll have prepared your older child for the coming of the **Jealous feelings** baby by drawing her into the excitement and the planning, **are perfectly** but however carefully you do this the older child won't really **normal** understand what's involved until you bring your baby home. Even then, when she's tired of the baby she will want you to put him away in a cupboard or drawer like a toy until she wants to play with him again. When she realizes the baby is here for good, she will have very mixed feelings, and on balance would rather you sent him back where he came from. If you accept her feelings, and show sympathy and understanding towards her, giving her extra attention whenever you can, these feelings won't last. Small children are very adaptable, and your older child will soon accept that the baby is here to stay, and will forget the days when she was the only child in the house. If you get angry with her over her feelings, however, she'll end up confused and upset, resenting the baby and at the same time worried about the strong jealousy inside her which you tell her is naughty. By showing your anger, you'll only prolong the period of adjustment, making your older child genuinely unhappy about herself, and stacking the odds against your children becoming good friends in the years ahead.

How to help your child In addition to accepting your older child's feelings, you can help her by giving her set jobs to do in looking after the baby. She can't be as much help as a five-year-old, but she can be in charge of the talcum powder or responsible for fetching the clean nappies or for seeing that the toys are ready in the bath. Praise her, and tell her that you just don't know what you would do without her. Equally important, make sure there are occasions during the day when your time is *hers*. The baby isn't allowed priority on these occasions except in emergencies. Naturally these occasions have to be when both parents are in the house so there is somebody to look after the baby if need be. Your older child's bathtime and bedtime are two good examples, but there will also be television programmes which you watch together, and story-time and other similar shared experiences. If your baby cries during these times, let your older child hear you call to him that daddy/mummy/grandma/auntie or whoever will be along to see to him as you're busy with his sister. This will help the latter understand she counts too, and that just as she has to play second fiddle to the baby sometimes, so it works the other way round.

Properly handled, the worst evidence of jealousy will normally disappear by the time your baby has been home three months or so. There will still be subsequent sporadic outbursts, and even when your children are considerably older they will still have their moments, but after these early months your first child will have got used to the idea that the baby is a permanent part of the family. Provided the first child is reassured that she has your love and understanding just as she's always had, she'll soon take to the idea that like most of her friends she has a brother or sister of her own, and has every reason to feel proud of him.

Be warned though that for a time your first child may revert to babyish behaviour herself. Although she's toilet trained she may suddenly start wetting again. Or she may begin waking in the night or indulging in some irritable (if rather theatrical) crying. Be patient with her. She's part conscious of what's going on, part unconscious. What she's doing is trying to gain for herself the kind of attention the baby is receiving. Because she has a natural instinct for copying, she's also experimenting out of pure interest with babyish behaviour. Can she get you to attend to her at night if she cries? Can she wet her pants? Naturally you're unlikely to regard all this as a welcome addition to the day's frivolity, particularly as you have your hands full with the baby. But if you engage in a battle of wills with her over it, you only risk prolonging the phase. She can't understand why the baby receives loving care and attention for behaviour of this kind, while all she receives is cross words. So she'll tend to persist, at least until the baby is a little older and starts to learn more grown-up ways.

Reverting to babyish behaviour

Remember that a two- or three-year-old child still has only limited control over her own behaviour, and even less control over her moods and feelings. She genuinely wants to please you, but she can't understand the big changes that have come into her life with the arrival of the baby, and all her instincts are to try to recapture for herself the full care and attention she received from you when she was an only child. If she could put things into words, she'd explain to you that she's confused and unhappy about things. Confused because there seems to be a double standard for the baby and for herself, and unhappy because she wants you all to herself again.

When your older child reverts to babyish behaviour, adopt a kindly but matter-of-fact attitude. Tell her that now she's a big girl she doesn't need to wet her pants or cry for things instead of asking for them properly. She's far too clever for that. And be sure you make a fuss of her for *being* so clever.

How to treat such behaviour

115

Let her hear you telling the baby when nappy-changing that soon he will grow big and strong like your first child and won't need to wear a nappy. And what a help that will be for you.

Leave your first child in no doubt that you and she are on the same side, big people who know how to do things and who have to care for the baby until he's a big person too. When you're washing the nappies, say (with a deep sigh for dramatic effect if you like) how lucky you are that your first child is now such a big girl she doesn't need nappies any more. Let her hear you say things like this to neighbours and friends too, so that she'll realize she has every reason for being proud of the way she is, and doesn't need to try to copy the baby in order to get her full share of care and attention.

If you're a parent who finds small babies easier to relate to than toddlers, look particularly carefully at your own feelings and your own behaviour at this time. Plenty of people feel the way you do. They love the dependency and vulnerability of the small baby and feel a toddler, with her increasing independence, is already growing away from them. But a toddler needs love and patience as much as a baby. Be very careful not to let her lose out in favour of the baby. Be fair about it. Don't resent your toddler because she always seems to be demanding things just when you're having fun with the baby. See this as a sign that she wants to have fun with you too. She was your baby only a few months ago remember? Don't start telling her she's being 'selfish' and not giving the baby a chance of the same attention she had when she was small. You've two children to care for now, and they can both have enough of your time if you arrange things properly.

Older children   If you've other children in the family, older still, the chances are they'll be past the age when jealousy is a major problem. Get them to help with the baby as much as possible, but try to make this fun rather than a chore. Do this by allowing them to take the initiative where possible in offering help. When the baby first arrives, he'll be a novelty for everyone, and the older children will be only too ready to help. Let them do so at this crucial stage. Let them have a say as far as you can on how the baby is managed, how his room is arranged, what should be bought for him, when he's to have his bath, which toys he

116

should have. If you're bottle-feeding, let them, under supervision, take turns at giving the feeds. Let them help push the
pram when you're out. If they get into the habit of helping
early on, and of seeing the baby as *their* baby and not just
yours, then they'll be much more inclined to help later on,
when some of the novelty has worn off.

But remember older children have their rights too. If they're
at school, they'll want your attention when they come home.
They may have things to tell you. They may be troubled over
something. They may have news of some success they want
to share with you. Set aside time for all this. If the older
children feel that the baby has taken over the house, they'll
start feeling jealous too, and certainly won't want to play their
part in caring for him. Resist the temptation, also, to use them
as unpaid servants, running all your errands for you and going
upstairs to 'save my legs'. At the end of the school day they'll
be tired and will have had enough of being told what to do.
They'll want the chance to relax when they get home, just as
an adult does, and to have time to play and enjoy themselves.
So don't make immediate demands on them. You'll be tired
too, but give your children a chance to unwind a little before
you give them tasks to do. You'll be amply repaid in terms of
their willingness to pull their weight, both with the baby and
with other household jobs.

THE IMPORTANCE OF FATHERS

Most of the things said about baby care so far in this book
apply as much to fathers as to mothers. But this is a good
place to stress the father's role more fully. Gone are the days,
thankfully, when child-rearing was looked upon as women's
work, and when the man concentrated upon the bread-
winning and left the domestic jobs to the woman. Nevertheless, some fathers are still reluctant to involve themselves fully
with their small children, and confess to being awkward and
ill at ease with babies. As I said earlier (page 67) this is a social
rather than a biological reaction. Men have allowed themselves
to believe that small babies aren't for them. There's nothing in
nature to support this view, and the paternal instinct in

117

humans is a very strong one so long as cultural factors aren't allowed to interfere with it.

Taking his share in looking after the baby

In some households, where the woman is the bread-winner, the father may have more to do with the daily care of his baby than the mother, and if he does the job properly the baby will flourish happily under this arrangement. But where it's the mother who is chiefly responsible, it's important both for her and for the baby that the father is fully drawn into the experience of baby care. Particularly if the baby wakes regularly in the night, the early months of his life can be a very tiring experience for the mother; she may have had to give up her career to care for her baby, and she can feel very isolated and trapped if she's left to cope single-handed for much of the time. Some men insist that when they come home from work they're too tired to start caring for a baby, but the woman has been working hard all day too. By taking the baby off her hands the father is not only getting to know his own child, he's also showing his love and concern for his wife. This reassures her, and convinces her of the continuing warmth of his relationship with her. Having a baby is a major milestone in a woman's life, and she needs the knowledge that her partner still cares for her as much as ever.

Happy then the woman who receives that bit of extra attention from her partner at this time. In practical terms, this isn't demanding a great deal from a man. It simply means that when he comes home in the evening he shows interest in mother and baby's doings and in the excitements and minor crises that have been taking place. If the baby is sleeping, he goes up to peep at him, and later on he brings him down and if he's bottle-fed gives him his feed. He takes his turn with the nursing when his baby is suffering from irritable crying and if he's waking at night. These things can become a matter of routine, and the father will have the reward of a warm greeting from his baby, who will quickly come to associate him with these tasks and will look forward to the time spent together.

The responsibilities of fatherhood

I'm often surprised that some fathers get out of the house most evenings when they have a small baby. They come in for their meal, then disappear to the pub leaving wife and baby on their own until closing time. Often the argument is that this was their life-style in the days before the baby arrived, and they see no reason why they should change now. To change would be to admit that responsibilities are closing in on them, and that their carefree days are gone. The answer to this is that although 'closing in' is the wrong term, they do have responsibilities now that they didn't once have. With fatherhood comes an extra commitment to one's partner as well as a commitment to the baby itself. But with it also comes the chance to see that a close, loving family relationship is one of the greatest experiences life has to offer.

As mentioned in the Introduction, men also need reassurance when there's a small baby around. A man can be jealous as he watches so much care and attention lavished on the child, so the wife must make sure he receives a proper welcome when he comes home, and is given the chance to talk about the things that may have gone wrong with *his* day. She also has to be careful not to shut the father out of the baby's life. Sometimes a mother claims that the father is so awkward with the baby she doesn't like leaving them together. On other occasions, a mother will confess that she feels so possessive about her baby she resents anyone apart fom herself, even the father, having care of him. Feelings like this must be faced. They stem from a mother's natural concern for the well-being of her baby, but if they're allowed to dominate, then she isn't only being unfair to the father but also to her baby. A baby needs to make social contacts if he's to grow up confident and out-going, and an over-possessive mother will cramp his development. Possessiveness also stores up trouble for the years ahead, with a mother finding it harder and harder to accept that her children are growing up and have a right to increased independence.

In these early months, what should happen is the creation of a family unit, with both parents involved with the baby and sensitive towards each other's feelings and needs. Both parents need the reassurance of each other's love, and the reassurance of each other's love for the baby. They need to feel they both have a say in how the family operates and in how the baby is cared for, and to see themselves as equal partners in what happens in the home.

Including the father in the new family unit

OTHER PEOPLE

One of the pleasures of a small baby is to see her admired by other people, whether family or friends. Most people love a baby, and most parents are happy to share their own joy with others. But you have to be careful. Babies differ temperamentally in the readiness with which they take to strangers. Some beam delightedly at whoever picks them up, while others put on a great show of distaste towards anyone other than their parents. And what a source of embarrassment for all concerned that can be. The rule is, don't force your baby. Study her reactions. If she clearly feels uneasy with other people, don't rush to hand her to them. In any case, any adult who really cares for children knows that you should never impose youself on them when they're small. The secret is to hover in the background until their natural curiosity leads them to show interest in you and even make the first approaches. This is hard for grandparents coming from a distance and seeing the new baby for the first time, but from about six weeks on she's alert enough to know that you're strangers, and she just doesn't understand that as grandparents you've got a very special bond with her. This is something she learns as time goes by.

Babies should meet other people
But even with children who are wary of strangers, it's important they meet with other people. A child is far more likely to be nervous of others as she grows older if she's been deliberately shielded from them. Encourage your family and friends to call on you, but explain that your baby is unsure of herself with strangers as yet, and must be given time before they can successfully be allowed to hold her. And though you shouldn't rush to reclaim her from them the moment she starts fretting, don't leave her with them until she becomes distressed. One or two unhappy experiences with other people in the early months can make a child extra nervous for some time to come.

Other people's advice
Another area for caution is taking advice from others. Remember I said earlier, when talking about feeding, that although advice can be helpful, she is your baby and your responsibility. What worked for other babies won't necessarily work for yours. The best help is given by those people who've

successfully raised children of their own, and who tell you when asked how they went about things, without giving you the impression there's something wrong with you or your baby if you don't go about things in the same way. Such people are usually good listeners too. They'll hear you out when you want to tell them about your problems, instead of using them as an excuse to jump in and tell you about *their* children and *their* problems and how wonderful they were at coping with them.

If you have friends and relatives of the helpful sort nearby, they can be a great source of moral support and practical help. Moral support is important, because your worries and anxieties as a parent will be much less if you can talk them over with someone who understands. And practical help when it comes to baby-sitting or picking up something for you from the shops is equally valuable. But don't rely *too* much on others. The family unit has to be able to run itself. And don't let other people make you feel inadequate. Sometimes parents, particularly mothers, get the impression that other people find them wanting in all aspects of baby care. If your child is restless for example, or not feeding quite as she should, you're given the clear message that you're the one at fault.

Remember that it's much easier to criticize than to do the job yourself. Lots of folk feel they could handle other people's children better than the parents. But no one knows your child as you do, and no one has the emotional bond with her that you have. Don't waste time arguing with those who try to tell you what to do. Let them know politely but firmly whether you want their advice or not, and leave it at that. Grandparents can often be particularly hard to handle, since to your own parents you're still something of a child yourself. Understandably enough they still want to run your life for you, and they have to learn that it won't work. You're grateful for their help and interest and support, but in the final analysis your baby is your responsibility, and the important decisions on how to rear her must be taken by you.

The ultimate responsibility is yours

IF YOU'RE A SINGLE PARENT

The assistance of other people is particularly welcome if you're a single parent. I have more to say about single parents later on, when the older child is discussed (Chapter 7), but single-parent families are common these days, and they do raise special issues. Some single-parent families are created through divorce or the death of one of the marriage partners, but many come about when children are born outside marriage, intentionally or unintentionally. In the United Kingdom some 17 per cent of children are born this way.

The most obvious problem faced by the single parent in the early months of a baby's life is simply one of hard work. With no partner to share the responsibility, the single parent will find a restless child a particular strain. The absence of someone to talk to in the evenings if the single parent lives alone is another problem, and the feelings of isolation and loneliness can become a major worry. There may also be financial insecurities, and an uneasiness as to whether the baby is going to miss a second parent. But many single parents manage very successfully, and there is a recognizable pattern to their lives which we need to summarize briefly.

The successful single parent The first characteristic of the successful single parent is that they fully accept their position. This is easier if a mother has made a clear decision to become a single parent, and has become pregnant knowing exactly what is involved. But whatever the background, things will go better if she wastes no time regretting her lot, and simply gets on with bringing up her child. The second characteristic is that she organizes her life well. She makes the right domestic arrangements, so that while her baby receives every care he doesn't dominate her for twenty-four hours each day. She has her routine worked out, leaving time to herself and time to relax free of domestic chores. Whatever her source of income, she also has her finances under control, so that she knows what she can and cannot afford.

Importance of getting out Her next characteristic is that she makes contacts outside the home. There may be a single-parent support group which she can join, or a women's group. She may be a member of a local church, or of a local drama or music or sports society.

Whatever her contacts, they allow her to keep up a social life outside the home, and ensure her interests remain broad. She also has arrangements for baby-sitting. Since she can't sit for other people on a reciprocal basis as in a baby-sitting group, finding someone to be with her baby in the evenings so that she can get out can be something of a problem. Being a successful single parent depends in no small measure on finding ways to solve it.

Next she doesn't have too demanding a job outside the home. No single parent can easily cope with a baby and a job that involves long hours or carries major responsibilities. Unless she can afford to pay for full-time help in the house, this means that a single parent is going to find it very hard to pursue an ambitious career. At least until her child starts school, a single parent must make him her first priority. If she doesn't, her child is at a major disadvantage, and problems will be created now and in the years ahead.

A job that is not too demanding

Finally, though the effects of this aren't apparent until later on, a successful single parent avoids becoming too possessive about her child. Particularly if she has had to sacrifice a great deal for him, there is a strong temptation for her to become very bound up in her child, and to expect as he matures that he'll show her extra gratitude for all she's done for him. She invests everything she has in her child, and expects a return in the way of a special kind of love and sympathy in the future. If this return is not forthcoming, she feels bitter and betrayed. But in truth a child can't be expected to show gratitude for a state of affairs in which he has no say. He didn't choose to be raised in a single-parent family, and in fact may compare his circumstances unfavourably with those of friends from more conventional homes. Unless she wishes to store up resentment in her child and possibly heartbreak in herself, the single parent must accept from the start that her child will one day want his independence like any other child, and will thank her for the quality of her mothering rather than for the fact that she brought him up single-handed.

Don't become too possessive

Since most single parents are women, the above remarks have been directed at mothers. But they apply equally to single-parent fathers, who can have additional problems through lack of domestic skills and possibly through role confusion. This last owes much to the attitude of other men.

Single-parent fathers

123

The sight, for whatever reason, of one of their number deviating from traditional male behaviour can bring out the worst in many of them, showing how easily such behaviour makes them feel insecure about their own maleness. Not surprisingly, if your male friends feel looking after children isn't man's work, you as a single-parent father may feel it isn't either. Unless you can re-educate them, the answer is to find more understanding friends, perhaps through one of the male support groups springing up in some areas. If a local group doesn't exist, take the initiative and start one. A notice in the local paper or public library or through a local church or community association is one good way. But as with all single parents, don't let your need for help tempt you to leave your children with anyone who doesn't have your complete confidence.

COT DEATH

There can be no more devastating experience for a parent than to put a healthy baby to bed at night and to find in the morning that he's died in his sleep. Mercifully, cot deaths are extremely rare – only one in every 500 babies. Ninety per cent of these tragic deaths happen in children up to eight months, but they can occur up to age two. However, due to the publicity cot deaths have received in recent times, many parents confess to having it linger as a haunting fear in their minds.

In spite of extensive research, we're still not clear as to the cause (or causes, as there may be more than one) of cot deaths. The child may have an undetected virus infection (sometimes cot deaths seem to be associated with a mild attack of the snuffles) or, so the various theories go, the death may be associated with such diverse and contradictory factors as sudden drops in room temperature, too much crying during the day (which may interfere with the breathing reflex), an allergy, or one of a number of other possibilities. Or it may be simply that the breathing reflex stops during deep sleep, and doesn't re-start. We many of us hold our breath for quite long periods when asleep (the correct term for this is sleep *apnea*), and start breathing again when the body begins to register shortage of oxygen. With cot deaths, it's possible that this shortage doesn't register, and that what started as a normal episode of breath-holding becomes tragically fatal.

Cot deaths appear to run in families, which is why parents who have experienced the trauma of one death can be supplied with an apparatus that monitors their baby's breathing throughout the night, and wakes them at once if for any reason it stops. Going to the baby and picking him up immediately starts the reflex working again. If you're worried about the possibility of cot deaths, even though there's no obvious reason, talk it over with your doctor. Your fear may be irrational, but it's a real enough fear to *you*, and you've a right to have it put to rest. It may even be possible for you to have a breath-monitoring apparatus for your child during the brief period in his life during which he could be said to be at risk.

Precautions you can take

Other sensible precautions are to make sure the room does not drop in temperature during the night, that any chest or bronchial infections are reported to your doctor, that you check up on whether there has been any incidence of cot death amongst members of the families of either parent, that your baby is in no danger of suffocation from his bedclothes, and that you are near enough to him during the night to detect any sounds of distress. It's also worth keeping in mind that recent research shows there *may* be a link between smoking during pregnancy and an increased risk of cot death. If this is the case it's yet another reason for not smoking when pregnant. And an argument against having smokers in the house, especially during the at risk period, since even inhaling cigarette smoke could increase the risk.

IMMUNIZATION

The immunization programme begins at age three months. Your doctor and health visitor will advise you, but the main details of the programme are set out in Appendix 4.

[4]

The Second Six Months

IN THE SECOND SIX MONTHS of life, your baby will become much more of a person in her own right, with ways and mannerisms of her own. During this period, parents often show renewed interest in where such things come from. They can see that their baby is different from the baby next door. If she's their second or subsequent child, they can also see that she differs from her older brothers and sisters, just as they in turn differed from each other. By six months – and often indeed as early as six weeks – parents can see signs of a distinct personality in their baby.

Temperament

As we saw in Chapter 2, a child inherits the *temperament*, the raw material, from which this personality is formed. A child may have a temperament that looks similar to that of one or other of her parents, or she may have one that is more like that of her grandparents. But whoever in the family she happens to be like, the mechanisms of inheritance ensure that there will be a quality of uniqueness about her temperament. No one anywhere will have been born with a temperament exactly like hers.

'Temperament' means that she will have a tendency towards certain kinds of behaviour. She may, for example, be a placid baby, who doesn't easily get upset by things. Or she may be extra noisy or rather quiet. Or she may smile or chuckle a lot. She may be adaptable, friendly and regular in her habits, or she may be rather nervy and anxious, or rather easily put out by any changes in her routine or by the presence of strangers. These qualities, apparent in the early weeks of life, will tend to persist throughout childhood and even into adult life, though the way in which she learns to cope with her temperament, to develop certain aspects of it, to learn how to control others, to be happy or unhappy about herself, will depend very largely on how you as parents treat her.

Sensitivity towards a child's basic temperament from the early weeks onwards helps us as parents to decide more easily how to relate to our children, how to accept them for what they are and how to aid them in the business of coming to terms with their own dispositions. It also helps us not to judge our children too much. A child doesn't choose her temperament. *And many of the qualities that might make a child a little hard to handle in early life are the very qualities that we admire in adults.* A child may for example be a sensitive child who feels things very deeply, and who experiences the extremes of disappointment and of joy. She may also be determined, even wilful at times, causing us our fair share of traumas. But sensitivity, determination and a strong will are qualities we all welcome in adults. They help a person to understand the problems of others, and to stand up for what she knows to be right.

Work with your child's temperament

So don't make the mistake of imagining you must 'overcome' a child's will. Instead, learn how to work with it, how to channel it in desirable directions. Certainly your child must realize she can't always have her own way, and that the ability to understand and respect the rights of others is essential. But she will learn this more readily through skilled and careful parental guidance than through constant battles of wills, with the understanding and respect having always to come from her.

If you find a certain fractiousness and negativity of mood in your baby, the most important thing is for you to accept this. If she's easily upset at changes in routine, keep these changes to a sensible minimum. If she doesn't take readily to strangers, don't force them on her. If she has a low pain threshold and feels physical discomforts more readily than the next child, sympathize with her rather than accusing her of fussing over nothing. You don't have to be constantly dancing attendance on her. She has to learn gradually to put up with minor inconveniences. But don't make a habit of leaving her until she gets really upset about things. She may feel as badly about them in ten minutes as a more placid child would in twenty,

The fractious, negative baby

and it just isn't fair to leave her to put up with them for the same length of time. She'll grow up into as successful a human being as the more placid child, but she does need that bit more help and patience from you, both now and in the years to come.

The child with a cheerful, contented disposition
If, on the other hand, your child has a cheerful, contented disposition, your job as a parent is rather more straightforward. Your child will take her feeds at regular times, adapt happily to changes in routine, shrug off minor discomforts, and generally show a welcoming and sunny attitude to life. The only word of warning here is that you shouldn't presume too much on her good nature. Because she doesn't fuss greatly over things, there can be a temptation to leave her too much to her own devices, particularly if you're busy with older children or have other demands on your time. Resist this temptation. She isn't going to learn much if left on her own for long periods. And if she doesn't have plenty of your company she may be forced into becoming a rather self-sufficient person, instead of discovering that other people have a part to play in her life as well.

The withdrawn, solemn child
The same danger may also occur with a child who is rather withdrawn and solemn by temperament. Since she doesn't react as immediately or as dramatically as some other children, there may be a tendency to leave her also to her own devices for much of the time. Since she may need a generous minimum of stimulation if she's to become less withdrawn, long spells on her own are a big mistake. Both now and later in childhood, though, she should never be forced into things simply for the sake of it, she needs to be given as many opportunities to have her interests aroused as possible, and needs to be helped discover what an exciting place the world actually is. Help her widen her horizons, but do so by prompting her to *want* to do so rather than by pushing her into new experiences whether she likes them or not. And don't become impatient or discouraged if she doesn't seem to respond all that readily, or seems to have a rather short attention span. Let her take to things in her own time.

Temperament is the raw material of personality
With all children, let's repeat again that temperament is only the *raw material* of personality. The child's life experiences determine how that raw material will develop. If a child has a quick temper, for example, that's a temperamental thing, and

130

is likely to be with her throughout life. Punishing her for her temper isn't going to do much good. It won't help her get rid of it, and at best will only prompt her to bottle it up, suffering inner frustration and occasionally losing all control of herself quite unexpectedly. As a parent, you need to help her accept the fact of her temper, to get to know the circumstances in which she is likely to lose it and why, and to help her find ways of facing these circumstances without letting them bother her so much. Similarly the child who is by temperament easily upset and hurt by others needs help in understanding the reasons for her feelings, and in developing a more philosophical and realistic attitude towards life events. These again are matters to which I shall be returning when we discuss the older child, since it is in older children that these temperamental factors may cause most problems, but from the early weeks of your child's life onwards you'll make things much easier both for her and for yourself if you get to know her temperament in as much detail as possible. Don't waste time wishing she was temperamentally different from the way she is. If she seems to feel things deeply, or to become easily upset or cross, don't bother yourself with questions as to who she gets it from or why she isn't a straightforward character like the baby next door. Accept that's the way she is, and that your job is to help her develop the person she is into a successful and happy human being. Don't give yourself the idea it's in some way 'better' to be like the baby next door. The richness of human nature lies in its diversity. And as I've already stressed, the qualities that may make a baby or child rather difficult may be the very things that turn her into an effective and likeable adult. Whether they do or not depends very much upon the handling she receives in her childhood years.

The growth of love and trust

Now that your child is becoming a more definite person, you'll notice how his relationship with you is becoming closer all the time. In the first weeks and months of life he depended totally on you, and began to distinguish you from the other people in his life, but he didn't really look upon you as much more than the provider of his physical needs. All this is now changing, and many a mother says that in the second six months of his life her baby 'starts to come to know *me*'. Instead of loving his parents in a rather vague, indiscriminate way, his feelings for them become much more personal. He begins to see them as very special people in his life, and begins to study them as individuals.

Bonding between parents and child

If this process is to go ahead satisfactorily, much depends upon what has happened during the first six months. The whole of the first year, from birth onwards, is a period of *bonding* between parents and child. The child will bond with whoever carries out the parental tasks and whoever shows him the love and care of a good parent. Thus an adopted child will bond just as satisfactorily with adopted parents as a child with natural parents. Bonding works the other way too, and even parents who are rather unmoved by their baby when he first arrives soon feel the growth of love as bonding gets under way. Successful bonding depends upon close links between parents and child. It happens best where parents spend a lot of time with their child, pick him up and cuddle him frequently, play with him and talk to him, satisfy his physical and emotional needs, indeed do all those things that we've talked about so far as constituting good parenting. If bonding fails to take place during the first year – if the child is left in the care of numerous different people or is left largely to his own devices – then it becomes increasingly hard to make up for lost ground in the years to come.

The growth of trust

Together with successful bonding goes the growth of *trust*. In fact learning that he can trust you as parents is one of the most important lessons your child learns during this first year of life. If he knows he can trust you, your child has a secure base from which to reach out and explore the world. He learns that his home is a happy, safe place where he will be well looked after and treated with love and understanding. If he can trust you, he will also be favourably disposed to trust other people. The lessons he has learnt from you are that people are nice; they look after you, care for you, bring you fun and stimulation, and can be relied upon to be there when you need them. So the early experience of trust in his relationship with you helps make him sociable and welcoming towards others as well. Even if he's a little shy by temperament, basically he'll accept that other people are okay, and over the first year or so of life will gradually lose his hesitancy in dealing with them.

Obviously your child will best learn to trust you if in addition to treating him with all the necessary love and care you are also *consistent* in the way you go about things. Your child will quickly learn that he knows where he stands with you. There is a pattern about his life that he can recognize, and which makes him feel secure. It helps him understand the way the world works, and his own place in it. The fact that small babies, whatever their temperament, thrive best on routine is a clear sign of the importance of consistency to them. After all, they are setting out on a vast and in some ways daunting voyage of discovery. At birth they know nothing about life and have all their learning ahead of them. Even when we adults take on a new task we feel much more sure of things if we can identify some logic and pattern to the way things work. If everything is just a confused jumble, with important parts of the task behaving one way today and for no reason in a totally different way tomorrow, it makes our job of getting to grips with things much more difficult. In the end, it will probably lead us either to a screaming fit or to giving up in despair.

The need for consistency and order

Your child also likes to do his learning in a logical and coherent environment. He finds it hard to make sense of a confusing jumble. Help him find the world an understandable and manageable place by treating him consistently and arranging day-to-day affairs consistently. Later, when he starts to talk, you will notice he comments on anything that happens differently today from yesterday. If Daddy doesn't come home from work on time, or if bits are left out of a familiar bedtime story, or if meals are suddenly switched from the dining room to the kitchen. Needless to say, change and inconsistency are a part of life, and your child must learn this fact. You can't run the house like a machine with everything happening precisely the same way every day. But you can keep a pattern to things, and take time to explain the reasons for changes as they occur. You can also make sure that in your own relationship with your baby he can come to recognize and know the person you are and the way in which you go about life.

A child who learns to trust his parents will, whatever his temperament, have every chance of a confident and optimistic

A happy, secure family life gives him the best possible start start to life. If he's nervy, he'll be better able to live with his nerves, and to distinguish between real causes for anxiety and those occasions when we're inclined to worry over trivial things. If he's naturally placid and even of disposition, he'll end up even more self-possessed and well-balanced. Either way, he'll be able to give full rein to his natural curiosity and his desire to explore, and later on he'll be well placed to develop his sense of initiative and originality. Put yourself again in his shoes. As adults we're much readier to face the world if we have a happy and secure family life behind us. And if we have a job, we do it much better if we know it's secure, and if we know we can trust our employers not to turn against us for no reason, or treat us first one way and then another without warning. Even as grown-ups, we still therefore need to trust those who are close to us and important to us. How much more vital this is in the first year of life, when the child has nothing else to go on, and gets his total picture of the world from the relationship he has with those whose task it is to love and care for him.

Throughout childhood a child needs to know that this love and care are always available to him, that under no circumstances will they ever fail him. He needs to know that he inhabits a reasonably predictable and ordered world, where people's behaviour towards him, just like the objects of the physical environment, remains consistent and recognizable from day to day. This enables him to build up a clear picture of the world and to use that picture in learning how things happen and why. Above all it enables him to begin the vital business of seeing himself as a valued and cherished member of that world.

DAILY CARE

By the time she's into her second six months, your baby is becoming increasingly robust. She still needs special care, but as the weeks and months go by she's showing increasing signs of being able to meet the world on the same terms as everyone else. She's ready to try a mouthful or two of most of the food prepared for the rest of the family. Her eating utensils have to

134

be scrupulously clean but the need for sterilization has largely gone. She's long since given up her 2 a.m. feed and she's about to dispense with her 10 p.m. feed as well. Part of the family routine is now getting back to normal, and though you'll still lose sleep some nights and rise early to attend to her, you won't be as tired physically as in the early months. She'll be much more mobile physically now, much more alert to the world, much more interested in everything, much more ready to communicate through the use of sounds.

Feeding

As far as feeding is concerned, the first thing you notice is that although feeds are still important to your baby, they don't quite dominate her life (and yours) in the way they did in the first six months. She's taking so much more interest in the world that she's got other things to think about. She'll still fuss for her meals when she's hungry, but you can distract her from the inner baby rather more easily nowadays when she has to wait a few minutes for you to get things ready, which is a great relief for all concerned.

Weaning

As discussed in Chapter 3, during the second six months of life your baby is going to be weaned off the bottle and on to solid food. Many parents have the idea that feeding problems often start at around this time. They may also have studied the works of Freud, who saw dire consequences for later personality development if weaning involved traumas and battles of wills between child and parents. The truth is that weaning is a straightforward and enjoyable stage in your child's development provided you don't try to rush things and provided you take your cues from her.

Just as controversy has raged over whether we should feed a baby to a timetable or on demand during the first six months of life (Chapter 3), so controversy has raged over whether you should wean to a timetable or on demand. Those who advocate a timetable claim that unless you're strict with her your baby will still be demanding the breast or bottle when she goes to school, while those who advocate demand say that

Should you wean to a timetable or on demand?

135

unless you allow your baby to go on sucking as long as she wants she'll grow up with a deep sense of deprivation.

In fact, as long as your baby has had plenty of sucking in the first six months, the instinctive need for it begins to disappear during the second six months. Provide her with the opportunities for solid food, and of her own accord she'll come to a stage where she starts pushing the nipple or teat out of her mouth when you offer it to her. 'That's all very well,' she seems to say, 'and thanks very much, but I'm not quite so sold on this idea as I once was.' Usually you'll notice this first at the midday feed, and then at the morning one. The last to go is usually the bedtime breast or bottle, suggesting that she likes the comfort it gives her before she settles down for the night, and in any case it's less effort than taking things from a spoon. If your child goes on wanting the breast or bottle into her second year, don't worry. You can go on offering it to her quite happily. She'll almost certainly have had enough of it by age two.

You may have read of children in under-developed countries still being put to the breast at six years and even older, but this is less a matter of choice than of necessity. Without her mother's milk, there is a grave chance the child may be dangerously under-nourished.

From a practical point of view, therefore, weaning isn't difficult. From about four months your baby will probably already have been taking a little food from the spoon, and now gradually you increase this amount. At around six months, you'll find that usually she's ready to dispense with her 10 p.m. feed, and manage on three meals a day, though naturally the amount she takes at each will be increasing. Dispensing with the 10 p.m. feed (in rare cases it may be the 6 a.m. one instead) will in fact give a strong boost to the process of weaning, since a child cannot take this increasing amount on board at her three remaining meals unless she relies more and more on solids. As long as she seems to want it, give her the breast or the bottle first at each meal to take the edge off her hunger, then switch her to the spoon.

What food should you use? The great majority of parents these days use commercial ready-prepared food for their baby at this stage, and you can switch around and experiment until you find things she likes. But don't just confine her to commercial foods. After all, no adult would like to live exclusively out of tins. Taking care over hygiene, do prepare food for her yourself at least some of the time.

Keep in mind that whatever you give your baby *texture* is as important to her as *taste* at this stage. Many babies refuse food not because they dislike its taste but because they find something unpleasant about the texture. They've been on a liquid diet up to now, and suddenly to confront them with lumpy or stringy items comes as a shock. As mentioned in the previous chapter, their palate doesn't yet recognize this as food, and self-preservation sets off an instinctive gagging (half retching) response. The food is pushed out, not because your baby is ungrateful or wants to annoy you, but simply because her reflexes won't allow her to swallow it. Too many experiences of this kind may give her a rooted dislike for lumpy food which will persist throughout childhood.

Continue your wise policy of not forcing your baby to eat. **Never force your baby to eat** Give her gentle encouragement when necessary, but don't fuss if she clearly doesn't want to finish something. Her appetite will vary from meal to meal and from day to day, and she is the best judge of whether she has any room left. However much she enjoys her food, a baby of this age still has the good sense to stop as soon as she's full. So don't adopt the habit of praising her lavishly for leaving a 'nice clean plate' and scolding her for any waste. Words like 'ungrateful' or 'wicked waste' have no place at the meal table of a small child. If you make her force down more than she needs, you'll either turn her against food and create the very 'feeding problem' that you fear, or give her the idea that it's 'good' to finish each meal feeling bloated (thus establishing the overeating habit so disastrous in later life).

Once weaning is well and truly under way, it's time to think **Getting a high chair** about a high chair. But before you buy or borrow one, make sure your baby can support himself steadily when put in a sitting position. He can do this any time from about six months onwards, but don't worry if it takes him as long as nine months.

The high chair must have a safety harness that prevents him standing upright when he's older and overbalancing. But it must be a harness that doesn't slip up around his chest or worse still his neck. This is important, because your baby's usual way of signalling to you that he's had enough and wants to come out of the chair is to straighten his body and slide down the seat until he is supported only by his straps (rather like a parachutist caught in a tree, but much crosser). If his harness rides up round his neck, this could be dangerous. But even though he's safe, lift him out of the high chair when this happens. He may be bored or his back may be getting tired. Either way, if you leave him in the chair too long he'll come to dislike it, and you may have a dramatic altercation with him every time you want to lift him in.

Learning to feed himself

With his increasing physical skills your child now wants to take part in the feeding process. No longer is he content to sit there while you act as stoker. He wants to do it himself. To begin with he'll be happy using his fingers, but before long he'll get the idea of the spoon, though for some time to come he'll reserve the right to use his fingers when the going gets difficult or when he's very hungry. Let him get on with it. It's far too soon to start worrying about his table manners. Encourage him to play his full share in getting the food to his mouth. This doesn't apply when he's very hungry of course, since he'll quickly become frustrated at the effort to satisfy his grumbling tummy. But as soon as the first desperation has gone out of things, let him have a go himself.

Coping with mess Messiness goes with self-feeding as night follows day. Better to accept this right from the start. Put an old tablecloth under the high chair to gather up the generous helpings of food that find their way on to the floor, and position the chair so that sticky fingers can't leave graffiti on the walls and furniture (and sticky fingers can reach a long way). A rigid plastic bib with its own built-in tray is another sound precaution. As soon as your baby starts feeding himself most of what he is eating goes into the tray, allowing him to pick it out later with every sign of delight at this unexpected discovery. In other words, cope painlessly *with* mess, rather than fight *against* it. This way you'll be doing yourself a good turn now *and* helping prepare for the future, when mess will become an even more ubiquitous fact of domestic life.

Comfort yourself with the knowledge that your baby is in fact learning a great deal by making a mess (though a hollow

138

laugh is perhaps in order here). As soon as you put food in front of him he sees not only something nice to eat but a fascinating arrangement of colours and textures. What more natural than to explore it by poking fingers into it? The fact that in doing so he reduces an appetizing plateful into a sorry heap of goo matters to him not a whit. It tastes just as good, and it's much more fun.

From the start, the experience of eating solid food should be an enjoyable one for him, so that he continues to look forward to mealtimes. Let him have a go at feeding himself as soon as he wants to, and don't tell him accusingly afterwards that if that's the best he can do he'll have to go back to being fed by you. Sit with him and encourage him and talk to him. He's used to having you with him when he feeds, and despite his growing independence with the spoon he's still much happier if you're around to take notice of him. When an older child starts deliberately throwing food on the floor he often does it because he's been left to eat on his own and wants to reclaim your attention. **Mealtimes should be enjoyable**

Usually the ability to feed himself is well established in a baby by nine months. Take pleasure in this new skill, no matter how rough it still is around the edges. Think how far your baby has already come. Increasingly now he's able to take an active part in things and share experiences with you, instead of always being on the receiving end. Don't keep rushing to wipe his hands and face. He doesn't in the least mind if they're messy, and much prefers it in fact to the feel of a damp flannel across his mouth. Wait until the meal is over, and then do a major clean-up. Keep a flannel especially for this job, and boil it frequently to get rid of germs. Anything that has this amount of use is bound to need it!

How much sleep does your baby need?

In the second six months of life, some babies are already down to twelve hours of sleep in the twenty-four, and many want even less. So it's no good putting them down to sleep after every feed, as you once did. The chances are that by six months they'll be taking only two naps during the day, and soon after may object vigorously to one of these. By one year, some children refuse all sleep during the day, though most will take one nap up to and often beyond their second birthday.

Refusing a daytime nap Don't put a child down for a nap at a set time or times during the day if she shows clearly she doesn't like the idea. A small child will take the sleep she needs, and if she stays fretting and wakeful long after she's put into her cot this shows she's getting enough sleep at other times and doesn't require this particular nap at all. Certainly it may be convenient for you to have her tucked away at this time of the day so that you can get on with other work, but it isn't fair to her. No child throughout childhood (one of the very few sure facts!) likes being in bed when she isn't tired and when she's feeling fine. This particular addiction tends to creep up on us in adolescence. So it's unfair to keep your baby in her cot when she wants to be up and doing.

Babies tend to wake early Nor is it fair to expect her to sleep on in the mornings. Even in winter, when it's dark outside, babies have a natural tendency to wake at around 5.30 to 6 a.m. Probably this is nature's rhythm, built into all of us in spite of centuries of artificial light and going to bed and rising at all kinds of odd hours. Nature would prefer us to retire early and wake early, and probably we'd all be healthier physically and psychologically if we did. Your baby is a more natural person than we adults, and she can't help waking, bright and breezy and calling lustily for food and attention, at what the rest of us regard as a very ungodly hour.

In many children, the bad news is that this early waking goes on well into childhood, though there comes a time when they can be encouraged to play quietly or read in their room until the rest of the household is stirring. Only adolescence, with its foretaste of adult sloth, puts pay to this commendable eagerness to greet the day.

You can of course prompt your baby to sleep on a little by putting her to bed later the previous evening, but often she'll take matters into her own hands and fall asleep at her usual time, no matter where she happens to be. In any case, most parents, while wanting their baby to sleep on in the morning, also want to get her to bed in the evenings, so that they can have time to themselves. One of the many examples of our wanting to have our cake and eat it. Generally speaking, you'll have to be content to let your baby establish her own sleeping habits, and to arrange your life around them. Amazingly, it is possible to get to *like* going to bed early and getting up at 5 or 6 a.m. You can feel quite smug at being out of your bed while the rest of the world is still slumbering, and it's a good feeling to watch the sunrise and appreciate the freshness and stillness of things at this time of day. (Or so early risers tell me.)

From what we've said, it should be clear that you needn't worry that your baby isn't getting enough sleep. Provided she's otherwise healthy, the fact she sleeps less than other babies you know simply means she needs less. It's often true that a baby who wants less sleep than average is above average in intelligence too. Often babies who sleep relatively little are extra alert and interested in things, and their extra hours of wakefulness mean that they've more opportunity to be stimulated by their environment. But since no baby is silly enough to keep awake just for the sake of taking an interest in things, you needn't feel that it's a bad sign if she sleeps more than average. A lot depends on how much physical energy she uses. A baby who is always on the go during the day is bound to be more tired than one who prefers to watch the world go by. Hereditary factors probably also play a part. Just as some babies are hungrier than others, so some seem to need more sleep.

Babies need different amounts of sleep

Washing and bathing

One element of daily care that definitely needs more attention during the second six months of life is washing and bathing. Now that your baby is more active, and learning to roll or crawl (see page 144), inevitably he'll get grubbier than when he was small. Feeding, especially when he takes over the job himself, is also increasingly messy. Often parents feel their child has a genius for making an elaborate (and to the adult eye revolting) muck-heap of even the blandest fare. Nor is this genius confined to food. No matter what comes within range, your baby can be relied upon to rearrange it into unrecognizable form in the time taken to turn your back and go and fetch something from the other side of the room. And if it contains ingredients that can be smeared over his own person, so much the better. These skills

Grubbiness is a fact of life

141

are matched only by his ability to get his hands and knees black from the most spotless of floors, and to end up with sticky fingers even though he hasn't been near anything remotely sticky all day.

Since this is the way babies are, you might as well accept it along with all the other facts of life. Make sure the floor and the house generally are as clean as possible, that there are no potentially harmful items within his reach, and by and large let him enjoy himself. Don't follow him around all the time with a wet flannel to wipe him clean, and don't keep rushing to change his clothes every time he gets himself dirty. Put him in something serviceable, such as dungarees and jumper, and let him get on with the serious business of exploring and enjoying himself. And don't worry that if anyone calls they ought always to see him looking like a new pin.

Now that your baby is so active, the evening bath is more necessary than ever. It's also more fun. Babies and small children have a natural love of water, and nothing pleases your baby more than a really good splash. He enjoys the feel of the water and the sight and sound of it as he vigorously splashes away at it with the palm of his hand.

Children who dislike having a bath It's odd, then, that some parents claim their child starts to dislike his bath round about this time, and protests the moment they take him into the bathroom and begin to undress him. If this happens, think what may be going wrong. Perhaps the days are drawing in and the the bathroom feels chill and unpleasant to him. Perhaps the water is too cold or (far worse) too hot. Perhaps he just doesn't like the feel of the bath itself against his skin, though this is unlikely if the bath is fibreglass.

If you've checked these points and found nothing wrong, the answer probably lies with the way you're handling him. A frequent problem is that parents are a little too rough. Your baby's skin isn't as delicate as it was in the first six months, but he still doesn't take kindly to vigorous rubbing with a rough flannel. I'm surprised to see how briskly some parents rub their baby's face for example. They wouldn't treat their own faces in this way, and there's no reason they should do it to his. They seem to imagine he doesn't have the same sort of feelings as an adult, and even his wails of protest don't convince them otherwise.

If you're satisfied you aren't too rough, check that water

isn't getting in his eyes. Babies dislike this intensely, an over-reaction perhaps but one programmed into them by nature as a way of protecting these delicate organs. And if you've managed to get soap, however mild, in his eyes as well, you can hardly wonder he views bath-time with decreasing enthusiasm. Check also you aren't rushing things too much, and interpreting his desire to play as a lack of co-operation. Give him time to enjoy himself. Try not to take him out before he's ready. And don't worry if he splashes water on the floor.

Finally, check the bath isn't too full. If he feels himself buoyant and insecure, he'll find the experience frightening and will be reluctant to repeat it next time. Buoyancy can be a particular problem when you tip him back with one hand under his neck in order to wash his hair. He doesn't enjoy this position at the best of times, particularly if he has to look straight up at a bright electric light in the ceiling above him, but if he also feels unstable in the water it quickly convinces him that bath-time isn't all it's made out to be.

Going to the baby clinic

At this stage, you should still be keeping in close touch with your clinic and doctor. Many parents become rather casual about such things once their child is beyond the early months of life. But his rate of growth still needs to be regularly checked, and it's valuable to have an experienced eye cast over his general progress. Particularly if he's your first child, you may not have seen enough of small babies to know all the subtle things to look for in their development. Doctors and health visitors, on the other hand, know how alert your baby should be at a given age, how responsive to sights and sounds and other stimuli, how active physically and how generally thriving. Thus they'll quickly spot something that needs attention. So don't neglect their help. At the same time, remember that you're an expert on your baby too. Don't assume that everything the medics say is automatically right and everything you say automatically wrong. This is perhaps most important when it comes to feeding. A well-meaning health visitor may insist, for example, that you 'get more solids' into your baby, even though it's clear to you he isn't ready for

Your baby's progress still needs careful checking

them and finds them actively distressing. Provided he's gaining weight, is taking plenty of milk and is otherwise healthy, thank her for her advice but diplomatically point out that your baby is working to a slightly different timetable than usual.

PHYSICAL AND PSYCHOLOGICAL DEVELOPMENT

Starting to get about

Babies are nothing if not inventive. They look out at the world, find it's an interesting and exciting place, and very soon want to find ways of carrying out a closer inspection. From six months or so onwards, as soon as they are able to make attempts at sitting unaided, they show signs of wanting to move around on their own. This is always a fascinating time. Almost daily, parents see their child move a little closer to solving the problem of getting about, and can only marvel at the creative way in which she goes about it. There is no fixed pattern here. Each baby tackles matters in her own way. One will learn to crawl, another will find it easier to roll across the floor to get where she wants, another will discover she can move around on her bottom, pushing herself along with one hand and leaving the other free to explore.

One reason why all this is so fascinating is that you are being given visible evidence of your baby's ability to solve problems. In life, much learning comes through problem-solving. I can't emphasize that too strongly, and I'll return to the subject at various points later in the book. An individual is faced with a problem, and keeps at it until ways are found of solving it. In the case of your baby, she's been solving problems since birth as part of the process of making sense of the world, but you haven't always been able to observe her at it. Now you have the chance. She's surrounded by objects which to her look strange and fascinating, and she wants to get to them so that she can give them a proper once over. She knows she can move her body, so it's natural to try to find ways of moving it that will allow her to get around. She doesn't think all this out as you or I would, as she hasn't yet got the use of language. But she knows perfectly well what she wants to do, and she has her natural instinct for movement to help her. So you can watch her getting daily closer to finding a workable solution, helped by her rapidly developing physical abilities and powers of co-ordination.

You needn't worry if your baby seems a little slower than average in mastering all this. Some babies aren't moving around the room even at twelve months, and occasionally a baby will leave out this kind of movement altogether and go straight from sitting unaided to pulling herself into a standing position. There's no indication that babies who crawl early or who use one method of movement as opposed to another grow up more intelligent than those who crawl late or who choose not to crawl at all, and provided your doctor is satisfied your baby is physically fit, be patient and let her do things in her own time. Beyond giving her plenty of opportunities to move around if she wants to, there's nothing you can usefully do to 'teach' your baby how to get the better of this problem. **Some babies start to move later than others**

A typical crawling timetable goes like this. From six months, your baby showns signs of wanting to get around. You'll suddenly discover she can draw her knees up under her when lying on her tummy and get into a proper crawling position briefly, though she won't be able to move forward. During the next month or two, this position will become an established favourite with her, and she will rock backwards and forwards and even swivel around, but still find forward progress frustratingly difficult. Then lo and behold, sometime during the ninth month of life she'll discover how to do it, often moving backwards first, since she can push more strongly with her arms than with her legs, but getting the proper hang of things very shortly afterwards. Naturally she'll be pretty pleased with herself. The world is now her oyster, and you'll join happily in the celebrations, oblivious for the moment of the precise implications of this new development! **A typical crawling timetable**

As a variant on the usual crawling pattern, some babies get on to their feet instead of their knees, and move around on all fours. Others, as I've said, find it better to roll, while others favour the bottom shuffle. Good luck to them all. If you've carpeted floors, any of these methods can be managed in comfort, but if you haven't, make sure knees or bottom are well padded, so that she doesn't get the idea that you have to endure pain in order to move around.

Safety precautions you will need to take

It's unfair for me to spoil things for you, but from now on you must remove any breakable or dangerous objects from the crawling path. Watch out particularly for electrical appliances. Unplug them and take them out of the room. If you have a china cabinet or similar luxury in your lounge, secure the doors in some way. Prevention is better than cure. You can't blame your baby if she breaks things. She's no idea of value yet, and a broken object looks to her every bit as interesting as an intact one. So get vulnerable items out of the way. Leave her plenty of things that she can explore in safety, and as far as possible give her the run of the room. It's frustrating for her and for you to be constantly pulling her away from things, or whipping them from her the moment she gets them into her hands.

If she's crawling in the kitchen there's a real danger that she may get herself stuck between cupboards or under something, so guard against this. In any case, never leave her in a room on her own now that she can move around (except of course for her bedroom when she's safely in her cot). If it's summer and you want her to crawl around outside, be especially careful. Put her on a large rug or bedspread, and make sure she doesn't stray beyond it. A garden can be a very hazardous place for a small baby.

What about a playpen?

Once your baby starts to move around, a playpen can be a great boon. But don't force her to stay penned in when she's had enough. Psychologically it's very frustrating for a small child to be denied the opportunity to move around now that she's solved the problem of how to do it. Her piteous crying when she's bored with the pen comes straight from the heart. She's setting out on her voyage of discovery proper now, and it's unfair to keep holding her back. You want her to learn and make progress and be happy and contented, so the playpen has to be only a short-term expedient, there more for your convenience than for hers.

Learning to stand up . . .

'Fine', your baby seems to be telling himself, 'now I've learnt to crawl the next thing is to find out how to get up on my feet.' His legs have been strong enough to support him from about six months if he's held in a standing position on your lap, but he has no control over the process and will plonk

146

down if his knees bend just a little too far to support him properly. Around eleven months, however, he'll have progressed to the point where he can pull himself into a standing position. This is another joyful milestone in his progress. You may go into him in the morning and there he is, standing up in his cot and chortling away, pleased as punch with himself. Let your own enthusiasm show. It means a great deal to him to know that you share his pleasure, and that each of his achievements is a good and proper way to go about things.

Watch out for a minor problem though. He's learnt to pull himself into a standing position, but how on earth does he get back down again? The problem worries him. Suppose he has to spend the rest of his life standing up clinging to the bars of his cot? Very sensibly he cries to draw your attention to the problem, and you solve it for him by sitting him down. Once down, however, he wants to practise his new skill and get back up again, only to find himself faced once more with the problem of getting down. For a while you and he seem to be engaged in a mysterious ritual. He stands up, beams briefly, then cries; you sit him down. He stands up, beams briefly, then cries; you sit him down. And so it goes on. To him, it quickly becomes a kind of game, but you probably have a choicer term for it.

. . . and sitting down again

Fortunately, this new game doesn't last long. In no time he masters the mechanics of sitting down, and has no further use for your help. Especially as he's now learning yet another skill, holding on to things and moving along with their aid. At first he isn't too sure of what you do with your feet. He moves his hands along the bars of the cot or whatever he's clinging to, then moves one of his feet in the same direction. After that he's stumped, and stands straddle-legged, often as if he's deep in thought over the whole business, until his legs give out and he subsides down on to his bottom. Nothing daunted, he keeps at it, and in a matter of days you'll notice he has the knack of moving his hands, then first one foot sideways, and then the other to join it. 'Well,' he seems to be saying to himself, 'there's not so much to this business of using your legs after all.' Since even at a few weeks he can copy you when you pull faces at him, realizing that his tongue and other features correspond to yours (page 84), he knows perfectly well that his legs correspond to yours as well. He's noticed

Starting to move along on his feet

147

that everyone around him seems to use these strange objects as a way of getting about, and he wants to join in the fun and be like everyone else. It won't be long now before he's walking properly.

More safety measures Once your baby starts pulling himself up, extra safety measures are needed. He has the idea that anything above head height when he's on the floor will serve for his purpose, and there's the danger now that he'll grab hold of something insecure and pull it down on top of himself. Tablecloths hanging conveniently within reach are a particular hazard – many is the child who has tragically scalded himself by pulling cloth and brimming teapot down on his unprotected head. Anything projecting over the side of a table – or worse still a cooker – is also a hazard, not only now but in the years to come. Make a resolve *never* to leave saucepans with their handles projecting where he can reach them. He may be small now, but you'll be surprised how quickly he'll be able to get at things you thought were well beyond range. Now that your baby is moving around, get into the habit of looking around a room and thinking what he could possibly get at that might be dangerous. Don't worry yourself into a bundle of nerves. Simply be sensible, anticipate hazards, and move them to places of safety. Since many of the most hazardous and most fragile things in the home seem to exert a kind of mesmeric fascination for him, it's fairer to move them right out of sight, so that he won't constantly be hankering after them, than simply to put them on high shelves where they're a perpetual challenge to him. (See also Appendix 7.)

Don't hurry him into walking Don't be tempted, now your baby has got this far, to try and hurry him into proper walking. Not only will such efforts be fruitless (he's working to his timetable and not yours), they could be a source of frustration for him. The old idea that babies who walked too soon would end up with bandy legs is no longer accepted. No baby will support himself until his legs are ready for it. Bandiness in many babies is a perfectly natural stage in the growth of the bones, and will normally remedy itself. But your baby *will* become fed up at your constant attempts to prompt him to put one foot in front of the other. At the moment, he's able to get around well enough for his own purposes, and he'd much rather you didn't interfere. He'll master the next stage soon enough anyway.

One word of warning about footwear. If you have cold floors you may feel at this point you want to rush your baby into shoes or socks to keep his feet warm. This will actually make it harder for him to balance, and if you leave him just in socks he may take a tumble on your polished floors. Bare feet in the home are by far the best strategy at this stage, and indeed for some time to come.

Bare feet are best

Using her senses to explore

In the second six months of life, your baby will be getting a much better idea of what is going on around her. We don't know for sure how she sees the world, but it's likely that she's now seeing it very much as an adult does. She can focus on objects near and far, she can separate out sounds and tell where they're coming from, she can discriminate between things, distinguishing those that are familiar from those that are strange. She's also rapidly gaining control over her bodily movements and learning how to co-ordinate them and how to use them. We've just seen examples in the way in which she learns to crawl and stand, but there's a great deal else going on. Study her carefully. Watch what she does when you give her something to hold or when she comes into contact with something unfamiliar. Watch how she uses her developing abilities to help her explore the world. Take delight in her competence, and try to see the world through her eyes and through her experience.

One thing you'll notice is that she gets control of large muscles before small. This is particularly noticeable with the arms and hands, which at six months she still uses very much as a single unit, making broad sweeping gestures with the wrists locked and the fingers clenched. In the seventh or eighth month she starts to gain control of her elbows and to differentiate between her upper and lower arms, and by nine months she's usually starting to control her wrists. It's about now that you're intrigued to find she can start waving goodbye (how everyone loves this simple gesture!), and very soon she'll be able to involve the fingers too, opening and closing them from her palm as part of the grand gesture of farewell. Noticing how pleased you are with her, she'll produce this

Gaining control of her arms and hands

gesture happily on demand, and it's something of a milestone for you because you can now see her responding very definitely to the things you ask her to do.

Learning to use her fingers

Watch carefully for other examples of her developing skills. At six months she'll still be using her whole hand to grasp an object, as if she hasn't learnt that each finger is a separate part in its own right. But by eight months she'll show signs she's beginning to learn this important fact and to acquire the physical control that goes with it. If you hand her something now, instead of grasping it with the whole hand she'll curl her fingers around it, separating out her thumb, and by nine months she's usually able to separate out her index finger and to use it in the delightful gesture of pointing at things. Partly she learns this gesture from copying you, but it also seems to have an innate quality about it, since even children of parents with a handicap that prevents them from pointing manifest the habit, though rather later than normal.

By twelve months, your baby will be so skilled at using her fingers and thumbs separately that she'll pick up even the smallest objects from the floor or from the tray of her high chair. Notice the absorption with which she goes about this task, putting her whole mind to it as if it's the skill that captivates her rather than the object itself. By this time, she can use her hands so cleverly that they become her main method of exploration, and though she'll still explore things by putting them in her mouth, this lessens from now on. She'll also use her hands to explore textures, such as the pile on the carpet or the dog's coat, which shows that she's becoming increasingly sensitive to the sensation of touch, identifying the signals that are fed from her fingers to her brain and developing very definite likes and dislikes. Round about this age, she'll often become attached to a soft toy or to a piece of blanket (see Chapter 5 for more on comfort objects), and show a marked aversion to other sensations such as household rubber gloves or particularly rough or spiky objects.

Your baby's delight in her new skills

One of the joys of watching a small baby is to see the total fascination with which she experiences her own skills. She obviously takes enormous delight in her increasing mastery over her environment. Watch out for your spectacles every time you pick her up. Nothing will please her more than to be able to tweak them off your face. Watch what happens when she does. She grabs hold of them with a very definite and determined gesture, pulls them clear, then continues to look intently at your face. She's not really interested in the spectacles themselves, only in her skill at bringing about this strange transformation in your face. A moment ago you had those strange things on, now you haven't. Yet you still seem to have a face. She knows, in that mysterious way of hers, that there's no part of her own face that corresponds to your spectacles, so they set her a real puzzle. If no one in her household wears spectacles, and she meets a stranger who does, the experience will be particularly fascinating for her.

Another favourite trick during the second six months of life is to pick things up and throw them on the floor. There hasn't been a normal baby since man first walked the earth who hasn't wearied his parents with this one. You put something into his hand and bingo, away it goes over the side of his pram or high chair. You pick it up and at once away it goes again. Should you fail to restore it to him he'll become most indignant, in the end putting on quite a tantrum about the whole matter. Assuming he desperately wants the object on the floor you obligingly bend down and get it for him, only to have it hurling back past your ear while you're still in the process of straightening up. The point is he *doesn't* want the object at all. Any old thing would do. He just wants to practise his new skill of hurling it over the side of his pram or whatever. (Though I must say that as parents we all reach a point where we wonder darkly whether he isn't drunk with the sense of power at the sight of his poor parents groping around on the floor for him. Babies are canny people.)

Throwing things on to the floor – a favourite trick

Be that as it may, try to humour your baby in his games. Don't make yourself a slave to him but do try to enter into his fun. All these intriguing phases are over so quickly. In no time he'll be looking around for fresh worlds to conquer. Let him take pleasure in his new achievements, and look upon them as welcome signs that he's developing along the right lines. The more curious a baby is about the things around him, whether it's your spectacles, or the pen clipped in your top pocket or the sight of you stooping to pick up the things he's thrown down, the more sure you can be that he's mentally bright and alert and will learn essential lessons quickly and competently.

Encourage your baby's explorations

In addition to having a good laugh with him, you can also encourage your baby's explorations by making sure he has a variety of interesting but safe things to play with. There's no need for expensive objects. Simple household items such as cotton reels, wooden spoons, plastic containers, together with his own toys in the shape of wooden bricks, rattles, soft or squeaky toys, will all keep him busy. Since his attention span is still quite short, ensure that he has plenty of variety, so that when he tires of one thing he can go on to another. But do remember that as he hasn't yet abandoned the stage of exploring things with his mouth the objects you give him must be clean, and free of anything that could come off and be swallowed. Even a careful doctor friend of mine found that his nine-month-old son had swallowed the clip of a watch bracelet, which had somehow been left within reach. It passed through him in twenty-four hours, and he no doubt wondered what all the panic was about, but it was a nasty twenty-four hours for his parents.

You are still your child's best learning aid

Remember too that your child's most effective learning aid is still yourself. No amount of exciting hardware and software is much use unless you spend time down on your hands and knees playing with him. He also finds you a fascinating object. He'll want to pull your hair (and he can really hurt when he tries), and to feel your face. He's intrigued by your mouth when you talk, and will ram his fingers in it if you let him. He'll also have a good go at poking out your eyes if you give him half a chance, and at grabbing hold of your nose and giving it a firm and painful tweak. The first rule is to protect yourself from physical harm, but the second is not to keep drawing away from him unnecessarily. Don't worry about your hairdo, let him touch and explore you as much as he can. He wants to learn about you, and the experience of touching you and being close to you and finding you accept his advances is a further good way of forging the bonds of affection between you. His mother and father are his people, and it's important for him to know they like his attempts to get close to them and relate to them physically.

Don't worry about mess

Don't forget either that if he's going to explore he's not only going to get you messy, he's going to get himself messy too. Don't keep trying to polish him up like a new pin. Keep him out of the bathroom and the toilet, and make sure the floor is as clean as possible and that there are no unhygienic articles lying around; otherwise let him explore and get a little grubby. Often he'll seem more intent on exploring his food than eating it, for example, smearing it about his plate with his splayed fingers and wiping it over his face. Certainly it doesn't look too marvellous to the observer, but it will all wash off easily enough, and he's learning a lot about texture and shape (and colour too).

Babbling and the beginnings of language

We adults take language very much for granted. We live in a verbal world, and talking and listening are as natural a part of our behaviour as walking and breathing. But there's more to it than this. Language isn't just a convenient way of communicating with other people, it's a vital part of our identity as individuals. We use language to read and to learn, to record our ideas, and above all to think and make sense of the world, and to build up the self-concepts that define us to ourselves.

Throughout the early months of your baby's life you will have talked to her, sung to her, and generally accustomed her to the sound of the human voice. She'll have made sounds herself too, but these will mostly have been cooing noises (plus of course more lusty noises when she wants something rather badly). But somewhere between the fourth and sixth months of life one of the most magical developments in the whole of the early years will have occurred. Your baby will have entered the stage known both technically and popularly as 'babbling'. With this stage, she starts producing a wide range of delightful little sounds, voluntarily and often with great joy, as if she's thoroughly enjoying this new skill. Babbling is a natural, spontaneous occurrence in the developmental pattern of a young baby's life. Its emergence has nothing to do with the sounds she hears around her, since whatever the country of her birth she babbles in much the same way, reproducing in the process many of the sounds used in languages other than her own. Nor is babbling a social phenomenon, for though your baby will babble happily when you're around she'll also babble freely when she's on her own, and dull of soul would parents be if they didn't delight in

The beginning of babbling

listening outside the nursery door to the monologue of musical sounds coming from within.

From babbling to talking

Babbling is a pre-speech stage. Once your baby starts babbling, his first words usually won't be long delayed. But quite how he moves from babbling to talking is yet another of those intriguing mysteries that surround babyhood. Words are part of a very complex process. They're sounds which we use to *represent* the world of objects and events in which we live. To grasp the fact that these sounds stand for real experiences is a considerable feat of understanding, and we don't yet know the mental processes involved. On a purely descriptive level, what happens is that your baby quickly comes to realize that some of the sounds she's producing during her babbling correspond to the sounds you make when you're speaking to her. She then comes to retain and repeat these sounds, and to discard any sounds she doesn't hear around her. Thus although at the babbling stage she could pick up any language under the sun with a perfect accent, once she gets beyond the babbling stage and discards these unheard sounds, she begins to lose this facility. In future, if she learns a foreign language, she'll find great difficulty in speaking it without traces of her mother accent.

Sadly, babies born deaf, although they go through the babbling stage, gradually fall silent because they hear no sounds around them. For this reason, the earlier deafness is diagnosed the better. If a baby is not completely deaf, and if we can amplify sounds to a level at which she can hear them, her babbling stands a good chance of developing into speech. Denied the opportunity to hear language during the babbling stage, the speech a deaf child does eventually acquire sounds characteristically laboured and unnatural.

Keep talking to your baby

Once your baby starts to babble, then, the more speech she hears around her the better. Keep talking to her as much as you can, explaining to her what's going on, telling her how much you love her, commenting on life in general, and even asking her opinion on things. She won't exactly be able to understand your words, but she will quickly detect the differences in sound between them, and the different inflections you use when you're telling her something and when you're asking her a question. You'll notice her looking at you when you talk, carefully studying your lips as they move, and listening attentively. Sometimes she'll watch you with a puzzled expression, as if she's not quite sure what all the fuss is about, but at other times she'll have a very wise and knowing look, as if she's perfectly aware of what you're saying and could even reply if she chose.

But don't just stick to words when you talk to your baby. Repeat her sounds back to her, and notice how she'll copy you in turn. It's rather like the pulling faces game all over again (Chapter 3), and once more we musn't underrate what's going on. Somehow she knows that she can make sounds that correspond to yours, and somehow she knows how to use her speech organs to do so. It isn't a question of trial and error. She will often repeat exactly after you a whole 'sentence' of babbling sounds, getting each of the sounds exactly right first go and in the right order. Make the most of this. Hold long 'conversations' with her, each of you babbling in turn and waiting for the other to reply. This not only helps to reinforce her in her use of sound, it also shows her that babbling can be used socially. Making sounds is a way of communicating with other people, of holding their attention and getting them to make sounds back to you.

Of course, your baby won't acquire all her babbling sounds at one go. In the cooing noises produced before babbling started she was able to make 'aah' and 'oooh' sounds, but now she produces first a 'baba' sound then a 'meme', often stringing together several repetitions ('babababa', 'memememe'). Next usually come the 'dadadada' and 'nananana' and 'mamamama' sequences of sounds, and gradually the repertoire expands with vowels becoming established before consonants. You'll naturally be delighted when you hear 'mamama' and 'dadada' sounds, because you'll be convinced she's referring to her doting parents. To you this is a very special moment, and though your baby will be using these sounds quite spontaneously at first, she'll soon associate them with you if you repeat them back to her, and as a result they will be amongst her first proper words.

So the babbling stage is great fun, for your baby and for you. Enjoy it to the full. Some parents say they feel foolish babbling away at their babies as if they've gone soft in the head. Nonsense. Babble away to your heart's content. If other people start muttering about your state of mind, let them. **You too can babble**

They're missing the fun. And if you feel embarrassed even when there's only you and your baby around (and *he* won't start wondering about your mental state – just yet at least!), then use the experience as a way of unwinding and being more at ease with yourself. What if you do feel embarrassed? Let the feeling go. It's of no use. It shows that there's a part of yourself with which you don't feel comfortable, and a perfectly innocent and useful part too. A part that has to do with having fun, a natural part that makes us feel good and that helps both our physical and psychological health. A part that in our childhood is all too often lost, mostly because adults tell us we're being silly or childish or making an exhibition of ourselves. So we become self-conscious, inhibited, and something of our capacity to find life exhilarating goes. I shall return to this theme, since this book is about parents learning from children as well as about children learning from parents. But use your relationship with your baby as a marvellous opportunity to rediscover this part of yourself. There's nothing remotely self-conscious about *him*. He takes life exactly as it comes and his own feelings exactly as they come. Learn from his free spirit to find the same freedom in yourself. It's still there, no matter how deeply it's overlaid by your life experiences to date.

Some babies babble later   Incidentally, don't worry if your child starts babbling a little later than the average. As I said earlier, the phase usually starts around four to six months, but some babies are well into their second six months before things get moving. There's no relationship between how early a baby babbles and how quickly he acquires language, nor is there any relationship with the eventual quality of his language skills. Nor, looked at the other way, is there any guarantee that the emergence of babbling shows a baby is perfectly normal. As already indicated, even deaf children babble, as do many of those later found to have some form of mental or physical handicap. But babbling is a good sign nevertheless, quite apart from the enjoyment it gives, because it marks an important stage in development. A few babies never babble. This may be normal, or may signal the need for investigation. Consult your doctor.

The duration of babbling   The babbling stage usually lasts for eight months or so, disappearing progressively as a baby begins to use proper words. But even older children will babble at times, often to their dolls or to make-believe friends. Sometimes a child will revert to babbling along with other babyish behaviour when a baby brother or sister arrives in the family, (see Chapter 3), and there's no need to be alarmed if this happens. Don't comment on his babbling, except to agree with him in a matter-of-fact way that yes, that's the noise small babies make. Otherwise take it in your stride, and continue to use words to him as normal. He'll soon grow out of the phase of his own accord.

You may also see this reversion to babbling in an older child when he's upset. Maybe you're displeased with him, and you've told him to sit in the corner for a few minutes. He sits down, and starts babbling quietly to himself. This is because he finds the sounds comforting, just as older children sometimes start humming to themselves under similar circumstances. Don't attach much importance to this if it only happens occasionally, but if it's frequent it does mean your child is feeling unhappy with things. What's more his unhappiness is turning into a lonely experience, cut off psychologically from those he loves. End this unhappiness by re-examining your attitude towards him and the punishments which you may have been using (see Chapter 6). Make sure these punishments don't isolate him from you, pushing him into this withdrawn state.

ISSUES AND PROBLEMS IN THE SECOND SIX MONTHS

If your baby is physically healthy, receives plenty of love and attention, is treated kindly and consistently, and is given plenty of opportunities to explore and be stimulated by the environment, there should be no major psychological problems in the second six months of life. But minor crises are bound to occur, and these can cause anxiety. Your baby's daily experiences all play an important part in moulding her personality, and naturally you wonder at times whether you are coping correctly with these problems.

Let's repeat that an essential part of parenting in the first year of life is to help your child learn to trust you, and therefore to see the world as a secure place in which she can

Work with your child's innate temperament

157

develop the confidence to reach out and explore. Let's repeat also that good parenting involves studying a child, and recognizing her innate temperament and her individual way of doing things. She's a unique human being, (babies don't come on conveyer belts) and to relate well to her now and throughout childhood you must get to know her as a person, with a mind and will and rights of her own. Don't try to force her into a mould of your own making, to force her into the image you have of what a baby 'ought' to be like.

Sure, she has to learn acceptable forms of behaviour. She has to learn that other people have rights beside herself, that social living demands a compromise between what we want and what other people want, and that the ability to control our own behaviour when necessary is an essential part of growing up. But these things take time to learn. In the first year of life, your baby is too young to take decisions and consciously do as she's told. For all her cleverness and the feats of learning in her first year, she's still very much at the mercy of her own needs, and has no idea that you have a life of your own outside your role as a satisfier of these needs. And her eventual learning of the rules of social behaviour will be much influenced by the unique inborn qualities which *you* gave her at conception. We're each of us, throughout life, the product of our inborn qualities plus the way in which experience has shaped, developed and sometimes frustrated these qualities. Just as the area of a field is determined by the combination of length and breadth, so each individual human being is determined by inborn qualities interacting with life experience, and your baby is no exception.

When you come to deal with your baby's problems, work with her rather than against her. A potter can mould a lump of clay into any shape he or she likes, but a wood-carver has to work with the grain and the natural qualities of the wood. As a parent, you're more like the wood-carver than the potter. Study your material in the way the wood-carver does, aiming to develop its possibilities and to bring out the best in it, rather than sticking rigidly to some picture of how you think it ought to look when you've finished with it.

Dealing with crying

Let's see how this works in practical terms. One of the problems that occurs frequently in the second six months (as in the first) is how to cope when your baby cries for reasons other than obvious ones like hunger or thirst.

In the second six months, some crying is now a matter of habit. Your baby sets up a routine, token protest (when for example you put him down at night or when you wash or change him), but after a few minutes he gives up. Or there may be periods of silence, punctuated by half-hearted attempts to stir things up again. Such crying doesn't usually become distressed or last long, and has a 'going through the motions' feel about it. Some parents wonder whether it means their baby will grow up rather disagreeable, or whether it's a sign they themselves aren't getting things quite right. **Routine grumbling**

In fact it means neither. Your baby hasn't yet acquired the use of language, so he can't tell you what he thinks about things or carry on that internal running commentary in which adults indulge when doing a job they dislike ('Be glad when this job's over and done with', 'Much rather be doing something else', 'What a rotten waste of time', and so on). So instead he sets up his fussing routine. It's his way of grumbling about things, and of letting you know his very low opinion of what's going on. He's as much right to these grumbles as we have, particularly as he doesn't yet understand the *reason* why boring activities such as going to bed or having your face washed are necessary. Talk to him while he's grumbling, as if the grumbles are simply his end of the conversation. Tell him you see his point, but these things have to be done, so he may as well make the best of them. Be matter-of-fact about it. Avoid impatience, since this will only get him genuinely upset, and will give him, young as he is, the impression that he has no right to his opinion or to his say.

If the grumbling happens routinely at bedtime, talk to him in this way while you're putting him down, then say goodnight and leave him to go to sleep. Don't linger in his room. As long as you're sure he isn't really upset about something, he has to learn that though you sympathize with his views on bedtime, sleep is a part of life and he must reconcile himself to it. If he's had plenty to do during the day, and if you don't rush him to bed before he's tired, he'll soon settle down when he sees there's no alternative. Many babies in fact drop off to sleep literally in mid-grumble.

Crying for no obvious reason

More difficult to deal with are those occasions when the crying sounds genuine enough, but you can't spot the reason. By the second six months of life, your baby is well used to the business of living in the world. He's adapted to life outside the womb, and if memories of the intra-uterine environment still remain, they've sunk into his unconscious. He's become used to the sensation of clothes and of warm and cool air against his skin. He's become used to breathing for himself, and to the feel of fullness and emptiness in his stomach and to the rumbles of digestion. So the restless crying of the first six months, and particularly of three-month colic, is usually behind him. His genuine crying is now far more likely to be caused by real discomfort, or by boredom or loneliness or, with his greater awareness of what is going on around him, fear of some kind.

Night-time crying

This is particularly true at night. Thanks to his greater awareness, he is more easily disturbed by sounds and other sensations these days, and wakes more readily. Once he wakes, he finds himself disorientated. His familiar surroundings look different at night. He isn't quite sure where he is and he cries for reassurance. If he's awoken abruptly from a deep sleep he also won't feel too happy within himself. And once he's into the habit of waking in the night, he'll go on doing so even if there isn't anything actually to disturb him. So you may find that after weeks of unbroken nights, your baby now starts waking regularly at around two or three o'clock. Naturally you find this disappointing, and as none of us are at our best in the early hours, you find it hard to be as loving and sympathetic as you'd like.

Have a definite plan of campaign

It isn't easy to think properly when you're in this state, so have a definite plan of campaign for these nightly goings on, and put it into effect in your somnambulistic state with all the consistency you can muster. On being woken the first two or three nights of a restless spell, peep in at your baby to make sure everything is all right, but without letting him see you, in the hope that he'll soon settle of his own accord. If it's clear this isn't going to happen and that he's working himself into a state, let him know you're there by speaking gently and soothingly, staying with him until he drops off. On subsequent nights, since it's clear he won't settle without you, start the talking and the soothing earlier. You don't want to let him cry until he becomes really upset, as he'll then take longer to settle, and you'll be out of bed for an hour or more instead of ten to fifteen minutes. On the other hand, unless he's in pain, you don't want to lift him out if you can help it. As soon as you do, he'll stop crying, but get the idea that's the end of the cot, and as soon as you put him down again he'll protest in genuine surprise and indignation.

Sit at the head of his cot, so that he can hear but not see you. Don't put on extra light. Talk quietly and soothingly to him each time he frets, but don't talk more than you have to. The chances are he isn't properly awake, so don't rouse him further. Linger in his room a moment after he falls asleep, in case he stirs again, and only when you are reasonably sure this isn't going to happen go back to bed. It's less wearing for you to sit with him a little longer than to be back in bed and just falling asleep when he starts to whimper again.

Usually, periods of wakefulness in the second six months **Making a stand** end as mysteriously as they begin. You wake one morning and realize that everyone has had a good night's sleep at last. Whatever the reason for your baby rousing, he's suddenly grown out of it. But if the phase goes on indefinitely, and you have to make a stand, the best plan is to do this gradually. If you suddenly stop going to him, he'll be genuinely distressed at your non-appearance, and work himself into such a state you'll have to go to him in the end. So go to him as usual, reassure him, but sit with him a little less long each night. This will accustom him to the fact that when all's said and done, he has to manage this business of going back to sleep on his own. After a few nights of this, try leaving him altogether. This usually works. If if doesn't, there's no alternative but to sit with him. A baby should never be left to cry until he becomes frightened and desperate. Take it in turns, with each parent going to him on alternate nights, so that neither loses too much sleep. And comfort yourself that the phase will pass. Unless there's a good reason, it rarely lasts beyond the first year.

Crying from frustration

Crying during the day is a different matter. There's nearly always an obvious cause. For temperamental reasons, babies vary a great deal in the readiness with which they cry when things go wrong, but just because your child cries rather easily it doesn't mean she's making a fuss over nothing. She *feels* small things as deeply as another child feels big things. She's experiencing the same emotions, and although this makes more demands upon you, she's in as much need of help and comfort. But prevention is better than cure, and once you know your baby's reasons for crying, you can avoid many of them. Much of her crying is caused by simple frustration. She's becoming more and more interested in the world and in you and your doings, and more and more impatient with her own helplessness. She wants to be up and doing, and as yet she just hasn't the physical skills to match her enquiring mind.

Frustration can be useful Frustration of this kind isn't altogether bad for a baby. It's part of nature's way of encouraging her to learn. She wants something badly, finds she can't get it, and immediately searches for ways of putting things right. In other words, her frustration motivates her to start problem-solving, which, as we see later (Chapter 6), is at the root of much intelligent and creative behaviour. But a baby can only stand so much frustration, and if it rises above a certain level she realizes the task is beyond her and gives vent to understandable rage and despair.

When you see your baby trying to solve a problem, don't rush to help her straightaway. Watch how she sets about matters, and notice how she tries first one way and then another. Her eagerness to get at things is a necessary stimulation to her, and you'll be surprised to see just how ingenious she can be. But if she clearly can't cope, step in and help. A bad dose of frustration puts a baby in a difficult mood which can last all day. So strike the happy medium between letting her struggle too long on her own and intervening too readily.

The extra active child Much of her frustration may come through wanting things which you can't let her have. Once she starts to crawl, she wants whatever she sees. Whatever is available, she's into it. Some babies are a particular handful at this time. Never a minute still, they forage and explore relentlessly. Nothing is safe from them. Active and energetic, within two minutes of your picking them up or taking them into a strange environment, they want to get down on the floor and start pulling things to pieces. If your baby is one of these, coffee mornings and outings to friends' houses can become a nightmare. While other babies are content to sit and survey the scene from the comfort of a parental knee, your baby wants to rearrange the world. She struggles and kicks to be released from your grasp, and once she's on the floor it's only seconds before there are predictable shrieks of alarm from your hosts and a certain unspoken atmosphere of criticism and accusation ('Well really!' 'Wouldn't you think her mother could . . .?' '. . . makes it so difficult for the rest of us.' 'Well if she were *my* child . . .').

In point of fact, a busy baby of this kind is a delight (in her way . . . !) She's showing you what an alert, active mind she's got. Full of enthusiasm and drive, she wants to be fully involved in life from the word go. And since enthusiasm and drive are things we welcome in an adult, it's worth remembering, as I said earlier, that the very qualities we admire most in adults sometimes make them difficult as children. So if your baby is of the busy kind, give her an environment where she can work off her energies in safety. If you're forever pulling things away from her (or pulling her away from things) she's bound to become angry about it all. Constantly frustrated in the activities nature has programmed into her, life becomes one long struggle between her and other people. You can – make no mistake about it – turn your busy child, through these constant frustrations now and in the years to come, into a nervy, angry and confused person, torn between her love of doing and her efforts to obey the restrictions you impose upon her. Far from developing her interest in things, and helping her use it to achieve success, she will be turned into a problem for you, her teachers, and herself. She'll still be active. Her basic nature doesn't change that easily. But her activity will be of the aimless, random, nuisance variety, devoted more to disrupting and interfering with others than to anything constructive and useful.

If your child is naturally busy, see to it there are plenty of interesting, safe, unbreakable things she can explore around the house. Put vulnerable objects out of sight. Tie cupboard doors together so she can't open them if you must, but a better

Make sure there are plenty of things she can explore

idea is to put suitable objects in your cupboards and let her pull them out when she wishes. Your pots and pans have a particular fascination for her, and they're unlikely to come to harm. But do make sure there are no bottles of bleach or disinfectant about, or packets of soap powder or anything else that could be a danger. When you take her to see friends, warn them in advance how extra active she is, and give them a chance to put vulnerable items out of the way. Don't be apologetic about her when she sets out on her voyages of discovery. That's the way she is, and if history wasn't full of people like her the human race would probably still be sitting in caves. If your friends are clearly on tenterhooks from the moment you carry her (a smile wreathing her face and blissfully unaware of the havoc she'll soon cause) through the front door to the moment you take her home again, resolve to give them a miss until she's older. You may find the main criterion of friendship is whether people are prepared to welcome her into their homes and make *you* feel equally at ease. But no matter. This is at least one way of assessing whether the people you know have their priorities right or not.

Given the right scope and opportunities, a busy baby will grow up into a most willing and helpful child, with plenty of initiative and go. The extra work required from you now will therefore pay ample dividends for everyone in the future. This is an excellent instance of how applicable the maxim 'Cast your bread upon the waters, and thou shalt find it after many days' is to child-rearing. And find it (this is the point) with a healthy rate of interest.

Always keep frustrations to a minimum

Even if your child doesn't fall into the very busy category, she'll still want to be up and about, and will find plenty to frustrate her. Arrange the environment so that unnecessary frustrations are kept to a minimum. Concentrate on providing things she *can* do rather than things she *can't*. Don't put yourself in the position of constantly having to stop her doing what she wants to do. Nothing could be more tedious for you or her. With thought and planning, you can greatly reduce the number of occasions you have to put a stop to her activities, mainly by ensuring there are no dangerous or flimsy and breakable objects within reach.

Crying from fear

Assuming your baby is in good health and not suffering badly from teething, frustration and boredom are the major causes of daytime crying. But another significant cause is fear. Here again, babies differ greatly. Some are born with a nervous system extra ready to give a nasty jolt whenever something threatens. This doesn't mean that many fears aren't learnt. Certainly they are. But some of us are innately more likely to *respond* with fear when presented with potentially intimidating experiences, so we learn to be afraid of them more readily than the next person. And some of the things that frighten us do so right from the very first.

With small babies, some are noticeably more tense from birth than others. They hold themselves in a tighter, less relaxed fashion, and show more signs of a startle reflex (see Chapter 2). Some experts refer to these babies as 'hyper-tense', but there is no real need for terms like this. Once we get them into our heads, we see them as fixed aspects of our baby's personality, instead of simply as descriptions of the way he is at certain times. There is no reason why, with a stable and happy background, such children shouldn't learn to relax as well as anyone else. Their tenseness may be due to inborn factors, or to factors in the intra-uterine environment, but when such babies become used to the world and learn the important lesson of trust, they increasingly lose their extra tight muscle tone, and take life more as it comes. **Some babies are more tense than others**

When your baby cries through fear, it is usually because something unexpected has happened. As I stressed earlier, babies thrive best on a set routine, on a consistent environment which allows them to learn what to expect and what their immediate world is actually like (see page 133). If something crops up that doesn't fit this routine, particularly if it is introduced abruptly, your baby doesn't understand what's happening and his natural reaction is fear. If he wakes from sleep, for example, to find strangers in his room. Or if he hears a sudden unfamiliar noise. Or if he's handled in a novel way. Or if you take him out in a high wind or somebody extra tall towers over him. You can't protect him from all these things, but you can make sure you're quickly on hand to reassure and comfort him, and you can make sure that where **Fear because of something unexpected**

165

possible sensible precautions are taken to avoid unnecessary alarm.

Introducing your baby to strangers

For example, if you've asked someone he doesn't know well to baby-sit, ensure that he or she comes early, and that you yourself are ready in good time to introduce the baby-sitter to your baby and stay with them both until they're at ease with each other. Let the introductions take place in his bedroom, so that he associates the sitter with his room and isn't startled if he wakes and finds him or her there. Another precaution is to avoid crowded or noisy places if they intimidate him. When strangers visit (particularly if you have large friends with loud, booming voices!), let your baby get his first dose of their company from the safe haven of your arms. And let them come into the room where he is, rather than the other way around. Even the most equable baby finds it confusing to be taken into his lounge, which is so familiar to him, only to find it cluttered with people he's never seen before, all talking at the tops of their voices and intent on making a bee-line for him and sweeping him into their arms.

Far better for him to be safely ensconced in his own territory, and allowed to see the strangers shown into the room. You'll remember I've said your baby doesn't know you have a life of your own once you go out of his sight. This is even truer when it comes to strangers. If you take him into a familiar room and he finds it full of them, he doesn't know where they've come from or what they're doing or even whether this is the same room as last time around. The sense of disorientation he feels is similar to how we'd feel if we went into a room at home only to find the familiar furniture had been replaced by strange objects we'd never seen before.

Sudden fear of something familiar

In addition to fear of the unknown and the unexpected, babies in the second six months (and often earlier) can develop a sudden aversion to something which up to now they've lived with quite happily. The sound of the vacuum cleaner is an example. It may never have bothered him before, yet suddenly he finds it extremely upsetting. You may rack your brains to remember whether there's any reason for his fear, and come up with nothing. The true explanation may be a very subtle one. Perhaps he wanted you for something last time you used it, but couldn't make you hear, even when he became thoroughly distressed. The sound of the vacuum

166

cleaner is now associated with this distress. Or it may be you always put him in his pram or cot for safety when you begin to vacuum the floor, and he associates the sound with his own frustration at being cooped up when he really wants the run of the place. Or the explanation may be a physical one. His awareness may have developed to a point where the noise made by the vacuum cleaner goes through him, producing a very unpleasant sensation.

Whatever the reason, if your baby suddenly develops fears of this kind it's wise to protect him from them if you can. Use the offending appliances when he's sound asleep upstairs. Don't carry on as normal insisting he must just 'get used to it'. Give him a rest from the cause of his fear in this way, and next time you introduce it to him the chances are he'll have forgotten all about it and will be able to take the experience in his stride.

Crying because he wants something

Of course, since it is your baby's way of communicating to you that she wants something, much of her crying is still to do with hunger, discomfort, wanting to be lifted out of her cot, wanting your attention and wanting her own way if there's a battle of wills. You're bound to wonder how you should react to crying of this kind. If there's no desperate urgency about it, or if it's to do simply with wanting her own way, should you satisfy her request at once, or let her wait your convenience or even refuse outright to give her what she wants? In the second six months of life she's far more knowing than in the first six, and many parents feel that she'll quickly want to be top dog around the place if everyone is always at her beck and call.

This is the argument about spoiling coming up again, but you now feel she's at the stage when she can learn more of the realities of life. Should you therefore leave her to cry a little longer before you attend to her? Should you stick to your guns even over small matters if there's a clash of wills, simply to teach her who's really boss? The answer is that until she begins to have a command of language, and you can explain things to her and help her understand, she isn't going to learn the finer details of what's right and wrong, or about waiting her turn or seeing matters from someone else's point of view. So simply behave towards her in a common-sense way. If her

Once again, what about spoiling?

crying isn't urgent, and you're in the middle of something else, let her wait a few minutes until you're ready. On the other hand, if you're free, go to her at once. This isn't being inconsistent. She'll come to realize that although you're always there when she really needs you, you don't always materialize like magic at the very first signs of a whimper.

Similarly, if she wants her own way over something, be prepared to give way if it's a small thing, but to stand firm if it's out of the question. By wanting her own way, she's only showing she was a will of her own. Fine. She won't get far in life without it. And you'd probably complain if she turned into one of those children and adolescents who are easily led by others and can't stand up for their rights. Remember, once again, the point about those qualities which can be difficult in children being the very qualities we admire in adults. So don't give her the impression she has no right to her own will, and that every time she asserts it she's going to be met with firmness by the people around her, people who are much bigger and stronger than she is.

On the other hand, she must start to learn that other people have a will of their own too, and that social living demands we accommodate to each other, giving and taking and compromising as necessary. So when you have to stick to your guns, don't feel bad about it. But do it calmly as well as firmly. Don't turn matters into an angry confrontation each time.

Never bear grudges after a clash of wills
Always distract her from her unhappiness and reassure her of your love the moment the incident is over. Thus as soon as you've finished washing or dressing her (or whatever it is that's causing the trouble), pick her up and give her a good hug and take her over to something that will interest and divert her. This way you teach her (so important in child-rearing) that whatever passes between you doesn't alter one bit your love for her. You have a disagreement. Okay. That's part of life. But it's soon over and no one holds any grudges. There's always a temptation, when she's involved you in a clash of wills, to plonk her down in her cot as 'punishment', and to leave her to sob on her own while you go and attend to other jobs. Resist the temptation. She's upset and she wants to be near you, so make it up quickly. If she learns, now and in the future, that you never bear grudges, she won't bear them either. She'll forgive and forget every bit as readily as

you, and you'll avoid becoming one of those households in which 'atmospheres' so readily build up, to the detriment of everyone's peace of mind.

By quickly getting back to normal after these little quarrels you'll also be showing your child that the quarrel hasn't been about whether she should have a will or not, simply over whether she can be allowed to do whatever she wants whenever she wants. You've decided for good reason that she must see things your way this time, and that's the end of it.

A child who is allowed to express herself but shown at the same time the clear limits beyond which she isn't permitted to go, will start even in the first year of life to learn that she is respected as a person in her own right. This will help her one day not only to accept herself (so important, as we shall see later, to the development of a well-balanced personality) but also to accept that others are people in their own right too, with the same feelings and wishes and hopes as she has herself. From this acceptance stems a genuine concern for others, and a genuine sensitivity towards their needs and expectations.

Visiting others

However well your child is learning the early lessons of love and trust, he may still find it very strange to be anywhere other than at home. All babies are best in their own homes, and even a baby who usually takes his feeds and sleep like clockwork may play up when you take him to visit. This is particularly true if you're staying the night away from home, and can be very annoying for you. You've arranged a weekend away with friends, and after the hard work and the restricted social life of the first months of your baby's life you're very much looking forward to it. You're also naturally eager to show off your baby, and it never occurs to you he'll be on anything but his best behaviour.

In the event, he seems deliberately to want to spoil things for you. He won't take his feed, won't let your friends near him, and just when you get him down for the night and anticipate a pleasant evening he decides not only that he won't go to sleep but that he has to be where you are. So instead of

Going away for weekends

169

relaxing and laughing with your friends over dinner, you spend all your time trying to calm a grizzling, infuriating little baby. The precious evening ticks away while you sit upstairs with him, or while he frets and fusses on your shoulder in the lounge. Hardly a recipe for a happy weekend, and in spite of their attempts to pretend otherwise, your friends won't exactly enjoy it either. To cap it all, your baby insists on waking the whole house in the night and again in the early morning, ruining everyone's sleep and ensuring that you're all grumpy and bleary-eyed the next day. Though no one will admit it, everyone will be relieved when the weekend is over.

The best advice is that unless you have one of those very rare babies who take *any* change in routine very much in their stride, it's better not to go on overnight visits unless your friends are particularly understanding. Even with close friends and relatives, there's often the unspoken criticism that it's your fault the baby won't settle, and that if he was *their* child they'd have no difficulty in seeing to him. Such criticism can leave you very much on edge, just at a time when you need to be at your most relaxed and patient. So unless you're sure of yourself, better to wait until he's into his second year. And however much you may want to re-create the old carefree weekends you used to have with your friends before your baby arrived, things are different now and you have to think of your baby. He genuinely finds it very unsettling to be in unfamiliar surroundings and with strange people, and perhaps the wonder is he manages to adapt to it at all. It's rather as if his whole familiar little world of bedroom and cot and bathroom and the rest of it have suddenly been transformed into something strange and frightening. No wonder when he's a little older he'll be so ready to take stories of magic and of people and places being turned into something else so seriously.

Daytime visits When it comes to coffee mornings and afternoon visits, you'll probably still find your child acts up a little. Keep your visits short if he is overwhelmed by it all, and make sure you keep him within sight and sound of you all the time. But going out and meeting others is part of a child's social learning, and usually his own natural interest and curiosity will see to it that he takes things in his stride provided he isn't rushed into them too abruptly.

Separation anxiety

Separation from parents is a different kind of worry and always a problem with a small child who is old enough to be fully aware of the separation and yet not old enough fully to understand the reasons for it. In a confused way, she feels deeply let down by her parents, and this hinders the growth of trust which, as stressed earlier, is so vital at this stage. The feeling of being let down may linger as a general insecurity into the coming years, surfacing not just when her parents have to leave her again for any reason, but whenever she's faced with something new and unknown in life. Moving house, starting school and making new friends are all typical examples.

We call this anxiety *separation anxiety*, and it's more prevalent in children who are by temperament a little nervy than in children who are by nature cheerful and resilient. But as far as possible it must be guarded against in all children. The crucial factor isn't how to find ways of avoiding separation from your child – each parent has to look at their own circumstances and see how this can be done – but to recognize the existence of separation anxiety, and to realize it may be an issue even when children give little outward sign that they're distressed at being without you. Leaving a child in day care without adequate preparation (see later in this chapter) can induce separation anxiety, but it's more frequently caused by longer separations, especially if accompanied by some other trauma (for example, a child having to go into hospital). After the separation, a child often shows her feelings by being excessively clinging and weepy. If the separation can't be avoided, be extra loving and patient towards her at this time. She won't want to let you out of her sight until she's reassured herself that you're not going to be separated from her again, so let her stay as close as possible until this reassurance has taken place.

Conflicts between baby and older children

Now to another worry. Older children's activities are all too often reduced to a state resembling a natural disaster by an active baby. The result is that the older children become angry and vigorously try to repossess their vandalized territory, while the baby fights back grimly with yells and a tight grasp upon the sad remains of whatever favourite toy she's singled out for special attention. At such times many a parent thinks wistfully of the delights of celibacy, and can be excused for whisking the baby (still clutching the spoils of war) angrily into the playpen, or for packing the older children out of the room to play elsewhere. The fact that neither the baby nor the older children are particularly to blame for this kind of scene only makes the parental peace-keeping role all the harder.

The play of older children always exerts a particular fascination for a child in the first or second year of life. Unable to understand what's going on, she yet feels a closer affinity with this kind of activity even than with the doings of grown-ups. She learns a great deal from watching what's happening, and in no time is bursting to be allowed to join in. But the older children have their rights too, and fond as they may be of the baby, they weren't responsible for bringing her into the world, and therefore have every right to escape from her when they wish. Avoid conflicts as far as possible by giving the older children somewhere to play (warm bedrooms, another living room) where they won't be disturbed. This is increasingly difficult when the baby becomes a toddler, and is even keener to join in the older children's fun, but sympathies must as far as possible be extended to the older children. It's easy to see the logic of this. Keeping baby (or toddler) with you while the older children get on with their game will upset her temporarily, but it won't turn her against you. And you can soon find something to distract and amuse her. On the other hand, letting her run riot amongst her siblings will make the latter feel very resentful not only towards her but towards you. As I say elsewhere in the book, children have a remarkable eye for detecting unfairness (when it's directed against them!) By contrast, if they see you're protecting their interests, they'll be much easier to deal with in general, and will also be much readier to take the baby off your hands for a while when you really need their help.

THE WORKING PARENT

One of the issues that taxes many parents is whether or not their baby will suffer if they both return to work while he's still small and leave him during the day with someone else (whether relative, friend or baby-minder). Naturally they also wonder if it will influence their baby's feelings towards them.

Will your baby lose out if you return to work?

Usually this is thought of as the problem of the working mother, but it can be the problem of the working father if the mother is the bread-winner and it's the father who takes the main responsibility for baby care in the early weeks and months, and then finds a job outside the home. It's a problem that can occur soon after birth (as for example when the mother's maternity leave runs out), so although I'm dealing with it in the second six months of life, I'll also relate it to the baby's younger days.

The first important point is to recall that babies thrive best on consistency. So if both parents do return to work, they must avoid leaving their baby with a succession of different people. The ideal is a relative or friend who can care for your child in your own home and who has a natural love for and interest in him. The relative or friend should be able to enter into a definite commitment that they will take your baby from an agreed hour in the morning to an agreed hour in the evening, every day without fail. To be fair to the person concerned, and to play your own part in offering your baby consistency, you must be sure to stick to these hours yourself. Keeping him waiting in the evening, especially if you have agreed that you're going to be responsible for giving him his evening feed, is particularly unhelpful to him. Though he doesn't know the time, his inner biological clock will tell him when he can expect you, and he'll become confused and upset if you're not there.

Importance of consistency and routine

The second important point is that your baby doesn't know you've had a hard day at the office. When you come home he's pleased to see you and wants to be allowed to enjoy your relaxed attention. So if you are going to tackle a job outside the home, you must enter into a very clear agreement with yourself that your baby has priority when you're reunited with him. This isn't just an agreement for mothers either. Fathers

Your baby must have priority after work and at weekends

must enter into the same commitment. It isn't fair on the mother or the baby that she, after just as demanding a day out at work, should be expected to carry the full load of baby care in the evening while the father puts his feet up and relaxes. It's even less fair if the mother is also expected to help him relax by getting his meals and seeing to his needs as well.

By extension, the third important point is that your weekends must also belong as far as possible to your baby. This is the time when he has you to himself, and can make up for not seeing so much of you from Monday to Friday. I'm not saying you should over-indulge him. But I am saying that you shouldn't see him as something of a nuisance because you're extra tired after the week's work and want to spend the weekend either catching up on household jobs or sleeping. It's only fair that he has as much of your weekend as if you weren't tied to a job outside the home.

If all this sounds rather demanding, that is exactly what it is. If a woman takes on outside work, and her partner unfairly doesn't pull his weight, then a mother can find herself in effect trying to do three full-time jobs – caring for her baby, doing her paid work, and running the home. Unless she's bounding with energy, it's a very tall order, and not to be undertaken without a great deal of thought and planning.

Choosing a baby-minder The fourth important point, again in the interests of consistency, is that whoever cares for the baby during the day should have similar ideas on baby care to your own. It's difficult for your baby if he's treated one way by you and another by his baby-minder. The three of you (both parents should be involved) must talk this over and come to clear agreement on what's to be done if the baby cries, on how he's to be given his meals, on how often he's to be changed, on how much time is to be spent playing and talking with him. Moreover, if your house is a quiet place, without the TV or radio blaring all the time, then this is what your baby will be used to, and if possible the baby-minder should keep things equally peaceful. Particularly if the baby-minder can't come to your home and you have to take your baby to her, he's going to find it very confusing to be bundled each day from the tranquillity of one environment to the din of another or vice versa. He will adapt in time, but at first he's going to be upset by it all, and it's as well to avoid this upset if you can.

Next, be sure your baby is familiar with the baby-minder and feels comfortable with her before you go off and leave him for a full day. If she (it could easily be he) is a relative or close friend there's usually no problem, since your baby will already have come to know her well. But if you're leaving him with a stranger, then you must do some ground work first. Have the baby-minder visit you or take your baby to her house for informal visits. When he's used to her and to his surroundings let her hold him and make friends. If possible, leave him for an hour or so in her company on several separate occasions so he can get some practice.

Make sure your baby is familiar with the baby-minder

At the same time, reassure yourself that the baby-minder is a suitable person to care for your child. If she's doing the job professionally she'll probably have plenty of experience and will be able to advise you on the best routines for making your baby feel at home with her. But watch closely to see how she handles him. You'll want her to be sensible and efficient, but at the same time you'll want her to be gentle and show plenty of affection. In other words, you'll want to be sure she actually likes small babies and has patience and understanding. If you're leaving your baby at her home you'll want to be sure the home is clean and hygienic. You'll want to be sure that the surroundings are pleasant, and that the baby-minder will play with your baby and offer him sufficient stimulation. It isn't just a matter of keeping an eye on him while he lies most of the day in his carry-cot. His young mind needs the kind of fun and interest that you provide. So satisfy yourself that the baby-minder isn't taking on too much work, and that if she's caring for more than one child she really can devote attention to each one of them. Usually she'll be a mother herself, often with older children, and it's useful to see how well she's bringing them up. If you can talk to other mothers who use her services and listen to what they have to say about her, this is also valuable.

Make sure the baby-minder is suitable

However careful you are, when the first day of the experience proper comes, and you leave your baby behind and go off to work, you're bound to feel some pangs. If you've given yourself plenty of time that morning to get her ready, and stay with her a while instead of dumping her and rushing off, the chances are she'll settle happily. But even so you'll miss her and wonder if you're doing the right thing. Even if you're sure

The first day back at work

175

she'll be contented and well looked after, you'll still wonder what effect all this is going to have on her feelings for you. Will she blame you at some deep level for leaving her like this? Will the development of her love for you be affected? At the very least, will she have divided loyalties between the baby-minder and yourself? And will there be any long-term effects on her personality from this early experience of being deprived of parental care each day?

Most of these fears are groundless. Provided the baby-minder is good at the job neither your baby's intellectual nor emotional development will suffer damage. A professional baby-minder who has several children in her care can't give as much to your child during the day as would you or a relative or a friend devoting her whole time to her. But she'll probably receive the necessary minimum of attention and stimulation, and provided you spend enough of your own time with her at evenings and weekends, she'll manage well enough. Nor is she likely to blame you deep down. Provided the transition from home to baby-minder is managed smoothly, she'll accept that this is the way things are, just as one day she'll accept starting playgroup or school. She won't love you any the less either, provided again that she sees plenty of you at evenings and weekends.

What about divided loyalties? Divided loyalties are another matter though. Assuming the necessary bond of affection is created between her baby-minder and herself (and you wouldn't wish it otherwise) then yes, she's bound to cast the baby-minder in the role of an additional parent. This won't worry her, since just as she can love both mother and father without any conflict of feelings so she can love baby-minder and parents. But it may worry you, since it's natural to want to keep your own very special relationship with her. However, in the long run you are her parents, and she's going to see far more of you during her childhood than of anyone else. When the time comes for her to stop going to her baby-minder, her relationship with her will quickly and naturally become more distant. She may go on seeing her from time to time, particularly if she's a relative, but the place she occupies in her feelings will be much less central than your own.

A final question parents ask is what should you do if your baby *doesn't* settle with her baby-minder? Assuming you've prepared the ground as outlined above, and take plenty of time with her in the mornings, getting up earlier so that you don't have to rush getting her ready, this problem is unlikely to occur. In the first two months or so of life, your baby may not even seem to notice that you've left her with someone else. As she grows older and takes in more, so she's more aware of what's happening, but she still should be able to cope. If she frets a little the first few days on being left, a caring and experienced baby-minder will soon soothe her and will probably prefer you not to linger too long. While she can see you, she'll want to go to you, but she will quickly become more philosophical once you've left and she knows she's still in good hands. It's also amazing how quickly even young babies seem to sense their parents' anxiety and distress. If you're upset at leaving her, better to go before you've had time to communicate this.

What if your baby won't settle?

However, if your baby is one of those rare children who won't settle with anyone but you, or if it's difficult to find a suitable baby-minder, then you'll have to ask yourself seriously how necessary it is for you to go out to work. If there are economic reasons, then you may have no choice. But if the reasons are psychological, the situation is more complex. Maybe you have a career that means a great deal to you, and you don't wish to lose it by staying at home. Or maybe you need the stimulus of getting out of the house and meeting people. These considerations are perfectly legitimate. And an unhappy frustrated parent in the house all day isn't going to provide an ideal environment for a baby. Better that you should go out to work and feel fulfilled in your own life than mope around at home all day. And if you are fulfilled then you're more likely to be relaxed and to want to spend time with your baby when you *are* free.

Do you really need to go out to work?

But do examine your own motives carefully. Are you simply trying to hold on to the life you had before your baby arrived? And if so, have you adjusted yourself properly to the idea of parenthood? I have already stressed that once your baby arrives things aren't going to remain the same. You have responsibilities to your baby, and she's your prime consideration. For the most part, with careful planning, you can avoid any conflict between a career and your role as parent. But when you've adjusted to this role you'll see that if there *is* a conflict, your baby must come first. If she can't settle with a child-minder, or if a suitable person isn't available, you'll have to consider putting off your career until she's over this difficult phase, even if it means waiting until she's ready to go to nursery school. Or perhaps, if it's feasible, until you can find a suitable au pair who she can really get to know and who can live in and care for her in the security of her own home.

The issues involved in being a working parent change all the time as your child grows older, and I'll be returning to them later in the book. If it's helpful to think more fully about these issues now, you may like to turn to pages 564-8.

THE CHILD WITH A HANDICAP

Physical handicap

Many physical handicaps are apparent at birth, and if your child is one of the 2 per cent who has one of these handicaps he will already be receiving the necessary medical care and, where appropriate, treatment. However, some handicaps don't become apparent until the child is older, and may be identified as a result of parents reporting anxieties about their child to the doctor, or as a result of routine screening by the clinic or health visitor. With the majority of handicaps, the earlier the diagnosis the better the chances of remedial treatment. Some parents are reluctant to accept that their child may have a handicap, and as a result delay reporting any symptoms to their doctor, or delay taking their child for routine screening. Understandable as this reluctance is, it is unwise in the extreme. Delay could mean the difference between a child overcoming the handicap or being saddled with it for the rest of his life.

Parents should never attempt to take over the screening role for themselves. This is very much a job for experts, and requires professional training. But they can nevertheless carry out some of the simpler screening procedures in order to alert the doctor or health visitor to anomalies at the earliest possible moment, and enable more intensive screening to take place. During the second six months of life, two important areas where such parental pre-screening can take place are *hearing* and *vision*.

Hearing impairment

As early as six months, test your baby by presenting him with a range of everyday sounds. The human voice, a rattle, a spoon stroked against the side of a cup, a rustle of tissue paper, and a hand-bell are the sounds usually used, presented in this order. One parent sits in front of the baby, holding his attention, while the other stands to the side of the baby (up to a metre (3 ft) away and outside the line of vision) and makes the sounds. The speech sound is made at a quiet conversational level, and consists of the vowel sound 'oo' repeated two to four times in a deep voice, while the consonant sounds 'tit-tit-tit', 'pth-pth-pth' and 'ps-ps-ps' are repeated four to six times in a higher voice. The exercise should be repeated on both sides of the baby, and rattle, spoon/cup, tissue paper and hand-bell should all be sounded only gently. If the hearing in both ears is good, the child should turn in the direction of the sounds, but if he gives a clear-cut response to at least three sounds out of five (the five sounds together cover a wide range of frequencies), then he has enough hearing for speech to develop. If he fails to respond to any of the sounds it can be repeated two or three times, with an interval of two seconds between each repetition.

Keep a check on your child's hearing

If the child 'fails' the test (scores less than three out of five) it can be repeated a month later, but it is wiser to report this failure to your doctor at once (the test is called the Stycar Hearing Test by the way, just so that you can use the right terminology). The test is by no means foolproof, and 'failure' does not necessarily mean that your child is hearing-impaired. But your doctor will be able to carry out more sophisticated tests, just to clarify things.

What if your child 'fails' the test?

If there *is* impairment, it doesn't necessarily mean your child is going to grow up deaf. The impairment could be caused by a blockage in the outer or middle ear caused by fluid or catarrh (so-called 'sticky ear' or 'glue ear'), or even by an object such as cotton wool. This is called *conductive* deafness, since the neurological mechanisms of hearing are in good order, but the sound is failing to be conducted to them. Other forms of conductive deafness, caused by slight malformations in the structure of the outer or middle ear, can usually be cured by surgery. In others, the problem may simply disappear or reduce as the child grows older (though early diagnosis is still essential, so that he can have extra help with language during the period of deafness).

Less treatable is *sensori-neural* deafness, where the problem lies with the hearing nerve between the inner ear and the brain. In 50 per cent of cases, we don't know what causes this problem, but it rarely improves with time and cannot be operated upon. The other 50 per cent of cases can be divided between *congenital* (caused by *hereditary* problems, or *pre-natal* problems such as a disease in the pregnant mother like rubella, or *perinatal* problems such as prematurity, lack of oxygen at birth or rhesus incompatibility) and *acquired* (post-natal virus infections such as meningitis for example). Again there is little chance of improvement with time or of successful medical or surgical treatment.

Measuring your child's hearing loss
But even if your child is diagnosed as suffering from sensori-neural deafness, this doesn't mean he has no hearing. Careful testing when your child is a little older (typically from eighteen months onwards) will establish precisely the extent of his hearing loss compared with other children of his age. This loss is expressed in the form of decibels, that is, how many decibels louder would a sound have to be before your child could hear it as compared with the average child? This difference between your child and the average is known as his decibel loss. Children with varying degrees of decibel loss are usually classified as follows:

> Up to 40 decibel loss – slightly hearing-impaired
> 41–70 decibel loss – moderately hearing-impaired
> 71–95 decibel loss – severely hearing-impaired
> Over 96 decibel loss – profoundly hearing-impaired

Each ear will of course be tested separately, since a child may have less impairment in one ear than in the other. Looking ahead to school days, *any* child with a hearing loss, no matter how slight, is potentially at a disadvantage, and has a right to extra help and consideration. Children vary (depending upon such factors as their intelligence and the support and patience of their parents and teachers) in their ability to cope with the educational implications of deafness, but generally a loss of as little as 20 decibels signals the need for careful monitoring and possibly for additional educational help. A loss of 32 decibels or more makes this additional help essential, while a loss of 55 decibels or more indicates the need for more specialist intervention. Children with a hearing loss greater than 71 decibels (i.e. severely hearing-impaired) normally require education in a unit or school which has special provision for the deaf, and which has teachers specially trained in this work.

Reference has already been made to the importance of making use of a hearing-impaired child's residual hearing as early as possible if he is to stand the maximum chance of acquiring language successfully (see page 154). And there is a more extended discussion on how to relate to a child who has a handicap in Chapter 7. But it's appropriate to stress here some of the things to keep clearly in mind if your child has a significant degree of hearing loss. These things apply throughout childhood, but they are dealt with now rather than later so that parents can be aware of them right from the outset.

How you can help a hearing-impaired child

- As with any handicap, he's a child first and a child with a handicap second. He has all the needs of the unimpaired child. He needs love, understanding, and human company. And he needs – even more than the unimpaired child – stimulation and parental patience. It's harder for him to relate to the world than it is for an unimpaired child, and inevitably he'll be slower at learning many necessary lessons. Go to extra lengths therefore to interest and involve him, to draw him into the experiences of the rest of the family, to reassure him that he matters just as much as anyone else. And go to extra lengths to be patient with him, making full allowances for the additonal challenges with which life presents him.

- Though children born into a silent world accept their lot in a wonderfully courageous and full-hearted way, they are nevertheless bound to be frustrated at times by their inability to communicate as they would wish, and to join in with other children. Don't over-indulge. A hearing-impaired child has to learn the lessons of social living and self-control like any other. But at the same time do make full allowance for the emotional demands which your

181

child's deafness makes upon him. And help other children in the family to make the same allowances, while at the same time walking the narrow tightrope between favouring the deaf child over his siblings and vice versa.

- Stimulate and use whatever hearing your child may have as much as possible. Try to expose him to the same *range* of sounds as a normally-hearing child. Listen to the advice of the audiologist, and if possible make use of headphones with appropriate amplification so that your child can experience as much richness of sound as he can (including, vitally, music).

- At the same time, pay extra attention to the use of your child's other senses. Give him as much visual experience as possible – colours, shapes, three-dimensional structures. Give him tactile stimulation – the feel of different surfaces and textures. Exercise his sense of humour. As he can't hear you, make your jokes visual. Help him experience joy and laughter.

- Help him make the connection between movement and sound. Placing his hands on your throat as you talk will help him to link vibrations with words. Buy him percussion musical instruments so that he can feel the vibration of drums and cymbals and glockenspiel (and hang the noise while all this goes on!). Tap out the rhythms of nursery rhymes and simple tunes with him.

- As he may not be able to hear the words of stories, 'read' pictures with him. Choose sequences of pictures which show a narrative of events (some commercially produced material is excellent). Help him get the *idea* of stories, and to develop an early interest in books.

- Spend all the time you can with him. Listen carefully while he tries to articulate sounds and words. During the babbling stage, respond to him visually while he chortles and prattles away, so that he can *see* the effect he has upon others.

- When he is older and starts receiving specialist help from therapists and teachers of the deaf, take as active a role as you can in helping him, and show as much interest in his progress as you do in the schooling of your other children.

- Last but not least, take special care with his physical safety. He can't hear danger like other children can. Nor can he hear you when you call him back from danger. Ensure the house and the garden are even safer places for him to play and move around in than they would be for a normally-hearing child. Use your imagination and anticipate what *might* happen and then take steps to see that it can't.

One question that's often asked as the child grows older is whether he should be taught sign language or not. At one time sign language was widely used, but more recently its use has declined sharply, as experts felt it was more valuable for deaf people to focus upon lip-reading. Unfortunately, the experts never thought to consult deaf children themselves (or their parents). There is no doubting the value of lip-reading, since it allows the deaf to converse with normally-hearing people who are ignorant of sign language. On the other hand, sign language is an excellent adjunct to lip-reading, since it allows the deaf to communicate much more fluently and expressively amongst themselves and with those normally-hearing people who have mastered sign language. Much of the frustration felt by deaf people comes from the fact that their speech cannot keep pace with the need to express thoughts and feelings, and both deaf children and their parents testify to the new world of understanding and shared experience opened up through a command of sign language.

What about sign language?

Currently, this is being increasingly recognized, and sign language is once again being made generally available. My advice to parents is to learn sign language and use it, along with speech, to their deaf child. Your child will pick up the language very quickly, particularly if he sees you using it to each other and to any normally-hearing children within the family. Use a judicious blend of sign language and lip language, employing the former where necessary to explain the latter. On no account neglect lip language in favour of sign language, but on no account neglect the mental and emotional benefit your child dreives from the enhanced powers of communication sign language gives him. Start him on sign language at the same time as lip language. He'll be able to understand it long before he has the command of gesture necessary to use it for himself, but by the age of five most children can sign nearly as well as their parents.

Visual impairment

Keep a check on your child's sight

In the early weeks of life, check that your child's eyes appear normal. The lens and cornea should be clear, the pupils should be round, equal in size and responsive to light, and the child should blink in response to sudden movement. By two to three months check that she follows a horizontally moving object, and by four to eight months a vertically moving one. By nine months she should be capable of visually directed reaching towards small objects, down to the size of a small sweet. Failure to pass these tests by the upper age limits should be reported to your doctor.

At around three, you can try your child with a version of the Stycar Vision Test. Write any five letters on a card, then write them again in various sizes (down to a size which a normally-sighted person can read comfortably at 3 metres – 10 ft) on separate sheets of paper. Sit your child on the lap of one parent, while the other stands 3 metres away and holds up in turn each of the letters written on the separate sheets, going from large to small. Your child has the card on which the letters are printed on her lap, and each time you hold up a letter she is asked to point to its equivalent on the card. Each eye is tested separately, and if your child fails to recognize the smallest letters she should be referred for proper screening. She may need a little practice before she gets the right idea though, so you can try more than one trial, spaced out over a period of a few weeks, before deciding definitely that she needs referral.

Pre-screen for squint and colour-blindness too

It's worthwhile to pre-screen your child for squint as well as for vision. The procedure is to ask your child to fixate on a small object while you cover up each eye in turn. Then look if the uncovered eye has to move in order to keep fixating, and if there are signs of unsteady fixation. Another test is to hold a small torch about 30 centimetres (1 ft) away from your child's face and in line with the bridge of her nose. As she looks at the light the reflection of it in her cornea should be symmetrical and situated in the centre of the pupil.

It's worthwhile to test for colour-blindness too (more common in boys than girls). Colour-blindness is the inability to distinguish greens and reds, and for this you really need commercially prepared cards with green and red dots which the child has visually to discriminate from each other. But you can mix up identical green and red beads, and see if, by age three to four, your child can sort them into their correct colours.

None of these tests for visual defects is 100 per cent accurate, and even if your child 'fails' them there is still an even chance that everything is in order. But 'failure' does suggest the need for proper investigation, and if this is done before your child starts school she may escape many of the disadvantages faced by a visually-impaired child. Surprisingly, many children do not have their visual handicaps detected until they have been at school for some time, with the result that not only are they denied the opportunity for medical treatment, they also miss out unknowingly on many early learning experiences.

Measuring your child's visual impairment

If your child is visually impaired, the degree of impairment will be expressed medically in terms of a rating for each eye. The rating is given in the form of two numbers, with 6/6 representing normal vision. 6/6 means that at 6 metres (20 ft) the eye can see precisely what a normal eye can see at 6 metres. It thus scores, in effect, 6 out of 6. However, the larger the second number becomes in relation to the first, the poorer the vision. Thus 6/15 would mean that the eye has to be as close as 6 metres to see what the normal eye can see at 15 metres, while 6/30 would mean it has to be at 6 metres in order to see what the normal eye can see at 30 metres and so on. Conversely the smaller the second number becomes in relation to the first, the better the vision. Thus 6/5 would mean that the eye can see at 6 metres what the normal eye can only see at 5. For near (reading) vision, the standard is set at 33 centimetres (13 in.) rather than 6 metres, and vision better or worse than normal is expressed as a deviation from this standard, in just the same way.

Detailed diagnosis of this kind will of course not be done until your child is at least three or four years old, but it's mentioned here rather than later in the book in order to give a complete picture. Similarly some of the points mentioned below also apply more to an older child, though it's important for parents to be aware of them as early as possible. But

185

thankfully much can be done medically and surgically for most visually-impaired children, with the result that many of them are soon able to enjoy normal or near-normal sight.

How to help a visually-impaired child

With any visually-impaired child, however, the following are key points for parents:

- Once again, your child is a child first and a child with an impairment second. Make sure she doesn't miss out on any of the love and fun so necessary to normal development.
- If her impairment is severe, so that she cannot distinguish objects, keep the furniture and other household objects arranged in the same way, so that she can quickly find her way around once she becomes mobile.
- As she grows older, try to keep her appearance normal. As a partially-sighted child may not be able to distinguish her reflection in a mirror, or see other people clearly enough to compare herself with them, she cannot be expected to know when her clothes or hair or other physical features look a little odd. Help her, while at the same time giving her confidence in the way she looks. She may need extra reassurance, particularly if other children thoughtlessly tease her.
- Stimulate her visually as much as possible. If she can't see much for herself, describe things to her. Give details of size and shape and colour. Even severely visually-impaired children usually have some sight, even if only sufficient to distinguish light and dark. This vision can be put to excellent use if others help them by telling them where to look, how to distinguish this from that, how to recognize distinctive characteristics. Persevere. Act as your child's eyes, while at the same time prompting her gently to use her own sight wherever possible, instead of having everything done for her.
- Linked to this, help her to be independent wherever she can. There's a tendency to rush in and do things for a visually-impaired child. Blindness or near-blindness rightly raises the most profound feelings of compassion in us. But your child needs her independence as much as anyone else. She has a right to it. Decide what she can do and what she can't (and as she grows older listen to her

own views on the matter), and give her as many opportunities as possible to be independent and responsible, and to *demonstrate her usefulness to others*. Help her feel she has an important part to play in the family, and that she's valued not only for who she is but also for what she can do.

- Stimulate her other senses. Her senses of hearing and of touch will quickly become extra acute. Develop them with music, stories, poems, shapes, textures. Play games with her, seeing how quickly she can identify different sounds. Since she has difficulty with vision, help her develop mathematically by giving her sets of variously shaped objects which can be mixed and sorted and counted.
- Read to her as often as you can, and stimulate her memory and imagination by getting her to tell the stories back to you, and to add in bits of her own.
- Be careful not to underestimate her. She may be able to do far more than you think. And she may enjoy many 'visual' activities, such as scribbling and painting. Give her every chance.
- Give her plenty of scope for physical activity. She finds it harder than other children to get all the exercise she needs and, later on, to take part in sport and games. Make all the opportunities for her that you can.
- Be careful of her physical safety. Avoid sharp corners in the house, objects she can fall over once she starts toddling, things she can pull on top of her. Make sure the garden is safe and escape-proof.

Finally, with both hearing and visual handicaps, remember how crucially the development of intelligence and of thinking and creativity depends upon our experiences in the world. A very high proportion of these experiences are fed to us through our ears and our eyes. Denied the full use of these organs, even the brightest child will be held back, and will experience all the frustrations and emotional upsets that this involves. Any child with a hearing or visual handicap needs generous amounts of help in compensating for it. Given this help, it is enormously heart-warming to see how well even severely handicapped children can adapt and keep up with their peers. But so much depends upon parents and siblings. Without

Such help will be amply rewarded

their devoted support, the child stays in her own silent or dark world. No one should underestimate the demands this makes on parents and siblings, or the rewards that come to them from watching their child shrugging off her disadvantage and living life to the full.

Other physical handicaps

The norms for physical development given in Appendix 2 for children at various ages are a good way of monitoring your child's progress and making sure that all is well physically. Check his progress against these norms, and inform your doctor if he falls markedly behind in any area. Falling behind does not necessarily indicate the presence of problems, since there is wide variation between children, but it does suggest that further monitoring and perhaps more sophisticated screening are called for.

Cerebral palsy

Cerebral palsy is one of the main causes of physical (and often mental) handicap in children. The issues it raises are primarily medical, and lie largely outside the scope of this book. In addition, children with cerebral palsy are normally diagnosed at an early age, and parents given the guidance and help they need. Nevertheless, since the presence of cerebral palsy can have such a profound psychological effect upon a child and his family, some discussion of its cause and management is called for.

Cerebral palsy isn't a term for a specific disability. It's a collective term that covers brain damage caused by many things, of which intra-uterine problems, birth injuries and or childhood conditions such as encephalitis are among the most common. Typically it produces spastic paralysis (hence the terms 'spastic' and 'spastic diplegia', which derive from the word 'spasm'), a condition in which the large muscles twitch convulsively although the ability to move them at will is lost. One or both sides of the body can be affected, and sometimes there is also defective intelligence. Children with cerebral palsy vary enormously in the strength of their symptoms. In some, symptoms are so slight as to go virtually unnoticed, and the child leads a near-normal life. In others the spasticity is so severe, with speech and vision also affected, and the damage

Task 4

to intelligence so pronounced, that the child needs institutional care for at least some part of his life.

There is no proven 'cure' for cerebral palsy, in the sense that the brain damage which causes it can be put right. But there is interesting evidence from research institutes around the world that in many cases the child can be greatly helped by appropriate education and a carefully devised programmed of physical training. The twin assumptions behind work of this kind are that spastic children are capable of much more than we imagine, and that by repeatedly training (or *patterning*) the body in correct physical movement the brain eventually gets the 'message', and undamaged brain areas are able to take over from those which are malfunctioning. Thus children are on the one hand encouraged to do more and more for themselves, in their own time and in a stimulating, loving and supportive environment, and on the other put through an intensive daily physical programme in which their limbs are guided repeatedly by therapists through the normal patterns of movement (crawling, walking, etc.). As the brain begins to respond to these patterns, so the children are given specially designed equipment to help them take over more and more responsibility for their own movement. Special breathing exercises are also sometimes used, so that the child's brain is more richly provided with oxygen. Throughout the treatment, the emphasis is upon cheerfulness, optimism, playful challenge and mental alertness and interest.

New treatments for cerebral palsy

Work of this kind is in its relative infancy, and many medical authorities are still doubtful as to the results. It is also very demanding upon therapists (who have to be particularly well-trained and dedicated) and upon parents, who have to continue the treatment once their child is back home, often for hours each day and for many years. However, it is increasingly hard to ignore the slow but astonishing progress that very many children make under programmes of this kind, and faced with spasticity in a child no parent should lightly accept there's nothing that can be done.

It is unfortunate that parents of handicapped children, who already have their hands full caring for the special needs of their offspring, should also have to be the ones to find the time to lobby governments for better provision for the education and treatment of childhood disabilities. Nevertheless, if your child is physically disadvantaged, learn all you can about the nature of this disadvantage and the availability worldwide of new treatments, and then bombard doctors, politicians and charitable organizations with questions as to why more isn't being done for *your* child. I needn't emphasize that often things happen only when people make a thorough nuisance of themselves, and what better cause for nuisance than the welfare of a handicapped child?

Muscular dystrophy

Muscular dystrophy is a genetic disorder which causes the nerve cells in the spinal column to degenerate, leading to wasting of the muscles, particularly in the legs and hands. The gene responsible is carried in the X (or female) chromosome, yet only males suffer from the disorder. This is because in the female, who has two X chromosomes, the faulty gene is always recessive, while in the male (who has only one X chromosome) the X chromosome is dominant in terms of the relevant neuromuscular functions. Since males never pass on the X chromosomes to their sons, however, they cannot pass on the disease, although women, who do pass X chromosomes to their sons, can.

The distressing feature of muscular dystrophy is its progressive nature; it is harrowing for parents to watch a young boy gradually lose more and more strength from his body, with perhaps the prospect of death in early adult life. The sufferer's intelligence and personality are not affected though, and, as in so many cases of childhood handicap, his courage and acceptance of his condition can act as inspiration for the adults who care for him.

What you can do to help It is vital that the sufferer be given every possible chance to live a rich and meaningful life, and that his parents, while realistic, adopt a positive and optimistic outlook. The progress of the affliction is highly variable, and many boys confound the experts by living on into vigorous and useful adult life. Attitude may be a vital variable here, with those who are taught to face the future with determination and hope doing much better than those who are treated as invalids and taught to give up.

The prospect of increasingly effective treatment should also be kept in mind. In the meanwhile there is interesting evidence that if a child is taught regularly, frequently and vividly to *visualize* full and vigorous movement in his affected muscles, this may help his condition. The same could be true for children who suffer from arthritis and other rheumatic complaints (which can strike cripplingly in childhood as well as in adult life), who can be taught to visualize full movement in their stiffened joints.

With muscular dystrophy and rheumatism, the less the child can be taught to see himself as a cripple the better. Encourage him to move as much as he can, to believe in the possibility of movement, to utilize fully all the strength he has, to keep his mind lively and alert, to develop interests and hobbies, and to prize and value himself just as much as you prize and value him.

Spina bifida

The cause of this congenital condition, which is present at birth, is a failure in the embryo to close the area over the base of the spine. The consequences can be double incontinence and paralysis of the legs, and although surgery can close off the affected areas these consequences can be irreversible. However, unless the child develops hydrocephalus, in which spinal fluid gathers around and affects the brain (this condition is treated by the insertion of a valve behind the ear which draws off the fluid, but if it has developed before birth some irreversible damage may already have occurred), there need be no mental impairment, and the spina bifida child may be able to live a normal intellectual and emotional life.

Psychologically, as with any child born with a crippling condition of limbs or parts of the body, or who develops such a condition, the essential thing is to emphasize through an appropriately organized environment all the things the child *can* do as opposed to all the things he *can't*. Crippled children can become immensely resourceful and adaptive, and can also quickly develop all those abilities which are unaffected by their handicap. The other essentials remain the same as for all handicapped children – love, stimulation, acceptance, optimism, cheerfulness, and the unequivocal communication to the child that she is as valued and as useful a member of the family as anyone else.

191

Bronchial asthma

One of the most common handicaps, in which the child's bronchial muscles go into spasm (usually with accompanying swelling of the mucous membranes), making breathing difficult. In severe cases, a dangerous stress may be placed upon the heart, and even in mild attacks the child finds the condition very frightening and disturbing. The first attack can occur at almost any age, and the cause is still not certain, although there are many theories. One is that the child suffers an allergy to the dust mites present in bedding, furniture and even clothing, or to the hair and feathers of certain pets. Another theory is that the condition is emotional in origin, linked to a deep-seated insecurity brought about by excessive parental expectations, separation anxiety, or frustrations of some sort. Probably both these theories contain some truth, as asthmatic attacks often seem to be triggered on the one hand by the introduction of an allergen into the household, and by emotional upsets on the other. At times, it may even seem as if some children *will* their own attacks (perhaps at an unconscious level) as a means of getting their way or of avoiding an unwelcome situation.

What parents can do Asthma attacks should never be ignored, and medical help should be sought the first time you suspect your child is asthmatic. Your doctor will then advise you how to cope with future attacks, and prescribe the necessary medication. It's vital to keep calm when your child has one of these attacks, and to reassure her that it will pass. Your child's own panic will only make matters worse. Help her to relax the muscles of her shoulders, arms, chest, stomach and legs, since consciously relaxing these muscles helps to relax the spasm in the bronchial muscles which is causing the problem. Without being over-protective (a common error made by many parents of asthmatic children), try to avoid those situations which trigger an attack. Scenes and confrontations in the home perhaps, uncertainties as to parental whereabouts, unrealistic parental expectations, sudden unexpected challenges like surprise tests at school. At the same time, try to identify any allergens (you will have medical help in doing this), and avoid them as much as you can.

Asthmatic children often seem to improve markedly on holiday. Sometimes this is particularly noticeable if they go away without their parents. This may be because they are away from allergens in their own home, because something in the relationship with their parents is stressful, because the novelty helps them to forget their condition, or because they are unable to command parental sympathy. The possible explanations are legion, but they give food for thought in detecting the causes that may lie behind an individual child's condition. Thankfully, many children grow out of their asthma, while most of those who continue to have attacks learn how to control them without undue distress. Continuing improvements in treatment may mean that even these children will in the future be able to free themselves from this troublesome complaint.

Eczema

The red patches and irritation caused by eczema are troublesome both to a child and to her family. But most cases clear up by around age three, and in the meanwhile steroid creams help to control them. In really bad cases, your doctor will advise you on how to secure your child's arms to give her as much freedom as possible while at the same time preventing her from scratching. Advice will also be given on the use of soap and water and oils, and on other aspects of daily management. As with asthma, there is a strong possibility that persistent eczema may be triggered or worsened by allergens (possibly food – dairy products being particularly suspect), so again attention should be paid to identifying and avoiding the relevant substances. Where eczema persists in an older child, a vital aspect of management is the reassurance that physically she's acceptable and nice to be near. This involves plenty of hugging and physical contact, so that she's helped to develop a positive and confident self-image and attitude towards herself.

Cystic Fibrosis

This is a genetic disorder, with the genes concerned inherited from both parents. The symptoms are disorders in the lungs, pancreas and sweat glands, and the child failing to thrive and gain weight as he should. The condition can be diagnosed from the first stools passed by the baby, so it's usually spotted very early. There is no known cure, though pancreatic extracts, antibiotics (to combat the infections to which the child is particularly prone) and physiotherapy are all very helpful.

Children with cystic fibrosis are otherwise perfectly normal, and usually become hearteningly brave and resourceful in handling their condition. Parents and relatives often have to spend long hours patting and massaging their backs to help them bring up congestion in the lungs, but the children submit cheerfully to this, inspiring their parents and all those fortunate enough to know them. Psychologically, it is important to show a young sufferer that he is as quick and bright as other children, that his help in the house is of just as much value, and that in all possible respects you are going to treat him just as you would any other child. Carefully monitor his condition at all times, always heed your doctor's advice, and let your child feel the very special warmth of your love.

Epilepsy

Occasionally caused by brain damage at birth, in most cases no cause for epilepsy is ever found. Essentially what happens in an epileptic attack is that the child has a temporary alteration in his consciousness, as if briefly the brain moves into a different mode of functioning. The first attack can happen at any age, and the frequency of attacks may vary greatly from one sufferer to another. Two forms of epilepsy are recognized. In *petit mal* consciousness is lost for only a second or two, the child suddenly looking strange and vacant (perhaps even mid-sentence), then continuing as if nothing has happened. In *grand mal* he has convulsions which affect the whole body, and falls unconscious to the ground, shaking violently (and often rhythmically) while he clenches his teeth and foams at the mouth. It is as if his brain has produced a sudden and violent burst of electrical activity, sending the wrong signals to his limbs and body. While in this state he may urinate; he should be moved on his side and care taken that he does not choke or bite his tongue. (Note, though, that not all convulsions are caused by epilepsy; they can result, for example, from a high temperature. They should always be reported to your doctor immediately.)

There is no known cure as yet for epilepsy, but anti-convulsant drugs can lessen the number of fits in *grand mal* sufferers. Sometimes the incidence of such fits lessens naturally as the child grows older. Treat your epileptic child as normally as possible. His epilepsy doesn't affect his intelligence or personality or other areas of physical health or development, and most epileptic children are not held back by their condition. Explain to your child, when he's old enough to understand, that all brains emit electrical signals. That's how they communicate with the nerves and muscles of the body. In the case of the epileptic, it's just that the brain seems to get rather too enthusiastic at times. If he suffers from *grand mal*, reassure him that he doesn't do anything bizarre during his fits, or become violent or frighten his family. It's just like a very bad attack of shivering. Do make sure that he avoids activities which could be dangerous if he has a fit – cycling and climbing for example, or swimming unless he's in shallow water and watched all the time by a good swimmer. And do make sure that teachers and others who come into contact with him know he has fits and what to do if they occur. Unlike most other handicaps, the epileptic child gives no sign of his condition until a fit occurs, and this may leave others who don't know about it shocked and unprepared.

The epileptic child can lead a normal life

Diabetes

Diabetes is a complaint that tends to make its first appearance either in childhood or in middle adult life. The symptoms in a child are lack of energy, extreme thirst, frequent urination, failure to gain weight and, if the condition goes undetected, coma (which can prove fatal unless dealt with immediately). The management of diabetes depends upon regular monitoring of blood sugar levels and regular injections of insulin, since it is the body's inability to do its own monitoring and produce its own insulin (via the pituitary gland) that causes the problem. The details of this management are highly specialized and lie outside the scope of this book, but your doctor will explain them to you.

Once a diabetic child has had his condition stabilized (i.e. the correct amounts of insulin have been determined and are being administered), there is no reason why he should not lead a near-normal life, except that his diet has at all times to be carefully monitored, with carbohydrates and other key foods being given in meticulously weighed and measured

The importance of diet

195

amounts. The earlier a child develops diabetes, the more readily he accepts this routine, since he will have had little experience of any other. Once at school, teachers must be fully informed about his condition, and the doctor's advice heeded on the question of engaging in sport or games where cuts and bruises or other physical injury are likely (these can lead to complications in some diabetics). As a parent, you have to understand and accept fully the extra demands that a diabetic routine is going to place upon you – not always easy at first – and then get down to reassuring your child that apart from this routine he is just like anyone else.

The causes of diabetes are not really clear, though genetic factors (including perhaps small genetic mutations while the child is still in the womb) may be involved. But continuing advances in modern treatment, involving amongst other things the possible implantation under the skin of a capsule which will monitor blood chemistry and release insulin as needed, hold out good hope for the future.

Mental handicap

There's no very clear dividing line between physical and mental handicap, in that the one may often be associated with the other (as sometimes with cerebral palsy). Any physically handicapped child is bound to be at a certain *mental* disadvantage due to the limits placed by physical handicap upon opportunities for experience, even though she may have no actual loss of mental functioning. Similarly a child with mental handicap is bound to be at a certain *physical* disadvantage in that she's limited in the opportunities she has for using her body. However the term 'mental handicap' is usually taken to refer to specific mental disabilities such as those caused by Down's Syndrome and autism.

Down's Syndrome
Down's Syndrome (mongolism) is caused by an extra chromosome in the twenty-first of the twenty-three pairs of chromosomes that carry the genetic information in the human body. There are in fact three different forms of this syndrome, but these need not concern us here except to say that in one of the

forms (most usually found where the mother is over thirty-five) the chances of another child in the family suffering the same disability are slight (trisomia-21 mongolism), while in another the chances are significantly higher (translocation mongolism). The parents of a Down's Syndrome child will of course want to be clear on this distinction if they are contemplating further pregnancies.

The symptoms associated with Down's Syndrome are well-known. They include mental retardation, retarded physical development, small stature, slanting of the eyes, changes in the iris of the eyes, shortening or broadening of the skull, snub nose, open mouth and large fissured tongue, misshapen hands, and some malformation of the heart and skeleton. On the other hand, Down's Syndrome children are by nature almost invariably lively, cheerful and sociable, with a great capacity for warmth and affection, and for tackling their handicaps with realism and courage. Their families and friends testify to their sunny and trusting dispositions, and to the way in which they reward and enhance the lives of others through the sweetness of their temperaments.

Down's Syndrome is diagnosed at birth (or sometimes in the womb by taking a sample of the amniotic fluid), and parents receive appropriate help and guidance from that point onwards. From a psychological point of view, the important thing is not to limit unnecessarily the expectations one has of a Down's Syndrome child. In spite of the general picture of mental retardation, many Down's Syndrome children show near-normal intelligence, and can be encouraged and educated into living full and sometimes quite independent lives. Parents of Down's Syndrome children who reach this level of achievement are often very impatient over the way in which their children tend to be written off by society. They insist that with appropriate education and guidance the expectations we have of such children could be very successfully raised. They point out that, excellent and caring as the staff are in the special schools to which Down's Syndrome children are sent, there is a tendency to provide a rather stereotyped and unstimulating environment, with the emphasis upon protection and physical welfare rather than bringing out the full potential in each child. As with children with cerebral palsy, bringing out this full potential may mean a high level of personal attention over

Do not expect too little of a Down's Syndrome child

a number of years, but the results more than justify the effort involved.

Provide all the stimulation you can

As a parent, do all you can to provide extra stimulation for your Down's Syndrome child. Give her all the attention needed by an unhandicapped child, and then more besides. Use music, stories, bright colours, pictures. Talk and play with her as much as you possibly can. Respond to her efforts at movement (many Down's babies tend to be rather floppy) and later on at speech. Since her attention span will be short, provide a wide variety of things to interest and amuse her. Laugh and joke with her. Resist the temptation you may have to over-protect her and rather hide her away. Instead, give her plenty of opportunities to meet people, to see things, to be a full member of the human race. Encourage her as soon as possible to do things for herself, to take decisions and make choices, to be useful and helpful in the house, to gain confidence in herself and her abilities, to take appropriate responsibilities, to assert herself when she needs to. Above all, show her that what matters is that she's your child, not that she's disabled.

Autism

The term 'autism' comes from the Greek *'autos'*, meaning 'self', and suggests a child withdrawn into himself to such an extent that he is unable to make proper contact with the outside world. Though the condition was first recognized medically only in 1944, it has captured the popular imagination, and one frequently hears reference, even in children who are attending normal schools, to 'autistic behaviour' or 'autistic symptoms'. In fact, *genuine* autism is rare, so rare that some experts claim it occurs in only one in every 25,000 children. Other authorities put the incidence rather higher, but even where problem children are given the diagnosis of autism on their first medical or psychological examination, further exploration of their condition often fails to confirm the finding. The child's excessively withdrawn and uncommunicative behaviour is seen to be merely a symptom of some other psychological disturbance, and disappears when this disturbance is properly attended to.

Psychological and genetic explanations

The genuinely autistic child is not therefore a case of ordinary psychological withdrawal writ large. The causes of autism lie at a deeper and less accessible level, and remain less

198

susceptible to treatment. Some authorities suggest these causes are psychological. Parents of autistic children tend to be high in intelligence and drive, and it could be that the child realizes early on that he can't meet their expectations, and withdraws into himself at a crucial stage of early social development. Having done so, he can't profit from social experiences later on, and therefore can't develop normally. An alternative psychological explanation is that the child receives some profound psychological trauma (shock) in the early months of life, which terrifies him so totally that he withdraws from a world that can contain such fears.

Other authorities reject these psychological explanations, and consider instead that autism may be a crippling genetic deviation from what would otherwise manifest as high intelligence. Studies of blood serum have discovered serious metabolic defects in some autistic children, and suggest that the precise genetic abnormality may be a fault in body chemistry. This genetic explanation is currently gaining ground, and the divergence of opinion amongst experts as to whether autism is psychological or genetic in origin may be due either to faulty diagnosis (with only genetic autism being true autism), or to the fact that the autistic state in genetically susceptible children can be triggered off by psychological episodes which would leave other children unscathed.

One thing is clear, however, and that is that true autism makes a very early appearance in its victims. Sometimes it appears present at birth (which has inspired another set of explanations, namely that the trauma of birth itself may be a factor), and although a few cases appear normal until around the third year of life (perhaps because their parents have been unable or unwilling to recognize the symptoms), in no instances does it appear to have been first diagnosed after the age of three. Typically, the autistic child is physically normal, and may show certain signs of high intelligence. He may walk early and suddenly, without an intermediate crawling stage, and be very agile and graceful, with great finger dexterity. As he grows a little older, he often shows great skill in clambering up on to things (this skill in climbing frequently remains a feature of autism), rarely falling or hurting himself. Yet to the observant eye, all is clearly not well. Physically and emotionally he is unresponsive to others, failing to adapt himself to

Symptoms of autism

199

the body of his mother or father when held, and sometimes vigorously pushing himself away. He shows the same lack of response to the human voice, so much so that there may be early fears he is hearing-impaired, fears proved groundless by the fact that he responds readily to music. Fascinated by mechanical toys, he shows little interest (often aversion in fact) towards living things, whether people or animals. His facial expression is inwardly absorbed rather than open and alert, though he does take in his surroundings, as is shown by his early preoccupation with sameness, manifesting extreme agitation if furniture or playthings are rearranged, or if a different route is taken to the shops, or if different utensils are used at mealtimes. Often he develops rooted eccentricities in feeding, such as refusing – or accepting only – milk, or refusing food that has to be chewed.

Two types of autistic children In general behaviour, autistic children fall into two separate camps. Some remain passive and withdrawn most of the time, others are lively and alert (though never socially so), sometimes involving long unprovoked tantrums when the child will lie on the floor screaming and kicking and may even attempt to bite or in other ways injure himself. These two camps perhaps represent children who temperamentally would have been introverted on the one hand or extroverted on the other, had their personality development been normal. The passive, withdrawn children rarely develop speech, while the lively and alert sometimes do, though it is of an unusual sort and not readily used for communication. It tends to be monotonous and hollow ('puppet-like' is the description sometimes given), often consisting of repetitions of what other people say (*echolalia*). The words 'yes' and 'I' rarely appear before about the age of eight, the child indicating 'yes' by simply repeating the question, and 'I' by saying 'you'.

Prospects of recovery The outlook for autistic children is at present rather doubtful, though modern biochemical discoveries look increasingly promising for the future. The key variable is speech. Children who have some meaningful speech by around five and a half have a 50 per cent chance of at least partial recovery, while those without speech have the odds stacked more heavily against them. Thus the lively, alert autistic child tends to do better than the passive, withdrawn one. Occasionally, autistic children make a complete recovery, and have gone on to become gifted musicians or mathematicians. But whether recovery takes place or not, one often gets the impression of a ready intelligence imprisoned in a world of isolation and silence.

One of the mysteries of autism is the phenomenal gifts that some autistic children show in highly specialized and limited areas. Music, mathematics and drawing are the three most common examples, with autistic children showing abilities in these fields which leave us baffled, not only because of their superb quality, but because we have no real idea how the children do it.

If your child is diagnosed as autistic, she will need special help and eventually probably special schooling. In coping with her be prepared for disappointments as you try everything to assure her of your love and to get through to her. But don't let these disappointments deter you. Even if it seems impossible to get through to her, we don't know what she may be absorbing at her own deep level. She may show no sign of response, but this doesn't mean your efforts are wasted. In her private world she may be very much aware of you and of all you're teaching her, and even if you (and modern science) can't yet find the key that will open the door into this world and allow her to come out and join the rest of us, your influence may be profound.

How to cope with an autistic child

You'll find early on that it's no good trying to force things upon her. The more insistent you become, the more withdrawn and agitated she becomes, until it looks as if she perceives you as a threat (though her agitation may stem from her own inability to respond). So the answer is to make things available, knowing that she may be taking in the impressions offered and that she may in her own time make use of them, rather than pressing her. Often if left on their own autistic children suddenly open out and show normal pleasure in things (they may also do this when with other children), only to clam up again or become destructive when adults approach. Normal, relatively simple tasks like weaning and toilet training become many times more difficult with autistic children, and here you will need specialist help and advice.

Given that many autistic children are upset by rearrangements of furniture and by strangers and strange animals, it also makes sense to keep the environment as consistent as possible, with plenty of space for movement and for safe climbing. If the child is liable to tantrums, the calmer her environment the better. You can't stop her tantrums, and the best advice is often to let her work them out to her own satisfaction, but it's worth seeing what will soothe or comfort her. Sometimes it's music, sometimes it's certain colours, rarely is it people. You have to watch for self-injury during these tantrums, so organize things so that you can see without always being seen, and be ready to intervene at once if your child starts head-banging (which can cause brain damage) or anything else dangerous. As she may rarely approach you, try to socialize her by finding the things she likes and then making her come and take them from you rather than going across and giving them to her. Use these favoured objects as rewards too, so that if she does something she's asked or makes an approach response, she's able to see these actions bring desired results.

Implications for your social life
Your social life may also pose problems. People drawn to your child's physical beauty withdraw when they find their normal social overtures produce no response. Expect this, then plan ways to get round it. If friends understand the true position, those that are worth having will rally around. Since autistic children sometimes show outstanding gifts in mathematics, music or the visual arts, it helps if your friends include people who are knowledgeable in these areas. Autistic children do not seem to 'learn' these gifts or their development in the way of normal children, so your knowledgeable friends are unlikely to be able to use their conventional teaching skills (though some autistic children do take to formal music lessons, listening to their teacher play and then repeating the music after her). Instead, they should concentrate upon exposing your child to opportunities for creative or mathematical expression, or taking them to places where they can use their eyes and ears, and experience high levels of creative ability.

Do all you can to encourage speech
Help her all you can with her speech. Again, let her see that producing the right sounds brings good results. Sit her in a chair opposite you, hold up something she wants, and keep repeating a word you want her to learn. When she says it herself, give her the reward. Steer a line between being over-indulgent and giving her everything she wants too readily, and rigidly holding things back until she's learnt what you want her to learn. Look upon her echolalia as a good sign (at

least she's using speech), but concentrate your rewards primarily upon her attempts to produce speech of her own or to repeat words you specifically want her to learn. Don't look upon her remoteness as necessarily an indication of lack of interest, and don't look upon her coldness as necessarily an indication of lack of love. Try to see her as someone rather distinct from the rest of us, in that she can't follow the same 'rules' of understanding and communication. One day, perhaps sooner, perhaps later, she may be able to leave this private world and join us. Until she does, be sure of one thing. She isn't where she is from choice.

[5]

The Second and Third Years

THE SECOND AND THIRD YEARS are a delightful time in your child's life, for him and for you. During these years he develops more and more into a proper person. He learns to walk, he masters an amazing variety of skills, his language develops to a point where he has command of much of the vocabulary and grammar used by adults in everyday life, he becomes physically mobile and much more independent, and, most remarkable of all, he gains the ability to *think*. This means he's less at the mercy of his immediate physical needs, more in control of himself and his environment, more able to communicate with others, able even to form attitudes and ideas about the world, to ponder over experiences, to predict what is going to happen next.

But most of all during these years your child will become a real companion. He'll chat to you, and want to be involved in your activities. He'll ask questions, he'll have opinions and pass comments. He was good company in the first year of life, because he listened while you told him things just as if he understood, but now he'll begin to play a proper part in the conversation, amusing and cheering you with his spontaneous attitude to life and his efforts to bend language to his own use. He'll follow you around, copy the things you do, want to help, want to be like you. From now on, his contribution to the family will be an increasingly positive one. 'Whatever's happening,' he seems to be saying, 'count me in'. He's one of us. He's arrived, and wants everyone to know it.

Life is a magical journey of discovery For the child of this age, given a happy home and plenty of stimulation, life is a magical journey of discovery. He looks out at a world of infinite fascination, full of excitement and fun. Everything has a novel feel to it. Experience hasn't staled for him the pleasures of life. He feels the warmth of the sun,

206

he registers the bright colours of nature, he delights in animals and family pets, everything (not to wax too poetical about it) has a shining newness about it that would bowl us adults over if we could rediscover it. Even a trip to the shops is a big adventure. He takes in everything, eager for experience and delighted by what he finds.

But since he feels things so intensely, he also experiences disappointments and frustrations and boredom in the same overwhelming way. He hasn't learnt to put up with things, to be philosophical if he can't immediately have what he wants. For him, life is a matter of extremes. The high flights of joy which he experiences are counterbalanced by the depths of despair, and this is worth remembering when we're impatient with him for making 'such a fuss over nothing'.

Watching the emergence of your child from babyhood into this more mature and confident stage is one of the most rewarding experiences life has to offer. Sure there are ups and downs, and moments when you feel like sending him round to his doting grandparents for good, but the privilege of watching and guiding him from the restricted horizons of babyhood into the wide horizons of the outside world is a priceless one. And you needn't stop at watching and guiding. You can actually *share* this magical journey with your child. We've each of us forgotten virtually all our own experiences when we were this age. The earliest memories most people have date back to around age three, and even then they're fragmented and elusive, like half-remembered dreams. Though these first three years have a profound influence upon the children and adolescents we soon become, and upon the adults we now are, at a conscious level it is as if our lives began at around four or five years. Our memories go back firmly and clearly to then, but delve back further and we're met by a wall of forgetfulness, like a fairy spell.

You can experience this journey with your child

Some psychologists say there are good reasons for this forgetfulness. If we could really remember these early years, we'd be a trifle red-faced at our own helplessness, and at the way even our most intimate bodily needs had to be handled by others. It mattered nothing to us at the time, but looking back from adult life it would be a very different matter! Anyway, be this as it may, we forget almost totally what it was like to be one, two and three years old, and as a parent you now have the chance to re-enter this world through the eyes of your child. Playing with him, talking with him, getting down on the floor with him and becoming part of his experiences, you can witness the wonder and the joy, the anger and frustration with which he interacts with his environment. And by helping him, encouraging him, providing him with the right stimulation, you can see how daily he learns more about this environment and about how to respond to it and manipulate it, sometimes learning perforce to live with things as they are, sometimes learning how to change them to make them more as he wants.

Stimulate your child's imagination We know little about the early origins of imagination, since small children are unable to tell us much about what goes on inside their heads, but it's certain that these years see the rapid development of this vital inner resource. Imagination allows us to be creative, to think up new ways of doing things, to *add* to the physical realities in the outside world. Without imagination, mankind would still be back in prehistoric times, if he'd even managed to survive at all. During the years from one to three you have the chance to stimulate this resource in your child. I shall talk in detail later about how to do this, but one of the basic necessities is reading to her. Sharing books and stories with her is one of the happiest parts of a parent's job, and it begins in the years one to three. You can start the process of telling and reading stories to her from one year old onwards, and although she won't want to listen for very long at first, and won't understand a great deal, she'll love the experience, and you can set your own imagination free along with hers, absorbing yourself once more in the delightful story-book characters who were a part of your own childhood.

Don't divide life into 'her time' and 'my time' All this sounds time-consuming, and there's no doubt that it is. From now on, your child spends less and less time in her cot during the day and more and more time with you. Increasingly, her satisfactory development depends upon the time older people are able to spend with her. Right at this early stage, it's useful for parents to avoid the habit of dividing the clock into 'her time' and 'my time', the former being the dutiful minutes one spends playing with her and the latter the enjoyable adults-only hours spent pleasing oneself. Fathers are particularly prone to making this kind of distinction, with the result that when they're with their child their minds can often be elsewhere, planning what they're going to do the moment their child is put to bed or taken off their hands by her mother. It isn't that they don't love their child, it's just that they haven't got into the habit of counting her fully into their lives. If this description fits you as a father, get into the routine of thinking about '*my* time with my child', and put as much of yourself into this time as you do into the other things you enjoy. Since you're going to spend the time with your child anyway, give yourself (and her) the chance to get full value out of it.

In both fathers and mothers, the 'my time' and 'her time' distinction is often particularly noticeable when busy professional lives are lived outside the home. Teachers, doctors, social workers, business people often give themselves selflessly to their responsibilities at work, yet shift their own children (and sometimes partners) to the back of the queue. If you're one of these people, remember your child has rights too. She isn't old enough to tell you about them, but if you aren't able to give her the time and attention she needs now, you may have some unwelcome questions to put to yourself if avoidable problems loom up ahead.

DAILY CARE

On a more mundane level, the years from one to three see a big change in patterns of daily child care. Your child's growing desire for independence and her developing physical skills mean that increasingly she's able to do things for herself. She needs less in the way of special foods, and will soon be eating much like the rest of the family. Toilet training will soon mean no dirty nappies to change and wash. There'll be fewer disturbed nights, and she'll sleep on just that bit longer in the mornings. And she'll graduate from pram to pushchair, making shopping and journeys easier propositions.

Feeding your toddler

Let's look first at one of the most important of these changes, feeding. There is something particularly pleasing about preparing food for others, and seeing them polish it off enthusiastically. And something correspondingly irritating about seeing them greet your offering with disdain. In accepting the food you've prepared they're in a way showing their acceptance of *you*, while when they reject it they seem to reject you along with it. Food is a powerful symbol of our warm feelings for others, and in refusing the symbol our feelings are also refused.

So the psychology of giving and accepting food is an important one, and touches something very deep in us. Not for nothing is the symbol of food used so widely in the ceremonies of the world's great religions. Not for nothing is the breaking of bread together seen as a token of friendship between people, or as a sign of reconciliation after conflict. Not for nothing is the refusal of hospitality seen in some cultures as a deadly insult. Evidence of this kind shows how closely human beings associate food with friendship, unity and love.

You naturally enjoy seeing your child eat Naturally then, feeding your child is a sign of your love for him, and when he eats up with gusto you get as much pleasure out of the exercise as he does himself. Equally naturally, when he refuses to eat you feel hurt and resentful. Doesn't he want this tangible example of your care and concern for him, of your wish to share happy family experiences with him?

Of course, this isn't the only reason you enjoy seeing him tucking into his food, and feel anxious if he leaves it. You want him to grow strong and healthy, and to have all the vitamins and proteins he needs. You dislike seeing good food go to waste. Then there's always the worry that he's going to refuse food when you take him to visit friends, and show you up in front of them. And worst of all perhaps there's the feeling that if he is allowed to dictate to you over what he intends to eat and not eat, he's going to start dictating to you in other areas too, and end up a very defiant and troublesome proposition.

The toddler years seem to be a favourite battleground over food. Few children present no difficulties during this time, while some can be particularly awkward, rejecting everything with a cavalier disregard both for your feelings and for your clean floor, sometimes even spitting out selected half-chewed morsels to the stomach-turning discomfort of everyone else present. You try him first with one thing then with another, but the greater your ingenuity, the greater his contempt. At times, driven to distraction, you wonder how he swallows enough to keep alive, let alone thrive. And thrive he usually does. Anorexia (a condition in which people voluntarily starve themselves) is quite definitely a phenomenon of adolescent and adult life (see Chapter 8). The toddler, even if he knew of this strange-sounding complaint, would show a healthy disdain for it. Unless there is something physically wrong with him, he manages somehow to get what he needs, and although the faddy child (we'll call him this for want of a better term) usually remains on the thin and wiry side, he'll be as full of energy and as raring to go as most other youngsters of his age.

In dealing with faddy children, two points must be made clear. First, children vary in their need for food and in their temperamental attitude towards it. Second, whether a faddy child becomes a full-blown feeding problem depends not upon his temperament but upon you. It's in your hands whether mealtimes become a battleground or not. If you let yourself feel the emotional slight I mentioned earlier, and worry over wasting food and over whether your child is going to become self-willed in all things once you give way to him over food, then the scene is all set for conflict. You present him with his meal, he takes a mouthful or two and shows as far as he's concerned that's it, let's get down on the floor and resume the serious business of playing. You reject the idea, and turn his attention back to the unfinished food. He indicates this is not a good idea at all. You insist. He insists. You take over the spoon and try to insert a mouthful. He clamps tight shut, and the mouthful ends up spread liberally around his cheeks. You try again and this time he turns away, receiving the mouthful in his ear. You pass some choice remarks on life in general and him in particular, and he counters with an imperious sweep of the hand which banishes spoon, plate, food and all on to the floor.

After a few domestic dramas of this kind, each mealtime becomes a world war in miniature. Like two skilful generals,

How feeding problems begin

211

you each try to outsmart the other. You alternately try coaxing and demanding. He alternately tries rejecting happily and rejecting crossly. The battle lines are drawn, but the end result each time seems to be the same. You cross and him in tears (but tears behind which lurk an undeniable sense of triumph. As in the first year, he proves the old saw about taking a horse to water but decidedly *not* being able to make him drink).

How to prevent mealtimes becoming a battleground
So what is going wrong and what can be done to prevent it? The essential point to realize is that neither coaxing nor demanding are going to work. As parents we have jurisdiction over a large area of our small children's behaviour, but this doesn't extend to whether they swallow their food or not. Even an extra co-operative child, who does his best to please us, will often gag on his efforts to get down food he doesn't want. And if your child comes to associate mealtimes with unpleasant experiences of this kind, or with a constant battle of wills, he'll come to dread them as much as you do, and it may be years before he loses these unwelcome associations and comes really to enjoy his food.

Throughout childhood, a child's sensitivity to the taste and texture of food is far greater than our own. An adult can if necessary usually tackle food he doesn't enjoy, but a small child's stomach will heave at the very thought. If he doesn't like food, then it's a wretched experience for him to put it in his mouth let alone his stomach. When he's older you can stand over him and force him to eat in a way that you can't at the moment, but don't. He'll end up with a very dim view of food, and a dimmish view of you into the bargain.

Make mealtimes a happy occasion
The rule at mealtimes in the second and third years is to prepare a child small amounts, and put them in front of him without fuss. Have your own meal with him, so that he can see your example of a clean plate. Eating with him also makes mealtimes a shared experience, and not something babyish and special to himself. He's also less likely to become bored, and to leave his food not because he dislikes it but because he wants to get on the floor again and resume the much more interesting business of playing and moving around. If he refuses his food, or toys with it instead of eating, remind him that it will soon be cold and won't taste so good. If he still doesn't eat, carry on with your own food and chat to him normally. Don't keep reminding him to eat up. When you're

sure he won't eat any more, clear his plate away along with your own, without special comment. If there's a second course he can have his share, but keep any left-overs out of sight so he won't start asking for more. You've no intention of letting him fill up on the second course. If there's no second course, don't be in a hurry to lift him down from his chair. He can sit a little longer while you finish your own meal, but keep chatting to him so he won't become bored. Once it's plain he's had enough sitting, lift him down.

The lesson he learns from this experience is that while you enjoy your own food, you're not extra concerned whether he eats his up or not. So there's nothing much at stake. There's no battle and no one ends up defeated. Mealtimes are seen as a happy occasion when he has your company and attention, and there's no need for him to feel anxious if he finds he doesn't like his food. The question of anyone making him eat just doesn't arise. When one day he hears from other children how their parents force them to swallow things they hate he'll be very surprised. And grateful that his parents aren't like that.

But – and it's a big but – this isn't the end of the story. If she doesn't eat, then she's likely to be hungry between meals. This is the point at which you can remind her that she's hungry because she didn't finish her food. Don't sound accusing (or triumphant!) about it. Just announce it in the way in which you comment to her about things in general. If we don't eat when we've the chance, we're likely to be hungry before the next meal. It's a fact of life. And *don't* start giving her sweets and chocolate to tide her over. Parents tell of fearful scenes, of their child throwing a tantrum in her efforts to get sweets, and of having to give in for the sake of peace. The result is that, gorged on sweets, she isn't hungry when the next meal comes round. The way to avoid all this is to resist the habit of dishing out sweets and chocolates on demand. They contain little or no food value, and confuse her appetite and her hunger reflex. The craving for sweet things, once allowed to start in early childhood, grows steadily worse. If she is to have sweets, restrict them to set times during the day, say mid-morning or mid-afternoon, and keep the amounts small. Put the packet out of sight at the top of a cupboard, and give her one to suck (or a small piece of

Don't let your child eat between meals

chocolate) when you have your own coffee and biscuit. And that's that.

She'll soon realize that if she's hungry between meals it's no good expecting to fill up on sweets. Life isn't like that. She'll ask why she can't have more sweets, but rather in the way she asks why it's raining. She isn't expecting to change a fact of life, she's asking *why* it's a fact. Your answer is that too many sweets make our teeth go bad and make us fat. (When she asks is that why Uncle John is fat, hasten to tell her that people can be fat for other reasons too!)

If she really is suffering with hunger pangs, or if she's a child who becomes difficult and cranky whenever her blood sugar is low, then she can have a few raisins or a small piece of bread to tide her over until the next meal. Let her see that this is simply a tiding-over process, and it's only at mealtimes that we can really deal with hunger. If things nevertheless become desperate, then bring the next meal surreptitiously forward a little.

With fair, consistent behaviour from you, your child will learn that mealtimes have their special routine. You're allowed to choose whether to eat or not, and if you decide not, you must wait until the next meal before you make up for it. There's no question of anyone being strict. It's just the way life is. However, in introducing her to this routine, take into account that some children naturally thrive on smaller, more frequent meals. If you as a family normally eat an early breakfast and late lunch, your child may need a small meal mid-morning and a small lunch, rather than be expected to starve five hours and then have a feast. If she becomes too hungry, she may in any case still find if difficult to tell the difference between hunger pains and genuine stomach ache, with the result she won't feel like eating when her food does eventually appear.

Allow your child some choice over food

Usually if a faddy child leaves her food at one mealtime, she makes up for it at the next, not necessarily by eating a great deal but by at least eating enough for her needs. So by allowing her choice you avoid mealtime problems but still ensure she doesn't go short. See that she has equally nutritious food at each mealtime though. It's no use giving her all the essential foods at lunchtime, when she usually isn't hungry, and giving her only bread or cereals at other mealtimes when she usually is. This doesn't mean you have to cook for her each meal. Often it's cooked food that puts her off. She may be a child who prefers her vegetables raw or liquidized to the bland flavours produced by cooking. As for meat, if she dislikes the taste, don't offer it to her. Many children in the toddler stage seem natural vegetarians, and thrive perfectly well, but take medical advice if she's in this category, as she may need a vitamin supplement. (See Appendix 3 for vitamin needs.)

As your child grows older, increasingly ask her to say for herself what she would like for meals. Don't give her an open invitation. Select alternatives which are all equally good for her, and ask which she'd prefer. However, don't insist she eat everything up simply because it was her choice. If you do she'll associate 'choosing' with having to force things down, which will rob her of confidence in the whole choosing process. So let her choose, but accept that what may seem a good idea initially may appear less appealing when it's actually in front of her. And whether she chooses or not, stick to the principle of giving her only small amounts initially, so that she isn't over-faced by a vast mountain of food. Better she should have minute portions and finish them up than become accustomed to always leaving something on her plate. Once she's eaten up, she can always be given more if she wants it.

A question parents often ask is whether they should offer a child a bribe if she eats up. Finish your first course and you can have your second. Eat everything up and I'll find you some chocolates. The answer is that bribery is never a good idea. It works only rarely, because even though your child may dearly want her second course she literally *can't* get through her first. The price is therefore too high. And she then becomes very upset to find she's to be denied her pudding, and sees you in the role of a Scrooge. She'll also develop the idea that the nice things in life are always conditional, and are never given to you simply because people love you and like to see you enjoying yourself.

Don't bribe a child to eat

On the few occasions bribery *does* work, it quickly becomes a treadmill, with the rewards having to be increased time after time, and with your child prevented from developing the right attitude to food. So if there is a second course, give it your child whether she finishes the first or not. But remember what I said earlier about not giving second helpings or letting her see that seconds are available. Offer her a reasonable helping, and leave it at that. Very importantly, don't prepare a second course which is very sweet. If you do, this will encourage your child to focus more and more of her attention upon the second course at the expense of the first. The second course will become the fun part of meals, and the first a dreary prelude which needs to be got out of the way as quickly as possible. Fresh fruit should be the order of the day.

Food your child really dislikes Parents also ask whether food rejected at one meal should be warmed up and presented as a punishment at the next. Few adults would enjoy such treatment, and there's no virtue in inflicting it upon a child. If she enjoys a meal but can't manage it all, she may welcome its reappearance at a subsequent sitting, but if she hates it first time it's even more disgusting heated up second time. No, if she takes strongly against something, let that be the end of it.

The same is true if she can't face a particular food of some kind. When you're sure of this, leave it off the menu. Cabbage is a good example. Many of us think back to a childhood regularly blighted by a heap of greenstuff, stalks and all, menacing us from the plate planted firmly before us. There's no evidence that those who are allowed to escape this experience are any the worse in health because of it, or that those rare children who actually *like* greens are any the better.

Why the humble cabbage should so turn childish stomachs isn't clear. There's something in the combination of smell, taste and texture that disgusts them, but whether this is a sign they may not yet be able to digest it properly we don't know. Suffice it to say that most children grow out of this disgust given time and left to themselves, and provided your child likes other vegetables there's no need to try to hasten this natural course of events. (See Appendix 3 for more on diet.)

Meals as social occasions Taking meals together helps unite a family (I stressed at the beginning of this section the psychological importance of sharing food), and gives everyone a chance to catch up on the news, make plans, and debate the latest differences of opinion. Sadly, many parents choose to miss out on this. When their child is a toddler there's an urge to 'get his meal out of the way first so we can have ours in peace', and the habit persists into later childhood, with the family seldom coming together even at weekends. Not only does this hinder a child's social development, since it denies him adult company and the experience of being part of a family, it also holds him back in other ways. Children who eat with their parents tend to be more advanced in language, because they have more opportunity to hear adults talking and to join in adult conversation. They also tend to know more about their parents as people, and to have more general knowledge.

This doesn't mean never have a meal on your own, just the two of you, after the children have gone to bed. But it does mean that generally meals should be taken together. If the bread-winner is in too late for this to happen in the evenings until the children are older, make sure it happens at weekends.

Make sure that at table your child or children are allowed to take a full part in what goes on. Let them have their say. Listen when they want to join in. Use words they can understand. Explain things to them when they don't catch on. Answer their questions. Let them sit at the table as far as possible as equals. No constant reminders to 'keep quiet until Daddy has finished speaking'. Allow give and take. Show you like having them there and are interested in their point of view, from the toddler stage onwards. If you want them to keep quiet until someone else has finished speaking, ask them pleasantly, and show that *you're* not always interrupting *them* when they try to say something.

Let your child take a full part in the conversation

Once again, as with so much of parenting, showing warmth and interest towards your child at table pays rich dividends in the future. I've already remarked on the advantages for his social development, his relationship with you, his language development and his general knowledge, but there are other long-term gains. By knowing he can join in your conversation, his confidence increases and he learns he's someone with useful things to say. Since he isn't constantly frustrated when he wants to say something, he doesn't end up trying to capture your attention by bad behaviour. He also enjoys mealtimes more, is more likely to eat his food, and is less aware of the things he dislikes because his attention is held by the interesting things going on around him. And he's less likely to develop into the sullen teenager who has to be called half a dozen times to come to the table, and who sits through the meal in dogged silence longing to get down and leave these boring grown-ups to themselves. Include him in things when he's younger, and he'll include himself when he's older.

Don't worry about table manners

Don't fuss a toddler too much over his table manners. It's more important to let him enjoy his food. Time enough when he's a little older to impress on him there are certain standards which make life more pleasant for everyone. For the present, eating and good company are what matter. If you prevent mealtimes from becoming a battle of wills, then whether your child is faddy or whether he cheerfully tackles whatever you put in front of him, you and he will have a great deal of fun at the table. In the years to come, mealtimes are often the only occasion when a busy family comes together, and they should be a good experience for everyone, with plenty of chatter and laughter.

Toilet training

Next to feeding problems, the routine issue that causes most heart-searching during the toddler years is toilet training. All too easily, this too can become an emotional battleground. It can feel very uncomfortable if your child isn't clean and dry as early as others of her age, and the spectre of bed-wetting and of frequent all too public 'accidents' looms large. Due to the taboos surrounding natural functions, and the feeling there's something not quite nice about the subject, parents are often too embarrassed to discuss it even with their doctor or close friends. If they've studied the writings of Freud and Freudian psychologists, they can also have the idea that incorrect toilet training may have dire consequences for their child's developing personality.

Toilet training from the child's point of view

Let's start by looking at the whole procedure from the child's point of view. Up to now whenever there's a feeling of fullness in her bowels or bladder she's relieved it, with a fine disregard for place or the sensibilities of others. In the middle of feeding, in the bath, part-way through nappy changing, as soon as she's dressed to go out, the moment she's in the arms of a prim visitor. It matters not. And relieved it with every sign of enjoyment, as of a job well done. If she could understand the consternation her realistic approach sometimes causes, she would think it very strange indeed. Nature has

218

designed the body to get rid of waste easily and quickly, and by making the process a pleasant one has ensured it isn't unwittingly resisted. So what in the name of goodness are all these silly grown-ups getting so fussed about?

Up to the present, then, your baby has simply responded to her natural urges. But now suddenly, without warning, she's a toddler and people are trying to get her to regulate matters. They start sitting her on a cold hard receptacle and making strange encouraging noises. They inspect the interior of the receptable critically when she stands up, and if it's empty sit her down on it again. If it's full they're pleased, but they become curiously bashful when she wants to explore the object of their pleasure. If she insists, they hold her off and hurriedly empty the mysterious object into a contraption that makes a loud flushing noise and spirits it away. All very odd.

But odder things are to come. It seems now that the pleasant business of relieving yourself when nature calls is frowned on by the adults in your life. If you're clean and dry when they change you, they become very excited and shower you with praise. On the other hand, any evidence that you have obeyed nature at your own convenience is greeted with mutters and dark looks or worse still with a slap on the leg. As extra punishment, you find yourself plonked on the cold hard receptacle, and screwed back into it every time you try to get to your feet. Things, it seems, have come to a pretty pass.

This toddler's eye view isn't an argument against toilet training. Left to themselves, children would realize what is expected of them eventually, when they became aware of how everyone else goes about things. But naturally we want to hurry the process along, and there's no harm in that. On the other hand, it isn't a race, with a clean, dry toddler as the prize. Toilet training should be an unstressful, relatively enjoyable experience for toddler and parents, with nobody upset if things don't go quite to plan, and with no question of punishment if a child fails to understand immediately what's expected of him, or fails immediately to gain control over the complex set of reflexes and muscles involved. **Toilet training should be a relaxed and happy process**

Parents who don't realize this, create the very toilet training problems they most fear. Angry scenes, smacks, forced lengthy sessions on the potty confuse a child to the point where however much she wants to please you she just can't **Consequences of over-strict toilet training** do so. Quite apart from being upset and not understanding what you want from her, bladder and bowel control become much more difficult when you're frightened and nervous. Even adults are reminded of this from time to time! And even after a toddler begins to get the hang of things, strict toilet training should still be avoided. Though things may not be as extreme as Freud suggested, there's no doubt that a child who is frightened into toileting will remain anxious about this side of life for years to come, hedging the whole area with confused feelings of guilt and shame. This doesn't help the rest of her personality development, and if you're equally uncompromising with her in other areas will contribute towards a tightly repressed and over-controlled personality, bound by inhibitions not only about natural functions but about all areas of life. The excessively tidy, excessively clean and proper personality, obsessional and guilty about everything, seems to be a product of severe parenting of this kind. Strict and punitive toilet training by itself may not bring this about, but as part of a consistent pattern of over-fussy and controlling parental behaviour it plays an important part.

With a child who is temperamentally very determined and strong-willed, there will be other problems too. Such children are less prepared to conform to any parental discipline which they can't understand or which goes against their own inclinations. So when it comes to toilet training, battle is joined in earnest, and once she understands what's expected of her, the child deliberately decides to be defiant. Put on her potty she stubbornly refuses to perform, only to produce spectacular results the moment she's allowed free once more. Things go from bad to worse, with parents ending up in despair, and what should have been a simple and straightforward learning exercise is converted into a lengthy and emotional saga, souring all concerned.

How to avoid problems Since you want to avoid all this, how should you go about it? The important essential is to stay calm and unworried. The transition from nappies to potty demands, as I've said, a major adjustment from your child. So it's bound to take time. Attempts to rush matters are likely only to prolong them. Be patient, keep a sense of humour, and rest assured that everything will work out. Through this relaxed attitude you ensure your toddler stays relaxed. There's nothing to be gained by making her anxious. Let her see toilet training is a normal and happy process, in which she's the person who counts. When she performs to order praise her, but when accidents happen or the potty produces no results, keep things low-key. There's nothing at stake, and no need even to make a special comment. Should you feel disappointed don't show it. A child wetting her pants is behaving more naturally than an adult scolding her for it.

The next essential is to adopt a definite routine. I've already said children thrive on routine. It helps them see the world is an orderly place, and that they can learn to cope with it. If your routine fits into one that your child has already established, so much the better.

Learning bowel control

Since bowel control comes earlier and more easily than bladder control, let's take this routine first. Most babies fill their nappies after a feed, sometimes once or twice a day, sometimes after every feed. Make use of this fact. If your child shows his independence by performing between feeds, there'll still usually be favoured times of day that you can identify. When you know your baby is likely to go into action, place him on the pot and let him stay on it until the job is done or until he gets bored with it, whichever is the sooner.

You can start this procedure in the first year if you wish. The drill goes like this. Your child enjoys his feed, and then sitting on your knee you relieve him of his nappy and slide the pot under him. Potting thus becomes part of the pleasant interlude when, with tummy filled, he enjoys sitting with you and being talked and played with. After a few minutes he's usually done the necessary, and you can take him upstairs and wash and dress him. These early experiences won't stop him using his nappy when he wants, but they help him associate the potty with a bowel movement and also with a happy and relaxed time spent in your company.

Start potting at regular times

Once he's taking his meals in a high chair and has learnt to walk, he can be potted at the same regular times. Stay with him, and keep the experience a light-hearted and casual one. If he wants to get up, let him. But ask him to let you know when he feels the need to be potted again. When accidents happen, tell him that soon he'll be able to use the potty every time, like the bigger children do. When he performs as required, praise him but use terms like 'well done' rather than 'good boy'. As I shall discuss later (pages 269–70), we should be careful about using adjectives like 'good' and 'bad' to describe children. If he feels he's a 'good' boy for performing in the potty, he'll think he's 'bad' when he has an accident. So refer to the action rather than to the child himself. But don't be too lavish in your praise. You want to give your child the idea that this is a normal part of life, rather than an extra big deal.

What if he wants to look? This approach also stops him from wanting to explore the contents of the potty too minutely. If you heap praise on him he'll want to see what's caused all the fuss, and will be surprised at the speed with which the precious objects are banished down the toilet. Of course, even with this low-key approach, he'll still be interested in them. He's produced them, and his curiosity makes him want to make their acquaintance. You don't want him poring over them with the concentration of a research scientist, but it's better he satisfy this curiosity and then turn to more interesting things than see you abruptly change your mood from praise to disgust. This will strike him as a very strange piece of behaviour, and far from ending his curiosity will only make it worse.

The best procedure is to let him look, then tell him this is what's left when our bodies have taken the good things out of the food we eat. We don't need it any more, so we throw it away. Let him watch you flush it out of sight. Don't use terms like 'nasty' or 'dirty'. Not only are they out of place for a natural healthy function, they also confuse him. How can nasty, dirty things come out of his body? Does this mean his body is nasty and dirty inside? Keep your explanation short and factual, and use words which he understands.

What if he wants to touch? Most of us can manage this without trouble, but we're uncomfortable if he goes a step further and wants to touch, probably because we weren't allowed to come to terms with our own curiosity when we were children. There's nothing wrong with this curiosity in itself. It's part of a general desire to explore the world. It won't just go away. The best response is to let him touch, but then in the same brisk way as before take the potty away and empty it. Point out to him that we don't want to smear it everywhere because it's hard to clean

222

off, then wash his hands thoroughly. If he asks why we always wash our hands after the toilet tell him that when the food has been through our bodies it would upset our tummies if it got back inside again. So we wash our hands to make sure it doesn't.

Treated this way, a child's curiosity about his own faeces is short-lived. There are plenty of more interesting things about, and he's happy to turn his attention to them. The same applies to the puddles which he produces on the floor while learning bladder control. In a way these puddles are even more fascinating to him than faeces, since he can look down and see them actually being produced. One moment he feels a fullness in his bladder, the next moment water splashes from his body making a pool on the floor. If you watch him while this is going on you'll see him gazing floorwards with a pensive expression, then as if taking a weighty decision squatting down and prodding an exploratory forefinger in the puddle to see what it is he's just created. Say to him 'it's just like water isn't it?', then mop it up. Explain to him, once more in words he understands, that we always mop up water because otherwise we may slip over. Use a variant of this if the puddle happens to be on the carpet (but keep it printable), stressing once more the *practical* side of things rather than telling him there's anything 'naughty' or 'dirty' about what's just happened.

Learning bladder control
Bladder control takes longer to achieve than bowel control, so be prepared for these little accidents over a period of some weeks. Boys usually achieve full control rather later than girls, because the muscles concerned are harder to manage. But with both girls and boys the toilet training procedure is the same. Usually a small child will empty the bladder at the same time as the bowels, though naturally urination will also take place on other occasions. So once she's started having bowel movements in the potty she will also come to associate it with peeing. This is a help. But it doesn't yet signify she's achieving bladder control. It's simply that the relaxed position on the potty together with the emptying of the bowels is conducive to the emptying of the bladder.

The first real signs that a child is ready for bladder training

Keep the potty always handy come when the bladder is able to hold more liquid, and a nappy stays dry for two hours or more – sometimes even overnight. Usually this happens around sixteen to eighteen months. From now on the potty can be kept handy, and your child placed on it every two hours or so. But don't fuss her over it. If she doesn't produce anything, leave it at that. And don't rush to clamp her down again ten minutes later. She'll become fed up with the whole idea. Since they are easier to pull up and down, towelling trainer pants are better at this stage than nappies. But once a child begins to perform each time you pot her, it's best to leave her without pants while she's with you in the kitchen (though take care if she's too close while you're preparing food; particularly with boys a well-directed stream can put an abrupt end to evening dinner). She'll quickly get the idea that she can go to the potty and sit herself down when she needs to, and this makes toilet training a quicker job altogether. She'll become very proud of herself too, which is also a help.

Pants or no pants, your child will soon learn to tell you when things are becoming urgent. The best way to help this learning is to make a game of it. Suggests she calls out 'potty' (or whatever word you choose) at the appropriate moment, and rehearse it with her. She'll think it's no end of a joke, and although you'll have a few false alarms at first just for the fun of it, before long she'll realize you don't take much notice of these and only praise her when something actually happens.

Accidents are bound to happen Usually this signalling system works from the start with bowel movements, but with the bladder she'll sometimes give the signal and almost at once start to wet. Don't blame her for this. Her bladder becomes full, gives a sudden warning twinge, and in spite of her efforts to clamp down she fails. The muscles aren't strong enough yet. And until she felt the twinge, she wasn't aware she needed to go. Quite soon the muscles will become stronger, and she'll also become more sensitive to her bladder and receive earlier warning. Until this happens, simultaneous signalling and wetting are bound to occur. Sometimes she'll even wet first and then signal, genuinely unaware until the urine starts to flow that her bladder is full.

Problems also arise if she's very absorbed in something else. She can't yet give her attention to two things at once, and by the time she's aware of her bladder it's too late. The same thing happens if she's very excited about going, say, to a party. You ask her if she needs the toilet and she insists she doesn't. You may even sit her on the potty with no result. Then you take her to the party only to receive all too tangible proof on arrival that she did need it after all. You're embarrassed and angry in equal measure. Why on earth hadn't she the sense to go when she had the chance, instead of showing you up like this? The answer is that she can't always separate one bodily sensation from another. The feelings of excitement overlaid the warning feelings of fullness. Even at the last minute she wasn't aware of what was about to happen until it happened. Put a brave face on it – no one should be embarrassed at a toddler's accidents.

Bed-wetting

Your child should quickly gain bowel control at night – though you'll often have to get to him smartly in the morning to prevent a disaster. Some babies and toddlers have a habit of relieving themselves as soon as they wake. The action of waking and pulling themselves to their feet sets off the heave in the bowels that is a natural part of peristalsis (the undulating movements of the bowel that pass material along), and before they know where they are a crisis is upon them. If your ears are very sharp you may catch a despairing cry of 'potty', but it's probably better to set your alarm clock a bit earlier so that you can handle things in good time.

Wetting at night is less predictable. The weather plays a part – children wet more on cool nights than on warm. So does the amount of liquid consumed before bedtime. But don't make him go thirsty just to save a wet bed. Lift and pot him at your bedtime. Keep a nappy on him at night until you're reasonably sure it won't be needed (though don't insist beyond the point where battles ensue), and keep up the practice of placing a polythene sheet underneath his bottom sheet and blanket. Boys may need this precaution rather longer than girls.

If you are presented with a wet bed, there's no need for special comment beyond reassuring your child that accidents happen at first but that they don't go on for long. Don't make him nervous or embarrassed (the same applies to daytime accidents). The more nervous and anxious he becomes the

Never make an issue out of a wet bed

225

harder it is for him to gain control during sleep over the necessary muscles. It isn't even advisable to keep stressing that he'll be all right when he's 'older' or 'bigger'. Naturally he wants to be big and grown-up now, and if wet beds remind him that he's still a 'baby' he's bound to start worrying about himself.

With a relaxed attitude on your part, bed-wetting is soon a thing of the past. The psychological and medical evidence points strongly to the fact that, in the absence of physical cause, it persists only where the child is deeply troubled, either by the bed-wetting itself or by other problems in his life. In some cases, if there's frequent conflict between parent and child and if the former makes a great fuss about having to change the wet bed, the child may wet as a way of punishing his parent by giving extra work. He rarely does this deliberately, but during sleep and half-waking his conscious controls over his behaviour are relaxed, and his unconscious tendencies come to the surface.

If he *has* got into the habit of bed-wetting, being angry (or disgusted) with him just isn't going to work. Adopt a more casual attitude, as if you've really stopped taking much notice. Make a pleasant comment such as 'Well done, a nice dry bed' on his dry days, but don't be too lavish about it, and don't focus your praise on him rather than upon his actions. On wet days, change the bed as if this is just part of the day's routine and you don't feel strongly about it one way or another. Your whole aim is to play things down. By making less of an issue about it you help him become less anxious in turn, and the problem usually clears up of itself over the weeks.

What about star charts and electrical devices? Parents sometimes ask whether they should use a more positive approach to bed-wetting, either by putting up a star chart and awarding a star for each dry day, or by investing in an electrical device that goes under the lower sheet and sets off an alarm as soon as your child starts to wet, thus waking him up and stopping him mid-flow. Or a combination of the two methods, with a star for each night when he doesn't ring the bell. After he's collected a set number of stars, he's allowed a special treat of some kind, which increases his motivation.

The answer is that such strategies are rarely necessary. A high success rate is claimed for the electrical device, particularly when used in conjunction with stars and treats, but it's better both for your child and for yourself that he should gain bladder control naturally and within the context of your normal loving relationship with each other.

If this doesn't happen, ask yourself why this control hasn't come and what's worrying your child. The connection between anxiety and bed-wetting doesn't exist just with small children. Sometimes secondary school children, faced with a move to a new school or with undue pressures from teachers and parents, will suddenly revert to wetting, much to their own embarrassment. This can happen even in adult life if the going gets extra tough. In all such cases check first with your doctor that nothing is physically wrong, then reassure your child it doesn't matter and will soon clear up of its own accord. In the meantime, find out what he's worrying about, and try to ease things for him.

Children wet their beds when they are anxious or insecure

With small children, ask yourself firstly whether you've been placing too much emphasis upon toilet training. Has your child been given the impression that a great deal is at stake, that being 'good' or 'bad' depends upon being dry or wet? Or worse still that your love for him depends upon these things? If the answer is yes, take the pressure off. Show him these things aren't really important, and have nothing to do with whether he's good or not and nothing to do with your love for him.

If the answer is no, see if something else is to blame. Are you generally expecting too much from your child? Are you setting him standards which are beyond him? Have you been using punishment too freely? Is he unsettled at being left with strangers if you've started a new job outside the home? Are there quarrels between parents that have been upsetting him? Search out and put to rest these and any other fears and anxieties he may have. They've made him insecure, and the remedy is to reassure him he's safe and secure within his own home and the love of his parents.

Sometimes a child who's been dry for a while will start to wet again when a younger brother or sister arrives (see Chapter 3). This is due to a combination of sudden insecurity at the appearance of this rival plus a desire to copy the baby's behaviour in order to gain the same parental attention. Tell your child that wetting is something the baby will stop doing as soon as he learns to be like his big brother. And made sure

227

that your older child gets a full share of attention. The problem will then disappear.

The toilet training timetable There are no hard-and-fast rules, but generally a child understands the purpose of the potty by eighteen months, and may even have bowel control at this age (and almost always by the age of two). Around this time, he will also usually start asking for the potty when wetting, but often too late for effective action. By the age of two, most children are dry by day (and show bowel control at night), and dry by night six months later, though normally requiring lifting out once in the night, when they usually perform still half asleep. By three, they go through the night without lifting, and barring the odd accident, full toilet training is achieved.

Slipping back into old habits Progress isn't always smooth though. Quite apart from the reversion to earlier behaviour as a result of stress mentioned above, a child may slip back into old habits for no obvious reason. Sometimes he's just become bored with toileting, and forgets about it. Sometimes, especially at around two and soon after, his growing independence makes him want to do things his own way. Draw a fine line between showing him it doesn't matter and making too much of it. Avoid scenes, but tell him firmly that he does know the right behaviour, and he's much too big and clever to go back to being a baby again. Don't put him back into (or threaten him with) nappies if you can help it, but explain this may have to happen. Take the line not that he's letting you down but that he's letting himself down.

Slipping back into old habits in this way is almost always short-lived. Your child wants to be big and responsible like everyone else. And having learnt the comfort of being clean and dry, he doesn't really want to lose it.

Going to bed

No toddler wants to go to bed. This is almost a rule of nature. Whereas most adults regard tumbling into bed at the end of a hard day as one of the luxuries of life, for the toddler bed is a very unwelcome intrusion indeed into the business of living. She's so excited and curious about the world, so anxious not to miss out on any of the fun, that bed seems the most boring place imaginable. Both now and throughout much of her childhood, going to bed is a potential bone of contention between her and you. You think bedtime is a good idea, she thinks it isn't, and often the resulting disagreements are long and heated.

I can't pretend there's an easy answer, short of allowing her to stay up until she falls asleep on the floor. But there are a number of rules that keep disputes to a minimum. Let's summarize them.

- Never use the idea of bed as a punishment ('You do that once more and you go straight up to bed!'). You don't want unpleasant associations of this kind in her mind.
- On the contrary, do all you can to make bedtime actively pleasant. Let her enjoy a play in the bath beforehand. And read or tell her a story once she's tucked between the sheets.
- Don't rush these pleasant activities. Let her stay in the bath until she's had her fun. Make a game of rubbing her dry and tell her that she's got her story to look forward to. Have a routine over the story. Agree with her in advance how far you're going to read so she won't be too disappointed when you stop, then put a bookmark in that page and read up to it. If she's very immersed in the story and wants you to go further, compromise by going on for another page or two, but get clear agreement from her before you do that after this extra ration she must keep her side of the bargain and settle down.
- Co-operate with her in other rituals too, like putting her soft toys to bed. Many children find a great deal of comfort in having Teddy, or even a favourite piece of blanket or material in bed with them. Sometimes these comforters share much of their waking life as well. This is perfectly healthy, and a child should be allowed to grow out of these habits in her own time (comfort objects and thumb-sucking are discussed more fully later in the chapter).
- Gauge her sleep needs accurately. I've already said (Chapter 4) that children vary considerably in their need for sleep. By three, most children need approximately ten hours a night, but there are many who seem to need significantly less. It's unfair to insist your child goes to

bed early if it means she can't get to sleep and lies there bored and lonely. This will only encourage her to come downstairs (something I have more to say about shortly). You want to get her off to bed so that you can start your own evening, but if she needs less sleep than the average (see Appendix 6) this isn't possible. And having to battle with her every bedtime won't help you relax when you do take your well-earned rest.

- Make her bedroom an inviting place. This is discussed in Chapter 1, so there's no need to go over it again. But a bright, attractive bedroom, with plenty of favourite toys on hand, is an important part of the exercise. It also helps if her bedtime story involves some of the characters or scenes in the pictures on the walls. In winter, keep bedroom lighting warm and welcoming, and the bedroom at the right temperature, while in summer keep things shaded and cool.

- Be sympathetic to her likes and dislikes. If she wants a light left on, fine (though make sure it's safe). If she wants the door left open, fine again. And if she wants the curtains drawn back a little so that she can look out at the sky or the stars, that's all right too. Some parents think you should keep a child's room as dark as possible otherwise she won't go to sleep. This isn't so. Better she should lie there looking at the pictures on her walls or at the sky outside until she drops off than that she should lie unhappy in the dark.

- Keep to a set bedtime, but don't be too inflexible. If she's very absorbed in something or if there are other good reasons, give her an extra few minutes. Don't draw attention to this extension though, otherwise she'll start demanding it every night. Simply tell her it's bedtime when you feel the right moment has arrived. And don't refer to staying up late (on a birthday, for example) as being a special 'treat'. If staying up late is a treat this shows that going to bed at the usual time is a chore. Avoid value-loaded terms of this kind.

- Give her an 'early warning', especially if she's very occupied with something. This allows her time to wind down. If there are things to be put away, give her time for this too. But don't make a rule that she must always clear *everything* away before she goes up. Not only is clearing away a bind for a small child, which makes her associate bedtime with unpleasantness, she'll also get into the habit of spinning out the clearing up, both because she doesn't want to do it and because this postpones bedtime. Ask her to put away the easier things, then finish the job yourself after she's been tucked up for the night.

These rules help make bedtime a happy experience for a child. He'll particularly enjoy having the undivided attention of his mother or father as part of the routine. However, even though he'll go to bed happily, this doesn't mean he'll always fall asleep the moment his head touches the pillow. Once he's moved from his cot into a bed of his own (some time during his third year), you've no sooner bade him goodnight and gone downstairs than you hear a thump followed by the patter of feet as he exercises his new-found freedom. You're now faced with whether or not to go back upstairs and tuck him up again, to the accompaniment of a suitable lecture. And whether or not to go back a second time if he ignores the lecture and makes another bid for freedom. If you do go back upstairs and lay down the law the results are often inconclusive; he chooses to ignore you (and quickly learns to do it more stealthily so that you don't hear him), and you counter with threats of dire consequences. If you don't go back up, you may hear him padding around just above your head for an hour or more. What's the answer?

What if he gets out of bed again?

In parenting, as in any other walk of life, a law that can't be enforced is a bad law. Unless you linger outside his door like a policeman ready to pounce the moment you hear him stir, or unless you take the unwise course of frightening him into obedience, he's going to get out of bed on those evenings when sleep won't come. It isn't that he wants to disobey you. It's simply that at his age he responds to the call of the moment. When you tuck him up and tell him to stay in bed he really means to do as you say. But once you've gone and he finds himself bored, the lure of the world outside his bed becomes too strong. He's naturally physically active, and his mind is equally busy, and he just isn't able to let the *abstract* idea of what you told him a few minutes ago override the

A law that can't be enforced is a bad law

concrete wish to put this activity to proper use. Living in the present moment as small children do, he gives way to the enticements around him and hops out of bed.

Let him play in his room if he can't sleep

Rest assured that a child who does this regularly is likely to be an intelligent child, with plenty of initiative and imagination. So long as he's awake, he wants to be up and doing, and even if you could keep him in bed he'd find the experience very frustrating and upsetting. Some parents wonder whether the correct procedure is to keep his room bare of stimulation so there's nothing to jump out of bed *for*, but a bare room is an impoverished environment for a child, and besides, it won't stop him. Finding nothing worth playing with, he'll venture on to the landing to explore other rooms. Or failing that he'll look out of the window or pull the sheets off his bed to make a 'game' of some kind. No, let him pad around for a while as long as you know he's safe. Sometimes he'll pop back into bed when he's had enough, at other times you may find him asleep on the floor. Either way, he's been using his mind instead of lying in bed looking up at the ceiling. Don't worry he'll go short of sleep. A child of his age will take the sleep he needs, and if he keeps himself up late one night he'll drop off promptly the next.

This attitude towards the problem not only allows your child to use his active intelligence if he can't sleep, it avoids giving him the idea he can break your trust the moment your back is turned. Since you haven't made a big issue out of it, trust isn't involved. But if you insist he stay put and he then finds he can disobey you and get away with it as long as he's quiet and you don't hear, then he's learning an unfortunate lesson for the future. He's also learning to keep 'secrets' from you, instead of sharing his life with you.

What if he comes downstairs?

If your child enjoys his bedtime and doesn't feel you mind if he climbs out of bed to play, there should be little chance of his coming downstairs once you've said goodnight. A child who gets into the habit of coming back down can be the bane of a parent's life. No sooner have you sunk into your favourite chair than the door opens and a small figure in nightclothes, often clutching a favourite teddy bear, sidles into the room. When the small figure is questioned on his motives out comes a patently transparent excuse such as wanting a drink or hearing a 'funny noise'. Under protest, the small figure allows himself to be returned from whence he came, only to reappear, sheepish but determined, the moment you're back in your chair.

If a child comes downstairs regularly it shows he's bored upstairs, but more importantly still it shows he doesn't feel the day has ended properly. He still wants your company. He can't put it into words, but he wants the reassurance of knowing you're still there. He feels short of attention, and if you let the habit become established he'll curl up on your knee and watch whatever you're watching on television, with a docility that would amaze you if he produced it earlier in the day. He quickly learns that if he keeps quiet, and if you're watching your favourite programme, you're unlikely to take him back upstairs until it's finished. He may not care for the programme, but he cares very much for the company!

Does he need more attention during the day?

However much you love your child, you want a chance to unwind without him in the evening. So the habit of coming downstairs is unwelcome. It's also another way of giving your child the idea he can break your rules with impunity. The solution is simple. Give your child the attention he needs during the day, spend time with him at bedtime, don't insist he return to bed the moment you hear him padding around upstairs, and he'll be unlikely to come down. If in spite of everything he does so occasionally, pick him up firmly but kindly and take him back upstairs at once. If he asks for a drink give it him, but only when he's back in his bedroom. Don't let him stay downstairs to have it. Should you suspect he's frightened at being upstairs on his own, deal with this as suggested later in the chapter. *Never* lock or threaten to lock him in his room.

The child who calls out regularly from upstairs is a similar problem to the one who comes down. He's bored, and he also wants your attention for its own sake. Attend to these two factors, and the regular calling will cease. You don't of course want to stop him calling when he has real need. So if he still calls occasionally, go to the bottom of the stairs and ask what he wants. If possible, deal with his request without going up to him. If he asks for something definite like a drink, take it up to him, but indicate to him kindly that at the end of the day your legs are tired and you can't be climbing up and down stairs every five minutes. The following evening when he's

The child who calls out from his room

ready for bed ask him if he needs a drink and remind him that now is his chance, as you don't want to bring him one after he's been tucked up. If he refuses one and then calls for it later, remind him from the bottom of the stairs that he was offered a drink a short while ago and can't possibly be really thirsty now.

If he calls for the potty, keep it in the bathroom and allow him to go and use it when he needs, only calling you if the occasion demands bottom wiping. But as always, check that there are no safety hazards such as scissors, mirrors or razors within reach, and nothing on which he can climb. If there's the slightest doubt, keep the potty in his own room, putting it on a large polythene sheet in case of accidents.

PHYSICAL DEVELOPMENT

During the first year of life, your child was growing so quickly you could see the change week by week. In fact she was growing so quickly that, proportionately, she'll never match that rate again. But in the years one to three – the toddler years – she's still growing very fast. In terms of weight, she'll usually be putting on 25–50g (1–2 oz) a week, and in terms of height about 5 centimetres (2 in.) every six months (see Appendix 1). Her proportions are changing too. In relation to the rest of her body her head, from her first birthday onwards, begins to look smaller, and she starts to develop a visible neck. By now, her arms and legs are growing much faster than her trunk. The rolls of baby fat are disappearing, so she looks more graceful. Her bowed legs are beginning to straighten out, and arches (an essential aid to good balance) are developing in her feet. Her hands are taking on more adult-like proportions, and over the next two years she'll increasingly use them like an adult, mastering simple manipulative skills such as holding fiddly objects. Her hair will grow thicker and coarser, and will often begin to darken. Her teeth will fill out her mouth and jaw. Her nose, though it may stay snub until her teens, will grow longer, and the puffiness caused by extra fat around her eyes will disappear. Her control over her movements will increase daily. Once having learnt to walk she'll soon learn to run. Greater co-ordination will allow her by age three to be using her body as a unit, instead of as a set of separate parts. Physically and mentally, she'll become aware of herself as a person, as a 'self' who can move around as she wishes and use her body as a way of interacting with and controlling the environment. Between the ages of one and three years, physically and mentally she begins to look and act like a child and not a baby.

Learning to walk

The things that gives parents most pride in the early years are usually their child's first words and first steps. I've already said something about these first words in Chapter 4, and I shall be returning to the question of language later in this chapter, so let's concentrate for the moment on the first steps.

Although we describe these steps as 'learning to walk', there isn't much in the way of learning about them. In the early years of life, most of your baby's physical development follows a maturational timetable. She matures to the point where she suddenly starts doing things, without having to learn them first. Babbling is one example. As I said before, even deaf babies babble, so there's no question of their learning the activity from listening to and copying others. Crawling, pulling oneself up and pointing are also examples. Walking looks much more complicated than any of these, but experiments have shown that even where babies are deliberately prevented from doing it for a time, the skill still develops once the opportunities are there. And the children concerned easily catch up with other children who have been allowed to walk right from the start.

You won't need to teach your baby to walk

So you don't have to do anything to 'teach' your baby to walk. She'd do it on her own, and every bit as quickly. But this isn't quite the point. You want to be part of the experience, and she'll enjoy your pleasure at her first steps just as much as you will, and will benefit psychologically from these shared moments of delight. On average, babies take these first steps around fifteen months, though there is considerable variation. Some babies manage them at a year and a few even before this, while some wait as late as their second birthday. Walking

235

early doesn't mean your baby is going to be forward in other things too, but it does occur more frequently in babies who are physically active and curious about the world. Perhaps their curiosity prompts them to make use of this new ability just as soon as it becomes available to them, while other babies are content to wait a little longer.

The first steps   Often the first steps take place almost by accident. Your baby pulls herself into a standing position, and suddenly sees something she wants, not on the floor but at or near eye level. Face a picture of eagerness and concentration, she takes first one faltering step then another and another. If she manages to get to what she wants, the delight on her face is ample proof that it was all worth it. But her delight focuses on having got where she wants to be, rather than upon the walking itself. In fact she hardly seems aware this has taken place. You'll notice that she doesn't look down at her legs. All that matters is the objective ahead. Indeed, if something does make her look down, she immediately plumps on to her bottom. The walking seems to be incidental to the other matters in hand. This is just as it should be. Like most other natural activities, if we stop and think how to do it even we adults would find the actual mechanics of walking difficult. Far better to let the walking take care of itself while the mind focuses on other things.

The fact that your baby often takes not just one step but several at her first attempt is an indication that this skill arrives at a single go, rather than being laboriously built up. Nevertheless, there will already have been signs that her development has nearly reached the walking stage. From standing with help at around eight and a half months, to standing holding on to furniture at nine and a half, to crawling at ten and a half, to pulling herself up at around thirteen months, your baby's progress has followed a clear developmental pattern progressing towards greater and greater use of her legs. At twelve months, most babies will walk when led, setting each foot determinedly in front of the other and enjoying themselves no end, and in some cases will even take their first unaided steps.

Encouraging your child to walk   Once she can walk when led, you'll want to encourage her to do it on her own. As I've said, nothing will prompt her to walk before she's ready. But you may be able to get her to *use* her new ability a little sooner than she might if left to her own devices. The secret is to give her some attractive object at eye-level to look at when she's already standing up. She's aware at some level of understanding that it's much more effort to drop to the floor, crawl to her objective and then pull herself up again, than it is to strike out boldly from where she stands. A straight line is the shortest distance between two points she seems to muse, so here goes. Almost as effective is the traditional method of mother and father kneeling to face each other, one holding the baby upright and the other stretching out arms and calling to her. By going down on your knees you bring your face to her eye-level. Keeping eye contact off she sets, refusing, like a good tight-rope walker, to look down. It's also fun to use this method once your baby has already managed her first steps. There's no evidence she *needs* this kind of practice, since she'll soon be scampering away to such an extent that you'll begin to wonder whether walking was quite such a good idea after all. But it gives you lots of fun together, and it's nice she should come to associate the development of new skills with the enjoyment and encouragement of her parents.

Once she starts walking, there's sometimes a lull of a few days or even a week or two during which she forgets all about the new achievement, making you wonder whether you dreamt it all. But then something catches her attention at eye level once more and off she goes, and soon she's even getting to her feet when she wants to go across to something on the floor.

As walking comes so naturally to a child, it stands to reason there's no need for contraptions such as a baby-walker or a walking trolley. Baby-walkers are in fact positively dangerous, as a child can too easily topple over in them. Walking trolleys, on the other hand, are harmless, and if your baby enjoys one (and you don't mind the damage to the furniture) then all well and good.

Whether they can walk or not, children usually master stair **Stair climbing** climbing at about fourteen months, so sometimes this comes before walking and sometimes after. Either way, stair climbing is yet another example of maturation. One day your baby has never climbed a stair in his life, and the next he can go from bottom to top with the skill of an experienced mountaineer. If you're not prepared for this, and haven't taken the necessary precautions, you could be in for a shock. You leave your baby crawling happily in the hall, turn your back on him for a moment and hey presto he's disappeared. With mounting alarm you look first in the lounge then in the dining room. He can't, you tell yourself, have gone far. Under the sofa perhaps? Behind the chair? It isn't until you're out in the hall again and happen to glance up that you see his bright, pleased little face peering down at you from the top of the stairs. He's managed it all by himself, and he gets no end of fun from looking down at you from this strange angle.

Extra safety precautions you will need to take

Guarding the stairs Obviously stair climbing can be dangerous, and you need now to take the necessary precautions. Don't deprive him of his fun. Once he's gone up the stairs once on his own he'll want to do it again and again. But make sure you're with him when he does, walking behind to catch him if he falls. He's unlikely to do this, and you'll be surprised at how assured and skilful he is, nevertheless the risk isn't worth taking. Since you can't watch him every minute of the day, put something across the bottom of the stairs to prevent further unauthorized forays into the upper regions.

Check the house for possible hazards As far as walking is concerned, the main thing is to be on hand to pick him up when he falls, and to check there's nothing sharp or dangerous to fall against. Be extra careful if you have glass panels in doors, or tables with glass tops. Redouble your determination not to leave pans on the cooker with their handles pointing outwards, or hot food or drinks where he can reach up to them. A freshly made pot of tea pulled down on himself by a toddler can cause scalds which will scar for life if not kill. Check once more there are no electrical appliances that may be a hazard, and that there are no unguarded room heaters. Be even more careful than at the crawling stage that there are no outside doors left open. A door pulled shut but not properly secured can swing open or be pushed open by a toddler, and in a moment he can be out of the house. If your back is turned, that's long enough for him to be out in the street and under a car. Leave nothing to chance. If you're the kind of family who keep an outside door open for ventilation in summer, fix a gate across it and make sure the gate is properly designed for the job, not a makeshift device propped precariously in place. It's no good saying afterwards that you just didn't think he was strong enough to pull it open.

Check the garden too. Your toddler should never be left out there unsupervised, but even if you're on the spot accidents can happen if you haven't removed the possible cause. You'll be surprised how nimble your toddler will quickly become. In the time it takes you to get out of the garden chair he can be across the lawn and into trouble. The first necessity is to make sure the garden gate is secure and that he can't squeeze his way through a gap in the fence between you and your neighbour. At all costs, he mustn't get off home territory. Next, be sure there isn't a garden pond into which he can tumble. Though babies are born with a swimming reflex that allows them to dog-paddle with their chins above water, they've lost this reflex by the time they're toddling. A toddler can drown in only a few centimetres of water. He falls in, starts to cry, immediately draws water into his lungs, and that tragically is that. Next check there is no glass he can fall through, or heavy objects he can pull down on himself, or sharp or jagged rocks or garden appliances he can fall against. Even the most innocent garden gnome can be a hazard to a small child if he falls against it, while the blades of a stationary lawn mower can do devastating things to small fingers. Make sure at the same time there's nowhere he can wedge an enquiring head, nothing under which he can crawl and get stuck, or between which fingers can be pinched. If you've been unwise enough to keep an old fridge or freezer dumped at the bottom of the garden, phone the local council and arrange for them to come and collect it without delay.

Check that there are no poisonous leaves or berries in your garden. We all know that the leaves and to a lesser extent the berries of the yew tree are poisonous, but we're probably not aware that so are the leaves of the rhubarb plant, and those of the tomato and even the potato. Also poisonous are the white berries of the snowberry plant, the seeds of the laburnum tree and the native broom, the berries and leaves of the common privet, the seeds of the lupin, the leaves and flowers of the rhododendron, all parts of the monkshood, and the leaves, flowers and berries of many other garden favourites. Consult a garden book which deals with this wide range of hazards,

Check the garden too

239

and remember that when I say poisonous I'm not just talking about an upset stomach. The plants I've mentioned and some others can kill a toddler even in small doses. (Incidentally some common houseplants are poisonous too, such as hyacinths, poinsettia and both dieffenbachia and the castor oil plant; play safe and keep all houseplants way out of reach.)

Many small children die from accidents in the home

Always keep in mind that more people die each year from accidents in the home and garden than die on the roads. Tragically, many of these people are small children. Make sure your child isn't one of them. If you have a large rambling garden that you can't possibly make safe, fence in a secure area near the house and confine him to that. He'll want to get into the big wide world beckoning to him outside of course, but that will have to wait until he's older. Provided you give him plenty of appropriate toys, and a paddling pool in the summer, he won't miss out on too much fun.

Remember that even the most innocent things within or just outside the home *could* become deadly in certain circumstances. It may not be possible to guard against everything, however hard you try, and you don't want to worry yourself into a nervous wreck. But look around your house and use your imagination. Guard against every hazard you can. And never leave small children unattended where danger could lurk. An extensive list of possible hazards is given in Appendix 7.

If an accident does happen

The first rule is to foresee and prevent accidents. The second rule is to be prepared, so that if in spite of everything something does happen, you can cope. Get a good first aid manual, and familiarize yourself with it *before* things go wrong. Go to an evening class if necessary. In a single two-hour session you can be taught most of the practices a parent could reasonably use. Learn mouth-to-mouth resuscitation (there are special techniques for use with the delicate lungs of a small child), how to cope with choking, how to deal with burns, bruises, scalds and cuts. Learn how to deal with shock, concussion, household poisons, foreign bodies in the eye, nose-bleeds and other bleeding. Learn what to do if you suspect a fracture (with neck or spinal injuries, for example, it may be *vital* not to move the child). But remember these things are only *first* aid. Proper medical help must be summoned immediately if the accident is more than a minor one (give the

240

accident, not yourself, the benefit of the doubt – see Appendix 8). So know who to contact. Have the telephone number written down ready (in extreme anxiety we can easily forget numbers we've only committed to memory). Keep it by the telephone, together with second and third numbers that you can use if the first is unobtainable. If you haven't a telephone, keep the numbers handy, and know where to reach a *reliable* phone. As mentioned elsewhere, if this is a public callbox, check regularly to see if it's in use. If it's in a neighbour's house, be sure you have access to it even if the neighbour is out.

Prepare a first aid box with everything you need, and keep it handy. Don't let other members of the household 'borrow' important items from it and then not replace them. Organize everything so that the 'system' takes over if there's an accident. Remember that you will feel weak and shocked yourself if anything nasty happens to your child. The better your training, the better you'll be able to cope effectively in spite of yourself. Don't panic if the accident does happen. You know you're well-prepared. The accident may not be as bad as it looks at first, and the more promptly and efficiently you deal with it, the less the chance of lasting damage.

Language development

In the toddler years, your child's language usually forges ahead. The developmental norms given in Appendix 2 give an idea of the average number of words children use during this period. Psychologists recognize both an *active* and a *passive* vocabulary. The active vocabulary consists of those words a child actually uses, while her passive vocabulary is those words she understands. Naturally the passive vocabulary is bigger than the active, but she is constantly transferring words from passive to active as she gains in confidence and becomes clearer about what she wants to say.

Listen to how your child uses language, and you will also see that she quickly begins to master the rules of grammar. But she doesn't just learn grammar by copying you. She also adapts it for her own use. Many so-called grammatical errors in the language of small children are simply their attempts to apply the rules they've already learnt to new situations. Thus

Mastering the rules of grammar

241

a child will say 'catched' rather than 'caught' and 'bringed' rather than 'brought'. She's never heard you say 'catched' and 'bringed', but has already spotted that you usually add 'ed' when you want to talk about things that happened in the past. Far from being errors, episodes of this kind show you just how clever your child is. So when you correct her, do it gently. You don't want to discourage her from using her initiative in forming new words. Let her know you enjoy hearing her talk, and want to help her explore language and use it to express her ideas and feelings.

Always correct your child gently

Listen for other oddities too. For instance how she tackles the use of pronouns 'I', 'you', 'we', etc.) and possessive pronouns ('my', 'yours', 'ours', etc.). To begin with, she'll find it hard to understand that when you talk to her you use the words 'you' and 'yours', but that when she talks about herself she has to say 'I' and 'my'. To complicate matters further, when she talks about you she's supposed to say 'you' and 'yours' (i.e. the very words that *you* use to talk about *her*!) All very confusing, and hardly surprising that for a time she'll refer to herself as 'you' and 'your'. Don't make a great labour of correcting her over mistakes of this kind. She'll soon get the hang of things. And remember again that all correcting must be done gently and patiently. It's more important she should use language than that she should always be word-perfect.

The same rule applies to mispronunciation of words, and to the little words that she makes up (sometimes because she mishears the words you use, sometimes because she enjoys the sounds). Help her see that language is fun, and that it helps her communicate with the people around her. If she coins her own words, this shows she understands the way in which sounds symbolize the real objects of everyday life. Quite a feat. The acquisition of language is in fact not only one of the most important but also one of the most mysterious pieces of learning a child undertakes. After all, she has to learn that a sound like 'dog' can be used when we want to refer to the real live household pet, but that it can also be used when we refer to other dogs of all different shapes and sizes, and even to pictures of dogs in books. We're so used to language that we take it for granted, but imagine the feat of learning required from a small child, coming to all this for the first time. And imagine how much more difficult it is when we come to verbs, that is to words that stand for actions instead of for definite objects, and that through the use of tenses convey the idea of time. And when we come to adjectives and adverbs which are used for *describing* nouns and verbs. The more you ponder it, the more you realize how bright small children are.

Talking about words that children make up for themselves brings me to a question parents often ask, should you encourage a child in the use of baby talk? Some parents regard baby talk as a secret language between themselves and their child, and value it accordingly, while others are afraid it will lay their child open to ridicule when she mixes with people outside the home. The answer is that baby talk in moderation does no harm. Your child will quickly grow out of it when she meets other children, and if it helps her to use language, fine. On the other hand, if you overdo it, there's a danger you'll begin to see it as 'cute', and fall into the trap of wanting to keep your child a baby for too long. The best bet is to avoid using baby talk yourself once your child starts to use language, and gently offer the correct word when she manufactures one herself. In that way, baby talk won't become a problem.

What about baby talk?

But don't confuse baby talk with your child's sheer love of sound. All small children put together long strings of sounds from time to time, just for the fun of it. Usually this happens between ages three and seven, but there is no particular rule to it. Your child will hear a sound she likes (perhaps someone's name) and go on repeating it over and over, often introducing rhyming variations of her own. Thus 'John' might become 'don' 'bon' 'gon' 'ron' 'fon' and so on. This behaviour seems to come from a very deep-seated fascination with sound for its own sake, as opposed to sound as a means of communication. Don't discourage her ('Oh for goodness sake stop that silly noise; you're driving me barmy'). Her sound games may not mean she'll be a great poet one day, but they show creativity, and seem to satisfy an innate need.

Children are by their very nature noisy. Once you reconcile yourself fully to this, you'll save yourself a great deal of wasted effort. You'll rightly want your child to compromise between his desire to raise the roof and the preference of the rest of the family for a quiet life. But unless you become excessively strict with him, he'll never resemble a dormouse. Nor would it be a

Children are naturally noisy

good thing if he did. I've just mentioned the pleasure children take in sound for its own sake, and of even more importance is the fact that they use sound to release their feelings. When they're excited they shout. When they're cross they shout. And in between times they chatter away, both as a means of communicating with others and as a means of keeping up a running commentary on what they're doing.

So accept that having a child around the house means not just the patter of tiny footsteps but the yelling of a not so tiny voice. If you're constantly telling your child to keep quiet ('You're giving me such a splitting headache') you make it hard for him. He has to bottle up his energy, and becomes cross and irritable and vents his frustrations by destructive behaviour towards his toys and other possessions. Healthy small children are bursting with energy. On the go from morning till night, they need plenty of outlets. Physical activity is one, the use of the voice is another. Channel this activity into useful and constructive pursuits by all means when you can, but don't repress it, or give your child the idea he's just a darn nuisance for being so full of himself.

Letting off sudden loud shouts One of the earliest examples of letting off steam through the voice comes as early as one year to eighteen months, when your child goes through a phase of loosing off a sudden loud shout, just for the heck of it. It is said that advanced karate masters have a shout (called a *kiai*) which is so devastating in its effect that not only does it unnerve opponents it drops small animals dead in their tracks. Anyone with a youngster given to this early phase of shouting is excused for thinking the child was a karate master in a previous incarnation, and has lost nothing of his skill. Many is the plate (if not the large adult) that has gone crashing to the floor when a precocious one-year-old lets out his kiai. Worse, the young kiai master takes evident delight in the discomfort he causes, redoubling his efforts in an attempt to produce even greater carnage.

Most of us react with anger when startled, and there's a strong temptation to take immediate issue with the kiai master and demonstrate to him in no uncertain terms that we too have certain skills in the martial arts. But it's doubtful if he can stop himself, however much you try to make him. The shout is initially spontaneous, and even when he repeats it, intrigued by the havoc it causes, he hasn't yet sufficient control over

244

himself to hold back. Grit your teeth. The phase soon passes. On the other hand, don't encourage him by swapping shout for shout. If he gleefully gets the idea that it's a competition, he'll quickly show that you've met your match.

Chattering

Less of an assault on the nerves but equally tiring to many parents is the child who chatters a lot, particularly as he's always at his most conversational when you're trying to watch a favourite television programme. But as a small child very addicted to chattering once said to me, 'You can't stop people talking can you?' A child who talks does so usually because he's an outgoing character who wants to interact with the world. Don't worry he'll grow up to be one of those compulsive talkers who backs you into a corner and won't stop until he's drained the last bit of energy from you. Compulsive talkers of this kind are usually deeply inadequate people who have to talk to hold attention or to avoid staying with their own thoughts. This is a psychological problem, and your child isn't in that league. He talks for the sheer love of it, and because his enquiring mind is seeking information about the world. If you find this tiring, fortify yourself by remembering how much he's learning. And with the knowledge that the more you talk to him now, when he really wants to talk to you, the less likely he is to become one of those taciturn teenagers who finds talking to his parents the biggest bore around.

Answering 'why' questions

In the third or fourth year of life, your child's curiosity about the world takes the form of the celebrated 'why' question. 'Why you doing that?' 'Why grandma come?' 'Why the light on?' 'Why it rains?' And so on, a hundred times a day. Variants of the 'why' question are 'where' questions and 'what' questions. 'Where you go out?' 'Where Mummy gone?' 'What this/that/it/him/her, etc?' Often most tiresome for parents is the tendency to use 'why?' as a response to every request or instruction, or to develop it, a little later, into 'Do I have to?'

There is only one rule for dealing with a child's questions. See them as part of the learning process, and answer them as fairly and sensibly as you can. Give her the information she needs. Don't fall back on 'Because that's the way it is' or 'Because I say so'. And don't tell her she's nosy when she asks you what you're doing and where you've been and why you're looking like that. She's curious because the world is a big and mysterious place and she's a small child who doesn't know much about it yet and wants to find out more. Keep your answers simple and straightforward, and don't launch into elaborate attempts to explain the principles of atomic physics when she's only asked you why a stone sinks or why the stars shine.

Is 'Because I say so' sufficient? Some parents ask whether it's really necessary to explain to a child why she should do something they've just told her to do. Surely telling her should be enough, and the explanation 'Because I say so' quite sufficient. They feel this particularly when they suspect the child is only asking the question to delay doing whatever it is they want of her. But it's far better to have a child obey you because she sees and understands the reasons for your request. Obedience of this kind is more likely to produce a co-operative child, particularly when she's older. And even though she may not agree with your reasons, at least she'll appreciate your fairness in explaining them. If you simply insist 'Because I say so', she'll see you as an arbitrary authority who lays down the law and doesn't allow her to have any real understanding of (let alone say in) the events and actions that go to make up much of her life. This is a good place to stress – and I shall re-emphasize it later – that one of the things children prize most in their parents is fairness. Fairness means that you're prepared to take the trouble to talk things through, to be consistent, to see her point of view and to be prepared to change what you expect her to do if she comes up with good reasons to the contrary. If your child sees you as fair, you are well on the way to having a relationship with her that will weather the storms of childhood and beyond.

Answer her questions if you want her to answer yours Another major bonus for parents who answer their children's questions is that it prompts children to respond in kind. If you're open and honest with your child, take her questions seriously and don't regard them as irritating or an attempt to be nosy, she won't resent it when you put reasonable questions to her about her affairs in the future. Parents who grumble that their teenage children won't tell them anything about their lives usually confess that in earlier years they rarely responded to their children's natural curiosity. They shut their children out of large areas of their lives, and now they wonder why their children are treating them in the same way. The more you share with your children now, the more they'll share with you in the years to come. It would be too much to expect a teenager to tell you everything. She has a right to some privacy. But if you want her to confide in you, start confiding in her now.

Encouraging language

The early years play an important part in deciding how well your child is going to use language in the future. A good vocabulary, with a good command of sentence structure, will give your child a flying start. It will help him communicate thoughts and feelings, to develop powers of thinking, and to listen and understand when he's being spoken to. A verbally impoverished child is at a massive disadvantage in so many important areas. His progress at school will be slow, the impression he makes on others will be limited, his ability to express himself will be frustrated, and his enjoyment of pursuits such as reading and writing will be drastically reduced. Helping your child develop language is therefore one of the most valuable things you can do for him. The following guidelines will help you make a success of it.

- Talk to him as much as you can. Use language in his presence. Describe things to him. Give him explanations. Answer his questions. But at all times keep your language simple. Use words he can understand. He'll quickly become bored with long elaborate sentences and ideas that are beyond his grasp.
- Listen to him. When he tries to put things into words, don't hurry him, or give him the impression you're in a rush to go and do something more important. Be patient. Show interest in what he's trying to say. Don't make him feel he must gabble things quickly in order to hold your attention.
- Encourage him to use words whenever possible. Many children are very good at conveying their needs by pointing at things or shouting. Prompt him to put his wants and likes and dislikes into words. Don't take this to the point where he becomes frustrated. Keep things playful. But at the same time help him see that words

247

are a much more interesting and precise way of communicating.

- Praise his efforts. Don't overdo it so that he talks *only* to earn your praise. But smile and nod at him when he talks. And say 'Well done' and 'Yes that's good' when he comes out with the right words.
- Correct him gently. I've already mentioned this. But remember that if you tell him he's wrong every time he tries to say something, he'll give up the unequal struggle. And keep your corrections brief. If he makes several mistakes in a sentence, correct only one of them. Don't tell him he's wrong, simply give him the right version, or tell him 'We usually say . . .' He may repeat the correction after you, but don't insist. If he hears it on two or three occasions, he'll soon grasp it for himself.
- Don't rush to complete sentences for him, or to supply the missing words. Wait a few moments to see if he can find them for himself. If you think he knows them, remind him of when he last used them. Help him to use his mind.
- Read to him. Reading is a marvellous stimulus for language. The more your child hears you read, and the more he enjoys it, the more he'll pick up words and the more he'll realize that language is a marvellous tool which he'd like to use for himself.
- Don't pressurize him. Children learn language quickly, but there's a limit to the speed at which they can go. Your main task is to provide him with the *opportunities* within which his language can develop, rather than to try to be a formal language teacher. If you pressurize him, constantly trying to speed him up, he'll get the idea that language isn't fun, and he'll become nervous and anxious (or even plain obstinate) about it.

The child who's slow to talk

When to seek professional advice As in most aspects of development, children vary a great deal in the speed with which they acquire language. If your child is slower then average, this isn't necessarily worrying. Many great men and women (including Winston Churchill) were very late talkers, but spent the rest of their lives making up for lost time. There's no necessary connection between late talking and low intelligence or poor school performance in the years to come. But if you do think your child has special problems in this direction, discuss them with your doctor or health visitor. They will ask you a number of specific questions about your child, and will want to chat to her themselves and listen while she's chatting to you. There's no accurate test they can use with pre-school children, but they'll have in mind a timetable like the norms I've already mentioned (Appendix 2), and will look to see how far your child deviates from it.

The doctor and health visitor will rely on their experience of other children when assessing your child, but from your observation of your friends' children you will be able to get an idea for yourself. If you think your child lags far behind, it's right to seek professional advice. If, for example, she isn't able at age two to use the few recognizable words usually apparent at eighteen months, talk to your doctor about it. This is especially necessary if you think your child's slow speech development may be linked to other factors such as deafness (see Chapter 4). The earlier physical problems of this kind are diagnosed, the less the likelihood of their permanently handicapping your child's development. And of course if her late talking is only one of a range of late development symptoms (e.g. the inability to sit up or to focus her attention), then your doctor will already be aware of this and will be carrying out other tests to establish if there's something wrong.

But for the most part, if your child is a late talker your doctor will reassure you that speech will soon come, and that once it does your child will quickly catch up. Pay special attention to the guidelines already given if your child is a late talker though, and in particular ensure that she sees the *need* for language. If you constantly anticipate her wants and satisfy them for her without her having to ask, she may quite reasonably decide language isn't worth the effort. Enlist the help of the rest of the family in this. Often older brothers and sisters, kindness itself, over-indulge a toddler by waiting on her hand and foot. Point out to them they'll help her even more if they encourage her to put her wishes into words before they jump to satisfy them. Extra problems are sometimes caused if your child is one of twins or is very close in age to the next one in the family. Children in this position sometimes develop a private language of their own, communicating well

Most late talkers catch up of their own accord

enough with each other but failing to communicate with anyone else. It would be wrong to damage their relationship by keeping them apart as much as possible, but it is important to give each of them as much individual attention as you can, and to prompt them through games and reading to relate to you as well as to each other (see the end of this chapter for a more extended discussion on twins).

Nursery schools and pre-school playgroups are of obvious benefit to slow talkers. The need to interact with other children soon galvanizes them into using language, and their progress is usually rapid. If there isn't a suitable school or playgroup handy, do all you can to substitute for it by inviting other children home and by taking your child where she can meet playmates of her own age. But don't worry *her* about her speech. Once you've satisfied yourself there's nothing wrong, results won't be long in coming, and a build-up of anxiety on her part won't help.

Other speech problems
It sometimes happens that even though your child talks readily enough, you notice a speech defect of some kind. Mispronouncing words and muddling up sounds is natural enough, but you may perhaps notice your child has difficulty getting his words out, or is unable to say certain sounds (such as 'r'). Or he may lisp his words, or abbreviate them by leaving off endings. Don't be too alarmed by any of this. You don't want your child to grow up with a speech defect, but provided there's no physical reason for his problems, most of them soon clear up.

Stammering and stuttering   Let's take speech hesitancy first. Your child wants to say something, but try as he might no sound comes. When he does manage it, he may simply produce several repetitions of the sound, instead of going on to the next syllable in the word he's trying to say. We usually refer to the hesitancy as a stammer, and to the repetitions as a stutter. More common in boys than girls (as with most speech defects), stammering and stuttering are more psychological than physical. Often they occur suddenly in a child who up to now has managed language perfectly normally, since in the absence of a physical problem children rarely if ever stammer or stutter from the word go.

So what causes a child to start? Usually there's something wrong with the way in which other people are relating to him. He's become anxious about language. Perhaps he finds it hard to capture and hold the attention of others, and has to rush to get his words out before they turn away and attend to something else. And once the stammering starts, he finds it harder and harder to command this attention, and becomes more and more anxious about doing so. If anyone is heartless enough to tease him, this makes things rapidly worse, and he loses all confidence in his ability to get his words out and talk like other people.

What makes a child start?

It's said that stammering can also result from a sudden very violent shock, such as a child witnessing violence or having violence done to him, and although not a major cause of the problem this is sometimes true. More important, however, are those repeated incidents when a parent becomes angry with a child and scolds him soundly while he struggles to protest his innocence or to sob out apologies, or those times when a child is pressurized into attempting speech by an impatient and unthinking adult. The common belief that a child can start to stammer if he is made to change from left- to right-handedness probably also has some truth in it, not only because such a change may involve emotional scenes but because the areas of the brain that deal with speech and handedness are closely associated with each other.

If you do notice your child developing a stammer or stutter, look at what has been happening to him. Is he being unduly pressurized in any way, either to do with speech or with other aspects of behaviour? Is he nervous or anxious for some reason? Does he have to try to get out his words quickly in order to hold attention? If the answer to any of these questions is yes, then ease up on your child. Perhaps you've been expecting too much from him. Perhaps you've been too busy with other things. Perhaps something else in your life has been making you short-tempered and you've been taking it out on him. Be more patient. Give him more of your time. Show him you love him. Help him to feel secure and wanted. As for the stammering itself, never try to hurry him. Tell him there's plenty of time. Be relaxed about it, and listen to him with the same attention you'd show if he was talking normally. Don't indicate you're embarrassed or upset by his

What you can do to help

stammer, and don't complete his words for him out of a mistaken belief this is helping. Show him he's important enough to be allowed to say his own words, and to be listened to calmly and sympathetically while he does.

Encourage him to whisper and to sing
If he has real difficulty, encourage him to whisper. Few people stammer when they lower their voices. It isn't mouthing the words that is the problem, it's making the sounds that go with them. So make a game of it. Whisper away to each other. Once he finds he can talk perfectly normally in this way, his confidence will start to return. Singing is another helpful strategy. Most stammerers have no difficult with singing, so practise rhymes and songs together. And above all, never tease him or allow others to tease him. If an older brother or sister is involved, take them to one side and explain to them that no one likes to have difficulty with their words. If we're lucky enough not to have difficulty, it's our job to help those who do. The stammerer can't help it, and he deserves our sympathy. There are few crueller things than to see a child taunted by others for a speech defect (or for any other handicap), and you must explain to your older child that although he didn't mean to be cruel, if he goes on with his teasing now that he knows what is involved, he certainly *will* be cruel, and you're sure that isn't something he really wants.

With sympathetic and patient treatment, a stammer or a stutter is likely to clear up. But if it persists, ask your doctor to refer you to a speech therapist so that your child can be given specialist help.

Lisping and other minor problems
Other speech problems are less important. Provided you don't give him the impression that a lisp is in some way 'cute' (for example by fondly copying him and drawing the attention of others to it) your child will grow out of it in time as his mouth and speech organs develop. The same is sometimes true of his inability to say certain sounds, but this problem can persist (especially with the 'r' sound). It won't handicap him, but since children prefer to talk like everyone else, it's advisable to ask for help from a speech therapist. It may not be possible to overcome the difficulty entirely, but usually it can be sufficiently masked to be barely noticeable.

As for abbreviating words, this is often a sign your child is rather bright, and knows the meanings of words and wants to use them before he's able to remember how they end. He may also use abbreviations as a short-hand which cuts down on the labour of speaking and allows him to use language more readily and expressively. Leave him to it. The important thing is that he's using language. He'll grow out of abbreviating when he's older, and it'll probably be one of the little tricks of childhood that you'll miss most when he does.

Learning two languages

Parents who speak Welsh or Gaelic in the home, or who come from ethnic groups of non-British origin, often ask whether a child will suffer if she grows up in a bilingual household. Should they speak one language exclusively to the child until she's mastered it, then introduce her to the second one? Or should she pick up both languages side by side? Should there always be one 'main' language in the home, and one 'subsidiary' one? Will the child's command of language, or her thinking, or the growth of her intelligence be held back because she isn't concentrating just on one language? Will she suffer emotionally?

There's no doubt that some children do suffer from growing up in a bilingual household, but equally there's no doubt that some children gain a great deal from it. More important than the fact that they are bilingual is the way in which parents handle the languages and present them to the children. The rules to follow in order to help your child cope with (and benefit from) learning two languages go something like this:

How to help a child in a bilingual household

- Introduce a child initially to just one language. Two sets of words for everything will only confuse her. If you teach her English first, she's unlikely to pick up the second language very easily, as she can get by outside the home perfectly well without it. So it makes sense to begin with the non-English tongue.
- Nevertheless, *expose* her to English from the start, even though you don't actually speak it to her. Thus let her listen to English television, hear people talking English around her, hear English pop songs and radio broadcasts. This way she'll grasp from the outset that there *is* another way of speaking, and she'll accept this as the natural way of things.

253

- Once your child begins to master her first language, and to understand the proper functions of words, she'll begin to pick up English simply through her exposure to it. Once she's starting to use English along with her mother tongue, read and speak to her in both languages. This makes slightly more demands on you and on her, but get into the habit of saying something to her in her first language, then explaining how we would say it if we were talking English.

- Neither now nor later make the mistake of forcing your child to speak in one language rather than the other. Language is a very basic means of expression, and your child needs the freedom to say what she wants in the words which best suit her purpose. Sometimes you'll speak to her in one language and she'll answer in the other. There's nothing wrong with this. Obviously you'll want to give more emphasis to her first language within the home, since she'll hear enough English outside it, but she shouldn't be made to feel there's anything wrong or disloyal about using English. It's as much her personal possession as is her first language. Occasionally a child can be turned against her first language by being made to use it when she doesn't want to, and occasionally she can be made fanatical about it. Both these things are unfair to her.

- Make sure there are plenty of books in both languages available in the home. And where possible newspapers and television programmes too. This is particularly important with the non-English language, since your child needs to see that it has currency outside the home, and carries its own culture and richness of expression.

- Finally and vitally, make sure both parents agree on the language policy they are going to use, and remain consistent and amicable about it. No child flourishes, linguistically or otherwise, in an unstable or peevish environment.

With the right approach, two languages will enormously broaden your child's horizons, without risk to her intelligence or powers of thinking. And although the possession of two languages may not directly help her when she comes to tackle a third one later on in school, her early experience of switching with ease from one tongue to another will at least help her linguistic confidence and the readiness with which she approaches this new learning task.

Play and playthings

Now for the vital matter of children's play. And let's be clear that although play by definition is non-serious, we should never make the mistake of not *taking* it seriously. Play in young children matters. It is the means through which they carry out much of their learning. Because your child is having fun when he plays doesn't mean he isn't finding out all sorts of important things about the world. Playing with water or sand or dough, for example, teaches him how materials from which the physical environment is made actually behave. Playing with bricks teaches him about gravity and construction. Playing with soldiers or dolls helps him work out some of his feelings about human relationships. Playing with paints teaches him about colour and shape. The list is endless.

Children learn through play

So although a child doesn't play *in order* to learn, it's through play that much of his learning occurs. He plays for fun. To him, there is no distinction between playing and working. A thing is either fun and worth doing, or not fun and best avoided. But in the course of this fun he masters a vast amount of information about his environment, about other people, and most importantly of all about himself and about the things he can and can't do, and the skills he needs to operate effectively.

Through watching your child play, you learn a great deal about him. You see him master materials and the procedures for handling them. You see him meet problems, puzzle over and then triumphantly solve them. You see him daily adding to the repertoire of his talents. You see *how* and *why* he learns. And by watching him playing with his toys and with other children you gain an insight into his developing personality. Is he determined in the face of difficulties or does he give up easily? Is he learning how to share and to wait his turn or does

Learn about your child by watching him play

he demand everything for himself? Is he destructive or constructive? Is he rough or gentle? Does he show ingenuity in tackling problems or is he easily baffled? And when he *is* baffled, does he throw a tantrum or does he take things philosophically? And what happens when he sees other children succeed in such things as party games? Does he share their pleasure or is he angrily jealous?

Through watching your child in this way you see how he's developing. You see where he needs help and where he can be left to handle things for himself. You see where he needs more stimulation and where he's going along happily as he is. Above all you see how much play means to him, and how vital it is that he's given the opportunities he needs.

Stages in the development of play   Your child goes through a number of stages in the development of his play skills and interests. These stages stretch from birth to around sixteen, at which point there is usually a sharp drop in the *range* of activities in which he wants to take part. From this age onwards (earlier in many cases) children become much more specialist, concentrating mainly upon those things at which they show real competence, and in many cases losing the ability to 'play' at all.

In providing play materials for your young child, it's as well to remember the existence of these stages, so that you can be sure you're providing the appropriate things. Once he reaches school age this is less necessary since now he can tell you what interests him, based upon his growing understanding and upon the wide range of play experiences that are offered him at school.

Let's look at these stages up to age five. Actually, although I call them 'stages' there's nothing hard-and-fast about them, and children will vary to some extent one from another. So don't interpret them rigidly. Study your child, and experiment with a wide range of safe play materials. His reactions are the best guide to what he needs. Provided he shows interest in something, and wants to explore its possibilities (with a lengthening attention span as he grows older), this is a good sign that it's right for him.

Age	What attracts him	Best playthings
Stage 1 First 3 months	Movement around him Pleasant sounds Gentle touch	Mummy and Daddy! (this goes for all the stages)

Stage 2 3–6 months	His own movement
	His own body
	The human face
	Sounds and rhymes
	Mouthing
	Novelty
	Shapes and brightness
	Softness and warmth
	Your movement
		Objects to grasp and shake
		Mobiles and hanging toys
		  (especially ones to hit out
		  at)
		Soft toys and woolly balls
		Bags filled with crunchy
		  material
		Baby bouncer
		The floor to roll on
		Your knee to bounce on
		Your voice to listen to
		Your face to see and explore
		His own hands to move and
		  gaze at
		Safe objects to mouth
		A bright and airy room
		  around him

Stage 3 6 months to
      1 year
	The domestic
	  environment
	Things you do
	Physical activity
	Things that can be
	  moved
	Things that can be
	  explored
	Things that come apart
	Things which make a
	  noise
	Things which can be
	  thrown
	Repetition
	Recognizable objects
	Water
	Imitating others
	Shouting (when he's the
	  one who does it)
		Space in which to move and
		  explore
		Household objects
		Watching Mummy and
		  Daddy
		Toys which produce an
		  effect (squeals, musical
		  notes, ringing tones)
		Bath and bath toys
		Things that roll
		Things that surprise him
		  (now you see it, now you
		  don't)
		Things that can be pulled or
		  pushed
		Bricks to knock down
		Nests of containers
		People to imitate
		Things to pummel
		Things to throw down
		Things to tear up
		People who tolerate noise
		  and mess

Stage 4 1–3 years	Pouring and measuring Stacking and building Other children Pulling and pushing Sorting and matching	Walking trucks Rocking toys Hammering toys Toys to be pulled along behind him

Age	What attracts him	Best playthings
Stage 4 (cont.)	Hiding	Abacus or counting frame
	Fitting together and taking apart	Balls
		Soft toys
	Hammering	Bricks to build up
	'Helping'	People who read to him
	Supermarket shelves	People who sing to him
	His own body	People who get down on hands and knees
	Toileting	
	Exploring	Other children to watch and interfere with
	Speech sounds	
	Nursery rhymes	Things that are *his*
	Brief stories	Safe places to hide
	Television	Safe places to clamber on
	Walking	Safe places to creep through or under
	'Conversations'	
	Swimming	Safe knobs and switches to turn, pots and pans
	Music	
	Getting his own way	Water and sand to be poured
	Scribbling	Coloured and shaped objects to match and sort
		Toys that pull apart and fit together
		Children's television
		Picture books
		Paddling pools
		Swimming pool (first visits)
		Space to play and to arrange things as *he* wants
		People who listen to him
		'His' potty
		Shopping trips
		Pencils, paper and crayons
Stage 5 4–5 years	Make-believe	Dolls, cars, soldiers
	Social play	Mechanical toys
	Counting	Bat and ball
	Skipping and hopping	Football
	Cooking	Pets (hamsters and goldfish rather than cats and dogs – be sure you like them too)
	Colours	
	Musical instruments	
	Longer stories	Climbing frame
	Animals	Visits to playgrounds
	Climbing and swinging	Garden swing
	Drawing and painting	Big cardboard cartons for getting inside
	Modelling and making	
	Domestic jobs	Playmates
	The outdoors	Playgroup
	Dressing up	Lego and construction toys
	Constructing	Fingerpaints
	Ball games	Playdough
	Competition	Pastry (to shape and cook)

Age	What attracts him	Best playthings
Stage 5 *(cont.)*	Memory games Puzzles Collecting Other people's bodies Learning to read (perhaps) Learning to write (perhaps) The concept of time Planting and growing Manipulative skills Rhyming Inventing	Old magazines to cut out and paste (mosaics, montage) Glove puppets Marbles Jigsaws Sand trays Containers for water play Dressing up clothes Clothes horses and blankets for making 'houses' Plastic cups and plates for 'houses' Empty boxes and packets for 'shops' Toy money Dolls' house Toy fort Toy garage Board games Races and race games Bulbs, wires and batteries Toy toolset Toy clock to learn the time Books and more books Bedtime stories Beans to sprout in jars Seeds to sow 'His' garden plot Papier mâché Video games Nature walks Family outings (brief visits to museums and places of interest) Swimming pool (regular visits) Things to collect (stones, leaves, pictures, perhaps coins and stamps) Toy box or cupboard for storage Glockenspiel, drum, accordion, recorder (to blow and play with) Potato printing Tie-dying Flower press Drawing books and pencils

Many of the activities given for the earlier stages also apply to later ones, even though they haven't been repeated. For example, mother and father remain two of the best playthings throughout these years, while scope for exploration and for satisfying curiosity is essential (commensurate with age and safety) at all times. So is somewhere to play, and somewhere accessible to store playthings. So is toleration of a certain amount of noise and mess. But these things have been fully discussed earlier, and don't need further elaboration.

See the world through your child's eyes Let's re-emphasize that your child's play experiences depend to a large extent upon your ability to watch him and sense what he needs, and upon your ingenuity and imagination in supplying it. Try to see the world through his eyes. Things that an adult wouldn't look at twice are often full of magical possibilities for a child. See the world, literally, from your hands and knees at times. Getting down on to the floor often recaptures memories of how everything looked to us when we ourselves were small. It helps us pick up once more the essence and flavour of childhood, and allows us to understand more fully how our child feels and responds to what he sees and hears around him.

Providing your child with play materials

Everyday objects as playthings As you'll see from the lists in the previous section, the best play materials in the toddler stage as in the baby stage are often the materials of everyday life. Pans and strainers from the kitchen are ideal for water and sand play. Empty cartons make excellent boats. Notice how your child improvises. In the magic world of her imagination almost anything can be made to stand for anything else. Shoes dragged out from the hall cupboard become a fleet of lorries. Spoons and clothes pegs become people. An empty box becomes a house. Cotton reels become tanks. Unless there is a risk of danger or breakages, let her play with the objects she roots out for herself. Never pour scorn on her inventiveness. ('A car?!? That doesn't look anything like a car!'). Encourage and praise her wherever you can. If she says an old shoe is a boat, then of course it's a boat. Who could doubt it?

Don't interfere too much in her play But don't interfere too much in her play. If she's absorbed in what she's doing she may not want to have to tell you what it's about. And don't rush in too readily with suggestions as to how she can improve things. Let her experience the stimulation of setting up her own play situations and solving her own play problems. Step in with help only when she asks for it, or when it's clear things are beyond her. Wherever possible, let your help take the form of prompts and questions rather than ready-made instructions. Questions such as 'Now what would happen if you tried so-and-so?', 'What about the way you were doing it yesterday?', 'Would it help if you . . .?' and so on. Help her believe in her own ability to solve problems and to come to terms with difficulties, rather than give way to the temptation to leap in and do everything for her.

My emphasis on everyday objects as play materials doesn't **Bought toys** mean of course that bought toys are out of place. Many of them are excellent, and some are carefully designed to provide educational benefit, giving her practice in useful skills and problems to solve. But often the expense of many of the toys in the shops is hardly justified. And when you buy them, once the novelty has worn off she may find them very limited and consign them to the toy cupboard. Mindful of how you had to dig into your pocket in order to provide them you rather resent this, and end up blaming her ('Well you *are* an ungrateful girl', or 'What's the matter with you, can't you *see* how to play with it?'). The result is that your child plays with the toy dutifully for a few minutes, then abandons it the moment your back is turned. If you force it on her, she ends up hating it, and half-intentionally half-accidentally engineers its rapid destruction.

The fact that a child pesters you to buy a toy is no guarantee **You must judge** she's going to like it. She hasn't yet any clear idea of what toys **what toys are** will stand the test of time and what toys won't. She's easily **right for your** taken in by the clever way manufacturers present their prod- **child** ucts, and isn't always a good judge of what she likes and dislikes. Few people enjoy saying 'no' to a child who desperately wants a particular toy, but if you think it isn't right for her say so and stick to your guns. In spite of the tragedy this initially causes, the floods of tears are quickly forgotten. And if, stricken with remorse, you creep back to the shop the following day and buy it for her as a surprise, you'll be chagrined to see that often she's rather indifferent to it by now. She's already lost interest in the toy, and being totally honest at this age about her emotions she can't pretend to an enthusiasm which she doesn't really feel.

Your toddler's attention span is rapidly growing though, and when she does like a toy, she'll spend a fair chunk of time with it. As a baby, even a favourite toy was discarded after a few moments as her attention turned to something else. Now, as a toddler, she's able to explore the potential of things more fully, and to make them really hers.

Good toys fire the imagination and set puzzles I've said children quickly become bored with toys that provide them with limited opportunities. To this we can add that they quickly become bored with toys that confuse them with *too many* opportunities. Toys that bristle with complex gadgetry, for example, and fail to focus a child's attention properly. Some of the best toys are disarmingly simple, and their success lies in the fact that they stimulate the child's *imagination*. This is why she will often have as a favourite toy some everyday object she's found for herself – a stone, a curiously shaped piece of wood, a box in which she's made holes. She likes it because from the first she sees its possibilities. It whisks her into the world of ideas. Its ambiguous shape becomes a boat, a car, a gun, a spaceship, whatever the need of the moment.

Successful toys often set a child a puzzle. The enjoyment of puzzles, of mysteries, is a natural quality in the human race. If it weren't, we would never have developed our sciences and technologies. We learn through meeting puzzles and solving them, and your child is no exception. She also enjoys toys that give her a chance to develop and practise a skill, or which allow her the achievement of creating something such as a model or a picture. In the same way she enjoys taking part in adult 'games' such as baking a cake or making pastry.

It's the doing she enjoys rather than the finished product But note that with many of these things it's the doing rather than the finished product that appeals to her. Both now and later in childhood she'll spend long periods of time absorbed in painting or making something out of scraps of material, only to show little interest in what she's made. Similarly she'll help with the cooking, only to show indifference when the finished product comes out of the oven. For we adults, geared as we are towards achieving definite goals, this all looks very strange. But to a child the fun lies in the activity itself rather than in the result. It's the smearing of paint and the cutting of material and the kneading of dough that she enjoys, rather than whatever it is she ends up with. She's interested in the process, the active part of things, rather than in the product, the static part. Don't criticize her for this. It's often we adults, attached as we are to results, who miss out on the fun.

Most parents quickly come to appreciate the need to think carefully when buying toys for their children. They also understand that good toys are not a question of money. Often the best toys are the cheapest, as can be learnt to our cost when watching a child spend far more time with a cheap little item from the Christmas tree than with the expensive goodies we'd placed at the centre of attraction.

But parents confess to other problems as well. These have **Buying your** to do firstly with whether children should be bought toys **child a gun** associated with violence (soldiers, guns, toy swords), and secondly whether different toys should be bought for boys and girls. Don't agonize over such issues. There's no evidence that children who are bought toy guns grow up more violent than children who aren't allowed them. In any case, once your child mixes with other children she'll soon be introduced to these things. Very early on a child begins to distinguish between the make-believe of play and the real world outside. She knows her toy gun won't really hurt anyone, and that when she shoots her friends they'll quickly be back on their feet again. By forbidding her toy guns you'll spoil her fun and risk setting up a fascination for forbidden fruits. I'm not saying this will make her more prone to violence in later life, but it will make her more prone to hide the toy gun a friend swaps her at school, and to feel that there's something rather wicked about her interest in such things, as if there's a bad streak in her that she must keep out of everyone's sight. So avoid making a big deal out of toy guns either way. If she wants a toy gun she can have one, and it's of no more significance than the other make-believe items in the toy cupboard.

The same relaxed approach is needed when it comes to **Different toys** buying different toys for boys and girls. Start off by buying **for boys and** your child the same things whatever the sex. All babies like **girls** soft toys, and all toddlers like cars. As they grow older, if your girl toddler wants a soldiers' fort and your boy toddler a dolls' house, fine. Equally if the girl wants the dolls' house and the boy the fort. On the one hand there are parents who are terrified their son will grow up a sissy if he plays with girlish things and their daughter grow up a tomboy if she plays with boyish things. On the other hand there are parents who are anxious their children shouldn't be thrust into stereotyped male and female roles, and want them to inhabit a unisex world where all distinctions are banished. Both these extreme sets of anxieties are misplaced.

To take the question of sissies and tomboys first, research shows that children with older siblings of the opposite sex show more interest in the games and toys of the opposite sex than children with older siblings of the same sex. On the other hand, research shows equally that this interest doesn't lead to sissiness or tomboyishness in later life. So if a child enjoys the toys of the opposite sex, leave it at that. Usually this interest (for better or worse) fails to survive the first year or two at school.

By the same token, children who are given unisex treatment by their parents soon learn their respective male or female roles when they mix with other children outside the home. However hard we may try to avoid sex distinctions, the world beyond our doors doesn't share our enlightenment, and once our children come under its influence they quickly gravitate towards their appropriate sexual camps. To try to prevent this by insisting our children remain unisex in the face of ridicule from their friends is wrong and doomed to failure.

Parallel and social play
In the third year of life your child will play alongside another child ('parallel play' as psychologists call it), sometimes watching and copying, sometimes interacting briefly in order to claim a particular toy. This is a forerunner of social play, in which children join in activities together, each one contributing to the play of the other. True social play of this kind establishes itself usually in the fourth year of life, but we'll discuss it now because many of the issues it presents also apply to parallel play. Through parallel and social play your child greatly expands the value of play experience, and begins the task of learning to relate to other people of his own age. Playing with another child enormously expands the scope of his play; it opens up new horizons and possibilities, stimulates imagination, and encourages self-expression. At the same time it leads to frustrations,

battles of wills, and strong emotions. At this age, a child is basically selfish. Not because he wants to be or because he doesn't care about other people, but because he doesn't know any other way. He still looks at the world very much from his own standpoint, and can't yet appreciate that other people have feelings besides himself, or that he has to give as well as take if he is to get on well with the rest of the world.

Encourage parallel and social play by seeing to it that your toddler has every chance to mix with others of his age. Being a parent of a small child is a good opportunity to make new friends for yourself, since you come into ready contact with other parents. Invite them and their toddlers to your house so that the children can mix.

Avoid the temptation to rush in and sort out minor squabbles the moment they arise. Young children need to experiment in their relationships with each other, to find out what works and what doesn't, to experience their own emotions and those of others. But don't hang back when adult intervention is clearly necessary. You may notice that one child never has a fair chance, that another child dominates all the time, that a third is rather rough. Step in and ensure equality by helping children see the needs and rights of others, and be firm when necessary. Don't be seen to take sides, even when your own child is involved, and see that when children are taught to wait their turn they really *do* get their turn. If they wait patiently only to find that everyone has forgotten them, not only will they be disappointed, they'll learn that waiting your turn really isn't a good idea after all, and that next time it's better to jump in first.

When should parents intervene?

Problems can arise if there are other parents present who don't play their part too. We all feel extra protective towards our own child, and there's a natural inclination to jump to his defence when he's victimized, but to turn something of a blind eye when he's the victimizer. There's also an inclination to jump to his defence too quickly if another parent tells him what to do. Nevertheless, if you honestly feel your child is being treated unfairly by another child or group of children and that the other parents are making it difficult for you to put things right, avoid that particular social gathering in future. Your child has to learn to take a few knocks, and has to find that he can't always expect others to behave properly towards him, but on the other hand he's a vulnerable human being who looks to you for protection, and if he's constantly having advantage taken of him it's time to choose a more suitable set of friends.

Involving you in his play As he grows older, your child will also involve you more in his play. When he was a baby much of his play was what psychologists call solitary. That is, although he would laugh and romp with you, he was really reacting to you rather than playing with you in the true sense. Whatever was going on in his head was his own private affair. By the time he's into his third year of life, however, he's beginning to share things with you. He responds to your suggestions, even begins to make suggestions of his own, and to comment on what he's doing. By the fourth year of life these comments have become a running commentary, which includes descriptions of his own actions, of what dolls or toy soldiers are doing, and of what he thinks about their performance.

The young child's ideas about herself

Your child is learning all the time. From the moment she wakes up in the morning until the moment she drops to sleep at night she's learning how the world works. Learning not just about the things around her, but about people too. In the first two years of her life you've simply been the mother or father who provides her with food and comfort and daily care, someone she accepts and loves without question. Although she has been able to tell the difference between you and other grown-ups easily enough, she hasn't really known about you as *people*.

Finding out about you as a person By the third year, all this is changing. Your child is beginning to build upon her simple knowledge of you and to get some idea of the things that please you and the things that don't, and of your daily routine and the special way you have of doing things. The way you smile perhaps, the way you join in her fun, the way you read her a story, the funny voices you put on, the interesting things you find to do together, the way you introduce her to people as if she's a proper person who they will enjoy meeting, the way you have of comforting her when she's upset, the way you let her splash about in the bath or make a mess with flour and pastry in the kitchen without fussing her all the time, and a host of other characteristics that she will come to associate especially with you.

She's also increasingly able to compare you with the other individuals in her life, and this further helps her to distinguish you as separate human beings with your own features and qualities. Mummy has dark hair for example, while Grandma has grey hair and Grandad no hair at all. Daddy smiles and laughs a lot while Uncle Bob is rather serious. Mummy can drive a car while Auntie Ethel can only sit in the back seat and grumble. One parent puts you to bed at night and reads the bedtime story while the other gets you up in the morning and takes you to the shops. Mummy sometimes wears dresses and sometimes trousers, while Daddy sticks to trousers and seems rather against the idea of being seen in a dress.

By these and similar things your child comes to know you better each day, and will express interest in your doings and surprise at any big change in your appearance (a new hair style or pair of spectacles) or any break in routine (a working parent who stays at home for a day, or a meal served in the kitchen instead of the dining room). This is an important stage in her development, and marks the beginning of her real relationship with you. She is now starting to see you as a person in your own right, and the more you're prepared to share your life with her and talk to her about it the better she'll come to know and understand you.

But the most important piece of learning taking place at this stage is your child's developing knowledge of herself. Not only is she finding out that you're a person in your own right, she's finding out that she is too. Up to now, she's been aware of her own needs and of the way her body feels (happy, hungry, tired, warm, comfortable, thirsty and so on) but she hasn't had much idea of who or what she is. Somewhere between the ages of two and three, all this changes. It dawns on her that she is a separate individual, able to think things over, make choices, decide for herself how she wants to behave. She can't put this into words, even to herself, but it marks a vital stage in her development. We describe this as the growth of a sense of 'self'.

Developing her own sense of self

Much of this sense of self comes to the child from the way you handle her. She's getting the idea she's a separate person,

This sense of self comes largely from you

but she doesn't really know what *kind* of separate person. So if you tell her she's a good girl, and show you love and cherish her and think her important, she'll get the idea she really matters. On the other hand, if you keep telling her she's naughty or bad, and if you're impatient and off-hand with her and show her little physical affection she'll end up thinking she doesn't count much or even that she's downright unacceptable.

Depending upon her temperament, she'll either accept this bad view of herself and become dispirited and unhappy, or she'll do her best to assert herself and force you to take more notice of her. Through this assertion, which takes the form of aggressive and disobedient behaviour, she's saying to you I *do* count as a person and I *will* make you realize it. She can't express this. She simply wants you to give her the attention she needs, because without it she feels rejected and lonely. She wants to be on good terms with you, and to have you love and value her and help her to feel she's worthwhile, but she can't seem to find the way to do it, and nobody seems prepared to help.

Think about the words you use to your child

You can see how vital parents are in helping a child build up a satisfactory picture of himself. This doesn't mean you have to worry every time you speak sharply. As long as you show your child you love him and that he matters enough for you to go on loving him even when you have to be firm, you won't go far wrong. But you need to think about the words you use to express this firmness. Words are powerful things, and if you tell him he's bad or wicked or a liar or a bully he'll believe you. To a two- and three-year-old you're someone big and clever who knows all the answers, and once he understands what these words mean he'll add them to the list of things he knows about himself, and carry them around in his mind rather as he carries his own name. This won't stop him from doing the things you consider bad or wicked; he doesn't have that much control over his behaviour. But it will make him feel he isn't a very nice person to have around.

If you find this hard to believe, make a list of the words that describe you as a person. You'll probably start off with your relationship to others (wife, husband, parent and so on), then proceed to the kind of job you do and the way you look, (tall, slim, blond) and then go on to list the qualities you think you have (kind, friendly, humorous, sensitive, intelligent). Now go on and add words like 'bad', 'wicked', 'liar' and 'bully'. How does this make you feel? Even though you know these things are untrue, they don't exactly help you think the better of yourself. And remember that your child, unlike you, is unable to reject the truth of these words. He'll believe what you say, just as at his age he believes the other things you tell him.

When you speak disapprovingly to him, help him grasp that you don't mean there's anything wrong with him *as a person*. Draw attention to *what is amiss with his behaviour* rather than to *what is amiss with him*. Use expressions like 'That was a silly thing to do' rather than 'you are a silly boy'. Or 'That was too rough' rather than 'you're too rough', or 'That's a very cross way to behave' rather than 'What a cross child you are'.

Criticize the action, not the child

The difference may seem slight, but it's a profound and far-reaching one. Your task is to help your child accept himself as a person, and then on the basis of this learn to think about and control his behaviour. We all feel like being rough or cross at times. This is human nature. But we do ourselves no good by rejecting ourselves as evil or worthless. We have instead to face up to these emotions and learn to deal with them without hurting others. A three-year-old isn't going to be able to do this overnight. But he can start to learn, and start to learn from a basis of love and acceptance that will give him the confidence to learn how to handle himself.

So the rule is accept the child. Help him to feel good about himself and the person he is. Then together you and he can work sensibly on the business of developing this person into a happy, thoughtful, secure member of the community. The kind of person who has the power to weigh up his own behaviour and make wise choices. The kind of person who understands and respects himself just as he understands and respects others. And the kind of person who will relate warmly and openly to you now and in the years to come. The main reason for making a success of bringing up your child is that you will be giving him the best chance of a useful and happy life, but in so doing you will also be helping yourself. We all want to have a relationship with our children that brings us pleasure. A relationship in which children and parents can together produce a relaxed and contented home. We don't

Help your child see himself as a worthwhile person

269

want to spend the time in continual battles and hostility, or to feel that our children will never do anything unless we tell them half a dozen times. So though a relationship of this kind calls for extra thought and patience when children are small, it brings an increasingly rich return as the years go by. It allows us to enjoy parenthood, and allows our children to enjoy childhood.

Helping a child see himself as a worthwhile and secure person, someone who is working towards an understanding and control of his own behaviour, is an essential part of this relationship. So important is it in fact that I shall be returning to the subject again as the child grows older (Chapter 6).

Avoiding the double bind situation
Not only must your child be allowed to develop a clear picture of himself, he must also be allowed to develop a clear picture of your relationship with him. This brings us back to the importance of consistency. This time, the importance of using consistent parental behaviour in order to avoid what we call the *double bind*. A double bind is the situation where whatever a child does he's put in the wrong. He isn't allowed to develop any consistent idea of what you want from him. For example he plays happily (and noisily) in the lounge. 'You're driving me mad with that racket,' shouts his father, 'keep quiet.' An unnatural hush develops as the child does his best to co-operate. Irritated by this his father snaps at him a moment later, 'What's the matter with you – sulking or something?' 'Let me get in the house before you start strangling me,' says mother coming home laden from the shops and repulsing an affectionate greeting. Next time, the child remembers this rebuke and hangs back, only to be told, 'Other children hug their mummies when they come home to show they love them.' The poor kid can't win. He isn't allowed to see how relationships work, or what he has to do in order to gain approval. The double bind is particularly destructive of a child's developing personality, and not surprisingly the frequent use of it is linked by psychologists with all kinds of problems, both now and in later life.

ISSUES AND PROBLEMS IN THE SECOND AND THIRD YEARS

Negativism in the two-year-old

One indication that your child is learning she's a separate, distinct person is an outburst of very determined and rather difficult behaviour somewhere between ages two and three. Not all children go through this stage, but many do and it can be trying while it lasts.

It may start quite suddenly, with a child who has been co-operative up to now abruptly asserting herself and letting people know she can say 'no'. But usually it builds up more gradually. Up to now, your child has been quite capable of showing she's very cross about things. She may object strongly to being taken out of the bath while she's still enjoying herself, or she may become irritable if she's tired or bored, or jealous of a new arrival in the family. But this kind of angry behaviour comes from immediate physical causes. The child hits out emotionally at those around her in the way an older person speaks sharply to someone getting on his nerves. It's an immediate and unpremeditated response to a sudden irritation. But as your child starts to become aware of herself as a person and not just as a bundle of sensations and physical needs, so she becomes more aware she's someone who can *cause* things to happen and not just someone *to whom* things happen. Most adults find that their earliest memories of childhood date from around this period. At this point the child moves from the world of the baby and joins the rest of us.

How the negative phase begins

Many parents find this transition and the problem behaviours that accompany it difficult to take. Having come through the sleepless nights and hard work of bringing up a small baby they now find themselves locked into a series of running battles with a determined toddler. What makes things worse is that it often seems as if the toddler is saying a firm 'no' to everything for the sheer pleasure of being rebellious. Which isn't far from the truth. The child has discovered that she can refuse to do something not only because she doesn't like it (as in babyhood) but because saying no is a marvellous way of asserting this new and interesting person she is discovering inside herself.

Saying no for the sheer pleasure of saying it

271

Small wonder that some parents, at their wits' end, adopt a get-tough policy, which often makes things worse. The child launches into a fierce temper tantrum and goes through a range of behaviour well favoured by toddlers over the years. She lies on the floor kicking and screaming and imitates a limp sack of potatoes if you try to pick her up. Or she throws things across the room or goes rigid as a plank when you attempt to thread her legs into a high chair or push-chair. To add to your problems, the worst tantrums are usually reserved for public occasions such as when you have visitors or are in the middle of a supermarket at peak shopping times. The child yells and kicks and struggles and vetoes every suggestion put to her, no matter how reasonable, while you fuss around her hotly embarrassed and the world looks on disapprovingly.

Not surprisingly you have the feeling that in a previous existence the child must have been a skilful general, and still retains the cunning knack of choosing the battleground that best suits her, and of grasping the fact that although you succeed in the end in having your way, the wear and tear on your nerves makes it a hollow victory. And tomorrow is always another day, and another opportunity for your doughty little opponent to spy out the land and decide where you are most vulnerable to attack. What is really needed from you, therefore, is a clearer understanding of what is actually happening, and a better choice of tactics.

Your child needs to assert her independence   The first thing to bear in mind is that even if a get-tough policy were to work, and were to produce a docile 100 per cent co-operative child, this wouldn't benefit either the child or you in the long run. The child's behaviour at this stage is a bid for some independence in life. For some freedom in deciding what to do and what not to do. Unless this bid is accepted and guided by parents, the child ends up doubting whether she has the right or ability to be independent and assert her own wishes. Doubt of this kind leads to low self-confidence, and a lack of initiative and decisiveness which will hold her back in the future. In her dealings with other people, for example, in her school work, and one day in her career and family life. More important, it will hold her back in her relationship with herself, leaving her confused and guilty as to the person she is and the things she wants to achieve in the world.

This certainly doesn't mean that a child at this age should

do as she likes. But there has to be a balance, with decisions left to the child when possible, and care taken to explain to her why she must do as you say when not. Work with children shows that boys and girls who don't go through this negative or rebellious stage often end up described by parents in adolescence as weak-willed and easily led. So what looks like a difficult phase at the time is in fact better news when viewed long term.

Coping with negativism

This still leaves the problem of how to cope with these difficult months. It's one thing to say decisions should be left to the child when possible, and another to know how to go about it. Leaving decisions to the child really means giving him a taste of responsibility, and showing him that you value his opinion and want to take notice of it. In the matter of clothes (a favourite battleground), ask him what he'd prefer to wear, and take time to explain why, should his choice be unsuitable. He can't wear his thin summer shirt outdoors in mid-winter, but if you don't explain why he'll think his wishes don't count with you, and start a scene in which he tries to point out to you the error of your ways.

Give your child a choice where possible

Make things easier for yourself by cunningly hiding away unsuitable clothes, and only leaving him suitables ones from which to choose. He may of course see through this tactic and demonstrate his knack of remembering exactly what these unsuitable garments are, and exactly how much he wants to wear them. This is annoying and inconvenient and bad for your ego, but he's giving a good indication of his powers of observation and memory, excellent pointers for the future. Don't teach him observation and memory are out of place. Praise him (through gritted teeth if you will) for being clever, and while he's enjoying this approval explain that such a clever boy won't want to wear clothes not thick enough to keep out the cold. If he decides that such a clever boy is nevertheless determined to wear them, compromise by agreeing he can wear thin clothes provided something warm goes underneath. This isn't climbing down. Since you didn't start out by *insisting* he wear his warmer things, you're simply showing your ability to work out a solution acceptable to both parties.

273

What if he changes his mind?

Regrettably things aren't always as easy as this. You agree he can wear his red shirt, and he immediately wants the blue one. You agree to the blue one, only to have him shift back and want the red. Much as it looks like he's being plain cussed, he's in fact trying out a new skill called changing his mind. He's fascinated by this skill, and can't understand why it doesn't captivate you in the same way. Rather than terminating things abruptly by forcing the blue shirt over his unwilling head, make a game of it. Tell him you'll put the shirts behind your back and he can point to the one he wants. Then praise him for making a good choice, and slip the shirt on him before he has time to think up less convenient variants of this game.

Adopt a similar approach to food problems. As suggested earlier, give him a choice when possible, and keep the range of things on offer suitable. Once food is in front of him, don't let him change his mind about it. Remind him it was his choice, and that he'd better think more carefully next time. If he doesn't want it, he goes without, so that he sees choice also carries responsibility.

You can see that the strategy for dealing with negativity is a simple one. Allow choice when you can, and if he doesn't like what he's chosen, help him see this is the result of his own actions, and that next time he must choose more carefully. Where it isn't possible for him to have a choice, make your own decision and stick to it in a friendly but firm way, however cross he becomes. This way he learns there are times when decisions have to be made by other people. As long as these decisions are fair and sensible, and are explained clearly to him, he must learn to accept them. After all, there are many occasions in the adult world when we're unable to have things just as we like.

The importance of staying calm

By staying calm you avoid giving your child the idea he has no right to an opinion and even less right to express it. So although he may be pretty cross at not getting his own way, he doesn't end up feeling put down ('invalidated' is the word psychologists prefer to use) as a person.

At this point you may be thinking it isn't always easy to remain calm and patient with a two-year-old, particularly when he's throwing a tantrum in public. But being a parent, as I've said before, teaches us about ourselves as well as about our children, and gives us opportunities for change and development in our own personalities. Staying calm doesn't mean staying outwardly unconcerned while seething inside. It means thinking carefully, in between incidents and when you've time for this kind of reflection, exactly why you became angry and exactly what your anger meant. Don't feel guilty about anger, or inadequate compared to those parents who sail through life with never a fluster. See the anger as a chance to learn more about what's happening in your own emotional life.

When you think about it, you may see your anger was because you felt the child was challenging your authority. Or because he made you feel foolish in front of other people. Or because his behaviour stopped you carrying on with something you wanted to do. These things all make sense as reasons for anger. But do they make *that much sense*? Your child isn't really setting out to challenge your authority or to make you feel foolish or to stop you getting on with your work. He isn't big enough yet to know what 'authority' means to you, or that you're capable of feeling foolish, or that your job of work is really important. He's aware only of his own feelings, and doesn't even fully understand these as yet.

Think about why you got angry

And if other people see you as losing your authority or being made to look foolish, they don't know enough about childhood and parenthood to appreciate that dealing with awkward behaviour and temper tantrums in a two-year-old is never straightforward, and that in your position they'd probably be managing very much worse. It's no fun to feel other people are criticizing you as a parent, but this criticism rarely comes from people who've done the job successfully themselves. Such people will feel for you and remember when they went through much the kind of thing you're now experiencing.

So reason things out. This will help you keep cool just a little longer next time he throws a tantrum, and feel just a little less embarrassed if other people are watching. Soon you may be able to switch off the spurt of anger the moment you feel it, until you're able to see the child's behaviour simply as a problem that can be tackled successfully enough if you remain objective and clear-headed about it.

If the child goes on with her tantrum after you've explained

275

Ignore your child while she throws a tantrum

things to her or tried to divert her attention to calmer pastimes, don't engage in a desperate battle of wills, simply ignore her. While she lies on the kitchen floor howling, carry on with whatever you're doing. Don't worry she's doing herself harm by getting into such a state. It's far healthier for her to get her displeasure out of her system, and to see that you accept her anger without getting excited about it, than for her to bottle it up for fear of punishment if she doesn't stop.

Don't try bribes or punishment

Whatever you do, don't try bribing her into submission. Once you start this, she'll use her intelligence and realize that throwing a scene is a sure way of getting something nice. Divert her attention by all means, but do this in the matter-of-fact way you use when she isn't making a scene. Talk to her in a normal friendly way and ask if she'd like to come and help you with whatever you happen to be doing. Don't mention her tantrum, and if she doesn't take up your offer, shrug your shoulders and carry on without her. Don't punish her by putting her out of the room or worse still smacking her (see Chapter 6 for more on punishment). Punishment at this point only makes her cry harder and gives her the idea that self-assertion leads to trouble or banishment. Adopt the attitude that if she wants to make a scene that's her choice, but your choice is not to take much notice of her while she does. You're just not very interested.

Pay her attention when she starts to calm down

Once her anger is off her chest, and she sees that although you accept her feelings you're not going to have them used as a weapon against you, she'll become bored with herself and start to calm down. Now's the time to pay her attention and suggest something enjoyable that you and she can do together. By taking notice of her now, you're helping her learn it's calmness that brings rewards, not tantrums. If she should decide, however, that now she has your attention she may as well re-establish her tantrum, switch this attention away from her again and carry on once more with what you're doing. Tell her, if you like, that you'll have to put off whatever you were planning to do together until she's quiet again. But don't say until she's 'good' or 'behaves herself', as this implies that the emotion behind her tantrum is naughty or bad.

If she holds her breath in a tantrum, there's no cause for alarm. A child can't suffocate by deliberately holding her breath. But it can be frightening for you, and the best remedy is to tickle her, which makes her giggle and draw in air.

If the scene takes place outside your home, tackle it similarly. If it's the kind of tantrum where your child throws herself to the ground in a busy department store, don't drag her to her feet against her will. Tell her she can stay there if she likes, but you're going on with your shopping. As soon as she's in danger of being left on her own surrounded by strangers she'll soon be upright and scurrying after you. Again she's being given an element of choice, and helped to see the consequences of her choice, instead of being forced to do as she's told and left feeling rebellious and hostile. **Tantrums in public places**

Choice is still possible if the tantrum takes place in the home of friends or relatives. The dinner or tea table is a favourite setting for such extravagant outbursts. The child is given something to eat by her well-meaning hosts to which she takes strong exception. Or she may find herself bored with all these stuffy people and their chatter, and want to stage an attention-seeking diversion. Either way she does something spectacular like throwing (or spitting!) food to the floor, and in the ensuing shocked silence winds herself up for a thoroughly enjoyable bit of self-assertion. In fairness to family and friends you can't ignore her this time. But if you have a battle of wills with her, you'll end up much crosser than you intend, and regret the whole episode when you get home and have time to think it over. So with decision and what the onlookers hopefully recognize as admirable professionalism, pluck her out of her chair and carry her smartly out of the room. At one fell swoop you thus remove her from her audience and give yourself an opportunity to sort things out with just the two of you. **Tantrums when visiting friends or relatives**

Often the sheer surprise of being taken out of the room, coupled with regret at the loss of her captive audience, is enough to calm the child down. Explain to her that you'll take her back into the room with the others if she's going to be quiet, but that if she's going to make a noise then you and she will have your meal on your own. Even if she takes a little time to get the message, before long she'll be fit for returning to the table with a reasonable chance of a smooth run through to the end of the meal. If the tantrum arose over food, take the offending dish away (without comment) as soon as you've put her back at the table. It may be tempting to capitalize upon your success at quietening her by trying to get her to eat her food, but the chances are this will only spark off the problem again.

Tantrums are often a way of getting attention

Mention of the child's regret at losing her audience when you remove her from the table brings us to the important point that tantrums, in fact any kind of unwanted behaviour, are often used by a child as a sure way of getting attention. As she becomes more and more aware of herself as a separate person with a mind of her own, she comes increasingly to test out the effect she has upon other people. If no one takes much notice of her, it seems to her as if she doesn't count for much. So she tries harder to attract attention, and discovers through trial and error that one infallible way is to make a scene. Once she starts a scene (and the more dramatic the better), people stop what they're doing and she becomes the centre of attraction. Thus a child who receives scant attention when she's happy and co-operative learns to fall back upon being difficult. The point is that she needs attention and will try hard to get it, even if she has to make people angry in the process.

Children of course vary in the strength of this need, but they are sociable by nature, and by the third year will have learnt that most of the best things in life (food, warmth, comfort, pleasant sounds, touch) come when other people are around. A child of this age will also need the reassurance that other people think well of her and like having her near. After all, if other people don't think well of her, how can she think well of herself? Her sense of personal worth should come from the love and care and time that adults give her willingly, but if she can't get attention by fair means, her need to be noticed prompts her to resort to other tactics.

Not every tantrum is a bid for attention

This doesn't mean every tantrum is a simple bid for attention. As we've seen, the reason for behaviour of this kind often lies with the child trying out the person he is discovering himself to be. Nor does every tantrum show your child is being starved of attention. Quite apart from the need for self-assertion, the child from the most caring and attentive home will enjoy the heady feeling of getting everyone to look at him from time to time. But the child who is genuinely short of attention will quickly learn to use tantrums as a major weapon for being noticed. You may think that because you're speaking crossly to your child you're punishing him, but the fact is that if he's short of attention he'd rather have angry attention than none at all. So the strategy is to give him plenty of time and love when he's being sensible and co-operative, and take much less notice of him when he's trying out one of his scenes.

At the same time, particularly with tantrums in public places but with those in private too, you can do much to smooth things along by planning ahead. Try to avoid the situations that genuinely upset him. He may object to his push-chair in a busy department store, for example, because he wants to be that bit freer to look around and see what's going on. Or he may feel that in front of all these people he wants to be a big boy and stand on his own feet. If this is the case, let him walk while you're in the store, and put him in his push-chair again when you're outside and he's feeling tired. He may make a scene in other people's houses because he's bored with all these grown-ups who sit around talking and are far too busy to notice him. If so, decline those invitations that you know he'll find tedious, and let him take plenty of toys with him when you go to the others. Do your best as well to draw him into the activities that are going on, and leave for home before he starts becoming impatient.

Plan ahead to avoid scenes

Forethought of this kind makes life much easier for you, and teaches your child that, young as he is, you consider his wishes and his likes and dislikes whenever you can. This makes it easier for you to teach him that *you also* have likes and dislikes, and that it's fair as he grows older and begins to understand what these are that he should show consideration towards you in return. Many parents worry that by showing acceptance and respect for their child's wishes they'll be spoiling him and 'storing up trouble' for the years ahead. The reverse is the case. No child is spoilt by parents who show consideration and understanding, and who make it clear the child matters enough to have feelings of his own. The way to store up trouble for the future is to ignore these feelings, so that the child has no incentive to study your feelings in turn and no example of how to go about doing so. Or to let the child have everything he wants without helping him see the consequences of his actions and thus learn to discriminate between what's good and what's bad, what helps and what harms, what's important and what's trivial.

Show consideration for your child and he will show consideration for you

Lessons learnt during this difficult phase in the third year are of enormous importance in helping your child develop a confident and considerate personality. Don't lose sight of this even when things become extra trying and when people say things like 'I should give him a good hard smack if I were you'. They're not you, and your child is not their child. You and not they will have to live in the future with the damage done by the ill-considered 'good hard smack'. And conversely you and not they will have the joy of living with a child who has responded to your patience and understanding, and who repays you with mature and co-operative behaviour in the years to come.

But don't over-indulge him One of the manifestations of your child's growing self-will is an insistence upon getting the things he wants. He's really coming to know the world now, and when he sees sweets or toys he increasingly imagines the pleasure he'll get from them. So he demands you buy them, and won't listen to your refusal and your reasons for it. Though to begin with he may not have felt *that* strongly over the goodies concerned, the very fact that you're saying no converts them into the most desirable acquisitions under the sun.

In the face of his insistent demands (backed up by the usual rent-a-tantrum) there's a tendency to give in for the sake of peace. Don't. At this age, he has to learn that you don't say no for the fun of it, and once you say it you mean it. The thing he's demanding is unsuitable, and you're not buying it for him. Firmness now stands you in good stead in the months and years to come. It may take time, but once your child realizes you won't give way just to shut him up, the edge is taken off his pestering.

The third year of life is in any case time for your child to start learning he can't have everything he wants. It's from now on that a child can be spoilt by over-indulgence (buying him things to keep him quiet, or just for the sake of it). If he's given everything he wants, whether suitable or not, he'll have no opportunity to learn to appreciate gifts, or to care for them and get the most from them once he's got them. From now on, he's old enough to begin to discriminate, to make choices between something he'll really enjoy and something that's just fleetingly caught his eye. From now on he's ready to start learning that money doesn't grow on trees, and that we treasure things more if they don't come too easily. I can't over-emphasize the importance of this. Knowing how to discriminate and how to appreciate are lessons that start now, and continue throughout childhood.

Growing out of the negative phase

Whenever you meet with difficult behaviour from your child that begins suddenly and quickly establishes a definite pattern, you can be pretty sure it's only a phase and will probably disappear as quickly as it came. What's happening is that your child has reached a point where she can do things in a new and different way, and is trying out this new way to see what happens. Some children go through these phases more regularly than others. No sooner does one phase end than another begins, some of them welcome, others less so.

Such phases are part of the way a child learns, both about herself and about other people and their reactions to her. However difficult some of the phases are, they show the child is developing the variety and strength of personality that we value in people. Nobody wants to think their child is growing up colourless and lacking in spirit. And this means we have to pay the price from time to time of living with a particular shade of colour or a particular outburst of spirit that we don't find all that convenient.

Negativism is just a phase of your child's development

If your child has a naturally sunny, outgoing disposition, the chances are she will have fewer negative, stubborn phases that the more intense child, but no one can expect any child to be always plain sailing. The rule is to remember that the phase your child has just entered is a part of her development, and will soon pass and be replaced by something easier or (if you're a born pessimist) at least by something different. And if you need another thought to help you through these episodes, remember we were all children once and gave our own parents a thing or two to think about.

By the time a child reaches her third birthday, the particular negative phase we've been discussing (and it's probably the worst) is usually on its way out. Particularly if you have handled it successfully, the child will know you and herself very much better by now. She will be confident that you love her and accept her as a person, and that you're firm about the things she's not allowed to do and won't be budged by displays of temper. She will have learnt many of the limits within which she has to live, and that these limits are reasonably broad, fair and sensible, and thus acceptable to her.

Another sign that she is now recognizing you more and more as a special person is that she will show evidence of wanting to become like you, and to copy your behaviour. Often, as if to reward you for having put up with her baulky, negative phase, a child now becomes particularly co-operative and helpful. Welcome this phase, and allow her to help you whenever possible, even if it means jobs take twice as long and have to be surreptiously done again by you afterwards. Thank her for her help and tell her you don't know how you would manage without her. You thus make her feel a good and useful person, and prompt her to see that helping you is fun, that you're grateful to her, and that it's a worthwhile way of behaving both now and in the future.

She will still
want her own
way at times

Of course, even though she's become extra co-operative and biddable, your child will still want her own way at times. There is no going back to the days of babyhood. She knows she's a separate person, and likes to feel she's her own person at times. But she's better able to listen to reason now, and to take guidance from you, beause you've taught her this isn't a plot to deny her freedom or prevent her having a mind of her own. It's simply a way of showing your love and concern for her, and of helping her learn about life. And because she loves and admires you as a person, she'll be all the readier to listen to what you have to say. Before long, she'll be telling people that there is no one like you. And what is more she will mean it.

Night fears

Starting at age two or three, and through almost to adolescence, a child may suddenly show fears of the dark. Never minimize these fears. To the child they're real enough, however unfounded they seem to us. To a child, the world is a much stranger place than it is to an adult. Everything around us is so familiar we have to picture remote lonely places before we feel fear, but to your child the same remoteness and loneliness can be felt in his own bedroom once you've said goodnight and he's heard your footsteps retreating downstairs.

So take your child's fears seriously. Don't tell him he's silly or a baby. Don't laugh at him or dismiss everything as 'only your imagination'. A child's imagination is very strong, and it confuses him if you don't believe in his fears. To him the *feeling* of fear is real enough, whether the things he's afraid of are equally real or not. I stress later (Chapter 6) the great importance throughout childhood of helping your child recognize and accept his own feelings, and learn how to deal with the negative ones, rather than bottling them up or kidding himself they don't exist. This applies as much to fear as to anything else. If he says he's afraid, he really is afraid, and he needs to feel you understand and will help him handle the feeling. In his case, fear is to a great extent the fear of the unknown, of what may be hiding in the shadows under his bed or in the corner of his room, of what may be causing the creaking sound on the stairs, of what may be hovering in the dark outside his window.

Take your child's fears seriously

If your child is growing up in a happy home where he's secure and loved, and where he can trust and communicate with his parents, his fears can usually be put easily to rest. Let him talk to you about them. If he can't put them into words, don't insist that if he's afraid he must be afraid of *something*. Accept it's quite understandable to be afraid of the dark itself, and of something nameless and unspoken lurking there. Listen to him, and reassure him that most people feel the same when they're small. Without going into the kind of detail that might frighten him further, tell him that *you* certainly did, and help him to laugh reassuringly with you at the idea.

Then give him details of how carefully the house is locked at night, so that no one (and no *thing* can get in). If he's still unsure, tell him that any intruder would in any case have you to deal with, and *you'd* very quickly send him packing! Make sure also that you don't read him frightening stories at bedtime. Even well-known children's tales can be terrifying for a small child; not so when you're there with him perhaps, but the moment you've left and his imagination can get to work. Protect him as well from anything on television that could particularly bother him, and make sure the pictures on his walls don't contain hidden menace of some kind. As

Reassure him as much as you can

mentioned earlier, leave a light on in his room if this helps, leave his bedroom door open (unless he prefers it closed), and leave the landing light on as well, so there's no dark pool just outside his room.

Finally, talk to him about imagination. Explain to him it helps us enjoy stories and think up all kinds of nice happenings. But it also sometimes lets us think up things that aren't so nice, and we have to learn to take less notice of it when that happens.

His fear may be caused by anxiety

With some children, now and later in childhood, careful and sympathetic treatment of this kind doesn't entirely do the trick. The child still seems to feel threatened by a nameless dread which he can deal with in the daylight but which comes into its own at night. When this happens, the fear of the dark seems to be a symptom of a deeper fear. The child is anxious about something in his life, but can't identify what it is. So he needs your help. Think what may be wrong. Perhaps he's by temperament more timid than most, but this isn't the full answer. A timid child may be frightened more easily than average, but this doesn't explain what's actually frightening him *now*.

Think about his daily life. Are there arguments or quarrels in the house which may be upsetting him and making him insecure, with a deep fear of his parents' anger towards each other, or of losing one or other of them if the marriage breaks up (see Chapter 7 for a full discussion of the importance for a child of his parents' relationship with each other)? Or are you getting too angry with *him*? A small child finds it hard to reconcile the picture of his parents as providers of love and kindness with the picture of them as providers of punishment and fear. Which picture is his real parents? Because he can't make the two pictures fit together he tries to push the 'bad' one out of his mind, but the fear it causes remains, and his terrors of witches and evil monsters can be unconscious dramatizations of the angry and unpredictable side of his parents.

Or it may be his own anger he is afraid of

Another possibility is that he may not be allowed to accept and deal with his *own* feelings of anger. There are many times when a child feels cross with his parents for stopping him doing something he wants. If he's told his anger is wicked, or that he's spiteful or ungrateful, or worse still that he's got the

284

devil in him, he becomes very frightened of his own inner self. The feeling of anger that surges up and nearly overwhelms him becomes for him a kind of monster lurking inside. He goes in terror of those moments when it rises from the depths and threatens his self-control. At night, it can be this fear of himself that is projected outwards and causes imaginary unpleasant characters to lurk in the shadows.

Once you have identified the probable cause of his fears and anxieties, you can help him deal with them. I discuss these matters in detail in Chapter 6, but bear in mind that a child relies very much upon the adults in his life not only for his sense of security but also for his sense of who he is and what he is. If you tell him often enough he's bad he comes to believe it, and goes in fear of his own 'badness' and his inability to handle it. If on the other hand he's enabled to see that you understand and accept his feelings whatever they happen to be, and are there to help him learn to cope with them sensibly and without hurting others or himself, then he can see there's nothing to fear. He can see that anger is only an emotion, that emotions aren't bad in themselves, and that having emotions doesn't make us a bad person. It's what we *do* with our emotions that matters, and this 'doing' depends crucially upon the lessons the adults in our life help us learn.

Thumb-sucking and comfort objects

Children are born with a natural instinct to suck, and with a natural liking for soft warm objects. Both these instincts have survival value. Sucking is essential for feeding, and a liking for soft warm objects prompts a child to stay close to the safety of her mother's body. Sucking and cuddling also play a vital part in the bonding that takes place between child and parent (see Chapter 3), and quickly come to be associated in the mind of the former with security and relaxation and comfort.

It isn't surprising therefore that some children turn sucking and cuddling into a habit to be exercised even when they aren't in their parent's arms. Particularly when tired or distressed, a thumb finds its way into the mouth (alternatively some children 'dry suck' without the aid of the thumb) or a soft toy or piece of blanket is held against the cheek. Some children become so attached to these latter comfort objects that they show genuine distress if parted from them, and refuse to settle to sleep without them.

Does your child lack attention or feel in any way insecure? We mustn't generalize too strongly about sucking (with or without the thumb) and comfort objects. But these habits are seen rather more frequently amongst children who have reasons for feeling insecure than amongst children who are cheerful and sure of themselves. They give a child a reassurance that may be lacking at times in the rest of her life, and sometimes suggest the need for a little more adult attention and demonstrations of affection. Temperament also plays a part, in that some children have a greater *need* than others for this attention and affection if they're to feel good about themselves.

Sucking and an undue dependence upon comfort objects are less likely to occur if children are given full opportunity to satisfy their instincts for sucking and cuddling during the first two years or so of life. Children who are too hungry to linger over their feeds, for example, or who are weaned too rapidly, may not be able to experience enough sucking, while children of very busy parents who are put into their cots at the first opportunity may not experience enough cuddling. But even children who have had these needs fully satisfied may cling on to them (or revert to them) if circumstances make their lives rather difficult. And let me stress here I'm not talking about over-strict parents or parents who deliberately neglect their offspring. The youngest child in a large family, for example, or the child of extra industrious parents, may quite unwittingly be given less time and overt affection than she needs, or may be given the same amount as was an older brother or sister whereas temperamentally she needs significantly more.

This doesn't mean you have to start worrying or blaming yourself if your child sucks or spends a lot of time with her comfort object. Nor does it mean you have to try to break her of the habit. Look instead to see whether she is receiving the physical affection that she needs, and whether there is anything in the environment that may be affecting her security. Attend to any relevant factors in these areas, and allow your child to grow out of her sucking and comfort cuddling in her own good time.

Some parents are unduly alarmed by the warning that

sucking can alter the shape of a child's mouth and affect the position of her teeth, but this isn't likely to happen (if at all) until the appearance of second teeth at around age six, by which time most children have dropped or drastically reduced the habit. As to comfort objects, parental worries are usually confined to the thought that there's something 'babyish' about them. Not so. What adult doesn't enjoy the feel of warm soft sheets at night, or the feel of a favourite garment against the skin? Allow your child her comfort object, and notice how she comes to rely less and less upon it for emotional (as opposed to tactile) satisfaction as she grows older.

Will your child's teeth be affected?

Sometimes adults tell me there's a great battle of wills between them and their child when they spirit away the comfort object to wash it. The piece of white blanket has become grey, or the pink teddy bear has become the colour of old bricks. They miss the point that it's the very familiarity of the comfort object (smell as well as looks and feel) that gives it much of its appeal for their child. It may look better to you if it's restored to pristine condition, but to her it's lost some of its power to please. Either wash the object regularly right from the start, so she gets used to it that way, or leave it until she agrees it's time it had a bath. And if it can take its bath along with her, so much the better!

Washing the comfort object

Personalizing a comfort object

Many children give their comfort object a name, and talk about it as if it's alive. This is fine, and is part of a child's fantasy world, whether or not the comfort object takes on the extreme importance I've just been discussing. The teddy, the toy dog, even the piece of blanket takes on a personality of its own, and the child breathes life into it with her imagination. Parents worry though if their child as she grows older seems at times to prefer the comfort object to real people, or begins to talk about it as if it were she herself. Let's take these two situations separately.

If a child feels very upset, or very powerless in her life, then she may indeed occasionally prefer her comfort object to anything or anyone else. The comfort object doesn't answer back or tell her what to do (rather like a pet in this respect – see Chapter 6), and if she's been scolded and has no one else to whom she can turn, the comfort object is always there,

What if a child prefers her comfort object to real people?

undemanding, forgiving and sympathetic, and ready to give her the solace she can't find elsewhere.

If this is what's happening, the remedy is simple. Your child needs more scope to express herself, and more adult comfort when she's feeling down. She also needs the reassurance that you still love her even when you're angry with her (see pages 391–2), and never want her to feel isolated or abandoned.

What if she projects her own feelings on to the comfort object? The second situation, where a child begins to talk about a comfort object as if it's she herself, is rather more complex. What is happening is that the child is projecting her feelings and likes and dislikes on to the object, rather than own them herself. So she tells you that Teddy feels this or Teddy feels that, or Teddy wants this or Teddy wants that, rather than tell you she feels or wants these things herself. Sometimes this is just a brief phase. Your child finds it easy to substitute Teddy for herself, but soon tires of the game and forgets about it. But at other times it's more persistent, and your child needs help in owning her own emotions and preferences. If she can see that you accept these feelings (see Chapter 6), you're giving her the best help possible. Often her reluctance to own them stems from a feeling of uneasiness (and later on guilt) about them. If she's always expected to control her feelings, they seem alien and strange to her, and it's far easier to pretend they belong to Teddy. But if these feelings are accepted by you, then they will be accepted by her.

Help your child as well by responding to remarks such as 'Teddy feels cross' (or whatever) by firmly prompting, 'You mean *you* feel cross; yes I can see you do.' Don't make an issue out of it. Once she's sure she has your love and understanding no matter how she's feeling, she'll quickly leave this strange little phase behind.

Naughty talk

Children have a funny sense of humour. They take delight in things that to an adult have less comic possibilities than an income tax demand. One good example of this is the use of 'naughty' words. Your child has heard a word like 'bum' from other children, or a word like 'snot', and finds it so side-splitting that he has to use it at every available opportunity, most of all when there are visitors in the house.

This is an interesting psychological phenomenon, and shows quite clearly how children take their cues from adults. Since there is nothing especially funny about bums or snot in themselves, and since children are by nature matter-of-fact and unshockable about their own and other people's bodies, what has happened even by age three is that they have learnt that these words make grown-ups uncomfortable and embarrassed. The small child has no idea why this should be, but enjoys the spectacle none the less. Other children have told him that these are 'naughty' words, and when he tries them out in front of grown-ups to see for himself he notices their very odd reactions. All very curious, but an excellent way of making yourself feel important. *You* aren't bothered by these words, but you can make your parents act very strangely every time you repeat them. So you have undoubted power over your parents, and over other grown-ups. And seeing those in authority discomfited is, after all, one of the classic recipes for good comedy.

Children learn that some words make grown-ups embarrassed

One way of dealing with this problem is to ignore your child whenever he comes out with the dread words. This approach has its advantages. It shows him you really can't be bothered with his attempts at humour, and often it does discourage him from repeating them. But sometimes it has the opposite effect. Your child notices your uncharacteristic stiff-upper-lip behaviour, and deduces rightly that you're trying to show you're not shocked. Delighted, he redoubles his efforts. You still pretend not to hear. 'Bum bum bum' he shouts gleefully. Goaded to the limit you tell him sharply that's enough. Convinced by the abruptness of your reaction that his earlier deductions were correct, your child stores up the experience in his mind and brings out his 'naughty' words again at the next most inconvenient opportunity.

Ignoring it may not always work

A better response is simply to deal with the words as you would any other. He shouts 'bum' and seems all set for a good laugh; you tell him you can't see what's especially funny. After all, we'd all look very much funnier if we *didn't* have bums! And sitting down would be something of a problem (if he elaborates on other problems the absence of bums would cause, simply agree with him and go on to talk about something else). The same applies to his gleeful shouts of 'snot'. You point out to him that without snot the inside of our noses

Openness about the body will demystify the words

would be dry and breathing would be unpleasant, then change the conversation to something more interesting.

This approach quickly demystifies the words concerned, and your child will come to share your view that there's nothing special about any of them. Of equal importance, it shows him you're perfectly prepared to accept the body and its functions. That's the way the body is made, and it serves its purpose very well. There's no need to be shocked about the body, or to see it as something dirty or smutty. Ignorance and secrecy, rather than openness, are responsible for a fascination with 'naughty' words and 'naughty' talk. A straightforward attitude towards the body will also help you cope with the business of sex education, which many parents find one of the most difficult aspects of their task (see Chapter 6).

TWINS

Parents of twins nearly always say that in spite of the extra work they wouldn't have missed the experience for worlds. And as twins grow older, the burden of extra work tends to lessen, as they usually get on well together and amuse and occupy each other, (though care has to be taken that their opportunities to meet other children and to develop language are not hindered by their tendency always to play together).

Before enlarging on these points, something needs to be said about who twins are and why you've managed to produce two children for the price of one. Twins fall into two separate categories, *identical twins* and *fraternal twins*, and I'll explain the differences between them in a moment. In the Western world, about one pregnancy in a hundred produces twins, with roughly one-third of them being identical and two-thirds fraternal. Twins tend to run in families, and once you've had twins, you increase your chances of a repeat performance (spare a thought for the Florida mother who in 1961 produced her *seventh* set of twins!). Your chances also increase with each pregnancy and with age, though these increased chances apply only to fraternal and not to identical twins.

The difference between fraternal and identical twins is that the former are produced from separate ova (eggs) and sperm, while the latter are not. In the case of fraternal twins, what happens is that the mother's ovaries for some unknown reason produce two ova one month instead of only one. Both these ova pass into the womb and are ready for fertilization, and should both be fertilized (there are enough spare sperm around to do the job thousands of times over and to spare) the result is two children growing together in the womb instead of one. In the case of identical twins, the mother produces only one ovum as usual, and this is fertilized by only one sperm. However, early on in the process of cell division through which growth in the womb takes place, the cluster of cells splits up into two separate though identical clumps, each of which grows on as a separate child.

Identical twins and fraternal twins

You can see from this that fraternal twins are no more alike than any other siblings within the family. They've each been formed from a separate ovum and sperm, and it's just chance that they've been in the womb together instead of separated from each other by at least nine months. Identical twins on the other hand are literally identical (or virtually so; small genetic mutations may occur in the womb to make them very slightly different). Nature intended them to be one child, and it's just chance that they split up and developed as two separate human beings. Since they are no more alike than any other siblings, fraternal twins can be of the same sex or a boy and girl, while identical twins are always of the same sex. The latter are of course usually spitting images of each other, though occasionally they will be mirror images – one right-handed the other left, one with a crown on the right side of the head, the other with a crown on the left, and so on (interestingly, though, the *finger-prints* of identical twins are never exactly the same, even as mirror images).

In spite of their greater similarity, identical twins often look *less* alike than fraternal twins at birth. This is because, situated nearer to each other in the womb, one may have had a better supply of blood and oxygen than the other; although they quickly grow to resemble each other minutely, these differences in the intra-uterine environment are often responsible for the small differences in ability and personality that may develop later.

Parents with twins, whether fraternal or identical, obviously have their hands full, and here more than anywhere it's vital

Child-rearing must be a shared responsibility

that mother and father see child-rearing as a shared responsibility. Changing, feeding, bathing, amusing all take twice as long, and there's the added difficulty that if one twin is hard to settle she invariably sets the other one off as well. Unless they are unusually gifted, no one person on their own can effectively cope with twins. Here, more than ever, it's also vital to have a well-organized household, with everything to hand and set routines. Fraternal twins are often harder to manage than identical ones, because they may differ markedly in their eating and sleeping habits, one wanting her food on demand, the other happy to go by the clock, one happy to sleep at all the set times, the other with enough personal idiosyncrasies to confound a saint. However, most parents with twins report that the children mercifully seem to develop some synchronicity between their internal clocks, with the result that given good management and a slice of luck it's possible to get through the first year or so of their babies' lives without too many problems.

The problem of apportioning blame

The real questions start to occur in the second and third years of life, and these have to do primarily with discipline, language, socialization and individuality. Let's take discipline first – a problem that will of course persist throughout childhood. There's no evidence that twins are any naughtier than other siblings, or that they suffer from more psychological problems. Often they get on better together than children with two years between them, since they are closer in ability and interests. But parents complain that it's much harder to apportion blame when something goes wrong. Identical twins in particular have a very similar pattern of behaviour, so if an offence has been committed and the culprit won't own up you don't recognize whose hallmark it carries. Twins are usually more likely to stick up for each other too, and less likely to give each other away than other siblings, so you're faced with whether to punish them both or let them both off. The correct course of action depends upon the punishment. If a mess has been made, then both must clear it up. If there are arguments, then both must relinquish the activity they're arguing over. If instructions have been disobeyed, then both must forfeit any privileges that may have depended upon them.

As twins grow older, so the guilty one will be less ready to see the innocent one punished alongside her, and more inclined to confess. If it comes to things such as breakages, and the twins are old enough for pocket money and to make a contribution towards repairs, tell them both will have to pay unless the guilty one owns up, and give them a little time to talk it over between themselves. On the other hand, if you're inclined to give punishments which do not connect directly with the offence (reasons why such punishments are less advisable are given in Chapter 6), it would be quite wrong to punish the innocent along with the guilty. Some parents say that if one twin gets a slap on the leg, so does the other, regardless of who is to blame. This only leaves both twins with a feeling of how unjust you are. Better to lecture them both, saying that you know one is to blame and the other isn't. The guilty party will take the lecture more to heart than her twin, and may even own up during it.

Language sometimes becomes an issue with identical twins (rarely with fraternal twins) because of their habit of always being together. Able to communicate at a rudimentary though effective level with each other, they may not have the objective necessity to develop language which is such a stimulus for most children. Occasionally, identical twins will even produce their own language, incomprehensible to everyone but themselves. If language becomes an issue, so too does socialization. The twins spend so much time together that they may never meet other children, and by the time they start school this habit is so firmly ingrained that they may only be parted at the cost of great emotional upset. **Language and socialization**

The sensible way round this is to get the children used to being apart at an early age. You want to encourage their friendship with each other, but at the same time you want to strike the right balance. As babies, take them out and play with them separately a reasonable amount of the time (here again the involvement of both parents is vital). When they start playgroup, arrange for them to go on different mornings and afternoons at least some of the week. Explain that this helps other people to get to know which is which. Never separate them abruptly and without saying why. Try instead to let them grow up with the understanding that being apart from each other is the natural course of things sometimes. The earlier you start this, the easier for all concerned.

Similarly with identity. Fraternal twins can usually be given

The problem of identity in identical twins their separate identities from the word go. Always treat both twins alike in terms of your love for them. Give each the same amount of your time. And as with all siblings, never compare them with each other. But in other ways try to allow each twin to see herself as an individual, with a right to differ from her twin and make choices for herself. As I say, fraternal twins usually take to this without difficulty, particularly if they're of the opposite sex. But identical twins do tend to think and act alike, and need encouragement to develop the confidence to act independently. I'm not saying you should force independence upon them if they clearly find it unsettling, simply that you should give them all the right opportunities *from as early as possible*. Many parents actively withhold these opportunities, preferring to see their twins as a pair, and to dress them alike and do everything possible to stress their similarity.

Why is an independent identity of value to an identical twin? Why not simply treat them alike, especially if they seem happy with this? The answer is firstly that they have to be independent of each other one day, and secondly that without intending it each twin may be subtly restricting the other's freedom of choice. This second point is particularly important where, as so often happens with identical twins, one tends to dominate the other. This domination may not be very obvious, and it may not be intentional. But one twin is often (for reasons I've already given) slightly more forward than the other, slightly quicker, slightly better at games and school work, slightly more attractive. This domination is to the advantage of neither twin, and each should be given a full chance to be herself and relate to the world outside the close bond of twinship.

Encourage twins to express their individuality Encourage each twin, therefore, to express her individuality. Put them in different clothes from babyhood, so that they don't think of themselves simply as clones of each other. When they grow older and tend to choose the same things, buy them different colours, or at the very least different shades of the same colour. If they both like blue shirts or blouses best, find out their second favourite colour and buy some shirts in that and some shirts in blue. Then when one wears blue the other can wear the second favourite colour and vice versa. If they both take up musical instruments later on, encourage them to choose different ones. If they both play a team game, encourage them to play in different positions. When they go to the hairdresser, encourage them to choose different styles. If you've the space, put them in separate bedrooms when they're small, so that they grow up used to their own rooms and can each decorate them in their own way. Encourage other people (relatives, friends) to treat them as individuals too, and emphasize this further by choosing rather dissimilar names for them at birth (Andrew and Roger, for example, rather than Peter and Paul, Jennifer and Barbara rather than Susan and Sally).

Let me emphasize again that it's far easier to do all this if you start from birth onwards, and if you yourselves look for each sign of individuality instead of concentrating upon similarities. It's much harder to help each twin to become her own person if you start late, or if you yourselves tend to think of them always as two and the same. Explain your policy to neighbours, to playgroup leaders, and later on to teachers so that they back up your work. You needn't fear that your twins will grow up too remote from each other. They'll still be very close, whatever you do, and that's as it should be. But at the same time they will come to respect both the twin relationship and their individuality, and this is what you want.

[6]

The Fourth and Fifth Years

MANY PARENTS SAY THEY ENJOY the fourth and fifth years almost more than any others in their child's development. During these years the transition from babyhood into personhood is completed. Every day brings new signs of individuality. More and more, a child develops his own ways of doing things, his own ways of arranging and relating to his environment. His horizons widen rapidly. He's learning all the time. He makes an excellent companion, interested and involved in everything that goes on in the home, and genuinely helpful and resourceful. He begins to understand the needs of others, and that his parents get tired and have likes and dislikes just as he does. This is the age at which you can teach him the simple routines that contribute to the smooth running of the home. Taking off shoes at the door, carrying dirty plates to the kitchen, hanging up hat and coat. This is the age at which such tasks are fun, and once the habits become established they remain through childhood. Welcome his help, praise and encourage him, and he'll become part of the family team.

One of the major developments in these two years is his quantum leap from the early beginnings of language to a near-adult command of everyday words. With this leap goes a similar leap in his powers of thinking and in his ability to reason and to listen to reason. Along with this goes a growing interest in stories and in learning to read, and often by the age of five it's lack of experience rather than lack of brain power that stops him coping with virtually all aspects of daily life. With this growth in language and thought goes an ever-increasing awareness of self, and a particular need for those around to give him a picture of himself as a loved and valued person, with the necessary skills and qualities to make him acceptable to others.

PHYSICAL AND PSYCHOLOGICAL DEVELOPMENT

Physical Growth

During these years careful height and weight checks are no longer necessary. Provided your child looks to be developing normally, these checks are now usually only done twice yearly. The usual growth rate is about 7.5 centimetres (3 in.) in the fourth year and 6.5 centimetres (2½ in.) in the fifth, with a weight gain of about 2 kg (4½ lb) each year. Although the head is still large for the body, and the shoulders and hips very slim, your child's physique in these two years finally leaves the contours of babyhood behind, and increasingly resembles that of the pre-adolescent. Children of this age (and through into the seventh and eighth years) often have a lithe grace and an upright posture that puts us adults to shame. Study your child's straight lower back, the erect carriage of head and neck, the gentle curve of tummy, the upright relaxed shoulders, then take a surreptitious peek at your own naked body in a full-length mirror and ask yourself what's gone wrong!

Language development

So great is the quantum leap in language during these two years that almost daily your child adds new words and new concepts to his speech. Now more than ever it's vital you talk to him all you can, listen to him, question him, prompt him to put his wants into words, answer his questions fully and informatively. If he misses out on opportunities for language development during these crucial years he may never make up the lost ground. Language gives him *access* to the world in a way that nothing else can. Through language he enquires, conceptualizes, understands. As in the previous months, don't always rush to correct him when he makes mistakes in the way he puts things. These mistakes are often evidence of his skill in trying to construct grammar for himself; he'll soon learn by listening to you that he hasn't got it quite right. If you're constantly correcting him, you'll curb his enthusiasm

299

for language, make him hesitant and over-cautious, and put back his progress. When you do correct, use encouraging words such as, 'That's a clever way of saying it; though what we usually say is . . .' If he persists in his mistake, it normally means the correct way of putting it is rather beyond him as yet. His intelligence is running ahead of his memory for grammar. He knows what he wants to say, but can't recall exactly how to say it. With one or two reminders, he'll quickly grasp the idea. For the rest, continue the good language work of the first three years. Talk to him. Use a varied vocabulary. Stimulate and challenge him. Listen to him.

The beginnings of reading

Closely linked to language is learning to read. Of all the gifts you can give your child, helping her to master reading is one of the most precious. But don't make a big meal of it. Many parents, with the best of intentions, try to force reading on their child before she's ready. By 'ready', I mean before she wants to do it, and before she's matured enough to be able to master the visual and mental skills involved.

When is your child ready to read? Experts have argued a great deal down the years whether 'reading readiness' depends upon the child reaching a definite stage in her mental development or upon her learning experiences. Those who take the former view claim that it's a waste of time and possibly harmful (since it may turn her against books) to try to teach the child to read before this development occurs. Those who take the latter view claim that even babies can be taught to read provided you know how to do it.

Don't concern yourself with these arguments. Even if it's possible to teach babies to read, there's no evidence it makes them better or keener readers in the years to come. Nor is there evidence that you have to wait for a very definite stage to be reached in your child's developmental timetable. The best approach is to make books available to your child from an early age, and then as she shows signs of wanting to read introduce her to the necessary skills.

There's no great mystique about these skills. I discuss them in more detail when we talk about the school-age child, but the keys to reading are simply one patient and caring adult, one suitable reading book, and one happy and interested child. Bring all three together, and reading happens. Often so smoothly in fact that it seems a natural process, almost like walking or learning to talk.

I've already mentioned the value of reading to your child at bedtime. Start the practice at around the first birthday, and make it a regular habit every night. At first your child won't seem to take much in, and won't want to listen for more than a few minutes. That's fine. Don't scold her into attending. Read to her while she bounces around in her cot or on your knee. Keep the experience short, but help her associate it with the fun and games of going to bed. Very soon, she'll start to listen and to look forward to her story. Choose books that are suitable, and watch how certain tales so quickly become established favourites that your occasional attempts to speed things up by missing out chunks are quickly spotted and sternly admonished. Make sure the books have plenty of colourful pictures, and pause at these as you go along, so that your child associates words with pictures, and has her interest and imagination further aroused. **Read to your child from an early age**

When she's a little older, the next step is to place the book where she can watch the words as you read. Maybe she's on your knee, or when she's older and has moved into a bed she's snuggled against you. Watching the words helps her make the connection between the written word and sound. Let her turn the pages if she wishes, but help her realize that if she turns several at once just for the fun of turning pages, this loses your place in the reading. Look at the pictures with her, and ask her questions about them which focus her attention and help her get more from the story. ('Whose house is that do you think?' 'What's that girl's name?' 'Which one is Squirrel Nutkin?' 'What's that man doing?' 'Why is the lady looking cross?' 'Would you like to live in a tree like that?'). As her language improves, so she'll want to talk more and more about the pictures, 'reading' them by telling you exactly what they represent and what's happening in them. **Look at the pictures together**

A little later, start pointing to each of the words as you read, so that she sees the connection between specific words and sounds. Often she'll ask if she can point with you, and you can take her finger and use that instead of your own. The next step is to see if she can recognize any words for herself. If she can't, don't press her. You'll soon see whether she's interested yet in a task of this kind. If she isn't, leave it for a while and **Point to the individual words** ask her again in a few weeks' time. To begin with, it doesn't matter what words she recognizes and what words she doesn't. She may surprise you by picking out quite a large word, like the name of one of the characters in one of the stories, simply because she's interested in the character and because the name has a rather distinctive shape to it.

Don't push your child if she's not interested

Many children by age three are showing a definite interest in developing reading skills. But if your child isn't one of them, don't worry. Provided you're giving her the right opportunities she'll come to it in her own good time. It's only if a child still doesn't show any signs of wanting to read by age six that she may need extra help. And many later readers become great enthusiasts in the long run. So don't start making her anxious. Carry on reading to her as usual, and adopt a light-hearted approach to the whole thing. Reading is fun. One of the great pleasures in life. Don't give your child the impression that it's a difficult task she must grit her teeth and master at the same speed as an older brother or sister or her friend across the road.

Choosing books for your child

Later on I'll talk more about reading schemes that you can buy and use with your child (see Chapter 7), but in these early years the important thing is that the books you buy should contain language that she understands, stories that interest and amuse her, and pictures that give plenty of scope for discussion and chat. Don't feel you must quickly get your child on to 'serious' books, presenting her with potted versions of the classics as soon as she's out of nappies. At her age, she likes simple stories with happy adventures and characters with whom she can identify and be in sympathy. She isn't ready for stories about great human themes. These come later. And remember the earlier point that children can be frightened by stories that to adults seem very innocuous. Even stories you remember enjoying as a child may not be right for her. If she is frightened by them, not only is this unpleasant in itself, it may also turn her against books, at least for now. And she may wonder why you're choosing to make her feel bad. So select her stories with care, and watch her reactions to see what she likes and dislikes.

Starting to write

Reading and writing go together. Once your child begins to show an interest in reading, the chances are he'll do so in

302

writing as well. If he sees you writing frequently, this helps too – writing letters, shopping lists, birthday cards, Christmas cards. You may also have a board in the kitchen on which you jot down telephone numbers and bits of information and reminders to yourself. A child who sees his parents writing and reading and getting fun from these skills is much more motivated to acquire them himself than a child whose parents don't seem interested.

When your child has seen you writing a few times, he'll want to have a go. Find him a pencil or a fibre tip pen and plenty of scrap paper, and let him. He won't write proper words as yet, but simply try to copy the *action* of writing, drawing large scrawls across the paper and then proudly presenting them to you as 'writing'. Admire his work. Like all the other creative bits and pieces he produces for you, put it up in the kitchen on display. A pin-board is ideal for this purpose, and you can change the exhibits every day or so. Show him you're interested in what he's doing, and want other people to see it. **Let him scribble away as much as he wants**

Don't make the mistake of thinking that as soon as he starts to 'write' you should give him words to copy. That comes later. A small child doesn't have the concentration or the manipulative skill to copy proper letters, and if he thinks you expect this of him things will turn into a labour and he'll lose interest. Let him scribble away to his heart's content. Don't take him to task for 'wasting' paper. A child of his age has no real idea about what's waste and what isn't. He's concerned only with making marks on paper, and needs to have the freedom to go ahead.

But he can't always make a distinction between the paper you give him and the lounge wallpaper. Once he's discovered the thrill of using a pencil, any available surface will do as far as he's concerned. And he'll think it very odd that you should be encouraging him to write on one kind of paper only to react with horror when he has a go on another. Prevention, as so often, is better than cure. Explain to him from the start that we write on bits of paper kept specially for the purpose, and not on walls because walls are difficult to clean. At the same time, keep pencils and pens out of reach until he wants to use them. Tackled in this way, and provided there is never any **But not on the lounge wallpaper** shortage of paper when he asks for it, scribbling on walls shouldn't become a problem.

Helping your child to learn

You want your child to do well in life, and this means you hope she's going to be a bright person who learns quickly and will be a success when she starts school. Most people equate being 'bright' with being 'intelligent', and are anxious to know whether their child rates well on this ability or not. There's more to say about intelligence and how we define and measure it when we come to the school-age child, but some things must be clarified right away.

Intelligence tests for pre-school children are very inaccurate

First, we can't measure intelligence with much accuracy before about age six. There *are* intelligence tests for use with children as young as two years, but no great importance can be attached to them. They give you a 'score' for your child sure enough, but the level of agreement between this score and the score your child achieves in later years isn't usually very high. My advice to parents is not to bother about these early tests. If you use one and find your child has a high score, you could well be disappointed if she fails to live up to this when she's older. On the other hand, if she obtains a low score you're bound to feel depressed about it, often needlessly. The fault lies with the tests. They're simply not very appropriate. Child development goes in spurts in these early years, and a child who is behind the average at one point may race ahead a few weeks later. Early tests of intelligence are based mainly upon such things as a child's ability to react to various objects and experiences presented to her, and there's limited value in this because small children vary so much in the rate at which they acquire the perceptual and motor skills concerned. This variation tells us little about the speed of subsequent development. In any case, it's far too early to start tying labels like 'bright' or 'not-so-bright' on your child. Enjoy her and allow her to enjoy you, and don't start pressurizing her with expectations or disappointments.

Even when your child starts nursery school at age three or four there's little to be gained from asking teachers to arrange for intelligence tests. If she's at a state nursery school the local education authority educational psychologists can measure her abilities for you, but they'll only do so if there is real cause for concern about her progress. It's well understood that measurement at this age (except for specific disabilities such as sight or hearing defects or obvious mental handicap which I discuss in Chapter 4) still isn't very accurate.

There's always a risk that if a child is labelled as not-so-bright people will start reacting to her *as if* she's not-so-bright. Put more crudely, tell someone a child is dull and they'll treat her as if she's dull. This means that far from giving her the extra stimulus she needs they may give her less. 'After all', the argument often goes, 'if she hasn't got it you can't put it there.' This state of affairs is referred to by psychologists as a 'self-fulfilling prophecy'. Get the idea that someone is dull and your treatment of them from now on may help produce the very dullness you think has been identified.

Labelling a child as dull can be a self-fulfilling prophecy

So instead of labelling your child as bright or not-so-bright, accept her for what she is, and devote your energies to developing her potential by giving her as much stimulation and encouragement as you can. In the pre-school years this means widening her experience by introducing her to as many interesting and enjoyable opportunities as possible. Remember that she learns best when she's having a good time. As I stressed in Chapter 5, much of a child's learning takes place through play. And anything which is fun is play to her. So make the right experiences available to your child, and allow her to absorb them at her own pace, encouraging and praising her wherever you can and helping her to see how useful her new skills are.

Give your child all the stimulation and encouragement you can

Let's take an example from learning colours. Some children can name all the common colours by age three, but others still have problems even at age five. Since there's no connection between the age at which a child knows her colours and intelligence, it's simply a matter of maturing to the point where she's able to discriminate between the visual impressions made by the different colours, and to link these discriminations with the words she holds in her head. Some children show this kind of maturation early, in others it comes later. But if you spend a great deal of time trying to get her to recognize colours before this maturation has been reached, it's largely wasted effort. Certainly she can see that colours are

Learning colours

different from each other, but she can't turn this seeing into true discrimination because she can't retain the memory of these differences. It's almost as if she comes to them afresh each time. Thus, though she may know all the colour words, she can't match them up with the colours themselves.

If you want to help your child learn her colours, then, all you have to do is use the colour names often. 'Here's your *red* shirt.' 'Would you like the *blue* or the *green* ball?' 'Look how *white* the clouds are.' 'This is a *black* pencil.' For a time she won't seem to catch on, but then suddenly the penny drops, and apart from the odd mistake she has no further problems. She's learnt her colours easily and naturally, and without any great effort from anyone.

There are ideal times for learning particular skills

This example of learning colours illustrates a very important point about learning in general. There is often *a particular stage in a child's development when she can learn a certain lesson or skill more quickly than at any other time in her life.* The ability to acquire any language accent-perfect at the close of the babbling stage (see Chapter 4) is an example. So probably are other language skills, many physical and sporting skills, and many musical and creative skills. For this reason, the more chance you give your child to come into early contact with such skills the better. She'll have cause to thank you in later life when she watches other people struggling to learn what she picked up so effortlessly.

But don't expect too much of her

Your child is learning from the moment she wakes in the morning to the time she goes to sleep at night. She learns from the things you tell her. She learns from listening to the conversations of others. She learns from playing and experimenting with the materials around her. She learns so quickly in fact that there is sometimes a temptation to expect too much of her. She recognizes a neighbour's car in the street, and we immediately think she should recognize the cars of all our friends. She knows the way to the shops so we immediately think she should know the way to the playgroup. She uses new words every day, so we think she should remember all the names we tell her. Perhaps above all we think she should remember all the do's and don'ts that we pass on to her and think she's being disobedient when she doesn't. Remember just how much there is for a small child to learn. If we sat down and made a list it would fill a book even longer than this one and show us what a daunting, well-nigh impossible task faces her, even before she gets to school and starts on more formal learning. So be realistic about what she can and what she can't do. A little understanding, a little patience and a little dash of humour are as valuable to any adult engaged in teaching children as a whole clutch of more formal qualifications.

Encouraging intelligence

It's plain from all I've just been saying, therefore, that when we talk about encouraging intelligence we're not talking about sitting a child in front of some boring task and telling him not to get up until it's finished. We mean helping him to use his curiosity, to find out about things, to use his ears and his eyes, to use his hands and his body, to ask questions and listen to answers, to see how things work, to see how things are linked together by a chain of cause and effect. 'You do this, and it causes that to happen.' 'That happens, and it makes this work.'

Intelligence is essentially a matter of understanding how the world works, how cause and effect operate, how you can influence the environment in order to obtain a desired result. Put another way, it's the ability to see how the objects and events around us are related to each other, and then to use our knowledge of this relationship to solve problems. Look at any written test of intelligence, and you'll see it incorporates this two-stage process. 'Insert the missing number: 2 5 8 11 – ' 'Insert a word in the brackets meaning the same as the words outside: dance (. . .) sphere' and so on. These problems are solved when we see a relationship within the given information and use it to identify what's missing. Thus when encouraging your child to use his intelligence provide him with opportunities that allow him to see relationships. Even simple jigsaw puzzles help him do this, as do puzzles where he has to fit a number of different plastic shapes into slots in a plastic box. In both cases he has to see relationships between two sets of shapes, and in the case of the jigsaw he also has to see the relationship between the picture on an individual piece of the jigsaw and the picture that he is trying to construct.

Anything which stimulates your child to think is going to be of help to him. Anything which stimulates him to see a puzzle

Intelligence is a matter of seeing how things relate to each other

307

Intelligence versus creativity

and want to solve it. Anything which stimulates him to ask questions, to explore, to look behind the appearance of things and understand how they're made or how they work. At this early age, there's no need to make hard-and-fast distinctions between experiences of this kind and the experiences we will discuss later in the section on creativity. Psychologists consider that although intelligence and creativity may stem from separate groups of abilities, they're closely related in a number of ways, and that what stimulates the one will also (at this age at least) stimulate the other. Both involve aspects of problem-solving. The main difference between them is simply that intelligence involves situations where there is a single right answer on which the mind must *converge*, while creativity involves situations where there is a range of answers and the mind can *diverge* and throw up varied and novel solutions. To understand this distinction, contrast the two intelligence test items on page 307 with a typical item from a creativity test, namely 'How many uses can you think of for a house brick?' In the intelligence items there is only one right answer. In the creativity item there are as many right answers as you can dream up. With the intelligence items your mind narrows down on the solutions, with the creativity items your mind opens out and has licence to be fluent and original.

As your child grows older, he comes to recognize which problem demands thinking of the convergent, intelligent kind, which demands thinking of the divergent, creative kind, and which demands a combination of the two. But for the present, simply provide him with experiences inside and outside the home that encourage his curiosity and stimulate him to find answers to the questions he is beginning to ask.

Let your child find the answers for himself

And a vital point here. Though you will often have to provide verbal answers to your child's questions, it is of even more value where possible to help him find answers *for himself*. Don't allow him to become irritated by problems that are too difficult for him, but if you can prompt him to think where the answer can be found (in a book, by a simple experiment, by watching carefully) he'll understand and remember better than when he's supplied with answers ready-made. The old Chinese proverb 'I hear and I forget, I see and I remember, I do and I understand' is worth remembering. It isn't a rule to be slavishly followed. Often a verbal explanation in clear and simple language is ideal. But the principle of *doing* rather than just hearing is a good one, and should lie behind many of the learning experiences you offer your child.

In mathematics and reading and any thinking skills your child still can't think like an adult. As I mentioned earlier, you still mustn't expect too much of him. The speed at which he's progressing can trick you into believing he sees and interprets the world in exactly the way we do. The truth is he doesn't. For two reasons. First, because his experience is so much more limited than ours. He's learnt a great deal about the world, but he hasn't had time to learn more than a fraction of what we carry in our conscious and unconscious minds. Second, because there may be biological factors involved. There is much debate amongst biologists and psychologists as to what these factors might be, but one simple way of looking at them is that although your child's brain is well developed at birth, the neurological connections between the various parts of it may not yet be complete. Thus certain kinds of thinking may be difficult or impossible for him until he's matured to a certain point.

Remember his thinking is still limited

One well-known approach to the matter is to see the development of a child's thinking as passing through several definite stages. At each stage, he finds it hard to cope with the kind of thinking possible at the stages that lie ahead. Some psychologists believe that these stages are relatively fixed, and that a child passes through them in a set order and according to an identifiable timetable. Other psychologists think that matters are more flexible, and that with the right opportunities a child may be accelerated through the stages and perhaps miss certain of them altogether. Other psychologists believe that the real problem is our inability as adults to ask children the kind of questions that would really reveal their level of understanding. Thus they believe children are restricted in their thinking simply because our way of exploring this thinking doesn't take account of their limited experience and their misunderstanding of many of the words and concepts we use.

The parent needn't become too involved in this debate. From a practical viewpoint the important thing is that your child's failure to grasp something which seems to you ludicrously simple is usually due not to stubbornness or obtuseness but simply to the fact that he isn't yet at the level where

Make his experiences as concrete as possible

he knows properly what you're talking about. Abstract concepts like 'time' and 'distance', so familiar to us, are very mysterious to him. If we want the pre-school child to understand them, we must try to find a way of *showing* him what we mean. 'Look, this brick is that far away from this one. Now we can take another brick and put it further away still.' 'Grandma lives a long way away. That means beyond the next house and the next house and the next house and the next house and lots and lots more houses.' 'We leave it to cook for three hours. That means if we put it in the oven just after breakfast we can take it out again just before lunch.' 'Your birthday is 20 days away. Let's put a mark on the calendar for each of those days. Then we can cross them off one by one until we get to your birthday.'

The secret with the pre-school child is to make his experiences as concrete as possible. This ties in with what I've already said about doing and understanding. But it also means that when you give him a verbal explanation you should relate it to a concrete experience he's already had. 'Why don't we have floods when it rains?' would therefore be answered by saying 'You know what happens to the water when we pull out the plug in the bath. Well these drains in the road are like big plug holes, and the rain water can run away.' 'How long ago is last year?' would be answered by 'You remember when we went to the seaside last summer? Well it's all that time ago.' 'Why do I have to wash my hands?' would be answered by 'You remember my hands when I've been in the garden? Well yours would get like that if you never washed.'

Concrete explanations of this kind won't always give your child a *precise* idea of things like time and distance. But they'll give him a good working knowledge. They'll also stimulate him to want to find out more, something that won't happen if he doesn't understand your answers. For example, they'll stimulate him to ask questions like 'What happens to the water when it goes down the drains?' 'Does Daddy like getting his hands dirty?' and so on. The more you relate your answers to simple concrete experiences, the more your child will gain confidence that the world is a place he can understand, and that you can be trusted to give him the answers about it that he needs.

Further evidence that your child doesn't yet interpret the world in the way we do comes from the way he draws. A house, for example, is always a flat object. Your child doesn't understand the idea of perspective or depth. And time spent trying to teach it to him at this stage is wasted. Similarly people are often just heads and legs. Skirts are stiff triangles imposed on a strange object called 'Mummy'. Hands are all fingers. The sun is a spiky object up aloft. Hills always end in a point. The sky is like a ceiling. Hair is a sort of halo and so on. By studying the way your child draws you can see that he isn't a miniature adult (awful term) but a little person in his own right who can't be expected to deal with everything in the way we do (see Chapter 7 for more on children's drawing). We must present him with experiences and explanations in a form which makes sense to him and which he can absorb into his picture of the world.

Your child doesn't yet see the world exactly as you do

Encouraging mathematical skills

Much of your child's learning is carried out through language. But don't forget that non-verbal language called mathematics. All children are mathematicians. If you don't like maths now, this isn't because you've no natural bent for it. You have a mathematical bent just as you have an artisitic and a musical bent. The fact that all three may lie dusty and neglected at the bottom of your mind is due more to the way these subjects were presented to you in childhood than to any lack of innate ability. All children love counting, just as they love drawing and painting and making music. Though their natural aptitude varies, no child without a mental handicap lacks what it takes to tackle these areas successfully.

So make sure you give your child mathematical experiences. At her young age, it's helpful to think of these experiences as falling into two broad areas:

1. *Identical objects*. Provide your child with several objects of the same kind. Identical buttons for example. Or dominoes, or bricks, or things to eat. She'll learn the idea of counting much more quickly if she sees that all the things she's counting are the same. Counting 1, 2, 3, 4, 5 dominoes, for example, is much easier than counting a motley collection of different sized, shaped and coloured items.

2. *Sets of objects*. Provide her with opportunities for playing with sets of objects, each set identical within itself but different from the other sets. Five blue bricks and five red bricks for example. Or five large and five small. Or five apples and five oranges. Experiences of this kind introduce her to the important mathematical concepts of sorting and categorizing.

Children who are introduced to mathematical experiences of this kind not only acquire important concepts at a time when they may be particularly ready to learn, they also gain confidence in their own abilities. Both these things give them a good start to more formal learning later in school. But keep these experiences fun for your child. They're part of play. Non-serious activity done for enjoyment. For this reason don't neglect rhymes and number games. Children love these. 'One potato, two potatoes, three potatoes, four . . .' will teach her more about counting than any number of more earnest lessons. So will 'One man went to mow, went to mow a meadow, . . .' and 'Ten green bottles hanging on the wall, . . .' though she won't fully grasp the idea of counting backwards just yet.

Impatience from you will only discourage her   There is no particular timetable for acquiring number skills, so don't worry if your child doesn't seem to grasp the ideas you're offering her right away. As I've said before, children's development goes in bursts during these early years. For weeks nothing much seems to happen, then all of a sudden she races ahead. Never give your child the impression (in mathematics or any other skill) that you're impatient and disappointed with her progress. It's all too easy to fall into the 'But-surely-you-*must*-understand-this-it's-so-simple' syndrome. If she *could* understand it she *would*. Pressurizing her in this way only makes her discouraged with herself, and gives her the idea she can't do it. It also turns her against the subject, and her defeatist attitude will hold her back in the future. Be patient. Don't make her stick at something when she's clearly had enough. Praise her when she succeeds, but if she can't understand simply say 'Don't worry dear; you'll soon get it' or 'I couldn't understand it at your age but it soon came' and then turn to another activity, returning to the original problem when she's older.

Encouraging creativity

Creativity has to do with producing exciting and original ideas and ways of doing things, either to solve problems or for the sheer joy of it. By 'original' I don't mean original for the human race as a whole. Your child is being original if he's thinking up things which are new for *him*, instead of simply copying others or repeating himself.

Children have a natural potential to be creative. Drawing, painting, modelling, cutting out, helping in the house, dressing dolls, building with bricks. The list is endless. And the more scope you give your child, not just from the fourth year of life onwards but as soon as he's sitting up and taking notice, the better chance he'll have of developing this potential. Certainly children differ in the strength and direction of their creative potential, just as they differ in their potential for physical skills. But in each individual much depends upon exposing him to the right environment at the time this potential is ready to begin expressing itself.

It's helpful to discuss creativity within the context of the 'bored' child, the child who's constantly pestering his parents for something to do. No child need be bored. If we lived out of doors he'd find no end of things with which to occupy himself. He's bored because he's in the limiting environment of the house, and because he has a busy mind that wants fresh challenges. This is where creativity comes in. Keep ready a range of stimulating activities for him. Don't protest you're 'not in the least creative' and don't know what to offer. I'm not talking about great art or spending a lot of money. I'm talking about reading to him, playing with him, enjoying fantasy and make-believe, using the right questions to prompt him to generate ideas.

No child need be bored

And I'm talking about laying in a stock of creative material. This needn't involve a trip to the art shop. The modern home generates enough useful throwaway materials each day to keep a child happy for a year. Artists refer to these as 'junk materials', and prize them highly. Newspapers which can be rolled into spills and used for paper sculpture. Cardboard boxes which can become houses, ships, blocks of flats, cars. Washing-up liquid containers which can become lighthouses, the towers of a fort, the body of a space ship. Matchboxes,

Keep a stock of 'junk materials'

313

cartons, plastic lids, egg boxes which can become doll's furniture. Larger boxes which can become garages and aeroplane
hangars. Pictures from colour supplements which can be cut
up to make mosaics. The big carton that housed the new
washing machine or television and which is big enough to
hold a small pirate or spaceman. Old clothes which he can use
for dressing up (a special favourite). Carpet offcuts, bottle
tops, cotton reels, empty containers from the kitchen cupboard
which can be put to a hundred and one good uses.

Modelling materials are good too
Don't neglect modelling materials either. Plasticine, pastry
and modelling clay, household fillers which can be painted
when hard to make permanent models. Paints can be impro-
vised from cocoa or food dyes or saffron (but make sure
everything he uses is harmless). Since children tire more
quickly at the table than on the floor, put a polythene sheet
down where he can make a mess to his heart's content. He
wants to be near you, so this should be in the kitchen or living
room, but if it can be left out so he can return to it later, so
much the better. At first he won't stick at anything for long
anyway, so if you leave it out you're saved the trouble of
setting him up all over again tomorrow. Don't insist he stick
at something simply because you've gone to the labour of
getting it all ready. His attention span is very short as yet.
Prompt him to explore the possibilities of his materials, but
when it's clear he's had enough, clean him up and let him
turn to something else.

Useful things you can buy
In addition to junk materials you can buy all sorts of useful
bits and pieces for next to nothing. Safe round-ended scissors.
Paint brushes (though let him finger-paint too). Pipe cleaners
which can be turned into people and animals. Sets of buttons.
Stockinet. Velcro, ribbons and tape. Button thread, elastic
bands and plastic paper fasteners. Cake decorations and icing
sets. Jigsaw puzzles. Nor should you neglect outdoor
materials. Acorns, pine cones, berries (if non-poisonous),
catkins, flowers to be dried and pressed, leaves, anything else
in season. The only limitations, as with all junk and natural
materials, are your imagination in supplying them and his
safety in using them. Use natural materials not only for making
things but also for growing. Plant pips in flowerpots, grow
beans in jam-jars on damp blotting paper, sprout carrot tops
in saucers of water. Make your child a full partner in these

experiences, letting him do the planting and the cutting out and the pasting. Never keep him a frustrated onlooker while you do all the 'messy' (and thus most enjoyable!) bits for him.

Ordinary kitchen items such as bowls and strainers and measuring jugs are also excellent for stimulating creativity. Creativity doesn't have to have an end-product. In any case, your child is often more interested in the business of making than in what he actually makes. So he can play creatively with water, watching it pour from one beaker to another (water play probably keeps him happier for longer than almost any other activity available), or with dry sand or lumps of dough. Where he does produce an end-product, put it on display. Have a piece of pin-boarding in the kitchen, or a special window sill, and make sure everyone gets a chance to see and admire his painting or his model (when he isn't busy taking it to pieces again!).

But creativity isn't only a matter of the right materials. Creativity develops best in an environment where originality and initiative are allowed to flourish. I don't mean go overboard and turn the house into a kind of artists' colony where everyone goes around cultivating their artistic temperament. Like everything else worth doing, creativity involves good sense and (ultimately) hard work and self-discipline. But allow your child where possible to do things in his own way without always having to conform to other people. This applies not only to the creative activities themselves, but to life in general. Where it's reasonable for your child to make a choice or have his say, let him go ahead. As we shall see later, this helps not only his creativity but the development of his intelligence and his personality.

Let your child do things his own way

Creativity always involves a certain amount of risk. Not physical risk, but the risk of trying a new way instead of doing it like everyone else. It involves the ability to think *divergently*, that is to think with the freedom and confidence that allow the mind to experiment with different ways of doing things. If your child is to be creative, he needs a little elbow room. He needs to be allowed to put something of himself into what he's doing, without worrying too much whether it's going to look neat or perfect. He needs you to prefer a lop-sided house *he's* made to a perfect one *you've* made with just a little help

315

from him. Happy creative folk (we're not talking about tortured geniuses) are people who've been allowed to believe in themselves and in their own originality. Far from making them stubbornly independent, this belief helps them to know when to ask for help. The person who grimly struggles on alone rather than turn to anyone else is more likely to have been told over and over in childhood, 'There, I *told* you so; now if you'd done it *my* way . . . !' Small wonder such a person, if he has any spirit, would rather die than rely on others.

Since the possibilities of misunderstanding are so great, let's stress again I'm *not* saying your child should do just as he pleases. That won't work. He has to learn the rules of social living, and learn that these rules are there for everyone's benefit. What I'm saying is that within clear consistent standards and guidelines your child should have scope for individuality. Often there are many different ways of doing things, none of them necessarily 'right' or 'wrong'. Allow your child where feasible to explore and decide which he prefers. Even when you know there's a quicker way, don't always jump in and insist he uses it. His way may be slower, but it's *his* way, and helps him to understand the task he's working with. You want him one day to take decisions for himself, to be original where originality is called for, to use his own judgement. These things don't just happen magically when he's older and when they become more convenient for the adults around him. They have to be fostered and guided in childhood.

Learning physical skills

Learning to ride a bicycle With many early skills, we don't *teach* them to children so much as provide children with the right environment to *learn*. A good example is helping your child to balance a two-wheel bicycle. Usually at around age four a child is eager to tackle something more than the three-wheeler to which she's been accustomed. Some children at this age sit on a miniature two-wheeler and balance it at the first attempt, but usually the bike is provided with two small extra wheels as stabilizers. Once she is thoroughly at home on it the stabilizers are removed and the child is away on her own. If you think about it there's in fact no way in which we could *teach* a child to balance a bicycle. She learns by adjusting her balance, through trial and error, until she gets it right. And once learnt, the skill remains with her for a lifetime.

Swimming is another example. Put a new-born baby in a warm bath of water and she'll dog-paddle strongly enough to keep her chin above water. Within a short while after birth, however, she loses this skill, and when you introduce her to the swimming baths she has to start from scratch. But the learning comes easily enough. Take her along to the baths at around her second birthday (or even earlier). Equip her with a pair of arm bands – every bit as good as more expensive flotation aids – and take her into the water with you, allowing her to cling round your neck just as you would if you were carrying her on dry land. At this age she will normally have little fear of the water, and provided she can hold on to you and her arm bands are properly inflated there's no risk.

Learning to swim

When you're satisfied she's used to the water allow her to float on her own, with you in close attendance. The fact that she can't feel the bottom with her feet won't trouble her and she'll learn to swim more quickly this way than in a shallow pool with her feet on the ground. At first she'll hold her arms out in front of her and make walking movements with her feet, but she'll soon progress to a dog-paddle. From now on stay very close and put a little less air in her arm bands each visit to the baths (weekly, or more often if you can), so that each time she has to do just that bit more to keep herself afloat. Within a matter of weeks she'll dispense with her arm bands altogether and be a swimmer.

Playgroup – yes or no?

If, as I've been stressing, it's so important to encourage your child's learning and thinking skills (to say nothing of the social learning that comes from mixing with other children), parents often ask whether after the third birthday they should start their child at a pre-school playgroup, where he can broaden his experiences still further. On balance, the answer is yes. But I say 'on balance' because if a child receives plenty of attention at home and has good opportunities for mixing, the need for a playgroup diminishes. In fact he may do even better at home, especially if he has extra resourceful parents and plenty of attention and stimulation.

In most cases, try your child at playgroup and see what

Take a good look at the playgroup happens. If he likes it and enjoys going, that's an excellent sign it's doing him good. But take a look around. Is the playgroup well-organized, with a leader who seems to know what he or she's doing? Is there plenty of equipment and is it accessible so the children can use it properly? Is there sufficient range of activities, with children able to choose between apparatus, toys, books, puzzles and arts and crafts? Is there a story time for those children who are ready to listen? Is there plenty of space and is the playroom attractive? Can the children go outdoors in summer? Is everything safe and are the children properly supervised? Does the leader allow children to initiate and explore their own activities or is she always interfering and directing things for them? Does she deal sensibly and sympathetically with children's individual problems and with disputes? Does she know how to involve the rather solitary child in group activities, at the same time not forcing him into mixing if it clearly upsets him? Above all, does she seem genuinely to like children, to understand them, and to enjoy being with them and helping them have fun?

Few playgroups score high marks on everything, but carry out a fair assessment and if you're in doubt then find another group which may be more suitable for your child. If there isn't one, don't work on the assumption that even an unsatisfactory playgroup is better than none. Unless your child very much wants to keep going, let him stay at home. A child who has bad experiences in a playgroup will carry these over into his first days at school, and will find it harder to settle in when the time comes.

Most children learn a lot from playgroup However, most playgroups do a good job, and most children enjoy them and learn valuable lessons from them. They learn there are plenty of exciting things going on outside the home. They learn how to mix with other children and learn from them, how to relate to adults besides their parents, and how to accept guidance and instruction from them. They learn they can still feel secure even when their parents aren't there. Even though there aren't formal lessons, they also learn a tremendous amount from the leader's interaction with them, and from the new toys and apparatus. Finally, playgroup gives them wider opportunities for the use of language, and extra things to talk to you about when they come home.

Starting a child at playgroup usually presents no problem.

Most playgroup leaders are happy to have you stay with your child for the first few days. If you like the atmosphere and want to help, you are usually only too welcome to stay longer if you wish. In fact if the leader objects to your presence, this is a good sign that she doesn't really understand children, and a good indication that your child will be better off elsewhere.

However, some children fail to settle even in the very best playgroups. Sometimes they find the bustle and noise intimidating. Sometimes they just find home more fun. Sometimes they have one or two unhappy experiences such as being accidentally bowled over by more robust specimens. Sometimes there are deeper reasons, such as jealousy of a younger brother or sister left at home or a feeling of anxiety and insecurity about life in general or about their relationship with you in particular. If after giving the group a fair trial it's obvious your child won't fit in or refuses to be separated from you, accept this and withdraw him. Some parents worry this means he's going to be a poor mixer, but the worry is usually groundless. Certainly some children tend by temperament to be more attached to their own company and to their home than others, but this isn't necessarily a bad thing. We can't all be the life and soul of the party. But your child is far more likely to turn into a bad mixer if he's forced to join in now, before he's ready, than if he's allowed to wait until he's older. Keep him at home, and let him meet and play with other children on more secure territory. He needs time to adjust to others, and this adjustment needs to take place in a less hectic environment.

The child who doesn't settle

If you yourself find it difficult to mix with others, and rely very much upon your child's company, there is always a temptation to retreat with him into the home and turn your back on the outside world. So you may feel relief if your child doesn't like playgroup, and reckon that now you have a good reason for keeping him to yourself. These reactions are understandable, but they're unrealistic and in the long run will handicap your child's social development. Maybe you find it hard to mix because when you were a child your parents kept *you* to themselves. Or maybe you had bad experiences at school. But nervousness when with others is a big handicap in life. The well-rounded person is the one who is at ease both in his own company and in the company of others. As a good

Don't try to keep your child to yourself

319

parent you want your child to be like this, even though it means you have to sacrifice keeping him all to yourself. So resolve that even though he may not be going to playgroup, he'll nevertheless have all the right opportunities to make friends outside the home and enjoy the experience of widening his social circle.

What about nursery school?

Many of the things I have said about playgroup apply equally to nursery school. The difference between playgroup and school is that the latter is usually part of the state educational system (though there are many private nursery schools, particularly in London) and as such is run by qualified staff and supervised by the local education authority. It therefore offers a more planned curriculum, with more conscious effort made to educate children in both social behaviour and even (if they're ready) in preliminary reading and writing skills. Nursery schools are also sometimes able to take children for the whole day, since they keep normal school hours, whereas most playgroups operate half-days only.

Official policy towards nursery schools is that they should mainly be sited in areas where social and economic conditions are below the national average, and where children are likely to be deprived of appropriate facilities and stimulation within the home. Thus whether or not your child has a chance of attending nursery school may depend upon where you live. If he does have a chance to go, then as with playgroups you should make use of it unless your child clearly prefers otherwise or unless you have reason to think the school is unsatisfactory.

The advantages of nursery education Since state nursery schools are free, and often cater for the less well-off, this gives children from economically more favoured backgrounds the valuable chance to widen their social horizons. Thus they can understand from an early age that many others have fewer advantages in life than they have, yet nevertheless have just the same qualities and strengths.

On the other hand, if you are from a less economically privileged environment, the opportunities provided for your child by nursery school will be an excellent source of additional stimulation for him, and will give him a useful start to his formal education. Research evidence shows that although nursery school children don't necessarily do better at the basic subjects once they start infant school than children who've missed nursery education, nevertheless the lessons they learn there are very helpful for the future. In adolescence they are much less likely to be in trouble with the police or cause their parents problems, and once they leave school they are better able both to find and to keep worthwhile employment. So there's no doubting the value of nursery education, provided a child takes to it and enjoys the experience.

Knowing and understanding herself

Your child first realized she was a separate person in the third year of life (see Chapter 5). In the fourth and fifth years, in a more sociable and co-operative way, this realization develops apace. Children aren't born knowing who they are. They aren't born knowing whether they'll be popular or successful, whether they're going to be thought of as 'good' or not, what sort of feelings they're going to have, whether they're going to feel happy with themselves. These and other issues to do with the *self* have to be learnt. Yet they're vital to our well-being as people. If we grow up with self-understanding, and the ability to accept ourselves, we've a good chance of being psychologically healthy individuals, able to use our talents effectively and cope with the problems thrown at us. On the other hand, if we grow up rejecting ourselves, confused and guilty about who we are and hating ourselves all the same, life will hold out much unhappiness.

Your child needs to grow up at ease with herself and the world, a confident assured person who can recognize her own strengths and weaknesses without conceit or self-deprecation, and who can meet life on equal terms. To do so she must have the strength to be honest with herself and others, the self-insight to know where there's room for improvement, and the peace of mind to accept criticism without becoming defensive and aggressive on the one hand or cowed and submissive on the other. She must have the courage of her convictions and the scope to make full use of herself, and she must experience life, with all its ups and downs, as a pleasant and rewarding experience.

Your child needs to be at ease with herself and the world

If your child is to develop these qualities, much depends upon the experiences of the pre-school and school years. These experiencs should leave your child feeling she's a worthwhile person and can be herself without constantly striving to be the person other people think she 'ought' to be. I earlier stressed the importance of helping your child feel the world is a place in which she can trust those close to her, and that provides her with a secure base within her home and family from which to reach out and explore. I also stressed that she needs to feel her independence and individuality are acceptable to those around her, and aren't going to be crushed or condemned (see Chapter 5).

Her self-image depends very much on you

Building on this knowledge, you can now help your child towards healthy self-acceptance, and the development of a concept of 'self' which allows her to feel good about the person she is. She takes her early picture of herself very much from what you tell her, which is why it's so vital you give her a positive and happy self-image. Help her to like herself. Not to see herself as 'goody-goody' of course, because that's unrealistic, but to see herself as a nice person to have around, with all sorts of good and useful qualities to enjoy within herself and share with others.

This means giving your child the right sort of praise and encouragement, and avoiding *personal* labels like 'bad' or 'naughty'. Remember that the way to avoid these labels is to draw attention to the unacceptable action rather than to the child herself ('That was a silly thing to do' rather than 'You are a silly girl'). But it means more than this. It means helping your child accept the existence of her emotions, instead of feeling frightened and guilty about them.

Anger

Let's take the example of anger. Your child is playing happily with his bricks on the floor. You decide it's time he came and put his hat and coat on because you have to go to the shops. Far more interested in his bricks than in hat, coat and shops he refuses. You insist, he insists. You get angry, he gets angry. The upshot is that one cross parent hauls one cross child off to do the shopping, telling him in the process exactly what he or she thinks of him.

But analyse the incident. He's enjoying playing with his

bricks, which are a nice outlet for his creativity. He doesn't want to be interrupted. If in addition he doesn't feel like a trip to the shops, all the more reason why he feels put out. So his anger is natural. For that matter so is yours. You've got a great deal to do during the day, and you don't feel much like a trip to the shops either, so you're resentful your child won't co-operate. The two sets of anger meet head-on, and your child receives some home truths, to which he responds with some home truths of his own. Things go from bad to worse, and you both end up feeling unhappy with each other, and with yourselves as well. **His anger is perfectly natural**

The truth of the matter is that no one is really in the 'wrong'. There's been a clash of interests, and there's no reason your child should feel he's naughty simply because he feels cross at having to do as he's told. Tell him, 'I know you're angry. I feel angry when somebody stops me doing something I'm enjoying. But we can't always do as we like. So let's try to make the best of it.' This won't turn off his anger by magic. You'll still have to insist he does as he's told. But it will show him you understand how he feels and that *these feelings are perfectly natural*. This helps him accept them in himself, which frees him as time goes by to work on them and learn how to handle them. The problem to his psychological development arises if he's made to feel he isn't acceptable to you if he's 'the kind of boy who has a temper'. Since everyone has a temper (saints are rare creatures) he will, depending on his temperament and self-control, either continue to lose it and feel bad about it afterwards, or bottle it up and repress it and feel even worse.

Repressed emotions don't just go away. If your child is denied the safety valve of emotional expression, psychological problems can be the consequence. He's at risk of developing into an over-controlled child who never shows his feelings and lives with a constant sense of guilt. But whether the anger forces its way out or is repressed, the child now has an inner conflict, with the 'good' part of him at war to keep down the 'bad'. No wonder he's at risk of growing up with what psychologists call a fragmented personality, never able to bring the various parts of himself into harmony and create a whole person. **The dangers of repressing emotions**

There may be physical problems too, since mind and body

are closely linked. The obvious signs of these physical problems are tenseness and an inability to relax, but there may be others. Both psychologists and medical doctors are coming to accept that many serious physical ailments – even perhaps cancer and heart disease – may in some people be linked to an inability to express emotions and communicate feelings, and at a deeper level an inability to accept and value oneself. The high toll of mental illness in the Western world (one woman in eight and one man in twelve will need medical treatment for psychiatric problems at some stage in their lives) seems also significantly due to the failure by individuals to come to proper terms with themselves as people, to free themselves from unacceptable burdens of guilt, and to deal with life's problems without undue stress or frustration.

How to react to your child's anger

As I mentioned when talking about the negative phase through which many children go in the third year, it isn't always easy for you to accept your child's feelings. Her anger makes you angry, not just because it may be hindering you in something you want to do but because it seems to carry a threat to you as a person. This is particularly so if your child makes a verbal attack on you. 'I hate you I hate you,' she screams, or 'Go away I wish you were dead'. Hurt and outraged, you respond with 'What a terrible *terrible* thing to say; I don't know what gets into you at times'. Or maybe you use even stronger language, ending up by telling her that you really don't know what's going to become of her 'if you don't get rid of that evil streak in you'.

Don't over-react to words like 'hate' and 'dead'

You're only human and you don't enjoy being told you're hated, or wishfully consigned to your grave before you feel quite ready. But a small child can't choose her words with the care you or I use. She doesn't know that 'hate', used angrily, carries with it wounding connotations for an adult. All she knows is that she's heard you say casually 'Oh I hate walking in this wind' or 'I do hate the misuse of the word "fantastic"' or 'I hate doing this but I've got to knock you back' when playing ludo. Most of the time, we adults use the word 'hate' lightly, and it's only when we scream it at someone in the midst of a rage that it's really used as a way of hurting. So when your child tells you she hates you, she's using a word she's picked up, and which for her is a way of saying she's very angry with you. She doesn't *hate* you in the full meaning of the word. Nor does she want her words to hurt you, as she's too young to know you can be hurt by what she says. She's simply giving vent to the frustration she feels towards you for stopping her doing something she enjoys, or for refusing her something she very much wants.

Similarly your child has no idea what being 'dead' means. She's never seen a dead person, and though she may have seen a dead animal she isn't yet able to transfer that experience to human beings. All she knows is that old Mr Smith across the road died recently, and he isn't around any more. Being 'dead' simply means not being around, and when she wishes it on you she's saying she wishes you'd go away so that she could get on with doing what she wants. She's frustrated with you and is trying somehow to put this feeling of frustration into words.

By over-reacting to words like 'hate' or 'dead' you are attributing emotions and motives to your child which she isn't experiencing. By telling her how terrible her words are you make her think her feelings of frustration are terrible. What a wicked girl she must be, she tells herself, to have such feelings. Good girls must be people who not only obey their parents but don't even *feel* like disobeying them, and who certainly never feel angry towards them. She'd like to be like that, but she isn't. So she ends up doubting her right to have any feelings when she's deprived of what she wants.

Incidentally, by being upset or by adopting a 'How *dare* you say that to *me*!' attitude every time your child tries to communicate her disapproval of you, you're lessening the chances of having an honest relationship with her in the years to come. **Allow your child to express her feelings to you** By making her censor carefully what she can and cannot say to you now, it will be hard for her ever to feel really at ease with you. Some parents are horrified that they should be expected sometimes to tolerate their child speaking crossly to them, and take the view that she must be put in her place. But there's a price to pay for this unyielding attitude in the years ahead. A child *can't* be allowed to say what she likes when she likes, but she *can* be allowed to see that from where she's sitting on the floor, with her bricks whisked away by an adult who wants to take her to the shops, her cross feelings are justified. This puts her in a better position to learn how to handle them, and to learn that your cross feelings are equally justified, and that successful human relationships depend upon this kind of mutual understanding.

When she shouts she hates you, respond with 'I expect you do for the moment, but we've still got to go to the shops.' Don't worry that she'll go on using the word. When she's older and realizes its full meaning she'll keep it for more appropriate use. Use the same approach if she says she wishes you were dead, but since this is a more factual word you can help her to understand its proper meaning. Tell her, 'That isn't a very nice thing to say; when people are dead it means they go away and you never see them again. Is that really what you want? Who'd look after you then?' Since children have a very sensible awareness of how much they depend upon their parents, this is quite enough to help her realize your death is the last thing she wants.

Your child's emotional development is of vital importance
Since the issues in this section are so important, let me re-emphasize them. Feelings are a vitally important area of our lives. Thinking is fine, but it's *feelings* that really decide whether we're enjoying life or not. People who hate themselves or are constantly guilty, anxious or fearful, people who are full of frustrated emotions, people who are at war with themselves, are never going to get much joy from life (or bring much joy to others). So in raising your child you must pay attention not only to his mental abilities, but to his emotions as well. We all like to feel our children are bright and alert and developing well mentally, but we must be equally concerned with their emotional development and the self-understanding that goes with it.

Don't let him harm others
This doesn't mean we should be soft with them of course. There are clear limits to what a child can be allowed to *do* with his emotions. He can have his tantrum on the floor for example, but if he tries hitting out at others he's restrained or removed from the room (see page 361 onwards for more details). There's no reason why he should – and every reason why he shouldn't – be allowed to use his emotions to harm others, especially children smaller or weaker.

If he breaks a toy in his anger
Similarly if he acts destructively towards possessions he must be prompted to see that breakages lead to going without, or in the case of someone else's property to paying (symbolically at this stage by perhaps foregoing the money that was to have been spent on a small treat of some kind) for the damage.

The aim here is to let your child see the consequences of his actions. If he becomes cross with a toy because it won't do what he wants, and throws it across the room, the result is a broken toy that's no use for anything at all. The crossness is understandable, but if it's vented on the defenceless toy this only makes things worse. If you can warn him in time of the consequences of his actions all well and good, but often these incidents happen in the heat of the moment. So he has to learn the hard way that it's one thing to feel cross, and quite another to vent his cross feelings unwisely.

There's no need to add your crossness to his. If he gets the impression *you're* now cross about the whole incident he may divert his anger to you, and you'll have a real tantrum on your hands. He'll learn his lesson more quickly if you confine yourself to pointing out that throwing his toy down wasn't very sensible because now it's broken and won't work at all. If he's distressed, comfort him and assure him you know how he feels. You often want to throw things across the room when they won't work properly too. But you've learnt by experience that if you do you usually end up making things worse. Better to find some other way of getting rid of cross feelings. Make a game of it and run through all the ways you can both think of for showing you're cross. Jumping up and down, running round the room, beating your fists on the floor and so on. This is a good exercise, because when your child thinks of unacceptable ways like hitting the cat you can have a good laugh, and point out that of course we can't *really* do things like that because it isn't the poor old cat's fault, and it isn't fair she should be the one to suffer.

As for the broken toy, if your child's upset put it on one side and promise you'll mend it or replace it for him, but that when you do he mustn't break it again because you won't do that every time. Should your child show no remorse about the damage, and insist it was a stupid toy anyway, leave it at that. Don't mend or replace it. Tell him 'It's your toy; if you want to break it and go without, that's up to you. But you can't expect people to go on buying you things if that's the way you're going to treat them.' And of course if the toy was a gift from someone else, remind your child he's now going to have to explain to him or her how it came to be broken.

Fear

Don't dismiss
your child's
fear

Fear raises much the same issues as anger. If a child tells you she's afraid of the dark or of bogey men under the bed and you tell her she's a 'great big baby' or laugh at her or say 'of course you're not afraid', she's made to doubt her own feelings. It *feels* as if she's afraid, but you tell her she isn't, so what *are* her feelings? Are they really there or not? And if they are, obviously they're something to be ashamed of. Thus the child isn't helped to recognize and come to terms with her fear, and to realize that grown-ups understand it and see it as natural.

Your child needs you to listen to her fears and say, 'Yes I used to feel like that when I was your age. But there never *was* a bogey man under the bed' and then go down on hands and knees with her and look under the bed and check that all is well. And then offer to leave the light on and the bedroom door open as you did when she was smaller.

Adults must keep in mind that young children can find the world a very threatening and frightening place. They're very aware of how small and vulnerable they are, and how much they depend upon other people. So they can be afraid of physical harm on the one hand, or of losing their parents and being left alone on the other. Pretty harrowing fears. But children can't always express these fears in direct form. Often they don't fully understand them themselves. So their fear of physical harm may be expressed as a fear of imaginary things like monsters and witches, and their fear of losing their parents as a fear of being left alone at night.

Fear of physical
harm may
come partly
from fear of you

As parents we must accept, however unpalatable it may be, that a child's fear of physical harm comes in part from her fear of us (see the section on night fears on page 282). Yes, I know you love your child and wouldn't do anything really to hurt her, but we all of us from time to time use our greater physical strength to get a child to do as we want. We may or may not smack her, but there are certainly occasions when we take her by the arm and *make* her do as we want. There are also occasions when she's totally absorbed in something, only to find us suddenly leaping across to stop her because she's in danger or doing something forbidden. Both sets of occasions are a shock to a child. Hers is a small world, and adults tower over her at the best of times. Imagine someone twice your height towering over you, and this will give you some idea of how you might look to a small child. So a sudden grab at her when she's lost in an activity is frightening for her, and fills her with very mixed feelings towards you. (Notice how *you* feel towards someone who, however inadvertently, gives you one heck of a fright!)

If you follow up by speaking angrily to her, her fright is redoubled, and for the time being she sees you as a rather terrifying person. But she can't reconcile this picture of you as a terrifying person with her picture of you as the person she loves and depends upon most in the world. How can you be one and the same? Most of the time you're warm and loving towards her; if anything *else* threatens her, you're the one she runs to for protection and comfort. But then sometimes you frighten her, and she doesn't know what to make of it, particularly as she then has *no one* to run to, and is left isolated and troubled.

Because she can't reconcile the two sides of you, your child tries to push away the frightening side, and projects it on to imaginary beings like witches and goblins. These are things for which it's 'legitimate' to feel fear, and thus they help her handle her feelings. This doesn't mean you should think badly of yourself for ever frightening your child. Certainly it's important to remember how vulnerable she is, but you have to be firm with her when necessary and there are bound to be occasions when she feels a stab of fear in consequence. And of course there are other things, unconnected with you, that are also responsible for frightening her. Television programmes, pictures in books, stories, loud and overbearing visitors, people who pick her up and hug her when she doesn't know them, elder brothers or sisters who get angry with her. No child is a stranger to fear. But if your child has an *excessive* fear of imaginary creatures waiting round corners or lurking in her bedroom, think what real fears these imaginary terrors may be symbolizing. Are there things going on in the house which are frightening her? Have you startled her frequently of late? Have older children been unfair to her?

Are there real fears behind her imaginary terrors?

Often with a little imagination the real reasons for your child's fear can be pinpointed. We're often quite resistant to the idea that she may be frightened of us ('Of *course* that couldn't have frightened her!'), but we must accept the fact

329

that it may have happened. If someone else is frightening her, avoid that person until your child is older. If it's a story or a television programme, avoid that too. And get her to speak about her fears if possible. If she can put them into words, they become more familiar, more manageable.

Fear of losing her parents Where a child is frightened of losing her parents, and shows this either directly or through a fear of being left alone at night, identify how this fear has arisen. A child who feels secure in her home and with her family shouldn't be too troubled by fears of terrible things happening to her parents, or of being abandoned by them. She feels so safe with you that she can't really imagine the possibility of losing you (though she might overhear and misinterpret a chance remark you make about going away somewhere, and want to discuss it with you). It's the insecure child who worries that something awful might happen to the people she loves and on whom she depends.

If your child has these insecure feelings, find out why. Have you threatened her that if she isn't good you'll leave her or send her away? Are there problems within your marriage that may have alarmed her? Do you leave her frequently with different baby-sitters while you go out in the evenings? Run through these and other possibilities until you hit upon what's troubling her, and try to put it right.

A child can also be made insecure if she gets the impression that although you won't leave her physically you may withdraw your love for her. I return to this when we discuss punishments later in the chapter, but let me stress that if a child is ever to feel really secure she must be sure she has your love at all times. Nothing can take that love away. Even if she's naughty you never stop loving her. She's your child, and your love isn't negotiable.

Dealing with fear Even if you do your best to find out the real cause of your child's fear, and try to remove that cause, you still have to accept that he's going to meet other fears in the future, and must be helped to learn how to handle them. Fear is a very powerful emotion, and the psychologist meets plenty of children and adults whose whole lives are dominated by it. Fear, and the worry and anxiety that are an inseparable part of it, is an ever-present feature of their lives. Even when they've got nothing concrete to worry about they still torture themselves with what *might* happen, and with all the things that *might* go wrong.

Some fathers are sympathetic about generalized anxiety of this kind in their daughters but less so in their sons. They want a boy of theirs to learn how to stand up for himself. But you can't expect a small boy to be a man before he's even learnt to be a child. Accept his fears first, then help him deal with them. And remember that small boys aren't all the same. Some take readily to rough play and enjoy a physical challenge. Others don't. Your child has a right to be himself. If you enjoy physical activity and risky sports and pastimes you may want your son to grow up like you. But it's only fair to accept his right to be different. Your son isn't you. He can't help the differences in temperament. He must work with the person he is, rather than be pushed into a role he can't live up to.

With your support, your child will learn that fears can be faced and understood, and that when they are, they lose some of their power. Part of the reason why our fears unsettle us is that they seem to be uncontrollable forces just waiting to overwhelm us. Thus we become afraid of fear itself. Once we acknowledge and confront our fears, instead of trying to push them away and pretend they're not there, we begin to see that after all they're nothing we can't handle. Fear is a natural reaction to things we don't understand or against which we feel ourselves defenceless, and the more we recognize it for what it is, the less it behaves like an enemy towards us. **Acknowledging our fears is the first step**

Your child can be helped to see that many of his fears are groundless, and that even those that have substance can be kept in perspective. The valuable lesson to learn is that to be afraid is human. And that deep down humans have plenty of strengths. Each of us has to be helped to find and use these strengths. We don't have to be the victims of our own fear, just as we don't have to be the victims of our own anger.

Phobias are no less 'real' to the child than his other fears (in that he experiences the full strength of the fear reaction), but the term stands for those fears which have no rational basis. We're all prone to the odd phobia. A fear of spiders or mice or crawling insects is a good example. There's no way in which any of these humble creatures can directly harm us, yet some people react to them much more intensely than they do to real **Phobias** physical dangers such as breaking the speed limit on a crowded motorway or taking an overdose of alcohol. A phobia about heights is another example, while claustrophobia (fear of confined spaces) and agoraphobia (fear of open spaces) are yet others. In fact one can have a phobia about virtually anything, the defining characteristic being that the fear is out of all proportion to the threat involved. Thus it's rational to be afraid of scaling a high ladder, but irrational to be afraid of mounting an ordinary step-ladder; the former is a fear, the latter is a phobia.

Phobias can make their appearance at virtually any age, and in young children they're not uncommon from the third year of life onwards. Your child may have a phobia about flowers for example, or about your rubber kitchen gloves, or about the cat, or even about harmless Aunt Ethel. When the object is brought near him, he shows every sign of genuine distress, and requires not only its prompt removal but also a great deal of comforting before he's back to normal again. In most cases, these early phobias are short-lived, clearing up as suddenly and mysteriously as they appeared. The cause of a phobia in a young child is usually that the offending object is associated in his mind with a severe fright of some kind. You may not have been aware of this fright (children cry for so many incidents during the day that you can't go diagnosing them all), but it was sufficient of a shock to have left a lasting impression on him. The object may itself have been the cause of his fright (for example the cat may have jumped up on him when he was asleep) or may have been only incidental to it (you may have been wearing your rubber gloves when he slipped and fell while having his bath), but either way the object and the fright were in close enough proximity to be associated in the child's mind. He doesn't understand the connection himself, he simply responds with fear each time he sees the object.

Childhood phobias usually disappear of their own accord

The standard treatment for phobias in adults is to break this connection by judiciously associating the cause of the phobia with something pleasant. However, this is rarely necessary for most children. Given time, the connection usually fades of its own accord. In the meantime, keep your child away from the phobic object if you can, and if you can't, make sure it isn't forced upon him in any way, and that it's accompanied as far as possible by pleasant associations.

As to your own phobia about spiders or mice, that's a little harder to explain. Probably these things weren't directly associated with fear in childhood, but their speed of movement maybe evokes forgotten childhood incidents when you were terrified by such movement in people or things that really did threaten you (an angry or frightened parent grabbing at you suddenly when you were least expecting it, an older child riding a bicycle straight at you). Or perhaps you took the fear over, ready made, from seeing the terrified reactions of adults to these creatures. And while we're on the subject, your claustrophobia may have been caused by a genuine near-suffocation experience in childhood, while your agoraphobia may come from early experiences of being thrust, vulnerable and unprepared, into the spotlight. However, as I've already said, most childhood phobias don't last long, and even those that persist into adult life are usually mild idiosyncrasies rather than anything more serious.

Unhappiness

Another powerful emotion which children have to learn to handle is being hurt and upset. If a small child is upset the natural reaction is to cry. Crying is a good emotional outlet, and we all feel better for it when we're very down in the dumps. But if a child (particularly a boy) is told briskly that she is being a silly baby, or that big boys and girls don't cry, she has to learn to choke back her emotions and pretend she doesn't feel vulnerable. Certainly you don't want your child to grow up a cry-baby, open to the taunts of other children. Nor do you want her to use tears as a way of getting what she wants. But you do want her to express her feelings when she's genuinely upset, and to know she's got nothing to be ashamed of. Satisfactory personality development in a child means that she has to be able to cry as well as laugh when the occasion demands it, and not feel she has to reject the emotions concerned, or pretend she doesn't have them.

Little children's moods are quickly up and down. A child may be laughing one minute, crying the next, and laughing again a few moments later. Compared to the adult, a child's moods surface much more readily. And she can't disguise them like the adult. If she's happy she shows it. If she's disappointed she shows it. If she's excited she shows it. If she's heartbroken she shows it. And although to the adult her moods may seem out of keeping with the actual events concerned ('Oh surely you can't be crying over a little thing like *that*!' or 'Goodness it's not *that* exciting!'), to a child her feelings are perfectly genuine. She wears her heart on her sleeve, no matter what emotion it happens to be registering.

Don't expect toughness from your son
Since this is the way children are, it's far better for your child to get unhappiness or disappointment out of her system and have a good cry about them. Throughout childhood, tears are an excellent safety valve. There's evidence, both psychological and medical, that even the adult who has a cry when things go wrong suffers less from the effects of stress than the adult who bottles it all up and pretends everything is okay. This applies just as much to men as to women. As I said in the last section (page 331), it's wrong to expect a toughness from your small son he isn't capable of delivering. If he's upset, he's as much in need of tears and a warm hug from a loving parent as your small daughter. We rightly hear a lot about the unfair way girls and women are treated in our society, but less about the unfairness that sometimes faces boys and men. The image of 'toughness' which they're supposed to match up to is a good example. Don't make the mistake of imposing it on your son. He's as vulnerable as your daughter, and needs sympathy just as much when things go wrong. So allow him to get it off his chest when he's genuinely unhappy.

Don't encourage helplessness in your daughter
But – and it's an important but – some children quickly discover they can use tears as a means of getting their own way. Perhaps to win sympathy or attention (in which case are they short of sympathy and attention at other times?). Perhaps to persuade you to buy or do something for them. You know your own child, and you can tell the difference between when she's genuinely upset and when she's turning on tears just for effect. You can't blame her for 'acting' upset; we all like to find strategies for getting our own way. But you can indicate to her that sorry, it just won't work. If it works with you, she'll soon be using it with others, and could even carry the practice through into adult life.

This is an example of where girls are more often unfairly treated than boys. We say, 'Oh well, she's only a little *girl* after all!', and we give her what she wants. So instead of learning to win the day by reason or perseverance, she lets tears say it for her. This is a kind of *acquired helplessness*. The girl learns that by breaking down or acting helpless others will rush to do things for her. She's denied the opportunity to develop her own skills and to show she's every bit as capable as the next person. So she's denied the opportunity of becoming an effective human being. And unless she finds people throughout life (a husband, her own children) who are prepared to go along with her act, she'll one day find the world running out of patience. Irrespective of sex, encourage your child to develop competence in the face of challenge. To have a cry first by all means if it helps, but then to tackle what needs to be done realistically and competently.

Of course, both boys and girls have to discover that they can't go through life never feeling unhappy. Crying and being comforted are necessary things, but we have gradually to become more philosophical in the face of setbacks, and not to become 'addicted' to sadness and weepiness simply for the pleasure of having it all kissed better. As a child grows older, she'll meet more and more things that can't be 'kissed better' (made magically all right again), but which have to be coped with as they are. A child who's encouraged to be too soft will throughout life hark back to childhood when a loving adult was always able to make the world suddenly into a happy place once again.

All children must learn to accept setbacks

So once your child has had any necessary comforting, she must forget about it and get on with life. Most children learn this lesson quickly, because little children live mostly in the present, not the past. But it's worth emphasizing they'll learn the lesson best if they feel that whenever things *are* genuinely distressing they're allowed first to have their cry and their bit of sympathy. We brood over things far more if we think no one cares about us, or if we feel we haven't had the chance to let others know what we're going through.

A final word on emotions

If you've more than one child, don't expect each of them to have the same emotional responses. Temperaments differ, as we've seen. So what devastates one child will hardly ruffle another, and what excites one child will scarcely raise a smile

Different children have different emotional responses

from the next. Some children just feel things more deeply than the rest. That's the way it is. It's no good expecting an emotional child to show the same tranquil disposition as his brothers and sisters. He doesn't choose to be the way he is, and he's the one who suffers his own moods most keenly. Show the patience and understanding *he* needs. If he's over-doing it even for him, chivvy him out of his mood instead of becoming irritated with him. Show him you appreciate how he feels, but that at the same time he has to play his part in coming to terms with the way he is.

Children may respond differently at different times of day
Children's moods often vary depending upon the time of day. A child is more inclined to be difficult at the end of the day when he's tired, but some children are also not at their best in the mornings. Others are at their worst just before a meal, while others seem to go through mid-morning dol-drums. Sometimes these phases have to do with a child's blood-sugar levels, which may be low when he wakes or just before a meal. Your doctor can check these for you, and give necessary advice (like allowing your child to eat little and often). But usually it's just part of his daily rhythm. We all of us have a 24-hour rhythm (called technically a *circadian* rhythm) which dictates at what time of the day we're likely to be at our best, at what time we're going to have most physical energy and so on. Many of us have a low point some time during the day (certain of us may feel it extends for 48 hours), and around 1 or 2 a.m. is a period of low metabolism for us all.

Your child may seem tired all day but brighten up in the evening, getting into his stride when it's time for bed. Or he may wake bright as a button but be good for nothing come teatime. Or he may be quite impossible before each meal but a little saint once he's been fed. Unless there is an identifiable physical reason behind it, there's nothing you can do to alter your child's circadian rhythm. Often it changes slowly as he grows older, so that the five-year-old who can't sleep beyond 6 a.m. becomes the teenager who can't wake by midday. But in the meantime the only thing to do is to learn to live with it, identifying those points in the day when your child is going to be more difficult to handle, and those times in the day when you can expect plain sailing.

Children aren't the only ones with emotions and moods.

336

Adults aren't immune from them either. And there's a ten- **Your moods** dency when we feel ragged round the edges to snap at our **vary too** children over minor things. Be aware of these moods in yourself and try not to take them out on your child. Not only is this unfair to him, it makes things worse for you. You snap at him, he feels aggrieved and snaps back. You become angrier, he becomes angrier. You make more demands for his co-operation, he becomes less co-operative. All reasonable communication between parent and child breaks down, and the latter is packed wailing and protesting up to bed, leaving the former to collapse in a chair calling for sedatives. Avoid this kind of situation by being more sensitive to your own moods, and by not giving your child an angry earful that he has done nothing to deserve. Tell him you're tired or that your head aches or that you're having a bad day. Small children respond with great sympathy if their parents are unwell and (for five minutes at least) are exaggeratedly considerate and helpful. Informing them of your moods also helps them understand you're a human being too, like them. And allows you to say, 'Sorry I snapped at you, but we all feel a bit snappy when we're tired.'

Keep in mind finally that your child is learning a great deal about his emotions without necessarily showing it in his daily behaviour. Many of the lessons which he internalizes have no visible effect until weeks, months or even years later. Parents often say in surprise to their children 'Fancy you remembering *that*!' over some small incident which appeared to make no impression on the child at the time. You can multiply this many times over in all areas of your child's learning. Much of the influence you're having upon him will only become obvious in the time ahead. You're building for the future.

Moral development

Learning right and wrong

I have already mentioned the young child's inability some-times to understand abstract adult concepts. Nowhere is this inability more obvious than in matters of right and wrong. But before we look at this, a word of warning. Often with children we think of right and wrong rather in terms of what's convenient or inconvenient for us as parents. 'Right' means a child being instantly obedient, keeping quiet when we're talking or watching television, keeping clean, not making a mess, not waking too early in the mornings, not wanting us to do things when we'd far rather snooze in the chair, not upsetting visiting relatives, not tearing clothes, not losing a glove when we're out for a walk, not pestering to be bought things when we go to the shops, not 'letting me down' when we go visiting, not persisting with questions, and not answering back. This approach to right and wrong is understandable, but it mustn't be taken too far. Quite apart from the child's need for a reasonable amount of freedom and autonomy in her life, we must realize that in these early years she's going to take her ideas of right and wrong ready-made from us. Thus she feels 'good' when she's doing as she's told, and 'bad' when she isn't, *irrespective of whether the things we're demanding of her are fair or unfair.*

You want your child to be able to think for herself   You want your child to grow up with the ability to think for herself, to do the right things in life because these *are* the right things, not to go through life ruled by the strict conditioning she received in early childhood. A person who receives this conditioning still carries at an unconscious level all the prohibitions and guilt her parents kindled in her when she was too young to have much of a mind of her own. Thus she may go through life believing that untidiness and mess are 'bad' (i.e. morally wrong) in themselves. Or feeling guilty every time she tries to defend her point of view against those in authority. Or terrified at the thought of 'upsetting' others, or of what the neighbours will think, or of being original or being herself. She doesn't really know *why* these things are wrong. She invents reasons and comes to believe in them herself, but the actual cause of her behaviour lies back in childhood, at an age when she was deeply impressionable and really believed her parents when they told her it was 'naughty' to speak with her mouth full or have her say or romp with her friends or make a noise at inconvenient times.

A child must learn to respect the rights of others and to show thoughtfulness. But this learning comes not from telling her how bad and wicked she is every time she transgresses, but from rules which are simple, sensible, and properly explained and understood. It comes too from showing her she has rights as well as everyone else, and that it's her home as much as yours, and you want her to enjoy it. Make things easier for everyone by organizing the household so that it takes account of the fact there's a small child around. New furniture and carpets are a doubtful asset if you have to spend every second of the day telling her to be careful of them; better to postpone them until she's a little older and more restrained.

Take the trouble to show your child the difference between things that are simply inconvenient for you and things that are morally wrong. Stopping a noisy game because you're resting, and taking off a pair of muddy shoes at the door are simply convenient for you. There's nothing wrong with noisy games or muddy shoes *in themselves*. It's just that there's a time and place for them. On the other hand cruelty to another child or to an animal or insect is morally wrong, whatever the occasion. Explain this to your child by indicating that the noisy game can be resumed later and the muddy shoes put on again next time she goes out into the garden, but the cruelty is out of the question, now and at any time and in any place. When she asks why, tell her it's because we wouldn't like cruel things done to us. At this age, she responds best if she's helped to understand that other people and even animals and insects have feelings just like she has, and suffer from cruelty just as she would.

Distinguish between what is convenient and what is right

It's often easier in fact to explain reasons for moral issues like cruelty and stealing and telling lies than for convenience issues like noisy games and muddy shoes. With the former she can understand that she wouldn't like it if other people did these things to her, but she finds it hard to put herself in your place as the person who has to put up with the noise or clean the muddy footmarks. The last thing she wants is peace and quiet during the day, and she can't understand why you do. Nor can she understand why you mind cleaning up mud. Most household chores are still games to her, and if you ask her to clean up the floor she'll do it with a will, having fun and making twice as much work for you in the process.

So it's a particular temptation with convenience issues to tell her to do as she's told simply because she *is* told. Avoid it nevertheless. Explain to her that you're tired, and that when grown-ups are tired they don't have the energy children have.

Don't fall back on 'Because I told you'

So letting them relax or keeping the floor clean for them is simply a way of being kind. Point out that the family is happier when people try to think of each other. Don't expect miracles. She'll see your point, but in the urge to resume her game a few minutes later she may well forget it. Children at this age haven't the memory or the self-control to stop themselves easily from going against your wishes. But don't see this as proof that she 'just *won't* co-operate'. It's the way she is at this age. Remind her again, and if she still forgets tell her you'll have to take the game (or whatever) away from her now, and she can have it back later. There's no need to do this accusingly. She knows the reason for your actions, and she's far more likely to learn the lesson if you agree it's hard for her to keep quiet but she knows why it's necessary, than if you start telling her what a thoughtless or worse still wicked child she is. And having taken the game away from her, find her another activity she can do without raising the rafters.

This approach is also less likely to make her feel resentful. She won't like having to stop her game, but at least she sees you're being fair. This is particularly important if you've a relative living with you who needs special consideration. A child who is constantly getting into trouble for doing normal childish things simply because they disturb Grandma or Grandad is going to build up fierce antagonisms. It's much fairer to let her know you realize she's having difficult demands made of her, but that Grandma can't help being tired any more than she can help wanting to make a noise. We can't blame Grandma and we can't blame her. All we have to do is to find ways of being as thoughtful towards each other as possible, and of living together as best we can under one roof.

Learning to be polite
We most of us like to think that our children are growing up well-mannered towards others. Courtesy costs nothing, and it does oil the wheels of the social machine. If your children are polite to people, they're more likely to be thought well of, particularly by teachers, adult relatives and other people of importance in their lives.

The best kind of politeness comes from a genuine thoughtfulness and sensitivity towards others. If we understand and respect the wishes and needs of other people, then we show a natural consideration towards them which is of far more value than the mere observance of social etiquette. So if you encourage your child to develop this understanding and respect, he's well on the way towards good manners. But he does need help in learning and using the right forms of words, with 'please' and 'thank you' being the obvious examples. The best teaching, as is so often the case, consists of setting a good example. If you use these and similar words in your dealings within and outside the home he'll pick them up much more rapidly than if you expect them exclusively from him.

Politeness should stem from thoughtfulness

Prompt him from an early age, however, into using such words himself. Most parents start with the word 'ta', which the small baby rapidly cottons on to and thinks great fun. 'Please' comes later, as his vocabulary widens, and 'may I' rather than 'I want' comes later still. Having mastered the use of 'ta', and used it happily for some little while, a baby will then often drop it, and perversely refuse to use it no matter what blandishments are offered by parents captivated with his new skill. The reason is that 'ta' is a game to a small baby, and there comes a point where he develops a healthy boredom with it. Better not to press the point at this stage, but instead to re-introduce the word later, when he's forgotten about it and greets it as a novelty. Some parents then make the mistake of using 'ta' when they want to take something from the baby, instead of 'please', so the use of 'please' doesn't become so easily and naturally established. Other parents make the mistake of insisting too early upon 'please' and 'ta' every time their baby wants or receives anything, with the result that he comes to see the satisfaction of his needs as conditional upon the use of these two strange sounds, rather than as a natural expression of the bond between his parents and himself. So introduce your child to these words as early and as naturally as possible, but don't overdo it. Introduced in this way, he'll be using them much of the time and without prompting by age three.

Teaching a baby to say 'ta'

But around three he may rebel against them as part of his general assertion of independence, which means that the years from three until he starts school are the vital ones for establishing politeness on a firm and properly understood basis. Help your child to see that 'please' and 'thank you' are ways of showing our appreciation for what others do for us. They

Establishing politeness on a proper basis

show we realize that others go to some trouble on our behalf, and that we're asking for things rather than demanding them always as of right. In turn, the use of these words makes other people more willing to do things for us, so both parties benefit equally. However, don't expect him always to remember to use them. The tone of voice in which we ask for things often says more about our attitude towards others than the mechanical use of 'please' and 'thank you'. But settle on a reasonable minimum, and expect him to keep to it.

When you do need to prompt him, it's often better to do so by ignoring his request until he says 'please', rather than by always saying the word for him or by reminding him with phrases such as 'Haven't you forgotten something?' or 'How do you ask?' or 'Now what do you say?' Ignoring his request makes him think for himself what's missing, reminding him only sets up a mechanical ritual which wearies you and has little effect upon him. But throughout, don't forget the earlier point about setting him a good example. Use 'please' and 'thank you' to him in direct proportion to the number of times you expect him to use them to you.

Good manners and subservience are not the same thing

I do occasionally have parents say to me that if you teach your child good manners, he only gets trampled on by others. What he needs is to be taught to assert himself. Unfortunately, such parents are confusing good manners with subservience. Being polite to people doesn't mean you automatically see them as superior to yourself. It simply demonstrates the thoughtfulness I referred to earlier. Teach your child that being polite doesn't mean he mustn't stick up for his rights when necessary. It means learning a social skill, which is often far more effective and leaves everyone feeling much better than a blunt demand for what you want. Having asked nicely to begin with also leaves you scope for becoming more insistent if people unreasonably refuse you. Starting off in a truculent way often makes others equally truculent, and means you've played your full hand right at the outset instead of keeping some of your cards in reserve. These are points that children come to appreciate more fully as they grow older, but they're essential factors in knowing how to deal with people, and even the four-year-old will quickly understand the principles behind them.

Distinguishing fiction and reality

The more imaginative your child, the more creative and usually the more intelligent. And the more imaginative your child, the more fun she gets from stories, and the more inventive and resourceful she is in occupying herself during the day and (if she wakes) during the night. Even a relatively unimaginative child has enormous potential in this direction; stimulate it not only through stories and games of make-believe but also by asking her puzzle questions such as 'What do you think would happen if . . . ?', 'What do you think we shall see when . . . ?', 'What do you think it will be like when . . . ?', 'How do you think we can . . . ?' and so on. Remember that children don't all express their imagination in the same way. One child invents games. Another loves books. Another prefers instead to imagine how things work, often taking them apart to see if she's right. The early beginnings of a bent towards the arts or the sciences can often be seen in these different approaches.

But parents worry sometimes that their child's imagination is too vivid. They may catch her inventing involved and colourful stories to get herself out of trouble, and they're anxious she may turn into an incorrigible liar or that there may be something 'wrong' with her psychologically. This is particularly the case if she invents imaginary playmates, and seems to believe wholeheartedly in them, even feeding them at table, scolding or praising them, and at times blaming them for her own misdeeds. Interestingly, parents rarely worry about behaviour of this kind when it's directed towards a doll or a teddy bear. It's only when it happens in the child's mind that they have qualms about it. **Is your child's imagination too vivid?**

Let's take story-telling (or fibbing) first. You discover some minor disaster area in a room where your child has just been playing, and suspicion falls upon her. You put your suspicion to her, and are nonplussed when she looks at you with touching innocence and insists she had nothing to do with it. She may even offer a plausible explanation of how it might have happened, mentioning the household pet or even a younger brother or sister at the crawling stage. You end up very puzzled. She *could* be right. You don't want to blame her unfairly. On the other hand she *could* be making it up. The awful thought comes to you that you can't trust her, followed **Story-telling**

343

by the guilty thought that maybe it's *you* who are at fault for harbouring unworthy suspicions. A cloud descends upon the day. The incident keeps coming back to worry you.

In reality, nothing terrible has happened. She isn't embarking on a life of crime. Your relationship with her isn't under threat. It's simply that at her age she can't yet understand the full difference between imagination and reality. 'Truth' and 'falsehood' don't have for her the clear-cut meanings they have for you. She enjoys listening to stories you read her and letting her imagination play upon them, and now she has the chance to make up a story herself. Even as she tells it she half believes it. Her memory isn't yet very sharp, and the imagined incident may soon be much clearer in her mind than the real one.

This isn't an argument for not caring whether she tells you the truth or not. It's an argument for realizing the matter needs appropriate handling. It's no use getting cross with her. If you do, you may find she ends up very stubborn indeed, and sticks to her story no matter what. Your anger confuses her, and her need to avoid punishment becomes so strong that she quickly comes to believe implicitly in her story. Nor is it much use telling her that if she admits her guilt you won't punish her, but that if she doesn't admit it you will. This may make her own up even if she *isn't* guilty, thus being forced into lying to you in a different way.

Teach your child the importance of truthfulness

The right tactics are to use this as an opportunity to help her begin learning the difference between fact and fiction. You can't allow her to get away with fiction. If she does, she'll learn that fiction is a good way of avoiding blame. Just as she learns other lessons on how to handle the world, so she'll learn this one. It's not a question of wickedness, simply of learning that lying is a good way to cope. So if you suspect her of untruth, explain to her seriously that in life we have to know what *really* happens. Remind her that if she asks you what you've been doing or why you've been doing it, she'd think you were a very funny person if you kept telling her made up stories. You can become less serious now and insist that she'd very quickly say, 'Come *on* Mummy, don't tell such *stories!*' Point out to her that if she really committed the deed in question, far better to tell you now. That way you'll be able to believe what she says in future. Introduce the term 'trust' and explain that this is what we mean by it.

Don't be deceived by people who tell you a child can't understand explanations of this kind. Provided you keep the explanation short, use simple words, and give her one or two *practical examples* to illustrate what you mean, she'll soon catch on. Children have an extraordinary ability to grasp concepts as long as we follow these three simple rules. And if after everything she still sticks to her story, give her the benefit of the doubt this time. She could simply have forgotten what really happened by now. But whether you get the truth from her on this occasion or not, she'll still need to have the lesson repeated frequently in the future. Even though she's grasped the idea behind it readily enough, in the excitement of the moment she's perfectly capable of forgetting it until she's two or three years older.

It's also good policy to ask her from time to time to tell you what she's been doing when you already know the answer. Don't do this just when things go wrong. Do it for nice things too. If she strays from the truth, gently prompt her. Praise her for getting things right, and don't punish her if she gets things wrong. She's still learning. And you're trying to encourage openness and accuracy on her part, not playing a stern game of trying to catch her out and teach her she can't fool you. Helped in this way, your child will realize the difference between imagination and reality, and that recognizing this difference and sharing it with you is the right way of doing things. Reinforce this by avoiding dire punishments when she owns up to misdeeds. If telling the truth gets her into trouble, she'll quickly slip back into fibbing, though this time the fibbing will be real; she'll know she's deliberately misleading you, and she'll be doing it through fear. Of course, you can't always ignore the misdeeds just because she's owned up. But talk them through with her. Find out how and why things went wrong, and how similar mistakes can be avoided in future. Always praise her for the truth and tell her how important it was for you to hear it from her and that if you'd found out some other way, you really would have been cross.

Occasionally parents say all this is demanding too much of them. They complain they haven't the time or the patience. Or that it's much better to punish a child severely each time

Encourage her to be open and truthful with you

you catch her out. She'll soon learn then. But I can't repeat too often that in the long run you make things much easier for yourself in child-rearing if you tackle the groundwork properly in these early years. Once a child learns *why* we need to tell the truth, and that you aren't going to come down on her even though the truth means owning up to some misdeed, you'll be avoiding much trouble and heartache in the future. Your child will have realized that truthfulness and openness are a key part of any loving and trusting relationship. Within that relationship, she has nothing to fear from the truth. And one day, if she's unfortunate enough to get into serious trouble of some kind, she'll know she can come and confide in you, and be greeted with sympathy and help instead of anger and blame.

When you need to find out the truth immediately
One point remains. Occasionally your child may be involved in something where you can't give him the benefit of the doubt. You have to find the truth out now. Perhaps he has brought something home from nursery school which he says he was 'given' but which you're pretty sure he may have taken from another child. Or (though usually this happens when a child is rather older) you may find some money in his possession for which you can't account. This is always an unpleasant experience. Small children can succumb readily to the temptation of taking something they want, because the rights of property don't yet mean a great deal to them.

On these occasions, a patient, systematic approach is needed. Explain to him that you know he didn't think he was doing wrong, and that we all sometimes feel like taking things that don't belong to us. Nevertheless, we wouldn't like it if other people came and took our things, so we mustn't take theirs. You think he may have taken something that wasn't his; you're not angry about it, but you need to know. (Don't bribe him by the way – i.e. through offering to buy him a toy like the one he's taken; this will tempt him to repeat the same exercise in the future in order to be bribed again.) If the truth doesn't come out, return to the topic again later so he realizes that you won't let the matter drop. If you do get the truth, give him a hug, tell him it's good to speak up, and then see to it that the toy or money is returned to its rightful owner. But do this diplomatically, so that your child isn't shown up, or punished or scolded by some over-zealous third party. The whole incident is a matter between you and your child, nobody else. And since prevention is better than cure, make sure that in the home money and possessions aren't left around in a way that offers temptation to his still fragile moral sense. If in spite of everything you *can't* get a clear story from him, give him the benefit of the doubt but tell him the other child probably didn't mean him to keep the toy (or money), then return it in just the same way.

Imaginary friends are a different matter altogether. Even though your child may speak of his companion as though he really exists, don't treat this as a falsehood. Go along with it, though indicating that although you accept the friend is important to your child, you know it's only a game. A good game mind, and perfectly understandable, but a game nevertheless. If your child blames his own misdeeds on his friend, be matter-of-fact about it and announce, 'That's another way of saying you did it.' Don't try and drive the imaginary friend underground by refusing to talk about him. Enter into the spirit of things, but make it clear that in this as in everything else there's a line between imagination and reality, important though both of them are in their different ways.

Imaginary playmates

Usually, imaginary friendships become less and less intense as a child grows older, and fade out once school proper starts. There are various psychological explanations for them, and often different ones fit different children. Sometimes the imaginary friend compensates a lonely child for the lack of real playmates. Sometimes, if you're rather strict with your child and demand high standards from him, the imaginary friend lessens his feelings of guilt and unworthiness at falling short of your expectations. The imaginary friend is seen as someone inferior in behaviour to your child himself, and your child gains comfort from the feeling that here's someone less able to cope even than he. Sometimes the imaginary friend makes up for possessions or experiences which are missing from your child's own life. In this case the imaginary friend is usually presented as cleverer and more successful. But sometimes the friend is merely a way of exercising the imagination, and of personalizing the stories and fantasies that pass through a child's head. Very occasionally, if a child is punished a great deal, and is unhappy with his life, the friend is a provider of sympathy and understanding.

Children have imaginary friends for different reasons

By seeing which of the above reasons best fits your child,

347

you learn important lessons about him. If the friend is there as compensation or comfort, find ways of providing him with these through real-life relationships. Remember you can also learn these lessons from children who don't have imaginary friends. Watch how they relate to their dolls and teddy bears. Are they constantly lecturing them? Do they retreat to them if you're angry, and say things like 'Teddy isn't cross with me are you Teddy?' Do they criticize them for the dirty hands or bad manners for which they themselves are being criticized? If your child is externalizing his own problems in this way, it's time to stop being quite so strict or demanding, and to bring more warmth and understanding into your dealings with him. But there's only cause for real concern if this kind of behaviour is very marked. It's natural for your child to act out with his toys events that happen in real life, and to give them 'characters' of their own which are based on the people he knows. Exaggerated behaviour, or behaviour which always seems to be reflecting aggression or unhappiness, is the thing to watch out for.

Learning about sex

We've all laughed at those cartoons of a red-faced father trying to tell his adolescent son the facts of life, only to find he knows them already and can't understand why his father is so coy. But as in most cartoons, there's an element of truth behind the humour. Sex can be a pretty embarrassing topic, and parents who would cheerfully discuss anything else with their children find themselves painfully tongue-tied when it comes to human (and even animal) genitals, let alone the mechanics of using them.

Importance of coming to terms with our own bodies and our sexuality

This is partly because there's more to it than the sex act itself. Sex education also involves helping a child come to terms with her own body and the bodies of other people, and with her sex drive and the issues surrounding it. If you have come across Freud's work, you'll know some psychologists think this education is so important that mistakes made during it have a permanent effect upon a child's personality. And by 'mistakes' they mean children being taught there's something dirty or wicked about sex, which leads them to see their own sexual curiosities and desires as sinful, and as powerful emotional forces constantly threatening to overpower them. Or children being denied proper sex education and left at the mercy of the taboos, misinformation, or sexual exploitation of whoever happens to chance by.

Other psychologists are more cautious than Freud. But there's no doubt that unless a child is helped to accept her sexuality as a normal part of life, a part which must be channelled into socially acceptable forms but which is a potential source of great joy, she is never going to be a psychologically whole person. If we load her with feelings of disgust about her own and other people's bodies, if we teach her to see nudity as obscene, and if we teach her the sex act is revolting, then we are teaching her to reject an important aspect of herself. The point is that her sex drive won't just go away. We can teach her to suppress it ruthlessly, to pretend it isn't there, but this is to put her perpetually at war with herself. Part of her personality has to fight a constant battle against another part. Worse, part of her personality has to see another part as a sinful force that must be subdued at all costs. But since it can't be wholly subdued, the emotional energy associated with the sex drive finds other outlets. In Freudian theory these other outlets are such things as ungovernable rage and anger, harsh repressive authoritarianism, cruelty masquerading under the banner of social good, exaggerated and unnatural prudery, or any one of a range of psychologically unhealthy conditions. Be this as it may, there's no doubt that sexual feelings are enormously potent, and unless we handle them properly they inevitably have a damaging effect upon the personality. At the very least, they lead to inner turmoil and confusion, and to the risk of a rigid inner censorship that threatens the growth of self-knowledge and self-acceptance.

When providing children with sex education, we need first to take a look at our own attitudes. If the subject of sex makes us uncomfortable, and if we have a sense of shame about the human body, we must be careful about passing these reactions on to our children. Largely they come from lessons taught us in our own childhood when we were too young to consider them rationally, and accepted because they came from those in authority and were often backed up by punishments and

Look at your own attitudes first

disapproval. Think before this legacy is passed on to your children. Remember how impressionable children are, and about the duty we have to help them know and understand their own bodies and emotions.

What about morality? But what about our duty to give children a moral education? Are psychologists saying that children should be taught sex is okay at any time and in any place, and that there are no rules and standards to follow? In a civilized society surely there must be restrictions upon the sex drive and its expression? Surely there must be values, religious or otherwise, we want to teach our children? The answer to these questions is that of course there must be standards and values and restrictions. Of course morality is important. Nothing I say should be taken to contradict this. But there is a difference between a child who is helped to know herself, and to see how she can consciously and sensibly apply standards to her behaviour, and a child who is taught standards that must be rigidly imposed, and taught that to question and discuss any of them is morally wrong.

It is what we do with our sex drive that matters In sex education our starting point must be that the sex drive isn't bad in itself. On the contrary. Not only does our presence on this planet depend upon it, but it is in its own right a joyful and joyous way for people to express their love for each other. However, it is what we *do* (or don't do) with that drive that can be criticized. Learn to accept the drive in the first place, to recognize that it is there for good reasons, and you are free to decide how morally you should put it to use.

Our obsession in the Western world with sex stems partly from an inability to realize this. Because sex is something on which children are either left in ignorance since we're too embarrassed to talk about it, or something around which so many restrictions are placed that an open, sensible attitude towards it becomes impossible, we become over-preoccupied with sex. We intrude it in disguised forms into almost every corner of life, instead of keeping our sense of proportion and seeing it as only one of the many important aspects of who we are. The result is that it's increasingly difficult for many people to view sex simply as part of a loving relationship between individuals that draws them closer and allows them to express their feelings for each other in a tender and intimate way. To some it becomes the be-all and end-all of life, to others it becomes the cause of all our moral (and many of our physical) ills. Small wonder so many people are unable properly to accept their own sexuality and the sexuality of others, and sex becomes a matter of greed and exploitation on the one hand, or of shame and disgust on the other.

If we forget all the conditioning we've received on the subject, and take an objective look at our children, we find they're robustly curious about sex from an early age. Sexual interests and emotions don't start like magic at puberty. They're present in children from the early years onwards. So it's important to get things off to a good start by answering your child's questions about sex as soon as she begins to ask them. And not only is this right for her, it's also right for you. Remember those cartoons of the red-faced father and adolescent son? Well it's much much less embarrassing to discuss sex with a there-year-old than it is with a thirteen-year-old. Help your child to know about sex from an early age. Help her to grow up with the knowledge, accepting it in the same sensible and straightforward way she accepts knowledge about everything else. In that way you'll also help her not to see sex as a giggle in the corner with other children, something to make parents go stern and red-faced (remember the delighted shouts of 'bum' we talked about in Chapter 5?).

Answer your small child's questions about sex

How to tell him

So how do you tackle telling your child what sex is about? The answer is simple. When he asks you questions, you give him the information he wants. To him, sex is like all the other intriguing things he's curious about. 'Where do babies come from?' is an early demand. When you answer it ('From a special place inside Mummy's tummy') the next demand is 'How do they get there?' All right, how *do* they get there? He has a right to know. They get there because Daddy puts his penis inside Mummy's body and leaves a seed there. The seed meets another seed inside Mummy, and they become one and grow into a baby. A child will accept this information as naturally as the other things you tell him. Often, curiosity satisfied, he'll turn to more interesting things. If he does, leave it at that. Time enough to give him more details when he asks for them. But if other questions occur, deal with them in the same way, always keeping your answers simple and direct (and accurate), and not confusing him with concepts that are beyond him. Even if you do feel a little uncomfortable about it all, don't show it. Don't give him the idea that sex is something to be talked about abruptly and the subject quickly changed. Talk to him about sex in the way you talk about what happens to food when we swallow it or why our bodies need milk and fruit if we're to grow big and strong.

If he asks whether Daddy putting a seed in Mummy's body hurts, explain no it doesn't, it's an enjoyable experience and people do it even when they're not planning a family. If he asks how the baby gets out from inside Mummy, explain it's through the vagina, which is a special opening made by nature for the purpose. It's the same hole through which Daddy's seed enters Mummy. If at this point he asks earthy questions like 'Is it the same hole Mummy wees out of?' don't be shocked. This is a perfectly natural question. He no more intends to be 'dirty' than if he was asking whether we breathe and swallow through the same opening in the throat. Answer him easily and naturally. No it isn't the same hole, though the two are close together.

This brings us to another aspect of sex education and of our own attitudes. Some people say it's a joke on the part of the Almighty to put the organs of reproduction and the organs of excretion together. Any feelings of dirt or unpleasantness which we may have about the latter become bound up with our attitudes towards the former. But the problem lies not with a design fault by the Almighty but with our own approach to the human body. As I said when discussing toilet training, children should be allowed to realize that excretion is a perfectly natural and healthy process. There's nothing to be ashamed of about it. And although rules of hygiene are necessary, this isn't because there's anything disgusting about excretion. It's because, as with other waste products, there are germs around which could upset our stomachs. A child who learns to accept excretion without shame won't transfer any shame over to sex. Nature manages things pretty well. It's only our adult inability to come to proper terms with her processes that causes problems.

So discuss sex freely and openly with your child whenever

he wants to talk about it. Don't make a big deal of it. A matter-of-fact approach prevents sex from becoming an exaggerated preoccupation for your child, and he'll be surprised one day when he realizes what a fuss other people make about it, and how they nudge and titter (children) or become unable to cope (adults) whenever it's mentioned.

Should your child see you naked?

However, talking sensibly about sex is only part of the process of sex education. If you help your child accept his own body, yet nevertheless furiously cover yourself and thrust him out of the bathroom if he wanders in when you're under the shower, he's going to be very puzzled. Have his parents something special to hide? Is there something wrong with them? Aren't they made like he is? Questions of this kind feed his curiosity. And if he does catch a brief glimpse of you before you cover up, he may indeed wonder if something strange has happened to your body, and be quite frightened by the experience. Pubic hair in particular, unless he's able to see that it's only hair like that which grows elsewhere on the body, is likely to worry him. Things that are only glimpsed, and not seen clearly enough to be properly understood, can have a lasting effect upon a young mind.

No one has anything to be ashamed of in nudity. If from a very young age a child sees you naked, casually and naturally in bathroom or bedroom, he'll grow up accepting the sight and without being disturbed by it. If on the other hand he's given to understand in no uncertain fashion that when you're undressed he gets out of the room and stays out until you tell him to return, he'll battle with all kinds of uncertainties and confusions. What *is* so special about your body? Why is he so rigidly excluded when you're undressed if at all other times you welcome having him around? And if he's an only child and never sees a member of the opposite sex undressed, what *do* they look like? Children are naturally interested in the anatomical differences between male and female, and if they can see (and talk and ask questions about) these differences at an early age, they'll take them in their stride.

Some books insist children are unsettled by parental nudity, but this is only if they haven't grown up with it, and accepted it as natural. Some books also say that if a child is allowed to

What about touching?

353

look he may also want to touch. But this isn't a problem provided there's a matter-of-fact approach to nudity. You're obviously not going to flaunt yourself in front of your small child, so you aren't usually going to be around long enough for him to get concerned about touching. But if he does touch, don't over-react or give him the idea he's done something wrong. Keep the encounter brief by moving away, but do it casually. You're simply in the middle of washing or dressing and haven't time to stand around.

In adolescence, just as some children want more privacy over their own bodies, so some children become rather more reticent about parental nudity, and start to avoid situations where it can occur. This is perfectly understandable, and the child's wishes must be respected. Nudity has become a big issue to himself and his friends, and he suddenly finds it more difficult to handle in everyone, parents included. But sensible attitudes towards the whole subject, developed now early in childhood, ensure that the adolescent can cope with this phase and mature into equally well-balanced adult attitudes.

Oedipus and Electra complexes

At this point some mention is needed of the so-called Oedipus and Electra complexes. Most people seem to have heard of these in one form or another, and they do cause anxiety to some parents. Both the Oedipus and the Electra complexes belong to the theories advanced by Sigmund Freud on the early personality development of children, and suggest that the young boy forms a strong erotic attachment to his mother (the Oedipus complex) while the young girl forms a similar attachment to her father. Freud considered that these attachments are particularly strong up to about age six, and that the way in which they are handled and resolved has a profound influence upon the growth of the healthy personality. The boy who fails to mature out of the Oedipus complex may, for example, find it hard ever to develop a mature sexual relationship with other women later in life, while the boy who is made to feel excessively guilty about his erotic feelings towards his mother may grow up with inner conflict and feelings of rejection and worthlessness. The girl who similarly fails to mature out of her early erotic attachment may seek always to be dominated by a male father-figure, or if faced with excessive guilt may (like the boy) grow up divided against herself and with doubts over her own sexuality.

Freud was one of the major figures in psychology in the first part of this century, and he did much to help us towards an awareness of the great importance of early experiences for a child's later development. Since his work is so well-known, it's hardly surprising that many parents (particularly parents bringing up children of the opposite sex single-handed) wonder if unwittingly they are creating or mishandling Oedipus or Electra complexes in their children. They wonder, for example, whether parental nudity or hugging and kissing may be stimulating erotic feelings in their children. The position is further complicated by the very proper concern these days with sexual abuse in children. 'May I', a parent increasingly asks, 'unintentionally be guilty of sexual abuse if I take a bath with my small child, allow her to sleep with me when she's unwell or when we're cramped for space?' 'And what about my own feelings?' the same parent often asks. 'I enjoy the soft feel of my child's body against my own, the feel of her silk-smooth skin. Does this mean that *I'm* being erotically stimulated by my child? Am I storing up trouble for us both without knowing it?'

Who said being a parent is uncomplicated! But in fact these fears (and Freud's theories) are over-exaggerated. Certainly, in a good family relationship, a child feels drawn towards the parent of the opposite sex (as well as towards the parent of the same sex). But these feelings are only likely to cause problems where sexuality is something hidden and secret. Adults who in psychotherapy confess to troubling memories from childhood about parents' bodies are far more likely to recall that these were illicit experiences on the one hand, or the result of direct sexual abuse on the other, than that they were simple things like everyday nudity or a shared bed. Parental bodies spied on surreptitiously, or suddenly and threateningly revealed, are the things that leave deep impressions upon young minds, not the familiar and unremarkable sight of parents in the bath or the shower. As to bathing with a small child, provided this is natural and innocent, there's no evidence that this does anyone any harm, and the restricted size of most baths and bathrooms will in any case mean that the practice fades out of its own accord at some point during the pre-school years.

With matter-of-fact attitudes there should be no problem

What is 'natural and innocent'? But what is 'natural and innocent'? Which brings us back to the parental question as to whether *parents* are obtaining illicit erotic sensations from the feel of a small child's body against their own. The rules in all such matters are fairly simple. First and foremost, always study the child's own wishes. Anything that makes a child feel uncomfortable, and which could be interpreted as in any way sexual (irrespective of the fact that your motives aren't sexual), should be discontinued. Second, study and be honest about your own feelings. There should be a difference between the sensual, innocent pleasure of feeling your child's body against you as you pick her dripping and happy out of the bath, and actual sexual arousal. Anything that produces what you know to be a sexual response in you is out. Third, avoid anything which seems to be stimulating your child sexually. An over-lengthy handling of the genitals while washing them could be one example. *Don't* give her the impression that there is something embarrassing or 'dirty' about her genitals. Simply make a note to yourself not to focus special attention on them.

Fathers and daughters Some parents ask whether, in view of the fact that it is possible for adults to be aroused by children's bodies, fathers should avoid seeing their daughters unclothed after the very early years of life. My own view is that fathers who abuse their daughters are far more likely to do so if their daughters' bodies are allowed to become mysterious and alluring to them. This is one reason perhaps why step-fathers are more likely to be involved in abuse than natural fathers. Their step-daughter may come as a novelty to them. Familiarity, on the other hand, reduces erotic feelings. Of course, when a daughter reaches the age where she wishes to be more private about her body, her wishes must be respected. This may happen at puberty, and it may happen well before. A lot depends upon the conditioning she receives from other girls at school. In families which have always adopted a natural and unprudish attitude towards such matters, it is very unusual for a girl to become obsessional about her modesty, but she has a right to her own feelings and to expect proper notice to be taken of them.

Infantile masturbation

Different issues are involved when it comes to a child erotically stimulating herself. All children go through this stage, usually referred to as infantile masturbation, somewhere between the third and sixth years of life. They've discovered their genitals, and find the sensations they get from touching them are pleasant. So they touch quite often, sometimes through the clothes but more usually by sliding a hand inside trousers or knickers. Mostly, the action is an almost absent-minded one, with the child focusing her attention elsewhere and toying with herself much as an adult toys with glasses or a stray lock of hair. Half the time the child doesn't really know what she's doing, and hasn't set out with any particular intention of giving herself a special sensation. It's doubtful indeed whether at her undeveloped age she experiences much beyond a pleasant tickling feeling. Certainly there's no question of an orgasm, or of pronounced erection in little boys.

Infantile masturbation happens equally in boys and girls, though girls may indulge rather more frequently because their clothes make their genitals more accessible. Many parents become quite angry at the sight. Others say it makes them feel uncomfortable. Either way, the tendency is to tell the child sharply to stop it, sometimes smacking the hand or pulling it away, or worse still threatening to harm the genitals (or that the child will herself harm them) if the practice continues. The child is given the firm impression there's something wrong with what she's doing, and that it's dirty and disgusting. Since she's strongly motivated to go on doing it, like all pleasant things, and since she can't see what all the fuss is about, she ends up with confused feelings about her body. She can touch any time she likes the parts that don't give pleasure, but the parts that feel nice are apparently out of bounds. Worse, she's made to feel unclean even for wanting to touch them. There must be something wrong both with them and with her, but she can't understand what it is. And requests for explanations are met with anger or silence or the sharp retort 'Because it isn't nice'. To her it *is* nice, so it looks as if nice things are wrong, or that she's to blame for finding them nice.

Don't make your child feel dirty and disgusting

The right response to infantile masturbation is to ignore it. Left to herself, she'll soon grow out of it. It's a phase, like so many others, in her development. A phase during which she's exploring herself physically, and which she'll leave behind as more interesting things come along. Infantile masturbation doesn't mean, as some parents fear, that their child is wildly

The best approach is to ignore it

357

over-sexed and is bent already on a life of promiscuity. There is no known relationship between frequency of infantile masturbation and strength of adult sex drive. The only way in which infantile masturbation leads to trouble later on is if you impress on your child it's wrong, and thus draw attention to it and give it an 'importance' it doesn't merit.

The only time infantile masturation should really concern you is if your child resorts to it as a form of comfort after you've been angry with her. Not because the masturbation is wrong but because if she has to use it to find comfort you're probably being too hard on her, or are allowing angry scenes to smoulder on instead of getting things back on a pleasant footing as soon as possible (pages 168–9/391–2). Ease up on her a little and give her more in the way of physical affection.

Sex play between children

As children are so curious about their own bodies, they're naturally curious about those of other children as well. And once having seen another child's body, they may want to touch. If such behaviour is frowned upon by their elders, they invent games like doctors and nurses, since they've learnt that doctors and nurses *are* allowed to touch and examine even the most intimate parts of the body, and such games therefore give a dubious kind of respectability to their own explorations. In their sex play, young children rarely go very far with each other, however, and there's little evidence that they're actually sexually aroused by what goes on. Having satisfied their curiosity they become quickly bored by the game, and turn to other more interesting pursuits.

Sex play is less likely to happen where children (particularly children of the opposite sex) are allowed to bath together and become used to each other's bodies from an early age. It's also less likely to happen in families where there is good sex education, and where the body is seen as something natural rather than as something furtive and naughty. If you do come upon your children looking at each other's bodies or involved in sex play of some kind, don't be shocked. Your attitude will only convey itself to them and redouble their curiosity (and the sense of delicious 'naughtiness' that can go with it). If they seem over-preoccupied with sex play, you could say in passing, 'I should have thought you've seen quite enough of each

other's bottoms in the bath. Now come on, let's get on with
. . .' (whatever other occupation you have in mind). You thus
stop the sex play, without indicating that you're stopping it
because it's sex play. Handled thus, your children are unlikely
to become too preoccupied with it.

There's no reason, by the way, why you should normally
have to make rules as to when brothers and sisters are too old
to see each other naked any longer. If one child objects to the
other before age six or seven, he or she is only responding to
the influence of other children at school. Say, 'Goodness,
you've nothing to be ashamed of about your body; it doesn't
matter at all within the family.' After six or seven, children
develop more need for privacy, and if this extends to keeping
a brother or sister out of the bathroom the child's wishes
should be respected. But usually children don't become particularly sensitive to such matters until they're in their teens,
when by mutual unspoken consent they gradually come to
keep themselves more to themselves. Even at this age, in a
family where attitudes are sensible, the entry of one child into
the bathroom while the other is under the shower doesn't
cause any special drama.

When should brothers and sisters stop seeing each other naked?

You do have to be more careful with sex play between your
child and other children, however, if they're a lot older than
him. A child with an open attitude towards his own body can
easily have advantage taken of him by older children, whose
over-preoccupation with sex lies outside his experience. As
with the need to protect your child from any form of sexual
abuse (discussed later in this chapter), impress upon him, as
soon as he's able to understand, that his body is his, and that
only he or his parents when washing and bathing him have
any right to touch it in intimate ways. If older children want
to touch him or ask him to undress, he must refuse. Without
being too suspicious, be on your guard if an older child is in the
house with your child, especially if there are sudden silences
from upstairs. If you find sex play does take place, there's no
need to send the other child packing. Use the same brisk manner
you would with two of your own children ('Come on, let's go
downstairs; I've got something else for you to do').

Your child and older children

Sex play between pre-school children of the same age on the
other hand is normally perfectly innocent, and consists usually
of nothing more than inspecting and (more rarely) touching

359

Sex play and exhibitionism in pre-school children

each other's genitals. Once curiosity is satisfied, there's no more to it than that. Adult intervention isn't usually necessary, and children should certainly never be given the idea that there's anything 'naughty' or 'dirty' about this curiosity. The same applies to exhibitionism in pre-school children. They are as curious about another child's reactions to their genitals as they are about inspecting his. And of course if adults give them the impression that this, too, isn't 'nice', the curiosity is naturally increased. The child would dearly like to know why the sight of his genitals should have this effect upon others, and he goes on experimenting in an attempt to find out. The exhibitionism also gives him a sense of importance. Rather like the use of 'naughty' words (see Chapter 5), the ability to provoke an embarrassed or shocked reaction in others carries with it a feeling of personal power. Treat this exhibitionism in the matter-of-fact way you treat the other examples of sex play I've mentioned and your child will usually outgrow it before he reaches school age.

ISSUES AND PROBLEMS IN THE FOURTH AND FIFTH YEARS

Keeping pets

A child's short attention span at this age can present problems when it comes to the keeping of pets. All children love animals. Even at the toddler stage, your child may start asking for a cat or a dog or a rabbit (or a horse or baboon or elephant if she's ambitious), and show remarkable persistence in pressing her request ('Oh Mummy/Daddy *can* I have a horse/baboon/elephant? Oh *please*.'). Think carefully before you agree. To a small child a pet animal is rather like a toy. We said the same thing, remember, about a baby brother or sister (pages 113–14). She wants to play with it, and when she's tired of it to put it in the toy cupboard and forget about it.

Convenient as this would be at times, living creatures aren't like that. Buying your child a pet means a big commitment for you. One day she'll take full responsibility for it, but until that time comes you're the one who'll have to feed it and take it for walks once the novelty has worn off. And you're the one who will have to house train it and clean up the mess. Are you really prepared to take all this on? If the answer is no, then no pets. Even if the answer is yes, remember that you may be planning to go back to a job outside the home once your child is at school. If everyone is out all day, is it fair to leave a cat or a dog on their own? Perhaps a rabbit or guinea pig would be a better idea (preferably stuffed you may be muttering). The situation can be reviewed when your child's older. Once she knows what she's taking on, she's in a position to give you a promise that she'll be responsible for daily care. And if she does show a genuine love of animals, it wouldn't be fair to go on denying her.

But I'm never impressed by the argument that all children *need* pets as a way of relating to something more helpless than themselves. If a child is unhappy at home, and is denied any responsibility over her own life, then a pet would be useful therapy. But this isn't so in a home which already provides the right environment. Pets are fine for children if you and your family have the time and the living space to give them a happy life. But you needn't feel guilty if circumstances force you to say no, or if you have to settle for something smaller and less dramatic than the Great Dane or Irish Wolf Hound that has caught your child's fancy.

Behaviour problems

We must be careful about the term 'behaviour problems'. It's all too easy for anxious parents to develop the idea they have a 'problem' child simply because the child doesn't behave exactly like other children, or because she's got a strong will or because she's a little slow at learning. As I've said many times, all children are individuals, and it's a mistake to expect them to fall neatly into expected patterns. So if your child shows any of the symptoms I'm going to discuss (and most children show at least *some* of them for *some* of the time) don't assume you've got a problem with a capital 'P'. Patience, good sense, and the realization that much difficult behaviour by small children is part of a phase in their development which helps them to learn will see you through. Though I'm discussing these problems in the context of the fourth and fifth year there's no hard-and-fast dividing line, and many of them will already be apparent in the first three years.

Destructiveness

All small children can be destructive at times, mainly because they just don't understand how easily things can be broken. When they're very small, they don't even understand what 'broken' means, and confidently expect something that's damaged to be back to normal next time they want it. But as they grow older, they can be destructive on purpose, and this naturally concerns you because destructiveness seems to indicate a lack of respect for property and perhaps an aggressive nature.

The causes of destructiveness Deliberate destructiveness has three main causes. First, the child may be frustrated with the object concerned. It won't do as she wants, and in a fit of rage she throws it to the floor. Or, if she's frequently destructive, she may be frustrated with life in general. For example if she's a naturally busy child and people keep demanding restrained behaviour from her. Second, she may break something simply to see how it works. Her natural curiosity prompts her to see what's inside, and if seeing what's inside means breaking it open, she goes ahead.

She lives very much in the moment, and doesn't think far enough ahead to worry that she's depriving herself of the future use of the toy.

Third, she may destroy something as a way of hurting another person. For example she's angry with a brother or sister, but has learnt she mustn't hit out physically, so takes out her anger instead on one of their possessions. Add to this that some children (often but not always busy children) are naturally rather boisterous in the way they handle things, and you can see it's no surprise things sometimes come unglued.

Try to deal with the cause You want your child to take good care of her possessions, but you don't want constantly to be standing over her. The answer is to deal with the cause of destructive behaviour. If she's destructive through frustration, has she toys and games that are too difficult for her, or is she made always to play with them in the way *you* say instead of being able to explore their possibilities for herself? Or is she generally frustrated because everyone makes too many demands of her, and expects behaviour she isn't yet self-controlled enough to

362

produce? If she's destructive because she wants to see how things work, has she toys that can be taken apart and are specially designed to stimulate curiosity and inventiveness? If she's destructive because she's angry with other children in the family, is she being helped to express her anger in other ways, for example by telling you about it and seeing that you're prepared to listen and to appreciate her point of view? And if she's destructive simply because she's extra boisterous and hasn't the more delicate physical skills other children have, has she robust equipment that will stand up to the treatment she hands out?

When a child does break things, she has to see that now the toy is broken, it's no use to her and she'll have to go without. Don't rush to replace it. Point out to her that because she didn't take care of it she's lost the benefit of it, and discuss with her how and why things went wrong. A sentence or two, keeping it matter-of-fact, is quite enough ('That's a silly way to behave isn't it? You can see why that broke can't you?'). The loss of the toy in itself is sufficient for her to cope with. If you become angry she'll start relating to your anger rather than to her own actions and the broken toy. As a result she'll either be more concerned about upsetting you than about learning the lesson of why the breakage happened, or she may become angry in her turn and say she doesn't care about the 'stupid toy'.

Children need to see the consequences of their actions

When you're sure she's understood how to avoid the same thing happening again, the toy can be replaced. But with all her possessions, remind her to think what she's doing when she becomes too rough or tries to force open a toy that isn't meant to come apart. A word from you in the right place can save her a great deal of anguish. As a child grows older, she becomes more able to reflect upon her behaviour, and to think out the future consequences of her actions before doing them. Though it's good to act spontaneously at times, it's also good to be able to think ahead. Some children are able to do this naturally, others need more help.

Aggressiveness
As I've said earlier, aggression is a survival reflex, put there so we can defend ourselves when attacked and assert ourselves in competition with others. But aggression has to be socialized.

We have to learn that life isn't just a matter of strong people taking advantage of those weaker than themselves. Children differ a great deal in natural aggression. Boys are often (though by no means always) more aggressive than girls, and even in the same family there can be wide differences between individuals. But everyone, no matter what his nature, has to come to terms with his aggressive instincts and learn how to handle them in the face of the inevitable frustrations that life throws up.

Help him deal with his aggressive feelings

I've talked already about helping your child accept his emotions, and thus not feel guilty about the fact that he *feels* aggressive. He can't help aggressive feelings, but he *can* help what he does with these feelings. Working from this baseline of acceptance, make it plain to your child there are things he isn't allowed to do with his aggression. He isn't allowed to hit out at others smaller and weaker than himself, for example. He isn't allowed to be deliberately destructive. He isn't allowed to get his own way just by shouting louder than anyone else. Decide for yourself on other prohibitions; make sure they're realistic and within the control of a young child, then stick to them. If he starts hitting someone smaller than himself, you're going to restrain him physically. If he breaks things, he has to go without something to help pay for them. If he shouts and throws his weight about, he doesn't get what he wants.

Don't meet aggression with aggression

In addition to this, help your child through your own example. Aggressive parents tend to have aggressive children, because seeing a significant adult behaving aggressively makes a child think aggression is okay. The less aggressive you are, the less aggressive your children are likely to be. Restrain a physically aggressive child certainly, but if you meet his aggression with your aggression you won't be helping him to see that aggression is unacceptable. True, you may frighten him to such an extent that he isn't aggressive when you're around any more, but he'll make up for it when your back is turned. And the lesson that big people can hit smaller people (as with smacking – see later in the chapter) is a bad one to offer him. The idea that through hitting him you'll be giving him a 'taste of his own medicine' is also pretty crude. Psychological research shows plainly enough that aggression doesn't

364

cure aggression. If you're aggressive to him, he'll pass that aggression on, with interest, to someone else.

Don't confuse aggression in your child with boisterous behaviour though. Small boys in particular enjoy pitting their physical strength against other children. This is healthy enough. It's a way of working off surplus energy, and of finding out about one's own physical abilities. 'Am I stronger than he is?' 'Can I get on top of him?' Don't rush to intervene in behaviour of this kind. It's an inborn need that most small children have. All young primates do it. Lion cubs and wolf cubs do it. Even young rodents do it. If you're forever breaking up this rough and tumble, your child will be denied a natural learning experience. But naturally you must intervene if as sometimes happens it becomes serious, and one child gets hurt. This can happen without warning. One moment it's a game, the next moment a battle. The usual cause is that one child accidentally takes a hard knock, feels upset and threatened, and hits wildly back. But otherwise it's best to let little boys and girls get this boisterous behaviour harmlessly out of their systems.

Don't confuse aggression and boisterousness

Real aggression is when a child deliberately sets out to get what he wants by force, or when he habitually responds to disappointments or challenges by hitting out. Be firm with him. Indicate that although you sympathize with his cross feelings, he must realize hitting out isn't the answer. There are better ways of solving disputes. But help him by being scrupulously fair. If you're trying to teach him to show patience instead of immediate retaliation, see to it this improved behaviour meets with proper rewards. If it gets him nowhere, no wonder if he resorts once more to direct tactics.

Particular problems arise if you have more than one child, and one of them comes to you and reports aggression by the other, often sporting physical proof in the form of a red mark or the imprint of small teeth. You didn't see the incident, you're in the middle of something else, and you feel understandable exasperation that in spite of all your patience and guidance your children still present you with problems like this.

Aggression amongst siblings

In dealing with aggression of this kind you have to accept that as you didn't see the incident you don't know what led up to it. One child may have provoked the other, perhaps deliberately, in order to goad her into physical aggression and then 'get her into trouble'. Or the one who came off worse may have struck the first blow, only to find she couldn't handle the results. Or the children may just have been romping and let things go too far. Don't automatically blame the child who came out on top. Try to get a straight story out of your children as to what exactly happened, remembering *not* to punish them for coming up with the truth (pages 345/ 397). Calm things down, help them see what went wrong and why, and help them understand they must take responsibility for their behaviour. If you can't get a straight story out of them, separate them for a short time. One must play in one room, the other in another. They have to see that the natural consequence of their inability to play sensibly together is that they have to play apart. There's no need to make this separation a lengthy one. Like sitting in the corner or on a special chair (more on this and other forms of punishment later on), the lesson sinks in quickly. Keep them segregated for too long, and they'll forget the reason why you parted them, and each become absorbed in her own game and stop bothering about being alone.

Incidentally, if you always sort out squabbles of this kind by making your children come and play where you can keep an eye on them, this is using your presence as a punishment. As a result, your children will look forward to the moment when they can get away from you and back to their own pursuits. Do it when necessary, but don't make a habit of it. Show your children instead you believe they *can* play responsibly together without being under your eye, and that being with you in any case is fun rather than punishment.

Biting   Mention of teeth marks a moment ago brings me to one particularly difficult aspect of aggression, namely biting. All small children have a tendency to bite at times. It doesn't necessarily mean they want to inflict pain. In a very small child, biting is a pleasant activity in itself. She bites into things she likes. So when she gives a playmate a painful nip, she often does it without thinking, as she's excited and having fun.

So this presents you with a dilemma. You can't allow her to go round taking chunks out of people, but at the same time you can't punish her if she didn't mean any harm. The only answer is to show her that biting is painful. The best way is to bite your arm very gently and say to her 'But if we do that hard it hurts; now you try with your arm.' There's no risk she'll do it too hard. The feel of her teeth will be quite enough to convince her that biting others isn't such a good idea after all. The lesson may have to be repeated once or twice, but once learnt there will be no further problems.

Biting in an older child, with the definite intention of hurting, is a different matter altogether, and should be treated like any other piece of aggression. Don't bite her in her turn, though you may be tempted to. This is treating aggression with aggression. Insist she understand just how nasty biting is for the person on the receiving end. Ask her firmly would she like to be bitten? Invite her to try biting herself. No? Then why does she assume other people like it any more than she does? Leave her in no doubt that biting is a spiteful action, and that you know her well enough to expect much better behaviour from her.

If your child is particularly aggressive in spite of your best efforts, think what the cause might be. She may be the youngest child in a family of older children, and may have found she has to be determined if she's to claim her fair share of things. Or her older brothers and sisters may be teasing her, goading her into outbursts of unhappy fury. Or she may be playing with children from outside the home who are setting her a bad example of aggressive behaviour. Or she may be 'acting out' the things she hears in books or sees on television, though usually this is make-believe aggression rather than the real thing (see Chapter 7 for a discussion of violence on television). Or she may even be following an example of aggression set by other adults in the extended family or even at nursery school or playgroup. If other children in the home are the problem, protect her interests more. If it's children outside the home, choose her playmates more carefully. If it's other adults, reduce contact with them. Encourage your child to talk to you about her angry feelings and her aggressive behaviour. At the age of four or five she won't be able to put much into words, but she can be encouraged to see that talking about problems always helps. She has a sympathetic audience in you, and there are ways to solve problems other than fighting about them.

Look for causes of continuing aggression

Insolence

There aren't many things more guaranteed to irritate than a child who constantly answers back. We make a perfectly reasonable request, yet he must make an issue out of it. He wants the last word, and often his last word looks suspiciously like deliberate cheek. He seems to feel he has to score off us all the time. This isn't just a problem that happens with older children, though it's often seen at its worst in adolescents. It can start as soon as a child acquires sufficient use of language, and from the third year of life onwards can be a major trial for some parents. The more they try to curb their child's tongue, the more insolent he becomes. So it's important from the start to have a strategy for dealing with this and preventing it from developing into something you feel you can't handle.

When a small child is insolent, he's showing you he's found a new way of using language. He's found he can use it to express nice acceptable sentiments, but he can also use it to express more negative feelings. He's discovered what a useful and flexible tool language is. In no time he becomes intrigued by his own cleverness. In some ways it's rather like a game. You say something to him which he doesn't like, and he finds he can say something unpleasant back. And since he's taught he can't use physical aggression, this becomes a good way of hitting out. The trouble is this threatens your authority, and whenever our authority is threatened we feel insecure, which makes us defensive and cross. We want to reassert our authority and show who's boss.

Don't react with anger But an emotional reaction on your part simply shows him he's more skilful at playing this new game than you are. Like it or not, he's won the argument. There's an old story of two Chinese sages berating each other over an important issue. A bystander listening to the accusations they're levelling at each other wonders how they're able to keep from becoming heated. 'Ah,' he's told, 'the one who first loses his temper would be admitting he's lost the argument.' So if you react angrily to your child's insolence, you may put an abrupt stop to it but he's nevertheless registering for the future that he knows how to score off you if he wishes. Which leads to a subtle change in his motivation. Initially, answering back isn't really an attempt to hurt *you*. It's an attempt to defend *him*, by

using his new-found verbal skill and enjoying his own cleverness. But it may develop into a deliberate attempt to wound
you if you show him you're vulnerable.

It follows that the way to deal with insolence *and* stop it
from developing in this way is to beat your child at his own
game. 'Come and clear up your mess,' you say. 'I don't want
to,' answers junior. 'Then think how much less I want to clear
up other people's mess,' you say, 'Now come and do it.' 'Go
indoors it's raining,' you say. 'No I'm not going to,' answers
junior. 'Pity you weren't born a duck then,' you say, ushering
him briskly on to dry land. 'Put on your coat,' you say. 'No I
won't, it's horrid,' answers junior. 'Then let's wear it out
quickly so we can buy a new one,' you say, helping him into
it. Examples of this kind show that by thinking up a good
reply, and showing your child he has to do as he's told
anyway, you win hands down. Insolence neither gets your
child his own way nor upsets you. And usually he's so
nonplussed by your quick reply he finds himself doing as he's
told long before he can think of a way to cap it.

Beat your child at his own game

When discussing this strategy with parents the point is
sometimes made that you just *can't* keep calm when a small
child cheeks you. You can't help getting angry. The answer is
that by regularly and predictably getting angry you store up
trouble for youself in the future. There are too many parents
locked in a hopeless battle with their children in later childhood and adolescence, with each party doing its very best to
wound the other, to doubt it. Whenever we trace these
relationships back to the early years, we find things started to
go wrong there. Parents show themselves unable to cope with
insolence, and the child uses this vulnerability against them.
Things go from bad to worse, and repairing these battered
relationships once the real damage has been done is never
going to be easy.

Children find it very difficult to respect a parent who can't
outsmart them and who is goaded easily into extravagant
exhibitions of anger. The days when children automatically
respected their parents, if they ever existed, are gone. True
respect comes from an admiration of the way in which another
person copes with life. If a child is aware that he's better at
coping than his parents, it isn't easy for him to feel respect for
them, however much he may want to do so.

Hyperactivity

Some children are extra 'busy'

As already discussed, some children are extra 'busy' in their behaviour. On the go from morning to night, they find it difficult to keep still for two minutes together. Sit them in front of their favourite television programme and in no time they'll be squirming and wriggling and distracting anyone else within range. Upstairs, downstairs, indoors and out, their hands are never empty. Compulsive fiddlers, they pick up anything movable, only to put it down as soon as they spot something more promising. They have to be watched every minute of their waking lives, and baffled parents end each day as exhausted as if they've been living with a whirlwind.

Small wonder that when these parents hear the term 'hyperactive' they apply it at once to their child. And as soon as we give children labels, whether 'hyperactive', 'very intelligent', 'slow learner' or whatever, we begin to respond to them in terms of those labels. 'There you are, she's at it again; it's because she's hyperactive'; 'What can you expect of a hyperactive child?'; 'She's going to be a real handful at school as she's so hyperactive', and so on. The child now hasn't a chance to be seen as anything *but* hyperactive. Even when she's just running around normally we interpret it as yet another example of her 'hyperactivity', and try to calm her down. Alternatively, if she won't settle long to any task, we give up trying on the grounds that her 'hyperactivity' makes it impossible for her to concentrate on anything.

Most busy children are not hyperactive

The truth is that most busy children are not 'hyperactive' at all, but simply full of physical energy and find it hard to sit still for any length of time. Equally active mentally, they want constantly to interact with the world, to touch things, feel their weight and texture, pull things apart to see how they work, prod and poke other people to see how they react, open cupboards to see what's inside and for the sheer pleasure of opening doors, get down from chairs as soon as they're put up on them because there are so many more interesting things to do. With the world so full of fascinating opportunities, it's small wonder they can't settle for any length of time, and keep everyone around them on tenter-hooks.

You may have heard that hyperactivity is a symptom of 'maladjustment'. And if you feel that your child is hyperactive, naturally this will worry you. Let me put your mind at rest.

Hyperactivity is neither an invariable cause nor symptom of maladjustment. The reason why some hyperactive children become maladjusted is usually that parents and teachers try too hard to curb their restless energy. The result is the children end up frustrated and in perpetual conflict with themselves and everyone else. One half of them wants to be active, the other half wants to obey parents and teachers and keep still. Because of its strength, the active side wins, but the child is now deeply unhappy, and begins to see herself in the same negative terms that other people use to describe her. At odds with herself and the world, she becomes more and more difficult to control until her behaviour attracts the description maladjusted.

But we haven't yet dealt fully with the term 'hyperactivity'. Like many terms in psychology it doesn't have a precise definition, but the way to distinguish between very active behaviour which is simply a sign of a 'busy' child and very active behaviour which may reasonably be called hyperactive is that the former usually has a purpose about it while the latter is more frequently aimless. In other words, the busy child has an objective behind her behaviour, the hyperactive child does not. In addition, when something fully captures the busy child's attention she concentrates on it and isn't too easily distracted, whereas the hyperactive child has a very short attention span and is readily distracted. In consequence, whereas the busy child's intelligence usually develops at a good rate, that of the hyperactive child is retarded, since she never gives herself time to learn from her experiences. So you don't really have to worry about a child's active behaviour *unless* it looks to be random and inconsequential and associated with a very poor attention span, high distractibility and slow learning.

How to distinguish hyperactive and merely active

Even then, you can do a great deal to help her cope. With all very active children, and particularly with those who cross the dividing line into hyperactivity, a high premium must be placed upon parental patience and understanding. Accept that you can best help your child by working with her nature rather than against it. Organize your house so that there's a minimum of hazardous objects within reach, and see to it that your child is provided with plenty of things to interest and stimulate her. Don't force her to sit still for longer than she

How to help a hyperactive child

371

can reasonably manage, and don't give her the idea that there's something 'wrong' with her for being so active. Lengthen her attention span by encouraging her to stick at a task for that little bit longer than she otherwise might, and point out to her the interesting features in it. By directing her attention and praising and encouraging her for keeping at something, you'll help her to see more of the potential in whatever it is she's doing.

Protect her from frustration

At the same time, as with any busy child, protect her from too much frustration. Other people who misunderstand her nature may become impatient with her or make demands upon her that she just can't meet. Try not to let her feel she's hedged around with restrictions which she doesn't understand and to which she can't adapt. If she starts nursery school or playgroup, talk to the teacher, and see if he's likely to be sympathetic towards your child. If he isn't, the school's not for her. Some parents of busy children hope the experience of nursery school or playgroup will 'quieten her down'. It may help, but only if the teacher understands the child and knows the importance of giving her plenty to keep her occupied. If he just tries to control her by being over-strict and refusing to 'stand for any nonsense', then not only will the child be unhappy, she'll be even harder to control when she gets home. All the pent-up energy that's been accumulating during the hours in school will explode the moment she arrives indoors.

Encourage her language development

Another factor to watch with a very active child is the development of language. Some extra busy children seem to be that way because they're rather slow in language development. It's as if they can't communicate with the world through speech, so have to do it physically instead. Once such children start to develop a good command of language, they often calm down. So if your child's busy behaviour goes with poor speech, talk to her as much as you can and encourage her to respond. You can't force language on her. In her own time she'll probably spurt ahead. But you can make language available to her whenever possible, so that she hears words and can come to understand that physical activity is only one way of expressing herself.

If your child's busy behaviour is still a problem when she reaches age five and starts infant school, again talk it over with her teacher and see he's fully in the picture. If he feels the problem is a real one, your child will be referred to the school psychological service who will assess her behaviour and give both the school and yourself necessary advice. But they'll only suggest your child is given special help if she's also a slow learner and has speech problems, or if her behaviour is seriously distracting the rest of the class. Otherwise they will simply repeat the advice given in this section. Be patient, provide plenty of stimulation, don't frustrate her by expecting too much from her, and encourage her language and the gradual extension of her attention span. And comfort yourself with the knowledge that busyness is often a sign of high intelligence, and that many a child who is in perpetual motion in the early years has calmed quite naturally into a model of sober industry by the time she's into her teens!

Nervous habits

From the third year of life and on through the primary years children often express their emotions by developing nervous habits. Nail-biting, bed-wetting (dealt with elsewhere), hair-twisting and chewing, exaggerated blinking and even night-mares and sleep-walking, to name a few. Some of these habits are simply copied from friends, and disappear of their own accord after one or two gentle reminders. Others are more persistent, and require you to look more closely for the reasons for your child's anxiety, along the guidelines already discussed e.g. pages 328–335.

But while the nervous habits persist they can be annoying for you and (with sleep-walking and nightmares) even fright-ening. The trouble is the less relaxed *you* are about them, the less relaxed your child. These habits are a sign of tension. The body is geared up, through emotional energy, to do something physical (shouting, fighting, running away) to deal with the cause of its anxiety, but since it may not know the cause and since physical action may be forbidden, it releases the pent-up energy by nail-biting or nose-picking or hair-twisting or blink-ing or whatever. The more tense the child becomes, the stronger the habit. And trying to put a stop to the habit by threats or punishment only makes matters worse, not only because it adds yet another anxiety but because the highly charged emotional energy will only seek another restless outlet.

Nightmares and sleep-walking

With nightmares and sleep-walking, the child in any case has no conscious control over his behaviour, and ends up distressed if people become irritated with him or refuse to take his fears seriously. If your child wakes you in the night with a bad dream, or if you find him blundering about on the landing fast asleep, gently reassure him. If it's a nightmare, often he seems very disorientated, not knowing who you are or where he is, and slow to respond to your voice. This is because the dream is so real to him that he takes time to come back to the present. Stay calm and keep talking to him, and the moment will pass. If he's sleep-walking, lead him gently back to bed (often he won't wake and will remember nothing of the experience in the morning), and make sure that safety precautions are taken so he can't harm himself if it happens again.

Most children have bad dreams at some point in their childhood, and many sleep-walk. Occasional incidents of this kind are simply signs that the child's mind is still active in sleep or his body still charged with energy, and are no cause for alarm. It's only if they're repeated frequently that you need identify the reasons and ensure your child has a more relaxed and stress-free environment in future. Some experts suggest you shouldn't encourage a child to talk about the content of his nightmares, but simply allow him to forget them. Others say it helps to talk. My advice is be guided by your child. If he wants to talk, listen sympathetically and explain that everyone has bad dreams. It's simply the mind being busy and making up stories. When we're awake, we can decide for ourselves how to use our imagination, in sleep we can't. But though dreams seem real, they can't really hurt us. This won't stop his bad dreams or his sleep-walking immediately, but it will help him understand what's going on and be less alarmed and helpless about it. Most nightmares and sleep-walking gradually disappear by adolescence, though research shows that even in adults more people have (or at least recall) 'bad' dreams than 'good' dreams.

Other nervous habits

Children also simply grow out of most other nervous habits. The more relaxed their environment, the quicker this happens. Rather than nag your child about a nervous habit, question him in an interested but casual way. 'Why do you keep blinking like that?' 'Do you know you're twisting your hair?' Once he's aware other people are conscious of what he's doing, this often prompts him to stop. Mention his appearance too – 'Can you see you're spoiling the look of your nails?' Notice *when* he engages most in his habit, and use this as a pointer towards the situations that make him anxious. Be sympathetic. Encourage him to talk about his worries. But don't harp too much on his habit. Taking *too* much notice of it can lead him to use it as a way of getting your attention, or can make him feel rebellious ('They're *my* nails; why can't I bite them if I want?'). Provided your child agrees (such things shouldn't be used as a punishment) you can try painting the nails of a nail biter with bitter aloes, or you can cut the hair of a hair chewer and twister rather shorter, or you can award a point or a star for each day the nails remain unbitten or the hair unchewed or unmatted. But these strategies only work if the child genuinely wants to break the habit himself, so should only be used alongside sustained attempts to lower anxiety levels in his life generally.

If your child is sexually abused

We all hope our children will not meet people who take advantage of their sexual innocence, lack of physical strength, and natural obedience to adults in order to misuse them sexually. But the grim fact is that all children are at risk. At greatest risk are those children brought up in homes either where there is extreme licence in sexual behaviour or where there is excessive reticence and prudery. Children who are brought up in homes where there is a common-sense attitude to sex are less likely to be sexually assaulted, and are more likely if such assaults do happen to be able to tell their parents and to survive the incident without too much trauma. In a home where sexual licence reigns children can sometimes be seen as fair game, while in excessively prudish homes they often haven't the knowledge to realize what's going on, particularly if they're taken advantage of by someone out-wardly 'respectable' who tells them there's nothing wrong in it and swears them to secrecy.

Always be on your guard

The first thing you can do to protect your child is to give her a good sex education from the start. But in itself this isn't enough. Without alarming her, always be on your guard, because the majority of sexual assaults on small children are carried out by members of their own family, or people well-known to them. Cousins or uncles or grandparents or even parents themselves, or next-door neighbours or close friends of the family or boyfriends or girlfriends of older siblings. Nor need the assault come from an adult. Older children and of course brothers and sisters can be involved. Sometimes the incident starts out as a game, and then becomes serious as strong and unfamiliar emotions are aroused. Sometimes the child is told that what is going on is simply a form of 'exercise', and although the child may not actually be physically harmed her body could be used for feeling and caressing in a way which is upsetting and confusing.

Your child is also at risk from strangers. The majority of assaults come from members of the family simply because members of the family have more opportunity. But children are at great risk when left with people you don't know, of either sex, so don't leave your child with a baby-sitter unless you're sure you can trust him or her. Don't let your child be taken out by older children unless you know them well and are sure they'll behave sensibly and caringly. Don't leave your child (this applies equally to babies) untended inside or outside a shop, even for a few minutes. Don't let her out to play with other children if playing means wandering out of your sight. You may know she's safe from busy roads, but she may not be safe from undesirable people.

Tell your child never to go off with a stranger

Stress to your child as soon as she can understand that she must never go off with a stranger for any reason unless you tell her to. This is a difficult concept. You don't want to frighten your child that evil is lurking around every street corner. The great majority of people are kind-hearted and would never dream of taking advantage of a small child. But at the same time you do want to impress upon her that strangers are a potential danger. Small children can be very trusting, and can easily be won over by offers of being taken somewhere to be given a nice present. The best approach is to tell your child the simple truth. Most people are fine, but there are a few who may want to steal her away, so you're not going

376

to give them the chance. You don't have to tell her that such people have sexual motives. It's enough for her to know they want to take her away from you and her home. Fairy stories are a help here. If you've been reading to her regularly she'll know that even in the nicest of stories there are people who are a bad lot, and little children must keep clear of them.

Impress on her in addition that if anyone suggests to her that she goes off with them, or if anyone touches her genitals or anywhere else that upsets her, she's to tell you. If she asks why explain that her body is *hers*. It belongs to her, and no one has any business to touch it in intimate ways except her parents when they're bathing her. She'll usually be perfectly satisfied with this explanation. She already understands that people shouldn't mess about with things that don't belong to them without permission, and she'll have no difficulty in realizing that her body falls into this category.

If in spite of all your precautions you think someone has been interfering with your child, take action. Even if you feel your child hasn't been harmed in any way, the person concerned may try again or may try with other children. Something must be done to put a stop to the possibility. But remember that your first duty is to your child, and to see that in the follow-up to the incident he isn't allowed to suffer. If you show extreme horror, or a violent emotional outburst, or suddenly smother your child with over-protective affection, he'll get the idea something terrible has happened, and this could make him anxious and affect his feelings about his body long into the future. Instead, try to be objective. Don't cross-examine your child in a way that gives him the feeling that somehow *he's* been at fault. Don't rush to bring in other people to hear his story or to question him. Be patient and loving and make sure nothing is done to frighten him.

If your child is abused

He's also far more likely to give you the necessary details and be accurate about them if you don't pressurize him. Children become very confused when adults start cross-questioning them aggressively, and can end up genuinely not knowing precisely what *did* happen. They may also become upset or clam up and refuse to tell you anything, particularly if they think that in some way you're blaming them. Keep your questions light, almost casual. Concentrate on asking what X *did*, not on vaguer matters such as what was said or felt.

Once you've got a clear story, you must decide what to do next. Unless there's been physical damage, it may be hard to prove your child's story is true. You believe it, but if the adult or other children involved have a good reputation, and if they deny it point-blank, things will become difficult. And your child may have mixed up two different people, or may unwittingly have got important facts wrong. So proceed cautiously.

If a member of the family is involved Assuming the person concerned is another member of the family, you may decide the best thing to do is to tell him or her that you know about the act, but that you're not yet quite sure who was responsible. Name no names, but make it clear that when you do find out, or if the incident happens again or your child makes any further complaints, you'll go straight to the police. A veiled threat of this kind could have the desired effect. However, if you're sure of the person concerned, a face-to-face confrontation, however unnerving, is called for. Even if he or she denies the incident, tell them you believe your child, and that though you have no proof you can still go to the police and they will question the person concerned, in itself an unpleasant experience.

Always take your child's allegations seriously No matter how close a member of the family is involved, or how unlikely your child's story seems at first hearing, don't be too hasty in dismissing the alleged incident as fantasy. Often the younger the child, the less the likelihood of fantasy over things of this kind. Your child isn't old enough to have sufficient knowledge of sexual assault to make up the details. Nor is he old enough deliberately to set out to get an adult or older child 'into trouble'. *Always* take anything your child tells you about sexual assault seriously. Your refusal to believe him or do something to protect him will upset and confuse him. He knows you usually help him when he's in trouble, so why not now? It must be because it's somehow his fault. And if you reinforce this by telling him he's making up 'wicked stories' or worse still actively punish him, the psychological harm inflicted on him will go very deep indeed.

You'll also be making it easier for the sexual assault to be repeated. Not only has the culprit got away with it the first time, but your child now feels unable to report further offences to you, and will have to suffer them in silence. And whoever is doing these things to your child may convince him or herself that there's nothing wrong with them, even that your child enjoys them, and may go on to even worse behaviour in future. So listen to your child, follow up his story, and put his interests first. If you feel unable to go to the police, contact the NSPCC. They have abundant experience of these sad cases, and know that although they're more liable in overcrowded homes where children share bedrooms and even beds with adults and older siblings they're nevertheless a common occurrence in even the most respectable families.

If a relative is involved and you feel you can't seek outside help of any kind, talk instead to another member of your family whose judgement you trust. Doing nothing simply isn't an option. You have to be sure, by whatever means necessary, that the assault doesn't occur again, even if this means causing permanent rifts in the family. Solemn promises by the person concerned that the assault won't recur may not be enough. He or she has given way to temptation once, and may do so again. Whatever happens, there must be no further risk to your child.

If the offender is a stranger, your course of action is much more clear-cut. Go to the police at once, no matter how incomplete your evidence. The chances are they will have had complaints from other parents about similar incidents, and your small piece of proof could be just what they need to identify the man or woman concerned. If you have been taking the precautions outlined earlier, there's little fear of strangers having the opportunity to molest your child, but all too often parents say that 'I only let her out of my sight for two minutes' or 'The playgroup is only a few doors away; I thought she'd be perfectly all right coming home on her own' or 'He only went to the corner shop to buy some sweets' or 'She was with older children and I *told* them not to let her go off on her own' or 'I thought it was only little girls who were at risk'. Protests and self-reproaches of this kind after the event show how easy it is for even the most careful parents to relax their own hard-and-fast safety rules. Don't fall into the trap. Your child is far too precious.

If a stranger is involved

PUNISHMENT

We come now to the question of punishment, and what is said here applies not just to the pre-school years but right through to adolescence. Punishment is an unpleasant word, but children can't be good all the time, and sometimes sanctions are needed.

Why do we punish our children?

Before discussing these sanctions, let's ask *why* we punish a child. Is it:

1. to stop her being naughty in future?
2. to pay her back for being naughty now?
3. to relieve our own feelings?

Most parents, when pressed, say it's usually a combination of all three. They'd like to feel it was reason (1), and that their sole aim was to help her learn for the future. But they have to admit that there's usually an element of reason (2) about it ('There: *that* will show you I mean what I say') and that reason (3) comes into it too ('I just get so *mad* with her'). Not surprisingly they tend to be a little shame-faced about it. We all like to see ourselves as people who wouldn't hurt our children for the world, and this self-image is hard to sustain when we see the outline of our hand etched in red on a small arm or leg, and know it was done in revenge or anger.

So let's dispose of reasons (2) and (3) before we come to reason (1), the only justifiable reason for punishment. To be a human being does mean getting angry at times, and children can try our patience to the limit. So if you punish your child in anger sometimes this doesn't mean you're a terrible person. Nor does it mean you should fill yourself with guilt and lavish treats on your child in an attempt to make it up to her. On the other hand, you shouldn't just shrug off the incident. Think objectively about the affair. What sparked things off? Were you in a cross mood to start with? Had your child been particularly difficult all day? Did you feel she was deliberately

Punishing your child in anger

defying you? Were you trying to work and did she get in the way? Did you feel she was challenging your authority? Did this hurt your pride?

If reason (3) was involved, look as well at your reactions as you handed out the punishment. Some parents confess not only were they aware of relieving their feelings, they also felt a disturbing stab of pleasure at their power to hurt their child. This surprised and shamed them. Other parents, while not feeling this pleasure, report equal surprise at the strength of the anger they felt at their child, and at the violent streak which they seemed to glimpse in themselves.

These are sensitive issues, and touch on something deep in us all. When threatened in any way we tend to lash out. As we have seen, this is a survivial response, and one which has helped the human race to survive. And defiant and dis-obedient children can seem to pose a very real threat to us. Not a physical threat, but a psychological threat that if we can't even handle a small child, we can't surely be much of a person. Such a threat to our self-esteem isn't an easy one to deal with. Things are often made worse by the fact that you may be doing your level best to be patient, and far from appreciating this your child only tries you the harder. In the end something snaps, you lose your temper and punish her, only to feel bad about it afterwards. Far from helping your self-esteem, you are now faced with the thought that not only couldn't you handle your child, you couldn't handle your own temper either.

Learning to control our emotions

The problem is that in modern society the tendency to lash out physically when under threat no longer has a survival value most of the time. In our highly civilized way of life physical violence is more likely to cause us trouble than to save us from it. So our bodies gear us up for sudden action, only to find that sudden action is inappropriate. We have to control our emotion and handle it in other ways.

Inconveniently, however, modern society gives us within the home increased possibilities for conflict between parent and child. If we lived as our ancestors did, close to the land and with plenty to do outside the home and only the barest of necessities inside, life might be much harder but there would certainly be fewer rules for children to obey. No fragile objects to be broken, no carpets to get dirty, no artificial lighting to

Remove some of the potential causes of conflict

make you want to stay up late, no television programmes to argue over, no electrical hazards, no stairs to fall down, no toys to squabble over. Truly, within the modern home, we make any number of rods for our own backs. So if you find yourself punishing your child for reasons (2) and (3), remove some of the potential causes of discord within the home or resolve to take a more reasonable attitude over them.

On the more sensitive issue of feeling a guilty pleasure at punishing your child, accept that if nature has programmed us to lash out when threatened she's also programmed us to get satisfaction from doing so. The satisfaction comes from a feeling of power at asserting ourselves over another person. Once identified and seen as natural, you needn't worry about the feeling, though you certainly will want to avoid indulging it. The same goes for the violent streak you may think you see in yourself. Even the most docile person has violence in them, and since we control it rigorously most of the time, when it does break out it tends to carry a lot of repressed energy in it. All the more reason for avoiding punishing our children physically whenever we can.

Punishing a child to get one's own back
Reason (2) on its own, punishing a child to pay her back for wrong-doing, is less of a problem than reason (2) mixed with reason (3). But it's a problem nevertheless. Revenge – since this is what it is – is never a helpful way of tackling transgressions. The best way is to avoid the circumstances that led to the offence, and to help your child learn the reasons for your insistence upon good behaviour. If you've tended to punish your child as a means of getting back at her for wrong-doing, you'll have noticed it isn't in fact very effective in ensuring good future behaviour. It leaves her rebellious and hard done-by, and doesn't motivate her to want to understand *why* what she's done is wrong.

Once you start seeing punishment not as a means of revenge but as an aid towards understanding, you begin to appreciate that in many cases it isn't really necessary. There are other and better ways of helping a child learn, ways that involve guidance and that strengthen the relationship between you and your child instead of threatening it. But when a mild form of punishment is necessary, what form should it take? Let's run through the options.

The options for punishment

Smacking

In the Western world this is the traditional way of doing things, though in many Eastern cultures it's held to be a barbaric business. Smacking has the advantage of being immediate, and provided it isn't severe tends to be quickly over and done with. It's also convenient, for the parent at least.

Unfortunately, the disadvantages outweigh these questionable advantages. Smacking teaches a child that it's okay for big people to hit small people. It causes pain, and it may make your child genuinely afraid of you, with the consequences discussed earlier (pages 328–30). So if you rely on smacking you can't wonder when your child in turn hits children smaller and weaker than himself. Nor can you wonder if his attitude towards you is less spontaneously affectionate than you'd like, or that if he's a spirited child, he tries to hit you back. The natural defensive response in any of us is to meet physical aggression with physical aggression. Violence breeds violence.

The dangers of smacking

A further danger with smacking is that you run the risk of physically harming your child. Needless to say you must never hit a child around the head or with an implement of any kind. The same physical dangers are present if you give your child a hard shake. Shaking can cause brain damage if the brain comes in contact with the inside of the skull as the head is shaken back and forth. Children are physically more vulnerable than we think. And of course never hit a child with a closed fist. If you must smack, a slap with the open hand on the arm or leg is the very most you can allow yourself.

But once you start the practice of smacking you find yourself on a slippery slope, not only getting into the *habit* of smacking instead of thinking what's gone wrong and what can be done to put it right, but getting him into the habit of *expecting to be smacked*. As a result, he'll both come to associate you with physical aggression and to ignore you when you tell him to stop something, on the grounds that you don't really mean what you say unless you accompany it with a smack. If he's a tough character and finds that your smacks don't bother him, where does this leave you in your attempts at discipline?

Sending up to bed

Apart from removing the child out of harm's way if you're really angry with him (some hard-pressed parents confess this is the reason for 'getting him out of my sight') sending to bed has nothing to commend it. First, it makes your child associate bed with punishment, so no wonder he starts playing up come bedtime proper. Second, it separates him from you just at a time when he knows you're cross with him and most needs the reassurance that you still love him. It isn't good for your child to get the idea that when he's miserable he has to cry alone and sort out his bad feelings by himself. A child who is banished crying to his room, or even put to wait outside your door, feels very isolated from those he loves. Let him stay with you, even though you're at odds with each other for the moment. And I hope it doesn't need saying you must *never* put a child in a dark room on his own as punishment, or lock the door on him. A dark room or a locked bedroom door are terrifying experiences for a child. So much so that psychologists label such experiences *traumas*, that is single horrifying events that leave a deep scar on the child's mind. Consciously he may appear to forget a trauma, but it remains embedded in his unconscious, helping cause the nameless fears and anxieties that can haunt people in later life.

Withholding treats

Most parents fall back on this from time to time. The treat may be anything from next week's pocket money to a trip to the zoo, and the effectiveness of withholding it varies greatly from child to child. Children who feel deeply about things may be devastated to be told you're not going to buy sweets on the way home after all, while other more cheerful characters will take it in their stride. It does seem rather unfair that a child should be made to suffer just because he has the temperament that makes him feel disappointments keenly. So it's best to withhold treats sparingly. Besides, it makes the world a very uncertain place to a child if it happens often. One moment you think you're going to have something nice, and the next, often for no reason you can fully understand, you're told you're not. It makes you the victim of fate. It may also lead you to question the value of adult promises. 'Oh but you *promised*' wails the disappointed child, and one can hardly wonder if he grows up not too particular about keeping his own promises either.

When you do withhold treats, it's better if it happens as a direct result of the child's misbehaviour. This is a form of the law of natural consequences, discussed later. For example the treat may be something nice for tea, but because your child misbehaves and causes you extra work there isn't time to prepare it. The connection between his misbehaviour and the loss of the treat is then clear to the child, and he can't blame you for being unfair. Even when things are not as neatly connected as this, a child can still be brought to see the connection between his failure to co-operate with you and your refusal to co-operate with him. Wherever possible, make sure your child understands in advance exactly how the treat is dependent upon his behaviour, and that he receives a timely reminder when needed.

Let withholding be a natural consequence of the misdeed

Deprivation

Not dissimilar from withholding treats is the practice of taking something away from a child if she's naughty. Don't take a favourite toy away as punishment for something quite unconnected with it. This is arbitrary, and leaves her resentful. On the other hand, if she misuses something or inflicts damage with it then it's perfectly reasonable to take it away. If it's a household gadget of some kind and you've decided she mustn't have it any more, put it out of sight so she forgets about it. On the other hand, if it's something of her own that you're planning to return to her, put it out of reach but within view. This will give her an opportunity to ponder over her loss and feel suitably chastened over it. Don't deprive her of it for too long. Often a few minutes is enough, though sometimes up to a day or two is appropriate. Leave it much longer and the impact of the whole affair will have worn off by the time she gets it back, and she will be less likely to have learnt her lesson.

Going without a meal

If the writers of autobiographies are to be believed, this used to be a common punishment in bygone days. I doubt if it's very widely used today. Going without an occasional meal may not do a child a great deal of harm if she's physically healthy, but it won't do her a great deal of good either. It's another example of an arbitrary punishment which usually has nothing to do with the actual misdemeanour itself. And since your child depends upon you for her food and the other necessities of life, it's heartless to say the least. Once again, this isn't likely to help the loving, trusting relationship you want between your child and yourself. So, as the consumer magazine says about a bad buy, definitely not recommended.

Doing an imposition of some kind

Another favourite in bygone days. The child who misbehaves is made to carry out a hated task, like weeding the garden or wiping the dishes. And another punishment that's not recommended. You don't want your child to learn that jobs in house and garden are a punishment. The ideal is to encourage her so that she'll *want* to do these things for you! The same applies to jobs which are for her own good, such as tidying her bedroom or toy cupboard.

You could invent a special imposition for her, especially when she's older, like the writing of lines which used to be so popular with schoolteachers. But there isn't much to commend this. A child is hardly using her time productively copying out a set of lines. And there's the risk that if she's made to use her new-found writing skill in this way she'll come to dislike writing, associating it with unpleasant activities instead of things that are fun.

Banning television

Since children enjoy television so much, one obvious form of punishment is to stop them watching a favourite programme, or watching at all for a specified period. Again the snag is that the punishment is unlikely to be connected with the actual offence for which the child is being punished. And whenever there's a lack of connection your child inevitably sees you as unfair. I can't stress too often that because they live in a world dominated by the authority of other people, children place a major premium upon fairness. They're very much at the mercy of powerful people in their lives like parents and teachers, and they come to respect most those who treat them with a justice which they can understand and appreciate.

If you have more than one child and they're squabbling over

THE FOURTH AND FIFTH YEARS

which programme to watch, you can quite reasonably switch the set off while you arbitrate over the dispute. But having arbitrated and settled matters between them, it's better to switch back on again than to make both children go without. Making them both go without means you're reacting purely to their squabbling, instead of to their problem. Except for these situations, there's little to be gained from using television as a punishment (restricting television because you doubt the value of too much watching is quite another matter – see Chapter 7). If you have television in the house, it's part of everyone's life, and the important thing is to use it sensibly, not to keep it as a treat which can be snatched away from a child when she isn't being 'good'.

Help your children sort out their squabbles

Equally important, if you stop your child from watching her favourite programme you have to decide what to do with her during the time she isn't watching it. She won't be feeling at her most loving and co-operative, and the whole thing is a perfect recipe for more conflict. She feels she's now got nothing to lose, and the threat that she'll miss her favourite programme again next time won't mean a great deal to her. She'll be too pre-occupied with what she's missing *now* to think much about the future. And though she may not consciously set out to get her own back (she's a little young for such machiavellian tactics), her resentment towards you will ensure that things remain fraught for some time.

Withdrawal of approval

We come now to the really effective actions on your part. And of these, withdrawal of approval is one of the most important. Your child loves you and wants to please you. His ideas of what are right and wrong come largely from you. So if you make it clear to him that you disapprove of a particular action, and can't approve of him while he goes on doing it, this has a powerful effect in shaping his behaviour.

This doesn't mean withholding approval from him *as a person* (see pages 322/388–9). You don't want to make him think he's wicked or bad. You want him to think of himself as a sensible person who can make decisions to avoid unwanted behaviour. So direct your criticisms at his actions rather than directly at him. Remember from our earlier discussion that 'That was a silly thing to do' is much better than 'You are a

Criticize his actions rather than him

silly boy'. 'That's much too noisy' is better than 'What a noisy child you are'. 'That's just being destructive' is better than 'You destructive little hooligan'. By using words in this way you indicate that he and his behaviour are not one and the same thing, and that he has some *choice* over his behaviour. He can't be expected always to exercise it fully yet, but you want him to learn. Tie bad labels around his neck, and he'll come to believe in them. 'I do bad things because I *am* bad. I can't help it!' That isn't the kind of programme you want to give him.

Parents sometimes can't see much difference between saying to a child 'That was a silly thing to do' and 'You're a silly boy'. If you feel this way, think over the meaning of the verb 'to be'. It's the verb we use to assert our own existence. I *am* me. So it has a very powerful effect upon our self-concepts. Use it carefully and lovingly when you use it towards your child. If you're still not convinced, take two sequences of thought as an example. The first goes like this. 'I did a stupid thing this morning when I took a wrong turning in the car. I doubled the length of my journey. Usually I'm much more careful about following directions. I'll make sure I don't make the same mistake again.' The second one goes: 'I am a stupid person. I stupidly took a wrong turning this morning in the car and doubled the length of my journey. I'm so careless I'm always doing things like that. I'm bound to go wrong again next time.' Notice how the first sequence of thought separates you as a person from your actions. It helps you to feel confident about yourself and to know you have the power to avoid making the same mistake again. The second sequence identifies you with your mistake, and in consequence gives you the feeling that that's the kind of person you are and inevitably you'll mess things up again next time.

Your child will believe what you tell him about himself

This example illustrates the strength behind our choice of words. How much greater this strength when we're children and still learning the basics about ourselves! Come up against a parent or a teacher who keeps telling you how stupid you are, and because you accept they *know* these things you believe unquestioningly they're right. And no matter how much evidence to the contrary you meet with in the years to come, the belief goes so deeply into your unconscious that it remains with you, giving a persistent feeling of inadequacy and worth-lessness that may take specialist help to resolve.

So don't saddle your child with self-concepts that will weigh him down perhaps for the rest of his life. When you withhold approval from him, link it firmly with his actions and not with himself. Don't be deceived by the fact that he maybe doesn't *seem* upset when you call him silly or bad or stupid. This is a sign of how readily a child accepts these labels, and is no indication of the damage they do to him. Psychologists see far too much evidence of this damage, not only in children but in adults struggling to come to terms with themselves. No one can like himself much if he's made to think he's wicked or stupid; no one can believe in himself or have confidence in his strengths and abilities, or find the self-fulfilment in life that is his basic right.

When you withhold approval from your child's actions, he'll learn the behaviour you want from him more quickly if you help him to see what's gone wrong and why. You don't always have time to go into great detail when you're scolding him. And if you're irritated it isn't always easy to find the patience. But it pays good dividends if you can. When possible, ask him if he can himself tell you why what he's done is wrong, and what he should have done instead. Don't overdo it and make him feel confused or impatient in his own turn, but remarks like 'Now that was silly wasn't it; what should you have done?' or 'You can see what's gone wrong can't you?' or 'You know that's not the way to do it don't you?' prompt him into thinking about his behaviour. They're always preferable to simple statements that he's behaved badly.

Try to explain to him what he's done wrong

Natural consequences

Wherever it's possible (and safe) for a child to experience the actual consequences of her misbehaviour, she'll grasp the reasons for behaving sensibly more effectively. This doesn't mean rubbing her nose in it. Once she's got the message you can step in and help put things right. It simply means letting her see the connection between her actions and the results of her actions, and therefore the good sense of the guidance you're giving her. This is one of the most effective ways of helping her learn, and of helping her remember the lesson for the future. It's also fair, and helps her appreciate how the world works.

Sitting in the corner

On the occasions when you feel the necessity for direct physical punishment of some kind, it's usually enough to make your child sit down on a particular chair or at the side of the room or in a corner. Some parents keep a special chair for this purpose. Tell your child firmly to sit down, and not to get up again until she's told to do so. Usually a couple of minutes are long enough. Any longer and your child becomes too restless to stay put, and you've then got problems as to what further sanctions to use against this new act of disobedience. But she must stay seated until you tell her she can stand up again. The determined note in your voice leaves her in no doubt you mean business.

Why is this simple punishment so effective with most children? The answer is that children are extremely active, and sitting still is never easy for them. And while they're sitting still they have a chance to think about what they've just done and decide it really wasn't worth it. They also see it as your way of emphasizing disapproval, and their eagerness to get back into your good books mounts as they sit and reflect. They know they can't do this *until* they've served their stint in the cooler. If they've been angry about something, it also gives them a chance to calm down and think better of it, and gives you a chance to do the same.

There's no need to ignore your child completely while she's in the cooler. But the effect of the punishment is greater if you take only brief notice of her. Carry on with your own jobs, and leave her to sit it out until it's time to let her rejoin the mainstream of life. Once you let her rejoin go back immediately to normal behaviour. The incident is over and done with, and she's learnt her lesson and everyone can now put it behind them.

Do's and don'ts when punishing

Generally, keep punishments to a minimum. With some spirited children, the more you punish the more defiant they become. They see it as a battle of wills, and their strong nature makes them stand up for themselves. They also become resistant to punishment, and you have to get crosser and crosser before it has any effect. More naturally conformist children become cowed if you punish too often, and end up believing they've no right to their own wishes. *It's the attitude you use when you hand out punishment rather than the actual punishment itself that really matters.* Telling a child in a voice that brooks no nonsense to go and sit on the floor until you let him get up is of far more use than a stricter punishment handed out in a flustered and indecisive way. And remember that if you *have* to keep resorting to punishment, you're not being very successful at guiding your child to tell the difference between right and wrong for himself. Children learn best in a home where there's plenty of love and support, where parents set them a good example of the right behaviour, where parents have time for them and can explain things to them, where people behave consistently and reasonably towards them, and where they can understand for themselves the real purpose of good and thoughtful behaviour.

Let's list the other important points you should keep in mind:

1. Don't keep handing out threats of dire consequences if a child doesn't do as he's told. Threats soon lose their impact, especially if they aren't properly thought out and your child, young as he is, learns you're not likely to carry them through. Threaten seldom, and when you do, threaten sensibly and if the need arises stick to what you say.

Never hand out empty threats

2. Never *never* punish by telling a child you don't love him any more (or by threatening you'll stop loving him). This is a devastating experience for him. His whole sense of security and trust in life is based upon the knowledge that you love him, and that nothing can make you stop. 'Mummy/Daddy will love you whatever happens, and don't you ever forget it!' is a statement to a child which is full of joy and caring. 'Mummy/Daddy doesn't love you any more' is like a death-knell.

Never say you don't love him

3. Don't punish your child by being cold towards him once the incident is over. Get things back to normal as quickly as

possible. If your child is in tears, pick him up and comfort him and tell him that it's all finished and over and done with now. Show him your cross words of a moment ago have nothing to do with your love for him or your concern for his distress. Some parents protest that this encourages a child to start crying just as a way of stopping you being angry with him. But you can tell the difference in your own child between genuine distress and a put-up job. If it's the latter, tell him firmly that he knows it's no good crying for the sake of it. 'If you're really upset have a good cry by all means; but don't just cry as a way of getting out of it.' One or two reminders of this kind are usually all that's necessary.

Don't remain cool towards him
A long period of parental coldness towards a child after a misdemeanour is a deeply unsettling experience for him. He wants to be back to normal with you, but however good he tries to be nothing seems to work. It would serve his parents right if he decided to give it all up as a bad job, and ignore them or treat them coldly in return. But because their love and acceptance are so important to him he goes on trying, like some forlorn anchorite doing penance to appease wrathful household gods. It's a thoroughly bad experience for him, and if parents can turn off their good feelings and behaviour towards their child so easily and not turn them on again until the full pound of flesh has been exacted, it doesn't reflect the strength of the bond they have with their child.

Don't nag your child
4. Try not to nag. Nagging proceeds on the principle that if we keep on at somebody long enough eventually he's bound to learn. The trouble is there's no evidence that if someone doesn't learn after the first few tellings he's going to learn after the first few hundred. Having decided, consciously or unconsciously, that he isn't going to co-operate, he's prone to become more stubborn with each telling. Far from having the desired effect, he feels impatient with the nagger. So if after a few tellings your child still isn't doing as you want, change tactics. Figure out why he isn't co-operating. Are you expecting too much? Are your demands impractical or unreasonable for a child of his age? Does he see other children allowed to do the things you're forbidding him? Are you being inconsistent in your demands? Does he understand the reasons for them? Are his parents each asking contradictory things of him? Are there

392

grandparents or other relatives involved who may be confusing the issue? Does he see the benefit of doing as you ask? If none of these things apply, you may be focusing too much attention on what he shouldn't do rather than what he should. A child will do as he's told more readily if you *stress the do's rather than the don'ts*. 'Do play quietly' not 'Don't make that noise'. 'Come quickly' not 'Don't be so slow.'

5. Don't punish at second-hand. One parent threatening that the other will punish the child as soon as he/she gets home is unfair to the child and to the other parent. The child ends up dreading the latter's homecoming instead of looking forward to it. And the latter is put in the position of having to feel cross when they didn't see the misdemeanour they're supposed to be cross about. In this situation they may find discipline hard to enforce or, if they've had a hard day, may vent on the child their pent-up frustrations. The child thus either escapes leniently for behaviour which really requires firm handling, or is punished out of all proportion to the offence.

Don't punish at second-hand or use delayed punishments

6. Don't use delayed punishment. The 'Just you wait till I get you home' attitude shows your child that you're capable of harbouring resentment towards her over a long period. And it isn't effective in dealing with the unwanted behaviour. By the time you've got her home, your child will have half-forgotten what she's being punished for, and what the motivation and feelings that prompted her bad behaviour actually were. And it's the ability to examine her motivation and feelings and handle them better next time that best helps her change this behaviour. So to achieve results, punishment should follow as close to the misdemeanour and be as clearly connected with it as possible.

7. Don't make punishment too frightening. As already discussed, it would be unrealistic to think your child *never* feels fear when you're cross with her, but fear shouldn't be a deliberate part of the punishment. For illustration, think of a recent occasion when events punished you into learning a lesson. Maybe you ruined a car tyre by forgetting to check the pressures regularly. Or you flattened the car battery by leaving

Don't frighten your child

your headlights on all night. Or you took the wrong measurements for a dressmaking or woodworking job in the house,
and wasted money buying the wrong pieces of material. There
wasn't any physical fear involved, but the punishment of
having to buy the new tyre or being unable to start the car
next morning was nevertheless quite effective enough. If your
child looks frightened when you punish her, this is a sign that
the punishment is a bit too severe. And never terrify your
child there's someone who'll come and 'take her away' if she
isn't good, or with bogey men or other night-time terrors.

Try to avoid shouting and remain calm

8. Put authority in your voice without shouting. With both
parents and teachers who are good at keeping children in
order, correct use of the voice is one of the major factors. The
adult who's good with children knows how to speak to them
with a firm, decisive voice which shows he or she expects
obedience and expects it now. There's no screaming match.
Parents who shout all the time end up with children who
shout. You can put more authority into a brisk but contained
voice than you can into a voice that's trying to control others
but has clearly lost control of itself.

9. Keep calm whenever you can. Shouting and raised voices
often go with anger, but anger has other bad effects too. When
we're angry we often do things we wouldn't dream of doing
when we're our usual selves. Don't bottle up your anger until
volcano-like it explodes. But if you can keep calm you'll act
more effectively and avoid doing things you'll regret afterwards. Parents often confess 'I didn't really mean to hit her so
hard' or 'I know I shouldn't have said that to her', and then
add 'but I was just so mad'. The trouble is that things said or
done can't be undone. However, if you do fly off the handle,
don't be afraid to apologize to your child afterwards. Apologiz-
ing if we're in the wrong is a sign of strength, not weakness.
'I'm sorry, I shouldn't have spoken to you like that, but I was
really cross' shows your child you're human like everyone
else, and that she isn't the only one expected to admit she's
wrong. Explaining the reason for your actions ('I was really
cross') also helps her understand you better, and to realize the
value of explaining her own actions in turn.

10. Go easy on guilt. No one enjoys feeling guilty. So if you make your child feel guilty, this can help control his behaviour. But it's a two-edged sword. Feeling guilty means feeling we've fallen short of the person we ought to be. As adults we can cope with guilt (sometimes!) by accepting that no one's perfect, and all we can do is be honest about our actions and do our best. But as a small child it's more difficult. A child doesn't know whether the things we expect of him are reasonable or not. If we act towards him as if he should be perfect, he assumes perfection is possible, and that if he falls short he's the one to blame. Repeated experiences of this kind leave him with a poor opinion of himself, and unable, as he grows older, to look objectively at his life and recognize his real strengths and weaknesses. With the result that his actions become primarily determined by the desire to avoid adding to his guilt, and governed by the 'do's and don'ts' of childhood instead of by the responsible free will of the mature adult.

Go easy on the guilt

But there's another side to guilt. As a psychologist I often listen to the problems of adults who are still guilt-ridden in their relationships with their parents. They are unable to see their parents simply as human beings. To them their parents are above all agents of guilt. 'I'm never home for more than five minutes before my mother starts making me feel guilty,' they say, or 'My father just makes me feel so *awful* about myself every time I see him'. These unfortunate individuals find it hard to love their parents (yet another reason for guilt!) because they've come to associate them with these painful negative emotions. Most of us aren't as badly off as this, but we've experienced just enough of these emotions to know how bad they can be. So with your own children, go easy on the guilt. Let your child see where he's gone wrong, but indicate that you don't expect him to be perfect, and aren't trying to fool him into thinking you're perfect either. Mistakes are normal in life, and, as we see later (page 414), can often help us learn how to get things right next time.

Guilt can spoil the parent–child relationship

A final point is that if a child is made to feel deeply guilty he may deliberately seek punishment in order to deal with it. 'I'm a bad boy, but now I've been punished I don't feel so bad any more.' Thus he may go on goading you by repeating increasingly naughty behaviour until he *makes* you deal sharply with him. So on top of everything else, guilt can actually be a *cause* of bad behaviour in children!

Don't compare your child with other children

11. Equally important, don't keep comparing your child with other children. 'Little so-and-so across the road *always* does as her mother tells her first time.' 'Little so-and-so next door can read and he's *much* younger than you.' 'Little so-and-so round the corner *never* tells lies to her daddy.' Comparing him with the (probably fictitious) goody-goody image some other parents project of their children is unrealistic and unfair. Your child is a person in his own right, and he needs your help in getting to like this person and to develop the qualities that are uniquely his.

Think about the effects punishments may have

12. Think about the effects your punishment is having. Many punishments, far from improving children's behaviour, actually make it worse. Let's take an example. A small child darts into a busy road and you, terrified, call him back. Obediently back he comes, only to be rewarded with a hard smack to 'teach him a lesson' and relieve your feelings of fear and shock. But what in fact does your smack teach him? It teaches him that when you call him in that frightened voice he's better off not taking any notice, because if he goes to you he only gets punished. Far better for you to pick up your child and give him a big hug for being so obedient, before explaining to him seriously and fully the terrible dangers of running into the road.

Many parents say no matter *what* they do their child takes no notice of them. You can soon see why. They fail to grasp that when you punish a child, you prompt him to find ways of avoiding that punishment in future. Sometimes this avoidance takes the form of obedience, but all too often it manifests itself as keeping out of sight or as hiding what he's doing or as untruthfulness. When you catch him out you become angrier still and start accusing him of deceit, but all he's really doing is using his wits to avoid being punished (it isn't only children who get up to this game!). If he gets caught he's smacked. If he owns up he's smacked. If he does as he's told he's smacked. Small wonder these options soon lose their appeal.

So try to think about the effect any punishment is likely to have. If you see your child keeping things from you, maybe you've been too ready to punish him for whatever he's now concealing. If he refuses to own up to misdeeds, maybe you've been punishing him when he owns up, instead of first praising his courage and honesty (page 345). If he stops coming when you call him, maybe coming when you call usually means something unpleasant, like having to stop his game or get washed or be smacked or go up to bed. Children learn a great deal at this age simply through association. If your child associates doing as he's told or coming when you call with unpleasantness he's bound to be unenthusiastic about such responses in future. Help your child associate desirable actions like owning up and obedience with rewards rather than punishments. In this co-operative atmosphere all that will normally be necessary even after misdeeds is to talk to him firmly rather than to hand out nasty medicine.

Don't punish your child for owning up

Rewards

What I was really saying in the previous section is that you should make sure that good behaviour is rewarded, rather than (even unintentionally) punished. Actions like obedience and owning up deserve rewards, helping your child to associate them with pleasant things and thus want to repeat them. If you fail to reward and she ends up associating them with something unpleasant, you can hardly wonder if she becomes less co-operative in future. When you reward your child for good behaviour, it helps her think positively about herself, it improves the relationship between you, and it leaves *you* feeling happier too.

I often notice how parents with small children often miss opportunity after opportunity to reward good behaviour. They're quick at spotting things to grumble about, but seem unaware that much of what children do is very praiseworthy indeed. Most children produce acceptable behaviour most of the time, but receive scant thanks for it. Psychologists employ a useful phrase here, namely 'catching her being good'. This phrase reminds us that instead of catching a child being *bad* before we take notice of her we should try catching her being *good*. If we only catch her being bad, our relationship with her

Catch your child being good

will be dominated by scoldings. 'Catching her being good', on the other hand, serves to reinforce her good behaviour. Children like to know they've been noticed (don't we all?), and to know that the people they love approve of their actions. Research shows we can shape a child's behaviour in desirable directions much more readily if we catch her when she's producing good behaviour and praise and encourage her for it, than if we concentrate upon her mainly when she's doing wrong. And the more quickly our praise and encouragement follow her good behaviour, the better. A word of approval given as soon as a child has done well is more use than any number of words hours or days later, when she's almost forgotten about the behaviour and her motives for it.

We're not talking about material rewards

But don't get the wrong idea about rewards. We're not talking mainly about material things. For all children, the best rewards are the approval and thanks of their parents. At times you'll want to hand out a special treat, but your child's primary need is the encouragement that comes from knowing she's learning how to handle the world and herself in the right way.

Left to herself, your child certainly won't expect material rewards. Her face lights up from knowing she's helped you with a job, or that you're pleased with her or that she's been successful at something she set out to do. As she grows older, this develops into an inner motivation that comes from appreciating the value of co-operative, sensible behaviour. You don't want her to develop the idea that right actions are simply those that carry a pay-roll, or that the material things you give her are always dependent upon her producing the behaviour you want. You give her material gifts because you love her, and because they bring her pleasure.

Make sure a material reward is well chosen

When you do give your child a material reward, make sure it's well-chosen. You may be so pleased by her co-operation that you break one of your rules and give her something she isn't usually allowed. Extra-sticky sweets, for example, or staying up to watch an adult video, or a trip out with some older rather irresponsible children, or a rubbishy toy she's been nagging for, or being let off a necessary task like washing her hands. Once you start this practice, she'll get the idea that your usual rules aren't really important after all. If you can bend them for her as a special treat, you can bend them all the time. This undoes all the work you've put in explaining the whys and wherefores of these rules. Before you know where you are you'll have a nagging child on your hands, even one who tries to trade good behaviour for the things she wants. 'If I do it, can I have some sweets/watch the video/go to the park with the big children?' and so on.

Closely linked to this is the business of cupboard love. If your child learns she can get round you by producing particular behaviour such as affection, she'll start using it for these ends. Instead of allowing her affection for you to express itself naturally, she'll see it as part of a bargain. 'I tell Mummy I love her and Mummy goes and gets me something nice to eat.' If this happens often enough, your child's natural feelings for you become confused with the idea of wheedling something out of you. In the end, her love for you may even become conditional upon your giving her what she wants. Help her keep her feelings genuine and spontaneous by letting her see that just as your love for her isn't conditional, so there is no need for her love for you to be conditional either. Cupboard love is really an attempt by your child to bribe *you*, and the less you bribe her, the less chance of it becoming a problem.

Cupboard love

Bribing a child into being good is in any case disastrous, because when the bribes stop the good behaviour stops. Your child is only being good in order to receive her bribe, not because she appreciates the real reasons for being good. Certainly you can say things like 'If you hurry and finish the tidying we'll be able to see the TV programme from the beginning', or 'If you're in bed on time tonight we'll be able to read a whole chapter of the story', but these aren't bribes. They're attempts to show the child the natural consequences of her actions. Bribes refer to material perks that have no connection with the things you're asking your child to do. Keep them to a minimum.

Never bribe a child to be good

THE SICK CHILD

Sickness in children is always a worry, but the *practical* problems associated with it increase steadily as the child moves through the early years. True, as he moves from babyhood into early childhood so he can begin to tell you what's actually wrong with him, but whereas babies and very small children are 'content' to sleep or be nursed when they're unwell, the older, more active child hates the idea of being in bed during the day, craves amusement, and can have you racing up and down stairs like an enthusiastic Sherpa from morning to dusk. As he grows a bit older still, he may learn that he can also 'use' his illness as a way of getting what he wants, and if you're not adept at spotting innocent little excursions into fraud, he may be tempted to top things up with the odd imaginary indisposition just for good measure.

Short-term maladies But let's take genuine sickness first. This can of course be either temporary (e.g. colds, infections) or more long-term (e.g. asthma, eczema). With short-term maladies, the doctor will advise on just how long a child needs to stay in bed. But the vital thing is warmth and rest, rather than bed itself, and provided the room is adequately heated and the child can be swathed in blankets and tucked into a cosy armchair, the lounge is often just as acceptable a sickroom as the bedroom. It has the added advantage of being near you and of that godsend in times of childhood indispositions, the television set. But if your child does have to stay upstairs in bed, ensure the room is kept at around 18°C (70°F), and that the source of heating is safe (a sick child blundering out of bed and into an electric fire is a recipe for disaster). Keep a collection of toys, books and puzzles for use only in times of sickness (once used, add them to the normal store and lay up another secret cache for next time). And be prepared to spend time with your child. Naturally, you can't be with him all day. You have other things to attend to. But many adults speak with great warmth of the love and care their parents used to show them when they were confined to bed. These things stay in the mind because they matter. So show your child that he's important enough to be a priority when he's not well.

Once a child starts pestering you to be allowed up, this is usually a sign that he's on the mend. So unless the doctor forbids it, let him potter round the house a bit provided he keeps warm and doesn't overdo it. But don't let him outdoors, however much he pleads with you, until his temperature has been normal for at least a day or two. If he's had an infectious illness, your doctor will let you know when all risk of spreading germs is past.

While a child *is* ill, he'll need plenty of reassurance that all is well and that he'll soon be up and about again. Be sympathetic, but at the same time don't encourage him to feel extra sorry for himself. Provided he's sure of your sympathy whenever he needs it, even when he's in the best of rude health, a brisk sensible manner when he's ill will minimize the risk that he'll feign illness in the future as a way of getting what he wants from you. If his appetite has gone, tempt him with his favourite food (provided it's suitable for his invalid state!), but don't go to extremes. His appetite will quickly recover once he's back on his feet, and it's never a good thing to show a small child you're anxious about his food. Keep your other anxieties from him too while he's ill. If he sees you're worried he'll start worrying too, which will only delay his progress.

It's always good to try to introduce novelty into a sick child's life. I've already mentioned keeping a store of books and games to bring out at such a time. But make a list of other little things a child might like to do. Often these are things that are available to him any day of the week, but which he spurns when he's feeling energetic. Cutting out pictures from coloured magazines. Making figures and shapes out of dough. Rigging up a 'telephone' out of plastic beakers and a length of string so that he can talk to you. Shadow puppets for projection on to the wall as the evening draws in. Cardboard boxes which can be converted into toy theatres, houses, ships and garages. A tin full of buttons or beads which can be sorted (make sure they're not likely to be swallowed). Cotton reels which can be threaded. For an older child with nimble fingers knitting, or the long snake-like objects that can be produced from wool and a suitably prepared cotton reel. Cotton reel tanks made with the help of elastic bands and pieces of candle, and which can be made to climb hills in the bedclothes. You'll find that a large tray with high sides is an essential working surface for most of these activities, and that an even larger plastic sheet placed underneath to catch any mess is equally necessary.

Think of lots of things for him to do

When you consider how many other everyday activities there are which are also well suited to a sick child's needs (drawing and colouring for example), there's little need for

401

him to be bored. Variety is the key. His attention span will be shorter than usual, so the more things on offer the better. Don't let him have them all at once though. Produce each one as his interest in the last begins to wane.

Long-term sickness   So much for temporary sickness. Long-term sickness raises rather different problems. Your doctor will advise you on all aspects of nursing and sickness management, but at the psychological level the crucial factor is your child's attitude towards his illness. Help him to see himself as normal, as a child who happens to have an illness rather than as an illness that happens to have a child. Except where the doctor indicates otherwise, encourage your child to develop the same wide interests as any other child. Refer to his illness as little as possible when talking to other people in front of him, and when you do mention it, be matter-of-fact. Try not to let your child see himself as 'delicate', or as extra 'special'. Help him to take his illness in his stride. A positive, sensible attitude towards his own illness is much more likely to help a child achieve a cure than a negative, self-pitying one. And if the illness is not really susceptible to cure, a positive attitude will still be of much more help in learning to cope with it and lead as normal a life as possible.

With illnesses such as the two examples given earlier, asthma and eczema, your doctor may well tell you that the root cause could be a nervous one. If this is the case, try to identify the nature of any pressures your child may be under. His temperament may be a nervous one to begin with, but things in the environment may be acting as the actual trigger. So watch to see if there are particular incidents that trigger an attack. Can these incidents be avoided or modified? Can your child be taught to take a calmer attitude towards them, and a calmer attitude towards his malady as well? Does he need help in expressing his emotions, or in putting his thoughts into words? Does he fret over unnecessary trifles, and if so why? Are you perhaps demanding too much of your child, setting him standards he can't achieve? Is he being victimized by older children?

But no matter what your child's malady happens to be, remember that his attitude towards it will be formed very much by *your* attitude towards it. If you see it as something that's simply a part of life, and that can be handled as such, so will he.

It sometimes happens that a child finds her illness so useful she doesn't really want to let it go. Or, if it's been a lengthy illness, her confidence may have been eroded, so that she doesn't fancy the idea of mixing in with the rest of the world once more. There's nothing sinister about any of this, but it does make it hard for you, since you can't be *quite* sure whether your child is fully fit or not. Don't try challenging her on the one hand, or giving in on the other. Sympathize with her (which of us, in her shoes, wouldn't be trying to do exactly as she's doing?), accept that in part she doesn't *really* recognize where feeling ill ends and feeling sorry for herself begins, but be firm about getting her back to normal as quickly as possible. For all of us, and particularly for an active young child, good health is much more fun than being ill. Don't waste time telling her she isn't ill. She'll only insist she is. Find instead interesting things to do, and draw her into them. If she's started school and seems very reluctant to return, agree with her that she can stay off one more day *provided* she agrees to go back the day after without problems. A child of this age is quite old enough to understand that this is a bargain, and that she must keep her side of it. Let her understand that if she doesn't agree to the bargain, the alternative is to go back today, without further debate. This is enough to convince her that she'd better grab the best terms she can while they're on offer!

Getting back to normal after an illness

A rather different situation is presented by the child who 'invents' an illness just to avoid something she dislikes. This is dealt with elsewhere in the context of the child who doesn't want to go to school (Chapter 7). But the general rule is not to enter into a lengthy debate with your child over whether she's really ill or not. Make up your mind on the subject, and act accordingly. Showing her briskly and decisively that you've seen through her little ruse is a far more effective way of preventing her from trying it on again than any other strategy. Don't laugh at her over it, or make an issue out of it. Much of a small child's behaviour is experimental. She's in the process of finding out what works and what doesn't. Just concentrate on telling her that the thing she dislikes (whatever it is) has to be faced, and unfortunately there's no way out of it. But do resolve to find out *why* she dislikes it, and what can be done to put matters to rights.

Inventing an illness

Your child and pain

Any sick child who is in great pain will be under the doctor's supervision, so my remarks in this section apply only to minor pain, whether caused by illness or by the inevitable knocks and bumps that are part and parcel of a child's daily life. Pain isn't a pleasant experience for anyone, but we often don't realize quite how much of it is in the mind. If we're concentrating on something else, the pain is much less bothersome than if we're focusing on it with our full attention. Witness, for example, the knocks that people often take when engaged in sport, and which go unnoticed until after the game is over (not true, of course, for the professional footballer).

Kissing better really does work

So the time-honoured strategy of kissing a child better really does have an effect. The child now pays less attention to her pain, since you have told her that the kiss will put things right, and magically she finds it's gone. Distracting a child in other ways – for example with a favourite toy or story – often works equally well. If she can bear your hand on the painful part, touch also seems to help. A cool hand on a fevered brow doesn't just feel nice, it really does produce results. So does gentle stroking. Whether it's simply that we can convey our deep feelings of sympathy to each other by touching, or whether there's more to it than that (as many practitioners of alternative medicine claim), we don't know. But touching or rubbing a painful place is a natural reaction, and has stood the test of time. It's also suggested sometimes that certain colours have a soothing effect. The important thing again is probably simply belief. If you believe a blue handkerchief held against a painful spot is more likely to take the pain away than a red one, then it probably is.

Visualization is another way of helping, and some children, with their vivid imaginations, are excellent at this. The child is told to visualize white light streaming into her body with every in-breath, and then to visualize the light flowing towards the pain and washing it away with every out-breath. Finally, don't forget the power of simple reassurance. If you're able to tell a child that her cut or bump or whatever causes the pain is nothing much, then she'll forget it far more quickly than if you tell her it's awful. Sympathize with her of course, but let her know that no great damage has been done, and before long everything will once more be right as rain.

The child in hospital

Sickness and pain can sometimes be associated with a stay in hospital. Don't underestimate the potential impact of this stay upon your child. Many grown-ups retain graphic memories of their stays in hospital when children, and speak of the help-lessness they felt. I can't stress too often that children fre-quently feel very powerless, and their negative behaviour can be a result of their attempts to have at least *some* influence over what happens in their lives. This powerlessness is felt particu-larly during a stay in hospital and explains why children of any age find the experience of being in hospital initially a distressing one. Children worry much less about illness than adults, and confidently expect doctors and nurses will make them better. Nevertheless, the strangeness of the hospital environment, and the fact that they're sent there without any say in the matter and have little control over (or understanding of) what happens once they are there, all combine to make the child in hospital feel a pawn in the hands of others.

Of course, doctors and nurses understand this, and do all they can to make the atmosphere of a children's ward infor-mal, relaxed and friendly. In many cases, parents are able to stay with their children, particularly during the more acute phases of illness, and some children claim on discharge that once they settled down they thoroughly enjoyed their stay in the ward, and felt quite special during their time there. Rather more children, however, are reported by their parents to be subdued and tense when they get home from hospital, prone to night fears, tearfulness and dependent behaviour (reluctant to take initiative, to meet strangers, or to be parted from their parents even briefly).

Helping your child while he is in hospital

You can't necessarily make being in hospital a cheerful experience for your child, particularly if he's rather anxious by temperament. But you can help matters by explaining to him about hospital before he goes in, by staying with him as much as possible while he's there, and by seeing to it that he has a supply of exciting games and toys to stop him being bored.

Helping him get back to normal

You can also help by accepting any clinging behaviour once he comes home, easing him out of it gently rather than expecting him to be quickly back to normal. He needs the reassurance of knowing that you're around and that once more *you*, rather than doctors and nurses, are the person in charge of his life. Particularly in children under the age of five, who find it hard fully to understand what hospitals are all about, there's often a troubling feeling of being let down by their parents, of being deserted by them just when they were most needed (a feeling not dissimilar from that which a child may have when he first starts school – see Chapter 7). It takes a little time for trust to be fully re-established, so you will need to give your child extra support. But since life has to go on, and he must eventually get back to normal, don't allow the clinging behaviour to become a habit. The best way to do this is to assure your child that his bad feelings after being in hospital are perfectly normal, and that it's *equally normal for them to wear off*. Children quickly become anxious about being anxious. They hate to see themselves as 'different' from other children, and are fearful that their anxious feelings will persist, marking them off from their friends.

Put your child's fears at rest by telling him that most people feel 'down' after a spell in hospital, but that the feeling soon passes. Tell him the secret is not to take too much notice of it. Before long, his natural good spirits will reassert themselves. Help things along by arranging the odd treat and outing, and by inviting his quieter friends to play with him. Re-establish the comforting, secure routines of home as quickly as possible – the trips to the shops and the library, the leisurely bath-time, the 'something special' for tea, the bedtime story. If he persists in feeling sorry for himself, be gentle but firm and definite. 'Today we're going to . . .' rather than 'Today would you like to . . .?' And once you've made your intentions clear, stick to them.

7

The Years From Five to Eleven

THE YEARS FROM FIVE to eleven, the primary school years, see a big change in your child. From a dependent five-year-old, still bounded by the intimate world of home and still influenced at every point by his parents, your child will develop into an independent eleven-year-old, with views and interests of his own, a life outside the home, his own friends (and an increasing reliance upon their influence and upon that of his teachers), and on the verge of the adolescent growth spurt that in the next three or four years will take him almost into adulthood. But though you see your child growing up and in a sense growing away, the primary school years are a delightful time for parents. You can take pleasure and pride in your child's physical and mental skills; you can share in his new interests; you can watch him becoming more and more of an individual, with many of the attributes and characteristics that he'll carry with him through life; you can enjoy his ability to provide you with mature companionship and competent help around the house. From being a small child he becomes a full member of the family, a partner in what goes on and with the ability to make a full contribution.

PHYSICAL AND PSYCHOLOGICAL DEVELOPMENT

Physical growth

After the rapid growth during the early years of life, and before the adolescent growth spurt at puberty, the years from five to eleven see a steadier rate of development. There's none of the 'shooting up' that characterizes these other two phases of development. Children are growing fast certainly, but they don't quite grow out of their clothes overnight.

Nevertheless, shooting up or not, growth and weight must be carefully monitored during these years. Don't rely just on the routine medical examinations carried out in school. If you have *any* reason for feeling that your child is growing too slowly, or failing to put on weight as he should, consult your doctor immediately, and make sure he understands the extent of your concern. Occasionally, a child shows a deficiency in growth hormones, and the earlier this is diagnosed and treated the more chances there are of nudging his growth rate back to normal. It really is vital that you and your doctor don't delay. Once beyond a certain stage in development, there's little that can be done to help a child with a deficiency of this kind. Sadly, children are still occasionally sentenced to an under-sized future because appropriate action wasn't taken at the right time.

Generally, however, within the limits laid down by their inheritance, most children will grow at a satisfactory rate provided they are given adequate nutrition. The general rules for this nutrition (see Appendix 3) still apply, and in many ways require even more attention, because by the time a child is five he will usually have lost any natural ability to choose foods that are good for him. Artificial flavours and textures and colouring in foods will increasingly override any ability he has to make sensible choices between what he needs and what he doesn't, and your guidance and good sense in such matters become increasingly important, particularly as he's bombarded by television advertising and influenced by his friends into choosing an ever more unhealthy diet.

The importance of diet

Resist the argument that if you give your child a healthy diet he's going to find it 'boring'. There's no shortage of cookery books available these days that tell you how to make appetizing and varied menus from wholesome foods, and once your child has a taste for natural flavours and textures he'll take a poor view of the synthetic nonsense that passes for food in many modern homes. You'll make life much easier for yourself if you refuse to give such food house room. Once you start laying in stores of potato crisps, chocolate bars and convenience meals just for 'emergencies', you'll find that your children will start helping themselves before you've had a proper chance to educate them into correct eating habits.

Obesity Remember that the single most worrying physical growth problem in these years is childhood obesity. Estimates vary, but by even the least rigorous criteria 30 per cent of primary school children are significantly overweight for their age and height. Obesity and incorrect eating habits in childhood are increasingly linked by medical research with potentially fatal diseases in adult life. If you over-indulge your child's taste for sugary, fatty, and over-refined and processed foods in childhood, you could therefore be helping him on his way to ill-health and even early death. Dramatic but true. Some parents say helplessly, as they watch their children filling themselves with junk foods, 'Yes but what can you *do*? You can't just say "no" to them.' The answer is that if you value their lives you can and must. The years from five to eleven are particularly important in this respect because your child increasingly has a mind of his own. Spending more time outside the home, and usually with money in his pocket, he can fall quickly into bad eating habits. But he's unlikely to do so if he has your help. He's old enough now to understand the vital importance of what he eats. Explain to him the advantages of a good diet and the dangers of a bad one. Help him take a pride in his body, and understand that it can't work properly if it's given the wrong fuel. Above all, set him a good example in your own habits. If he sees you nibbling away between meals, eating sweets and chocolates, white bread and fatty sausages and chips he can't be expected to keep off such things himself.

To parents who claim they haven't the will-power to change their own habits, my answer is that if you haven't the will-power to change for your own sake, have the will-power to do it for your children. Your good health matters to them and so does your example. If they think *you* haven't the will-power, they'll find it hard to believe they have either. And the ability to discipline oneself into showing sense and proper organization in one's life are vital qualities in gaining and holding the good opinion of the young.

The growth of intelligence

As pointed out in Chapter 6, intelligence is essentially the ability to see relationships and to use these relationships to solve problems. Given this definition, it's clear that the more opportunities you give your child to see and know and understand how things relate to each other, and the more different experiences you offer her, the better her chances of developing the quality in herself. Some ways in which you can do this are suggested later in this chapter, when we discuss helping your child with her school work.

Here I must emphasize that psychologists don't see intelligence as a fixed characteristic, inherited at conception and largely uninfluenced by the environment. Such a view of intelligence is misguided and harmful, because it leads to the 'If she hasn't got it there you can't put it there' approach. A child at conception inherits a vast potential to behave in all kinds of intelligent and creative ways. True the range of this potential may vary from child to child, but given the right kind of teaching any child without a specific intellectual disability (such as brain damage before or after birth) can cope with amazingly complex activities. We're far too ready to write off children as 'unintelligent'. Some children need more help than their classmates. Some children are readier to experiment and come up with possible solutions than others. But it's a fair bet than no child ever reaches her full potential. There's always more to come if we're prepared to give that bit of extra guidance, or to show that extra patience, or to find the most appropriate teaching method for the child concerned. In any case, a great deal depends upon the extent of a child's belief in herself and upon her readiness to have a go at something without being too afraid of failure or too sensitive to the criticism or opinions of those around her.

Intelligence is not fixed at birth

One of the villains of the piece is the intelligence test itself. Children obtain scores on these tests, expressed as an Intellignece Quotient (IQ), with a score of 100 as average, a score of 90 to 110 showing a child is within the 'normal' range, and anything above 110 or below 90 showing signficantly above or below the average as the case may be. The trouble is that these IQ scores give the idea that intelligence is something definite and fixed (like height and weight) that can be accurately

IQ tests

411

measured. In fact 'intelligence' can't be directly observed at all. You can't show someone your intelligence in the way you can point to your nose. 'Intelligence' is really only a word we use to describe certain kinds of behaviour, in particular the problem-solving behaviour to which I've already drawn attention. To demonstrate this more clearly, imagine a foreigner having to solve the problems of finding his way around London in the height of the rush hour. He doesn't speak English, the streets are unfamiliar, he knows nothing about the underground or buses and taxis, he knows nothing about the currency, he doesn't know where to find a friendly face. He's completely unprepared for the shock of moving from his own culture into our very different one. Now this foreigner may be capable of very intelligent behaviour indeed in his own country. He may be a person of status and substance back home. But drop him out of the blue into London and an onlooker would describe his behaviour as very confused and unintelligent indeed. So where has his 'intelligence' gone? Whatever his IQ happens to be when measured on tests back in his own country, it means very little to him at the moment.

So IQ scores are really only a measure of how a person performs on the problem-solving items in an IQ test. True his or her behaviour on these items may give us a guide to how he'll behave with problems in real life, but we can't read too much into this. The problems used in an IQ test only sample a small range of the problems we meet in daily life. We're all familiar with the stereotype of the absent-minded professor, who is very good at solving problems within his own academic subject but hopeless at handling the simplest challenges in the world outside his study or laboratory. Or with the woman outstanding at languages who confesses herself incapable of learning the workings of her car. Or with the great writer who can hardly add up or the great scientist who is hopeless at putting his feelings into words. These examples show that people can be very proficient at dealing with one kind of problem, but hopeless when it comes to another. Perhaps the prime example is the person who is expert at dealing with problems at work, but quite incapable of solving the problems of how to relate to his family or to live in peace with his neighbours or with himself.

More recently a new kind of test has been devised – the

British Ability Scales – which recognizes these difficulties and which gives children scores on a wide range of different areas of problem-solving without attempting to add all the separate scores together to obtain an IQ. The test recognizes in other words that there are many different ways in which a child can show his ability, and in due course this more enlightened approach will probably do away with the whole idea of an 'IQ'.

So to come back to your role as parent. It's important to give your child wide opportunities to develop his interests and abilities and his capacity to solve problems. Don't build up unrealistic expectations, but at the same time don't get the idea that he's 'limited'. If he isn't doing too well in school, don't assume this means that educationally he's something of a write-off. Find things he *can* do. Spend a little extra time with him over the work he finds difficult at school. Build up his confidence. Show him that learning can be fun. Too often the difference between doing well in school and falling behind is very slender indeed. A missed lesson here. A piece of basic information misunderstood there. An argument with a teacher which leaves a child hurt and rebellious. A few bad marks that unsettle the confidence. All these things and many more, small in themselves, can begin the business of holding a child back. Or perhaps the failure to see any relevance in a particular lesson, or a difficulty in handling the concepts involved, or being laughed at by other children for making a mistake or two. Success and failure are separated by the smallest of margins in so many cases. Think back over your own school career if you want confirmation!

Your role in encouraging the growth of intelligence

Keep in mind that if you want to help your child, you must let him feel that whatever goes wrong outside the home as well as inside, he can come and talk to you about it. If your child feels you're likely to be angry if he reports bad marks in school or that he's had a misunderstanding with a teacher or that he's in trouble of some kind, then he'll do his best to keep these things from you. Telling you about them will only add to his difficulties, because he'll have your criticisms to deal with as well as those of the school. Show him that no matter what happens, he can come and tell you about it. You'll listen to him sympathetically, and you won't leap to pass judgements, on him or on anyone else. This doesn't mean you

He must feel he can always talk to you

413

won't prompt him to see where he's gone wrong and what he must do in the future to put things right, but it does mean you'll always be fair and supportive – and always ready to take his part when needed.

It also means you'll accept that a child's powers of decision-making in his own life are very limited. We tend to feel that if a child this age doesn't learn it's because he *chooses* not to learn, or that if he gets on the wrong side of his teacher it's because he *wants* to be on the wrong side of her. Thus if he chooses to do badly, then he can equally readily choose to do well, and all we have to do is nag him until he does. So the child receives all the blame, and whether he shows it or not ends up blaming himself. Don't fall into this trap. If things aren't going well at school, find out the real reason. Is it because the teacher isn't explaining things properly? Is it because your child is too frightened to go to her for help? Is it because he hasn't grasped some basic concepts and this is holding him back? Is he generally unhappy at school? Is he unhappy at home and carrying this unhappiness with him to school? (See page 448 for starting school.)

Making mistakes is part of learning

Often the root cause of a child's learning difficulties is that he can't ask the teacher for help. Some teachers are themselves to blame for this, either because they adopt a brisk manner which some children find intimidating, or because they weren't helped in their training to see that making mistakes is an essential part of the learning process. They confuse making mistakes with failure. The result of this attitude on the part of teachers is that children soon adopt the habit of hiding their mistakes, instead of asking the teacher to show them where they went wrong. They may resort to cheating, for example, or keep their hands down in self-assessment work when the teacher demands 'Who got that wrong?'. In addition to being intimidated by the teacher, they're only too well aware that their classmates are ever ready to pour scorn on their mistakes.

Perhaps you can't do much to change the teacher's behaviour, but you can reassure your child that he mustn't be ashamed of mistakes; we all make them, and the important thing is to use them as an opportunity for finding out why we went wrong and how we can avoid the same mistakes in future. Show him he doesn't need to hide things from you. Whether it's a matter of reporting poor marks in school or making mistakes within the home he can tell you about them and be confident of a proper hearing. Not only will this be a help in your child's education, it will do much to bring you and him closer together. Our best friends are those we can go to when we're in trouble, and know they're going to help rather than telling us how silly we've been. Too many parents say when they learn their child is in trouble, 'If only he'd told *us* about it earlier on', without stopping to think that the reason he didn't tell was that he knew from experience they'd only have created more problems for him!

The gifted child

Children of very high intelligence are often, semi-officially, referred to as *gifted*. There's no precise definition of giftedness, but usually it's taken to mean the sort of child who may one day be a candidate for a very good first-class honours degree at university. This suggests an IQ in the 140 region or above. But giftedness should also include the highly creative child, who may not reach this level in IQ but who more than makes up for it with her highly inventive and original approach to life.

All children are of course gifted in their own way, and it is perhaps unfortunate that the term is applied in this semi-official way to only about the top 1 per cent. But whether it's used for the top 1 per cent or the top 5 per cent, the concept of giftedness is an important one, because children within this bracket need a high level of stimulation if they are to reach their potential, and equally importantly need the understanding of parents and teachers. Due to their intellectual or creative gifts, these children even at a young age are often not just one jump ahead of their classmates but of the adults in their lives too. They may spot better ways of doing things than those currently employed by their parents or teachers, they may spot adult mistakes, they may be always eager to give their own views and ideas, they may seem critical of others slower than themselves, they may be bored by school work which is too easy for them and doesn't hold their attention.

What is a gifted child?

The stereotype of the misunderstood genius may belong more to fiction than to fact, but it's certainly true that the behaviour of the gifted child may be misconstrued at times by adults and classmates, who may see her as trying to be 'smart', or as refusing to mix or conform. Some gifted children speak of being very frustrated by the attitude of others towards them, and sadly (particularly in the case of girls) may deliberately try to play down their talents in order to make themselves more acceptable.

Having a gifted child is hard work

As I've just said, all children are gifted in their own way. But if your child is extra precocious, accept that having a budding genius in the family is very rewarding but means hard work for all concerned. Whatever you give her to do, she's finished in no time and looking for fresh worlds to conquer. Whenever you settle down in the armchair, she sees this as an excellent opportunity to ply you with all the questions to which her ready mind demands answers (and if you don't know the answers, then why don't you?), or to drag you off to the library or the museum or to hunt for fossils or to tramp through damp woods looking for insects and other specimens. Her bedroom becomes crammed with the results of her interests and hobbies. Every usable object in the house is likely to be pressed into service by her in her desire to build things, or set up experiments, or see how things are put together. Maddening and captivating by turns, she can't understand why other people don't see the world as she does, and don't share her enthusiasm for taking it to bits and re-assembling it in a more satisfactory way.

Since gifted people are only really happy when they're allowed to make full use of their gifts, it pays everyone in the long run to give the gifted child the scope she needs. And it pays adults to realize (not easy for some parents or for some teachers either!) that at times a gifted child *is* going to be quicker at solving things, or know more about things, or have more mature interests or more rewarding enthusiasms, than they do themselves. If you take a very active, energetic dog for a run you accept you're going to have to move a lot more quickly than usual, and if you have a very bright child you have to accept you're going to have to run hard to keep up with her. It's no good expecting the dog or the child to have to slow down to your pace all the time, and still get the exercise they need.

The gifted child at school

Keeping up with a gifted child means doing with her all the things we've discussed so far and will discuss later in this chapter by way of bringing out the best in your child, only

416

doing them more often and at greater depth. It also means watching her progress at school to make sure she's having the best brought out in her there too. It's all too easy for a busy teacher to develop a personality clash with a gifted child. He sees her as wanting to score off him all the time, she sees him as dull and limited. Both teacher and child have to be prompted to respect each other and to understand each other's difficulties. If you feel your child is under-performing, ask to have her assessed by the educational psychologist, so that there will be an IQ (or similar) score to back up your impression that she's gifted. Once you're sure she is, talk over with the school what can best be done to help her. The school should now see to it that she's given the stimulation (and the scope for initiative) that she needs, and should help you in contacting people outside school who can give her further support.

Local organizations and other activities

If you live in a city or large town, there may be a local group to help gifted children. Or there may be someone at the nearest university who takes a special interest in such children. Make enquiries at the central library and at the education department of the university (or polytechnic or college or institute of higher education), enrol your child in appropriate bookclubs, ask at your travel agent for details of holiday opportunities for gifted children, make a list of local scientific or historical or literary (or similar) societies which she might like to join, write to any organization in which she's interested to see if they will allow her to visit. If there isn't anyone locally interested in gifted children, start your own organization. Put an advertisement in the local paper or in the central library asking any parents interested in giftedness to contact you. Write to the National Children's Bureau (see Appendix 9) for the addresses of any national organizations that are involved with gifted children or with research into giftedness, and see if any of them can help you with local initiatives. Don't let time pass before you do anything. The earlier your child receives the extra stimulation she needs (just as with all children with special needs) the better.

Don't expect too much of your child

But some words of warning. Don't expect too much of your child just because he appears to be gifted. I've seen too many cases of very bright children who were pushed too hard too soon, or had their brilliant careers mapped out for them for the next fifty years by ambitious parents even before they'd left primary school. Such children may fail to fulfil their potential not because they haven't the ability, but because they were never given a chance to make any of their own decisions, to decide for themselves where their main interests lay, to go when necessary at their own pace. Their brains all too early became public property; geared only to expect success, they and their parents and teachers couldn't handle the inevitable set-backs when they came along, and what started out bright with promise ended in bitterness and disappointment.

Don't let him think too much of himself Just as important, don't let your gifted child come to think of himself as something extra special, and be impatient with those different from himself. Gifted children can become arrogantly self-centred, not because that's the natural way of things, but because they have had it instilled into them that they are a cut above the rest, and have never been helped to see that each person is different, and each person is equally important in his or her own way. Gifted children may need extra help in appreciating others (in this area they are much less 'gifted' than children who have had to contend with handicap and difficulty, and who early develop intense sensitivity and compassion towards their fellows), and in accepting that their own gifts are not of their own making, and must be seen as a trust to be used with responsibility and humility.

Given this help, gifted children are not only much more potential help to the community, they also avoid one of the drawbacks of giftedness, difficulty in making friends. Through their impatience and lack of understanding for others, many gifted children become all too easily isolated from their peers, caught in a spiral of mutual hostility and derision. But if we look at the lives of many of the most successful gifted people of our time, the lives of an Einstein or a Roosevelt or a Churchill, we find that they were at home with all types of people, able to relate with warmth and understanding to people with no education as readily as to statesmen and Nobel Prize-winners. The secret lies in the ability to see others as human beings first, and as anything else very much second.

Emotionally he's still a child Finally, remember that although a gifted child may be very advanced intellectually, emotionally he's still a child. He's just as subject to emotional upsets as other children, and needs just as much help in accepting his emotions and in accepting himself as a person as other children do. Don't expect that because he's able to do university level mathematics at the age of ten he has the emotions of a twenty-year-old. Or that because he's reading and enjoying the Shakespeare sonnets or playing the solo part in Mozart's Clarinet Concerto he knows all about love and suffering and joy. Emotional maturity doesn't correlate with intellectual or creative maturity. Your ten-year-old child still only has the life experience of a ten-year-old. Give him time. And remember that like any other child with special needs, he's a child first and a gifted one second. He needs the 'ordinary' experiences of childhood as well as the 'special' ones. Physical activity, the chance to romp around and make a noise, to play games, to swim and ride his bicycle, to take part in fantasy games and creative pursuits, to go for picnics and walks and seaside holidays.

Parents of gifted children sometimes say, 'But he's never shown any interest in those things.' I'm not so sure. Often he retreats into his books because he's got so used to being brighter than everyone else that he can't adjust to the fact that on the football field he's only average or below, or that there are other children who are stronger or more agile or who can run faster or who can express themselves more eloquently and spontaneously or swim better or look more fetching in swimsuits. Don't push a child into physical or any other leisure activities that he clearly dislikes, but make it clear to him at a very young age that he doesn't have (and mustn't expect) to be better than others all the time. Often it's the fun of taking part that's all that matters. And other children have their rights as well. They too want to be best at times. He can't expect to have all the limelight to himself!

Don't neglect physical activities

Personality development

If we think of personality development as involving amongst other things the learning of certain lessons, then in the years five to eleven the child has primarily to learn the lessons of initiative and competence. If her development went smoothly in the pre-school years, she will have learnt the lessons first of trust and then of selfhood. Now, building on these, she needs to learn how to take intiative and develop the skills to cope confidently with the challenges presented by her environment.

Initiative

If we take initiative first, we can see this is in part bound up with what I said in the last section about making mistakes. If a child is made to feel that she must always get things right first go, she'll become over-cautious, unwilling ever to take the independent and resourceful action so important if she's to develop creativity and the personal qualities necessary for her future. It's no good trying to teach your child initiative simply by telling her about it. She needs opportunities to *use* initiative in daily life. When you're doing jobs together, let her be a full partner and even take the lead wherever possible. If friends visit, let her speak up for herself instead of trying to prompt her to say what *you* want her to say. When she has pocket money, encourage her in thrift and wise spending but leave some of the decisions on how she spends it to her. Allow her to make decisions on how to arrange her room, and to have her fair say in what goes on in the rest of the house too.

Respect your child's need for privacy and independence

Respect the need for privacy that comes with the growth of initiative. From about age six onwards, most children need and want the chance to have some of their life to themselves, to tuck themselves happily away on their own from time to time and enjoy their own company and their own thoughts. This means that if your child can have a room to herself, somewhere she can go when she wants to enjoy her own company, so much the better. But if she has to share with a sibling, arrange it so that each child has a part of the room that is his or hers. Work it out with the children so that they each have a say in how the room is to be 'divided', and so that they each feel properly done by. If necessary, help them draw up a set of rules which ensure there isn't too much trespass on to each other's space. These rules should also cover noise levels (tape recorders, radios) and lighting (what time the lights go off, what time the curtains are drawn back in the mornings). Of course, your children will delight in goading each other from time to time by breaking the rules, but at least when you're called in to arbitrate you'll have something definite to go on. And children who do have an agreed set of rules produce far less conflict than children who live in a haphazard free-for-all.

So whether she has a room to herself or not, ensure that your child's growing need for independence and privacy is respected. Respect it too in the way in which the room is arranged and decorated. This issue comes to a particular head in adolescence, and is returned to in Chapter 8, but from age six and even younger your child should be given some responsibility for ordering her own immediate environment. This means allowing her to rearrange the furniture in her room (within reason; you don't want the bed half-way out of the window), and to have some say in what goes on the walls and in the choice of colour schemes. A strong proviso, however, is that she has to live with her choice. There can be no instant redecorating if she finds she's made a mistake. Independence carries with it certain consequences, and she must be early helped to see what these are and to recognize the need for forethought and planning which they involve.

Naturally granting your child sensible opportunities to exercise her growing initiative and independence will lead to problems sometimes. You and she won't always see eye to eye. She won't always present herself to the outside world as the docile, malleable little character other people often expect. But even when you have to overrule her, show her that you respect her right to her views and opinions. Show her that even when you have to curb her initiative you are ready to listen to her ideas and help her to see why this time they're impractical. Simple remarks like 'Yes I can see your point, but just think what would happen if . . .' or 'That's a good idea and maybe we can have a go at that next time' or 'Yes I can see why you said that but we need to think how Aunt Ada felt!' all help to reassure your child that you welcome her initiative and your main concern is to see she uses it wisely.

Overruling your child without being crushing

This means giving some thought to how you respond to your child. Some small children will go in for acts which are very kindly meant but which may look inappropriate in themselves. For example a child may try to press a 10p coin on an adult visitor when she hears it's his birthday, or try to give an expensive toy to another child or want to take a mug to school because she saw her teacher break hers yesterday. Embarrassed we tell her the visitor doesn't want her 10p.

Outraged we tell her how dare she give away a toy on which we've spent so much money. Unsure of ourselves we tell her her teacher would probably much prefer to buy the replacement mug herself. In each case, our child feels that her kindness and initiative have been snubbed. Not surprisingly, she's unlikely to be so ready with them next time.

The rule is always to praise the child's initiative (and kindness) first, regardless of whether we then have gently to talk her out of her idea. Words like 'That's a lovely idea' or 'I wish I'd thought of that' are vital. Small children are less concerned over whether their gift is accepted than with the reactions of people to the act of giving. A child will soon forget that the visitor didn't actually take her 10p, but she'll remember that he greeted the gift with delight and then said, 'But you know, I'd get far more fun out of it if I thought *you* were going to spend it on something exciting for yourself, than if I went and spent it on the boring old things grown-ups buy!'. Such a response is much better for a child than laughing or reacting with embarrassment.

Competence

Equal in importance to the development of initiative is the development of competence. Help your child develop competence by giving him both help and support in his general learning tasks and help with specific skills such as the three Rs (see later in this chapter). Help with his general knowledge too, so that he always has a ready answer when his teacher goes on to something new in class. This is done by taking him out and about and seeing that he has the right sort of reference material available in the house. Answering his questions and putting appropriate questions to him to stimulate his thinking are also invaluable, as is your *own* level of general knowledge. If you have wide and relevant interests, then he'll learn a great deal by being around you, and hearing what you say and watching what you do.

Encourage your child to think positively about himself

Encouragement is also essential to the development of competence. No child should be prompted to build up unrealistic expectations about his own abilities, but neither should he be left with the constant feeling that he can't do the things that other children can. Encourage him to think positively about himself. Draw attention to his successes rather than his failures. Show him you have confidence in him, and that there are always ways of tackling difficulties. Impress upon him that motivation and determination are often much more important than a natural bent for whatever it is he's trying to master. Don't become discouraged or allow him to become discouraged simply because he can't be perfect. Show him that our level of achievement matters less than the effort we put into that achievement and the fun and interest we get out of it. Above all help him see that he's a unique human being in his own right, and that competence comes in great measure from a recognition of this uniqueness and from the courage to be oneself.

I've heard children complain bitterly that no matter what they attempt, there's always someone who can do it better than they can. My answer is 'That's life. But there's one thing you're better at than anyone else, and that's being who *you* are. Don't keep comparing yourself with everyone else. They've all got different lives and have had different opportunities. Work at being yourself, at getting to know who you are, at recognizing the things you like and dislike, the things you can handle and the things you can't and the reasons for this, the things you want to do with your life and the things you feel are important.' The aim is to help children, once they start school and are faced with possible comparisons between themselves and others of their age, to realize that the only person who can live your life is *you*. You're the person inside your skin. You're the person who experiences your emotions, who looks out at the world through your eyes and listens through your ears. Get to know who you are and work with and feel good about that person, recognizing his strengths and weaknesses and making use of the former and seeking to remedy the latter.

No child is too young to start learning this lesson, and once he gets to school it becomes urgent. Psychologists work with people of all ages who confess that though often outwardly successful, whether at school or in adult life, they can't feel they have any real worth. They don't see themselves as valid human beings. All too often these negative feelings date back to early childhood and the experience that whatever they did they were never able to satisfy their parents or teachers, or perform as well as their siblings or friends. Pushed on by the

The main thing is to feel good about the person you are

423

need for ever more achievement, they came to judge themselves as wanting, and early on in life lost the opportunity of having the harmonious childhood that would enable them to develop into happy and harmonious adults.

By contrast there are people who, although in no sense high-flyers, are at home in their minds and bodies. They don't try to be anything they're not. They don't pretend. They're not driven by a constant indiscriminate desire to compete. They're simply being who they are. And because they aren't worried or over-preoccupied by themselves, they have time and energy to spend on others. They reach out to the environment, naturally and openly. They can afford to be unselfish, because they aren't constantly trying to buttress themselves against the world. These are the people who have learnt the true lesson of competence, namely that real competence means success at being a human being, not at desperately trying to outshine everyone else. And in and through this competence, they have gained the confidence to act independently and to make their own judgements. Their freedom from over-dependence on what others think of them allows them the freedom to find out who they really are.

Self-acceptance
People like this usually come from homes where as children they were prized and valued as people. Through learning trust and selfhood, and later on initiative and competence, they've learnt the vital overall lesson of personality development, namely *self-acceptance* (or self-esteem) – that is the ability to accept and value oneself. Not with complacency or conceit. Not as better or worse than the next person, but simply as oneself, with all the uniqueness we discussed in the last section.

Because of its vital importance to personality development and to the whole issue of psychological health, the subject of self-acceptance has been fully researched by psychologists. From the point of view of the parent, the most important findings have to do firstly with the qualities which children with high levels of self-acceptance seem to show, and secondly with the factors within the home which seem to help produce these levels. Let's take these two sets of findings in turn.

The high self-acceptance child tends to be confident and

friendly. She mixes well, she shows independence and initia- **High and low**
tive, she participates, she isn't troubled with shyness, she **self-acceptance**
takes criticisms without being unduly wounded, she isn't over- **children**
preoccupied with the opinions of others, she has a realistic
view of her own abilities and sets herself realistic goals with a
good chance of achieving them. By contrast the low self-
acceptance child tends to be fearful and often rather sad and
isolated. She worries deeply over failure and criticism, she's
anxious for approval and over-conforms, she's prone to shyness and participates in things often reluctantly and less for
the fun of it than to please others. She is a poor judge of her
own abilities and underestimates or, occasionally, wildly over-
estimates them. As a result she sets herself unrealistic standards, and fails to do herself justice. Her fear of failure and of
the damage it does to her already fragile self-esteem means
that she makes excuses for herself, often in advance of the
event, rather than face the prospect of finding she isn't good
at something. And when she does fail, unlike the high self-
acceptance child who is usually prepared to have another go,
she prefers to leave it at that and go away and brood over her
inadequacies.

Of course, not all children fall into one or other of these
extremes. Many have levels of self-acceptance somewhere
between the two, and many will fluctuate depending upon
circumstances, thinking well of themselves when working at
something they know they can do, and less well when faced
with uncertainties. Girls generally, because of the unfair social
conditioning which puts them into positions of inferiority,
have lower levels of self-acceptance than boys. And interestingly and perhaps unexpectedly, many children who have
extreme behaviour problems (including violent and delinquent
behaviour) have very low levels of self-acceptance, caring little
for themselves and using tough and anti-social behaviour as a
way of working off their hostility towards a society that fails
to value them or help them value themselves.

Which brings me to one of the most important rules in
understanding the behaviour of both children and adults.
Namely that we mustn't take behaviour always at its face
value. Because somebody acts aggressively doesn't necessarily
mean he's an aggressive personality. His aggression may be a
way of hiding his own inadequacy, hitting out at others to

hide or protect his low feelings of self-worth. Similarly a person who seems to have a conceited opinion of himself may often be hiding basic insecurities. He shows off as a way of trying to convince others and himself that he really is a big shot. The person with genuine self-acceptance doesn't need to go in for anything so foolish. He knows his own worth, and that it isn't based upon impressing all and sundry. He knows there are things he can do and things he can't do, and he's realistic enough to live with this knowledge. He isn't over-elated by his successes and he isn't devastated by his failures because he knows that neither of these is the true measure of himself. He accepts himself with the same good sense we all accept some days it'll be sunny and other days it'll rain. That's how life is, and the important thing is to live it, not to spend all our time worrying about success or agonizing over failure.

But don't let me give the impression that all people with low levels of self-acceptance compensate by anti-social behaviour or big-headedness. Many of them go through life trying to live up to some hopeless idealized picture of themselves, or feeling guilty and wretched because they imagine they're letting everyone down. A sad picture. And one which leads us to ask crucially what the factors are within a home that affect a child's level of self-acceptance.

Factors in the home that encourage self-acceptance The most obvious of these is that high self-acceptance children have the unconditional love of their parents. They're assured, by word and deed, that they're far too important ever to have this love withdrawn. Parental love in such homes in not negotiable. Almost as obvious is the fact that high self-acceptance children are helped to accept the existence of their emotions, in the way stressed very strongly in Chapter 6.

Next, they come from homes where there is plenty of discussion about family decisions, and where their views are invited and listened to. Their parents know the names of their playmates and friends, know their likes and dislikes, and share experiences with them. Their parents listen to what they have to say about school and about their lives outside the home. While respecting their privacy, their parents know them intimately and well, and show in every way that they matter as people, thus helping them to matter to themselves.

Since inconsistency makes a child insecure, the high self-acceptance child comes from a home where standards are clear, reasonable, and fully explained and understood. He knows where he stands with his parents, and knows that his world is a predictable one which allows him to identify what is acceptable behaviour and what is not. Interestingly, high self-acceptance children praise their parents' *fairness* – fairness being one of the things that a child (living as he does very much under the control of others) prizes most in adults, whether parents or teachers.

High self-acceptance children also come from homes where they aren't *invalidated* as people. A child is invalidated if the adults in his life constantly contradict him when he genuinely tries to put his own feelings and likes and dislikes into words. 'I'm afraid of the dark,' says the child. 'Don't be silly of course you're not,' snaps a parent. 'Do you like school?' asks a visitor. 'No,' answers the child – 'Yes you do', chimes in the parent. 'I like collecting insects,' the child tells a neighbour. 'Don't talk such nonsense,' butts in the parent, 'you don't like such nasty creepy things.' 'I'm sorry for that poor old man,' says the child. 'Then you're stupid,' says the parent, 'it's his own fault he's poor.' Treatment of this kind leaves the child feeling confused, and not knowing in the end what he *does* feel or what he *does* like. If people keep telling him he doesn't feel what he thinks he feels, or that only foolish people feel that way, he's left with not only a very muddled picture of himself but the conviction that he has no right to determine his own feelings and his own likes and dislikes anyway. This doesn't help him to get to know himself and accept and develop confidence in the person he really is.

Children must not be invalidated as people

Crucially, high self-acceptance children come from homes in which there is usually plenty of physical affection. Physical affection not only shows you're loved, it shows that *physically* you're nice to be near. You may not be the most beautiful or the most handsome person in the world, but no matter. If someone gives you a big hug, they're showing you you're okay, and this helps a child accept how he looks. Children can live with and adjust to even the most daunting physical disabilities provided they're given the assurance that other people accept how they are. And for most children, spared such disabilities, what's a lop-sided grin or big ears or freckles if it's clear from the start that your parents love you that way?

Importance of physical affection

Research with children shows that self-acceptance doesn't necessarily go with brains or good looks or plentiful pocket money. It goes with a home where the child is allowed to *see* he's loved, a home where the child is made to feel significant, where he's made to feel a full member of the family and not a rather messy little person who people would prefer kept quiet and out of the way. If a child is to develop his abilities and get on well with himself, he needs a home of this kind. He sees himself very much through the eyes of his parents. If it's clear they think he matters and that they feel the home and everything that goes with it is there for him as well as for them, then he'll matter to himself. He probably isn't going to set the world alight. He may never make a fortune or marry royalty. But he'll make himself and other people happy, and in the end put more into the world than he takes out. Let him know and respect himself, and he'll be set on the way to a psychologically healthy and productive life.

Techniques that help self-esteem
In addition to these vital principles, there are a number of techniques, which, though small in themselves, pay big dividends in helping a child develop confidence in herself. Don't try to teach them as formal techniques, but slip them in as and when appropriate.

- Encourage your child to use positive language about herself, not negative. 'I'm improving at this', not 'I'm no good at this'.
- Encourage her to use language that shows she's responsible for her own actions, not at the mercy of them. 'I won't do my homework', not 'I can't do my homework'. 'I won't make friends', not 'I can't make friends'. Alternatively 'I choose not to . . . (do homework, make friends, etc.)'. Once the situation is seen in proper perspective in this way, it can be tackled on its own merits.
- Prompt her to use the first person when she talks about herself, not 'one' or 'we'. This is a problem that usually surfaces in the teens rather than now, but by de-personalizing ourselves through language we duck responsibility for ourselves as individuals.
- Make a game of it when she uses the verb 'to be' deprecatingly about herself. For example she says 'I'm hopeless', you reply 'No you're not, you're Ann'. She

says 'All right, Ann is hopeless', you reply 'No she's not, Ann is Ann'. This may seem frivolous, but the verb 'to be' is a very powerful verb. Once I say '*I am* bored' or '*I am* hopeless' or '*I am* depressed', I am equating myself (and therefore identifying) with these conditions, and soon they become part of the way in which I see myself. In the final analysis, '*I am me*', and nothing else.

- Encourage her to change 'but' into 'and' if she's talking negatively about herself. Thus 'I'd like to be good at football like Tom, *but* I'm not' becomes 'I'd like to be good at football like Tom, *and* I'm not'. 'But' divides off the second half of the sentence from the first, suggesting that Tom's ability to play football and my own are two separate things, and are never going to be the same. 'And' includes both parts of the sentence together; Tom's ability and my ability are the same sort of thing, so one day mine may be as good as his.

- Prompt her to look people in the face when she talks. Not just as a sign of respect to them but as a sign of respect to herself. She's every bit as good as the next person, and has no need to look at the ground while she's talking to them.

- Help her use the power of suggestion. It sounds odd that repeating to yourself from time to time that you *can* do something, or that you're *getting better* at something, helps produce improvement, but it does. The unconscious mind gets the message (rather as we plant suggestions in the unconscious when we use hypnosis), and enables us to tackle life in a more purposeful and confident way.

- Let her write out these positive suggestions, colouring and decorating them in any way she likes, and put them on the bedroom wall. Seeing the suggestion 'I can do mathematics' attractively presented on the wall several times a day again helps get the message into her unconscious.

- Encourage her to set herself realistic goals. Goals where the chance of success outweighs that of failure, while at the same time reflecting her true potential. In this way she learns to associate herself with success rather than failure.

Prudery and exhibitionism

With the growing need for independence and privacy that develops from age six onwards, some children develop a growing shyness about their own bodies. However natural you are about such matters in the home, children learn prudery from their friends, and from around age six or seven may start to feel there is something 'naughty' about even their parents seeing them undressed. While of course children must be helped to see that nudity in front of strangers can be unwise, at the same time so is excessive prudery. A child should be able to accept the human body as something natural and beautiful, not as something dirty and sinful.

So how do you steer the correct dividing line? The important thing is not to make a major issue out of it, one way or the other. If your child starts covering himself up unnecessarily, tell him, 'Bodies are nice things; there's no need to cover yourself up all the time in the home.' On the other hand, if he's nude too readily when there are strangers in the house, tell him, 'Some people aren't used to seeing others without clothes on; so better not to walk around naked when there are strangers about.' (The more serious question of protecting your child from possible sexual molestation is dealt with in Chapter 6.)

If your child, in spite of everything, does become rather prudish, leave him to it. After all it's his body, and if he does feel excessively modest about it, then that is his right. But in most cases it's only a phase, and he'll soon come to have a more healthy attitude again. It's very rare for a child who has been brought up with a sensible approach towards his own and other people's bodies to grow up particularly embarrassed by such matters.

It's also rare for him to grow up too much of an exhibitionist. Most children go through an exhibitionist stage sometime from the third or fourth year onwards, when they rather enjoy showing their bodies or their underwear to anyone who happens to drop by. This is part of their natural discovery of their own bodies, and of the effect these bodies have on others. But the stage is much more likely to persist (or to re-emerge later) if they get the impression that exhibitionism can 'shock' their elders. At a loss to know why it should shock, they nevertheless feel enormously pleased at the reactions their bodies produce in grown-ups, and the consternation and attention which result. In some children, there is also a deep, illicit thrill at the thought that they are being in some way 'naughty'. Encouraging the child on the one hand, or punishing him on the other, only add to his feeling that there is something extra special about his behaviour. Encouragement prolongs this behaviour, punishment represses it and produces the worst kind of prudery (while at the same time storing up trouble for the future, as the child hasn't been allowed to come to terms with the interest in his own body which lies behind all this). The correct response to exhibitionism is 'Yes very interesting dear, now cover yourself up so that we can go out to the shops' (or whatever).

Moral development

The years from five to eleven are important ones for your child's moral development. During these years she develops a much clearer picture of what is meant by right and wrong. Up to now, the 'right' things are what you tell her to do, and the 'wrong' things are those which you forbid. But from age five onwards and the start of compulsory schooling, her horizons begin to widen and she sees that different people have different ideas on right and wrong. As her powers of thinking develop, she's also able to ponder more over the things she's asked to do, and to start judging others more objectively. Hitherto she's been angry with adults at times for stopping her from doing as she wanted, but she hasn't questioned their *right* to tell her what to do, or that however much fuss she makes over something her parents do ultimately know best.

Now all this begins to change, and we see the start of a process which will culminate at adolescence. A process in which a child comes increasingly to form her own opinions and to take her own personal view of the world. She's still very much tied up in what psychologists call the 'good boy/ girl syndrome' – that is she gears many of her actions towards gaining adult praise, and still thinks of herself as 'good' mainly when her parents or teacher tell her she is. But she is beginning to see that she has a mind of her own, and is gaining the independence to question the actions of others.

431

The challenge of primary school

(So morally the years five to eleven see a big change in children. Building upon the experiences of the first five years of life, the primary school child now has to resolve all sorts of new challenges. At home she's been taught to think of others and that considerate behaviour brings results. She's also been taught that no one is going to be allowed to be inconsiderate towards her either. She's been taught that she has certain rights along with everyone else, that those rights are going to be respected, and that when she feels unhappy about anything she has a sympathetic listener in you.

Now suddenly she's brought up against quite different moral codes. Her classmates may not show her the consideration she shows to them. Her teacher may not listen when she feels she's been hard done by. She may see actions going on that she knows to be wrong, and people getting away with them. Throughout her years in the primary school she'll come into conflict with sets of values that are alien to her own, and will often be tempted to adopt them herself. She'll hear language no one would dream of using at home, and she'll be introduced to early sexual experiences, if only through giggling talk and the half-innocent, half-knowing games that children play.

You'll naturally be concerned by all this. You don't want to see your child being hurt or led astray. But we can't always protect our children from the outside world. They have to learn that life will face them with decisions and choices, and that there's a great deal of unfairness around which they must learn to cope with. Provided they have a secure, happy base within the home, provided that they know their parents will listen and give support, then children will weather these stormy waters and emerge competent mariners.)

What if she comes home using bad language?

But what do you *do* when your child comes home using bad language, or when she tells you of some rather dubious activity in which she's been involved? Sometimes she'll announce these things to you guiltily, but at others with a proud innocence, offering them as evidence that she can keep up with the other children. If you react with shock or anger, you *may* intimidate her from similar escapades in the future. *Or* you may ensure that from now on she'll begin keeping things from you. The right response is to listen to what she

432

has to say, and then help her carefully to think through what she's been up to and whether it was the right way to behave.

Suppose she's just come out with some choice little expletive or other. Ask her matter-of-factly where she's heard it. When she tells you, enquire what's the point of the word. Does it add to what she wants to say? Isn't there a more accurate word she can use? Explain that swear words are a pretty poor way of saying what we mean. The English language is extraordinarily rich in words which convey exactly what we want to say. To go in for wearisome repetition of a few four-letter words is a very impoverished way of talking and thinking. Be realistic of course. Have a joke about it and admit that nearly everyone might use these words if they crack their heads against something or smack their thumb with a hammer. That's one way (though not necessarily the best way) of relieving your feelings. But it's very different from using swear words out of habit, just because the mind is too lazy to think up more appropriate alternatives.

If a child blasphemes rather than swears, your response is going to depend upon your own religious convictions. But here again anger and shock don't help. My own preference is for telling a child seriously to call upon God or Christ when she needs help, and not at other times. Even if you have no religious beliefs, it's hardly right to allow a child to use sacred names in a way that's likely to upset others, and in any case it's another example of the simple misuse of language.

If your child has been involved in a prank of some kind, or an activity of which you disapprove, hear her out and don't immediately deflate her. She's telling you about something that to her was innocent fun; she enjoyed it and wants to share her enjoyment with you. If you give her a prompt lecture on how thoughtless or foolish she's been, you give her the idea she either has to become a killjoy or make sure you don't find out what she gets up to in future. Listen to her, then agree that the events she's just described gave everyone a good laugh. But then prompt her to see that although she meant no harm, what must it have been like for the victim of the prank? Or, if there was no obvious victim, what would it be like if everyone went around behaving in a similar way? In each case, you're steering a careful line between on the one hand making her feel wretched over something that was

What if she gets involved in activities you disapprove of?

433

harmlessly meant and on the other appearing to condone her actions.

Why not just tell her what to do? If drawing such a line seems a difficult task, teaching a child a mature, responsible moral sense *is* difficult. Some parents say surely it's better simply to tell a child what to do, and to threaten her with dire consequences if she doesn't do it? But trying to frighten a child into being good rarely works. In many cases, as I've already said, she'll simply make sure you don't find her out in future. In other cases, if not now then at adolescence, she'll rebel against you and go her own way. And in other cases, if she's rather timid by temperament, she'll go through life fearful of thinking for herself and making her own moral decisions.

In moral development, your aim is to help your child see that care and concern for others, unselfishness, courage in resisting temptations, are right because they help people live together in peace and harmony, and not just because you tell her they're right. The world holds far more moral uncertainties and complexities than it did even a few decades ago, and you want your child to be able to recognize the real issues involved in these complexities, and be able to take sensible and courageous decisions and stick to them even in the face of the temptation to take the easy way out. She won't always have you to turn to. So teach her ways of thinking deeply and carefully about issues, of approaching life with humanity and compassion, of understanding the feelings of others.

Children's relationships with others

Relationships with friends

Your child must choose her own friends At this age children's friendships tend to be short-lived affairs, often much to our disappointment as parents. Your child brings home someone with whom she gets on famously and to whom you take immediately, and you're nonplussed when after a few appearances she disappears from the scene. There's no point in trying too hard to encourage particular friendships though. Your child has to learn how to make her own choices. Give her the opportunities she needs for friendships to flourish, then leave the details to her. In very young children, often these friendships involve members of the opposite sex. Before the age of seven or eight, children haven't been influenced by the repressive social attitudes that claim there's something 'odd' about boys who play with girls and girls who play with boys. Polarization into mutually exclusive sex-based groupings takes place in the later primary school years. Don't encourage it. The more children mix with the opposite sex, on sensible friendly terms, the better for their sexual adjustment in later years. People who are shy with members of the opposite sex almost invariably had little contact with them as children, and run the risk of either steering clear of them for good or of becoming infatuated by the first real acquaintance they make amongst the mysterious beings concerned (see Chapter 8).

In the wider context, and particularly when your child goes to secondary school, you can expect her to make lasting friendships usually only amongst those children with whom she has interests and personal qualities in common. Most children choose their friends from those who live nearby. This makes sense. Not only do they see more of these friends, they also often share a common environment and have parents who belong to similar occupational groups. Thus they're more likely to share the things that bring people together. By deciding where to live, and the interests and standards you want to encourage in your child, you are therefore playing an important part in helping decide on her friends. A far more effective part in fact than any deliberate attempts you may make in this direction.

Parents are sometimes anxious because their child chooses her friends consistently from amongst those in a different age group from herself. Let's take the question of older friends first. This is often a sign that a child is rather forward for her age. She hasn't much in common with her contemporaries, and prefers the stimulus of older children. But there is a problem here. Older children may take advantage of her innocence and lead her into mischief. And as older children can set useful examples through their greater skills, there is the risk that these frequent reminders to a child of her own more limited capabilities may make her feel inferior. An inferiority complex in a child stems from the realization that others can do things or expect her to do things that are beyond her scope. Thus even a clever child can develop an inferiority complex in the wrong circumstances. The younger or youngest

The child who chooses older friends

435

child in a very bright family is often at risk (as is any member of the family who is consistently outshone by the others), and the same applies to the child who plays always with older friends.

The child who chooses younger friends The child who chooses younger friends is a different matter. Sometimes this is a way of escaping from an inferiority complex. For one reason or other she finds it difficult to keep up with her own age group, and compensates by choosing younger friends. The difficulty now is that the child may be denied opportunities to develop behaviour more appropriate to her age, which distances her even further from her contemporaries and gives her less and less chance to catch up.

Once again, you can't choose your child's friends for her. But you can compensate her for the problems that may arise. If her friends are older, watch to see they don't involve her in exploits for which she isn't ready. And through your own relationship with her, make sure she's able to take a sensible view of her own abilities. If her friends are younger, provide her with the wider interests and the general stimulation they can't offer her. Help her avoid the trap of seeing herself as younger than her years. Make sure the toys, books and pastimes offered to her, while not beyond her competence, properly represent her age group. And give her the responsibilities and rights suitable to a child of her chronological age.

When your child brings his friends home If you welcome your child's friends into the house and show an interest in them, this will help him get on well with them. If you have to curb their behaviour, remember that a child who misbehaves in your home is probably only doing the things that are allowed by his own parents (the problem of genuinely unsuitable friends is returned to later). Naturally you won't accept bad behaviour in your home, but if you scold him too severely this sets up a conflict in his mind between his own home and yours, and comes between the relationship he has with your child. Avoid statements like 'I don't care what you do in your own home you're not going to do that here' or 'I can't understand your mother if she lets you get away with that' or 'I'm not having you bringing your bad habits into *my* home'. Instead, explain to him the behaviour you want from him, and give him the reason for it. 'If you make that kind of noise in the house I can't get on with my work' or 'That looks like a good game but it belongs in the

garden' or 'That isn't the way to speak to me if you want me
to be your friend'.

In addition to showing consideration to his friends, show **Don't show**
consideration to your child when he's with them. Often you'll **him up in front**
find that, though sensible enough when he's on his own, he **of his friends**
becomes irresponsible and silly when he's with them. There's
a strong temptation to let your child know in front of his
companions how annoyed you are with him for playing the
fool. But his behaviour, irritating as it is, represents the socially
variable behaviour to which we're all subject. Even we staid
adults tend to let down our hair when we're with certain of
our friends. We may not quite match the wilder excesses of
our children, but the principle is very much the same.

Seen in this light, a child's behaviour becomes less surprising. It doesn't mean you have to put up with it, but it does
make tolerance that bit easier! It also makes you less likely to
blame your child's *friends* for the unseemly goings-on. After
all, he's probably having the same sort of effect upon them, as
a word or two with their parents would reveal.

Whatever the context though, avoid showing your child up
in front of his friends. This rule should go through childhood
and into adult life. Making your child look small in front of his
friends delivers a blow to his esteem in their and his eyes
which takes a long time to heal. If you have to tell him off, do
it in a way which protects the good opinion his friends have
of him. 'Didn't we agree it would be a good idea not to do
that?' is much better than 'I've told you before not to do
anything so stupid'. 'I'm not sure that will hold your weight'
is much better than 'Get off there at once you idiot'. 'You
know that's not the right way to ask for something' is similarly
better than 'You make me so cross when you ask in that silly
way'.

If there's need to say more, ask your child to come out of
the room for a moment. Ask him pleasantly, so his friends
won't suspect he's in trouble, and don't send him back looking
crestfallen. Explain to him that you know he gets excited when
he has friends in, and that you don't want to show him up in
front of them. But he does know he shouldn't misbehave, and
if it goes on his friends will have to be sent home. Instead of
simply returning him to his friends ask him to invite them out
to the kitchen for a drink. This will give them all a chance to

calm down, and will make your child's earlier absence from the room look perfectly natural.

Don't discipline your child's friends through the use of phrases such as 'I don't allow my child to behave like that'. They give the impression your child has a very restricted life, and will lay him open to teasing remarks. The same applies if his friends ask him out to play when it's too late in the evening, or to do something unsuitable. Instead of saying 'I don't allow him out this late' or 'He isn't allowed to do things like that' say 'It's too late for you children to be playing' or 'That's a risky thing for you all to be doing'. In this way the onus is shifted off your child to a more general observation taking in all children of his age. His friends may still think you have rather strange ideas, but they won't see these as personalized towards your child.

When friendships break up In spite of everyone's best efforts, your child will sometimes lose a friendship she very much wants to keep. Girls at this age seem to take these losses rather harder than boys, and though it's surprising how quickly they get over them, the feeling of hurt at the time is real enough. Be prepared for a child to be a little snappy and difficult in the immediate aftermath of breaking with a friend or, if that's her temperament, to be tearful and withdrawn. There's a temptation to tease children at such a time, because with the benefit of our own experience we know that it isn't the end of the world. But teasing is out of place, and will give your child the feeling that you don't 'understand' her feelings. This will make it harder for her to come and tell you about them in the future, and will add to her present sense of isolation and distress. In a small but important way, her identity is bound up with being 'Sally's best friend', and readjustment is bound to take a little time.

It's always helpful to be able to tell your child, 'Yes I remember how badly *I* felt when I lost my best friend.' Listen to your child while she gives you all the details, if she wants to talk, but let her do most of the criticizing, if any, of the friend's behaviour. If you wade in with condemnations of your own, you'll be surprised at how readily your child will change sides and start sticking up for the friend. She's still confused in her feelings towards her. Half of her wants to dislike the girl, but the other half is still fond of her. Give your child a chance to work out her own attitudes, and incidentally to identify for herself whether any of the blame (and it probably does) happens in any case to lie on her own side of the fence.

There's usually no need to help your child forget the lost friendship by encouraging her to turn to other children. She'll do this of her own accord after the immediate pain has worn off. Sometimes, in any case, the broken friendship will repair itself, and be stronger than before. Sometimes the girls will make it up, though without regaining the old intensity. But whatever happens, these childhood friendships are both a preparation for more permanent relationships in the future, and precious experiences in their own right. Don't underestimate them.

Around the age of nine (it's rare before), some children develop a quite intense friendship with a member of the opposite sex of their own age. There's something touching (dare one say romantic?) about these early affairs, with the children caught up into a private adventure full of impossible hopes and dreams. Meeting each other secretly after school and walking home away from the prying eyes and jeering tongues of their classmates. Shy attempts at putting deep feelings into words. Yes, certainly rather touching, but also rather disturbing, at least for parents who have the worry that this early interest in the opposite sex may foreshadow even more intense teenage relationships (and perhaps even a wildly unsuitable early marriage!)

Boy–girl friendships

Because the children's relationship is important to them, they find attempts to criticize it hard to handle, as if this criticism is directed at something very deep within themselves. So it's better not to be hard upon them. And better not to take their relationship too seriously, or as too much of a pointer for the future. There's no real evidence that children who form early attachments of this kind are more prone to earlier or less successful marriages than their peers. In any case, marriage is looking impossibly far ahead. For the present, the important thing is that your child is having an opportunity to feel at ease with someone of the opposite sex, and to come to know her own developing emotions. It's best at this age to treat the relationship much as you would a relationship between friends of the same sex. If the children are happy together fine, though if their relationship means they're neglecting other important things, then restrict the times they see each other, just as you would with other friends. And be just as firm as you would normally be over coming in early and letting you know exactly where they're going. Usually these early affairs, like spring blossom, are soon a thing of the past, though not without leaving a memory or two to haunt the years ahead!

Relationships with siblings

It's a common saying that two children more than double the work of one. This may seem odd, but there's a lot of truth in it. The reason is that when you have two children they quarrel! Often endlessly and over the smallest things. It matters not whether the children are of the same sex or girl and boy. They'll find things to disagree about. Indeed, their inventiveness in finding such things would impress us no end if it didn't also drive us to distraction.

Young children enjoy quarrelling   But this very inventiveness is a clue to what is actually going on. Young children quarrel because they enjoy it. Though it may not look like it at times, they get a great deal from the give and take involved. Through quarrelling, they pit their wits (and all too often their physical strength) against another. They assert their individuality and independence. They learn about themselves and about conflict and about the kind of strategies that work and those that don't. They experience the thrill of emotional arousal, and the sense of triumph when they get the better of their opponent. They also experience the chagrin of being bested by the opposition. But even when they get the worst of it, quarrelling adds to the excitement of life, and most children are all the better from having someone at home against whom they can flex their psychological and physical muscles.

But all this doesn't make life easy for parents. Many of them confess to being worn out at constantly having to intervene to sort out disputes. Their ideal of a happy, contented home in which children play amicably together is shattered. Try as they might, they seem unable to keep the peace for more than two minutes together, and even get the feeling that at times their children are quarrelling as a deliberate ruse to annoy them. To make matters more exasperating, they find themselves having to take sides, only for the child whose side they're taking promptly to change camps and side with his sibling. All is sweetness and light between the two children, leaving the poor parent feeling very much the outsider, as if somehow it's he or she who's the cause of all the problems.

Of course children vary in the frequency and ferocity with which they pitch into each other. Some are the best of friends most of the time, others the best of enemies. But even in the most peaceful relationships flare-ups happen, and you're left trying to restore the peace. If you've more than two children the situation can be even worse, with two of them ganging up on the third, and no matter what the circumstances, you may also see emotions in your children, such as spite and hatred, which cause you a great deal of concern.

The first consideration when dealing with children's quarrels is a purely physical one. Is one child likely to hurt the other? If so, you have to intervene. Boys are more prone to sort things out physically than girls, while girls are more given to shouting matches. But these distinctions are partly learnt social roles ('Little girls don't fight'); both boys and girls can hand it out physically and verbally without much difference when they want to. But if one child looks like getting knocked about, or if you are afraid for fragile objects within range of flying fists, then you must put an immediate stop to proceedings. Not by catching someone a cuff of your own, but by a sharp word and pulling them apart if necessary. Remember that if you start hitting out as well, you're only engaging in the very thing you're trying to stop them doing.

If a quarrel comes to blows

Once you've restored the peace, spend a few minutes listening to how it all started. You'll get two wildly conflicting accounts of course, each presenting its author in the role of a little saint tried beyond the limits of human endurance, and you may find it impossible to decide which is correct. But it's more important to your children that you're prepared to let them have their say than actually to sort out every time who is to blame. If you listen to your children, you'll show them you're fair-minded and that you're prepared to let them get their feelings off their chest by non-violent means.

If the dispute doesn't involve blows, you needn't be too quick to step in and sort things out. As I've already said, children seem to have a need for a set-to from time to time. If you forbid it, then their repressed energies will find other

Don't rush to intervene unless you have to

outlets, such as destructive behaviour or unnecessary arguments with you. Let your children get at least a little of their instincts for confrontation out of their systems. Your children also need to create their own relationship with each other, to find out what they can do and say to each other, to explore their own feelings for each other. Since they're growing and changing rapidly, this inevitably means constant readjustments. If you're forever forbidding their quarrels and laying down the law as to how they should relate to each other they never have a proper chance to work out their own solutions. Thus their relationship isn't really theirs at all. It's an artificial thing, defined by you and sustained by the force of your authority. The result is that not only will your children have a good go at each other the moment your back is turned, they'll also seethe with repressed hostility towards each other throughout childhood. Rarely able to sort out their differences by direct means, they'll go on harbouring these differences, never missing an opportunity to get back at each other by more subtle and spiteful means. They'll never get on properly together, even when they're older, and will tend to drift apart the moment they've left home.

By contrast children who are allowed to argue things out when they're younger usually become good friends. By the time they've reached their teens, even the disputes have usually stopped. The children know each other well, know each other's territories, acknowledge each other's point of view. They've got rid of their irritation at each other, and now accept they have more to gain from friendship than from hostility.

Children must learn to settle their differences The rule is that unless your children are getting hurt, or damaging things, or one is dominating the other, don't feel you must *on principle* interfere every time they quarrel. Comfort yourself with the knowledge that things aren't nearly as bad as they sound to the listening adult. Of course, if the din gets too much, then you've every right to intervene. You're entitled to your peace and quiet when you want it. But make it clear to your children that you're not so much against them settling their differences as against them settling them in that noisy manner at that particular time. If they're at it again two minutes later, separate them temporarily as you did when they were younger. One of them plays in this room, or in this

442

corner of the room, the other plays in that. The separation needn't be for long. Just sufficient time to allow them to cool down and to realize that they'd much rather be playing together than playing on their own.

If the dispute is over a particular game or toy, take the item away from them and tell them they can have it back when they've worked out together how to play with it without arguing. Once they've done so they can explain their solution to you, and if you're happy with it and they promise to stick to it, they can have the game or toy back. This early lesson in helping them perfect the art of compromise helps their relationship along. You're not laying down the law, you're allowing them to work out the law for themselves. That way they learn how to discuss things properly, and they're far more likely to keep to a law agreed on between themselves than one imposed on them by you.

So far, I've been assuming that your two children are close in age and fairly evenly matched. There's more of a problem if one child is a lot bigger and stronger than the other, and likely to get too much of his own way. But a word of caution here. **Disputes between older and younger siblings** The bigger and stronger child does have an advantage, but younger and smaller children are often adept at teasing and annoying older ones, secure in the knowledge that if the older child retaliates you'll quickly put a stop to it. And they are skilful at getting your sympathy even when the older child is in the right. They can burst into tears and look pathetic and hard done-by. They can make the smallest bruise sound like a case for an emergency dash to the nearest casualty department. It isn't that the younger child is being wicked. It's just that he's learnt this is the most effective strategy for combating the greater strength of his big brother or sister, and having found his trump card he's going to play it for all he's worth.

So don't come down automatically on the side of either the younger or the older child. Try and identify exactly what has been going wrong. If you can't apportion the real blame, then help each one to see the other's point of view. **Don't automatically side with either child** Help the older child to see that he's bigger and stronger (which is good) and that big, strong people have a duty to show consideration to those who are smaller and weaker than themselves; not just within the family, but in life generally. Agree with him that you know this is hard, and that you understand how trying his little

443

brother or sister can be at times, but insist this is one of the lessons of responsibility that bigger people have to learn. Prompt him to show patience, but if his patience is tried too hard he must come and tell you and you'll put things right.

Help the younger child to see that his big brother or sister has rights too. A younger child has only himself to blame if he goads an older one into retaliation. He should realize as well that it's hardly fair to make a big fuss simply to get adult sympathy or to get an older child into trouble. If the older child has really been unfair, then the younger one must come and tell you, and you'll sort matters out. But it's no good just playing on your sympathy. That way you're likely to lose patience, and you may not side with him when he really does need you.

If they've received a clear lead from you along the lines indicated, children will know the correct standards of behaviour for relating to each other, and will use these as a guide in building up their own relationship. Probably the peak age gap for disputes between children is about two years. Children who are closer together than this are often too similar in interests and outlook to annoy each other overmuch, while if there is a larger age gap the older child is likely to be too mature to be much bothered by the little one, and too protective to want to come to blows with him.

Aim always to improve their relationship Whenever you can, try not to resolve disputes between your children by punishing the 'guilty' one too severely, particularly if you didn't actually see the incident that sparked things off. Punishing one child on the evidence presented by another builds up resentment between them and the desire for revenge. And if your punishment was directed at the wrong child, both children will come to doubt your judgement in future. Aim all the time to improve the relationship between your children, rather than to punish. Separate them, have your say, let them see that there are better ways of solving differences than coming to blows over them, and then leave things at that.

Never compare your children with each other One of the most insidious ways in which you can worsen your children's relationship is by comparing them with each other, particularly as usually one child (perhaps the younger) tends to come badly out of these comparisons. 'It's a pity you can't be more like your brother,' she's told. 'Your big sister

444

was doing twice what you can do when she was your age'. 'Your brother only needs telling once, not like you.' And so the comparisons go on, making the child concerned feel guilty and inadequate and fiercely resentful towards the sibling concerned. Things can be made even worse if the two children are compared in the same way by teachers once they get to school. By such comparisons, children are actively prevented from making their own evaluations of each other. Even if the nice things you say about his brother or sister are true, and if a child would be quite happy to acknowledge them in her own way and her own time, the constant attempt by adults to ram them down her throat will make it very hard for her to have a proper relationship with the sibling concerned.

Comparisons of this kind don't help your child's relationship with you either. She's bound to feel you're being unfair to her, and that you're deliberately trying to drive a wedge between her and her brother or sister, perhaps because you're jealous of their friendship. Nor do these comparisons actually help *you*. They're unlikely to make your child produce the behaviour you want. In fact, perversely, she may go to the opposite extreme, emphasizing unwanted behaviour as a way of hitting back at you and preserving her own identity. **Such comparisons help no one**

She wants to be herself, and your attempts to turn her into a carbon copy of her sibling threaten this sense of selfhood. I know that some adults say they remember as children longing to be like an older sibling who had all the qualities they seemed to lack in themselves, but this longing is only genuine where the child is allowed to choose it for herself. If she has it forced upon her by the expectations of others, it isn't part of her identity at all. It's an identity other people are trying to create for her, and will never lead to balanced and happy psychological development. And if she does choose it for herself, it's always qualified in some way. 'I want to have my big sister's hair or nose or charming manner,' thinks the little girl, 'but I don't want to stop being *me* when I have them.'

There's another way in which these comparisons are of no help to you. If you tend to think of one of your children unfavourably in comparison with another, you're harming your own attempts to love and accept her. You're consciously wishing she was something she's not. Each time you think she falls short of her sibling you mark her down further in your estimation, and then find yourself struggling to feel towards her as you should. I'm not suggesting any parent loves each of his or her children in exactly the same way. Each child is different and so is your love for them. But where things are going as they should, the love you feel for one child is never *greater* or *better* than the love you feel for another. They don't admit of comparison, just as your children don't admit of comparison. Trying to change one child into a replica of another should never occur to you, just as your children shouldn't wish to turn their mother into their father or vice versa.

Relationships with other relatives

The most important relationships are those that happen within the immediate family. But you want your children to get on well with other relatives, particularly grandparents, who probably dote on your children and very much want to be accepted and loved by them.

Let grandparents make their own relationship with your child

And herein lies a danger. Because we want our children to get on well with their grandparents and other relatives, we often try to school them in the kind of behaviour expected of them. 'Now remember to be nice to Grandad.' 'Now *don't* tease Grandma about her hat.' 'Don't you *dare* argue with Grandma when she says children don't behave properly these days.' 'Turn over channels at once when Grandad wants to watch his favourite programme' and so on. There's also a temptation to have an inquest when Grandad and Grandma have gone home. 'I really felt thoroughly ashamed of you when you told Grandad his pipe made you feel sick.' 'What on earth must Grandma have thought of you when you wouldn't eat a piece of her cake?' 'I really despair of you ever giving a good impression of yourself when Grandpa and Grandma are here.'

The trouble with this well-meaning badgering is that it doesn't allow your child to enjoy his grandparents' visits. He's so much on show that he can never be himself. And as with his relationship with a brother or sister, he's never going to be able to work things out honestly if you're always looking over his shoulder so to speak and telling him how the relationship ought to be going. Certainly you want to give him sensible guidance. Elderly people can be upset by the thoughtlessness of the young. But at the same time if Grandad and Grandma really care about your children then they want to get to know them as they really are and create their own relationship with them. It's no real help to them – nor much of a compliment – if their relationship with your children has to depend upon your frantic off-stage threats and warnings.

Another problem with relatives to which parents sometimes confess is the 'favourite uncle/aunt' syndrome. Your child has an uncle or aunt with whom they're particularly close, and at times you're left in little doubt that he prefers their company to your own. Not unnaturally you feel jealous, particularly as the uncle/aunt has the pleasure of your child without any of the responsibility. Ashamed to say anything to the adult concerned, you find yourself taking it out on your child, and end up feeling throughly miserable about the whole business. I suppose if we were saints we'd just be glad to see our child enjoying himself with the favoured relative, but we're not, especially as we may have the sneaking feeling that the relative is aware of our discomfort and rather enjoying it!

The favourite aunt or uncle

It would be unfair to stop the child seeing the aunt or uncle, or to try turning him against them. But where you can, it's always best to be frank about your feelings. Confess them to the relative, not accusingly but simply as a statement of fact. If the relative is worth the affection your child has for them, they should be able to accept your feelings and make sure they don't do anything to come between your child and yourself. If they can't accept your feelings, you've a right to wonder whether they *are* such a good influence upon your child after all, and you may justifiably be a little less encouraging towards them from now on. But be careful, whichever way things develop, not to let your child feel you're *competing* with the uncle/aunt for his affections. This will only confuse your child, in whose life you already have a special place anyway (though he doesn't always show it!), and make him feel you're forcing yourself upon him.

Frankness over your feelings in this case doesn't necessarily extend to pouring them out to your child. He has a right to make his own relationships with other members of the family, provided they're suitable people. But if you feel you must say something, make a joke out of it. Don't employ the weapon of guilt, or play on your child's sympathies. Most children respond readily to a parent who makes a rueful joke against himself ('Poor old Dad couldn't keep up with you and Uncle Bill; think of his ageing legs and go slower next time'), and while laughing over it are quick to see that there is a more serious side which calls for consideration in future.

STARTING SCHOOL

For most children and most families, starting and attending school represent the biggest changes that take place during the years five to eleven. Indeed many of the issues with which we have already dealt have been related to what happens in school and to the widening horizons that attending school opens up for a child.

What makes a good primary school?

Whether you have a choice of primary schools or not, you'll want to be sure that your child is going to a good school that will do its best for her. But what is a 'good' primary school? How can you as a parent assess what is on offer and whether it is going to be suitable for your child? Parents of children already at the school will of course be only too happy to give you the benefit of their opinions, and these are worth listening to, provided you don't always take them as gospel (parents differ widely in their impressions of schools and in what they expect from teachers). But make sure you have ample opportunity to look round the school, and to talk to the headteacher and staff. Most schools arrange to talk to parents in the term before their children start school, and to explain how the school is run and what is expected of children. Make full use of such opportunities, but don't necessarily leave it at that. If you want to see more of the school, and to talk in more detail to the headteacher, then make an appointment and go along when you can have more personal attention. It's always of value if both parents (where possible) make these visits. This allows you to swap notes with each other afterwards, and impresses upon the school that you're both interested in your child's education and will be looking carefully at her progress.

Although your child will be in the reception class, be sure to look at what happens throughout the school, with the older as well as the younger children.

In your visits to the school, look for the following things:

- Primary schools should be bright, lively places, which look welcoming and friendly. Does your school fill the bill? Is it colouful and well-cared for, and do the children look as if they enjoy it?
- Are there plenty of examples of the children's work on the walls of the corridors and classrooms? If children and teachers take a pride in work produced in lessons, then they want to see it up on the walls, attractively and tastefully displayed.
- Are there plenty of visual aids on the walls? Information pictures and posters which capture the attention and hold the interest? Children learn a great deal by seeing, and the good teacher goes to some trouble to present children with eye-catching displays of up-to-date and relevant material.
- Are there nature and science tables in the classrooms? Constantly changing collections of objects and little experiments for the children to use and explore?
- Does each classroom have its own little library of reading and reference books, suited to the children's interests, in good condition, and readily accessible to them? Books still remain the single most important educational aid next to the teacher in any primary school. And is there a school library, in a quiet room or a quiet comfortable corner, where children can sit and read?
- Are the sets of textbooks, or of work cards, up-to-date and in good, attractive condition?
- Is there ample evidence of good, exciting number work going on in each class? Look for graphs and charts on the wall, weighing and measuring apparatus, work cards which set the children interesting and challenging practical problems and projects, commercially produced counters, blocks and shapes which help the children with counting and setting.
- Is there evidence of ample opportunities in arts and crafts? Again look for examples of the children's work. Is

the work imaginative? Is it displayed in a way that indicates the teacher cares about it?

- In the reception class, is there plenty of good quality play equipment? Is it suited to the children and does it look as if it's well and properly used?

- Is there a good use of space within the school generally, and within each classroom in particular? Does it look as if the children have room in which to move and carry out their learning activities? Are there wet areas, where the children can engage in water play and water-based learning activities? Are these sensibly arranged so that they do not conflict with dry areas, and so that they give ample scope to the children using them?

- In the reception class and lower infants, are there sand trays, racks of clothes for dressing up, a corner for house-play activities (often called a Wendy Corner), and plenty of provision for cutting out, pasting, painting and other similar activities? Does it look as if the children are allowed to make the occasional mess, or is everything so neat and tidy it doesn't look as if children inhabit the place at all?

- Does it look as if the school recognizes that children in the 5–11 age range learn best through doing, rather than through sitting still and being talked to? Are there signs of relevant activity and experience, or is everything very static and teacher-orientated?

- Does it look as if the school recognizes and prizes each child's individuality? Look for example at the material on the walls. Is each child expected to produce the same sort of thing as everyone else, or does it look as if each child is helped to develop something of herself and of her own personality?

- Is the school well run and organized? There is always noise in a primary school, but does it seem purposeful and controlled, or are the children being allowed to run riot? Do the children seem to know what is expected of them? Are they taught to take a reasonable pride in their appearance, and do they show interest and involvement in their work?

- Are the relationships between teachers and children friendly and open, while at the same time showing a proper respect on both sides?

- Are there plenty of out-of-school activities for the older children, such as music and drama groups, PE clubs and hobby groups? Are there school trips and outings?
- Are the games facilities adequate and well-organized? Do the children have a spacious and pleasant environment in which to play during break and lunchtimes?
- Is there proper provision for children with learning difficulties, such as those children who are slow readers or slow at mathematics?
- Does the school have proper schemes of work (ask if you can see them), so that it is clear what ground they are expected to cover as they move through each of the classes? Is there a clear policy for the teaching of the basic skills like reading, writing and arithmetic (the so-called three Rs)? There are various different methods available, and since you cannot be expected to judge which is the best it is all the more important that you should satisfy yourself that whatever methods the school uses have a coherent and sensible plan behind them. If possible, ask to see examples of the children's work in the three Rs. Not just the best children's work, but a cross-section. Is the work neat? Are there more right answers than wrong ones? Are there good signs of progress from page to page? Do the children seem to have enjoyed their work and to take a pride in it?
- What is the school's attitude to parents? Are they welcome in the school (more on this later)? Is there an active Parent–Teacher Association?
- Does the school strive to teach through success (finding out and encouraging what a child can do) or failure (finding out and disparaging what she can't)? Too great a preponderance of wrong answers in books, too many star charts (on which only the names of the more able children appear), too much emphasis upon house points or other merit awards, too much talk about 'able' and 'less able' children, too much emphasis upon punishment and the loss of privileges, will suggest the latter rather than the former.
- Finally, do the headteacher and staff actually seem to *like* children? A strange question perhaps, but a necessary one. Some schools give the immediate impression that

each child is prized, others that children are there rather on sufferance.

You can't be expected to come up with answers to all these questions, but satisfy yourself on as many as you can. No school is perfect, but you can with a little perseverance tell the difference between a school that is well-run and well-equipped, and understands and cares about children, and a school that doesn't. Don't be too easily taken in by outward show, such as the presence of school uniforms or regular termly 'tests' in each class. These things have their good points, but when presented in the wrong way they can make a child nervous and fearful about all aspects of school. Far more important is a school's ability to welcome a child, and then to be perceptive enough to understand her strengths and weaknesses, to give her the help she needs, to teach her in a way suitable to young enquiring minds and young active bodies, to set her appropriate standards, and to help her develop confidence in herself and respect for others. All children can achieve. And where they fail to do so the responsibility often lies more with the adults entrusted with their progress than with the children themselves.

Early fears and problems

Most of us remember our first days at school. For something to stick in the memory like that it must have made a great impression, and it's not hard to see why. When we start school, we go in one leap from the secure, familiar territory of our home to the strange and intimidating world of the school. A world full of people and experiences that are new to us, and in which all kinds of new behaviour is expected of us. A world, what is more, from which the people who love and care for us at home are excluded.

If you think back to these early days, you may get some idea of what your own child is facing now that school is upon him. In my own case I seem to remember the physical hardness of everything. Desks and tables all seemed to have sharp square corners. The light seemed sharp and bright. The chairs and the floor we sat on hard and cold. The walls of the classroom stood out bleakly somehow, for all that I imagine they must have been decorated with pictures and drawings. Voices and sounds were loud and unsettling. And I think that my understanding of the strange expression a 'lump in the throat' dates from about this period.

Of course times have changed and schools are more welcoming places now. Often parents are able to stay with their children on the first few mornings, and in any case many four- and five-year-olds have had the experience of nursery school or playgroup before they begin school. But starting school is still a big and intimidating step for most children. So you must understand as much about it as you can if you are to play your part in making this step as painless as possible for your child, and in helping him adjust quickly.

In moving from the intimate world of the home to the less personal and supportive world of the school your child is faced with a major challenge. The way in which he copes with it will influence his feelings about school for some time to come, and as we shall see in a moment even perhaps his feelings about you. So prepare him for school by explaining to him what the children do there, and by walking past the school building as often as possible so that he becomes familiar with it and with the sight of the children at play. Many schools will make arrangements for you to visit along with your child, so that you can both look round the classrooms and meet the teachers.

But however well you prepare him, your child is still going to find the idea of school rather confusing. He knows he has to go there, because you've explained to him that's what big boys and girls do, but he doesn't fully understand why. You've told him there are lots of new and exciting things to play with there, but he may be happy enough with the things you've given him at home, and unable to grasp why he can't stay and play with them if the first days at school are not to his liking. You've told him there will be the chance to make new friends, but he may find some of his new 'friends' decidedly rough and strange in their behaviour. Perhaps you've told him school is a place where he can learn how to work and one day get a good job when he grows up, but being 'grown up' is still an impossibly long way ahead, and as we saw in Chapter 5 a young child sees no difference between

Your child may find the idea of school confusing

play and work. A thing is either play and fun and worth doing, or it isn't play and fun and much better avoided. And if school isn't play and fun then no amount of looking ahead to promised benefits in the future will make him want to go there. Even telling him he'll learn to read and write in school may not help much. Certainly he wants to read and write, but why can't you teach him? Why does he have to go to school to learn something that you yourself are doing all the time in the home?

One of the things that may confuse a child most is that the teacher has so little time for him. At home you spend hours in a one-to-one relationship with him. If he wants you for something, he only has to go up to you and ask. If he's having trouble over something or getting upset you sort things out. But in school he has to share a grown-up with twenty or more other children. And there seem to be rules about who he speaks to and where he is allowed to go in the school building. In spite of all the people around him, it's no surprise that he often ends up feeling lonely and wanting you.

He may feel let down by you Which brings us to one of the reasons why a child's experiences when starting school may affect his feelings for you, at least temporarily. However much we may tell him that school is there for his own good, a child quickly learns that no one takes any notice of whether *he* thinks it's for his own good or not. He has to stay there, whether he wants to or not. So although he may not be able to put it into words, he can feel badly let down. You told him school was going to be fun, and maybe it isn't fun at all. Worse still, when he feels unhappy and wants you, you aren't there. Up to now, you've seemed a very powerful person, far and away the most important person in his life. Anything that needs doing you seem able to do. Any dangers that threaten, you're able to cope. Now here you are suddenly handing him over to a strange person called a teacher in a strange building and with lots of strange children around, and treating this strange person moreover with unaccountable deference. Could it be that this 'teacher' is more powerful than you? Even worse, you now walk off without a backward glance, leaving him to the mercies of this stranger. You're off to the cosy world of home and shopping and cooking, while he's left to an interminable morning in this large and intimidating place. However kindly and understanding the teacher (and most infant school teachers are excellent), she is no substitute for you.

Perhaps it's just as well he doesn't know that you feel every bit as badly about it as he does! You too may feel you're letting him down, and leaving him when he needs you most. Many parents confess to shedding a tear or two when they get back home without the child who has shared their lives so closely for the last four or five years. The morning stretches for such parents just as interminably as it does for the child, and they find themselves wondering from minute to minute what he or she is doing. And all the while there is the knowledge that a stage in their own lives has ended, and nothing can bring it back.

You may feel badly too

Before we get too weepy about it, let's add that if you do feel bad when your child starts school you'll quickly get over it. Certainly a precious stage of your life and in that of your child has ended, but there are plenty of good things, every bit as exciting and joyful, just ahead. Before long you'll experience your horizons widening along with those of your child. You'll share the new enthusiasms he will soon be bringing home from school. You'll meet his new friends, and may well make new friends of your own amongst the other parents at the school gate. And you'll take a great pride in the progress and achievements of his school career and in the nice things that his teachers say about him.

Let's add that in spite of the great change in their lives that starting school represents, most children adapt quite quickly. It's difficult to get accurate figures, but even children who go through a particularly emotional patch in their first few days are usually over the worst by the end of the second week. And many children take to school without noticeable upset at all. Children who have cheerful temperaments and a secure and happy home background will find school particularly straightforward. And those children who are especially active and busy, and who have already outgrown many of the pastimes that home has to offer, will be very ready for the extra stimulation and new experiences that school holds out.

Even children who take to school like ducks to water may go through a phase of difficult behaviour at home. When they arrive back at lunchtime or at the end of the afternoon they

455

Your child may become more difficult at home may seem deliberately defiant and unco-operative. We may be reminded of the negative and obstinate behaviour of the third year of life (see Chapter 5). Or there may be a reversion to quite babyish behaviour, with the child rather clinging and tearful, and likely to fly into a rage at the least little thing. Parents who have missed their child all day and looked forward to home-time may find this behaviour hard to take, and become cross and upset in their turn. They may even feel surprised and guilty at a sudden longing for the quiet hours during the day when the child was out of the house.

Why she behaves like this The reason for the bad behaviour is that she's physically tired after the day or half-day at school. And even if school has been fun she's still had to cope with the different worlds of school and home. Moreover, even if she doesn't feel that you have abandoned her to the teacher, she's nevertheless been deprived of you during the day. So when she comes home she wants to reassert herself and demand attention. And if she *should* be feeling let down by you over the whole business of schooling, then in a confused way she will want to get her own back by awkward behaviour. After all, if we as adults feel let down by someone we trust, we also find it difficult to be as nice to them as usual.

On top of everything, there will probably have been frustrations at school, however well the day has gone. Your child will have wanted things and been told she can't have them or must wait her turn. The teacher may have scolded her for something. And there will have been disagreements with other children. All this will leave her wanting to take it out on someone, and who better than you? Then if there is a small brother or sister at home, she may resent the fact that they've had you to themselves while she's been banished to school. So she may be jealous or aggressive towards them, using them into the bargain as substitutes for the children who upset her at school.

If your child should revert to babyish behaviour during these early weeks, it's because part of her wants to go back to the dependent world of babyhood, when she was with you all the time and you gave her the security and love she needed. She doesn't fully realize that you can't put back the clock, and still associates babyish behaviour with the comfort and safety of a baby's life.

Though you may be exasperated at times, tolerate your **Be tolerant**
child's moods and outbursts. We expect a lot of four- and five- **with your child**
year-olds, packing them off to school as we do, and we must
help them learn how to cope. Don't be over-indulgent, which
may simply prolong things, but do show her she can have
plenty of extra attention if she is sensible and co-operative. Set
aside time to be with her when she comes home, and without
grilling her show that you're interested in her school day and
want to hear about it. When she's angry with you or with
younger siblings tell her it's good to get these things off her
chest but she can't expect to keep taking out on her family all
the things that have gone wrong at school. Make sure there is
plenty to occupy her, including little treats and surprises.

Tell her you've missed her, and bring her up to date with
what's been happening during the day. But don't start telling
her gloomily how lonely you've been without her. School is a
fact of life, and both you and she have to get used to it. If you
keep telling her how bad you feel you'll only make her feel
bad too, and oddly guilty that somehow she's been deserting
you. If she says she dislikes school and doesn't want to go any
more explain to her that lots of children feel like that. Maybe
you did yourself at her age. But the law says everyone must
go to school, and soon she'll find herself enjoying it. She may
not understand what you mean by the law, but she will
understand that school is a place where all children except
very little ones 'have' to go. Play a game and see who can
think of the most children nearby who go to school. Let her
ask you one by one whether the grown-ups in her life once
went to school. Did you go? Did Grandma? Did Auntie Flo?
Did the milkman? Did the teacher? She'll soon get the idea
that school is a fixture in her life, and with your help she's just
got to make the best of it.

Helping your child start school

Once you realize that starting school is something of an ordeal, **Give him all**
you'll want to do all you can before your child is of school age **the preparation**
to make it as easy as possible for him. If he has a friend next **you can**
door already at school this is a big help. You and your child
can go along with the friend's mother and meet him from
school. You can get him to tell you some of the things he's
done there, and show you his drawings and models. If you

457

know someone who is a teacher, your child can meet her and find out what nice people teachers are. Even if she teaches in a different school from the one your child will attend a visit there is always of value, both when it's empty and when there are children about.

Books and stories are also very useful. Read him stories in which the characters go to school, and show him pictures of their school and of the activities that go on there. The more realistic these stories and pictures the better. Tales of your own school days can also help, though avoid anything that might sound intimidating.

We talked about pre-school playgroups and nursery classes in Chapter 6, and provided they are well run and offer interesting activities these can be amongst the best preparations for school. They often have the added advantage of taking children for half-days only, breaking children in gently to being away from home and ensuring they don't become too tired and cross. One word of warning though. Attendance at playgroups and nursery classes is voluntary, and a child can be allowed to stop going if he wishes. But you must explain to him that schools aren't like that. Everyone has to go to school, and once he starts he will have to stick at it. School is for bigger children than playgroups and nurseries.

The importance of routine In earlier chapters we talked about the great importance of routine in the contented baby's life. But routine isn't only appreciated by babies. All young children, particularly if they are going through a difficult new experience like starting school, rely upon it. Routine gives the child a sense of security, a sense of the known, which helps him tackle the unknown confidently and surely. When he starts school, the wise parent makes sure he does it within an agreeable and consistent routine. Mother takes him to school and meets him from school, and is there on time ready with a warm greeting. Or mother takes him to school and father meets him. Or father does both journeys. The details are less important than the fact that in the first days and weeks (in fact until you are sure he's settled in) you stick to them as closely as possible. It's best also to avoid making major changes within the home during this time unless he's there to see them. Coming home from the strange environment of the school your child likes to find the house as he left it. If you grab the opportunity while he's out to move all the furniture round and change all the curtains he's bound to find it something of a shock, even if he can't explain this to you.

Once he is happily settled in school, your child will be able to take changes in routine without upset. But in the first rather anxious days a strange person to meet him at the gates, or even the sight of father when he has been expecting mother, can confuse him and make him feel he can't be certain about things any longer. If he's a worrier by nature, he may even become fearful that there will be nobody there to meet him, or that something terrible may happen to one of his parents while he is away from the house.

If you are a working single parent, or if neither parent can get there in time at the end of school, hand the job of meeting your child to a grandparent or a sympathetic neighbour who can be relied upon to turn up unfailingly. If you can make special arrangements to meet him for the first week or two so much the better, but have the grandparent or neighbour accompany you each day. That way there won't be an abrupt change when you eventually have to leave them to do it on their own. And be warned that if you make a special effort to leave work early on occasions in order to be outside school at home-time, he may seem more surprised than pleased to see you, and play you up a little on the way home. Not only have you upset the routine, you have also shown him that you *can* meet him if you want. So he's bound to feel somewhat peeved you don't do it every day. Like so much that happens in the early years of life, he may well not put this into words, or even be quite clear about it in his own mind, but his puzzlement at your behaviour will be none the less real for that.

In spite of your careful arrangements there may come a day **When you have** when you (or the person who does the job for you) are **to alter the** prevented from going to meet your child on time. Make sure **routine** he knows exactly what to do should this happen. Often the school will have an arrangement for children to wait in a parents' room or a designated classroom until their parents (or whoever else is collecting them) arrive. Make sure he knows this, and understands that if you are delayed it will not be for long. Better still, arrange for a friend or neighbour who knows him well and who is meeting her own child to collect him for you. And make sure he knows about this arrangement, so that he won't be taken by surprise should it occur. But it shouldn't happen until he's well settled in at school, when he has to be able to take the occasional change in arrangements in his stride.

He's too young to go home on his own

Impress upon him that he must never set off home on his own. However near school you live, and however well he knows the way, he isn't old enough to do the journey on his own. At the end of the school day, a four- or five-year-old child's head will be full of the things that have been happening and the things he's eager to do when he gets home. No matter how carefully you have taught him road sense, he can't be expected to concentrate fully when his thoughts are elsewhere. Even if he doesn't have a road to cross he still isn't safe. He may dart into the road without thinking, particularly if he sees a friend on the opposite pavement. Worse still, he may be suddenly frightened by a group of older children and run on to the road to get away from them. Or with a small child's fondness for animals he may stray out to pat a cat or dog.

We can't worry ourselves silly over the safety of our children every time they are out of our sight. But we can take every sensible precaution to see nothing happens to them. Children are particularly vulnerable when they have just been let out of school, and you will need to take extra care at this time.

Kitting your child out properly for school

You are not likely to forget the important matter of kitting your child out properly for school. You will see to it that she has appropriate clothes, that she takes a clean handkerchief, that her footwear is right for the weather, that everything is marked with her name, and that she knows how to take care of her belongings. In addition children are often asked by the teacher to take something home with them or to bring in or do something special. They may be given a note to take home, or asked to be especially smart for the visit of the photographer, or to bring in something to eat for the classroom party, or to take along money for a special outing. Help her to remember these special demands by asking her whether she's been given anything for you or got anything to tell you.

This is an early lesson for children in coping with the extra demands of the environment. If a child feels able to cope, and is seen by others to be coping, then she gains confidence in her own abilities. Because her parents are usually also involved in this coping (baking cakes for her to take to the party, remembering to give her money for the outing, sending an answer to the teacher's note), she will also see their competence as being on trial. It is difficult for a mere adult to remember how keenly a small child feels the humiliation of being the only one in the class to have forgotten to bring something for the party, or to have failed to have her costume made for the Christmas concert. At such times she experiences a sense of her own inadequacy and of that of her parents, and feels ashamed both for herself and for them.

On the other hand the child whose parents always help her rise to the occasion feels secure in the love and concern they show for her, and secure in the knowledge that she matters to them. She is left in no doubt they care enough about her to help her avoid unnecessary let-downs and disappointments. We are not talking about fussing over your child interminably. Still less about giving her the best of everything and wanting her to show up the other members of her class. We are talking simply about sending her to school properly equipped, so that she can take part in any activities that are going on and can see herself as an able person well prepared to match up to the demands made of her.

Getting to know your child's teacher right from the start is essential. Obviously she is a busy person and you don't wish to give the impression that you are one of those nuisance parents who thinks no one else understands their child. But neither are you one of those parents who believe their rights end the moment their child steps inside the school gate. Many adults, forceful enough in other walks of life, find themselves tongue-tied when they face a teacher. The conditioning we experienced from teachers in our own childhood dies hard. And some teachers have a brisk efficiency about them that's enough to daunt anyone. But schools exist for children, and most teachers are only too happy to have the co-operation and help of parents. They know that without this co-operation and help schools are very limited in what they can achieve.

Getting to know the teacher

So show your child's teacher that you're interested in your child's education and eager to see he makes a good start to his school career. If he has any particular characteristics that could lead to problems tell the teacher about them. He may be rather shy or particularly active, he may have special learning difficulties or have been kept back by illness. Don't expect the school necessarily to be able to put these problems right, but the more the teacher knows about them the better able she will be to take them into account and do what she can. Show the teacher that you are ready to play your own part at home in your child's education, and that you welcome any guidance she can give you. Be ready to accept criticisms she may make of him from time to time. No child is perfect, and many children find it difficult at first to adapt to the new social demands that school makes of them. On the other hand, if the teacher is constantly finding fault with your child, then it could be that she doesn't understand young children too well, perhaps because of inexperience. Listen carefully to what she has to say, but if you have good reason for disagreeing say so politely but firmly. He's your child, and you know him pretty well. If the teacher is doing her job properly, she will welcome the new insights that you are able to give her.

Schools that do not welcome parents

Just occasionally, even these days, parents are unlucky enough to have their child go to a school which seems intent on keeping them at arm's length. Parents are given the impression that education is something best left to professionals, and parents should stick to their role of caring for the child's physical needs. Such a school usually frowns on parents coming beyond the school gate let alone into the school building, and insists that parents make an 'appointment' if they wish to talk to the class teacher. There is no question of children being allowed to bring reading or other books home so that parents can help their progress, certainly no chance of parents staying with children who find it hard to settle during the first few days of school.

Excuses that may be offered Sometimes excuses are offered to the effect that it is 'unsafe' to allow parents through the school gate as they 'leave the gate open and children may wander into the street'. Or that teachers are far too occupied with after-school activities to talk to parents unless permission is given in advance. Or that children's 'work' is disrupted if they see someone's mother or father coming into the school building. Or that new children will settle more quickly if they understand from the start that they leave their parents behind at the school gate.

462

Obviously schools have to be careful that undesirable characters don't wander in and out pretending to be parents. And obviously it isn't always convenient for a teacher to talk to a parent after school or for parents to drop in on lessons just because they feel like it. But the good school is more than ready to welcome parents as partners in the education of young children. The minor inconveniences caused by some thoughtless parents who take advantage of the school's openness is more than offset by the benefits to the children of allowing parents to be part of the educational process. No good school has anything to hide from parents either. Teachers know that for every parent who snoops around the school looking for things to criticize there are dozens who like what they see and admire and respect teachers for the job they are doing.

If you feel parents are being unjustifiably barred from your child's school, you have a right to say so. Ask other parents how they feel and if they share your views then arrange to see the headteacher and make these views known. Don't make a confrontation out of it, but point out that parents would like to be more closely involved in school than they are. Indicate that you appreciate the difficulties, but wonder if a way can be found round them. If your approach is friendly and diplomatic, the head should be prepared to discuss the issues with you and agree to explore them with the teaching staff. But if you are sent away feeling that you had no right to open your mouth, then identify the parent representatives on the school board of governors or managers and raise the matter with them. If you are able to show that you have the support of other parents then these representatives will put the subject on the agenda for the next governors' meeting. The chances are they will already be aware of the problem, and will be grateful to have your backing and that of other parents whose names you give them. Anyway, let's hope you won't have to take on this role of dissatisfied parent. Everyone is much happier if teachers and parents can work together in harmony.

Arrange to see the headteacher

The child who does not settle at school
If after the first two weeks your child is still not going to school enthusiastically, he may have problems that go deeper than normal. If it is clear the school is doing everything reasonably

possible to help him settle, then you may have to look within the home for the source of his difficulties.

Problems at home may be the difficulty

The effect upon a child of upsets within the home are discussed in detail later in the chapter. These upsets can have a bad influence upon school progress at all ages, but particularly in the infant and junior years. Tension between parents, for example, with frequent quarrels and angry scenes in front of the whole family, can make a child disturbed and confused. His main source of security in life is his family and his love for his parents, and to witness domestic strife between the most important people in his world strikes at the very basis of this security. By the age of four and five years, a child is even able to sense unspoken tensions between his parents.

Without a secure home base from which to go out and explore the world, a child is especially vulnerable. The insecurities of starting school, on top of those already felt at home, will make him extra unsure of himself and extra prone to emotional outbursts. This is not the place to advise parents on the conduct of their marriage, but if there is discord within the home, make a special effort to keep it from the child during his early months at school. Help him to feel that home is a peaceful and loving place to which he can return at the end of the school day, and in which he can lay to rest any of the anxieties that have occurred during it. Who knows? You may even find that turning your attention away from the differences that have arisen within the marriage and uniting in the purpose of helping your child make a good start to school life will do the marriage a power of good.

Always give her a warm welcome when she comes home

And whatever happens, make sure that home offers your child a warm welcome when she comes in from school. If you have been extra busy during the day, try nevertheless to be free to spend a little time with her. Don't be tempted to sit her in front of the television as soon as she takes off her coat, or to send her next door to play with a friend. If she shows she wants to do these things, fine. Let her do them. Don't give her the impression she must have a chat with you every day whether she feels like it or not. But she's been out of your company all day, and usually there will be things she wants to tell you. Having your undivided attention for a while when she comes home also makes her feel you're glad to see her and that she's a special person and you want to hear about what she has been doing during the day.

Since she is likely to be hungry when she comes home, get her something nice to eat and drink, and sit down with her while she enjoys them. Tell her what you've been doing during the day as a way of encouraging her to tell you her doings. If there are things she wants to talk about usually they will be small routine happenings. Someone spilt their milk at playtime. The rain kept them indoors in the afternoon. Teacher praised her for some job she helped with. She had fun in the sandtray. Teacher read them a story about a goblin but she can't remember what happened.

Things that upset your child at school

From time to time, however, there may be things that have upset her. Another boy or girl may have taken something from her, or pushed ahead of her when waiting to play on some special piece of apparatus, or hit or pinched her for some reason. Or she may have found that some of the things you've taught her at home don't work at school. Asking another child nicely for something perhaps. Or waiting your turn. Or expecting people to say please and thank you. Maybe her teacher has been cross with her or has stopped her doing something for a reason she can't understand. Or maybe she has lost or broken or torn or spoilt something, or made a mistake of some sort and been laughed at by the other children. Perhaps she has had trouble with the toilets or with changing her clothes for PE. If she stays to lunch, perhaps she has been given food she dislikes and made to eat it up.

With these and similar problems it's often sufficient just to listen sympathetically to your child and let her get them off her chest. Once she has told you about them, and thus included you in her world of school experiences, she forgets them and turns her mind to other matters. Sometimes, however, she needs you to explain things to her. Teacher perhaps was very busy and didn't mean to forget about her turn on the apparatus. Being laughed at for making mistakes is a thing that happens to us all, and we have to learn to take no notice of it and remember not to laugh at other people's misfortunes. Whatever it was that she broke can be repaired or replaced, and she has learnt a valuable lesson in how to look after things. In future you'll make sure she doesn't have so many buttons to undo before the PE lesson. And so on.

Different standards of behaviour

A particular difficulty arises if she finds other children don't follow the standards of behaviour you have taught her. They snatch and grab for things, hit people, are rough with toys, and cheeky to the teacher. Hearing about all this can give you the uncomfortable feeling that your child is at a disadvantage with her classmates for showing the thoughtful behaviour you have taught her. Perhaps you have been unfair to her and should have encouraged her to grab like the rest. Don't worry. Your child has to learn that in life we do the right thing because it is right, and not because we hope it is the quickest route to getting our own way. Explain to her that some children haven't yet been taught to behave sociably and think of others, but that is one of the things they go to school to learn. And in any case there will be plenty of children in her class who *have* learnt these things and who try to behave as sensibly as she does.

Encourage your child to stand up for herself

At the same time, of course, your child has her rights, and must be helped to recognize what these are and how she can stand up for them. She's going to meet plenty of injustice in the world in the years ahead, and she needs to know what to do about it. Help her even at this early age to make a distinction between those minor injustices that we should not bother about and those more important ones where action is needed. Certainly she mustn't take the law into her own hands, but she must be sure to speak out and draw the teacher's attention where necessary to what is happening. All good reception class teachers in infant schools are well aware that their children come from a variety of backgrounds and have received quite different lessons in how to behave. So they are very alert to the fact that some children may take advantage of others, and will therefore be quick to intervene. But a teacher can't be everywhere, and your child must be encouraged to speak to him when she needs his help.

Have a word with the teacher if necessary

If your child feels her teacher hasn't given her a fair hearing, decide whether or not this is because your child is making a fuss over nothing. If she is, then explain to her that this is one of those occasions when we have to learn to ignore another child's silliness. We can't expect other people to behave always as we want them to, and probably the child concerned will learn his lesson as time goes by. On the other hand, if it's clear that the teacher should have taken your child's complaint seriously, and if the event concerned has happened before or may be repeated, have a word with the teacher about it. Naturally you don't want to play the role of over-anxious parent, and naturally you want your child to learn how to have her own say, but she needs to feel that she has your support in times of difficulty. And it is very confusing for a child if she tries to do as you tell her and finds that other children take advantage of her and no one seems to care.

It is also worthwhile talking to the teacher if you have a feeling that something is going wrong at school but your child seems unable to explain it to you. Ask her teacher if she seems to be getting on well with the other children and if she seems to be taking a full and enthusiastic part in all that is going on. Ask if she seems to know her way round and if she seems to be happy about the things she is asked to do. Even though the teacher can think of nothing that is going wrong, your child's difficulties may clear up quickly once you have spoken to him. Now that he knows you are anxious about her he'll be keeping a closer eye on her, and perhaps the extra attention is all she needs.

Sudden reluctance to go to school

Sometimes after making a good start to school life a child may suddenly show signs of losing enthusiasm. Maybe the length of the school day is beginning to tire him. Or perhaps the novelty is wearing off or he is starting to get bored. If you have given him a full and interesting life outside school he may find things at school rather tame. Or if you have started him on reading and writing he may become frustrated that his teacher is not bringing him on quickly enough in these skills. I discuss this issue later when we talk about the teaching of reading and writing, but it can be a problem and may need careful handling on your part.

Or perhaps he is suddenly aware that he is missing out on things at home, and is starting to feel jealous of a younger brother or sister. Or maybe he has just started staying to lunch, and finds he doesn't enjoy it and is missing seeing you midday. Or maybe his teacher has been away ill and there is a stranger taking his class, or some new piece of learning has been introduced into the school day and he finds difficulty in coping with it. Or perhaps a friend has moved to another school, or there has been some rearrangement of routine in the classroom which he dislikes.

Whatever the reason, your child may suddenly show a reluctance to go to school, even to the point of producing a tearful scene each morning. Sometimes he may back this up by telling you he doesn't feel well and wants to stay at home. He isn't setting out to trick you. He just worries about school, and wants to find a way of avoiding it. And once he tells you he isn't well he can quickly convince himself that he really *is* ill, and that you are pretty heartless if you turn him out of doors in spite of it.

Be sympathetic but firm If you are unable to find the reason for this sudden dislike of school, either by talking to the child or to his teacher, the only course is to be sympathetic but firm. He's already shown that he can cope with school, and he has to understand that we can't avoid things we're not too keen on simply by saying we're ill. Let him stay at home for a day or two to make sure there's nothing physically wrong with him, but make it clear that at the end of this short period he will be himself again and ready to get back to his schoolfriends. Don't make too much of the incident, but on the other hand don't tell him he's being silly. Stress to him the good things about school, and tell him that we all feel fed up with things from time to time, but that we have to stick at them and the feeling will soon pass. As long as your child is secure and happy at home episodes of this kind are usually short-lived.

Chronic school anxiety

However, a small number of children develop what is sometimes called chronic school anxiety. Both now and in some cases throughout their school careers they worry excessively about having the right games kit, the right books, the right science equipment, about being late, about minor problems with school uniform, about homework, and about a host of other small things. Such children usually perform well in school, so there is no clear reason for their worries. Yet the worries persist, in spite of everything you or the teachers say. You organize your child carefully, you listen to her anxieties, but to little avail. You try taking her anxieties seriously, you try making light of them, but nothing makes any lasting difference.

Children with chronic school anxiety usually worry about other things too, so they're probably worriers by nature. There's a difference, though, between an anxious child who stops worrying about specific issues once she's shown there's no need, and the child who in spite of everything can't seem to get free of them, or who as soon as one anxiety is laid to rest turns immediately to another. Sometimes the latter child shows signs of being obsessional. Everything has to be just so. Everything has to be in its right place. Every routine must be strictly kept to. Often obsessional (see page 551) children have parents who are themselves rather inflexible, in which case the answer is for parents to ease up a little. But more often still the obsessional behaviour is linked to some underlying insecurity. The child can only feel 'safe' if she's sure that everything is just as it always is. If your child is in this category, try to identify the reason for her insecurity. Was she left frequently with people she didn't know when she was younger? Was she upset by a stay in hospital? Have her parents separated, removing some of the certainties from her life and leaving her emotionally unsure of herself? Is there some deep tension in the family which makes her doubt its durability?

Is there any reason why your child should be insecure?

If none of these things seems to apply, then your child just has an anxious nature. But I must stress that it's very rare that nothing in the environment can be pinpointed as a factor. Some children are certainly more prone to anxiety than others, but it's their life experiences that turn them into chronically anxious people. Anyway, whatever the cause, help your child to feel she can communicate her anxieties to you, and as she gets older help you to understand what may lie behind them. Help her keep everything organized properly for school, and reassure her that your own love for her isn't conditional upon her school performance or anything else. Aim to increase her sense of security and of being needed and valued, and praise and encourage her every success.

With her specific anxieties, it helps to teach her to rate them on a ten-point scale, going from 1 (least anxious) to 10 (most anxious). A simple trick like this helps to make anxieties more tangible, and therefore easier to face and cope with. As an extension, teach her to think about these anxieties when she's

Helping her deal with her anxieties

469

in a relaxed state, and when she can run over them in her mind without feeling too worried by them. This applies to all anxieties. We try to push them out of our minds when we're feeling good, with the result that they pick the moments when we're feeling bad and our defences are down to come flooding back over us. When your child is in a relaxed, happy state she can be encouraged to recall category 1–3 anxieties, and allow herself to see it *is* possible to think about them without feeling distressed. When, over a period of time, she can handle anxieties low on her scale in this way, she can be encouraged to move to those which rank higher up. Work of this kind helps her associate anxieties with a relaxed state of mind rather than an overwrought one, at both conscious and (perhaps even more importantly) subconscious levels.

Finally, help her to see that anxiety isn't something 'silly', of which she must be ashamed. It's just a feeling, and like any other feeling must be acknowledged and accepted. Once accepted it can be kept in proportion and handled, and seen as part of who we are rather than as something which attacks us from outside or from deep down, and over which we can have no control.

Chronic school anxiety is rare Let's reassure ourselves in conclusion that chronic school anxiety is relatively rare, and that most children soon adapt to school and look forward to going. Your child will enjoy the company of other children, the attention of his teacher, the new toys and games, the new experiences and the opportunities to make progress in skills like reading and writing. Before long there will be Christmas parties and treats, class outings, and chances to show how grown-up and responsible he is becoming. And all along there will be your encouragement and assurance, the pleasure you take in the drawing and writing he brings home, and the knowledge that he is learning all kinds of new interests. School immeasurably widens a child's horizons, and widens yours too as you share the stages of his progress with him. The home still remains the major influence in your child's life, and the place where most of his learning takes place, but the school and your child's teacher are powerful allies in your pleasant task of teaching him the varied skills he will need to make a success of the years to come.

And remember that, much as you may miss him, the fact that he is out at school all day gives you a chance to catch up on the interests that have gone by the board while you gave him so much of your attention. This may be the time to take up a career again, or a new hobby, or some voluntary work. If he is your youngest child and there are no more left at home it can seem like the end of an era, with the house quiet all day. But it is also the start of a new era, both in your relationship with your new schoolboy son and in your relationship with your new and freer self.

The start of a new era

Changing school

No matter what his age, changing from one school to another is a very worrying experience for a child. He moves from a secure, familiar environment which he knows into an environment where everything is strange and threatening. He doesn't know anyone and he doesn't know what is expected of him. The teacher will have different rules from those he's been used to. There'll be different reading and number schemes, the class will be further on than he is in some things, and way behind in others. Little boys, in particular, find the new children unfriendly, often refusing to let them join in games. They have somehow to 'prove' themselves first, before they're accepted.

Since you may also have moved house (always a traumatic experience in itself for a young child, however much he copies you and say's he's 'looking forward to it'), and may perhaps be in a new job, you may have less time for your child just when he needs your support and reassurance most. Preoccupied with the problems of settling in, you may resent the extra demands he seems to be making on you, and the extra difficulties he's causing. But *he* didn't ask to move, and it isn't his fault he finds it upsetting and confusing. Try to make extra time for him. Listen to how he got on at school. Make yourself known to his teacher, and discuss with her the work he's been doing. If possible bring all the details of his progress from his old school (schools usually send on this material as a matter of course, but they can forget). Ask if he can bring home his new books so that you can help him familiarize himself with them.

Invite any neighbouring children round to your house so that they can get to know your child and integrate him into things. Establish quickly the whereabouts of library, parks and places of interest. Do all you can to make your child feel at home and get over his strangeness.

HELPING YOUR CHILD WITH SCHOOLWORK

As soon as your child has settled in at school, you'll start to wonder how well he's progressing. Is he keeping up with the other children? Is his teacher pleased with him? It's important not to pressurize him, but these are natural questions, and quite rightly you'll want to do everything you can to help your child make the best of the opportunities school has to offer.

Show him you care about his school life The golden rule right from the start is to show him you care about his school life, that it's part of *your* life too, and that simply because you're not with him in person doesn't mean you forget about him. Obviously this will be clear to him in part from the way you spend time with him at the end of the school day listening to all he has to tell you. But there's more to it than this.

Soon he'll start bringing home little drawings and paintings that he's done. On special occasions like Christmas and Easter there'll be cut-out shapes and simple little seasonal objects like a Christmas card or an Easter bonnet. In November there'll be a Guy Fawkes mask, and at Whitsun paper palm leaves. If he has an imaginative teacher interested in arts and crafts there'll be a constant stream of small items he's 'done' in school. Show him you value them. Keep a wall or a piece of pin-boarding in the kitchen where his work can be on display. Draw it to the attention of visitors. Help your child see that his efforts matter. Don't worry about the standard. The important thing is that they're his, and that you're proud of them.

Through your interest and encouragement you'll help him to take an interest in his own work. If he sees you care about it, then so will he. You'll also be bridging the gap between home and school. Things that are done in school find a welcome place within the home. Likewise, things from home should also find their way into school. So make sure that when his teacher asks the class to bring objects in for display, he has something he can take. It doesn't have to be perfect. Don't fall into the 'You're *not* taking *that* old thing to school!' trap. Your child wants to take part in the things happening in the classroom. He wants to help his teacher. He wants to be useful. Make sure he has the right opportunities, and receives due praise for being co-operative.

Helping with reading

But your interest and encouragement should extend to the more formal parts of the curriculum as well. And in this area there's nothing more important than reading. If you've been giving your child the pre-reading experiences we looked at in Chapter 6, then she will already be fully involved in reading and keen to acquire the skill for herself. She will already have mastered simple words by following the text with you as you read. By age five or soon after, she will normally have developed her perceptual abilities to the point where she can discriminate between the shapes of different letters and words, and understand that these stand for different sounds. Psychologists refer to this as having reached the stage of reading 'readiness'. Some children may even reach it by age three or four provided they've been given the right environment. 'Readiness' indicates your child is raring to go, and can make good use of the help adults offer her.

And here we come to an important point. Many parents say they would love to help their child learn to read, but don't know how. They're afraid of doing the wrong thing. They have the feeling that the teaching of reading should be left to 'experts'. They've got the idea that there is a mystique about teaching reading, and that unless you've received the right training you may do more harm than good. So let me assure you once again that the teaching of reading involves above all else one sympathetic patient adult listening to a child's efforts and prompting and encouraging her as the need arises. Certainly school teachers have special training for this task and most parents don't, but the basic requirement isn't special training. It's a caring attitude towards children, coupled with

You don't need to be an 'expert' to teach your child to read

473

a desire to help them into the magic world of books and an unhurried approach that allows children to go at their own speed and enjoy the activity to the full. And where parents score over teachers is that they can give a child individual attention, instead of attending to her against the background of demands from twenty-five or so classmates.

There are still a few infant schools, I know, that discourage parents from helping with the teaching of reading. They take the old-fashioned view that it's a job exclusively for experts. So if you ask whether your child can bring her reading book home for you to listen to her in the evening or at the weekend the answer is a disapproving 'no', together with an unspoken implication that you're being a nuisance. But such schools are a small minority. The infant teacher is usually only too happy to have the co-operation of parents, and will take time to explain to them the approach to reading adopted in class. Many schools even run special parents' evenings where parents are given specific advice on the reading schemes and methods used in schools, and on how they can best help their children at home, and the reading schemes used in some schools now have supplementary books designed specifically for parent/child use.

A few points to bear in mind But whether such advice is available or not, in helping your child read there are a few straightforward things to bear in mind if you are to be of maximum help. Let's summarize these:

- Select reading material that is at the *right level of simplicity* for your child and that *interests* him. I shall have more to say about this shortly.
- Set aside a few minutes that can be devoted exclusively to his reading. It's no good being in a rush between two important household jobs, or listening to him with your mind on something else. If he sees you're not concentrating on his reading, he won't concentrate either.
- Don't rush to correct him or to supply words for him. Encourage him to try again if he's made a mistake. Show you believe in his abilities. On the other hand, don't keep him focused on a word for too long. If he clearly doesn't know it, say it yourself and go on to the next word.

- Don't show impatience or tell him, 'Come on, you *must* know that word' or worse still 'Oh for goodness sake *think* boy!' If he knew the word he'd say it. Because reading looks so simple to adults we forget that for a small child it can look a very strange business indeed.

- Stop once he's had enough. You want above all to let him have fun with his reading. Keeping him at it if he's tired or has lost interest, in the mistaken notion that you're teaching him perseverance, is likely to turn him against reading.

- Give praise and encouragement. Even if you think he's a little slow compared to a brother or sister before him, never indicate this to him. He'll thrive on your encouragement. But he'll soon lose heart if he's made to feel inadequate. Always teach through success, never through failure.

- Take his occasional outbursts of frustration in your stride. However much he enjoys reading, there'll be moments when he feels impatient with himself for not learning more quickly. Let him get these feelings off his chest. Instead of telling him to 'control himself' say to him 'Okay, it's natural to feel cross sometimes when we can't get on as quickly as we'd like. Let's leave it for now; you'll feel better about it next time.'

- Always choose a good moment for reading. It's no good calling him to read when he's in the middle of an exciting game. He mustn't get the idea that reading is a chore. And it isn't much good if he's tired or cross. With some children a good time is when you've just been reading to them. They're interested and eager to have a shot themselves. With other children it's frustrating to stumble over words when they've just been hearing you read so fluently. Study your child and decide when is a good time for him.

- Show plenty of interest yourself in the story your child is reading. Show him that you depend upon his reading to find out what happens next. A remark such as 'I wonder what happens over the page?' or 'Let's keep on a minute or two longer because I want to know what they're going to get up to after this' are of great value in helping to motivate your child. He sees that his reading is something he's doing for both of you, not just for himself.

- Be careful and methodical in your approach. A regular programme of a few minutes at a time, using the same reading scheme and the same methods, is of far more value than sporadic, disorganized, lengthy sessions.

With these simple points in mind, you'll quickly see progress. Don't expect miracles though. Remember that in this as in everything else your child's development is likely to come in bursts. For a while nothing seems to happen, and he needs the same amount of help each time; words which he knew yesterday have been forgotten again today, and after only a few minutes he loses concentration. Then suddenly one day he races ahead; something seems to have clicked, as if he's spotted an important clue to mastering the code which reading represents. Then he may stay on another pleateau for a while, before once more making that exciting leap forward.

Reading schemes

As I've said, it's vital to offer your child reading material which both interests her and is at the right level. Material of this kind isn't as easy to find as you might think. It takes skill to prepare good reading books for young children. The illustrations must be lively and contemporary, the stories and events must tie in with a child's direct experience and provide her with characters with whom she can identify, and the vocabulary input must be at the right level. This last means introducing the child to the so-called 'key words' (the simplest and most frequently used words in the English language) in easy stages, while at the same time introducing just enough longer words to help capture interest. It also means the phased repetition of words, so that the child meets each word often enough to obtain the necessary practice at it, while not so often that it bores her and restricts the scope of the story.

Reading material must not be too dull or too difficult Once your child has started school, be guided by the reading schemes used by her teachers. But if she's ready for reading before then, choose from the various schemes readily available in the bookshops. You can always tell a reading scheme as opposed to the hundreds of simple books available for children by the fact that it contains a series of books at graded levels of difficulty, taking a child from a 'reading age' of five years through to a reading age of eleven or twelve. ('Reading age' is simply a term that denotes a child is reading up to the average for children of that age; thus a five-year-old with a reading age of seven years is performing at the level expected of a seven-year-old.) You're not likely to go far wrong with any of the widely available schemes currently on the market, but in making your choice keep in mind criteria mentioned in the last paragraph. A book which is too dull or too difficult will only bore and frustrate your child.

Reading methods

Over the last decades, various new methods for teaching children to read have been introduced (actually 'new' is the wrong word; most methods are simply variations on ones that have been around for years, and testify more to the vagaries of fashion than to anything more substantial). Each method is claimed by its supporters as *the* way to approach reading, and scorn is poured on anyone 'misguided' enough to take a different view. There's no need for parents to be too concerned about the variations between one method and another, or too impressed by experts' rival claims. Children have been learning to read successfully and happily enough for centuries, in spite of the experts, and provided a method involves the essentials of interest, correct level of difficulty, adult encouragement and regular practice, it won't be slow to show results.

Shorn of their complexities, most methods reduce either to helping a child recognize the individual sounds made by letters and groups of letters, and then use these to read new words (a 'phonic' approach), or to helping her recognize complete words (or groups of words) by their outline shape (a 'whole word' approach). Sensibly, most teachers use a combination of these approaches, helping children at first to recognize whole words or groups of words then prompting them to use this knowledge to grasp the fact that words are constructed from individual units of sound (letters or groups of letters). Armed with this realization, children can then tackle unfamiliar words by breaking them into these units of sound. Thus, for example, a child who has learnt the words 'the' and 'hat' by their outline shape is able to see what sound 'th' and 'at' each make on their own, and use these sounds to read a new word like 'that'.

The 'phonic' and 'whole word' approaches

Reading with your child

Let's see how you can put this into practice with your child. Assuming you've been reading to your child since his second year, he'll already be familiar with the idea that printed shapes on a page represent words. If you've been pointing to the words as you read, he may even be able to recognize some of the most common ones. Having chosen the right reading book and an appropriate time when you've got his interest, sit down together and show him the book, looking first at the pictures and building up his anticipation by discussing them with him and talking about the characters. Then suggest to him that as it looks so exciting maybe he'd like to read a bit of it himself (if you think he's likely to reject this suggestion, you can be rather more directive and tell him he's so interested in books you're sure he's now ready to start to read; don't use the word 'learn' – keep things light and playful).

When he's ready to read With his agreement, turn to the first page and read the first group of words to him. Then point to each in turn and let him repeat them to you. ('Now you say them . . . good, that's very good'). Then proceed to the next sentence, and repeat the process. If he can't manage a word, use what is sometimes called the 'three P' approach of *pause, prompt* and *praise*. Pause briefly to see if he remembers the word, prompt with the opening sound if he doesn't, and praise him when he gets the word right. If he doesn't remember it after the prompt, simply read the word yourself and go on to the next one. If he's happy to repeat it after you, fine, but don't make a labour of this. Some children are too eager for the next word to want to do this, and it's better not to insist. If the child reads the word incorrectly, never say 'wrong', simply read it correctly yourself. If he finds difficulty in repeating a whole sentence after you, break it down into smaller chunks.

After the first two or three sentences, check with your child whether he wants to go on any further. It's important to stop before he becomes tired, since this leaves him looking forward to the next session. In any case, in these early days, you're still confirming that he's ready to start reading. If he tires easily or loses concentration, he probably isn't, and it's better to put the book away for now, and try him again with it in a few weeks. But whether he wants to read or not, don't make the mistake of reading a page or two for him yourself. This is *his* book, and you're only here to help him, not to take things into your own hands.

At the next reading session, go back over the sentences he's already read ('Let's see if we can read from the beginning again so that you can help me remember what's already happened'). Don't expect him to be word-perfect. Then go on to the next three sentences or so, tackling them in the way you tackled the first three. If he can't recognize a word, remember to pause, prompt and praise. If he misreads a word, read it correctly ('That says . . . now what does it say?'). Once you've got beyond the first page, don't ask him to read from the beginning again each time. It's vital he doesn't become bored. Either pick out odd words or sentences and see if he remembers them, or point to an earlier example of a word he's just read successfully and ask him what it says. Another variant is to ask *him* to point to an earlier word that is the same as one he's just read.

Don't worry if he doesn't seem to pick up much at first. For example, he may repeat the words after you, but when he meets them in the next sentence he doesn't know them. As long as he's keen to carry on, keep up the short daily sessions. As I said earlier, things will come quickly all of a sudden, when you least expect it. You can, however, experiment with a set of flash cards if you wish. These are a set of cards, about 15 x 7.5 centimetres (6 x 3 in.), on each of which you print one of the words he's been meeting in his book. Make your print exactly like that used in the book. Then make a game of it by shuffling the cards and seeing if he can read whichever one you hold up. Or point to a word in the book and ask him to find a card which has the same word, or give him the card and ask him to find the word in the book. Most children enjoy this game, but if your child isn't one of them put the cards away and forget about them. If he doesn't like them, they do more harm than good. And never be tempted to introduce him to cards *before* he's met the actual words in his reading. Flash cards should only be used (if at all) as a game to help him practise what he already knows.

Using flash cards

Usually, quite early on, you'll realize he's learning some of the words in his book by heart. He can rattle them off to you with no difficulty, but when you point to the same words elsewhere in the book he's stumped. This learning by heart is

Learning words by heart

natural, and there's nothing wrong with it. Your child enjoys it and it gives him confidence. Let him 'read' sentences to you by heart if he wishes, and let him show the skill off to visitors (don't deflate him by announcing 'He's only learnt it by heart you know'). Very soon he'll find out the limitations of learning by heart for himself, and will abandon it as his skill increases. But it seems a necessary stage for many children, and helps them maintain interest in the proceedings.

Breaking words up into sounds   As soon as your child has started to recognize words in earnest, you can help him see how to break them up into separate sounds. So if you come to a new word – 'hat' for example – you would tell him 'That word says h-a-t (pronouncing each letter phonetically, i.e. just as it sounds), *hat*'. Then when he's said the word after you, point to the letter 'h' and say, 'So what does that letter sound?' When he tells you, ask him to find other words on the page that start with that letter, and then read these words with him so that he can grasp that whenever the letter 'h' appears at the front of a word it can be sounded the same way. The procedure can be repeated with the other letters in the word, so that he can build up an idea of the way in which words are constructed from individual units of sound, each of them represented by a letter or group of letters.

If he suddenly loses interest   Sometimes, after showing enthusiasm and good progress over a number of days, your child will suddenly say he doesn't want to read when you ask him. If this happens, leave it for a few days before asking him again. If he once more turns you down, allow another few days to go by. Children have crazes, and once the first novelty wears off find themselves less interested. Continue reading to him yourself as usual, and after a short break he'll normally be happy to carry on once more. If he still isn't, then tell him, 'It's a pity really because you were doing so well.' Reinforced by such words he'll be ready to tackle a few sentences. Don't expect too much of him for a while though. Perhaps you've been pressurizing him a little, even though unintentionally.

Exceptions to the rules   Once you start introducing your child to phonics, you'll come across exceptions to the rules he's learnt so far. These exceptions will be few in number in the early books, but they'll soon build up. Look at them carefully, both in terms of pronunciation and in terms of spelling, and you'll find that in

480

fact these exceptions often obey a clear set of rules of their own. Point these out to your child. Explain to him that once upon a time people pronounced the word just as it's spelt, but that this was rather difficult for people to say, so they changed the pronunciation over the years but still kept the original spelling. Agree with him that this is pretty silly!

Occasionally people say small children aren't interested in and can't understand explanations of this sort. Not true. Children usually think it great fun to try to pronounce the word as people once used to say it, and quickly cotton on to the fact that we say it differently these days to make life easier. It's vital that children should be helped to see how the language is changing all the time, and that there are reasons for all the exceptions in spelling and pronunciation they come across. If they don't receive this help, the whole thing remains very confusing for them, and they'll be tempted to give up in disgust.

The reading timetable

Your child may have made a good start to her reading by school age. Or she may not take to it until her sixth year. But unless there are problems, such as difficulties in vision or mental retardation, it's rare for a child to be unable to cope with simple reading skills by the end of her seventh year, and where such inability exists it's usually a sign that something has gone wrong. Perhaps she comes from a home where reading isn't encouraged, or perhaps she's had problems with her teachers. Either way, there's a clear need for extra help, and I'll return to this shortly.

Let the teacher know she can read

If your child has started to read before she begins school, be sure to let her teacher know. If she's made to start again from scratch there's always the risk she'll find it boring. Worse still, she may be held back because the busy teacher doesn't have time to hear her read as often as she needs, and she has to stay on a book she can read blind-folded because she can't move to the next level until the teacher says so. Discuss these matters with the teacher. He should then allow your child to move at her own pace, just listening to her when he can in order to check her progress is genuine. But if he's adamant that she must work at *his* pace, help your child accept that this is simply something with which she has to live. Explain to her that the teacher is very busy and is doing his best, and that in the meanwhile she can have all the new and exciting books she needs at home. Before long she'll be moving up into the next class, where the emphasis upon reading will be greater and where the teacher, fully occupied with helping the slower readers to get started, will welcome the fact that the fast readers can carry on under their own steam.

Listen to her as often as you can

Once your child has made a start with reading, listen to her as often as you can. You'll probably find that if she's very keen she'll bring her book up to you frequently. If for some reason you're too busy, arrange to hear her as soon as you're free. But remember that young children are very much guided by the feelings of the moment; she wants to read *now*, and if you have to put her off until later, she may by then have her mind fixed on something else and be much less enthusiastic.

As she grows in skill, prompt her to tackle new words by giving her only the initial sound and seeing if she can read the rest. Never leave her to struggle though. If she can't get the word reasonably easily, say it for her, ask her to repeat it, then go on to the next one. Another important way of prompting her is by context. If she can't get a word, see if she can pick it up from the context of the rest of the sentence. If she hesitates over a word that she's managed successfully on the previous page, turn back to it and say, 'I think you know this word; look, you read it there; so what does it say?' Still keep in mind the necessity to work through encouragement and through building up confidence and interest though. Never let her feel that reading is something she 'can't do'.

Reading problems

Nevertheless, there *are* children who have more difficulties than most. These difficulties become particularly apparent in children in the 7–10 age range. If a child isn't showing good signs of progress by the time he transfers from the infant to the junior school, his teachers will feel he has difficulties.

Backward and retarded readers

Here we must make an important distinction. Psychologists often divide such children into two categories, called *backward* and *retarded* readers respectively. A backward reader is one who, through limited ability, falls significantly behind his age group, the usual criterion being that by age ten or eleven he is two years and four months behind the average reading level of other ten- or eleven-year-olds. A retarded reader meets exactly the same criterion, but in his case the backwardness isn't explicable in terms of general intelligence. In other words he's just as intelligent as the rest of his age group, and he's fallen behind because of some specific problem. Maybe he's missed a lot of school through illness, or maybe he has some problem of perception or memory which is only apparent when it comes to reading.

Current figures in the UK suggest that by age ten some 20 per cent of children fall into the backward category, while up to 10 per cent may be retarded. Children in inner cities show a much higher incidence of reading difficulties than children in more favoured parts of the country. Backward readers are divided roughly 50:50 between boys and girls, and usually show backwardness in other areas of their school work. Retarded readers on the other hand are more often boys than girls (75:25), and may be well up with the rest of the class in all work that doesn't involve reading.

In many ways backward readers are easier to help than retarded readers, in that their main need is for patient help and encouragement. They experience difficulties in their work because they are a little slower than others in under-standing the various skills required of them, and with guid-ance they can usually become proficient readers in the long run. Retarded readers, on the other hand, unless they have been held back by simple problems such as absences from school, have some specific mental blockage (for want of a better term) which makes reading a mystery to them. They can do everything else. In fact they may be very bright indeed in all other areas. But they can't seem to make the mental connection between the printed shapes on the page and the verbal sounds that go with them. Sometimes this disorder appears linked to other language difficulties, and sometimes to a genuine inability to *remember* the shapes of letters and words.

At one time, teachers and parents would often be impatient with the retarded reader. The view was: 'He's a bright child; if he isn't reading it's because he refuses to read!' We now know better. He'd read if he could; in fact his slowness may be a major cause of frustration for him. He needs extra help and extra practice. And because he's a bright child in other ways, the books we give him must be sufficiently advanced in content to capture his interests. One of the big difficulties is

Suitable reading material for the retarded reader

that although on the one hand he needs books with simple words, on the other he needs books with stories and information that appeal to his ready intelligence. Not many books combine the two, and often children in this category have been put off reading because they've been supplied only with reading material suitable for a child of five.

More suitable reading schemes are now available, and if your child falls into the retarded reader category hunt around in addition for material in everyday life that seems suitable. That is, material which is simply written but which contains adult ideas. Travel brochures often fall into this category, as do certain newspapers and journals. At all costs, keep him interested in reading, and believing in his own ability to master the skill. Research sadly shows that a higher percentage of retarded than backward raders still have reading problems in their teens, and this is largely due to the difficulty of finding material that fully stimulates them. ('Dyslexia', which is often a factor in retarded reading, is dealt with later in the chapter).

The sooner he is given extra help the better If you believe that by age seven your child may be either a backward or retarded reader talk this over with his teacher. The chances are she will already have identified the problem for herself, but the sooner a seven-year-old is given help he needs the better. Indicate to the teacher your own readiness to help with any special reading programme she may decide to use, and ask whether, if your child's problems are severe, he can be referred to the school psychological service for specialist assessment.

There is no magic formula for helping a backward or retarded reader catch up. The method for helping him is very much the one I've outlined for the normal reader, except that, as I've already stressed, he needs extra time and patience on the part of those listening to him read, and special care in selecting suitable reading material. But one supplementary exercise that is often useful is tracing. The child is given words on cards, in suitably large print, and asked to trace round them with his finger. In this way he is able to use muscular memory to supplement visual memory. You can easily give him tracing at home, and if he enjoys working with a pencil he can also use tracing paper, either tracing from special cards or from the words in his reading book. Let him trace pictures as well, so that he doesn't become bored, and don't keep him at it when he's had enough. And – a golden rule – never refer to your child, espeically in his hearing, as a poor or backward reader. Show him you have confidence in his ability. He *will* learn to read in time; it's simply that he's going at his own pace. Don't hold him up for comparison with other children, and don't do anything that will stop him associating books and reading with fun.

Spelling

Although spelling problems are associated more with older children, it's appropriate to deal with them here since they do have links with reading. Both backward and retarded readers are unable to spell correctly. Since they can't remember words well enough to read, there's no chance they can remember the letters which make them up. But there's another class of slow speller, and that is the child who learns to read very quickly and with no problems, but who does so exclusively by recognizing the outline shape of words instead of breaking them down into their individual letters.

Many teachers are puzzled by this kind of poor spelling. 'She's such a good reader,' they say, 'I can't understand why she can't spell.' The reason she's a poor speller is precisely *because* she's such a good reader. She reads so quickly and with such enjoyment that she never needs to look at how words are constructed, and thus has no idea whether the 'i' comes before the 'e' or whether there's a 'ch' or an 'sh' and so on. This doesn't mean all fast readers are poor spellers. But it does mean that when the two things go together a good reader may be inhibited in her written work by a teacher who insists on correct spelling, and who as a consequence forces her to play safe and use only the words she 'knows'.

The fast reader who can't spell

If poor spelling is associated with backward or remedial reading, usually it corrects itself gradually as the reading improves. No special help is needed. But if it's associated with fast reading the best way to help is to ask the child concerned from time to time to take a page in her reading book and read it through very slowly, looking carefully at the construction of each word as she reads. This is far better than making her sweat over long spelling lists, and usually helps children make dramatic progress. A child should never be made to feel bad about her poor spelling though. There are few good readers who can't spell adequately by the time they leave school. Hounding a child over her poor spelling, as still happens in some schools, doesn't help her improve and is only likely to make her nervous and anxious about her work.

Encouraging reading in the older child

Once a child reaches book three or four of a reading scheme she'll be ready to do some reading on her own. She'll do this aloud of course, but reading will become on occasions a private experience for her. She'll curl up in a chair or on the floor, and pointing carefully to each word she'll lose herself in the story. This is an excellent sign, and most parents enjoy watching it take place. Don't spoil it for her by expecting her to read quietly. Hearing her own voice helps her, and when she's ready to read quietly in a few months' time, she'll do it without any prompting from you.

Going to the library Now that your child is discovering the magic of books, make sure she has plenty to choose from. Join the public library, and enjoy outings with her on Saturday mornings or after school to change her books. Browse through the children's shelves with her to show you're interested, but don't be tempted to keep finding books for her. Advise her on her choice by all means, but make sure it is *her* choice. A few encouraging words from you when she's made it ('Yes that looks interesting; I think you'll enjoy that') are invaluable in strengthening her love of books and in building up that delightful anticipation with which each of us, as children, hurried home from the library, clutching our treasures and longing to get started on them.

If a child is a very quick reader and is through her books in no time and eager to return to the library, some parents see this as a nuisance ('Oh I can't keep up with you; you *can't* have read it properly . . . Yes I know you say you have but you just can't . . . Well read it again then!'). This leaves the child with the feeling that she's done something wrong. She thinks she's read the book properly, but perhaps that isn't how you should read it. Perhaps you shouldn't rush excitedly from one page to the next, unable to put it down. Perhaps you should plod through, repressing your excitement. Or perhaps you should ration it out, reading only a few lines each day. Oh dear, reading can't be such fun after all!

Clearly this isn't the result you want with your child. So if she devours one book after another, fine. You want her to be a good reader, and that means she must have something she can use reading *for*. Reading isn't an abstract skill. It's there to be used, which in the case of small children mean exciting story books and more exciting story books.

One thing though. Don't let my references to the library suggest you shouldn't also *buy* books for your child. Unless there are major restraints on the family budget, help your child to experience the thrill of owning books. I know as her reading skills improve they'll quickly in theory be too 'young' for her, but children enjoy returning again and again to a much-loved book, even when they've apparently outgrown it. The book gives them a sense of security, that the good things of childhood are still there. Which of us even as adults can't still enjoy *The Wind in the Willows* or *Alice in Wonderland*, or leafing through the pages of old Rupert annuals? Outgrown them we may have, but they still have a strong emotional appeal for us. Your child has a right to build up her own library, and if later on she decides she no longer wants to keep some of it, then the books can always be given away to the school or to other children who aren't fortunate enough to have books bought for them.

Buying books

Finally, it's a great stimulus to a child's reading if she also sees her parents with their heads frequently in a book. If reading is a part of family life, and if there are always books around, books suitable for all ages, books of information and books of stories, then she'll grow up with the reading habit in a way that would otherwise be denied to her. And how nice it is, as she grows older and comes home with work to do for school or with questions to ask, if you can always say, 'Yes, we have a book that tells us about that; let's look it out.' I don't mean you should fill the house with expensive encyclopaedias. I advise parents against this. You spend a great deal of money on them, and then feel aggrieved if your child doesn't like them. They cost you so much, you feel she jolly well *ought* to like them, and set out to make her guilty about the fact that she doesn't. No; I mean relatively inexpensive reference books, books you like to have to hand yourself as well as books which you buy specially for her. Books which

Seeing you read

487

enrich life and widen the horizons of the home and which, like good friends, are there when you need them.

Writing

Along with reading, you'll probably have introduced your child to writing before he started school (see Chapter 6). Now that he's at school, he'll be given more formal work to do, and before long will be bringing home pieces of paper with an elongated, spidery scrawl on them which he'll proudly announce as his 'name' or a 'story' or more frequently 'what Miss told us to do'. At this stage his attempts at writing are usually combined with drawing. He's been told to draw something, and then 'write' underneath it. This is a good strategy. All small children love drawing, and to combine this pleasurable activity with writing is a good way of developing interest in the latter, particularly with children who haven't received much encouragement at home.

Writing is a complex skill
An important basic point is that writing in fact involves two skills not one – or to be more precise two *sets* of skills. The first set has to do with physical manipulation; your child has to hold his pencil and guide his hand into making the correct shapes. The second set is concerned with mental and visual skills. Your child has to know what it is he wants to write and remember the visual shape of it. All this makes writing into a complex activity, harder to master in many ways than reading. And whereas reading introduces him to interesting stories, writing has fewer immediate benefits for him. Small wonder that, apart from an initial novelty appeal, many children don't seem to find writing a very appealing prospect.

Show your child how useful it is
Help your child by showing him how useful writing is. Let him see you making shopping lists, writing letters, writing notes for the milkman, signing your name on cheques, jotting down ideas or information you want to remember. Have a white board on the kitchen wall on which you write in attractive colours the various things you need to keep in mind. He can have a white board too and make his own 'lists'. Keep plenty of scrap paper and pencils handy as well so that he always has something on which to write and something with which to write. From an early age, let him 'sign' any Christmas

or birthday cards you're sending, and any letters, making a mark next to your own signature so that he's part of the experience. Once he starts school, write down words which you and he use. He's talking about the dog next door for example, and you say, 'Let's see how we write "dog" shall we?', and write it down on the white board. Let him have a shot at copying it. Don't guide his hand. Let him do it himself even though his early efforts many not much resemble yours. Don't correct his efforts in a direct sense, but say to him, 'That's very good; now look, we can make it even better if we get this line to go straight up (or down) like this – here, you have a go.'

As usual, keep all activities of this kind light-hearted. Some parents, with the best of intentions, think they have to make great efforts to help their child 'get ahead'. The result of these efforts is often to make him bored and discouraged. A few minutes every so often, when the activity of writing arises naturally out of other things you're doing together, are of far more value than long concentrated stints when you formally set out to give him a writing 'lesson'.

Left-handedness

What should you do if your child show signs of being left-handed? She may well have shown these signs from a younger age, but when they're small some children are able to switch from left to right with no trouble. Sometimes they'll tend to favour the right hand for a while, then the left, and then back to the right again (or vice versa). But by the time they're ready to tackle writing, hand dominance is becoming fixed and more obvious. If you see your child picking up the pencil with her left hand prompt her gently with 'Let's try it with the other hand; that's the hand most people use.' Being left-handed is fine, but the world is designed for right-handed people, and if she can change without problems then it's better for her. But if it's obvious after the first few weeks that she prefers the left hand, leave her to it. And encourage yourself with the thought that although it's a right-handed world, in sports such as tennis being left-handed may be a definite advantage!

We're not quite sure what causes a preference for the right or left hand in people. Some children can use either, and if they tend to use the left can therefore easily be encouraged to

Factors in the brain that may cause left-handedness

use the right instead. With others, however, it may depend upon factors within the brain itself. The brain consists of two equal hemispheres, joined at the centure by a thick bundle of nerve fibres. Although the hemispheres resemble each other closely they do in fact have different functions. In most people the *left* hemisphere (due to a cross-over effect in the nerve fibres coming from it) controls the *right* side of the body, while the *right* hemisphere controls the *left* side. In addition the left hemisphere controls language and speech and rational thinking and is therefore said to be *dominant* over the right side which is concerned more with spatial ability and perhaps with intuition and artistic and mystical thinking.

If a child is a little unusual in that the right hemisphere of her brain does some of the work usually carried out by the left, then this may lead her to be left-handed. Should she be unusual in this way, it's best to leave her with her left-handedness. Changing to the right will be a big struggle for her, and could lead to emotional upsets and antagonism towards writing. So should she persist in using her left hand after you've made your gentle attempts at correction, it's a fair bet that brain hemisphere factors may be playing a part. Probably there are genetic influences at work here, since left-handedness does seem to run in families, though it may skip a generation.

Don't force your child to become right-handed

You may have heard that changing a child from left- to right-handedness causes her to stammer. The actual evidence for this is conflicting, but since both handedness and speech seem influenced by brain hemisphere dominance there could be a link. The emotional upset involved in having to change from a clearly dominant left hand to the right hand could also play a part. Both speaking and writing are forms of communication, and if a child becomes confused and hesitant about the latter this could prompt confusion in the former too. So if nature intended your child to be left-handed, accept the fact and allow her to get on with the business of learning the small adaptations necessary to cope with a right-handed environment.

More formal help with writing

Sometimes parents ask whether there's anything more they can do to help a child with his writing. If he's making a good start and if his reading is coming along well, thus giving him plenty of experience with words, then there's usually no need. His writing skills will more than keep pace with his growing need for them. But nevertheless if he's very keen, then you can offer him topics for stories which he can use. He may even enjoy, by the time he's six or seven, writing little poems, though a child shouldn't be asked to write poetry against his will. Poetry is very much a matter of inspiration, in small children as in adults, and the quickest way to kill a love for it is to be made to write it. Don't place too much emphasis upon your child being word-perfect in his writing either. At this stage, it's the writing itself that matters rather than the accuracy. Time enough for corrections when he's older and has a longer attention span.

If you think your child is rather *slow* in writing, however, then a little extra regular help is going to benefit him. One good way of providing this is to make up stories together, with each of you taking a share in the writing. Start by saying to your child, 'Let's write a story. What shall it be about?' If he says 'a dragon' you ask him to give the dragon a name, and then you write 'Once upon a time there was a dragon called . . .' and your child with your help writes in the dragon's name. Then, 'Where did the dragon live?' 'In a castle,' says your child. 'Okay, he lived in a castle', – and you write down the first part of the sentence, helping your child complete it with the words he's supplied. And so the story goes on, the pair of you working on it together using different coloured inks to make it look attractive. Once it's finished, it can be put on the kitchen wall, and shown to visitors. To keep up the link between writing and drawing, your child can do a picture of the dragon and his castle and the other characters and events in the story, and that can go on the kitchen wall as well.

Making up stories together

Memory games can also be a great help. Start off with something like 'In the shop they've got some bread'. Then your child says, 'In the shop they've got some bread and some cake.' Now it's your turn and you say, 'In the shop they've got some bread and some cake and some butter' and so on. Each time you come to a simple word say 'Let's write that down on our shopping list', and down it goes on the white board in coloured ink. If it's a word he can tackle, say 'You

Memory games

have a go at that one', or if he can't manage it write it down for him and ask him to copy it. Using your ingenuity you can dream up many little games of this kind. But since you want to make sure he's mastering the necessary basic writing vocabulary, make sure the games incorporate the words used in his reading scheme. Or you can buy a copy of the book *Key Words to Literacy*, which is the book upon which some reading schemes are based, and which lists the most commonly used words in the language.

Writing thank-you letters One last point on early writing experiences. As soon as a child masters the basics of writing, we want him to write his own 'thank-you' letters for gifts received at Christmas and birthdays. There's a danger that this can become too much of a chore for him though (did *you* enjoy writing thank-you letters?). They have to be done of course, and he has to learn the discipline of thanking people properly when they give him things, but both now and throughout childhood keep the experience a *relatively* painless one. The trouble usually starts when parents insist that the letters must be in 'best writing' and word-perfect. Faced with having to make a fair copy when you've corrected his original efforts, your child rapidly feels that the fun has somehow gone out of things. And the final result, though it looks pretty, is a stilted and formal affair, with your wording obviously dominating his own creative endeavours.

Don't insist that they're word-perfect Especially when children are small, most recipients of thank-you letters would much rather have something in a child's own words, mistakes and all, than a thinly disguised parental document, full of prim sentiments and grammar. So the best procedure, and the best learning experience for a small child, is to ask him to tell you what *he* wants to say, write it down word for word, keeping the whole thing very short, and then let him copy it in any colours he likes and put in drawings and any other decorations he fancies. As he grows older, so he can be left to take over more of the writing himself, with you spelling words to him as he needs them. Don't worry if the finished product is less than a visual masterpiece. Better to send it as it stands than to make him write the whole thing out again. When he's older still and you feel mistakes should now be kept to a minimum, it's perfectly good practice to make the corrections yourself, with a deft stroke of the pen, as long as he's with and you can explain to him what the corrections are and why they have to be made.

Some parents are horrified at this idea and feel that it's 'good' for the child to have to write out corrections himself, even if he has to make several drafts of the letter before it's fit to pass the parental censor. But the result is that as the child grows older there are more and more battles to get him to do his letters at all. He keeps groaning and putting them off every time you remind him, and finally turns to them with a bad grace and with every sign of further skirmishes ahead before the wretched things eventually find their way into the post. The point is that the letters now have nothing to do with gratitude and thanks at all, and have simply become a bind for everyone concerned. You may never be able to help your child actually *enjoy* doing his thank-you letters, but with sense and humour you can help him to do them with a good grace, and to keep in mind that the real reason for doing them is to tell someone he appreciates their kindness.

Dyslexia

You've probably heard the term 'dyslexia' used in connection with retarded readers and writers, so it's appropriate to deal with the problem here. The term 'dyslexia' doesn't have a precise definition, but it's usually taken to refer to *problems of laterality*. That is, to difficulties in knowing left from right. As a consequence of these difficulties, a child will tend to write letters and words the wrong way around. Looking at her writing, it often makes no sense at all. It's as if she's invented a code of her own, except that usually (though not always) she isn't able to read it herself either! You may hear this writing referred to as 'mirror writing', because if you hold it up to a mirror some of the words may be more intelligible than when read normally.

We're not sure of the cause of dyslexia, but it doesn't seem to represent any one single condition with any one single underlying neurological cause to account for it. In fact many psychologists think the term may be too vague to have a great deal of value. We do know, however, that dyslexia isn't linked to intelligence. Many otherwise bright children suffer from it, which suggests that it arises from some problem of perception and not from any difficulties with thinking. That is, the

Dyslexia isn't linked to intelligence

493

message received by the eyes and transmitted to the brain arrives scrambled in some way, before the brain has a proper chance to make use of it. Dyslexic children should therefore never be allowed to feel that they are less able than their fellows. Though more far-reaching in its effect, dyslexia is more on a level with colour-blindness and other perceptual problems than with mental backwardness.

Signs that your child is dyslexic

If your child is dyslexic, this will become apparent early on, when she first starts to write. You'll notice that although she scribbles and makes shapes like other children, when she reaches the stage of actually forming letters she'll either find great difficulty in copying them at all, or will *consistently* (most children do it occasionally) reverse them. She'll also show great difficulty in distinguishing right from left, pointing or looking in one direction when you ask her to indicate the other. Some children are made to go through a very unhappy time by adults who think they are being deliberately obtuse, but the truth is that they can't readily orientate their writing, objects, or themselves in space. However, the degree of dyslexia varies greatly from child to child. In some children, it will be so mild as to go virtually unrecognized until they tell you one day, perhaps years later, that they have to glance down at their hands for clues when asked to decide between left and right. In others it will be so marked that the child may find great difficulty in coping with much of her school learning.

In addition to problems with writing, the dyslexic child will have difficulties with reading, spelling, and any games that involve laterality. The extent of these difficulties will depend upon the extent of the dyslexia, but the vital factor is that the child should never be discouraged, through fear of failure, from taking an interest in these skills and from making the necessary efforts to master them. With patience and extra help, even the severely dyslexic child can make at least enough progress to cope adequately with these skills, and to develop a belief in her own capabilities. So if you have reason to think your child is dyslexic, draw this to her teacher's attention as soon as she starts school. At around age six, he will ask the educational psychologist to assess her, using tests specially designed for the purpose, and to establish the extent of her disability and the amount of special help she may be going to need.

The readiness with which this special help is available varies from one part of the country to another though, so be prepared to make a nuisance of yourself if you feel that your child is missing out. But because there is no 'cure' for dyslexia, much of this specialist help simply takes the form of extra patient and sympathetic teaching, involving primarily the techniques for helping with reading and writing that I've already discussed. And here you can do a great deal to help at home, because no very advanced teaching skills are involved. Your child needs above all an adult who will spend extra time with her over her writing and reading, who will invent little games to keep up her interest, and who will give her confidence that she is going to succeed. Often tracing over the outline of letters (as already mentioned with any child who has reading or writing difficulties) is a great help; the child through repetition gradually gets the hang of the way the letters go. Making designs and patterns based upon the shape of letters, and then colouring them in, also helps. So does the simple expedient (with the child's consent, and not when other children are likely to see it and tease her) of putting an 'r' for right on the back of her right hand, and an 'l' for left on the back of her left. Colours can be used to make the lesson even more effective, red for right perhaps, and blue for left. The colour coding can then be used in the child's bedroom, with red objects on the right side of her bed, and blue on the left. Use any other expedients that occur to you to differentiate right from left, such as different coloured socks and different coloured gloves.

But do remember to keep everything game-like and relaxed. And be prepared for constant set-backs. With a severely dyslexic child she may seem to have grasped things one day, and be all at sea again the next. Keep telling yourself that if she could get things right, she would. She'll be particularly prone to confusion when she's faced with anxiety, as in school examinations. So make sure her teachers are reminded of the fact whenever necessary. In public examinations, like GCSE, examination boards should be told by the school of a child's difficulties *before* she's taken the examination. It's less effective if they're told afterwards, when she's already got poor marks.

Specialist help and help at home

Don't let her use her dyslexia as an excuse

But as with *any* childhood disability, it's important not to let your child use her dyslexia as an excuse for not doing unpopular things, or as an emotional let-out if you and she are at odds with each other. See that she takes a sensible attitude towards it. If she's being given all the help and sympathy she needs, she's unlikely to make a habit of excusing herself, but if she does, remind her that it's *because* of her dyslexia that she must try that little bit harder than others, and that she's due extra credit when she succeeds. Don't let her wear 'dyslexia' as a badge on her chest. Show her you fully understand the demands it makes upon her, but that with determination and perseverance she can and will learn to cope with it.

Mathematics and number work

Once upon a time education used to be based upon what were called the three Rs – namely reading, writing and arithmetic. Though this set a puzzle to small children wanting to know how to spell the last two words, there was a great deal to be said for this. Reading, writing and arithmetic, the three basic subjects, lie at the centre of most educational activities. And although in more recent years there has been a reaction within schools, the reaction has been more against the formal way in which the three Rs were once taught than against the subjects themselves. Armed with competence in reading, writing and arithmetic, a child has an excellent start to his educational career.

Having looked at reading and writing, let's turn our attention to the third member of the trio, arithmetic (or 'number work' as it is usually called in infant schools). As with reading and writing, a child starts life with a natural interest in numbers. I've stressed throughout the book that a child is born curious. He wants to find out about the world and how it works, and to grow in the competence and skills that will allow him to master his environment. So to him, learning starts off being fun. He enjoys it. It's part of play. He learns quickly and naturally, not by setting out to master something in a formal sense, but by *doing*, by exploring and experimenting, by seeing for himself what makes this work, what that's made of, how these two things relate to each other.

At a very early age then, almost as soon as he begins to build up a working vocabulary, a child realizes that one way in which the world is organized is through *counting*. People put two or more things together and give them strange sets of names. Moreover, these strange sets of names seem to apply no matter what the objects themselves happen to be. You can have one, two, three apples, or you can have one, two, three bricks, or you can have one, two, three stories and so on. All very intriguing. You can even add quite different things together and still call them one, two, three, as for example when a parent puts three quite separate items in a shopping bag and says 'I've got three things to carry'.

Added to all this, a child early realizes that he carries around with him the most marvellous visual aid to number skills, namely his own body. Even before he knows the special words for them he can see that he has two of certain items, like hands and arms and legs, and a greater number of other items like fingers and toes. So he's naturally geared towards number skills, and once he's introduced to counting he'll usually catch on very quickly.

So why is it that once they start school many children get the idea that they're 'no good' at number work, and often carry this notion with them through school and into adult life? The answer is that their early delight in mathematics is killed off by the way in which it's so often presented. Provided he can understand the way in which he is being taught to use numbers, and provided he can see the purpose behind the mathematical skills, there's no reason why any child shouldn't go on enjoying maths and gain a competent knowledge of how it works. Part of the secret lies in helping him *discover* mathematics for himself, by giving him mathematical games and puzzles, rather than simply presenting him with a set of mathematical rules which he has to learn without proper understanding.

As a parent, you may still be suffering from the mathematical education you yourself received when young, and may be very doubtful of your ability to give your child any useful help. Don't be discouraged. You know quite enough to give him a good start, and you can easily discover for yourself, alongside him, all the maths you're likely to need to help him throughout his primary school career. I know this doesn't

Children catch on to counting easily and naturally

Children who say they are 'no good' at maths?

apply necessarily to computer mathematics, but if you have a good grasp of basic mathematical skills, then computer maths is simple enough. This book isn't the place to tackle computer maths, but there are plenty of specialist texts that will give you the help you need. Learn this new branch of maths step by step with him, and give each other the encouragement you both need.

Counting and settling

But to return to ordinary number skills. In the pre-school years, and especially if you've given her early experiences of the kind mentioned in Chapter 6, your child will quickly master two essential basic concepts, *counting* and *setting*. Counting refers to the progression of numbers from one upwards, while setting refers to the different categories into which things can be grouped. This is a set of red objects for example, this is a set of blue. This is a set of oranges, this is a set of apples. This is a set of fingers, this is a set of toes. Almost simultaneously with grasping the ideas of counting and setting, the child learns that the two things can be brought together. We can have four apples in this set and we can have three oranges in that set. We can have five fingers in this set and five toes in that. We can have six houses in the set on this side of the street, and seven houses in the set on the other side.

Adding and subtracting

By the time she starts infant school, your child will usually be able to grasp the idea of adding as well. If we already have two chocolate bars in our set and we add another two, this gives us four chocolate bars. And, since the idea of subtraction comes almost as quickly, if we take two of them away again then we're left with only two. Learning of this kind comes primarily from simple everyday experiences in the home. I've already emphasized the vital importance of talking to your child as much as you can from babyhood onwards. Now let's emphasize that this talking should include references to numbers. When you're out shopping together, when you're cooking, when you're playing with her, bring numbers into the conversation. Just as she gets the idea of reading from watching you read to her and point to each word as you go along, so she'll get the idea of numbers and sets from your casual chatter. A child who hears you saying, as you pause at the supermarket shelves, 'I think we need four of those' or 'No I think we need six, so I'd better take another two' or

498

'We've got six but I think four will do, so we'd better put two back' gets priceless early experiences in counting, setting, adding and subtracting. It's only a small step from this to asking her, 'We've got four and we need six, so how many more shall we take?' or 'If we've got six and I put two back how many do we have now?'. If she doesn't know, give her the answer. Remember that in addition to the importance of making learning fun, little children have an independent streak in them. If they get the idea we're very keen for them to learn something they can dig in their heels and refuse to co-operate. Alternatively, they can become over-anxious to please us, and in their very anxiety find that learning refuses to come easily. So keep number work as a normal, natural part of life; her natural curiosity will more than guarantee the arousal of her interest.

If your child has a good grasp of counting, setting, adding and subtracting at age five, she'll soon be ready for multiplication and division. Though the ages at which these two skills are introduced to children varies from school to school, many children are perfectly able to cope with them in infant school. Help your child to *understand* these skills though. Many children learn them without really comprehending the simple principles that lie behind them. They can 'do' multiplication and division because they've learnt the rules, but they have no idea how the rules work or what the underlying principles are. Use counters or buttons so they can concretely observe these principles. **Multiplication and division**

In the case of multiplication, this principle is simply addition. Four times two is just another (quicker) way of saying four sets of two. Add them up to show this to your child. Four sets of two gives us $2 + 2 + 2 + 2 = 8$, while $4 \times 2 = 8$. It's the same principle. The only difference is that to save us doing the addition we learn multiplication tables. Help your child see the truth of this by getting her to 'invent' the two times table for herself. She can construct each of the number bonds ($2 \times 2 = 4$, $3 \times 2 = 6$, $4 \times 2 = 8$ and so on) by doing the simple additions for herself, thus 'proving' that multiplication is only a glorified form of addition.

Children, by the way, thoroughly enjoy multiplication tables as long as they're kept light-hearted. The prejudice against teaching tables in schools, which came about as a reaction to **Learning tables** the grim way in which tables had been ground into children in the past, has all but disappeared. Knowing one's tables is an excellent way to gain confidence in handling numbers, and provided they're not made to feel anxious over it most children find the effort of memory involved in learning tables well within their scope. I'm greatly in favour of letting a child 'invent' each table for herself before she's actually asked to learn it. This inventing helps her see the link between addition and multiplication, and by the time the invention is completed she's usually half-way to knowing the table anyway.

Another great help is to prompt your child to see the *pattern* that develops in each of the tables. The ten times table is very easy because the pattern is that the tens column goes up by one each time while the units column remains zero. Similarly the five times is easy because the units column goes up alternatively by five and zero, while the tens column goes up one each time the units column is zero. In the nine times table you take one from the units column and add it to the tens column each time. The eleven and twelve times also have easily identified patterns. The patterns in the other tables are more complex, and aren't much use as an aid to memory, but they're still useful to spot because they help your child to get a feeling for how numbers behave.

Helping with division Division is simply multiplication in reverse. Whereas in multiplication we were asking how many have we in four lots of two, in division we take the answer to this question (i.e. eight) and say how many sets of two does this give us? Small children find it hard to understand this principle at first, because it involves reversibility (reversing a process so that you put things back as they were), and reversibility is something they can only grasp when they've reached an appropriate point in their mental development. But by the time they are introduced to division in schools they should be able to handle it. As with all rules in mathematics and in so much of learning, prompt your child to try to discover the principle behind division for herself. Give her the conditions under which the principle should be clear, and then ask her to tell you what the principle is.

One way of doing this is to ask her to tell you again what the principle of multiplication is. 'Four times two is just another way of saying . . .?' When she provides the answer

('Four lots of two') then ask her, 'And what do four lots of two come to?' When she answers 'eight', say, 'Now if I give you eight and ask you how many lots of two you could split that into, what would you say?' Once she's worked this out, you're ready to tell her that what she's just done is to *divide*. She knows how to multiply, which is a quick way of adding up, now she's learning to divide, which is a quick way of breaking things down again. Illustrate this further by taking a multiplication number bond, say $2 \times 2 = 4$, and showing the relationship between this and $4 \div 2 = 2$. We can take any multiplication table and turn it into a division table simply by reversing the order of the numbers and changing the multiplication sign to a division sign. Thus $2 \times 2 = 4$ becomes $4 \div 2 = 2$, and $2 \times 4 = 8$ becomes $8 \div 2 = 4$ and so on. If she can't quite grasp it, this means she isn't yet fully ready. Leave it a few weeks then try again. Show you have confidence in her though. Introduce the topic with words such as, 'You remember when we were talking about division the other day and you were nearly able to see what I meant? Well I wonder if I can make it clearer this time'. Don't give her the impression that she was slow in grasping it. She wasn't. It was simply that she wasn't yet quite old enough. When the moment is right, she won't have any real problems.

In all the mathematical experiences discussed so far, a young child will learn much more quickly (and often will only learn at all) if you give him actual objects with which to work. Mathematics is an abstract language (numbers themselves are ideas rather than physical objects) until we relate it to things a child can actually see and touch. So it's no good talking to him about 'three' or 'four'. We need to talk about 'three dogs' or 'four balls'. When it comes to counting and setting he needs to have things in front of him that he can physically count and group into sets. And when it comes to adding and subtracting, multiplying and dividing, he needs the same sort of direct, concrete experience. He's too young for abstract thinking. Unless he's actually involved in concrete experience, or has memories of it upon which he can draw, he finds it hard to make sense of whatever it is you are explaining to him. **Keep his experiences concrete**

So make sure that, in addition to the household objects and the items of shopping that you can count with him, he also has plenty of counters or blocks, with different colour sets or **Give him objects he can sort and count** different size sets, which he can use to represent the number experiences that you are giving him. An abacus or counting frame can be useful with the very young, but as soon as your child reaches the stage of setting it's better if he can group things for himself. Make sure that in addition to counters or blocks he has many other interesting objects which will help to stimulate his interest in numbers and the way they behave. A large button box, full of different sets, colours and sizes of buttons is invaluable (though things like this should be kept away from children until you're sure they won't swallow them). So are sets of glass marbles and beads. If you're fond of natural foods you'll have a cupboard full of different kinds of beans. Handfuls of each mixed together and given to your child to sort into separate piles provide him with fun and the right kind of experience. Sets of toy soldiers and toy animals, sets of wood screws, sets of paper clips and paper fasteners can all be used in the same way. The emphasis in each case remains the same. Interest and diversity, and a set of tasks which your child enjoys doing and out of which mathematical experiences arise naturally.

You can also make special apparatus of one kind or another. A piece of peg-boarding into which coloured pegs can be fitted is helpful in teaching multiplication and division. Use different coloured pegs for the hundreds, tens and units, and when he reaches the stage of writing down his sums show him how the process of carrying from one column to the next actually works. Number stairs, which are exactly like the wooden triangles used to group the red balls on a snooker table, are also useful in the early stages of counting. You can also buy educational toys and educational equipment of the kind used in schools.

Mathematical experiences from everyday life are best But on the whole mathematical experiences drawn from the happenings and objects of everyday life, in the way already described, are the best introduction to mathematics. They're not only readily available, with each day throwing up new opportunities, they show your child that mathematics isn't a special, separate skill. Mathematics is part of the fabric of living. In the home, at the shops, in the car, almost everything is linked in some way with numbers and the manipulation of numbers. From the ten fingers on our hands to the language of the home computer, numbers are as natural a part of each day as are speech and music. And what's more there's nothing mysterious about them. Given opportunities to understand how numbers behave and the principles we use when we handle them, no child should lose his early interest in them or find them beyond his ability. Certainly children will vary, probably innately, in their aptitude for more advanced work. Some children will quantify things almost from the word go ('How far is it?' How many are there?', 'How heavy is it?'), and will race ahead when they get to school. Others will simply use maths as a useful tool in helping them cope with necessities. But no child should ever feel that there's anything about mathematics that puts the subject beyond him.

Written mathematics

Once a child's started writing words and individual letters she can have a go at numbers. When a number is mentioned, tell her, 'I'll show you how we write that down', and then give her the pencil so that she can have a go herself. As soon as this process is well under way, write down the numbers from one to ten, with the appropriate number of dots against each one, and put the chart up on the kitchen wall. Make it big and colourful, so that she'll be attracted to look at it, and will quickly learn which written number goes with which set of dots. Children love little puzzles, so make out some cards with sets of dots on each, and ask her to write down the appropriate number each time you show her a card. Let her 'test' you too, and make the odd deliberate mistake so that she can have the fun of correcting you and showing how clever she is.

When she comes on to addition and subtraction, explain to her that we can keep a record of what we're doing. So when we add two marbles to another two marbles we can write this down by drawing a picture of two marbles and two marbles equals four marbles, and then write down the numbers themselves ($2 + 2 = 4$). At this early stage, it's important that you talk about 'keeping a record of what we're doing' rather than 'writing down a sum'. This helps emphasize again that mathematics is about real events in the real world. Written sums are merely ways of recording these events, just as written words are ways of recording real language. I can't stress too often that your child mustn't be given the false impression that mathematics is divorced from direct experience. Once children get this impression, many of them end up believing

Keeping a record of what you're doing

503

that maths has no relevance to their lives, and that it's beyond their understanding anyway.

Writing down sums   Most children find no difficulty in learning and writing numbers, and the four function symbols (+ − × ÷) that go with them. Nor do they have any problem grasping the idea this this is quicker than actually drawing pictures of the objects we're adding up and taking away, etc. They can build on this knowledge by writing down more advanced sums when they are introduced to them at school. Help your child to see, though, that if she writes down a sum incorrectly she spoils her chances of working it out. This is particularly important when she comes to writing down sums using columns instead of lines (i.e. $\begin{array}{r} 4 \\ +4 \\ \hline 8 \end{array}$ instead of 4 + 4 = 8). Many children get off

to a very confusing start with tens and units simply because they allow the tens column to wander into the units and vice versa. A little care and accuracy at this early stage pay handsome dividends later. Once a child begins to get her sums 'wrong' at school and gets the idea that she 'can't do' mathematics the trouble really starts.

Mathematics at school

If your child is familiar with numbers before he starts school, and if he receives the necessary support and encouragement from home, he'll usually make good progress. But many parents still feel they want to give him that bit of extra help, just as they want to help with his reading and writing. The problem is that of the three Rs, mathematics is often the one they feel least sure about. Even when their child comes home with specific questions about his number work they're at a loss how to help. They know the mathematics well enough, but they don't know the methods used by the school to teach them, and their uncertainty becomes worse when their child tries to show them these methods. 'We did things differently when I was at school,' says the puzzled parent, 'I may only confuse you.' They may also have heard reference in educational circles to something called the 'new' mathematics, and imagine that this represents completely fresh knowledge about numbers and the way they behave.

The truth is that there's no such thing as 'new' mathematics. Mathematics is mathematics, and although fashions for teaching them (some good, some less so) come and go, the basic principles remain the same. New methods when they come along are simply someone's idea for teaching these principles to children in a form which they can perhaps more readily understand.

Since different schools use different methods and work from different textbooks, this isn't the place to try to outline the details of what goes on. But there are certain things which you can bear in mind when trying to understand what is happening in your child's school and what you can do to help him. The first is that in many infant classes the teacher uses work cards rather than text books. Usually these are cards which she has prepared herself, though there are commercial sets available. Ask if you can see these cards and get some idea of what your child is doing. Most infant teachers are happy to co-operate, and on parents' evening will in any case put out these cards and other teaching materials for you to browse through. Once you see the kind of thing that is being used, you can make similar cards at home, and run through them with your child, laying the emphasis not only upon the right answer but more importantly on understanding how the right answer is arrived at. A few minutes a week of work of this kind is of enormous benefit for a child. Remember that if he doesn't fathom out how to do something in school he has to wait his turn for the teacher's attention in a class of other children.

Have a look at your child's work cards

The second thing to bear in mind is that once a child goes on to a mathematics textbook, he may be able to understand the maths well enough but not understand the language in which the book is written. In an attempt to make all mathematics practical and interesting, the most widely used textbooks these days present sums to children in the form of written problems drawn from everyday life. This is laudable enough, but the difficulty arises with the child who is racing ahead in mathematics but whose reading is a little slow. He literally cannot understand what he is required to do. And when he does cotton on, he's often disappointed to find out how simple the actual mathematics contained in the problem turns out to be. If your child falls into this category, discuss the matter with his teacher. It's unfair for a child to be held back in his maths simply because his reading isn't up to the

Some children have difficulty reading the textbook

same standard. Many children who are good at maths and get less fun than they might out of reading actually enjoy seeing a page in front of them containing numbers and no words. Though some teachers are slow to accept the fact, once a child has mastered the basic principles behind the four rules of number (adding and the other three), he often thoroughly enjoys the 'old-fashioned' sums which used to be the staple diet of mathematics textbooks. Even the child who is good at reading may get the same pleasure out of them. For these children, there's no need to wrap number work up in a smoke-screen of written language. They already understand the important lesson that maths is about real life, and are now eager to use the shorthand that written numbers represent.

If you can't convince your child's teacher that his maths book isn't suitable for him (and she may say, 'Yes you're right but the headteacher *insists* we use this wretched scheme of books'), then give him plenty of practice with his sums at home. Write out a page for him; within five minutes he's usually back clamouring for another page.

You can buy textbooks yourself The third point to keep in mind is that all books used in school are available to you through your own bookshop. None of them is restricted for sale to schools. Ask your child's teacher if he can bring his book home, and if the answer is 'no' (as it often is for maths books) then make a note of the title and order it from your bookshop. I know there's a danger here that if your child forges ahead at home, and his teacher insists he go through it all again in school, he's going to find classwork rather dull. But at least he'll have the satisfaction of getting all his work right, which will do wonders for his confidence, and you can make sure he fully understands his work and can help with the reading problems which the book may raise. Familiarizing yourself with his textbook will also give you an opportunity to understand the methods your child's teacher is using, and to impress other parents with your knowledge!

Is the maths teaching at your child's school up to scratch? Of course, there's no need to go to these lengths if you're happy your child is coping with his number work, and that the school he attends does a good job compared with other schools in the district. This latter point is vital, since your child will transfer one day to the secondary school (or to middle school and then secondary school if that's the local pattern), and it will be a daunting experience for him if he finds the children from his school way behind those from other primary schools in the catchment area. True most secondary schools try to ensure that all their children are at a common minimum standard by the end of the first year, but so much of educational success depends upon confidence and a belief in one's own abilities. Once a child is behind the others, it's hard for him to regain his conviction that he's as good as they are.

As with all other areas of your child's education, don't be afraid to sound the opinion of other parents and to take the matter up with the school if you think the maths teaching is below standard. If a child isn't given the right start in mathematics in the primary school his chances of making an eventual success of the subject are slim, which means that by the age of eleven he'll already have a range of eventual career opportunities closed to him. You can't be a scientist or an engineer without maths, to say nothing of accountancy or computing. If he turns out not to want a career involving maths all well and good. But you want him to be in a position one day to make that choice for himself.

Early scientific experiences

Science is about building theories about how the world works, and using these theories to control the environment. I've already indicated that children are born scientists. Their natural curiosity and their need to cope with life see to that. So unless they're turned against it, as with mathematics, they should take readily to the subject once they start school.

Your child will already have been given a good start in the pre-school years by the way in which you answered her questions, and the way in which you gave her opportunities through play to explore how things work and how materials behave, how you can see what happens if you do this and how you can find ways of stopping that. But the years from five to eleven are the real time to establish a grasp of basic scientific ideas and interests. This is the period when your child's curiosity about the world outside the home is really taking off, but when she's still sufficiently dependent upon

Much depends on what happens in the home

you to want to do things together. This is the peak period for family outings, for making models and pieces of apparatus in the home, for working on 'projects' for school, for collecting everything from acorns to grass snakes, and for enthusiasms about a hundred and one impractical and glorious schemes.

Much of the difference between children at this age, in terms of their interests and abilities, depends upon what happens in the home. Often parents bemoan the lack of progress or of hobbies in their primary school child, but when questioned reveal they've done nothing themselves to stimulate and encourage these things. They seem to expect, in some miraculous way, that it's all just going to 'happen' on its own, without any active participation on their part. When questioned further they say, 'Well she did show an interest in foreign stamps/bird watching/fishing/keeping rabbits, but we don't know anything about it so we couldn't help. Anyway, I didn't want her making a mess in her room/spending her pocket money/bringing the filthy things into the house.' It's little wonder that these interests, one by one, come to nothing.

Make sure your child has the right experiences

With science then, it's important you play your part in giving your child the right experiences. You don't need to be an expert yourself. Far from it. Let her help you open up a whole new area of interest for yourself. Learn alongside her. Listen to her and read the books she brings home. Spend a little time and money visiting libraries and bookshops and laying in a stock of useful pieces of science equipment. Not expensive chemistry sets but bulbs and batteries and lengths of wire, measuring flasks and containers, a soldering iron (to be used with care and under strict parental supervision), tools suitable for a child to use, magnets, battery-operated electric motors, modelling equipment and glue, and a little later on simple micro-chips, buzzers and bells and things that will add an extra dimension to her fun and her understanding.

Never miss a good learning opportunity

All these things are cheap enough, and should be bought not all at once but in response to her developing interests or as a result of something you've seen and want to try to build at home or in response to a new subject she's studying at school. Be imaginative and try to see the possibilities in each new experience. One of the most important qualities of a good schoolteacher is that they never miss a learning opportunity for their children, and the same is true of a good parent.

508

Throughout childhood, you remain your child's most important teacher. Whatever crops up, if there is a chance to use it to help widen your child's knowledge, then do so.

If, for example, your child is at a school where there's a good emphasis upon arts and crafts, then from the age of seven or eight onwards she'll be making a constant stream of models and projects for school. Small houses for a model village; castles and forts; lighthouses and lightships; aeroplanes and boats. Whenever the class tackles something new in school, the teacher will ask them to explore some aspect of it through arts and crafts, showing the class how to use throwaway household items like washing-up liquid containers, newspapers, cartons and matchboxes. Help your child link these arts and crafts experiences with science. With the aid of batteries, bulbs and a few pieces of wire she can give her lighthouse a real light, or illuminate her houses or her boats. With the help of a bell-push wired into the circuit her castle can have a signalling beacon, or her fire station an alarm buzzer. By experimenting in this way a child of eight can master all she needs to know about simple electrical circuits.

Make sure this kind of fun is encouraged as much in daughters as in sons. Too often girls learn that science and everything connected with it isn't really for them. Their place is with the less exciting, more mundane things of life. The really important jobs have to be left to the boys. As I pointed out earlier, we must make experiences available equally to both sexes. The time to convince girls they have as much right as boys to careers in science, technology and engineering is not when they're making their choice of GCSE subjects but now, in early childhood. **This applies to girls as much as to boys**

I'm not suggesting of course that you should try to force science on either your daughters or your sons. Although all children have wide interests, some gravitate naturally towards the arts, some towards science, some towards the social sciences and so on. There may well be a temperamental, inborn factor here. Some children start trying to build the Severn Bridge at age three, others prefer to concentrate on writing their major symphonies or on putting Rembrandt and Picasso in the shade. Children must be allowed to develop their own direction in these matters. But the important thing is to make scientific experiences available to them. If, after satisfying their initial curiosity, they gradually move away from this field, all well and good. But at least they will have had the chance to explore it, and will have grasped many of the basic principles upon which more advanced work is based.

Art and music

Just as children must be given these opportunities in science, so must they be given them in the arts. If your own interests are mainly scientific and if there isn't much emphasis upon pictures or music or poetry in the home, try to redress the balance a little. I talked earlier about the importance of pictures in your child's room (Chapter 1), but the colour and life that pictures bring shouldn't be confined to his bedroom. If your child grows up in a house that provides an aesthetically pleasing environment, then although he may not seem to take much conscious notice of it, there will nevertheless be a deep impression upon him at a subconscious level. As he grows up he'll find more and more benefit in the pleasing, harmonious atmosphere with which he's surrounded, to the benefit of his own psychological growth.

Music

Make music part of his life As in the earlier years, make sure your child has plenty of materials for arts and crafts, and introduce him to music not only through the songs and rhymes that you sing with him but also through the record player and the tape recorder. If you play a musical instrument yourself so much the better; draw him into the experience by playing to him and allowing him to request his favourite tunes. But whether you play yourself or not, give him the chance to learn. Many schools start children on the recorder, and there are often opportunities later for violin lessons. But try to provide these experiences through the home as well. A glockenspiel or a small xylophone are excellent buys for a young child, and he'll quickly learn to pick out simple tunes for himself. If you have a piano, arrange lessons for him from age seven or eight (even earlier if he shows special interest), and the same applies if you have other suitable instruments in the home.

Some parents find music lessons something of a worry.

They cost money, require parents to fetch and carry, and often lead to endless battles in the home when the child neglects or rushes his practice. Parents ask is it worth it, and how long should they keep their child at it if he isn't interested? The answer is that most certainly it's worth it. The ability to play a musical instrument can bring great joy in life, and the earlier a child starts the better. But if, after a reasonable time (I recommend a year or two but there's no hard-and-fast rule), and given that your child has a good teacher whom he likes, it's clear he's getting very little out of it and would prefer to give up, then let him do so. He's been given the opportunity, but it isn't for him. He just isn't musical in that way, or at least not yet. And once you've received this clear signal, it isn't fair to him or his teacher (or your own pocket) to keep him at it any longer.

Are music lessons worth it?

But when your child *is* taking music lessons, it's vital for him to see that you're interested in his progress. Set aside a definite time for his daily practice, so that he'll get into the habit of doing it. If he has a good teacher, he or she will give your child specific pieces to practise, and this acts as a good incentive since he won't want to go to his next lesson unable to play them. A good teacher will also see to it that the pieces are carefully selected with your child's age and ability in mind. It's important he should enjoy his music. On the other hand mastering an instrument does require self-discipline, and your child has to learn that he must put in a basic commitment if he's to make progress. Sit with your child while he practises, not in order to pick him up over his mistakes but to share your own enthusiasm with him. In the early stages, developing a good attitude towards music and towards the practice sessions is far more important than being note-perfect. And of course there's no need to rush your child into taking music examinations. His teacher will know when he's ready; far better to leave each examination a little later than necessary, and be sure he's going to pass, than to enter him for it too early and expose him to the disappointment of failure.

Sit with your child while he practises

If your child is particularly gifted in music or in any branch of the arts, it's worth making sacrifices to see that he receives the proper tuition. On the other hand, simply because he's gifted don't assume that he's bound to want to go on and make a career in the area concerned. A child may become an

He doesn't have to make a career out of it

outstanding musician or dancer (or sportsman or woman come to that), and yet show no interest in taking it up professionally. The important thing is that he enjoys his music or singing or acting or sport *now*. Childhood isn't just a preparation for adult life. It's a stage of life in its own right. You may spend time and money on a musical training for your child and then feel they've been wasted because he only keeps it as a hobby (or gives it up altogether) when he's an adult. This is the wrong way to look at it. If the musical experience enriched his childhood and gave him fun, that's what matters. Certainly it's nice if he goes on and develops the interest further in adult life, but this isn't essential. It isn't necessary as 'proof' that you made a good investment. I remember a small girl being asked recently, on the strength of her great success in her ballet class, if she was 'going to be a dancer' when she grew up. Her response was a very definite 'But I'm a dancer *now*', which taught the questioner a very valuable lesson about childhood!

Drawing and painting

Children's drawing shows an interesting progression from early scribbles to mature, representational work. It's sad that although every child loves to draw, very few adults do (unlike music, which often remains a creative interest throughout life). The reason for this seems to lie in the fact that most children are given the idea by adults that they 'can't draw'. Avoid this by allowing your child the freedom to experiment with her own style and technique. The same is true of painting. Children love to daub and smear paint. They're often less interested in the finished product than in the activity itself. It's only later, when people tell them their painting ought to look 'like' something, or gaze critically over their shoulder ('Yes dear it's very nice, but it doesn't look much like a boat does it?') that children begin to think of themselves as failed artists, and turn to more prosaic pastimes.

Your child's earliest scribbles In the pre-school years, your child will not have been interested in drawing or painting as we understand the terms, simply in the mysterious business of moving a pencil or a painting implement across a blank piece of paper and watching the changes that take place. Nevertheless, there will have been some 'method' in what she was doing. Even children's earliest scribbles (from around age one and a half years) are often done in the form of a circle (an oval really). The pencil goes round and round time and time again, until the child tires of it. Next usually come lines that cross over each other, then circles and lines combined, which by age three can often be used to represent 'Mummy' or 'Daddy' or 'me' or 'our dog'. By around three and a half a second circle is added to act as a head (some children go directly to this stage), and by age four details like fingers, buttons, ears, eyes, hair and feet are all being added. The inclusion of varied and accurate detail at an early age is often a good indication of above average intelligence.

By age five children are drawing groups of people, and soon after they start to add in trees and other landscape details. Attempts at 'my house' often start at age three or a little later, and by age five often contain windows, door and chimneys. You'll see, though, that with both people and houses your child is drawing an *idea* rather than an object. All people look alike, and so do all houses. There's no attempt to capture the details of a particular person or a particular house. You'll notice as well that the sky is always 'up there', and is represented by a strip of blue at the top of the paper. The ground is always 'down here', so much so that when hills are drawn the people stick off them at angles of 90 degrees. A child isn't drawing what he actually sees, but the ideas (and quite scientific they are too) that he has about them.

By about six or seven years, a child begins to be more representational, adding in more detail and more accuracy, and drawings are often discarded in disgust because they 'don't look right'. This quest for accuracy peaks at about age eleven or twelve, and a sharp decline in all interest in the subject then sets in, so that soon a child has to be coaxed into even putting pencil to paper. Prompted by teachers, parents and the deluge of representational illustrations she sees in newspapers, magazines and television, the child has tried to draw like a photograph, finds she can't do it, and gives up in disgust.

Attempts to be more representational

Painting follows similar lines, except that it lags a little behind. It's much harder for a child to be representational in paint, and once the early delight of painting for the sake of painting (abstract art we could call it) goes, then the child

513

quickly learns she can't reproduce what she wants to reproduce, and tells herself she just isn't cut out to be an artist.

How sad all this is. *Everyone* can draw and paint. Even accurate representational drawing and painting if we wish. All the information we need is right there in front of us. We go wrong by trying too hard, by trying to fathom out logically where this line should go and that line should go, instead of simply seeing them as abstract lines and drawing them. And we go wrong by trying always to draw or paint objects, instead of responding equally to the empty space bounded by the objects, and concentrating on drawing boundary lines.

Try not to crush your child's love of drawing and painting

Don't persuade your child too early into representational drawing and painting by insisting she tell you what her drawing or painting is 'supposed' to be ('Oh come on; it must be *something*'). Or by giving her set tasks to perform ('Draw our house/draw a man/draw a car'). Let the representational images come in her own time. If you feel the need to prompt her, prompt her to use her eyes, to see what she's trying to draw or paint as a fascinating interlocking jigsaw of shapes and spaces in between shapes. Don't encourage her to 'think' about what she's drawing or painting, simply to 'see' it. And never belittle, even in fun, what she produces. Whenever we create something (the same applies to her later attempts to do sums and produce solutions to her school work), we put something of ourselves into it. It represents, in no matter how humble a way, part of our identity. To have it laughed at or scorned is therefore deeply wounding. See how upset even older children are when something they've made is over-criticized (adults feel the same but they get better at hiding their feelings!). So encourage first; only afterwards add in any suggestions for improvement. And remember that these suggestions are only statements of how *you* would do it. Particularly in the creative field, children often need to explore and develop their own techniques, or simply just to disagree with you. After all, even professional art critics don't always see eye to eye!

Other childhood interests

I mentioned earlier that the years from five to eleven are the peak years for family outings. Once a child goes to secondary school and becomes more independent, family outings feature less and less. So make the most of these years and of your chances to go to places together, using these visits as a source of fun and as a way of introducing your child to new interests. Museums, old houses, sporting events, country walks, art galleries, all offer potentially exciting experiences for children.

While you're visiting these places, help your child use his eyes and his wits. Point out things to look for, encourage him to ask questions. If you visit places of historical interest, help him develop a feeling for the past, for how people lived, for how they earned their living. If you go into the country, help him identify trees and wild flowers, to listen to birds, to watch out for wild animals and insects, to look for natural materials like pine cones and curiously shaped twigs and stones which can be carried home and put on display. Teach him how to press leaves and flowers, to carry a sketch pad with him if he enjoys drawing and to have a go at recording the things he sees. Teach him how to use a camera and a tape recorder, and how to hunt for blackberries and nuts in season.

Getting the most out of family outings

If you don't enjoy these activities yourself, the chances are you were never introduced properly to them when you were young. Try to see them now through your child's eyes. Many is the adult who has discovered a love of nature through taking their child on country rambles, or who has found an enthusiasm for history through visiting old places, or an interest in animals or science through trips to the zoo or the science museum. And provided you choose experiences that are suitable to your child's age (and allow him to have his say in making the choice), and provided you don't linger beyond his attention span, you won't find him short of enthusiasm either.

Focus this enthusiasm by discussing in advance with him the things he is likely to see, and preparing a few short questions to which he has to find the answers. Make a small project book together, as he does before a school outing, and show the book to friends and relatives so that he shares his discoveries with others.

Make a project book and treasure the souvenirs

This principle of sharing new knowledge with others is vital in helping children remember what they've learnt. Don't consign the souvenirs of your outings to the waste bin or the back of the toy cupboard when you get home. Put them on display, just as you display the items he makes in school. Maybe you've found some fossils, or an interesting piece of wood; maybe you've done some brass rubbings, or taken photographs or bought postcards; or maybe you've drawn a picture or found feathers or sheep's wool. Make sure they go on show so that your child can take a pride in them and go on learning from them.

PROBLEMS AND ISSUES IN THE YEARS FIVE TO ELEVEN

Watching television

Much is written these days about the long hours young children spend in front of the television set (over twenty hours a week on average for children in this age range) and about the possible harm it may be doing them. With the wide availability of video recordings, the problem has come even more into focus. Parents wonder whether they should censor their children's viewing, whether they should restrict it in terms of time, whether they should even banish the television set altogether. They also wonder whether they should give up all hope of remaining sane in the face of interminable quarrels between their children as to what channel to watch, (see pages 386–7/442–3).

The positive and negative sides of television First let's start with the positive side of television viewing. There's no doubt that today's children are much better informed than were children in the days before television. Moving pictures are an excellent way of teaching, and there are many highly informative programmes going out every day. Today's children, through television, know more about the rest of the world, about political issues, about human relationships and about a host of other issues than ever before. This is all to the good. Television can also be splendid entertainment, especially the more thoughtful drama, music and comedy programmes. It also allows children to watch important sporting events, be a part of exploits of heroism and courage, see faraway places, watch epoch-making events as they happen. Television has helped enrich modern life, and as children and adults we're in many ways the better for it.

But television also has its negative side. It's a great thief of time. It cuts into family life. It can present unsuitable and frightening or disturbing programmes. And, perhaps most worrying of all, it can discourage the use of imagination. When a child has both moving pictures and words presented to her there's no need for the glorious flights of fantasy which come from reading stories or looking at the still images in a picture book. So instead of having to bring something of herself to the experience, she sits back and is spoon-fed by it, never stirring out of her armchair either physically or in the magic world of the mind.

How much time should a child spend watching TV?

Weighing the positive and the negative sides of television, you need have no qualms about keeping a television set in the house. But you should have qualms about the use your child is allowed to make of it. Let's start by taking the issue of time. How much time should a child in the 5 – 11 age range spend viewing? If you restrict her too severely she's going to miss out on many of the things watched and talked about by her friends, and she's going to feel isolated and resentful about it. So there has to be *some* element of compromise between what you think is right for a child of her age and what other families think is right. One useful approach is that a child in the 5 – 11 age group should ideally spend no more than about one-third of her free time (waking hours outside school and not including mealtimes) watching television, and two-thirds doing other things.

For example, if you think she should be in bed by eight thirty each evening during the week, this gives her roughly three hours free time each evening, which suggests one hour of television viewing and two hours doing other things. However, she'll protest vigorously at this if most of her friends watch for much longer, so a reasonable compromise might be to allow her to view for half her free time, say one and a half hours. Obviously there needn't be any hard-and-fast rule

Decide how much she is allowed to watch each day

about this. If there are good programmes she might watch rather more some days, and rather less on others.

You'll avoid a great deal of trouble if at least some of her viewing is done to routine. Thus she may play outside with her friends for an hour when she comes home, then watch half an hour of children's television, then have a family tea, and watch for another half hour to an hour afterwards. If you feel she isn't allowing herself enough time for reading or playing games, and is becoming addicted to television to the exclusion of other leisure experiences, then settle on a relatively early bedtime for her and allow her to read in bed or get her toys out on the bedroom floor, on the understanding that when you come up to turn off her light (or to draw her curtains if it's summertime) she must settle down.

Avoiding unsuitable programmes

At weekends, the routine is going to be different. But remember that after 9 p.m. many of the programmes are unsuitable for young children, so make this her bedtime even on Friday and Saturday nights. Never be afraid to stop her from watching something unsuitable. Be firm, and always try to make your decision *before* the programme starts. It's frustrating for a child to have the set suddenly switched off just when she's starting to enjoy what's on offer. Get into the habit of looking at the programme details beforehand, and make your decisions accordingly.

This raises the question just what *is* suitable for your children and what isn't. I've already said that television programmers regard 9 p.m. as the watershed between 'family' and 'adult' viewing, but even before that time there may be items on the screen which make parents uneasy. Is it all right for children to see violence? Is it all right for them to see sex scenes, explicit or not? Is it all right for them to see adult nudity? Parents agonize a great deal over these issues. But the answers aren't always as clear-cut as one might think.

Violence on television

Does it make children more violent in real life?

To take violence first. We know from research that children do tend to *act out in their play* the violent scenes they watch on television. But there is no hard evidence that this make-believe renders them more likely to be *violent in real life*.

For example, although children acted out the scenes they saw on newsreels during the Second World War, this was a time of very little domestic violence. And currently, although Japanese television is one of the most violent in the world, Japanese society is markedly violence-free. So even if the scenes on television are of real violence as opposed to dramatized violence, this doesn't mean it will make children want to go and literally do likewise. Their playing at violence is very different in their own minds from the real thing and they also draw a distinction in their own minds between the second-hand experience of violence that comes from watching television, and the first-hand experience of violence that comes from being brought up in a violent home.

Some psychologists think that there's another aspect to the problem though. If we want to help someone deal with a psychologically disabling fear, say a fear of domestic cats, then one effective technique we use is called 'systematic desensitization'. The person who is to be treated is put in a relaxed frame of mind, in comfortable, friendly surroundings, and then over several treatment sessions introduced in easy stages to the object of his or her fear. Thus the person would first be shown pictures of cats, then realistic models of cats, then finally the real thing (initially at a distance and eventually close to). At each stage, the psychologist ensures that the person concerned is thoroughly at ease before going on to the next. The treatment works because the person comes to associate cats with pleasant events, thus gradually losing any fear of them. The worry is that introducing children to violent televised scenes in the relaxed security of their own homes may amount to systematic desensitization, blunting their shock at real-life violence. The result could be that society gradually develops a casual attitude towards all violence, with a consequent lessening of the social controls which operate to keep it in check.

Does it desensitize them towards violence?

So we have in fact two worries about televised violence. First, that it may directly stimulate violence in children, and second that it may desensitize them towards it. As I've said, the evidence isn't clear-cut on the first of these worries, and it's just as unclear on the second. We must also take into account the fact that many children appear to be turned *against* violence by seeing it on television, though less often where the violence is carried out by a heroic or socially acceptable character such as a police officer. Overall, the best advice to parents is to use common sense. The human race has a morbid over-preoccupation with violence. This goes for verbal violence (the constant slanging matches in which televised drama revels) as well as physical violence, and this is hardly the right way to teach children how to relate to others. So keep the viewing of avoidable violence to a minimum, and indicate by your own comments the need to be *very critical of what's on offer*. This is the age at which children can begin to develop a critical awareness, and realize they don't just have to accept passively whatever appears on the screen.

Sex on television

The depiction of sex on television is a different issue, and it is unfortunate that in some people's mind it gets lumped together with violence. Sex is in and of itself a life-enhancing activity, violence is in and of itself a life-denying one. Sex, at its deeper level, is an expression of love. Violence is an expression of hate. Certainly sex can be and often is misused, but this is the result primarily of poor sex education in the home and in the school, rather than of problems inherent in sex itself. So the presentation of sex on television within the context of a loving and tender relationship can't be regarded as harmful.

It is often the parents' attitudes that make it a problem

Many parents accept this, but say that nevertheless it embarrasses them to watch sex scenes if their children are present. They say the same thing if adult nudity is depicted. They acknowledge that no one should be shocked at the sight of the human body, but even so find it an uncomfortable experience if the children are there.

Sexual issues and nudity in other adults shouldn't be the subject of taboos between you and your children. If your children see that such things embarrass you, they won't be able to discuss frankly with you their own questions about sex, or come to you with any problems they meet. There's no good reason why sexual matters shouldn't be discussed as openly and sensibly between you and your children as any other important aspect of human behaviour. If early sex education has gone well, children should be neither over-preoccupied with nor prudish about sex. Both these reactions stem from wrong or inadequate teaching when children are small. Sex is an aspect of life, and must be put into and kept within its proper perspective.

Your own feelings of uneasiness at sex scenes on the television if your children are present may stem from shortcomings in your own sex education (or from fear your children may see you actually quite enjoy these scenes!). Most of us had passed on to us in childhood the problems which our own parents had over sexuality, problems which they in their turn acquired from their parents. The important thing in adult life is to examine our own feelings, and to reason ourselves out of any which are left over from our early conditioning, and which prevent us from accepting both the realities of sex and the need for clear thinking on moral issues.

But you will need to keep a careful control over any video recordings which you may hire for home viewing. Many of these recordings aren't suitable for children, and you'll want to see them in the evenings when the children have gone to bed. But it's unfair to the children to whet their appetites by letting them know you've got something on hire, and you risk the likelihood of their coming downstairs on some implausible excuse just to take a peep at what you're viewing.

As a result of their exposure to sex and to sexual issues on television, your child may be much better informed about such matters than you were at his age. Publicity about homosexuality and about sexually transmitted diseases (especially AIDS and hepatitis) may lead him to ask you questions about sexual practices and about condoms and about the morality of it all that you find embarrassing. But follow the principles you've already adopted towards sexual matters. If a child asks questions, then he has a right to accurate and simple answers. If he doesn't get these answers from you, he'll only look for them elsewhere, and risk not only being misinformed but also filled with fears and associations between sex and something unpleasant. If he asks the meaning of anal intercourse or oral sex for example, tell him the first is when the penis is placed in the bottom and the second when the genitals are stimulated by the mouth. When he asks about condoms, tell him they're rubber sheaths placed over the penis before intercourse to prevent sperm from reaching the ovum and infection being transmitted from one person to another. You may feel the need to pass judgement on the morality of each of these things, but it's important not to fill your child with disgust

Children's questions about sex

521

about them. Judgements about morality are more likely to be helpful if they're objective rather than emotional.

Make sure sex is as open to discussion as anything else

Use the opportunity of questions like these to correct any misconceptions your child may already have picked up. He may have the idea that you can contract a sexually transmitted disease just from holding hands for instance, or alternatively that you can't catch a sexually transmitted disease unless you engage in practices like anal or oral sex. He isn't going to be sexually active for years yet, but it's vital he understands clearly and calmly as much about sex as possible, so that the subject is de-mystified and as open to discussion and debate as any other important area of human behaviour.

While we're on the subject, remember that he's going to pick up ideas about sex from sources other than the television. Newspapers and magazines are full of sexual issues, and so is playground conversation at school. Make sure he feels free at all times to talk about what he's read and heard, and about his anxieties and interests. Fear thrives upon ignorance, and so one day when he's older does sexual disaster. As always, don't confuse him with details or with language that's beyond his understanding, but leave him in no doubt that you are a ready and accurate source of information for him, in this as in other areas that bear crucially upon modern living.

Handling money

Once your child starts school, and sees other children with money, he'll come increasingly to want some of his own. All parents are only too familiar with a child's demands to have money spent on him during the pre-school years (sweets, toys, ice-cream, outings – the list is endless), but come the school years he now wants money to spend for himself. The problem grows steadily more acute as he grows older, especially when he's big enough to come home from school on his own and passes each day the enticing delights of cake or sweet shops (or even newsagents, which seem to have an irresistible fascination for most children). Before long, you will be treated daily to colourful tales of how much money *other* children have to spend, and of how (by implication) mean you are not to see that his rightful needs are similarly provided for.

Children have an astonishing gift for identifying just where the thorn of guilt hurts most in their parents, and having identified it for applying regular and painful pressure. The area marked 'money' is particularly sensitive in most parents, for we hate the idea that our children are being denied benefits enjoyed by all their friends. We also feel that our inability or refusal to stump up the necessary cash reflects back on the quality of our love for our children and therefore on our adequacy as parents and providers.

Faced with these sharp digs of guilt, the temptation is either to give way and hand out blood money on demand, or to become defensive and angry about it and blame our child for asking. Either way, we've missed a vital opportunity to introduce him to the value of money and to the necessary skills in handling it. Make use of this opportunity by starting your child on a weekly sum of pocket money *before* he begins to ask for it. This may be when he first starts school, or it may be a little later. But by starting him on pocket money before the actual need for it arises, you keep the initiative. Pocket money is now something which you recognize as necessary and something which you can be relied upon to take proper decisions about, rather than something which is yielded under duress and which leaves the initiative with him.

Give your child pocket money before he asks

Explain to your child that pocket money is a sum of cash which is given to him each week, and which is his to decide how to spend. If he spends it sensibly, then the sum be will increased regularly as he grows older. Keep the sum very small to start with, and try to give it to him at the same time each week and in low denomination coins (e.g. ten 1p pieces rather than one 10p coin). This will not only seem more to a very young child, it will also stimulate his interest in counting, and in adding and subtracting. Buy him an attractive money box as well, so that he can see his money grow if he saves it. Help him to target small items in the shops that he would like to buy, and then to work out how many weeks he will need to save in order to be able to buy them. Try not to veto his choice of purchase too often (though this may be necessary from time to time), as you want him to get the idea that this is *his* money and that it is his responsibility to spend it wisely. If he wastes it, he has none left to buy the things he really wants. And if he wastes it, then it won't be increased as he gets older.

Make small increases frequently

To begin with, it is best to make these increases quite frequently, and in very small amounts. If you've decided that he starts with 10p a week, and that this will be increased by 10p a year so that he will be on 80p a week by the time he leaves primary school (at which point you'll increase it to £1 for when he starts secondary school), explain this to him by showing him the relevant number of coins, and then give him his 10p rise in small instalments throughout the year. A young child finds it hard to grasp the idea that he's going to get another 10p a week next year, but he can more readily understand that at much more frequent intervals he's going to get extra pennies added on. Mark the 'increase' dates on the calendar to help him understand what calendars are for, and to help again with his skills in counting ('How much pocket money will you be getting each week by the time of Grandma's birthday in May?' 'How much pocket money will you be getting by our holidays in August?' 'How much pocket money will you be getting by *your* birthday?' 'and by Christmas?').

If other children have more to spend

Usually children who are treated in this way don't grumble if they find later on that other children are more flush with funds than they are. But if they do, point out that people who manage their money well when they're grown-up are usually those who learnt its proper value when they were children. Having money to waste when you're young doesn't teach you to be clever with it when you're older. Praise your child for the good sense he's shown so far in his spending and saving, and help him to recognize the way in which other children with more money in their pockets seem to be throwing it away on rubbish.

The child who has an appropriate amount of money to handle from an early age quickly comes to appreciate the need to think carefully before spending it, and to appreciate the advantages of saving it for something he really wants. He also comes to appreciate the value of things for which he's saved, and the good feelings that come from spending your money on gifts for other people, gifts that really come from *you*, rather than gifts bought with your parents' money and that do nothing more than carry your name.

Peer group comparisons

I've mentioned in connection both with pocket money and with television watching that children may compare themselves with other children of their own age. In fact, this happens with any number of things during the years from five to eleven. Up to now, your child has accepted that the way things are done at home is the right (even the only) way. Now that her horizons are expanding, she's able to see that this isn't so. She listens to her friends, she visits their homes, and she learns that their parents seem at times to do things rather better than you do. She also learns (she's getting very good at sizing you up by now) that comparing her own home unfavourably with the homes of her friends is a good way of making you doubt yourself and either of getting you to give her what she wants or (as punishment for your heart of flint) of making you feel guilty and inadequate.

There's nothing wrong with a child making such comparisons. It shows she's observant, and it shows that she holds promise of developing into a pretty good psychologist one day. But there's also nothing wrong in laughing them off and refusing to play her game. Be fair about the comparisons. Maybe she has got a point. We all have a few prejudices about what children should or should not be allowed to do, and it's quite useful to hear how the parents of their friends handle similar matters. If you're convinced by her arguments, show you're ready to be fair and flexible. But if her arguments merely confirm that her friends' parents take the line of least resistance, or haven't really thought things through, or have got more money than sense, stand firm. Whether the issue is pocket money or television viewing, clothes or fashions, video recorders in every room or skiing holidays in the Rocky Mountains, tell your child that the simple fact 'they' are doing things a certain way doesn't mean we should follow suit. Give your reasons, but also leave her in no doubt that although comparisons can be helpful, they also have their negative side. We're all individuals, and our circumstances differ, and she has to understand that comparisons between dissimilar sets of things can be unfair and misleading.

Stand firm if you feel your line is right

It's also a useful opportunity to point out to her that on

Don't be made
to feel guilty
occasions it's good *not* to be over-influenced by others. Sometimes it's right to conform, and sometimes it's right to do
things our own way. Fashions and fancies have their appeal,
but the really successful people in life are the ones who can
make objective judgements about what to do and what not to
do. Don't read her a sermon though on all the advantages *she's*
got and all the deprived children in the world who should be
envying her. She doesn't choose her advantages and disadvantages, and in a child who is materially better off than most,
comparisons risk leading to smugness. Focus more on the fact
that we're all different. And if she persists beyond the limits of
reasonable discussion, focus on the fact that this is a matter of
judgement, yours and the parents of her friends. And you're
backing your judgement *and* (conveyed by manner rather than
words) you've no intention of feeling guilty about it either!

How much should you tell your children?

If you've answered your child's questions fully and openly
right from the start, and been prepared to discuss the issues
that go to make up daily life (she needs to know when you've
had a difficult day at work, when you're extra tired, when
you're looking forward to something, when you're having a
good time), talking to your child should come easily. You
discuss things together like friends, and share each other's
views and opinions, plans and expectations. But there come
times when deeper issues are involved, and you find yourself
unsure whether it's right to talk to your child about them or
not. There may be strains between parents for example, or
strains between the parents of her friends, or financial problems, or worries over employment or health or in-laws or
housing or drinking or religious beliefs or a host of other
things. Seriously troubled yourself, you wonder whether to
unburden yourself to your child or not, especially as you feel
your preoccupation with these issues is affecting your mood
even when you're with her.

Alternatively she may ask you direct questions which you're
unsure how to answer. 'Why aren't you fun any more?' 'Why
doesn't the family go out together as it used to do?' 'Why was
your friend crying when she visited you?' 'Why isn't there

enough money?' 'Why are you not working any more?' 'What was all the shouting about?' Your dilemma is that you want to be open with your child, as you are about other matters, but at the same time you don't want to burden her with worries with which she can't cope. You're unsure what to do for the best, and this makes your worries all the worse.

The answer is simple (which isn't the same thing as saying it's always easy!). Your child needs – and has a right – to know enough to enable her to make sense of the situation. At the same time, she has an equal need and right not to be used as an emotional prop for adult problems. The key guideline therefore is to talk to her for *her* sake and not for your own. Children can cope remarkably well with upheavals in their environment as long as they understand what's happening and why it's happening. So if the upheavals are affecting your child, she needs to be told enough about them to help this understanding, and she needs to have her questions answered as openly as possible. If the upheavals have to do with strains in the relationship between her parents, she's fully involved in the consequences already, and it's better she should adjust to these consequences as and where they affect her than that she should be left to worry about them in the dark, and then perhaps be faced with abrupt trauma when her parents in due course decide to separate.

Talk to your child for her sake not yours

I'm talking about this problem in connection with the five-to eleven-year-old child, but obviously it can crop up at any time. Adjust your explanations to the level of your child's understanding and to her emotional strengths and vulnerabilities, and tell her simply as much as she needs to know. The nature and extent of her questions will give you a good guide as to what to say and when. Don't go into unnecessary detail, and if the problems *are* concerned with strains between parents, try to agree between the two parents that you'll give similar accounts of what's going wrong and won't each try to win the child over to your side. Trying to win her over will only cause a painful conflict of loyalties, and will threaten her respect for you as she reflects upon things now or when she's older. She'll see that you were trying to use her, and may also blame you for destroying a valued relationship with her other parent. Explain to her that because two adults can no longer get along well with each other, this doesn't mean that one of

Tell her as much as she needs to know

them is 'good' and the other 'bad'. As time passes, people change, and though her mother and father once wanted to be partners, this doesn't necessarily mean their partnership will last for ever. In fact, dissolving the partnership may be better for everyone than keeping it going now that it's no longer working.

Try to give facts rather than judgements

Use the same approach if you're talking about the parents of any of her friends who are going through difficult times. Unless the issues are very clear-cut, don't apportion blame or make one parent out to be innocent and the other guilty. Through an understanding of how relationships go wrong, your child will at this age be learning a great deal about adult life and how people get along with each other. She mustn't be prompted to see things always in terms of black and white. Human psychology is rarely that simple. In the real world, we all of us make mistakes at times, we all of us misunderstand each other (and ourselves), we are all of us prone to behave irrationally and thoughtlessly. On the other hand, we all of us behave postively just as often, and are capable of great warmth and unselfishness. Help your child to see people for what they are by giving her facts wherever possible rather than judgements. And you'll be surprised at how mature and sensible she is at drawing her own conclusions.

Follow the same rules if you're talking about money problems or the unemployment of one of her parents or any of the other issues I mentioned earlier on. Tell her what she needs to know to understand the situation. Accept that the situation affects her as much as anyone else, and she has a right to have you spend time and patience with her in an attempt to help her understand. Reassure her that what's happening in no way threatens your feelings for her, and listen sympathetically to any misgivings *she* may have. Many children confess to obscure anxieties that whatever is going wrong is in some way their fault. Don't dismiss such misgivings as silly. They're real enough to the child. Reassure her, and accept that during this difficult time she's going to need extra love and attention, however distracted you feel about your own worries.

Telling a child about a new relationship

The rules apply also if you're a single parent and starting a relationship with another partner. I discuss the issues raised by step-parents later in the chapter, so all I want to stress now is that as soon as this relationship begins to impinge upon your child, he needs to have it explained to him. One difficulty here is that children find it hard to understand that a parent has emotional and sexual needs, and that these needs require the support of another adult. To the child, the one-parent family may seem to be working very well, and if their parent looks for another partner they find this not only unsettling (How will I relate to the new partner? How will the partnership affect my relationship with my parent?), but also a threat to their own feelings of adequacy. Why isn't my parent's relationship with *me* enough for him/her? Aren't I good enough? Have I been failing him/her in some way?

The only way to handle this is to accept that this new relationship is potentially as important to your child as it is to yourself. Carried away perhaps by the heady feelings of the relationship, it's natural you should feel a little impatient that your child doesn't quite see things the way you do, and may even seem intent upon 'spoiling' things for you. Slow down a little, so that your child can catch up with where you are. The best way to explain the relationship to your child is to help him see that love between adults is as natural and necessary as love between adults and children. One day he'll be grown-up and will fall in love, and then he'll be able to see that this love doesn't come between him and his parent. We don't just have a fixed amount of love, which we have to divide up between the various important people in our lives. Love is an inexhaustible store, and nothing is going to take away the love that belongs to your child.

Your new relationship is important to him too

It's also helpful to explain to your child that one day he's going to leave home and start a home of his own. It's right and proper that he should. And when that time comes, he'll feel much better about it if he knows that his parent has a partner to share life with, and so won't be quite so lonely without him. Much as children may love their parents, it's rare for them to feel they want to be responsible for their parents once they're grown up. A child likes to feel that he's going to have a period of independence when he leaves school, so that he can decide for himself where to go and what to do with his life. Looking ahead, your child will usually be able to see that the idea of your having a new partner isn't such a bad one after all, provided he likes the partner and knows that whatever happens no one is going to replace him in your affections.

Don't unburden yourself to your child

To return now to my second proviso about talking to children, namely that your child has a need and a right not to be used as an emotional prop for adult problems. If you find yourself wanting to talk to him for your sake rather than for his, hold back. However mature he may seem for his years, he hasn't yet the resources to handle your emotional needs. If he can see you're unhappy, he needs to know why, but he emphatically doesn't need to have your deepest feelings poured out to him, or to see you in tears or at the end of your emotional tether. Such experiences are profoundly disturbing for a child. His security is very much bound up in you, and if he sees you crumbling so visibly, this security is destroyed at a very traumatic level. His fears for you and his fears for himself put him through a profound distress and confusion way beyond his ability to cope. Crumble by all means, but do so with a sympathetic adult and not with your child.

He can't yet handle your deepest feelings

I don't mean by this that your child must always see you as an invincible tower of strength. If you're honest with him about the ordinary events of daily life he'll know this isn't the case anyway. He'll know you get tired and dispirited at times like everyone else, that you don't pretend always to get things right, that you do or say things which afterwards you regret. But I do mean that there is a big gulf between being a child and being an adult. Your child's understanding and his emotions still aren't mature. His experience is still limited. He just isn't ready to handle your deepest vulnerabilities. If you ask him to do so, not only is he likely to find the experience devastating, he may also defend against it in future by recoiling from emotionality altogether. Many men, in particular, report being impatient as adults with the emotions of others because they found them to be so messy and disturbing in childhood. Allow your child to mature into an understanding of other people's deepest feelings rather than force him into contact with them long before he's ready.

Mention of men in the above paragraph leads me to stress that in all the rest of what I've been saying on the subject of talking to children I'm referring equally to both sexes. Don't feel that boys are 'tougher' than girls and can be told more, or that girls are more 'sympathetic' than boys and can be told more. Or that fathers can speak best to sons and mothers to daughters. At least until adolescence, the sexes vary very little from each other in their deeper emotions.

Also, don't feel that if a child doesn't *appear* to be upset when you're pouring out your troubles to him, it's okay to go ahead. Adults frequently speak about their childhood traumas over their parents' problems and confess that they were quite incapable of showing what they were going through at the time. Unable to understand his own emotional turmoil properly, a young child finds it difficult to put this turmoil into words (though it may seek expression in disturbed behaviour in other areas of his life). Keep always in mind the fact that much more goes on in your child's inner life than he can show on the surface.

Your child may be more upset than he appears

Telling your child about God

We may no longer be a religious country in terms of church attendance, but surveys show that over 80 per cent of people believe in some spiritual or life force to which they give the name God. This belief isn't confined to the less sophisticated either. In a study conducted amongst students in higher education more than 90 per cent were prepared to admit to it.

For many people, the question arises what should one teach young children about God. Maybe they attend a primary school where some good religious education goes on, or maybe they attend church or the local Sunday school. In these cases, your job is made easier. But often you're left to your own resources. The great Christian festivals of Christmas and Easter and those of other faiths invite questions from your child, and you feel the need to give her guidance. But what do you teach her? And how do you go about it? A careful re-examination of your own belief is often of help. It's unlikely that we can ever reduce the God in whom we believe to a simple formula, but we can often make our belief coherent.

Since Christ refers to God as 'Father', many children take to the idea of God as a wise old man, a kind of Father Christmas figure somewhere above the bright blue sky, looking down benevolently upon his world. This is where the idea of God as an old man with a long white beard, so ridiculed by atheists and modern theologians, originates. But if a child (or an adult

Different symbols may suit different stages

531

for that matter) finds it helpful to symbolize love and wisdom by the form of an old man with a beard, so be it. If God is omnipotent and infinite, then his reality certainly includes these symbols, and if people find them helpful in providing an image of perfect love and wisdom and compassion, there is every reason to use them.

Problems only arise if, as the child grows older, she mistakes the symbol for the reality it represents. If she thinks God is *only* an old man with a white beard, then she may well stop believing in him. Questions as to where this old man lives and how he can stay up in the sky inevitably arise. If a child doesn't have a good relationship with her earthly father, then the symbol of a heavenly one won't appeal to her either. This is where a more abstract concept of God as perfect love and perfect wisdom comes in, not symbolized in human form but as the force that fills and is conscious of all things. At this level, our relationship with God becomes a personal one. Each man and woman has to experience for themselves what this divine force means in their own lives, and how to live in harmony with it instead of in the conflicts and ignorance that are the real meaning of sin.

What I'm suggesting is that you should help your child see as she grows older that our ideas about God develop and change, just as do our ideas about ourselves, and that she doesn't have to abandon her religious enquiries just because she grows out of the symbols that proved to be of help earlier on.

At any rate help your child keep an open mind If you aren't happy with this approach, or if you have no religious beliefs and don't want to teach any to your child, then I recommend simply helping her keep an open mind. The scientific materialism of the nineteenth century, which took the view that science could explain existence and leave no room for a God, is no longer credible to many of our leading scientists. The universe is a very strange place indeed. Scientific 'laws' which hold good in some areas of existence (for example the everyday world around us) are found not to apply in the same way in others (for example the sub-atomic world or the world of outer space).

Where you feel God fits into this, if at all, is up to you. But you'll do your child a disservice if you teach her to close her mind to spiritual possibilities. If you ask why, the answer is that in work with troubled adults many psychologists (myself included) find them frequently to be searching for some spiritual doctrine or spiritual experience that would give meaning to their lives. We also see the inner transformation that discovery of such doctrines and experiences can bring, and the impetus it gives people to live lives of value to themselves and others. At the very least, your child has the right to have these possibilities left open to her.

Dealing with death and bereavement

Often linked to questions about God are questions about how to help children come to terms with death and bereavement. A child who is faced with the death of a loved one, or even with the death of a cat or dog or other pet, wants to know what's happened. He feels the sadness of parting, and he wants help in trying to understand where the departed person has *gone*. He may see the lifeless body. In fact, there is evidence that this helps, and although I would never recommend that a small child should see the dead body of a loved relative unless you're sure he can cope with the experience, seeing that of a dead household pet helps to bring home to him the finality of what's happened. What a short while ago was animated by life is now still and cold, and isn't going to be around any more.

The first essential, with a child as with an adult, is to allow the full expression of grief. There's nothing to be ashamed of in tears when we've lost someone we love. Tears are nature's way of helping us release a surge of emotion which otherwise would be almost unbearable. Through tears we express our sadness, and in some way do homage to the one we've lost. So let your child have a good cry, and let his grief run its course. Don't feel you have to rush him back into normality. Tell him gently that life has to go on, but don't give him the impression that there's anything wrong with his sorrow. If you're grieving too, then grieve together. Normally it isn't a good thing for children to see their parents in tears. It upsets and confuses the child, and can strike deep at his sense of security in you. But grief over a death is another matter. If your child sees you share his grief it enables him to accept it

Allow your child to express his grief fully

more fully, and as you come out of your grief so you teach him a valuable lesson in how to accept the fact that life is still there to be lived.

Don't present death as a terrifying prospect

When it comes to discussing the meaning of death with your child, the need is for the right combination of sensitivity and openness. In the death of a loved relative or even of a pet he comes face to face with the fact that everyone must one day die. Both you and he himself. This can be a frightening prospect to a child if he's made to see death as something dark and terrible. If he sees it in this way, then he equates it with being taken forcibly away from you and locked up somewhere for ever. Help him to see death as a natural process. Just as the leaves fall from the tree or the petals from the flower, men and women leave the world. If you have religious faith, tell him this isn't the end of things, any more than the passing of summer is the end for ever of summertime. Explain to him that the great religious teachers have taught that life goes on, that life uses the body for a while and then leaves it and goes elsewhere. We may not fully understand what happens to life when it leaves the body, just as we don't fully understand what life is in the first place, but we know that it continues its pilgrimage in other dimensions, which can be symbolized for us in the concept of worlds which embody the love and wisdom that we identify with God. Needless to say, no small child should ever be terrified with the prospects of a hell or hells.

Admit you don't know what happens after death

If you haven't any religious beliefs, it's better simply to admit that as you don't know what life is when it's in the body, so you don't know what happens to it after death. Parents who have no religious belief tell me that they're anxious not to fill the heads of their children with 'fairy stories' or wishful thinking. Nevertheless it's inaccurate for them to say they know death is the end of the person concerned. It's fairer to leave the matter open, at the same time helping the child to see the deceased (human or animal) as one who brought happiness to others, and as one for whose life we can feel grateful.

Psychologists working with both adults and children find that the fear of death can be a potent factor in the distress suffered by many anxious and troubled individuals. Often this fear goes back to the early years when adults or older children

534

scorned the youngster for his beliefs and terrified him with tales either of annihilation or of torments in all too vividly imagined hells. Naturally you won't want to give your child explanations in which you yourself don't believe, and if you are not convinced there is a life after death you'll want to be honest about it. But it would seem fair to indicate to your child that other people do have views different from your own, and that one day he must make up his own mind as to what he believes.

Problems with friends

Parents' worries about their children's friendships (and getting into 'bad company') take two forms. On the one hand there is the friend who is quite clearly a bad lot. She may swear, be mischievous and destructive, and quite clearly capable of leading your child into very undesirable ways. On the other hand, the friend may be law-abiding enough, but you have an uncomfortable feeling about her. Most parents admit rather apologetically that these feelings are usually because the friend comes from a quite different background from their own child (socially, intellectually or ethnically).

Unsuitable friends
To take the problem of the bad hat first. The poor kid probably has a disturbed and difficult background. Circumstances have dealt her a raw deal compared to your child, and she's hardly to be blamed for the flaws in her character. Having a friend like your child, and coming into your home, may be an excellent influence upon her. On the other hand, your concern for your own child is natural enough. She may be very trusting and you may see that advantage is being taken of her. And you may have a real fear that your child will be encouraged to develop bad habits and be led into mischief and even physical danger. You can't just stand benevolently by in the hope that your child will 'reform' her rather shady little friend.

Make a start by telling the friend, kindly but firmly, that while she's in your house you don't want to hear bad language and you don't want to see any rough behaviour (see also page 436). If she responds to this, it shows she's ready to learn. If

Allow the child to your house but don't let them go out together

things go well subsequently, keep a careful eye on her but let her feel welcome. Take her on outings with your child, both to offer her the opportunities she probably doesn't get at home, and to watch how she and your child get on together. But don't allow the two children to go off on their own, or allow your child to go to her friend's home where you can't see what's going on. If your child objects, explain that she can bring her friend home but she can't go out with her. That's the bargain. If your child can't agree to it, then she can't see her friend at all. You're doing your bit by welcoming her into the home, and your child must do her bit by accepting there's no question of jaunts off on their own together.

Unless the friendship is a genuine one, the friend will quickly get bored with these restrictions, and will fade out of the picture. If, on the other hand, she really has an affinity with your child she'll accept them. But should she try to tempt your child into breaking your rules, or should she refuse in the first place to accept your prohibition on swearing and rough behaviour, then your child must be told firmly she can't bring her home any more. After an initial protest your child will see that she has no option but to accept this. The chances are in any case the glamour of her friend's wild ways will be wearing off by now.

Why not forbid the friendship from the start?

Some parents ask why go to this trouble? Why not say right from the start the friend isn't suitable and have done with it? The answer is that your child probably sees her in school anyway. If you forbid the friendship it may persist without your knowing it. Better to allow your child to bring the friend home, and to assess within the context of her own background whether she's actually got anything in common with her. Your child will thus learn a useful lesson on how to pick her friends. It's no good being attracted to someone because of her bold devil-may-care attitude, only to find you have quite different standards and values. On the other hand, if the new friend is influenced by your child, then coming into your home may help her. At the very least, it will show her the terms on which a continuing friendship is going to be possible.

If in the end you have to forbid the friendship, but feel your child is still being adversely influenced by the friend when at school, then speak to the teacher. Usually teachers are keenly aware of the friendship patterns amongst the children in their class, and diplomatically split up these friendship if they feel one child is taking advantage of another. So she will move the children apart in class, put them to work in different groups, keep an eye on them when they're out at play and so on. Speak to the teacher too if you feel your child is getting in with a bad group. Find out more about the group, and why it is attractive to your child. Is she lacking 'adventure' in her ordinary life? Does the group help her feel 'big'? Are they teasing her or frightening her into joining them? Try to remedy whatever problems are making your child seek the friendship of the group. But be firm that she isn't to go out with them. One unsuitable friend you can handle, but not a whole group. And group behaviour is often much worse than the behaviour of each child left to herself. Explain your reasons, but insist your child and the group keep their distance from each other.

Friends with different backgrounds

Now for the second issue, namely the friend who is perfectly law-abiding but who comes from a quite different background from your child. This often makes you (let's be open about it) confront your own prejudices. The child may simply come from a rather deprived home. You sympathize with him, you want to be friendly, but at the same time you worry that the friend isn't quite 'suitable' for your child. Which means in effect that you wouldn't want your child to be like him, or to become identified with him and his background.

These misgivings are often natural enough. But learning to mix socially is an important part of your child's education. One of the functions of a school is to bring together children from different backgrounds so that they can get to know more about each other, to the benefit of everyone. As soon as he starts school your child is entering into a wider social environment. He has to learn to see the point of view of children from social and ethnic backgrounds which differ from his own. He has to learn to appreciate life from a wider perspective than that offered by his own home and family.

Your child needs to learn to mix socially

So by trying to restrict your child's circle of friends to people just like himself you'll be holding back important aspects of his learning. Keep an eye on his friends, encourage your child to bring them home, get to know them yourself. As mentioned earlier in the chapter, children's friendships change very rapidly, particularly in the primary school years. For a week or two your child may be inseparable from a particular companion, then as abruptly as the relationship started (and often for as little obvious reason) it ends, and your child looks at you in genuine surprise when you ask why he isn't playing with Peter any more. For your child, the friendship with Peter already belongs in the past. They've learnt what they had to learn from each other, and moved on.

Friends can lead your child into mischief

Always know where your child is

During the years five to eleven, children (particularly boys) grow increasingly daring, and show a growing tendency to behave in ways that can get them into trouble with the 'authorities' (teachers, headteachers, sometimes even the police). In such matters, prevention is much better than cure. So make sure throughout childhood that you are fully aware of your child's life outside the home, and ready to exercise proper supervision over it. He's far too young to be out late, or to be out at all unless you know exactly where he is. As he grows in independence, he'll want increasingly to go round and play at the houses of his friends. This is fine as long as you know who the friends are and where they live, and as long as your child understands he mustn't go off anywhere else unless he lets you know and gets your permission. It's far too easy for a child to go and visit a friend, and then go with that friend to the house of another friend, and then all three of them decide to go off to the woods together and so on. You easily lose track, and find afterwards your child went somewhere unsuitable because the mother of one of his friends said it was okay.

Always know who your child's friends are

Make sure as well that you know exactly who his friends are, so that if your child asks if he can go somewhere with one of the unsuitable ones you can say no and stick to it. He's welcome to bring Dick home with him if he likes, but there's no question of going off with Dick on his overland trip to China. As already pointed out, children often get into mischief when together in a way they never would if on their own. Even with suitable friends, one child eggs the other on, one tries to outdo the other, one child is afraid of looking 'soft', one sparks off inventive ideas in the other, and so it goes on.

Before each child properly knows what is happening, something silly has taken place, and when parents hear of it they're shocked their children could act so apparently out of character. What to do when children get into real trouble is dealt with in the next chapter, but for the moment, remember always that the potential for mischief in a pair or group of children is much greater than the sum total of the individual parts!

The lonely child

We all like to think that our children are popular and make plenty of friends. So we're disconcerted if we find they spend most of their time on their own, and don't seem to have any close companions. We wonder if this means they haven't the knack of relating to others, and we worry they'll miss out on the fun that comes from mixing well. Questions of this kind come to a head when children are about seven. Before that, their friendships tend to be made for them by parents and teachers, and in any case they're unlikely to form close attachments to anyone outside their own family. But with the growing independence that comes from seven onwards children begin to form relationships for themselves. Some children prefer to have a circle of friends, others to have one or two companions with whom they're very intimate. But some children don't seem to have anyone much, and these are the ones who concern us.

Let's make it clear that there are no hard-and-fast psychological rules on how a child should form her friendships. Much depends upon her temperament. A child who is naturally outgoing and energetic will tend to go for a wide circle, while a quieter, more withdrawn child will prefer to make fewer, closer friends. Both approaches are perfectly okay. It's equally wrong to nag a child over why she doesn't stick to one friend all the time (her 'best friend' may change almost daily) or to nag her over why she doesn't get to know more people. Give children plenty of opportunities to form both wide friendships and close friendships, and then leave them to establish their own preferred patterns.

Similarly, it's wrong to want to change a child just because she's a bit of a loner. Some children are very self-sufficient.

Is your child happy the way she is? They have their own interests and their own pursuits, and may find they simply don't have that much in common with other children of their age. On the other hand, some children desperately want friends, and are deeply hurt at the way others reject them. The golden rule is does your child seem happy with the way she is? If she does, and if she's well-adjusted and has a good relationship with her family, then fine. Many highly creative people tended to be loners when they were children, and just because your child is a loner now it doesn't mean she won't make good friends when she's older, when she finds people who operate on her own level and to whom she can talk freely. On the other hand if your child is clearly being spurned by other children, or worse still teased or picked on, then she needs help.

Children who become victims

Unfortunately, research shows there are certain children who through no fault of their own tend to be made 'victims' by their schoolmates. Such children usually have something which marks them off from others of their age and which makes it difficult for them to fit in. Maybe the difference is physical. The child is plump perhaps, or has protruding ears, or some actual handicap. Maybe it's social. The child comes from a different background from everyone else, and speaks with a different accent. Maybe it's ethnic, maybe it's religious. Maybe it's educational, with the child much brighter or slower than the rest of the class. But whatever the difference is, it signals to the other children that the child isn't one of them, and they turn on or shun her accordingly. Children can be very cruel over such things; often thoughtlessly so, but cruel nevertheless.

Having a victim enhances the other children's security It isn't just that they get a rather disreputable excitement from seeing one of their number persecuted. It's that by making one of their number an outsider they confirm their own acceptability to the group. Most children have an element of insecurity in their make-up, and by all turning on one unfortunate they experience the security of their own group membership.

We see something of the same thing in the awed delight with which children watch one of their classmates being punished by the teacher or receiving low marks in class. By avoiding punishment themselves they are able to revel in their own security. Many adults aren't exempt from this kind of feeling either – witness the fascination with which they watch or hear accounts of the tragedies which befall others.

So there's something in children which makes them almost hunt for a victim from within their midst. And if there's no obvious physical, socio-ethnic or educational characteristic which prompts them to pick on someone, they'll often find another excuse. Psychologists recognize that there are some very subtle reasons which can make a child a victim. One of them is a certain helplessness. A child almost invites persecution if she shows she has no defences against it. These defences needn't be physical strength. They can simply be a confident manner, a sharp tongue, or a happy serenity which shows that nothing very much bothers her. Another quality which can make a child a victim is if she shows she's easily upset. Once any animal is wounded, the more insensitive members of the pack are only too ready to turn on it. The child who is upset by teasing or bullying, even if she can defend herself quite vigorously, is likely to invite just this kind of cruelty from her fellows.

Reasons why a child becomes a victim

The reverse of the coin is that some children are marked out to be popular. A popular child is usually one with a ready wit, popular skills (such as proficiency at games), self-confidence, and the ability to help other children develop a sense of identity. 'I'm one of so-and-so's friends' is a good way for a child to think about herself, and get a picture of the kind of person she is. Sadly, no one wants to define herself by being the friend of an unpopular child.

If you think your child *is* genuinely unpopular or short of friends, go through the reasons I've just discussed and think why this should be. Many of the reasons can be remedied. If your child sticks out from the group because of his clothes or accent or background, help him make the necessary adjustments. You may not want him to pick up the local accent, but children whose parents speak differently from their classmates can usually contrive quite happily to develop two different ways of talking, one for home and one for school. If you really feel your child is at a school where children not only speak differently from him but have quite different standards and values, see if its possible to move to a more appropriate area.

Many reasons can be remedied

It isn't fair to subject a child to conflicting sets of values amongst classmates and at home. If he behaves as you've taught him to behave he is victimized at school, and if he behaves acceptably to his classmates you disapprove of him.

Some physical reasons for a child's unpopularity can also be remedied. If your child is overweight, keep him on an appropriate diet. The problem is more difficult if he's small and underweight, but have a talk to your doctor about the extra nutritious foods that might help. If his ears are a problem, growing his hair longer will make a big difference. If he wears glasses with thick lenses, see he's provided with attractive spectacle frames which won't emphasize the problem.

Is the problem a vulnerable or defenceless manner? If your child's unpopularity is due to a vulnerable or defenceless manner, things may be harder to put right, but there is much that can be done. The first essential is to show your child that he has you on his side. Don't scold him for not being able to stand up for himself. Don't suggest you're disappointed in him. Don't refuse to listen when he tries to tell you of his unhappy experiences at school ('Oh no, I'm sick and tired of your moaning and whining'). This doesn't mean you're encouraging him to go on being vulnerable. It means that you're giving him a firm base at home from which he can gather the confidence to face the world.

Have you been over-protective? The second essential is to check whether *you yourself* have been contributing towards your child's defencelessness. Have you been encouraging the 'acquired helplessness' mentioned earlier (page 334)? Are you being over-protective, for example insisting on taking your child to the school gate and meeting him after school long after the need has passed? Are you doing anything that holds him up to ridicule by his schoolmates? Do you treat him as a semi-invalid when he has the slightest thing wrong with him in order to increase his dependence upon you? Sometimes it's an only child who suffers in this way. Sometimes it's the child of a single parent. Sometimes it's the youngest child, or a boy in a household of women and girls. But whatever it is, recognize it and talk it over with your child. Be frank. Tell him you hadn't realized how big he was growing. Encourage him to think of himself as more independent, more in charge of things, less in need of you.

If it isn't your over-protective behaviour that's to blame,

look further. Have you tended to curb your child's attempts at self-assertion? If your child is dominated by others within the home, it isn't surprising he's dominated by others outside it as well (though some children – temperament is at work again here – will become extra aggressive outside the home to make up for lack of freedom within). Find ways of giving him more responsibilities. Allow him to speak up for himself more often. Show him he has a right to be himself. You don't want him to be a doormat at school, so make sure he isn't one at home.

Has he been dominated by others at home?

If he comes from a large family, maybe it's his brothers and sisters who have been keeping him too firmly in his place. Help them understand the long-term harm they may be doing to his belief in himself. Find ways of giving him obvious and important little responsibilities around the house, so that everyone has a chance to see what he can do and to encourage and praise him. Comment favourably upon his abilities when visitors and the rest of the family can hear. Make opportunities for conceding points to him in discussions so that he'll start thinking more highly of his own point of view.

Next, coach him in verbal skills. The child who comes up with a ready answer when someone makes an unpleasant remark often leaves his opponent nonplussed. If your child is being teased by other children, prompt him to tell you some of the things they say to him, and then work out with him what would have been a good quick reply. Children learn readily enough, and once your child gets the idea that there *is* a good answer to the jibes he's been suffering, he'll begin to develop the knack of thinking of it when needed.

Coach him in verbal skills

Then help him realize that one of the reasons he is picked on is that he lets other children see he's been hurt. If he can hide his feelings, and then release them in the safety and security of his own home, things will be much better. Sometimes a better response to teasing even than a ready answer is to ignore it altogether. At the very least, he must try not to show he's angry or tearful. The other children will soon tire of picking on him if he shows it's water off a duck's back. Children are helped if you play a little game with them, each of you teasing the other in a very light-hearted way. They're also helped immeasurably if they see you understand how they feel, accept and sympathize with it, and are now working with them to find ways of putting things right.

Teach him not to show he's hurt

Speak to the teacher   As usual when there are problems, speak also to your child's teacher. No teacher likes to think that one of 'her' children is unhappy, and she may already have noticed what was going on. If a teacher appears to side with a particular child, this can make things even worse for him, since his classmates now see him as the teacher's pet. But if the teacher has a good relationship with her class she can find appropriate ways of handling things. Her aim should be not to punish the other children (and thus antagonize them further against your child) but to get their support. She does this by refusing to blame or name names, but by indicating that there is teasing going on ('good-naturedly perhaps, but you children don't realize that some people find it unpleasant') and that she relies upon everyone's common sense to see it doesn't happen any more. Careful to give the impression that there are probably several people being teased, the teacher avoids personalizing matters and drawing attention specifically to your child.

This approach usually works, but if it doesn't the teacher may have to single out the ring-leaders and talk to them. If this is done in private, so that the children aren't humiliated in front of the rest of the class and prompted to go on teasing your child as a way of reasserting themselves, that should be the end of the affair. Compare notes with the teacher and watch to see that there is no recurrence of the trouble. However, if the teacher is one of those individuals who takes a robust view on teasing and thinks that a child should fight his own battles, then take the matter to the headteacher. Teasing (and worse still bullying) isn't a minor inconvenience that a child just has to put up with. It's a bitter experience that can make a misery of childhood and leave its mark on a person for life. Don't allow it to do that to your child.

Sissies and tomboys

One of the ways in which a child can invite teasing is by identifying with the opposite sex. So-called sissies and tomboys show by their interests and mannerisms that they're more at home with the opposite sex than with their own. Many parents find that in addition to getting their children teased this invites doubts in their own minds as to the eventual sexual preferences of their children. Does being a sissy or a tomboy mean a child will grow up homosexual? At the very least, does it mean a boy isn't going to share interests with his father and a girl with her mother? Nursing a happy picture of shared interests, many parents find this worrying.

In fact there's no real evidence that sissies and tomboys are likely to grow up unusual. Most children, if they're exposed mainly to the opposite sex (boys in all-female households or girls in all-male), will pick up many of their interests, as will boys who have especially close relationships with their mothers and girls with their fathers. This is in many ways a healthy sign, since it means they grow up with a sympathy and understanding for the oppostie sex. The only danger is that if a boy, say, is brought up in an all-female household, acquiring female interests and values, he may find it hard to adjust to a male environment when he grows older. And by making other boys tease him, his feminine ways could result in his avoiding male company and identifying more and more with females, thus making matters worse for him.

The remedy is to ensure that your children have plenty of opportunities to meet and relate to both sexes. The aggressive masculinity of a boy brought up in an all-male environment is just as one-sided as the femininity of a boy brought up in a female one. Children grow up best if they have ample chance to mix with both men and women, both boys and girls. So if you have an all-female or all-male household, give your child the benefit of the company of the opposite sex. Help him or her to see that each of us has both male and female sides to our natures, and that healthy development depends on our recognizing both. Sissiness and tomboyishness on the one hand, aggressive masculinity and defenceles femininity on the other, are all signs that an individual's learning experiences have been limited. He or she hasn't learnt the balance that allows us to be human beings first and men and women second.

Children need to mix with both sexes

Taking money that isn't hers

I prefer this term to 'stealing' when we're discussing small children, because stealing presupposes that the individual knows exactly what she's doing and why she's doing it. To a small child, watching her mother or father doing the shopping, money seems to have an almost magical quality. You hand over a few of these coins or notes (which look intrinsically rather uninteresting) and lo and behold you're able to walk away with something you really want. Not surprisingly, she may well feel that transactions of this kind are much to be admired, and that the sooner she gets some of these coins and notes in her possession the better.

So if you find that a small child has some of the contents of your handbag or wallet salted away in her room, this doesn't mean she has the makings of an international currency thief. Repossess the money without fuss, and explain to her that money is something over which you have to have very tight control, because you only have a limited amount and if it disappears you won't have any left to buy food for the family, 'and then where will we all be?'. Impress on her that she must never take money belonging to anyone else, and that similarly other people mustn't be allowed to come and take any money belonging to her (it will be some years yet before she has to learn about the activities of the Inland Revenue).

Give your child pocket money and don't leave your money lying around Starting her early on pocket money, as suggested earlier in this chapter, will quickly help her to master the niceties of all this, as will explanations of where money comes from (employment outside the home, interest on savings). But it makes good sense not to leave money lying around the house where a child can see it. Even though she's beginning to understand the value of money, the temptation to boost her small savings with the occasional injection of extra funds may well be beyond her. Very young children haven't yet the strength to handle strong temptation, or to look ahead to the retribution that may lie in wait for them. The innocence with which they fail to hide their illicit gains from parental eyes is proof enough of this. So don't put temptation in their way. Keep your money safe and out of sight.

At the same time, by giving your child a reasonable sum of pocket money, you decrease her need to take cash that isn't hers. Sometimes children with particularly generous natures will take money in order to spend it on presents for others, and where this happens it's a clear sign that they don't have enough funds to satisfy their urge towards generosity. You can't condone the taking of money even for laudable reasons like this, but explain to your child that you love her generosity, even though she must take care that it doesn't get her into trouble. Re-appraise the amount of pocket money she receives if it seems too little for her reasonable needs, and don't be afraid to give her an unscheduled increase if this is called for. Tell her, though, that if she should take money again, for whatever reason, she'll lose the increase. You don't want to take it from her, but she'll leave you no choice.

Don't treat any of these early attempts to take money as a crime. As I said earlier, they don't mean your child has the makings of a thief. Treat them as learning experiences. She has to learn about money and the rights of possession. She isn't born with this knowledge. Some parents tell me that they gave their child a severe punishment when they first caught her taking something that wasn't hers, and that 'she never tried it again'. Possibly not. Or possibly she just got smarter at covering her tracks. Or possibly she'll grow up quite happy to take money whenever there's no risk, since the only thing to stop her is the fear of punishment. For a child to grow up with a real moral sense about money, a sense which means she wouldn't dream of taking anything that doesn't belong to her irrespective of whether there's a risk involved or not, she has to understand the real facts about possession, that our lives as we know them would be impossible if people could just walk around taking what they liked from each other when they liked, with the strongest and cleverest victimizing the weakest and most helpless.

Don't treat taking money as a crime

If you do suspect your child has taken money that isn't hers, but you can't find the evidence, try to get the truth out of her. Not by threatening what will happen to her if she doesn't 'confess'. She may admit to anything, whether she's really guilty or not, in order to get herself off the hook. But by questioning her in the way in which you'd question her about anything you happen to have mislaid ('Have *you* seen it?'). If she professes innocence, ask her directly whether she's taken it. Don't give her the impression that if she owns up she's in for terrible punishment. If she has taken it and admits it, praise her for her honesty, and then explain to her why it mustn't happen again. If she denies it and you're sure she's the culprit, make it clear to her why taking the money and then not telling you the truth about it makes it doubly wrong.

If you think your child has taken money that isn't hers

As explained in Chapter 6, lying in children isn't the same

as lying in adults. A small child doesn't fully understand the difference between fact and fiction, and to her lying just seems like a convenient strategy to avoid unpleasantness. She has to learn otherwise of course, but this comes through explaining the reasons for truthfulness ('If you asked me something, and I made up answers instead of telling you the truth, you'd be pretty fed up with me. If you asked me where Teddy was and I said he was upstairs when I knew he was downstairs you'd soon tell me not to be so silly. Or if you asked me if I'd taken your toys and I said I hadn't when really I had. If people don't tell the truth we never know when to believe them, and we say that people like that can't be trusted').

If your child denies taking the money, and you *aren't* sure she's the culprit, there's little to be gained by pushing her too hard. Her denial may in fact *be* the truth, and if she sees you don't believe her, this will sour for a time at least the trust between you. On the other hand, if she isn't telling you the truth, she may become too worried and confused to go back on her original story, no matter how many times you ask her. Take a different course and tell her how wrong it would be if she *had* taken the money, how pleased you are that she hasn't, and how sure you are that she won't do such a thing in the future. Then let the matter drop, without holding it against her. But do resolve to keep a more watchful eye on things in future, and to reinforce the lesson on honesty by strategically dropping comments on the theme and by reading appropriate stories which have honesty as an important issue.

Tackled in this way, a child by age seven should have a very clear idea of why she shouldn't take things that aren't hers, and be sufficiently strong to resist the temptation to do so. It's still common sense not to leave sums of money lying around (quite apart from anything else this shows how careless *you* are, and weakens your attempts to teach her proper care of her own money), but the early lessons will now be firmly fixed in her mind.

If an older child takes money   If an older child hasn't had the chance to learn these lessons, and does take money, then once again the vital thing is to explain to him why taking other people's things is wrong. But the lesson can now be reinforced by consequences of some kind. Not harsh words or punishment that will brand him permanently in his own eyes as a thief, but something related directly to his transgression and his ability to understand why it was wrong. In the context of a good parent–child relationship, the best approach is: 'I can see you're sorry for what you did, and that you appreciate it must never happen again. That's very good. But you know, when grown-ups do something wrong they get taken to court, and the court doesn't let them off even if they are sorry. So what do you think you ought to do to make up for taking the money?' Most children respond well to this, and suggest something sensible (often they are harder on themselves than their parents would be). Losing pocket money for a certain time perhaps. Or losing other privileges. Since this is the child's own suggestion, he feels it's fair and it leaves him without feeling aggrieved at you or too badly about himself. You may decide it's now appropriate to let him off or reduce his suggested punishment, and this is fine. But in any case make sure the punishment doesn't drag on too long, and make sure your child understands that honesty isn't just a way of avoiding punishment. It's an essential virtue in social and moral living.

Cruel behaviour in a child

Cruel behaviour in children isn't necessarily linked to aggression. Some aggressive children have no real intention of hurting others. Their feelings get the better of them and they hit out, only to be aghast a moment later at what they've done. On the other hand some very non-aggressive children can seem cruel, particularly towards animals or insects who can't express their own feelings or hit back.

This gives us a clue to the nature of some cruelty in children. **The child is** It often isn't an emotional thing at all. The child is experiment- **experimenting** ing with the environment, rather than deliberately setting out **with his** to be vicious. What will happen if I do this to the cat, or do **environment** that to a captured beetle, or do that to an earthworm? Having completed his 'experiment' he feels nothing beyond satisfied curiosity. He doesn't attribute 'feelings' to the cat or the beetle or the earthworm in the way in which he has feelings himself. The poor creatures are simply the objects of his experiments (which isn't *all* that different from the way some branches of science approach their material!)

Even when cruelty is more obviously vindictive, as when a child squeezes the baby's arm to make him cry, he still isn't fully attributing his own feelings to the baby. Until the age of five or six, a child is very egocentric. He doesn't realize that the world 'out there' is in some ways very similar to the world 'in here', that other creatures and other people feel pain the way he does, and want their own way, and prefer to be treated the way he prefers to be treated.

He is also exploring his own emotions

Once beyond this egocentric stage, the child becomes better able to appreciate and sympathize with the feelings of others, but he's still curious about the effects of cruelty upon them (all primary school teachers are well aware of the rapt attention shown by their young innocents the moment there's some mention of torture or executions or other unpleasant goings-on), and about the emotions which such cruelty can arouse in him. He's still a stranger to some parts of his emotional life, and the thrill of horror that goes through him at the mention of cruelty is something he may feel he wants to explore and get to know rather better. To add to this, causing pain in others *can* give him a sense of power, which is another new emotion in his relatively powerless life, and another emotion which he wants to explore in more detail.

Teach him that other creatures have feelings too

So if you see an example of cruelty in your child, it doesn't mean he has the makings of a sadist. It mustn't be equated with a similar example of cruelty perpetrated by an adult. On the other hand, it has to be dealt with. Your child has to learn as early as possible respect for life, in no matter how 'humble' an insect. He won't learn this lesson through punishment. You can't teach him it's wrong to be cruel by being 'cruel' to him in your own turn (even 'There; now see how *you* like it when it's done to you!' doesn't exactly demonstrate our respect for another person's sensibilities). But you can teach him through his vivid imagination. Asking him to put himself in the place of the creature he's been harming is usually enough. How would *he* like to be a butterfly, enjoying flying up into the air, and then having his wings pulled off by an enormous giant? The answer is he wouldn't, and the lesson very soon goes home. And goes home all the quicker if he sees that you too have a respect for life, preferring to sweep insects into the dustpan and put them outside rather than thoughtlessly squash them. Insects, children and grown-ups all have rights, and if your child has each of these sets of rights demonstrated to him by someone he loves and trusts and wants to be like, he soon makes the lesson a part of him.

The obsessional child

'Obsessional' might seem rather a strong word for a young child. It's a term we usually reserve for adults, but many parents talk anxiously about obsessional habits even in children as young as eight, and my own observation of the 8–11 age group has shown me that these anxieties have some justification. By obsessional behaviour in children I mean behaviour which emphasizes one particular personality trait out of all proportion to its importance. This trait frequently has something to do with cleanliness, neatness or tidiness, but can also cover such things as punctuality or an emphasis upon sameness or order or precision in the environment. Children who show these personality traits can become quite unreasonably upset if things aren't just as they like them, and may remain unhappy until they're put to rights.

Another feature that often crops up is a liking for ritual. The child has to go through things in a set order (as for example when undressing, or eating, or bathing), or may have to touch certain objects twice whenever coming into contact with them, or may have to use a set form of words when asking for things or when answering certain questions. Any interruption to the ritual can cause genuine distress, especially if other people tease the child about it, or accuse her of silliness.

As with almost all psychological states, there isn't a sharp dividing line between children with obsessional traits and those without them. All children can show mild obsessionality at times, and all children enjoy a certain amount of ritual, particularly up to the age of six or seven. Ritual gives consistency to a child's life, and makes things seem secure and predictable. We're only concerned about obsessionality if it takes on an exaggerated importance for a child, and interferes with her normal life. When this happens, it usually seems to be associated with the child who has a rather intense, serious nature, and perhaps a somewhat anxious approach to life in general.

The need for security and predictability is usually the cause

The cause of exaggerated obsessions of this kind is the same as the cause of the mild obsessions we see in most children, namely the need for security and predictability. The only difference is that in the exaggerated child this need is very much greater. The child feels she has, in a sense, to hold her world together. Unsure of herself and perhaps of those she loves, and with a strong sense of her own powerlessness over events, the child tries to find safety in keeping things always the same way, in resisting change, in making things clear-cut rather than ambiguous and therefore uncertain and threatening. Usually averse to risk-taking, the child clings to what she knows rather than face the challenge of strangeness or newness.

Where the obsessional trait has to do with excessive cleanliness or tidiness, some psychologists think the child may also have been toilet-trained too strictly, thus making her guilty and uncertain about anything that suggests 'dirt' or 'mess'. Others feel the excessive cleanliness may be a way of relieving more general feelings of guilt. Be this as it may, the obsessional child often does seem tense and over-controlled in her attitude towards herself and others, which suggests she may not have been allowed to express herself freely in either physical or emotional ways when smaller. However, this is by no means always the case, and in some instances the child's obsessionality appears suddenly and apparently spontaneously, as a response to an upheaval in life circumstances, such as the break-up of the family, starting a new school, or even moving house. Part of the child's identity was bound up in things as they were, and in the face of the sudden change she tries to make everything consistent and recognizable again through her obsessional and ritualistic behaviour.

What you can do

Many children grow out of an obsessional phase once they learn how to live with the upheavals in their lives, or once these upheavals calm down again. If this doesn't happen, specialist psychological help may be needed. But the treatment for obsessional behaviour follows clearly enough from the things I've just been saying about the cause. Remove if possible the factors that are making the child's life seem uncertain, and try to provide her with the security that she appears to lack. Do this by showing her your love in word and deed, by keeping any promises you make to her, by planning ahead with her and sticking to the plans, and in general by adopting a much more understanding approach to your child's feelings. Take care not to raise guilt levels unnecessarily by constantly emphasizing how much you disapprove of her behaviour – obsessional children always experience enough guilt anyway. Don't tackle the obsessions head-on. If your child is obsessional about cleanliness or tidiness or food (sometimes such a child finds it hard even to eat with her family, and takes her meals alone in another room), then accept this as a fact of life for the moment. Don't tease her about it or pay much obvious attention to it. Make sure you don't yourself nag her too often about punctiliousness and correctness, or focus too much upon these things in your own life, and allow your child to grow out of her phase as she becomes more sure of herself.

If her confidence is lacking this may also need bolstering, and judicious words of praise when she produces behaviours opposite to the obsessional ones are also in order (for example tell her she looks nice when you catch her a little untidy, or that her room looks properly lived in when it's in a bit of a mess). Creative experience is also invaluable, so long as it involves free expression (abstract painting, blank verse), as are physical activities (especially swimming and muddy games). Given the right environment, obsessional behaviour usually disappears or reduces to a manageable level quite quickly in children. It's much more resistant to treatment in adults. So don't neglect this kind of behaviour in the belief that it's just your child's 'nature'.

RELATIONSHIPS BETWEEN PARENTS

The relationship parents have with each other is in its way as vital to your child as the parent–child relationship itself. Children flourish best in an environment where parents have a happy marriage and laugh together, show consideration for each other, talk things over, share responsibilities, help each other and generally set an example of how a mutually enriching and harmonious relationship should work.

Brought up in such an environment, children experience a

Constant strife between parents is deeply upsetting for the child

sense of deep security. They not only have a valuable lesson in how to relate to others, they have the happy knowledge that home is a place of safety. By contrast, children brought up in homes where there is constant strife between parents, where voices are constantly raised in anger, where one or other parent is frequently reduced to tears by the other, where there is bitterness and distrust, have a wounding time of it. For one thing, their loyalties are divided. They love both parents, so whose side should they be on? For another, they fear their parents may separate, breaking up the home and the life they know. For another, they rarely find themselves able to enjoy family events. Mealtimes and outings, instead of being cheerful occasions, are reduced to feuds and angry silences. Lying in bed at night they hear their parents rowing away downstairs. They come home to a heavy, emotionally charged atmosphere. And troubled, hurt and preoccupied by their marital problems, neither parent is able to relate to the children in the free and relaxed way they should.

Yes I know, most marriages have their ups and downs, and children can't always be protected from angry exchanges between their parents. Often in any case these exchanges are better than each parent bottling things up and seething away under the surface. Families work best where people are open with each other, and can each have their say. Some parents in any case confess they enjoy arguing, just as children themselves relish a good old set-to. But the best environment for a child is a home in which each parent respects the other's point of view, and is ready, through mutual respect and understanding, to give him or her the emotional and physical 'space' within the home upon which a valid sense of personal worth and identity depend. A home, moreover, where such differences as do arise are debated frankly and sensibly instead of argued and shouted over.

One of the big problems with trying to settle matters by arguing and shouting is that people become polarized into opposite camps. What starts out at as a minor incident, and with nothing needed other than mild give and take, becomes inflated into a major incident. Because they entrench themselves in opposed positions with emotions running high, and because 'winning' the battle and hurting the opponent become of paramount importance, neither party is prepared to give way. The result is that we have a confrontation which for sheer unnecessary silliness would rival anything the children themselves can muster. Such a confrontation leaves the smoke of battle hanging around for days. Things are said in the heat of the moment which aren't meant but which are taken up and remembered by the opposition, fuelling resentment which waits only for the next minor incident to break out again in full force.

Children who are exposed to these running battles, and to the uneasy periods of truce which punctuate them, suffer greatly. They remember into adult life the way in which every nerve in their body seemed stretched tight by the hostility and bitterness around them. The more sensitive the child the worse the suffering, but even hardy children who seem to take it all in their stride don't emerge unscarred.

Children can be permanently affected by the trauma

Children don't expect life to be perfect. They take it as it is. They have nothing with which to compare their lives, and they tend to view their own experiences as the norm, trying hard to adapt and cope with unhappiness. This often leads us to think: 'Oh, it hasn't harmed the kids; they're used to that kind of thing.' Or: 'Kids are all the better for growing up able to take a few domestic knocks.' Or: 'That's life isn't it?' But because the harm done to children isn't visible on the surface it doesn't mean it isn't there. The trauma of watching their parents tear each other apart causes insecurity, confusion and despair in children which can mark them for life.

This doesn't mean you have to feel guilty because your children see the occasional tiff. But it does mean you have to think carefully if yours is the kind of marriage that leads to frequent domestic ructions. Even the occasional angry set-to, if it blows up abruptly and fiercely, can be very frightening for a child. If your marriage falls into this category, both marriage partners should sit down together and talk about ways of improving things. With fair-mindedness on both sides many of the small incidents that lead to rows can be anticipated and avoided. More thought can be given to keeping quiet over disagreements if the children are present, and talking them over later when the children aren't there and when both sides have in any case had a chance to cool down.

A domestic contract

These issues are major ones, and I haven't the space to go into them in the necessary detail. But marriage works more smoothly if each partner respects the right of the other to be an individual. Once this right is established, the next step is to look at those areas where both partners have to work together, and to see how compromises can be effected so that things go smoothly. If necessary, these areas of compromise can be defined on paper, in the form of a *domestic contract*. This isn't being formal, it's simply showing good sense. The partners to a marriage have to live together under the same roof and share their lives with each other, taking up all sorts of important roles (housekeeper, gardener, bread-winner, accountant, car mechanic, chauffeur, lover, confidant, nurse, therapist and all the rest). Inevitably at times there are conflicting interests, and they have to work out ways of harmonizing these interests, and then putting the results on paper, leaving both partners knowing exactly how things stand.

For example, one partner may feel the other isn't helping enough in the house, while the other resents not receiving help with the garden. Or there could be disagreements over sexual relationships or evenings out or time spent at work or tidiness or cleanliness. Whatever the problem, each partner contracts to help the other in clearly defined ways in return for specified help with his or her own problems. Not only do contracts of this kind lead to greater harmony and give and take, they allow each partner to see the other's point of view. Marriage guidance counsellors report that after drawing up contracts married people often say, 'I never realized he/she felt so strongly about that' or 'I just didn't know how much work he/she has to do' or 'I hadn't realized how thoughtless I was being.'

The contract must have top priority Some parents say the contracts work smoothly for a week or two, then suddenly they find themselves confronted by other priorities which make them go back on their side of the bargain. The question is, *how much priority do you assign to the contract?* If the contract has top priority, then other things must fit in around it. And if both parties honour the contract trust develops between them, together with respect for each other's commitment. Where a contract breaks down, it's often because people who would never dream of breaking agreements made with folk outside the home think nothing of doing so when it comes to their partner. If written contracts aren't necessary, use verbal ones. But these must be every bit as binding. And both parents must understand that both their marriage and the happiness of their children may depend upon keeping their side of the bargain.

Further, their child's success in school may also depend upon it. A child who is preoccupied with anxieties and insecurities at home will inevitably lack concentration and energy in class. Depending on temperament he may also take out his unhappiness on others, becoming aggressive and disruptive and making himself unpopular with teachers and classmates. Or, in an attempt to attract the attention of his parents away from their quarrels and back to himself (consciously or unconsciously), he may get into trouble through stealing or vandalism or other anti-social acts. **Your child's school work may be affected**

Young children are fiercely loyal towards their parents and often they don't reveal the source of their troubles to their teachers. In any case, they often find it hard to identify and communicate inner fears and anxieties. Thus the teacher may unwittingly write them off as 'just lazy' or 'troublemakers' or 'spiteful and aggressive'. What then happens is that a child who already has all he can handle at home is faced with further worries at school. In their turn, parents now see their child's problems as contributing to *their* difficulties, and things go from bad to worse. The family falls apart, leaving each member isolated and without the support and understanding of the very people who matter most to him or her in life.

Most families, it must be said, never let themselves get into this state. But when they have children, parents have responsibilities not only towards one another for making the marriage work but also towards the children. Children have a right not to be caught up in parental quarrels, and a right not to have their loyalties played on, with each parent in turn trying to get them on their side. They also have a right not to be used as weapons by one parent against the other, as when for example one parent threatens the other with taking the children away, or alternatively with leaving home and forcing the other to cope with the children single-handed. They also have a right to expect parents to have time and energy to devote to them, rather than see everything draining away in constant marital feuding.

Separation

Knowing the harm that an unhappy home life can do to a child, parents whose marriages are going wrong inevitably wonder whether it is better for the children if they separate or if they try and hang on. Is it better for a child to be brought up living with one parent and seeing the other only on set occasions, or to be brought up by two parents who can't provide a happy home?

Children may be better off if you separate I know that if a marriage is going badly wrong there aren't only the children to consider. The parents also have to think about the physical and emotional strain they themselves are undergoing. But if we concentrate upon the children, the answer is that if the home really is falling apart, then the great majority of children would be better off if their parents separated, assuming the parent with custody provides a good home. Certainly the split-up will be traumatic for them, especially if it involves moving from the area and from their school and friends. And certainly it will lead to confused loyalties. But these traumas are preferable to the strains of living in an emotional battlefield.

Nor should parents stay together in the belief that unaided their children can 'save' the marriage for them, or that a new baby will miraculously do the trick. It's unfair to bring a child into the world expecting him to be a kind of glue to mend the marriage. All too often he simply becomes yet another issue to row about. It's equally unfair to expect an older child to listen to both parents and try and arbitrate between them. Young children are far too emotionally involved and far too inexperienced to take on demands of this kind, though in their heart of hearts they may see clearly how foolish their parents are being.

Difficulties after the separation I've already talked several times about the single parent and some of his or her problems. Much of what I've said applies now to the separated parent who has custody. Similarly, much of what I say now applies to those who are single parents from the outset or through bereavement. But a particular problem of the separated parent is that they have the influence of the non-custodial parent to take into account. Sometimes things work well. The children see the latter parent regularly, enjoy the experience, and find no emotional conflict. But sometimes the arrangement leads to friction. The non-custodial parent, seeing the children only weekly, is able always to be relaxed and friendly and to spoil them with treats and outings. He or she may also criticize, openly or by implication, the custodial parent and give the children the idea they'd be much better off if custody were reversed. If the children are very attached to the non-custodial parent they may also blame the custodial parent for the separation, and there may be sullen, resentful and disobedient behaviour as a result.

If as a single parent you're in this position, don't blame the children. It's simply one of the sad consequences that often follows the break-up of a marriage. And resist the temptation to get your own back by forcing your own side of the story on the children at every available opportunity. This may simply turn them against you. They're bound to see you're turning it into a tug-of-war, and they'll quickly weary of the whole business. They'll see your point of view much more readily if you can make a joke out of it, a joke which nevertheless brings home to them all the work that falls on your shoulders. So if they seem to be comparing you unfavourably with their other parent remind them, 'Yes that's fine, but I tell you what, take all your week's dirty washing along with you to Daddy (Mummy) next time and see what they say' or, 'Okay, but Mum (Dad) wasn't up half the night with you helping you with your homework'. **Don't let a tug-of-war develop**

Hard as it is, the important thing is not to appear martyred and resentful. If you show your irritation or your hurt your children can use them as a weapon against you. Children live in a world where they have very little power as of right. So they can become adept at finding subtle ways of asserting themselves or of hitting back at a parent. Shrug things off and you'll find your children won't ply you with flattering stories about their other parent. Show you're hurt, and you'll find yourself either having to forbid any mention of him or her (a challenge your children will soon find ways round) or having to 'defend' yourself against negative comparisons. **Don't show you're resentful**

Don't feel you must compete with the other parent. Do your

Don't compete with the other parent

best for your children, but be yourself and let them in the end make up their own minds who does most for them. Children aren't really fooled by extravagant displays of affection from a parent they see only once a week. They know on whom they most rely. Provided you don't drive your children emotionally away from you by attacking their love for their other parent, or put on competing displays of privileges and treats which you can't possibly keep up, your children will value you for what you are, and won't try to play one parent off against the other.

Don't expect extra gratitude

As for your children themselves, it isn't their fault you're a single parent, or that more duties and responsibilities fall upon you than if there were two of you. Don't necessarily expect your children to feel extra gratitude to you for the way you've struggled along on your own. This may seem hard, but children do take good parenting for granted. This doesn't mean they're not grateful, it's simply that you and all you do for them are part of their lives. They can't always be standing back and looking at your efforts objectively.

In later years they'll see you had a special kind of struggle, but for now they'll relate better to you if they're not constantly being told how much they owe you. And remember, they're not the ones who decided you had to be a single parent. But they'll accept the situation and be happy enough with it as long as they're allowed to find their own level within it, just as other children find their own level within a two-parent family.

If you remarry

More potential problems arise if you remarry or have close friends amongst the opposite sex. Naturally your children will feel jealous. If they have good relationships with their non-custodial parent, or warm memories of a parent who has sadly died, then they may also think that your new partner is trying to take the place of the old. For your part, you may feel your children are deliberately trying to sabotage your new relationship. You want them to get on well with your new partner, and may in your turn resent what you see as their attempts to rob you of deserved happiness. Divided loyalties between your children and your new partner also won't help, and there'll be the anxiety that perhaps the children will drive the partner away. After all, he or she is taking on a lot, and if the children continue to be rude and unco-operative then there's the real possibility the partner will up sticks and look elsewhere.

Minimize the problem by persuading your partner to keep a low profile at first. Allow him or her to grow on the children, rather than be forced on them. This means that he or she comes into the home as a guest, with the children's rights under no threat. Make sure that the relationship doesn't clash with obligations to your children – as for example if a date with your partner interferes with a long-standing arrangement with one of them. Let the children see they still hold the same place in your life they have always held. And although the new partner may accompany you on family outings, they must come along as a guest and not as boss. Importantly, they must also understand that displays of physical affection between you and them will for some time to come risk making your children embarrassed and jealous.

Persuade your new partner to keep a low profile

Advise them too not to try to take the place of the missing parent, or demand obedience from the children as the missing parent would. Children can have excellent relationships with step-parents, but they must come to love them for themselves, not as substitutes for their original mother and father. If the relationships with the step-parent are allowed to develop naturally, with the children left to make the necessary moves of friendship in their own time and with no one berating them for not being nice enough to the new member of the family, things will work out. But if your children have to act out warm feelings that aren't yet genuine simply for the sake of keeping the step-parent happy, or if they keep coming into conflict with you over the absence of these feelings, then they're bound to feel unhappy for themselves and unhappy for you too. After all, it doesn't say much for the step-parent's feelings for you if he/she has constantly to be kept happy to stop them from running away.

Single parents often complain that their children won't give them any real space to develop new friendships. Whoever they bring home their children are against them on principle. This isn't really surprising. If the children are happy with you

Don't expect your children to welcome your new partner immediately

then they're bound to feel threatened by the intrusion of a stranger (and if they're *unhappy* they'll use him or her as an excuse to get back at you). And if they've seen the effects of one disastrous marriage they won't want to run the risk of experiencing the same traumas again. Until they themselves are adults, it's also hard for them to realize the need one adult may have for another, though they'll usually understand how lonely you'll be when they grow up and leave home.

So your children are working from the basis of their life experiences to date. Give them time. Children are adaptable creatures. They'll gradually become more welcoming, particularly if in spite of themselves they realize your partner is quite human after all and kind to you and them. Patience doesn't always come easily, and children can be very obstructive at times, but the foundations of the new family life have to be properly laid. If they're not, then you're going to need even more patience in the years ahead!

The step-parent's authority must be a matter of consent

A vital point is that the new step-parent must accept that his or her powers of authority over the children are ultimately a matter of *consent*. If the children and step-parent get on well together, they'll accept he or she has the right to tell them what to do. If they don't get on well, or if the new step-parent tries to lay down the law from the start like a natural parent, the children will resent it and rebel. In the early days, the real authority must lie with you, and only as he or she becomes increasingly accepted should the step-parent begin gradually and sensibly to share some of this authority. If step-parents can't accept this gradual process, then they've only themselves to blame if your children confront them with 'You're not my Mummy (or Daddy), and you can't tell me what to do!'.

A particular problem sometimes arises if the step-parent is a man, and considers the children have 'lacked a man's hand' and become unruly. Or if he has quite different ideas on child-rearing from you. Ideally these things should all have been sorted out before marriage or living together. But once married, a step-father must accept that if the children have lacked a 'man's hand' they're not exactly going to welcome feeling the weight of one now. Better for the new father to build up a relationship with his children by introducing them to the activities and interests they've missed out on without a father. By helping his new children to enjoy his company they'll gradually become prepared to take notice of his wishes without his having to lay down the law. A step-father laying down the law from the word go seldom works. At best it leads to fear and hostility in the children, at worst to open defiance. Talking to step-fathers who try this strategy, it often becomes clear they're reacting to their own anger or jealousy towards the child rather than to any genuine desire to have a proper relationship with him.

A final challenge to a step-relationship is if you and your new partner have a baby. Should the step-parent bring children of his or her own into the family, usually your children will accept them provided the children are each given their own space and not forced upon each other. But if a new baby arrives, then your child may feel you and the step-parent now have something in your relationship from which she's excluded, and she may fiercely resent the time you spend with the baby. Treat this as you would the arrival of any new baby in the family (see Chapter 3 for a discussion of older children's reactions to a new baby), but accept that your child will need extra help in preparing emotionally for the birth and extra attention and love afterwards.

If you and your new partner have a baby

A particular problem that arises is that once a new baby has appeared on the scene, your child has to face the fact that the step-parent has come to stay. Previously, there was always the thought that if things didn't work out he or she could be sent packing. Moreover, now that the step-parent is father or mother to the new baby, they also have more of a stake in the household, and move to the centre of things instead of being seen as rather peripheral. These changes may be difficult for your child to handle. They entail a closer (though not necessarily warmer) relationship between her and the step-parent, and pose for her new questions about her own identity. Does she now see herself as a 'daughter' to the step-parent (in addition to being a 'sister' to the new baby)? Who is now the 'head' of the household and therefore the main aribiter in her life?

Young children can't always put these uncertainties into words. It's sometimes only when they look back from adolescence or adult life that they fully understand what was happening at the time. Thus you may notice they become sullen or even hostile, or begin to behave rudely towards the step-parent or yourself, while maintaining hotly when asked that '*nothing's* wrong'. It's better not to insist your child unburdens herself to you at such a time. Tell her, 'You're bound to feel unsettled for a bit, but don't force your feelings; things will settle down.' However, much depends upon the patience and understanding of the step-parent. Mistakes made during these sensitive months are hard to undo later. Without understanding (and a little forbearance by parent and step-parent in the face of uncharacteristically difficult behaviour) the awkward period of adjustment is going to be unnecessarily prolonged.

Show your child you love her as much as ever And remember that when there *are* tensions between your child and her step-parent, this is part of your child's process of testing your love for her. Who will you side with, her or the step-parent? This is a difficult situation for you. If you side with the step-parent, your child is left feeling isolated and alone. If you side with the child, she gets the impression your relationship with the step-parent isn't that good after all, and may use her behaviour to drive a further wedge between you. Show you can see both sides of any issue. And leave your child in no doubt that your love for her is as strong as ever.

WORKING PARENTS

Some of what I have to say in the following paragraphs applies equally to the single parent, because with both working and single parents there's often the worry that your child is missing out on the home life you ought to be providing. A home life in which he's seen off to school each morning with a parental hug and greeted in the same way when he comes home. Certainly children respond well to this kind of family life. But it's better for them to have parents with work and interests outside the home than to have parents stranded indoors all day and hating it. As they grow older and want more independence they can also feel rather smothered by parents who have nothing in their lives beyond their children, and who take an intense and intrusive interest in their every little doing. Children like to feel their parents aren't reliant upon them for *all* their happiness. It's a daunting prospect to have to carry that kind of responsibility.

This is a special danger in the single-parent family or in a family where one parent is away much of the time. The parent who has the care of the children looks to them to play a role in his or her life and provide the emotional support that should really come from another adult. The children have demands made upon them and pressures put upon them which are confusing and unfair, and which get in the way of their independence and their own emotional development. Some psychologists in fact identify this as one of the most serious threats to a child's psychological health; it's certainly an important one.

It's unfair to make too many emotional demands on children

So if you feel you need an outlet beyond the home, it'll be better for your children if you satisfy this need than if you stay at home unwillingly or focus your life solely upon them. Far more important than the bald fact of whether a parent stays at home or goes out to work is that a parent should feel sufficiently fulfilled in life to enjoy his or her children and to provide them with caring and stimulating companionship.

However, if you do have a job outside the home it's vital that proper arrangements are made for the children at each end of the school day, and that one or other parent can be reached during the day in case of need. Proper arrangements must also be made for the time when a child is off school sick. Ad hoc arrangements, which sometimes work and sometimes don't, are deeply unsettling for a child. They show him he's low on your list of priorities, and it's small wonder he presents behaviour problems which *make* you take due notice of him.

Proper arrangements are vital

Where problems arise with working parents they're usually caused less by the work itself than by the fact that the work is allowed to prevent the parent from being a parent. Your child won't be jealous of your job, and will be interested to hear about it. But what *will* trouble him is the feeling that he has to compete with your job for your time and your energies. Provided he knows he comes first and you'd sacrifice the job for him if the need ever arose, he'll be happy enough. He won't try to 'test' you by constantly feigning illness (and no hypochondriac ever came to believe in his affliction more readily than a small child) just to see if you're prepared to stay off work and look after him. He won't cause difficulties in the

Your child must feel he comes first

day so that the school will have to keep phoning you. He'll know you're there if he wants you, and that frees him to get on with his own life.

It helps if you take him with you to work occasionally, so that he can share that part of your life with you. But he shouldn't be taken to work simply because there's nowhere else for him (as for example in the school holidays), and then spend the time bored and miserable. He should be allowed to see your work as fun, so that he can understand why you enjoy doing it and prefer it to just sitting at home. If you have to go out to work to balance the household budget, still help him to think positively of your job if you can, and to be happy at the thought of your doing it.

There's no need for lavish presents As long as things are handled in this way and your child is allowed to feel he comes first, there's no need for parents to feel guilty about taking jobs outside the home. Excessive guilt in this area leaves parents unsure of how they should relate to their child. They want to 'make up' to him for what they fear he's missing because of their work. So they buy him lavish presents and over-indulge him, trying to show him the *material* benefits that come from their earning power. They're unsure how to control his behaviour, and let him get away with things as a way of lessening their own guilt. They try to buy from him the affection they feel they've forfeited by not being at home all day.

His needs are those of any other child Whatever your circumstances and those of your child, always see him as a child first, and as anything else second. So in this case he's a child first, and a child of working parents second. What are his real needs, as opposed to those your guilty feelings are projecting on him? He needs your time. He needs you to do things with him like the parents of his friends. He needs you to be free of excuses, and of inconsistent behaviour as you veer between short temper at the end of a tiring day and over-indulgence as you try and make up for the short temper. He doesn't need extra pocket money. He doesn't need to be 'let off' usual standards of behaviour because you're afraid of giving him yet another reason to be angry with you.

If being fair to your child and having a job sounds hard, this is because having two jobs *is* harder than having one. Perhaps hardest of all is to realize that your child sees life through his own inexperienced eyes and not yours. He's too young fully to understand the extra pressures two jobs may be putting upon you, or that you're maybe doing your outside job mainly for his benefit. So he can't always appreciate the need to co-operate with you to ease the pressures. Handle things by good organization and forward planning rather than by constant appeals to him to stop adding to your difficulties. Research shows that children with both parents working are generally just as happy and well-adjusted and do just as well at school as children with one parent at home. The important variable isn't whether you work or not, but whether you understand your child.

If both parents work outside the home, responsibilities must be shared within it. Young girls may rate charm and person-ality as the most important qualities in a man, but surveys of married women show that 'help in the house' quickly rises to the top or near the top of the list! With both parents working, dividing lines between 'his' and 'her' chores must disappear if women aren't to be put under excessive physical and psycho-logical pressure. Many fathers admit that not only do they feel it 'unmanly' to help in the house, they also feel threatened by their wives' financial independence and widening social hori-zons once she goes out to work. Not only are they no longer the bread-winner, their wives now have other interests than home and husband. The male ego can be a pretty fragile thing!

Sharing responsibilities within the home

All this can cause tensions between parents, with the children caught in the middle. And the paradox is that the more stubbornly a man protects his male 'role' and refuses to help in the house, the less time and energy (and goodwill) his wife has to give him the attention he wants. Remember the domestic contracts I talked about in the last section? This is an ideal opportunity for their use. They set out clearly what each parent agrees to do, and quickly highlight (and correct) ine-qualities in the way domestic responsibilities have so far been shared out. If a man still feels that helping in the house is a threat to his male identity, he must seriously ask himself whether he's got a true picture of what this identity should be. He must also ask whether he's using the idea of his identity simply as an excuse for getting out of what can at times be rather routine and boring tasks.

As for the feeling of threat which comes from a wife's

A woman's identity outside the roles of wife and mother

financial independence and her interests outside the home, this brings us to the question of a *wife's* identity. Many women put so much of themselves into their domestic role they've no time left to explore and develop their own personalities. When their children grow up and leave home, and when their marriage loses some of its early freshness, they suddenly awaken to the fact that they've no real idea of who they are or what they want from life. They've spent so long filling the roles of 'mother' and 'wife' that when the immediacy of these roles decreases they're not sure what's left. In a way this is a tribute to their selflessness over the years, but there's no real need for a woman to lose sight of herself just because she has a family to care for. A great deal depends upon her partner. If he accepts her rights to independence, does his bit to see she's not submerged in domestic chores, and supports her moves to develop outside interests, then she has the same opportunities for personal development that he enjoys himself.

One of the signs that a wife has difficulty in finding an identity outside the role of mother is when, having seen all her children start school, she immediately yearns for another baby. This could be because she loves small babies, but often it's an indication that only when she has a small baby dependent upon her can she feel needed and significant. Another sign is the mother who keeps her youngest child a baby for too long, denying him the independence that the passing years should bring. In both instances mother and child suffer alike. Is the mother who needs a small baby around in order to feel whole as a person still going to feel whole when the baby grows older and needs her in a quite different way? And is the child going to be wanted throughout childhood and adolescence, or only when he's small and helpless? Questions of this kind show how necessary it is for both husband and wife to realize the full extent and implications of the latter's need for her own life.

THE HANDICAPPED CHILD

Specific forms of handicap are dealt with in Chapter 5, but as the handicapped child grows older new issues, particularly those relating to self-acceptance and social acceptance, become increasingly important. Let's introduce these by re-emphasizing that 'handicapped' is a relative term. Nearly all children are 'handicapped' in some way. One child may have a physical disability. Another may be a slow learner. Another may be over-anxious. Another may have an unhappy home background. Another may have low self-acceptance. Another may come from an under-privileged home. Another may be bullied. Another may have suffered bereavements in the family. And so the list goes on.

So using the term 'handicapped' only for specific mental and physical disabilities is therefore rather misleading. It also makes us lose sight of the fact that all children are children first and anything else second. They all have the developing minds of children, the needs and interests of children, and the joys and heartbreaks of children. Rightly, the trend is now to educate so-called 'handicapped' children where possible in normal schools, and to offer them normal challenges and opportunities.

When they're small, children with handicaps are unaware they're different from others, but by the time they're of school age they're increasingly conscious of the attitudes of other people towards them. Children who grow up with physical or mental disabilities are almost invariably courageous and matter-or-fact about them. In their determination to cope with their problems and to accept them without bitterness, they put most of the rest of us to shame. It's fair to say that it isn't the fact of his or her disability that daunts the handicapped child, it's other people's attitudes. If other people take the same determined attitude towards her disability as the child herself does, and accept it without questioning or resentment while looking for constructive ways of coping with it, the child will have a good chance of living a full and rewarding life.

Other people's attitudes can be daunting to a handicapped child

Parents who provide their child with this kind of environment say it becomes easier for them if in addition they accept *themselves* as parents of a child with a disability. Parents can often load guilt on themselves if they have a disabled child, seeing themselves somehow as responsible. This is being quite unfair to themselves. If they can drop this burden and feelings of bitterness, however hard this proves to be, they're that bit freer to get on with life and organize things for the best.

If you accept her, she'll find it easier to accept herself

As with any child, if your 'handicapped' child sees that *you* accept her and accept yourself in relation to her, she'll have fewer problems accepting herself. If she's slower physically or mentally than others of her age, she can handle this as long as she knows you love and cherish her just as she is. It's only if she feels *you* reject her that she'll start rejecting herself. Don't over-compensate by being unnecessarily protective and solicitous. If she's able to have a go at something and there's no great physical risk, let her. If she can't manage it, encourage her to have another go. And whether she manages it fully or not, give her all the praise and credit you can. The important thing is that she's participated, not that she's able or unable to match the performance of other children.

Thoughtlessness is usually the result of ignorance

Provided they understand the real nature of a child's disability, other children are usually very sympathetic and helpful. Thoughtlessness and teasing come primarily from ignorance of what it's like to have the disability in question. One of the most heartening things about disabled youngsters is the spontaneous care and concern they show for each other. Children with severe disabilities will go to enormous lengths to help other children, whatever their problems. The disabled child knows what it's like to have to cope, and this frees the natural goodness in her to do its work. If you feel that able-bodied children aren't showing the consideration they might towards your child, prompt them to consider how they themselves would feel if they had her disadvantage. Enlist the co-operation of their parents and teachers in further emphasizing the lesson. It's no good blaming children for thoughtlessness unless they've been given full opportunity to appreciate how tough things are for a child with a disability. Help your child to take this view as well. If she's been the victim of thoughtlessness, explain to her that these people haven't been helped to imagine how they'd feel if they had her problem. Remind her how kind and considerate 'handicapped' people are towards each other. This is human nature at its best.

All parents should help their children understand the problems of the disabled. Simple lessons like 'Never ever make fun of somebody for something they can't help' or 'Think how you would feel if that was you' offered to a child, and backed up by your own example, will stay with her throughout life. If a young child makes fun of someone with a physical or mental problem, it's really the parents who are to blame rather than the child. The same goes if she is slow to offer help.

Finally, as stressed in Chapter 5, for any parent with a 'handicapped' child the support of relatives, friends and national and local organizations is vital. Don't be afraid to ask for help. Often people don't realize the strains and restrictions that a disabled child can mean for a parent until it's made clear to them. The support of others can make a crucial difference, not only to the parent but to the child herself. If she's unable to get out and about, the visits of neighbours and friends are a vital way of bringing the world into her home and providing her with the company and stimulation that all growing children need.

Don't be afraid to ask for help

WHEN TO SEEK PROFESSIONAL HELP

With some of the problems we've been looking at in this chapter you may need professional help. In the case of the handicapped child, early diagnosis will have meant that this help is already being given. But with the other areas we've covered, which have to do with less obvious things like learning difficulties and behaviour problems, it's not so apparent when you should take the initiative and ask for professional advice. So let's look at the way in which educational psychologists and to some extent child psychiatrists and medical doctors recognize and group the symptoms in children which may want looking into in more detail.

Generally the following headings are used, with the most common symptoms grouped under them as shown.

1. **Learning difficulties**. These are subdivided into *mild* (six months to a year behind the averge for the child's age), *moderate* (one to two years behind), and *severe* (more

than two years behind). They can either be *general* difficulties (covering most of the curriculum) or *specific* (apparent in only certain of the subjects the child is studying).

Under learning difficulties are included not just obvious symptoms such as an inability to keep up with the rest of the class, but such things as irrational dislike for certain subjects, unusual or bizarre responses to certain learning situations, and wild fluctuations in performance.

2. **Behaviour difficulties**. Virtually any item of behaviour in a child which goes contrary to what is considered reasonable and acceptable by responsible adults could be classified as a behaviour difficulty. But the most generally recognized are:

    Aggressiveness (cruel or bullying behaviour towards others, destructive behaviour, compulsive need to dominate others).
    Violent or ungovernable temper.
    Excessive demands for attention.
    Stealing or excessive begging or cadging.
    Unmanageable behaviour (flouting of all rules and discipline, rudeness, disobedience, excessive hyperactivity).
    Lying and romancing (especially if done deliberately to cheat others).
    Self-destructive behaviour (self-inflicted wounds, complete disregard for physical safety, continuous and unwarranted risk-taking, excessive proneness to accidents).
    Extreme jealousy (usually of siblings but possibly of classmates).
    Persistent truanting (or wandering from home or staying out late).
    Sex difficulties (over-preoccupation with sex, unsuitable sexual liaisons or attractions).

3. **Emotional difficulties**. These overlap with behaviour difficulties, but generally psychologists take behaviour problems to refer to more outward-directed behaviour, often involving other people, while emotional problems

are more inner-directed, and may go unnoticed by the casual observer. Emotional problems include:

Fears (timidity, phobias, anxiety, extremes of embarrassment).

Depression (prolonged periods of low spirits and brooding, particularly when there is no obvious cause).

Extreme excitability (pronounced over-reaction to minor events).

Mood swings (unpredictable and extreme fluctuations of mood, particularly between depression and excitement).

Withdrawal (unsociability, extreme shyness, over-solitary behaviour, friendlessness).

Excessive fantasizing (to compensate for inner inadequacies).

Apathy (lack of interest, lethargy, unresponsiveness).

Obsessions (abnormal incidence of rituals and compulsions).

Hysterical fits (paroxysms of weeping, screaming, physical outbursts).

Hallucinations and delusions (not to be confused with lying; become a problem only if extreme and allowed to interfere with normal life).

Excessive and unaccountable memory losses.

4. **Habit disorders**. These again overlap, in that they may be linked to behaviour or emotional difficulties. They include:

Speech defects (stammering, stuttering).

Sleep difficulties (nightmares, sleep-walking, sleeplessness).

Excretion (incontinence of bladder or bowels).

Nervous pains and paralysis (headaches, stomach aches, pains in arms and legs; must be checked by your doctor for physical illness).

Uncontrolled movements (nervous tics and twitches, head-banging, persistent rocking, savage nail-biting).

Feeding (excessive faddiness, indiscriminate eating, nervous vomiting).

Physical problems (asthma, allergies).

5. **Physical and sensory difficulties**. These are self-evident, and cover handicap (including hearing, speech and vision disorders), and also disabilities arising from physical injuries or from spasmodic afflictions such as epilepsy.

Don't worry unless symptoms are severe and prolonged

Don't get the idea that if your child shows any of the symptoms in the above five categories you must immediately rush out and get professional help. Children quite often show one or more of them for a short time, particularly if their lives have suddenly become very stressful. Apart from physical symptoms which may be linked to actual illness, you only need worry if the symptoms are severe, prolonged, or if they are causing actual harm to the child or others. If there is real cause for concern, consult your doctor and your child's teacher. Give them as much detail as you can, including when the symptoms first appeared, whether they fluctuate from day to day or are pretty consistent, whether they seem to be linked to any definite circumstances in your child's life, and the way in which you as parents have been reacting to them. You should also be ready to give as much detail as necessary about your child's life (friends, interests, school progress, physical health) and about the conditions of his home environment.

No one is going to pry unnecessarily into your private affairs, but effective professional help can only be given if the relevant people are in possession of the necessary facts. Confidentiality will of course be observed (it's as well to reassure yourself on this point before giving any particularly sensitive details), and the more interested doctors and teachers are in your child, the more trouble they will take to put themselves fully in the picture. Don't allow yourself to be too easily convinced that your anxieties over your child are groundless. Particularly if your child's problem is an unobtrusive one (such as depression or withdrawal), an extra busy teacher or doctor may be prompt to reassure you that everything is in order, and to tell you to see what happens in a month or two, but if you feel strongly that something is wrong, make this clear without fail.

Learning difficulties

Once it's decided that your child needs special help, then what happens next depends upon the nature of his difficulties. If he's facing learning difficulties, the help will usually be given at school level. In the case of mild difficulties, his own teacher will give him extra help, often receiving guidance in how best to do so from remedial teachers within the school as well as from advisers in remedial teaching appointed by the local education authority, and from the educational psychologist. If his difficulties are moderate or severe, he may be assigned to a special remedial group within the school for the relevant subject or subjects. Make a point of discovering exactly what provision is being made for your child, and exactly how his progress is being monitored. Ask for an interview with the teacher or teachers concerned, and ask what special help you can give your child at home. A child who has fallen behind in his work is in need more than anything of adults who will help him rebuild his confidence in himself and his belief that he *can* do the work. So the good remedial teacher is only too happy to work in partnership with the parent, allowing the child to take work home which can be supervised and guided by the parent.

The remedial teacher will ensure that the golden rules of good remedial teaching are followed, namely that:

The golden rules of remedial teaching

- the child is given work at which he can succeed rather than work at which he will fail;
- the work is presented to him in small steps, so that progress can be checked frequently and the child be reassured that things are going well;
- the work, while being at the right level of difficulty, is nevertheless mature enough to hold the child's interest;
- the child is given the opportunity to ask for the help he needs;
- the emphasis is upon encouragement and patience rather than blaming and impatience.

Within the home, the same rules should be followed. Agree with the teacher how much work will be covered at home, and set aside a special time each evening to attend to it. If a child

The backward child and the slow learner

has fallen behind simply through absence from school or through dislike of a certain subject (such children are usually referred to as *retarded*; they're perfectly able to keep up with the rest of the class once they've made up the lost ground), he's usually able to work quite intensively to catch up. On the other hand, if a child is *backward*, the chances are he can't rattle along at too brisk a pace. In carrying out his assessment, the psychologist will have established which of the two categories fits your child, and you will have been informed accordingly. Many slow learners have a relatively short attention span, which means that short regular periods of work are of much more benefit to them than long irregular periods. I have seen slow-learning children make remarkable progress in a few short months if they are fortunate enough to have parents prepared to spend just ten minutes with them on school work each evening.

Helping your child at home Discuss with your child what particular time in the evening he wants to devote to his work, and make this *his* time and keep to it. In a two-parent family, both parents should be involved. This spreads the load, and also shows the child that both his mother and his father care about his progress. Keep reminding yourself that if your child *could* do the work he *would*. No matter how simple the work looks to you, if your child can't do it this means it isn't simple to him. Keep a sense of humour, but don't laugh at him. Praise him frequently, and prompt him to keep at his work rather than becoming too easily discouraged. 'This takes a bit of thinking out, but I'm sure you can do it' is much better than 'But this is so *easy*, surely you *must* be able to do it.' Use graphs and star charts to give him a tangible sign of his progress, but don't try to bribe him into doing well with lavish promises which he is never likely to see fulfilled. By all means, give him little treats from time to time associated with his work, but for the most part let his interest in the work and his desire for progress speak for itself.

The techniques involved in remedial teaching are very much the same as those I've already outlined in connection with reading and writing and the other basic skills. All that is needed in addition is a special sensitivity towards your child's difficulties and a quiet but steady confidence in his ability eventually to overcome them.

Behaviour and emotional difficulties

If your child's problems are more in the nature of behaviour and emotional difficulties, the special help is likely to be forthcoming from an educational psychologist or clinical psychologist. The dividing line between educational and clinical is somewhat arbitrary, and varies from one part of the country to another, but generally the educational psychologist (who is employed by the local education authority) deals with behaviour problems while the clinical psychologist (who is employed by the health authority) deals with emotional and habit problems. Both educational and clinical psychologists are qualified to carry out careful assessment of your child, and either may refer him to a child psychiatrist.

Don't be alarmed by the word 'psychiatrist'. A psychiatrist differs from a psychologist in that he or she is medically qualified, and has charge of the mentally ill, but they see a very wide range of problems across the whole spectrum from simple anxiety states and personality problems (the kind of things we're talking about) to people who actually need hospital treatment. It is very rare indeed for a child to need hospital treatment for emotional problems, and the psychiatrist will simply help by making an even more thorough diagnosis of your child and advising you how best to proceed. Psychologists and psychiatrists are all highly trained in how to relate to children, and children find that visits to them are fun and never in the least intimidating.

You'll probably find that the psychologist or psychiatrist interviews you together with your child initially, and then sees the child on her own. Sometimes, particularly if the psychologist or psychiatrist is also a family therapist, he or she will ask to see your child together with everyone else within your home. This is to give him an idea of how the family relates to one another and to the child. Strictly speaking, there is no such thing as a child with a behaviour problem, there is only a family with a behaviour problem. By watching you all together, the psychologist/psychiatrist will be able to get an idea of what may be the cause of the problem. For example, do the family all treat the 'problem' child as if she's still a baby? Do they unwittingly make her feel small or rejected? Are they all much brighter than she is, making her feel

Your child will be seen with you as well, and perhaps the rest of the family

577

inadequate and inferior? Are there tensions between other members of the family that may have been upsetting the child? Are parents over-protective, or over-strict, or do they have difficulty in showing their feelings (particularly their love for the child)? Is the child brighter and more creative than the rest of the family, making them feel unsure how to cope with her? Is there a lack of understanding between different members of the family? And so on.

The aim of work of this kind isn't to apportion blame. Most problems arise not through family members deliberately setting out to hurt each other, but simply through lack of understanding (and sometimes communication) between the people concerned. Once the psychologist/psychiatrist gets an idea of what has been going wrong, he or she talks this through with the family, so that in future everyone is better able to relate to everyone else. But whether the psychologist/psychiatrist sees you all together or not, he will try to identify what lies behind your child's difficulties, and will advise you how best to handle them. He may also ask to see your child at regular intervals, so that he can help her to communicate her troubles and rethink her own behaviour. Often a child with behaviour problems just isn't aware of the extent to which her behaviour is upsetting and alienating others. Preoccupied with her own difficulties, she needs help in appreciating those of others. Parents and teachers often don't realize how deeply a child becomes 'locked in' to her behaviour patterns. Her desire for attention, her desire for acceptance, her desire to defend herself and her feelings may all lead to behaviour which produces many of the very problems she's trying hardest to solve. But without the help of a trained professional it's often impossible for her to realize this and to understand exactly why it is that her life is going wrong and what she needs to do to put things right. Just as without such help it's often difficult for parents to see that they too are helping to create the problems that worry them most.

Never give her the idea she has a 'problem' One final point. Although you should always discuss your child's difficulties with her in a frank and supportive way, never give her the impression that she has something called a 'problem', to carry around with her like a badge. All too often children are either worried by their 'problem', or come to enjoy it and begin to use it as an excuse for not doing things they dislike. So make it clear to your child that everyone has their ups and downs in life, and that there's nothing special about them in any way. Avoid discussing your child's 'problem' with others when she's around, and don't give her the impression that it's causing you any great anxiety. If she knows you're extra anxious this will make her worry all the more, or in certain circumstances it could prompt her to use the 'problem' as a weapon against you. Be matter-of-fact about it, assure her of your love and support, help her to see herself as 'normal' like everyone else, and if the problem is likely to be of a temporary nature, help her to see that with good sense and patience it will pass just like other phases in childhood.

8

The Years From Eleven to Eighteen

MANY PSYCHOLOGISTS CONSIDER that the years of adolescence are second only to the first five or six years of life in terms of the influence they have upon a child's development. Certainly in many ways they pose parents with equally challenging issues. In the years of adolescence, your child changes from childhood to adulthood. Both you and he have learnt how to cope with his childhood, now both you and he have to learn a new set of rules. Nearly everything changes, and with a rapidity that takes everyone by surprise. One moment you're looking at a child, and the next moment you're looking at a strapping near-adult, who wants to be treated as grown-up and who indicates that it's now time to put away childish things. Many parents find the whole experience stressful and disturbing. They feel their authority being challenged at every turn. The youngster who a few months ago seemed happy to have all major decisions taken by others now emerges as someone who wants to go his own way. Someone in fact who they describe as a stranger to them, with new and unpredictable moods. Someone who seems to treat his home like a kind of transit camp, and who is usually surrounded by an entourage of noisy fellow-travellers on the road to the heady freedoms of adult life.

'I wouldn't mind', such parents complain, 'if he hadn't *changed* so much. He used to be so friendly. Now he snaps my head off if I even look at him.' Or, 'He won't so much as lift a finger to help me these days.' Or, 'She used to be always smiling, now she just mooches around.' Or, quite simply, 'She just argues with me over *everything* these days.'

Other parents, by contrast, don't seem to find their adolescent offspring much of a problem, and sail through with no more than a minor skirmish or two. In fact, everyone seems to get even more out of the family relationship. The parents find that the new young adults who have come into their lives are interesting and worthwhile people, full of exciting new interests, and as ready with help as they are with their opinions! With justifiable pride, parents watch these young adults fulfilling the promise of earlier years, and holding out bright hopes for the future.

Are these parents simply lucky? And are the parents who remain locked in combat with their children unlucky? The answer is by and large no. So much depends upon the willingness of parents to accept the rapidly changing status of their adolescent children, and to accept their own changing role in relation to it. Three or four years are a short time to adults. We don't usually notice much change in ourselves over this period. But to the adolescent, three or four years mean the difference between childhood and being grown-up. When we look at our adolescents we see in them the children they recently were, and we tend to think of them and react towards them in terms of these children. But to adolescents the memory of childhood already seems remote. They're busy looking to the future instead of back towards the past. I know that we adults sometimes think longingly of our young days, but that comes later. To the adolescent, it's the years that lie ahead that matter.

Parents must accept their child's rapidly changing status

Of course, much will *depend* upon the years that have gone before. If your relationship with your children has been a good one, then the transition from childhood to adulthood usually goes well. But some parents who have thoroughly enjoyed young children find it difficult to face the fact that they're young children no longer, and this can cause even a very happy bond between parent and child to go wrong. Conversely, some parents who've found it difficult to relate to young children now discover they can talk to adolescents. The relationship of equals comes more readily to them, and they find a new companionship entering their lives.

As I shall emphasize throughout this chapter, adolescence is a period in which the teenager is finding a new identity for himself, an identity which is increasingly independent of his parents and which, even in the closest families, is in some ways a mystery to them. He's learnt how to be a child, now he has to learn how to be an adult, and to think about himself

Much adolescent behaviour is experimental

in new and challenging ways. Much of his behaviour therefore
has an experimental quality to it. He is trying out the new
person he is becoming. Trying out new ways of relating to
others. Trying out new ways of asserting his independence.
Trying out new ways of looking and talking. Trying out new
goals and objectives in life, new ambitions, new beliefs, new
feelings. Often tough and dogmatic on the surface, inside he
is vulnerable and uncertain, unsure whether the adult he is
growing into is going to be a success or not, whether he's
going to be liked by his peers, whether he's going to be
accepted by the opposite sex, whether his manhood (or her
womanhood) is going to stand the test. Not always an easy
time for either the teenager or his parents, adolescence is
nevertheless one of the most exciting experiences in life for all
concerned (provided there is sufficient understanding of what
exactly is taking place!).

PHYSICAL AND PSYCHOLOGICAL DEVELOPMENT

Physical development

In adolescence, the body changes from the contours of childhood to those of adulthood. In the boy, this means broader
shoulders and increased muscularity, while in the girl it means
breasts and the broadening of the hips. In both sexes hair
appears in the pubic region and under the arms, usually from
age twelve onwards, and most boys show signs of facial hair
at around seventeen. In girls the first period can come at any
time from eleven onwards, and a year or two later boys show
signs of the huskiness which foreshadows the voice breaking.

The adolescent growth spurt   But the most dramatic physical symptom of adolescence is
the adolescent growth spurt. After the rapid development in
the first three or four years of life, children's growth steadies
down in the primary school years, only to surge ahead again
in the years from thirteen to sixteen. So marked is this surge
that some children seem to do all their growing in a period of
twelve months, bursting out of everything they own. Unaccus-
tomed to the sudden lengthening of their arms and legs such

children often appear maddeningly clumsy, constantly knocking things over and getting in everyone's way. What looks like sheer carelessness is in fact an inability to judge length of reach or the position of bodily extremities, and the phase soon passes as the brain learns to adapt to the new physical dimensions of its owner.

Along with the growth spurt goes in most cases a very definite change in facial features. The soft, unformed face of the child hardens into the more definite physiognomy of the adult, often causing a great deal of distress to the person who looks at it in the mirror every morning! The problem is that in the transition from childhood to adulthood the face often doesn't develop evenly. Thus the chin, for example, may grow more quickly than the rest of the face, giving the adolescent for some months the exaggerated look of a lantern-jawed Wild West movie star. Or it may be the nose that outstrips the rest. Or the face may broaden without the features quite keeping pace, or the forehead may take on a noble but slightly disconcerting depth. These things even out in the long run, but for a time they may cause heartache for their owners.

Changes in facial features

Normally girls mature at adolescence rather earlier than boys. Their growth spurt usually begins at a younger age (sometimes making girls taller than boys for a few months), as do all the other physical changes, including the ability to conceive children. By sixteen, most girls are fully grown, and although growth in boys is usually slowing down by this age, many of them go on adding inches up to eighteen and beyond. In both sexes, the growth spurt and the onset of physical and sexual maturity come earlier than they once did. So much so in fact that in the years between the end of the Second World War and the 1980s the average age for the onset of the first period in girls advanced six months for every decade that passed. We're not sure of the reason for this. It could be 'improved' nutrition or it could be something else in the environment. Theories range from artifical growth hormones in meat to the aluminium in cooking utensils or the prevalence of artifical lighting. But whatever the reason, it does mean that problems of physical adjustment which used to be faced later in the teens are now often faced near the beginning.

Variations in speed of development

It's right to emphasize, though, that there is still a great variety amongst children in the speed of development during the teenage years. Some children are left behind by their classmates in the adult growth spurt, only to catch up later. Some girls still haven't had their first period at a time when all their friends seem to be talking about the menopause. Some boys are still squeaking away when everyone else is growling in his boots. Apart from the self-conscious feelings of the child who is left behind in this way, there's usually nothing to worry about. His or her body is simply working to a slightly different biological clock from everyone else. But speak to your doctor if the difference is marked; usually he or she will reassure all concerned that everything is fine and that the only prescription is a dash of patience.

Sexual development

Most girls are able to conceive children from their early teens and most boys by age sixteen. Taken together with the questions and anxieties which a teenager can have about the changes taking place in her body, this emphasizes the need for good sex education in adolescence. If you've answered your child's questions about sex fully and without embarrassment from the early years onwards, and if the human body has been treated sensibly within the home (see Chapter 6), then the queries she has now will be brief and easily answered. But if sex has been hidden behind a veil of secrecy, then it may be hard to deal with it properly, and the best solution is sometimes to buy a good book on the subject and give it to her to read. Don't fall back on the comforting thought that children are very worldly-wise these days, and pick it all up from school and their friends. They pick up a great deal from these sources, but it isn't always accurate information and it doesn't always have the right attitudes behind it. Whatever your child may have learnt from others, she still needs to feel she can bring her queries to you.

If the human body has been dealt with at home without prudery, then your child won't be surprised by the changes now taking place in her own. Nor will she be over-curious about the bodies of the opposite sex. Sex will be important, naturally enough. The sex drive appears to reach its peak in adolescent boys in the years sixteen to eighteen, and probably at round about the same time for girls. But she will be less likely to have the desperate over-preoccupation with the subject that comes from shrouding it in too much mystery and secrecy.

In the case of girls, there's the added necessity to explain **Menstruation** menstruation well before the stage is actually reached. A sudden, unprepared discovery of menstrual blood by a girl at an impressionable age can be a frightening experience, as can some of the stories she will hear from other girls unless she's first heard the full facts at home.

These facts, like all the details of sexuality and reproduction, can be conveyed in a sentence of two. But now more than ever it's important that the *spirit* behind the sex education is right. Discuss sexuality and reproduction with your adolescent son or daughter in a relaxed and caring way, helping them to develop informed opinions and realistic expectations. Help them to see the sex act itself as a natural extension of the touching and hugging that go on between people with good feelings for each other. Obviously your own views on the morality of sex before marriage will come in here, and you will want rightly to make these views plain. In the end, though, your adolescent will make up her own mind. And in any case morality is only morality if the individual is free to choose it for herself.

Make sure your adolescent is fully aware of the risks and consequences of unwanted pregnancies, and of the threat of sexually transmitted diseases such as AIDS, VD and genital herpes. Leave your child in no doubt that quite apart from the moral issues, casual sex carries very grave and even fatal dangers – dangers of which she must be fully aware and against which she must develop the necessary self-control. An adolescent who is unprepared for it can find sudden exposure to sexual temptation almost overwhelming, and it is only by sensible schooling before this temptation occurs that she can handle it.

Just as the first period can be a source of surprise and **Wet dreams** embarrassment to the young girl if she hasn't been prepared for it, so can the first nocturnal emission (wet dream) for the boy. All young boys are well used to penile erections even in the pre-puberty years, but at puberty these erections become much more frequent and dramatic, and are often in themselves sources of great embarrassment, particularly as they can strike

587

without warning (or erotic feelings) and at times of maximum inconvenience to the reluctant participant. Struggling with what he feels is the all too public evidence of his manhood, the young boy develops frantic subterfuges for hiding what's going on. But this becomes much more difficult if the erection is accompanied in sleep by actual orgasm and the emission of semen. Faced with the fact of his wet bed, the sheepish young man wonders how on earth he's going to explain things to his parents.

Of course, both the erections and the nocturnal emissions are simply nature at work testing out the apparatus. Nature is without shame of any kind. She goes on with her creative work, heedless of the artificial embarrassments felt by we humans. Help your children to cope with these embarrassments by explaining to them the facts of menstruation and nocturnal emissions, and that there's nothing remotely dirty or disgusting about them. Both menstruation and nocturnal emissions are simply reassuring signs that all is working well, and the same applies to the erotic dreams, with or without orgasm, often experienced by young girls at this stage.

Masturbation   The same sensible approach should be adopted towards masturbation. The evidence suggests that over 90 per cent of boys and 70 per cent of girls masturbate to some extent in adolescence. Masturbation at this time happens primarily because society asks adolescents to delay regular sexual intercourse until adult life and way past the age at which they first experience strong sexual urges. Masturbation is the adolescent's way of relieving these urges in the absence of other outlets. And no amount of preaching makes much difference. In the face of such preaching adolescents will still masturbate; the only difference is that now they'll feel guilty about it, and this guilt may in later life attach itself to the sexual act itself.

The best advice to parents is to leave masturbation as a private matter for the adolescent. Usually it will happen discreetly, when no one else is around, but if you should come on the scene at the wrong moment, don't act embarrassed or shocked, and don't embarrass the adolescent. Feelings of embarrassment or shame at such a time can have a traumatic effect upon a sensitive adolescent. Apologize in the same brief way you would if you'd interrupted her in any other private activity, and don't refer to the incident later unless she wants to.

The hormonal changes in the adolescent's body which accompany the onset of puberty go some way towards explaining the moodiness and abrupt mood changes which many adolescents experience. Adolescents feel things deeply, though they often try to hide it behind a 'tough' or 'cool' façade. Thus what may often look like an outburst over a very trivial incident is for the adolescent a sudden surge of feeling which she can't handle any other way. If she hates something or somebody, she really hates them. If she loves she really loves. If she's disappointed, she's really disappointed. If she's embarrassed, she's really embarrassed. There are no half measures. And the more we insist she control herself the worse things can become. Confused by the strength and suddenness of her own feelings, she's left with the impression we don't understand her, and are just put in the world to make her feel awkward and inadequate.

Moodiness and mood changes in adolescents

These stormy moods usually pass in the late teens or early twenties, as the hormonal changes in the adolescent's body begin to settle down. If we've shown that even when we have to be firm we do understand the strength of her feelings, then the moods will leave no legacy of bitterness on either side. The relationship between parent and child becomes stronger because of this tact and understanding. The adolescent sees that her parents are with her, and her respect for them (and her tolerance for *their* fusty little idiosyncrasies!) grows. If on the other hand we've seen her moods as deliberate cussedness, then the squabbles that will have resulted and the things that will have been said in the heat of the moment will remain, rankling with both sides and souring relationships.

The adolescent's worries over his appearance

As adults we can look back and laugh at the worries we had over our appearance in adolescence. But to the adolescent, concern over the way he looks is no laughing matter. Body image, the picture he has of himself, plays an important part in his new sense of identity, and in his self-acceptance and the way he feels about himself. So as he looks each day in the mirror and sees his face and body changing from the contours of childhood to the harder, more defined outlines of adulthood, he's often intensely preoccupied by what he sees. Although young children sometimes have worries about their appearance, they can always be comforted by the thought that things will be okay when they grow up. But the adolescent virtually *is* grown-up. And he's worried that what he sees in the mirror is what he's stuck with for the rest of his life. And if it doesn't appeal to him, it's a tragedy indeed!

Take his worries seriously So accept that your adolescent is extra sensitive about his appearance. Don't laugh at him, even in kindness. Take his worries seriously, and don't keep telling him they're groundless if he's convinced they're not. He'll only accuse you of not understanding, or of humouring him, or of being hopelessly out of touch. Point out to him that adolescence is a period of such rapid development that the face and body change from month to month and even sometimes from week to week. This means, as I mentioned earlier, that physical features often get out of proportion to each other for a short time. Point out as well that faults in his appearance which to him stand out a mile go mostly unnoticed by other people. I've had youngsters confess to me for instance that they're considering (wildly and impractically) plastic surgery for some minor defect which attracts not a glance from the rest of the world.

Strategies for hiding 'bad' features Help your adolescent realize that it's only when the individual himself is worried and embarrassed about some physical feature, and goes to great lengths to hide it, that the attention of the rest of us is drawn to it. A tall girl begins to hunch her shoulders for example. Or the boy with acne won't look us in the face. Or the girl with one 'good' and one 'bad' profile tries to keep the same side of her face towards us all the time. Or the boy with a large chin speaks half the time with a hand over his jaw, or the girl with a small bust improbably pads out her bra. Strategies of this kind are all self-defeating, and can even hold the unfortunate individual up to ridicule. At the very least, they broadcast his or her lack of self-confidence and poise.

But if your adolescent adopts one of these strategies, be careful how you point out its self-defeating nature to him. If you briskly tell him he's being silly, you risk an emotional outburst. He's dissatisfied with himself as it is, and if you inform him that what he thought was a clever strategy for covering up his bad features is in fact making him a laughing stock, he'll try to deflect this further blow to his self-esteem by hitting back. He may already be taking his troubles out on you, because he needs *someone* to blame for his imagined predicament, so don't go and make things worse!

It's all too easy to make a list of the physical qualities the adolescent finds to worry about. Many of them have to do with things being too large or too small, particularly facial and sexual features. In general, adolescents who are confident in other ways are much less likely to take their worries too seriously. But where these worries exist, far better that the adolescent should be able to grouse about them to his parents than that he should brood unhappily over them in private. Over certain things, you can reassure your adolescent with medical evidence. For example, there's no evidence that women with small breasts are any less effective at feeding their children (or at attracting men) than women with large breasts. Nor is there any evidence that men with shorter penises make less good lovers than men with longer ones. In any case, apparent differences in length of penis from one man to another are due more to variations in the volume of blood contained in the flaccid organ than to any real differences in size. (You can further console your son with the information that most men think they've been a little short-changed in this area when compared with others, simply because they get a foreshortened view of their own equipment when looking down!)

Worries that things are too large or too small

Another set of worries has to do with skin blemishes, in particular those caused by acne. These days, a bad case of acne belongs in the doctor's surgery and can be cleared up, at least temporarily, by modern treatments. But most cases are relatively minor, and unlikely to leave scarring of the skin. It's certainly unfortunate that acne should strike just at the very age when the adolescent boy or girl is most concerned about looking good, but that's the way it is. Exercise, fresh air and a diet low in fats are all said to help treatment, but the evidence is variable and inconclusive. Often there are specific foods that trigger off an attack though, and these should be avoided. Peanuts and peanut butter are amongst the worst, but chocolate isn't far behind. It's certainly sensible for the adolescent to keep a record of diet, so that these trigger foods can be

Worries about acne and facial hair

591

identified and avoided. Anxiety and stress can also prompt an attack. But acne is mainly a consequence of the hormonal changes taking place in the body during adolescence, and it clears up once the body settles down.

A different kind of blemish is that caused by facial hair. Though boys welcome this sign of manhood, to the young girl the sight even of fine down on her hitherto flawless skin can seem a direct challenge to her femininity. Let's stress then that the presence of minor amounts of facial hair in women tells us nothing at all about sexuality or the lack of it. But if it's troublesome the doctor should certainly be consulted, with a view to having it removed permanently. Fine down is best left alone, but there are discreet ladies' razors on the market these days, and there's nothing unfeminine about having one on the dressing table. Thankfully, there's no truth at all in the old rumour that shaving hair makes it grow thicker or darker.

Need for increased personal hygiene

Unfortunately there is truth in the notion that people can't smell their own scent as readily as they can smell that of others. In adolescence the sweat glands develop and become more active, while with puberty the sexual organs start to give off their own characteristic odours. In girls, menstruation also makes a contribution. You certainly don't want to make your adolescent feel he's only once removed from a compost heap, but it is important to point out the increased need for personal hygiene in adult life. It's said that there are certain things even your best friends can't tell you, but though best friends can enjoy the luxury of keeping silent, parents certainly can't. Be diplomatic, but make it clear to your adolescent that if he wants to keep his best friends, a daily appointment with the shower and with the deodorant is a must.

Help him accept the way he looks

In all matters of appearance, the better your adolescent feels about himself, the better he'll feel about life in general. So help him accept and value the way he looks. Helping him towards self-acceptance in all areas has been one of your main parental tasks all along, but now it takes a new form. When he was small, your child took for granted that you were a good judge of things. Now he's older, he questions this judgement more, and is increasingly influenced by the opinions of people outside the home. So his self-esteem is more dependent on others. Thus if you insist he looks okay when he imagines everyone is laughing at him, he'll round on you and indicate you're simply showing your lack of judgement (yet again!). So your approach has to be more subtle. Agree with him you understand what he's getting at. But point out that everyone worries about their appearance in adolescence, no matter how confident they seem, and that everyone has *something* about themselves with which they're not happy. It's a help if you can tell him you yourself were worried in adolescence about one of your own features, though it's obvious to you now how groundless these worries were. Stress the fact that other people usually don't notice the things which to us stand out a mile, and that it's poise and confidence that make people physically attractive, not just face and form.

Talking to adolescents

Now that she's an adolescent, your youngster's powers of thinking have developed to the point where they're very much like those of the adult. Measured intelligence doesn't increase much after the age of sixteen. By that age, our mental apparatus is at or near its peak. We've loads still to learn, but our ability to learn at age sixteen is as good as it's ever going to be.

You'll notice this particularly in the way your adolescent uses abstract ideas. In the pre-teen years her thinking tended to be more concrete, more related to her own direct experience. Now she's moved beyond that. Concepts like 'freedom', 'justice', 'love', 'peace' and the like begin to take on a fuller meaning for her. Your adolescent child may suddenly become idealistic, and very critical of her elders and the state into which they've got the world. Together with her increasing need for independence and for an identity of her own, this is one of the main reasons why adolescents seem rebellious and radical in their outlook. They can see more clearly what is going on around them (often without realizing the practical difficulties that may lie in the way of realizing one's ideals!) and can see what's 'wrong' and how to put it 'right'. Adolescents often believe they can change the world, and get very impatient with their elders for failing to see it their way.

Idealism and cynicism in adolescents

This idealism can be uncomfortable to live with. So too can its opposite, cynicism. Instead of idealism, some adolescents use their new powers of thinking as a way of deflating the

593

views and beliefs of others. They may turn against religion, against the political system, against many of the things which up to now they've held dear. Especially if it happens to be the fashion amongst their friends, this cynicism can be taken to the point at which the adolescent seems to believe in nothing and care about nothing, sneering not only at parents but at younger brothers and sisters for their 'stupid' ideas.

The adolescent is spoiling for a fight

To make matters worse, though the adolescent is now capable of handling abstract ideas in a mature way, *emotionally* she's still some way from maturity. So in spite of the way she criticizes others, she's often manifestly incapable of regulating her own behaviour. She preaches, but she can't practise what she preaches. And the temptation to point this out to her is almost as great as the temptation to tell her you thought as she did when you were 'her age', but you've got more sense now you're older!

In many ways your adolescent is spoiling for a fight. She wants to challenge your authority. She wants to pit her wits against yours. She wants the opportunity to air her opinions and show how clever she is. That's why she often argues for the sake of it, taking up one inconsistent position after another simply to oppose you. And if she can see you're rattled and forced to stand on your parental dignity, then so much the better. It shows her she's won, and her opinion of herself receives a welcome boost.

Teachers who get on well with adolescents

When working in schools I notice how some teachers get on well with adolescents. The adolescents respect them, like them, enjoy their company, enjoy listening to them and debating with them. On the other hand some teachers are constantly at odds with their class. One battle follows another, with the teacher ending up the target of derisory laugher. It's clear the teenagers not only dislike him, they have something of contempt for him. They know he can't handle them and can't communicate with them, and they reckon it's a sign he's no great shakes as a human being.

The difference between the teacher who does well with adolescents and the teacher who doesn't lies in the extent to which the teacher understands what's going on at this stage of development. As already stressed, much of the behaviour of the adolescent is experimental. He's experimenting with an adult identity, he's experimenting with ideas and behaviours, he's experimenting with relationships. The smart teacher knows this and enjoys it. He enjoys seeing children turning into adults. He has fun with them. He likes and respects their idealism, he understands their cynicism. He knows that these things are a necessary – and temporary – phase in the process of growing up. He can be firm when necessary, but he's prepared to listen. He's prepared to concede points in debate, or stick to his guns when he feels he's right. He wants to encourage ideas, to encourage his teenagers to think about life and about themselves, to formulate their own views instead of having to take them over ready-made from others. And he knows crucially that if he listens to his teenagers, they're going to listen to him in return. Respect breeds respect. Show others they have a right to be heard, and they're ready to learn that you have the same right too.

As with teachers so with parents. When I work with parents who are having problems with their adolescents, it becomes clear the two generations just don't understand each other. It's not so much that they have different ideas about life, it's that they're not ready to respect these different ideas, or even to give them a hearing. A few words are spoken on one side or the other, and in a moment a blazing row develops. Each side digs in deeper and deeper. They may not have cared much about their particular point of view when the argument started, but after the first few exchanges they're prepared to defend it to the death if need be. The ego becomes involved on both sides. To concede the other's point of view, or even their right to it, would be to lose face. Sometimes the argument rumbles on for days, with periods of uneasy truce punctuated by sudden outbursts of verbal warfare which make reconciliation harder and harder.

Parents who have problems with teenage children

When I see problems of this kind, I ask parents to think about their own behaviour. Is their self-esteem so fragile that it depends upon their winning a rather senseless argument with an adolescent son or daughter, particularly when it's clear that the son or daughter doesn't really have the experience or breadth of outlook as yet to see the parent's side of things? How much more valuable the interchange between a parent and adolescent would be if the former could says things like 'Yes that's a good point; I see what you mean. But my view is that . . .' or 'We're going to have to agree to differ on

Do you need to win every argument with your teenage child?

Help him learn how to debate this one; we both have our own ideas and we're both going to stick to them' or 'I don't see it your way but you've a right to your opinion and it's good to see how well you argue it'. Once they're persuaded to take this line, parents confess in no time their adolescent is using similar words back to them. Yes he now sees that his parents have a right to their views too. Whatever is being discussed, he sees that people are bound to differ, and that one of the most valuable things about a debate is not that you convince your opponent but that the very process of debating helps you to clarify your own thinking and decide what it is you really believe. It's okay for people to agree to differ. It isn't 'losing' or 'climbing down'. It's being perceptive enough to understand your fellow men and women and that the human race consists of individuals, each with his or her own way of seeing the world.

By handling debates with your adolescent in this mature way, you're also helping him learn how to relate to others without riling them or getting angry himself. This is a lesson that's going to stand him in good stead in the years to come, and one which will help him see he isn't the only one who's interested in ideas and in bouncing them off others.

Importance of the peer group

Friendships are of vital importance to the adolescent. In fact from around the age of transfer to the secondary school onwards, the adolescent's circle of friends and acquaintances becomes in many ways more important to her than her parents and teachers. Up to now, parents and teachers have set her standards and been the major influence on her life. Now all that changes. On the threshold of adult life, the teenager wants independence from her elders, and it's to her contemporaries (called the *peer group* by psychologists) that she now looks. All this is healthy enough. The human race would quickly stagnate if each generation merely looked to the previous one and took over all their values and standards and behaviour. It's right that the young should want to create their own distinctive style and attitudes. We did when we were their age. And provided we accept this, and work on a basis of mutual respect and tolerance with our adolescents, there need be no real conflict between the generations.

But to return to the peer group. Your adolescent will take over not only their fashions in appearance but also their fashions in speech and opinions. What 'they' say and do will suddenly become all-important, and nothing must on any account be done to get her 'shown up' in front of them. If 'they' start carrying all their possessions to and from school in plastic carrier bags branded with the name of the local super-market, then that's what she'll start doing, and reminders about the expensive school bag lying idle in the hall cupboard will have no effect. If 'they' spurn anoraks, she'll spurn anoraks. If 'they' stop eating school lunches, she'll stop eating school lunches. Is isn't that she's being easily led. Doubtless she plays just as much part in setting the pace as anyone else. It's simply that she wants to feel she belongs. The peer group help her to find her identity (of which more shortly). If the peer group think well of her, she thinks well of herself. If the peer group feel she doesn't rate, then in her own eyes she doesn't rate either.

The adolescent needs to feel she belongs

Usually the peer group will consist of individuals who live nearby, just as it was these individuals who made up your child's friends when she was younger. So the chances are the peer group will have a similar background to hers and there'll be no fear she's keeping bad company. But if you do have anxieties on this score, you're still responsible for her up to the age of eighteen, and you can still insist she takes note of what you say. Indicate to her the freedom she can have provided she agrees not to go with the undesirable element concerned. If she doesn't agree, then her freedom will be curtailed. It's in the form of a contract really. As long as both sides stick to their end of the bargain, all will be well. If either side goes back on the deal, the deal collapses.

But, as in everything else during adolescence, co-operation and consideration on both sides are far better than confrontation (I'll have more to say about this shortly).

Clothes and fashions

Not all adolescents have the extreme anxieties about face and figure referred to earlier in the chapter, but almost all are deeply concerned about another aspect of their appearance, namely clothes and fashions. Since the adolescent is finding his adult identity and isn't yet sure what kind of adult he's growing into, it's vitally important for him to feel he's fully accepted by his friends. In the attitude of his friends towards him he gains a picture of who he is and who he's going to become. So he'll want to wear clothes and choose a hair-style that will appeal to them. This means he'll want to follow their latest fashion. You may feel some of his older clothes still fit and are still serviceable, that he ought to buy for comfort and durability and not just for looks, and that he looks much nicer with a different hair-style. But to him, the all-important consideration is what are his friends going to say? If they approve, fine. He'll wedge himself into ridiculous trousers, wear absurd shoes, and have his hair cropped quite happily as long as that's what all his friends are doing.

Let him make his own choices   All this is harmless enough. Let him make his own choices whenever you can. He's on the threshold of adult life, and soon he'll have to decide things for himself anyway. Let him experiment a little. Fashion is a temporary business, and very much a matter of personal choice. We all laugh at pictures of the clothes our parents and grandparents wore, and even at the clothes we ourselves were so proud of a few years back. There are very few hard-and-fast rules about fashion, and your adolescent is just working to a different rule of thumb from your own. Parents and teachers sometimes claim that the clothes an individual wears are symptoms of the kind of person he really is. But in fact with the exception of socially alienated groups, who wear distinctive clothes as a sign of their rejection of everyone else's values, there's little evidence that the clothes an adolescent wears tell you anything lasting about his character. He'll go through phases of outrageous fashions because they're all the rage with his friends, or because he deliberately wants to challenge the fusty attitude of his elders. But the phases won't last, particularly if you show your attitudes aren't fusty at all and you're quite happy to take his ever-changing tastes in your stride. So parents' worries over an adolescent's appearance are largely groundless.

This doesn't mean you shouldn't make your own views felt though. Provided you don't take things too seriously, your son or daughter is going to be interested to know your views. It's fair as well to point out that, however much they dislike the idea, other people are nevertheless influenced by the way they look when it comes to job interviews, and it's self-defeating to spoil one's chances simply by refusing to compromise a little.

However, adolescents sometimes want to go further and make rather drastic changes to their own bodies. Shaving parts of the head goes in and out of fashion over the years, as does tattooing and ear piercing. There's an obvious distinction to be made here between changes that are reversible and changes that are not. Thus a bizarre hair–style, however unnerving to parents initially, will grow out one day, whereas a lover's name tastefully tattooed on the forearm won't. Assert your parental right of veto over permanent changes if you think they're unsightly and that your adolescent will come to regret them when it's too late. Any mutilation of the human body, even a very minor one such as ear piercing, needs careful thought before it's undertaken, and it's all too easy for a teenager to be carried along by the current fashions and feel sorry about it afterwards. As for temporary changes like a weird hair–style, the best advice is to weigh up what the change will mean for your child's life and for the way in which other people see him. If their attitudes are going to be negative (and remember that they may long outlive the hair–style itself), then stand firm against it and explain your reasons.

Head shaving, tattoos, etc.

One way you can keep the initiative in the matter of your adolescent's clothes is by buying them yourself. Parents who take this approach usually confess that it leads to endless arguments. They buy something nice, only to have it thrown furiously across the room. Naturally they react angrily to this ingratitude, and everyone ends up aggrieved. On the other hand, many parents hand over the money and leave everything to the child herself, with disastrous consequences of a different kind.

Starting choosing her clothes together

The best procedure is to introduce children early to the responsibilities of buying their own clothes. The first year in the secondary school is ideal, and often you can begin things even earlier. Go with the child to the shops, explain how much you're prepared to spend, and then do the choosing together. Let her know that although she can have her say, she must take serviceability and value for money into account. As she grows older, so she can take over more of the decision-making, always provided the twin essentials of serviceability and value for money figure in her thinking. If she buys foolishly, then she runs the risk of your taking over all the buying again.

This gradual process means that by the time an adolescent is in her mid-teens she should be able to handle things for herself, making judicious compromises between the height of fashion and what she knows is acceptable to you. Work out how much you expect to pay for her clothes every year, and give it to her by monthly instalments. Don't let her think that if she over-spends she can have an advance on next month's allowance. Unless it means she'll miss a sales bargain, leave her to save up until she has enough to buy what she wants. This will help her learn sensible money management. Being in debt is no fun, and the more training an adolescent receives is balancing her books the better.

Money management is best learnt where the individual is given a set sum of money each month and is then allowed to develop a responsible attitude towards it. If you're looking over her shoulder all the time the money is never really hers. And when one days she does start earning for herself, instead of carrying on with the sensible policies she's already learnt, she'll be inclined to waste it for the sheer pleasure of at last having money of her own to spend.

Crazes, fads and passions

One of the features of the experimental behaviour and search for identity which characterize the adolescent is that she's looking for people whose behaviour she can copy. Up to now, her role models, the people she looks up to and upon whom she models her behaviour, have been those close to her, such as her parents and teachers. Now she starts looking beyond them. They're still important to her, particularly if she likes and respects them, but her horizons are widening. Sportsmen and women, pop musicians, politicians and national leaders, writers and artists, older adolescents, all capture more and more of her interest. It doesn't matter very much whether her idols are living or dead, whether they're contemporaries or drawn from history. It's the idea of them, often the romanticized idea of them, that matters rather than the actuality. She sees in them some quality that she would like to see in herself. Or if the idol is a member of the opposite sex she sees in them some symbol of what she'd like to find in a lover. These idols often take on further importance in that they become part of the corporate identity of the peer group to which your child belongs.

Sometimes hero worship of this kind can approach idolatry, but usually it's harmless enough. The difference between idolatry and harmlessness lies in whether the adolescent passion interferes with reality or not. If the passion seems to get in the way of normal friendships, or of a sensible appraisal by the adolescent of her own skills and abilities, then there's something potentially unhealthy about it. If she moons over the picture of her fantasy lover instead of meeting real boys, or if she wants to emulate her pop idol when it's quite clear she's painfully tone deaf, then the imaginary relationship is getting in the way. Ask yourself why she isn't making friends as she should. Has she been given sufficient opportunities in the past to develop social confidence? Have her friends been made welcome in the home? Has she realistic role models to whom she can look in her search for personal identity? (See later this chapter for discussions of how to bring a shy adolescent out of herself.)

Sexual relationships

First love and the opposite sex

Many adolescents are lucky, and have a peer group that contains members of both sexes. This is likely to happen if the youngsters go to a co-educational school, or have a meeting place such as a local church or youth club. With puberty there comes a powerful upsurge of interest in the opposite sex (often a year or two earlier for girls than for boys), and individuals without the chance of mixing regularly with the opposite sex often have difficulties in adjusting. Sometimes these difficulties emerge as shyness and embarrassment. Sometimes as an exaggerated (and artificial) indifference towards the other sex. Sometimes as hostility or aggression towards them. Sometimes there is a lack of balance and the risk of a sudden headlong fall into an intense relationship which everyone finds hard to handle while it lasts.

The exaggerated nature of many adolescent boy–girl relationships mustn't make us lose sight of the fact that the

**Be sympathetic
and
understanding
if he is rejected
in love**

emotions involved are genuine enough. Perhaps only in the first five years of life does the individual feel so strongly about things as in adolescence, and the break-up of a relationship can cause deep wounds that may take some time to heal. To be rejected in love at this age is one of the greatest blows to self-esteem one can suffer. The adolescent's sense of identity is still a fragile, uncertain quantity, and to have demonstrated to him that his identity is unacceptable to the person whose opinion currently matters most in the world, can deal it a painful blow. So the adolescent not only has to cope with the loss of the beloved, but also with the rejection of the person he thought he was. Not easy to take, when you're poised in the uncertain divide between childhood and adulthood.

**Even if he takes
it out on you**

Obviously your adolescent badly needs your understanding and support if he goes through a trauma of this kind. But he doesn't always make things easy for you because in his confusion of emotions he often hits out at whatever target happens to be at hand. In a way, he wants someone to blame for his predicament, because this helps shift the blame from himself, thus helping him cope with damage to his self-esteem. And who easier to blame than his parents? He knows *really* it's nothing to do with you, but he may pick on trivial incidents in which you were involved and blow them up out of all proportion, as if it was these incidents that led to the end of the relationship. Or if he has nothing even as tenuous as this to fall back on, he may simply be sullen and snappy, spoiling the domestic atmosphere, as if to say that if *he's* suffering, then everyone else might as well suffer too. Paradoxically, alienating his family in this way lessens his sense of isolation, because everyone is now going through a bad time, not just him!

Much easier to cope with is the adolescent who wants to talk about his feelings, and have a sympathetic shoulder to cry on. He wants reassurance that other people have gone through what's he's going through, and managed to survive, and that therefore his own suffering is temporary. He also wants his confidence repairing, so that he can believe in the possibility of another close relationship in the future.

But don't press your adolescent if he doesn't want to talk. Individuals differ in how they handle emotional problems, and the idea that a person must talk about these problems if he's going to lay them to rest isn't by any means a universal rule. Some adolescents are already mature enough to see that, in the end, one has to work through these problems oneself. Nobody else can wave a magic wand and make things better *for* you. So if talking helps, they talk. If on the other hand they want their own company, then they may say very little. The important thing is that they should know both how to communicate their feelings if they wish to do so, and that they're assured of a sympathetic and understanding ear.

Don't press him if he doesn't want to talk

Be considerate towards your adolescent, and accept that his behaviour, whatever form it takes, is his way of dealing with things. And that he's learning valuable lessons in the process about the opposite sex, about his family, and most of all about himself. The very intensity of their feelings ensures that most adolescents won't stay in the dumps for too long. One can only live at that level for a short period, and soon a natural reaction sets in and the spirits begin to pick up again. Much to everyone's relief!

But generally, adolescents who have been brought up with the opposite sex escape the worst of these traumas because they don't feel the need to pair off too abruptly. They realize that you can have warm and supportive relationships between men and women without romance always coming along to complicate the issue. This usually means that when romance *does* arrive, it's far more likely to be between compatible individuals. Once a steady relationship develops, however, parents tend to ask two main questions. What if we don't like the boy or girl, and is the relationship likely to involve sexual intercourse? Let's take these two issues in turn.

If you don't like the boyfriend/girlfriend?

If you don't like your adolescent's boyfriend or girlfriend, and you make your dislike too apparent, you may simply strengthen the relationship, with the young lovers taking up a 'we two against the world' stance. On the other hand, if you don't make your views felt, the relationship may end one day in an unsuitable marriage. So be cautious. Do your best to be friendly with whoever your adolescent insists on bringing home, however wildly unsuitable they may seem at first sight. Once you've got over the shock, you may find you take to

603

them after all. And if you don't then you can always comfort yourself with the thought that first love is very rarely last love!

Encourage her to bring her boyfriend home

Coldness or open hostility towards them will only embarrass your son or daughter, and make the latter prefer to carry on the relationship elsewhere, so that you can have no influence on it. As with friends earlier in life, it's always better if boyfriends or girlfriends are brought home, so that your adolescent can see them against her domestic background, and have the chance to decide whether she really has much in common with them. Should the relationship develop, and turn out ultimately to be suitable, this attitude of polite welcome on your part will also bring excellent long-term benefits. If you're decidedly frosty in your welcome the partner (and your own child) will remember this far into the future, and however friendly you ultimately become, this will still tend to rankle below the surface.

This doesn't mean you mustn't convey your misgivings to your child. But it does mean you have to be sensible and thoughtful about them. Don't keep nagging her the moment her boyfriend has left the house and the smile you've kept clamped to your face can be allowed to slip. Give her a chance to weigh things up for herself. And when you do raise the issue with her, use *questions* rather than *statements*. 'Does he share your interest in hot air balloons?', rather than 'He doesn't care a fig for hot air ballooning'. 'Is he always as outspoken as that?', rather than 'He is the rudest person I've ever met'. If you make categorical statements you invite categorical statements back. If you use questions, you prompt your adolescent to think whether she's made a good choice or is simply infatuated. If you're able to ask your questions innocently and casually rather than in a good imitation of a judicial enquiry, you'll disarm her and show you're open-minded enough to reserve your opinion until you've got to know the new boyfriend better.

Affairs with older partners

We have already talked about the infatuation (crush) that some adolescents have with older people, either of the same or the opposite sex. This infatuation is usually a sign that the adolescent is looking for a role model, either 'the person I'd like to be' (if the infatuation is for someone of the same sex) or 'the person I'd like to live with' (if it's someone of the opposite sex). The infatuation is temporary and usually quite harmless.

In fact, if the role model is a good one, it can provide a valuable learning experience. The role model is often blissfully unaware of what is going on, and in any case is far too mature either to be flattered by it or to want to take advantage of a teenager's vulnerability.

It's a different state of affairs, however, if in these or other circumstances an older person returns the affections of a teenager, and an affair develops. Usually this is between a teenage girl and an older man, though it can happen the other way around. It's wrong to be too dogmatic, but generally these affairs are inappropriate. A gap of even five or six years in age at this time of life can mean a vast divide in terms of life experience. The teenager is still learning her identity, testing out her feelings, getting to know what she wants from life and what she has to give, while the older man has had a fair chance to work through these issues. There's also the question why is he attracted to a girl so much younger than himself? Does he like the feeling of being the senior partner? Is his ego flattered? Or isn't he adequate enough to relate to maturer women? A further complication may arise if he feels ready for marriage, and convinces the young girl she is too, whereas in fact she still has much learning ahead of her.

Such affairs are usually inappropriate

As to why a young girl goes for an older man, she too may find the relationship flattering. It may seem to give her status in the eyes of her friends. And if the man has been working a few years, he may have money to spend, and take her to exciting places way beyond the means of boys of her own age. On the other hand, the reason may lie deeper. She may, especially if her relationship with her own father hasn't been good, want a father-substitute. Someone who seems able to look after her and take all the big decisions in life for her. And if she lives in an area of high unemployment, or with only dull, poorly paid jobs available, the idea of an early marriage may seem not just romantic but also an ideal way round this dismal prospect.

If you're sure that the relationship between your child and an older man is wildly inappropriate, you should meet him alone (but with your daughter's knowledge) and point this out to him. If he's genuinely fond of her, he'll agree not to see her for a specified period, to allow her time to think things over and be more with boys of her own age. If he refuses, it's a fair

Meet your daughter's boyfriend and talk to him

sign he hasn't got your daughter's interests most at heart. In which case, point this out firmly to your daughter, and ask her to insist upon a trial separation. Your room for manoeuvre is limited, since she's free to marry at eighteen if she wishes (and to go and live with her boyfriend before then), but make your views perfectly clear and give your reasons.

One thing I must stress though. Don't alienate your daughter or her boyfriend. You've got reasoned arguments on your side; use these and not emotional ones. If the marriage or living together does take place, you don't want to lose your relationship with your daughter. And of course *should* things work out well, you face the prospect, as with any affair you bitterly oppose, of having resentment held against you for years to come.

What about sexual intercourse?
Turning to the question whether the relationship is likely to involve sexual intercourse, problems of a different kind emerge. In any intense teenage relationship the chances are sexual exploration of some kind will be taking place. This may involve so-called 'heavy petting', rather than actual intercourse. But it's vital that young people of this age should be fully aware of the risks they may be running. They're in the grip of powerful sexual urges which they haven't as yet learnt to handle, and however moral their background and firmly held their views, in the excitement of the moment both male and female resistance can often be broken down. Afterwards, the individuals concerned may be very ashamed and confess they don't know what came over them, but in the throes of sexual arousal moral qualms and sound sense sometimes stand little chance.

Try to discuss matters with your adolescent Even with a good sex education adolescents are private people and may be reluctant to discuss matters with you, while for your part you may feel embarrassed at raising them yourself. But the best and most effective discussion between adults and adolescents on these issues occurs when everyone has a good laugh about them. Laughter helps people to open up and forget their shyness. Indicate that you're not asking your adolescent what he and his partner actually do. They're hardly likely to tell you anyway. You're simply emphasizing the need for good sense. Certainly indicate that 'As you know,

I'm against the idea of sex before marriage', if this is how you feel. Indicate as well that 'I wouldn't like to think of anyone taking advantage of . . .; she's such a nice girl', but avoid laying down a rigid law. Not because laying down the law is wrong, but because in sexual matters there isn't any evidence it's usually effective. Far better to make your views clear, but keep the avenues of communication open between you and your adolescent, than to drive him into secrecy and a fearful showdown if and when the damage is done.

With young girls, the problem arises as to whether they should be prescribed contraceptive pills if they have a steady relationship with a boy. This is something for you to decide, together with her. Your decisions will be influenced by your moral beliefs and by your assessment of the health risks of going on the pill as opposed to the risks of pregnancy if she stays off it. If you decide that morally it's the right thing to do, talk it over with your doctor and allow him to make the risks clear. Include your daughter in these discussions and allow her to make her own views known. She's the one who is most closely affected. But young people, both girls and boys, do need guidance in sexual matters. They may be physically mature, but emotionally and intellectually they've still some way to go. As mentioned already, the risks associated with intercourse itself must also be spelt out without pulling punches. Venereal disease, genital herpes, and these days the menace of AIDS all threaten the health and even lives of both partners. Medically, the risks are at their greatest when youngsters engage in *casual sex with whoever happens to be available,* and for these reasons if for no other casual sex should be firmly discouraged.

Should girls be given the pill?

Take particular care to give the right kind of advice if your adolescent is going off on holiday with friends. This applies even if it's a supervised school trip. When parties of friends get together their behaviour often becomes that of the lowest denominator in the group. Particularly given the importance of the peer group, there's a great deal of pressure brought to bear upon the individual to keep up with everyone else. If there's alcohol involved, the ability of the individual to withstand group pressures becomes even weaker. 'I would never have thought it of him (or her),' bemoan the distressed parents when the damage is done. Of course you wouldn't. And left

Anything can happen on a holiday with friends

to himself or in sensible company you'd be quite right. It isn't that he was 'just waiting for the opportunity to get out of my sight'. It's simply that at such an impressionable age, with the sex drive and the drive to have fun at their very height, he isn't always his own master.

Teenage pregnancies

The possibility of an unplanned pregnancy is a worry that lurks in the back of many parents' minds. Because pregnancy doesn't mean your daugther is promiscuous. In fact sometimes the very opposite is the case. The promiscuous person goes prepared, and takes all the necessary precautions. It's the more innocent girl who's likely to be caught out, either from a petting session that gets out of hand with a regular boyfriend, or from a rare lapse while out at a party and perhaps under the influence of drink.

It's natural to feel upset   In these more humane times, you aren't likely to banish your daughter, baby clasped to her breast, out into the snow. But you are going to feel devastated by the whole business, and by the collapse of your plans for your daughter's future (and for your own future, since you're likely to be heavily involved in helping). You may also feel betrayed, as if your daughter has gone against everything you've taught her, and stopped to think neither of herself nor of you.

It's right to recognize these feelings in yourself, and to accept them as perfectly natural. Talk them over with your partner, and with anyone else who's close to you. Then make a number of sensible resolutions. First, avoid recriminations. You don't have to pretend to your daughter you're not upset, but don't waste time apportioning blame. What's happened has happened. Second, don't keep the whole business a guilty secret. People are bound to find out, however hard you try to keep it from them. Far better they should hear about it from you rather than through gossip, and the sooner the better. Third, plan what's going to be done.

Deciding what is to be done   The last is the hardest of the three. I'm assuming your daughter intends to go through with the birth, and has to decide whether to place the baby for adoption or keep it, and if the latter whether to remain a single parent or marry (or live with) the father. Adoption is very much a personal matter, and your daughter needs to consider both her own feelings and the future of her child. If she decides to keep the baby, then arrangements must be made as to who is to care for it, and as to money, accommodation and the rest. And here an important point must be made. In the end, the baby is your daughter's responsibility, and she must face up to the fact. Much as you want to help, and much as you may dislike the idea of your daughter abruptly having to take on an adult role, nevertheless your daughter must take control of her own future, not retreat (or be coaxed or pressed back) into the role of dependent child.

This means your daughter must take many of her own key decisions, and must avoid making unfair demands upon you. If she's to live at home, arrangements must be made so that everyone else's life isn't too disrupted. Your daughter needs all the love, support and understanding from you that she's always had in times of need, but in turn she must appreciate the strain that's being placed upon the rest of the family, and must accept that the main commitment to the baby must be her own.

It isn't necessary to add that it's unfair to hold any resentment against the baby (the unwitting party in all this). In any case you'll probably find that no matter how unlooked for the pregnancy, the moment the baby arrives you'll act towards it just like any other doting grandparents!

Finally, let's remember that in every unlooked for pregnancy there's a father involved as well as a mother. So although I've been talking so far about teenage daughters, it's almost as likely that a teenage son will be involved. With both daughter and son, marriage or living together simply because a baby has arrived isn't advisable. Unless there's a bond of love between the young parents, things won't work out, and the baby is likely to be the one who suffers most. But a teenage son must face up to the reality of the situation just as much as a teenage daughter. He has responsibilities, financial and otherwise, both to the child and to the mother. Again recriminations do little good. Far more productive is the line that what is done is done, and now what matters is how mature you are in facing the consequences of your behaviour. No son should feel he's lost the respect of his parents because of the unfortunate fact of a teenage pregnancy, but he should be helped to understand that the continuation of that respect

If it's your teenage son who is involved

now depends very much on how he shoulders the demands that are rightfully going to be made of him.

What about homosexuality?

This isn't the place to become involved in a discussion about the moral issues surrounding homosexuality. You and your child will make up your own minds about these. But parents sometimes ask about the facts surrounding homosexuality. How does it arise, how common is it, and what do you do if you think that your child has homosexual tendencies which concern you?

How does homosexuality arise? Let's take these three parts of the question separately. Studies of animals, and of both developed and undeveloped human communities, suggest that sexual attraction towards members of one's own sex occurs frequently in both males and females where heterosexual relationships are unavailable. Thus one would expect such attraction to take place at adolescence, when the sex drive is at its peak, in for example single-sex boarding schools. The result may be nothing more physically intimate than verbal expressions of affection, and even where something more intense does develop it is unlikely to be more than fondling or perhaps mutual masturbation.

Once heterosexual relationships become possible, this attraction to one's own sex usually fades (though the memories involved can often be enduring and precious), and there is no useful sense in which it can be called homosexual. In their early sexual experiments, siblings of the same sex will often go through a similar phase, and again this isn't usefully called homosexuality. By homosexual, we usually mean the individual who over a long period consistently finds sexual arousal only possible (or eminently preferable) with his or her own sex. This stands in contrast to heterosexuality, where arousal happens only (or eminently preferably) with the opposite sex. Poised somewhere in between is so-called bisexuality, where the individual may be aroused equally by either sex. But just to make definition more difficult, there are other individuals who experience strong emotional ties with their own sex (perhaps much stronger than they can experience with the opposite sex), yet who do not feel the need for a sexual relationship, or who perhaps prefer heterosexual sex.

The reason why some individuals remain drawn sexually to

their own sex even when heterosexual relationships are available to them may be to do with the balance of male and female hormones in their bodies (though research doesn't strongly support this), or it may be due to some element in the early parent–child relationship (some male homosexuals, for example, had very powerful relationships with their mothers, making it difficult thereafter for them to see women as sexual objects), or it may be due to the fact that at impressionable stages in their development many people see only the naked bodies of their own sex, and thus focus sexual desire upon them to the exclusion of the oppposite sex. Or there may be a fear of the opposite sex involved, or attraction towards prestigious acquaintances, themselves homosexuals, who serve as role models.

As to the second part of the question, how common is homosexuality, estimates vary. There's some consensus that maybe 10 per cent of males and rather fewer females (perhaps because of their greater concern with child-bearing) have significant homosexual tendencies, but a lot may depend upon one's age group, society's current attitudes towards homosexuality, opportunity, and other environmental factors. There's not much evidence that homosexuality runs in families (which suggests genetic explanations may be inappropriate), though too much importance mustn't be attached to this evidence as precise data is so hard to come by. Many homosexuals want to keep their sex lives private, while many families are reluctant to discuss openly such personal affairs. There may be truth in the popular idea that homosexuality is more common in artistic, creative professions, though this may simply be because such professions attach less stigma to it, and the individuals concerned can be more open about themselves. It's possible that in addition some male homosexuals may be drawn towards jobs which allow fuller expression to the feminine side of their natures and vice versa for females, but again firm evidence is difficult to come by. **How common is homosexuality?**

The third part of the question sometimes posed by parents is what do you do if you think your child has homosexual tendencies which concern you? If homosexuality does have psychological origins, you can prevent the query arising by ensuring that throughout childhood your child isn't over-dominated by either parent, and that he or she experiences **If you think your child has homosexual tendencies** open, sensible sexual attitudes, and has ample opportunity for mixing with members of the opposite sex. Any sexual attraction towards members of the same sex that does occur is then likely only to be temporary, as explained a few paragraphs ago. But if in spite of everything you feel that something more deep-seated is involved there's little to be served by accusing your adolescent and filling them with guilt. If it *is* deep-seated, then it probably isn't a matter of choice on their part at all. They may wish things were otherwise, or be happy with them as they are. Far better to be able to discuss it with them with honesty and understanding on both sides, than cause a rift between you which may never heal.

Understand your child's feelings
The point is that many of the ingredients for a happy and stable heterosexual relationship apply equally to a homosexual one. Love, responsibility and unselfishness are the qualities that make relationships work, and all partnerships should be approached with these qualities firmly in mind. People's feelings can be just as intense and just as vulnerable within a homosexual relationship as within a heterosexual one. If a child feels love for a member of his or her own sex, whether the love is physically expressed or not, he or she is just as much in need of understanding as if the love is for someone of the opposite sex. Whatever your own views and your own preferences may be, respond first and foremost to the fact that your child is experiencing deep and powerful emotions, and needs your help in learning how to express them and cope with them. Provided your own love for your child is never compromised, you will continue to be in a position to offer the necessary guidance and support. If your child agrees, discuss things by all means with your doctor, but never let your child feel in some way odd or an outcast.

Teenage daughters

It surprises some people to know that parents seek advice more often over their teenage daughters than over their sons. Does this mean girls are really more of a problem than boys? The figures for delinquency don't bear this out. Boys are more likely than girls to get in trouble with the police and to find themselves before the courts, at schools for the maladjusted or in detention centres. So why do parents worry more about their daughters?

Partly this is because girls are seen to be more vulnerable, and so are protected more carefully. Thus parents are more likely to have conflicts with their daughters over such things as staying out late than they are with their sons. But there's more to it than this, and it stems from the fact that as parents we're less fair to our daughters than to our sons. We expect more of them. We demand more in the way of domestic help. We're more likely to dictate to them what they should wear and how they should look. Mothers in particular are less likely to be indulgent towards them. Whereas a mother will happily pick up her son's dirty laundry from his bedroom floor, she'll demand her daughter do the job for herself. And she's much more likely to ask her to help in the house or mind the younger children or do the ironing or go to the shops.

Parents demand more of their daughters

Particularly if she has a brother at home who gets away with things, a teenage girl will feel this is unjust. She will also recall that when she was younger she still had much less freedom than boys of her age. Even with toddlers in the park, research shows that parents allow little boys to wander that bit further away than little girls before calling them back. Much of this has nothing to do with safety and all to do with social role. We expect little girls to be more dependent, more obedient, less adventurous, less individualistic, less determined than little boys. We have a picture in our minds of the ideal woman – pretty, demure, caring, loving, and more concerned with the needs of others than with her own. Interestingly, this picture is held by men and women alike. It isn't just men who force women into being feminine. (Though it's fair to say that mothers demand this femininity of their daughters not necessarily because it's how they want their daughters to be, but because it's how they feel *men* want them to be.)

Adolescent girls are often resentful because they feel that everyone, from their mother onwards, demands they serve, conform, be unselfish. And remember girls have even less time than boys to experience that freedom from responsibility that is possible when childhood is left behind and full adult responsibilities have not yet been taken on. The gap between the end of childhood and the start of married life and family

We give them little space to discover their own identity

responsibilities is shorter for girls than for boys, because on average they marry sooner. And once married, they carry more domestic responsibilities than men. Even if they have a full-time job outside the home, they're still expected all too often to carry the brunt of child-rearing and home-making. They spend so much of their time servicing children and husbands they have no time to get to know their own wants. When I talk to parents about giving adolescent sons and daughters some space which is theirs, mothers sometimes ask, 'Yes but what about some space for *me*?' They feel there's nowhere in the house that's uniquely theirs, no part of their lives that belongs just to them. Small wonder they say they've never solved for their own selves the questions about personal identity now confronting their offspring. On the few occasions when they do get away on their own they confess that much as they love their familes the experience is an exhilarating one and allows them to discover quite an interesting person lying beneath all the domesticity!

Don't force your daughter into a mould So although you must usually show more concern for the physical safety of adolescent girls than boys, they must in other matters be given as much opportunity to discover themselves and what they really want from life. Simply because she's a girl doesn't automatically mean your daughter enjoys household chores or minding young children or looking after the elderly. Women often confess to the psychologist that deep down they feel a surprising amount of anger and aggression towards a world which has made them conform always to other people's expectations of what a woman *ought* to be like. To cap it all, they feel guilty about their anger, and experience a sense of failure as a woman, since they can't rid themselves of the idea that a successful woman wouldn't want anything other than domesticity.

Avoid forcing your daughter into this mould; show her she does have rights and that you respect them. Don't ask too much of her. If she has brothers, they should be expected to do as much in the house as she does. If she genuinely gets more fun out of household tasks than they do, fine. Let her go ahead. But give her the choice. Show as much interest in her needs, in her opinions, in her making the full use of her potential as you do with her brothers. Let her see that being a human being is what counts, not which sex one is. And if she

614

feels resentment towards the things she's expected to do or to be, encourage her to talk about it. Give her confidence in her right as she becomes an adult to run her own life, to assert her own feelings and her own views, and to expect the same independence as a man.

SECONDARY SCHOOL

Though delayed until twelve or thirteen in some parts of the country, for most children eleven years of age still marks the transition from primary to secondary school. In a single bound, the child goes from the cosy, supportive, small world of the primary school into the much bigger and more impersonal world of the secondary school. Many parents experience this as a major wrench, an end to childhood proper in a sense, and a further milestone in the movement of their children away from them. They may also be anxious about the increased distance a child has to travel to school, the size of the school, whether he or she will be put with a group of friends from primary school days, the extent to which the new school will 'understand' the child, possible bullying, new teachers and new subjects, examinations, homework, and a host of other matters.

These anxieties are perfectly natural. There'd be something odd if they weren't there. But just as in the days when your child first started school, don't convey them to him. He needs you to take as much interest in his schooling now as ever, but if he knows you're anxious, this will only increase his own fears. At the same time (and it's a fine line to draw), do show that you understand and accept these fears, and want him to tell you about them. Sympathize with him, but reassure him that all children feel apprehensive when going to secondary school for the first time. If there's a choice of school, take his preferences into account before making a decision. If he knows which friends he wants to be with, contact the school and ask for this to be arranged (no school should refuse if they really care about putting new children at their ease). If both parents are working, try to fix it so that at least one will be there to see him off in the mornings and to greet him when he comes

Do all you can to smooth his path

615

home, if only for the first few days. Make sure that difficulties such as transport to and from school are sorted out, and that he has all the kit and equipment he's going to need. Don't fuss over him, but do make every effort to smooth his path. If he's still worried, try to make contact through a mutual friend with one of the teachers at the school, who will agree to keep an eye on him in the first week or so.

What your child will and won't realize about secondary school

Most primary schools arrange for children in their final year to visit the secondary school to which they will be transferring, so the chances are your child will already know something of his new environment. He will know that the secondary school is much bigger than the primary school, draws from a wider area, and therefore has a much greater social mix. He will be aware that discipline is going to be stricter, that he will have different teachers for many of his subjects, and that teaching methods and teacher–pupil relationships are going to be more formal. In spite of his feelings of apprehension, he'll probably be looking forward to secondary school life. To be in primary school is to be 'small', to be in secondary school is to be 'big'. Going to secondary school also means starting new subjects and meeting new opportunities. What he won't be so aware of is that to be a first former in a secondary school is in some ways to go back to being *very* 'small' again, with less status and less power over his own life than he had in the top class of primary school. Equally he'll be unaware that some of his lessons are going to be a disappointment, with much time perhaps spent going over work he already knows. It's as well to prepare your child for these facts of life, so that he doesn't build up unrealistic expectations. And assure him that he has your full support and interest, just as in his primary school days.

It will only make things harder if he takes days off

Once they start secondary school, it's surprising how quickly most children settle down, and begin to view their primary school days as through the wrong end of a telescope. Be prepared for some signs of insecurity during the first weeks though. Vague feelings of being 'unwell', and pleas to stay at home. The reappearance perhaps of earlier anxiety symptoms such as bed-wetting. Tears, anger and emotional scenes over minor incidents. Worries over the ability to cope with new work. Be patient, and most of these things will clear up of their own accord. Remember that even adults take a while to settle down when facing major upheavals in life, like changing jobs or moving house. And adults at least make most of these changes of their own free will. Your child has no say in whether he goes to secondary school or not. But go he must, and although it's fair to give him the benefit of the doubt on the odd day or two when he complains of feeling off-colour and being unable to go, be sympathetic but firm before this becomes a habit.

Just like problems with starting school at age five, a child has to learn that we can't duck out of duties and responsibilities in life just because they're uncomfortable. The more he skips school, the harder it will be for him to catch up with the work and to fit in with classmates. Discuss any real problems he has, and see what can be done to put them right. If he's been bullied by other children, report it to the headteacher at once. If he doesn't understand some of the work, go over it with him, and if the problem persists, contact the school and ask for extra help. I'm constantly surprised at just how few parents bring their children's difficulties to the attention of the school. It isn't making a nuisance of yourself, it's helping the school to do its duty by your child. But once you've taken these necessary steps, insist school has to be faced. The more we run away from problems the worse they become. Don't meet his emotional scene with one of your own. You and he are really both on the same side. Simply tell him that you don't make the laws of the land, but the law says he must go to school, and that's that. Do inform the school of his continuing reluctance though, so that they can take extra trouble to help him settle in.

What makes a good secondary school?

You may have had a choice as to which secondary school your child attends, or you may not. But either way, you'll want to know how to recognize a good secondary school (and what kind of improvements to suggest if your child attends one that doesn't come up to standard!)

Here are the things to look for:

- Is the building cared for? Shortage of funds may limit what can be done in the way of redecorating, but children

617

and teachers who respect and value their school take a pride in keeping it tidy, bright and cheerful.

- Are noise levels acceptable? A silent school is as suspect as a rowdy one, but in a well-organized school noise is kept to a level which indicates purposeful, well-directed activity. Those areas where noise is necessarily generated (music rooms, gymnasiums, drama studios) are situated where they won't disrupt everyone else. And even in these areas, there should be no sign that children either want or are allowed to run riot.
- Is the children's appearance acceptable? There are arguments for and against school uniform, and there are strong arguments against schools which set out to curb all signs of individuality in children, but in a good school you expect to see a premium placed upon cleanliness and tidiness (and that goes for teachers as well as children!).
- Are the facilities good? This applies especially to science laboratories, library, craft workshops, sports facilities, drama, art and music areas.
- Is the equipment up-to-date, well-cared for and abundant? Enquire (and ask to see) not just obvious things like science equipment but textbooks, musical instruments and sports apparatus.
- Are facilities for staff adequate? A happy, efficient staff need ample quiet areas for marking and preparation, and for relaxing during breaks and lunchtimes. Crowded, untidy staff rooms are a bad sign.
- Does the school offer an adequate breadth of subject choice? Are the children prevented from taking certain attractive subject combinations because of the vagaries of the timetable?
- Is the school well-organized in terms of how it sets and streams children, and how it identifies those in need of special help? Is this special help readily and appropriately available? Good organization is more important than whether a school is large or small.
- Are there equal opportunities for both sexes, or are children faced with sexual stereotyping?
- What are the school's examination results? Don't make the mistake of seeing these as the only measure of a

school's quality, but naturally you want your child to have the best chance of fulfilling his or her potential.

- What extra-curricular activities does the school offer? Is there a wide choice of organized activities at lunchtime and after school? Or are the children ordered promptly out of the building at these times and left to fend for themselves?
- What steps does the school take to prevent bullying? Are these adequate?
- What sort of pastoral care network does the school have? That is, how does the school ensure each child has proper opportunities to have his troubles (and his grumbles) listened to and put right? Vague talk about 'every child has a form teacher to whom they can go' isn't enough. A good school has a committed and properly organized pastoral care network involving teachers with special responsibilities (and often training) in pastoral care and with a recognized procedure for referring children's problems through the chain of command right up to the headteacher.
- Does the school offer its older pupils appropriate opportunities for vocational guidance and work experience?
- Is the school's policy on discipline (and punishments) humane, well-reasoned and effective?
- Are there recognized procedures for parents to consult staff about their children's progress whenever appropriate (and not just at organized parents' evenings)?
- Do the headteacher and his or her staff appear interested in your child and in you? Are their attitudes enthusiastic, caring, perceptive and well-informed? Schools are only as good as their teachers. Do you get the impression that the headteacher and staff know what they're doing, are genuinely concerned about children, have a warm and friendly approach, and see parents as allies in the educational process rather than as something of a nuisance?

All the above points are relatively easy to check on. If there aren't organized opportunities to visit the school your child will be attending before term starts, then make an appointment and go along there under your own steam. Talk to the headteacher (is he or she prepared to spend time with you, or only too anxious to pass you on to somebody else?), and ask to be shown round. Have your questions ready, and make sure they're direct and receive direct answers. On balance, is it the kind of school *you* would like to have attended at your child's age? Is the atmosphere industrious but happy? Are there plenty of examples of the children's work on the walls? Are the classrooms pleasant, bright places in which to work? Do they have a distinct character about them, or are they anonymous and boring? Get the *feel* of the school. Either on this or on a subsequent occasion make sure your child also has a chance to look around; listen carefully to what he or she has to say about the place. Talk to other parents whose children go to the school too, and listen to what they have to say. However good the school, some parents will criticize it, so listen carefully to their reasons rather than be satisfied with their vague impressions. Some of the things other parents dislike about a school may be unimportant to you, while some of the things they like may strike you as of little value. So weigh up the pros and cons for yourself, and don't be too easily influenced by what others say.

Private or state school?

One of the hardest decisions you may have to face is whether to plump for a state school or go private. Whichever way you're inclined, look at the list of things I've already outlined. Don't assume that because a school is private (and is going to cost you a great deal of money) it's necessarily going to be better than a state school. And don't assume that because a school is small and has an intimate atmosphere it's necessarily going to provide your child with better opportunities than a large school. Many state schools are better equipped and offer children a much wider range of facilities and subject options than all but the most expensive private schools. They may also have a more able staff, drawn from a much wider range of backgrounds. And they may be more sympathetic and caring towards their children, with more respect for individuality and personal expression.

Since a private school may well be a strain upon the family budget, you also need to ask yourself whether the money you're spending on fees might not benefit your child more if it was spent in other ways. And whether the very restricted social and perhaps ethnic mix she is going to find in a private school is really the best preparation for the world in which one day she is going to have to make her way. And whether private education is what *she* wants (she has a right to be consulted). But if you do go private, make sure your child gets full benefit from what is on offer. In a private school she may be in smaller classes, but that doesn't necessarily mean she'll get more individual attention and more preparation for public examinations. Keep just as close an eye on her progress as you would if she were in a state school, and be just as ready to consult with and make your views known to the staff whenever the need arises.

Helping your child's progress

While she's settling into her new school, your child will need help in organizing herself properly, remembering to take to school the things she needs, getting her homework done in good time, ensuring she knows how to take care of her possessions during the school day. But at the same time, your child has to realize that she must now take an increasing responsibility for her own life. I deal with such things as getting up in the morning later in the chapter, but in most matters your child has to understand the growing need to stand on her own feet. Help her draw up a timetable showing clearly and in different coloured inks her regular weekly commitments. Pin it somewhere prominent, either in the kitchen or where she puts on her shoes each morning before leaving home. Put a piece of pin-boarding there solely for her use. Encourage her to write a note to herself every time she has to remember something outside her usual routine, and get her to pin the note on the board under her timetable.

Homework

Now that he has more books and more homework, he needs somewhere where he can leave his things and know they won't be disturbed, and somewhere quiet where he can work. If there's nowhere downstairs buy him a desk and put it in his bedroom. Make sure there's adequate lighting, by day and in the evenings. Then leave him to organize his desk for himself.

However untidy it becomes, don't be tempted to interfere. I talk about tidiness later, but if his desk gets in such a mess that he can't find anything, then he has to learn the inefficiency of this for himself. Remember that untidiness is often in the eye of the beholder. Those of us (myself included) who work with a desk piled high with books and papers may look disorganized to anyone else, but usually we can find things when we need them since we've created the untidiness ourselves, and are well aware where each item has been placed. Let your child develop his own system, and if it doesn't work for him he'll have to improve it.

He needs a quiet place to work

Another reason for letting your child have somewhere he can leave his work undisturbed is that if he has to get out his books and papers every evening before he can begin his homework this is a powerful incentive not to begin at all. Far better to be able to sit down and carry on from where he left off last time.

As to a quiet room in which to work, children these days are brought up with the record player and the tape recorder and the television. Often they seem able to work through it quite happily, as long as it's *their* noise. However, a child who will work with his own tape recorder blaring in his ears will object vehemently to the noise made by a brother or sister in the room next door. As long as he's in control of the noise it's okay. But if someone else is responsible for it he'll quickly be goaded into paroxysms of self-righteous rage. The same with interruptions. Once he's working he'll break off cheerfully enough when *he* wants to, but if someone else interferes with him it's a very different story. So give him somewhere he can tuck himself away. Ask the rest of the family to co-operate, and remember that if he isn't enjoying his work he'll often be only too ready to seize on interruptions as a reason for packing up.

There's no best time for doing homework

As to when he does his homework, some children become adept at knocking it off during break and lunchtime at school, or in quiet moments in between (or even during) lessons. Their work isn't necessarily the worse for this, and if they're receiving good marks don't feel you *must* interfere. It points to an efficient use of time if nothing else! Other children prefer to work as soon as they arrive home. Others leave it until later. There's no 'best' time, and a lot will depend upon the child himself and upon how you as a family organize your evenings. Some children also work more quickly than others. If your child's work is going well don't worry if his system is different from the one you'd be using in his place.

If a child isn't doing his homework you'll have to intervene, but think carefully how you do it. If you take over full responsibility for seeing he gets it done you'll put yourself on a treadmill. Often the *natural consequences* I talked about on pages 389–90 are a better alternative. If a child doesn't do his homework, and if he comes from a home where he's expected to do well, the experience of confessing to his teacher he hasn't done it or of getting low marks will be very unpleasant consequences for him. He'll want to avoid them next time. So ask him if he's done his homework, and if he hasn't tell him, 'Well it's up to you. I'm not going to spend time chasing you. But you know how you'll feel when you have to tell Mr . . . tomorrow that you haven't done it.'

If your child isn't getting his homework done

Nine times out of ten this works. If it doesn't, then set aside a time in the evening for his homework and insist he can't watch television (or whatever else he likes doing) until it's finished. It's more effective if the television is off altogether during this time, so that he won't sit at his desk feeling you're watching it when he can't. But if there are younger children in the home this isn't fair on them, so tell him they'll be treated the same when they move to secondary school.

Give help with his homework if he needs it, but teaching methods change and the way you did things when you were in school may not be the same as the way he does them. So when he asks for help prompt him to tell you what he knows, rather than rush in and try to sort things out straightaway. If you can understand his method, then work with that. If you can't, study the textbook from which he's working so that you can see how he does things. If he's really in trouble, find out from his teacher what books you can buy to give him the help he needs.

Setting and streaming

By the end of her second year and often by the end of her first, your child's school may begin the process of putting children into *sets*, based upon ability, for at least basic subjects like English and mathematics. Children with special learning difficulties will also be identified and placed in remedial sets with teachers who understand such difficulties. Few state schools *stream* these days, that is put children in A, B and C streams that remain together for all their work. Streaming quickly produces the idea of an élite (the A streamers) and the strugglers (the C streamers).

As soon as the process of setting begins, most parents want their child to be in the top sets. They're worried that if she isn't her work in the vital basic subjects is going to suffer. But it will suffer much more if she's put in a set beyond her current level of ability. She won't be able to understand the work, she'll compare herself unfavourably with the other children, and she'll get one lot of poor marks after another. As long as you're satisfied that the school is using the right methods to decide who goes in which set, it's better to leave decisions of this kind to them, and be confident that your child is working at the right speed for her. There should be movement between the sets though, so if your child works hard she can be moved up. Give her what help you can at home, don't build up unnecessary anxiety or unrealistic expectations, but help her to set her sights as high as is right for her. Remind her that she doesn't want to fall behind in important areas of her work, and that if she can move up a set she may find the ground being covered is of more interest.

If you feel your child's been put in too low a set If you feel she's been wrongly assigned to a lower set, discuss it with the school. Do it at once. Don't wait for the next parents' evening, by which time she'll have missed out on crucial parts of the more advanced work. Make an appointment and go and explain your anxieties. If you have evidence she was progressing well in the subjects concerned in earlier years, make sure you raise this. The school is far more likely to listen to you if you have your facts correct and carefully marshalled. Schools know that parents tend to overestimate the abilities of their children, and they are therefore more likely to be swayed by thoughtful arguments than by emotional appeals!

Always have your facts correct and well marshalled Having your facts correct and carefully marshalled is, by the way, essential when talking to secondary school teachers about any subject. Most secondary school teachers, because they teach a number of different classes and because by now the children are more independent, do not have such a close relationship with their pupils as do primary school teachers. It usually follows that their relationship with parents isn't so close either. This makes it hard sometimes to get your point across to them. They also have a rather intimidating habit of cutting the ground from under your feet. Thus, for example, if you're questioning them on some aspect of school procedure about which your child is confused they're prone to answer briskly, 'Oh but that was made perfectly clear to all the children at the start of term', or if you're complaining about some injustice your child feels has been visited on her they're likely to say, 'Oh but that can't be true, because your child knows she should have given her book in to me the week before.' So be asbolutely sure of your position. Go over the details with your child until you're quite sure she's given you an accurate picture. Try to anticipate with your child what the teacher *might* say, and then be ready with your own response. When you do meet the teacher, be polite but confident, and stick to your guns. Things do go wrong in schools, and injustices do happen, not because teachers want it that way, but because they lead hectic lives and haven't always the time or the patience to sort things out as they go along. Have the facts at your finger-tips, and you're much more likely to emerge with a feeling that you've helped put matters to rights.

Attending parents' evenings

Important as parents' evenings were in the primary school they're even more important now. Even if you feel you've nothing very much to learn about your child's progress, it's still vital to go. If teachers meet you regularly and see that you're interested in your child this inevitably influences them favourably towards her. They may also have questions to put to you, and just by discussing your child together new and important issues may come to light. It helps your child's attitude towards school too if she knows you're interested enough in her to put up with the long queues and waiting about which parents' evenings inevitably entail.

Parents' evenings also give you the chance to get to know your child's teachers, so that you can refer to them by name when talking to her. If you never meet them, they remain vague distant figures, just as you remain vague and distant to them.

Subject choice

By the beginning of your child's fourth year in the secondary school, and often well before, he'll be faced with making choices between a range of school subjects. He may be able to take a second foreign language for example, or to drop some subjects altogether. He may be able to start new subjects such as technical drawing, or geology or economics. These choices require a lot of thought. Career prospects are opened up and closed down on the strength of them, and I'm often surprised how little foresight many children and parents show at this time. Teachers aren't always a great help either. The fact that a particular subject is on offer makes it hard for them to admit it may not be worth doing. Another factor is that teachers are often wary of appearing to criticize their colleagues, so even if they do privately feel a particular subject isn't a great deal of use to a child or isn't well taught in the school, they rarely come out and say so.

When helping your child to make his choice, there are certain points to keep in mind:

1. Does the subject open up eventual career prospects?
2. Is the school equipped to teach it, and do they place emphasis upon the subject?
3. Are the staff teaching it well qualified and good at their jobs?
4. Is there any obvious prospect of the subject being withdrawn from the timetable before your child has taken it through to examination level in the fifth form?
5. Is your child really interested in the subject? However valuable the subject, if your child dislikes it he may not make much of a success of it.
6. Does your child like the teacher concerned? If the subject is a valuable one and interests your child, advise him to take it even if he dislikes the teacher. An unpopular teacher has no right to decide your child's future for him.

Look to the future when making the choice

It's wrong to force a child into making a subject choice which he dislikes. On the other hand you don't want him to close down options and regret it later. Looking ahead to degree level, the latest available figures show that science and engineering graduates are (as they have been for many years) more in demand by employers than arts or social science graduates. The list goes from medical graduates at the top, almost all of whom find jobs soon after graduating, to philosophy and zoology graduates at the bottom, with only some 50 per cent in this happy position. After medical graduates come accountants, science teachers, electrical, civil and mechanical engineers (in that order).

If your child is wavering between the sciences and the arts, with a bent for both, then whenever he's faced with choosing between subjects, ask him to think ahead to the time when he'll be leaving school and thinking of a career. You can't make a convinced artist into a scientist or vice versa, but there's a large percentage of children who could go either way with equal success and enjoyment. There's little truth in the notion that if you're creative you go into the arts and if you're unimaginative (but highly intelligent) you go into the sciences. Though it's of a different kind, there's as much scope for creativity and imagination in the sciences as in the arts, while the arts offer just as much outlet for the use of intelligence and powers of reasoning as do the sciences. Enjoyment and career prospects should be the deciding factors, rather than mistaken notions of this kind.

School refusal

In certain inner city areas the truancy rate in secondary schools can be as high as 20 per cent. Children truant from school usually for one of three main reasons. They're bored, they're frightened, or they're worried about home. Boredom is self-explanatory. The child feels she's learning nothing from school, and that what's on offer has little relevance to her life or interests. Fear is less straightforward. The child may be afraid of her teachers, afraid because she hasn't completed an assignment or is facing trouble of some sort, or afraid of bullying or teasing by other children. Worries about home usually have to do with a feeling that there's something wrong with her parents' marriage. She may be anxious that one of her parents will go off with somebody else, or that one parent may be violent towards the other or that there'll be terrible rows if she isn't around to keep an eye on things.

**Find out why
your child is
truanting**

If you've reason to believe your child may be truanting, try to decide which of the possible causes applies. Traunting is rare in homes where the child feels secure and confident, though it's not unknown. A child who truants is always a child with a problem and most schools now realize that punishment isn't the answer. It only adds yet another problem to the one the child already has. Finding the cause and putting it right is what's needed. Where the problem is fear, forcing a child to go to school without first finding out and remedying the cause of her fear can cause school phobia, a disabling fear which requires patient long-term efforts on the part of the educational psychologist to put right.

The child who hates school

With or without school refusal, there are some children who take a rooted dislike to school and to almost everything associated with it. Though this dislike can start earlier, typically it starts around the first or second year of secondary school, and takes the form of repeated protests at 'boring old school', the 'soppy old teachers', 'rotten old' this subject and that subject and everything else on the timetable. Not surprisingly, this attitude almost always goes with bad school work and poor school reports. The child is characterized by her teachers as 'lazy', and it soon becomes clear that they will be even more delighted to see the back of her than she will be to see the back of them.

Let's be clear that no child is born lazy, no matter how fond we adults are of using the term. True, children vary temperamentally in their activity levels, but from the first weeks and months of life all children are curious about their environment and will attend to things that interest them. The 'lazy' child is, therefore, the child who has lost motivation; in the case of school work this usually happens because she's fallen behind in some way, gets low marks, can't understand what the teacher is saying, and decides the best thing is to give up. Her frequent references to 'boring' school are therefore partly true. She is bored by what goes on. But they are also a form of defence. She doesn't like to think she *can't* do the work, so she takes the line that she could do it if only it wasn't so dull.

If your child starts to dislike school, talk it over with her teachers to see how she can be helped. But talk it over with her too. She mustn't be allowed to develop the attitude that it's all 'their' fault. Get her to think about her own behaviour and the things she may be doing to upset her teachers. Often there's a measure of misunderstanding going on between teacher and child. The teacher misinterprets the child's attitude, the child misinterprets the teacher's attitude, small issues are allowed to become large issues, the child gets a bad name in the teacher's eyes, the teacher gets a bad name in the child's eyes, and things go from bad to worse. Once on the wrong side of one teacher, the child begins to get a bad name in the school generally, and before long she can do no right. But she has to see that she may have been as much to blame for the original incident or incidents as the teacher, and that her own subsequent stubbornness or resentfulness has been partly responsible for what's followed.

Talk to the teachers and to your child

What is needed is a kind of performance contract. If the child agrees to produce a certain form of improved behaviour, the teachers agree to change their behaviour too. Some schools actually put contracts of this kind down on paper, so that the child knows exactly where she stands and what is expected of her, and what the school is offering her in return. But whether things are formalized in this way or not, it's important that there's frank discussion between you and the teachers and your child, so that everyone is agreed upon what has been going wrong and what is needed to put it right. And once both teachers and child see that the new attitudes are beginning to bring results, they're encouraged to sustain and further develop their efforts. Your child may never admit to liking school (a grudging 'It's all right' may be as far as she's prepared to go), but at least *some* of the scorn will go out of her voice when she talks about it!

Draw up a performance contract

ISSUES AND PROBLEMS IN THE YEARS ELEVEN TO EIGHTEEN

The shy teenager

Adolescent shyness can manifest itself in a number of different ways. Lack of close friends. A neurotic over-emphasis upon studying and doing well at school. A choice of solitary rather than social pursuits. Exaggerated excuses for avoiding mixing with contemporaries. An unwillingness to look anyone in the eye. An inability to speak up for himself even with people he knows. The list is a long one. Most adolescents are shy to some extent, since they're unsure of their adult status and of just what sort of person they're developing into. And most adolescents grow out of this with the developing assurance that adulthood brings. But if the shyness is extreme it could persist, partly because just at the time when he needs to try out his developing personality and see what works for him and what doesn't he's cut off from others by his painful self-consciousness.

Don't be taken in by outward appearances In some adolescents, this shyness takes the form of an assumed indifference towards others, or even hostility. All attempts at communicating with him are met with abrupt, snappy responses. Because he finds the world threatening and difficult to handle, he snubs it as a way of retreating further into himself. Remember that with adolescents things are often not what they seem. Aggression may hide uncertainty. Brashness may hide vulnerability. And in the case of shyness, apparent self-sufficiency and impatience with others may hide a desperate need for them. Don't be taken in by these outward appearances. I don't mean you should confront the adolescent with 'I-know-more-about-you-than-you-know-about-yourself' attitude. He'll only deny hotly that he really feels as you think he feels. Simply note that he's uncomfortable with others, and do what you can unobtrusively to bring him out of himself. If you can get him to communicate his uncertainties to you, so much the better. But many adolescents are desperately anxious to hide their weaknesses, even from themselves, and this is one of the things that lies behind the inability to communicate. So your role is likely to remain an indirect rather than a direct one.

Giving the shy adolescent the confidence he needs and bringing him out of himself can be something of a challenge. Don't keep trying to push him into things. He'll retreat further into his shell. And don't make him feel there's something 'odd' or lacking about him. He's going to be self-conscious enough as it is. Instead, show him you believe in him. Think of ways you can encourage him to make friends (of both sexes). Back up your efforts by showing him in other ways that he's an effective human being. Give him the responsibilities and freedom to take his own decisions and have his views consulted. And don't expect an overnight transformation.

Blushing

Often coupled with shyness, many adolescents are martyrs to the habit of lighting up like reluctant beacons just at the moments when they most want to look suave and untroubled (the presence of an admired member of the opposite sex can often be counted on to produce the most dramatic illuminations). It's a curious fact that we still don't know the precise purpose served by blushing. It may be a misplaced sexual response. But what is clear is that the body suddenly produces a surge of blood to the surface of the skin in an effort to dissipate excess body heat. Intriguingly, we only ever blush as far down as the top of our clothes. The lower cut the dress or the more open the shirt or blouse the lower the spread of the blush, but it never extends under our clothes.

This suggests that the body tries to get rid of its excess heat in the most efficient way, through uncovered areas of the upper part of the body. Without clothes, we probably wouldn't blush as all, since the body would have a large enough area to dissipate heat without having to concentrate the blood supply into the face and neck. However, though this opens up intriguing research possibilities for psychologists, it isn't much help to the adolescent striving to control his blushes when first setting eyes on the partner of his dreams.

On the other hand it is some help to him to know that the more one struggles to control a blush the worse it gets. Self-consciousness, tension, fury with oneself all conspire to heat up the body even more and send more blood rushing to the unfortunate face. It isn't easy to achieve, but if one stops caring about blushing, the blush quickly subsides.

The best technique is to stop minding about blushing

The best way to work towards this not-caring attitude is to practise a technqiue called *paradoxical intention*, in which one deliberately tries to achieve the very effect one wants to avoid. That is, the adolescent practises *trying to make himself blush*. Initially in situations (e.g. when he is on his own) where blushing is virtually impossible anyway, and then in situations where blushing becomes progressively more likely. This

631

'tricks' the autonomic nervous system, which is responsible for the blushing mechanism, into thinking you enjoy blushing, and like a kill-joy it then begins refusing to oblige. Don't expect magic results with this technique. It takes time and practice, but it does work. It's helped greatly if the adolescent also tries to relax when a blush does spontaneously occur, and to tell himself he welcomes it or at the very least 'so what? it's only a blush anyway', and far less noticeable to other people than it is to himself. This strategy is doubly effective if the adolescent breaks himself of the physical actions that usually go with blushing, such as turning away and refusing to look people in the face. The more he can behave normally, the less importance he attaches to his blushing, the less likely it is to persist.

The unassertive teenager

Another issue sometimes linked to shyness in teenagers is a lack of assertiveness. Parents complain that the teenager is unable to stand up for herself, or is too easily led, or is chronically indecisive when it comes to taking even the smallest decision. Often temperament plays a part in this. Parents of such children usually report that they didn't go through the negative phase during the third year of life (Chapter 5) which denotes the emergence of a sense of independence, and that they've always tended to be rather docile and lacking in drive and direction.

Self-assertion depends on a belief in our rights

This is a salutary reminder of the fact that the qualities that can make children 'difficult' in earlier years are often the qualities we most admire when they're older, while the qualities that make them excessively obedient and co-operative as children are often the qualities we tend to criticize later. But temperament is only part of the answer. To be assertive when the need arises we have to be convinced deep down that we've a right to be assertive, that we've a right to our beliefs and to stick up for the things we consider important. When working with individuals (particularly women) who feel unable to speak out in defence of their legitimate interests, it's all too evident that they're locked into a process of constantly putting themselves in the wrong. Even though their head tells them differently, their heart tells them that in any disagreement with another person (be it parent or shopkeeper) they themselves are somehow the person at fault. Evident in adolescence, this form of self-denigration (for that's what it is) is all too likely to persist throughout life.

The remedy is simpler than one might think. It lies first and foremost in helping the individual *give herself permission* to assert herself. Her lack of it may be caused by low self-esteem, or by moral beliefs that tell her it's 'wrong' or 'selfish' to have one's say, but either way she needs to feel she's been granted permission to have this say. For one or other of these two causes, coupled with her obedient temperament, she's locked into the notion that she's denied this permission. Even the fear she experiences when called upon to speak out stems from this notion. She's afraid the person she's confronting will become angry or will think badly of her, thus confirming her sense of being the person to blame. Like a child being put in her place by an adult, she feels power and rectitude lie in reality with the other person, and never with herself.

Giving herself permission to be assertive

So get her to repeat to herself the simple formula 'I give myself permission to stand up for myself.' It may seem odd that such a mechanical process can help, but the power of suggestion is very strong. By repeating the formula several times a day, the individual gets the message across to her unconscious that it is *all right* for her to be assertive when the need really arises (if she's very unsure of herself you can give her your permission too, but in the long run it's better if she herself takes over responsibility for this area of her life). Once the message begins to sink in, she can be helped further by imagining the situations in which assertion is needed, and imagining herself calmly and firmly speaking up for herself. If you're good at role play, you can act out these scenes with her, sometimes letting her play herself and you the other person, and sometimes switching roles. But if acting isn't in your line or hers, then imagination alone can do the trick. Imagination can be as valuable as the power of suggestion in helping people change unwanted behaviour.

Let her grant herself permission in other areas of her life too. Often unassertive people find difficulty in expressing any of their emotions. Help her give herself permission to be angry when needed, or to cry, or to laugh, or to fall in love. If she

Giving herself permission to do other things

633

finds it hard to let herself go at a party, encourage her to give herself permission to enjoy herself, to let her hair down, to play the fool a little. We all need a responsible approach to our emotional lives, but this doesn't mean the rigid over-control that prevents us from ever letting go, from making our feelings plain to others, from having a good time. If her feelings have always been accepted in the home, the permission to let go should already be there, but all children come heavily under influences outside the home, and may need help in freeing themselves from some of the over-restrictive conditioning involved.

The unco-operative adolescent

Most adults when asked to do something mildly unwelcome usually contrive to make the best of it. So they find it hard to understand why an adolescent son or daughter, amenable enough over other things, makes such a fuss over certain minor requests. But to the adolescent, the effort involved, at the *emotional* rather than the *physical* level, seems gargantuan. An adolescent will confess for example that he just can't bring himself to greet his grandmother when she visits. He knows his sullen silence upsets her and angers his parents. The solution, to look at her and mutter 'hello', is so simple. Yet he can't do it. However much he decides to make the effort, the moment his grandmother arrives something inside takes over and stops him. He doesn't particularly want to be obstinate and difficult. The decision seems to be taken for him.

Incidents of this kind happen in the lives of most adolescents. In later life they can look back and wonder how on earth they could have been so silly, but at the time that's the way things are, and there seems no way round them. Parents who run up against these problems find it hard to make light of them, and to allow them to pass in their own good time. 'But I can't make light of it,' says the exasperated parent, 'he's got to learn to respect his grandmother/his home/whatever.' Certainly he has. But the question is, how successful are sterner methods in getting him to show this respect? Usually the answer is hardly at all, though they certainly succeed in leaving everyone shaken and upset! 'I just get so *mad* at him for not doing as he's asked,' says the parent. 'After all, we're not asking much. So I do think he should co-operate!'

The trouble is that both parent and adolescent are becoming firmly entrenched in their positions, and it is this entrenchment that is prolonging the whole situation. The parents don't want to climb down, because they feel their demands are reasonable and they're worried that their authority is being weakened. The adolescent *can't* climb down. And it's this *can't* that holds the key to things. The adolescent's position is in fact rather like that in the third year of life (see Chapter 5). In the third year the child suddenly realizes his separate existence, and needs to assert this separateness. It's a natural, inborn part of his development. Now in adolescence he suddenly realizes his separate identity, his adultness, his need to take his own decisions. This is just as natural and inborn.

Entrenched positions only make things worse

What's happened is that with the sudden strong feelings of adolescence his grandmother has irritated him over something. Perhaps its her entrenched opinions. Perhaps it's her age (adolescents, full of youth and vigour, often find old age aggravating). But whatever it is, left to himself he'd soon forget it. It isn't really that he can't stand saying hello to his grandmother, it's that he can't stand being *expected* to say hello to her. And he can't stand the guilt he's made to feel when he tries to assert his right to choose. He wants his own relationship with his grandmother, not a relationship decided for him by others, and he hates being made to feel guilty about it. At the same time he *does* feel guilty; he still wants to please others, and ends up feeling angry and frustrated with himself for not being able to give his parents what they want. But this strong urge to assert his independence won't go away, hence his sullen stubbornness. He doesn't 'know' whether it's right to stand up for himself or not. He's confused, and confused even more at the inability of his parents to understand how he feels. And the more rows there are, the worse things become.

Give an adolescent the assurance that he does have the right to his independence and wherever possible the right to make his own choices, and some of the need to be stubborn and awkward disappears. If we know we're free, we no longer have to fight for our freedom. In adolescence, your relationship with your child moves towards one of equality. You become partners, rather than one of you in firm authority over the other. The

Let him feel free to make his own choices

parent who can handle this change avoids many of the squalls that blow up at this time. I explain this to parents by saying that the best way to hang on to your children is to let them go. If you try to keep a tight grip on them, they can hardly wait for the moment when they can leave home. But if in a sensible way you allow them ordered access to the rights of adulthood, then they'll still feel good about their home.

In allowing your adolescent increasing freedom you don't cease to have a part to play in his life and to be necessary to him. Your role is still a vital one, and he needs you as much as ever. But both the role and the need are changing. He wants you there in his life, as a source of security and strength, but he doesn't want you sitting on top of him. He wants your advice and your guidance, but he doesn't want to be force-fed. He wants your love and your concern, but he doesn't want to be smothered. He wants you to see him as a near-adult, and not as an overgrown child. He wants to know what you think, but he doesn't want always to have to agree with you.

Don't make him feel you depend on him And – a vital point – he doesn't want to feel your need of *him* too intensely. He wants to feel you can rely on him, but he doesn't want to feel responsible for you. This is particularly important in the single-parent family, or in a family where the parental marriage isn't working well. There's an understandable tendency to look to the adolescent as a substitute for a good marriage partner. This means you want his company when he wants to be with people of his own age, and you make him guilty about leaving you on your own. You start showing him how much you depend on him, and in extreme cases even perhaps put on a show of physical or emotional weakness to force him into feeling sorry for you and giving you more of his time and attention.

I needn't stress how bad this is for the adolescent, and how unfair. As already mentioned, he has a right to be free of major responsibilities for a few years. He's just shaken off the restraints and restrictions of childhood, and soon he'll be enmeshed in the responsibilities of family life and a job and a home. He needs the freedom of the late teens and early twenties to find out about himself and develop his own interests and sense of direction. If he's denied this learning opportunity, it won't come again.

Helping in the house

If you've allowed your child to grow up with the idea that helping in the house is fun rather than a duty you shouldn't have much difficulty getting her co-operation in adolescence. And if you've always helped her when she needed help, then there's a good chance that she'll often come and offer help instead of waiting to be asked. But the nature of her role is changing. She'll appreciate being asked rather than being told. She'll appreciate being allowed to do things where possible in her own time rather than having to do them the moment you ask. And she'll appreciate being consulted about the way jobs are done and being allowed to use her own methods instead of having always to do as you say.

As a general rule, we all work best if our efforts are appreciated and if those who are working with or over us let us make as many decisions as feasible ourselves. Who wants to work for a boss who insists we always do things his way even when our way is preferable, and who doesn't seem to have the least appreciation for our feelings or our efforts? When I make points of this kind to parents, someone occasionally objects that I make it sound as if the teenager is always right. Not so. I'm simply saying that if you want to get the best out of your workers you must study how to be a good boss. An element of democracy achieves far higher productivity than a set-up where the word of the boss is always law. And what works on the shop floor works in the home as well. Be an autocrat and your adolescent, if she has any spirit, will at best perform grudgingly for you. She'll do the minimum, slowly and with bad grace, and she'll develop all kinds of strategies for not being there when you want her. You may even find you have a few sit-down strikes on your hands!

Let her do things her own way

Faced with difficulties in getting help in the house from a teenager, some parents ask whether they should offer payment as an inducement. So much per week for helping with the washing up, so much per week for hoovering and so on. The rule here is that you shouldn't pay for work that the teenager wouldn't be ready to do without payment. Once you start this, you're on the slippery slope of bribes and yet more bribes. If a teenager won't help with a particular job and you feel she should, then resolve to fight the battle on a question

What about paying teenagers for their help?

of principle rather than a question of money. Is it reasonable to expect the teenager to do the job? If so, then insist she does it. If it isn't reasonable, then don't ask her.

Don't encourage them to expect payment
However, payment is in order if your teenager is particularly willing, and does extra work cheerfully and undemandingly. When the job is finished, you may well feel it's right to give her a little something to spend on herself. But don't do it in such a way that she comes to expect payment. It's unfair to teach her that we should only work if there's a financial kick-back in it for us. Payment is also in order if both parents are out at work, and intend to pay someone to come in and help in the house (this goes for the single parent too). Since the jobs involved are over and above the call of duty, it's reasonable to ask teenagers if they'd like to take them on and receive the same terms as a domestic help. If they like the idea, fine. If they don't, drop it. But they must understand that a contract is involved. They have to do the jobs well and at the agreed time, and you have to pay them the agreed rates. If the contract doesn't work out, either side can terminate it with a week's notice.

A job outside the home
If arrangements of this kind aren't possible, your teenager may ask if she can take a weekend or evening job outside the home. In principle there's nothing wrong with this. Having her own money gives her more independence, and more experience in money management. It also gives her a chance to meet new people, and to see how those perhaps less fortunate than she is have to earn their livings. But if the job interferes with her school work, then you may have to think twice about it. Work out with her the exact nature of the commitment she's taking on, and whether it will leave enough time (and energy) for her studies. See how much travelling it involves, and whether it's going to be possible for her to get there and back in good time. Satisfy yourself that the job is suitable too. Is she going to be mixing with desirable company and, in the case of a girl, is she going to be free from harassment? Last but not least, look at the commitment it's going to demand of you. Will you have to get your child up at some unearthly hour at the weekend, or will you have to be

responsible for taking her to and from work? Are you able to handle these commitments?

If you feel all the indicators are positive, then certainly let your child take the job. But, again like an unwritten contract, make sure you both know and accept what is going to be demanded of you. If your child has to get up early and you need to sleep on, make it clear that getting up is going to be her own responsibility. If you're prepared to fetch her from work, make sure this is going to be a priority and that you won't let her down when other commitments come along. Agree on everything clearly and in advance, so that things go smoothly once the job starts. Agree also on the conditions under which it will be necessary to give up the job (too tiring, hints of exploitation, etc.), and satisfy yourself that your child is going to stick to them.

The untidy adolescent

Amusingly (or not as the case may be!) the single most frequent conflict parents have in their relationship with an adolescent son or daughter is over tidiness. 'She drives me mad,' says a parent, 'her room is always in such a *mess*,' or 'He *will* leave his clobber all over the house' or 'I've told him a thousand times not to leave his books all over the dining room table.' And so the complaints go on, with parents angry, resentful and baffled by turns. Surely it's easy enough to put things away when you've finished with them? Surely it makes them easier to find when you want them? Why doesn't the adolescent *see* this? Why does he *persist* in turning the place into a junk heap? Is he doing it just out of defiance? I've even had parents confess that their marriage was threatened by their teenage daughter's untidiness because they rowed continually over how to deal with her.

The situation is often made worse by the fact that the untidiness stretches to clothes and dirty linen. 'She *won't* put her dirty washing in the clothes basket,' says a parent, 'and then she blames *me* when things aren't washed when she wants them,' or 'He had to wear his muddy rugger kit because he'd forgotten to give it to me after the last match, and wasn't he *mad*!' Odd how quickly we forget that we were much the same at that age. 'Yes but my mother used to *make* me be tidy,' says a parent. Did she? Memory plays tricks. She probably did her best, and you recall the few occasions when she won. But the other times are conveniently forgotten!

If you really feel that tidiness is vital, and that dirty washing must always go in the clothes basket, then have a strict daily routine. It's no use waiting until the debris and washing pile up and then having a showdown. Have a regular routine, so that a few minutes are spent tidying at a set time each day and everyone puts their dirty clothes in the basket when they get undressed at night. Things still won't be easy, and there'll still be battles, but you stand a fair chance of success.

What about sanctions for untidiness? Sometimes parents ask me whether, as a sanction, they should stop pocket money if the tidying doesn't get done. My answer is to remind them that all punishments are *much* more effective if they're related in some specific way to the offence which is being punished (see Chapter 6). Punishment which is unrelated to the 'crime' only breeds resentment and is hard to sustain. If you stop pocket money this week are you going to stop it again next week and the week after and the week after that if the behaviour doesn't improve? Few parents really want this kind of running battle. The argument that surely it'll soon make the child see sense doesn't work. Adolescent stubbornness sees to that.

No, the only appropriate punishment is the law of natural consequences. If the dirty clothes are not put in the basket they don't get washed. Full stop. If they're left in a heap on the floor they stay in a heap on the floor, and if people tread on them, so much the worse. This means riding out the temper tantrums when the adolescent finds things aren't there, neatly washed and ironed, when they're needed, but that's his affair. However much he rants at you, he has enough understanding of fair play to know it's his own fault. (Though even when we know we're in the wrong it's human nature to cast around for someone else to blame, or at the very least to blame them for *letting* us be in the wrong!)

Is constant nagging really worth it? But if you don't feel *that* strongly about tidiness, review what's going on. Parents tell me they spend what seems like hours nagging their teenager each week (and hours feeling upset about it) over dirty linen which would take them two or three minutes to pick up and put in the basket themselves. It's a strange kind of arrangement. And the arguments that 'It's the principle of the thing' and 'I won't be treated as a doormat' are strange too, since the hours of nagging fail to produce results anyway. And there's another issue. With his growing need for independence and freedom the teenager more and more needs some space in the house which is *his*. Not space which is on loan to him and which can be invaded and rearranged by his parents whenever they feel like it, but a room which is really *his*. A room which he can turn into an obstacle course if he wishes. A room which no one else is going to tidy for him, but which no one else is going to make him tidy either.

Parents say, 'Yes that's fine, but I can't get in there to *clean* if the floor is covered with clutter.' All right, you can't get in there to clean. But if your teenager has been brought up to see that cleaning is something we do because it makes for a pleasant environment, then every so often he'll have a go at his room of his own accord. The same with tidiness. When things reach a certain point he'll see how inconvenient untidiness is for him. Sure the room will be as bad again in a few days, but he's learning bit by bit how to order and control his own environment. Interestingly, there's no particular relationship in young students away from home for the first time between how tidy they now keep their room and how tidy their parents tried to make them at home. In fact some students from very tidy homes go to the opposite extreme, living in cheerful chaos for the sheer joy of it. **His own bedroom**

Of course, you can't let him be that untidy in the rest of the house. The rest of the house is everyone's space, and there has to be consideration and co-operation. But he does have *some* rights to this space. To deny him these rights now that he's nearing adult life is to treat him as a lodger rather than a member of the family. Most of us like to leave a reasonable amount of clutter around. It shows we can relax in our own home. The home is there for us, and not the other way around. If the clutter becomes unreasonable, ask him to clear it away, but make a joke out of it. Far better to say 'What an untidy family *we* are' and to clear some of your own mess away at the same time he's asked to clear away his, than to take a 'look-how-tidy-I-am-and-what-a-pity-you-can't-be-more-like-me' attitude. Perfect people are all very well in their way, but they're awfully hard to live with. **The rest of the house**

As for the dirty linen, if you're going to do the washing and

And finally the dirty washing
the ironing anyway, picking up a few clothes from the floor adds almost nothing to the job. If you resent the idea, okay, let them lie and use the law of natural consequences. But looked at objectively, it demands little of you and it helps your teenager. We're only doormats over jobs like this if we make a great labour out of them. Far better to see it as good parenting. Tell your teenager it makes your job easier if he puts his dirty things in the basket. This encourages him to see he's doing it to help you, not because it's an arbitrary rule. But if he forgets, do it yourself without comment. Parents who try this find that in no time they're doing it less and less. Their teenager miraculously begins to 'remember' to do the job himself. He appreciates the fact that you're not making a big issue out of it, and that you make sure he has his clothes when he needs them. In turn he repays your kindness by co-operating. He sees you aren't forcing him to order his life in just the way you want it, and in consequence he's happy enough voluntarily to go along with you. The partnership is beginning to work.

Invading his space

Before we leave the subject of space, let me refer to a problem that taxes many parents. If you're in your son or daughter's room, and you find something obviously not meant for your eyes, what do you do? If it's a sex magazine, or an alcoholic drink, or what you consider to be an over-ardent love letter (should you be reading it anyway?), some parents say with great indignation that they burn them or flush them down the loo or throw them away, and then say nothing about them. Not surprisingly, the adolescent says nothing about them either. But this strategy is wrong for two reasons. First because, like it or not, the room belongs to the teenager and so does the property. In behind the embarrassment she is bound to feel hostile towards you and very much invaded. We can't draw an exact analogy, but the feeling isn't unlike the psychological shock you or I would feel if we had our homes broken into and something we prized stolen from us. Your child will also feel bad because although she suspects you of taking whatever it is you've taken, she can't talk to you about it. There will always be this unspoken question mark in your relationship with each other.

The second reason why confiscation of this kind is wrong is that it won't stop your child from reading sex magazines or receiving over-ardent love letters. It will simply make her more careful to hide them properly next time. This is such an obvious point that you may wonder why some parents adopt this tack. The answer is that firstly they're embarrassed at talking about their discovery to their child, and secondly they feel rather guilty at having found it at all. They know they shouldn't really be poking around in their child's room and they take the easy way out by drawing a veil over the matter.

If you do find something not meant for your eyes in your child's possession you may decide on reflection there's no real harm in it, and that it's best to leave it where it is and say nothing. But if you're worried by it, raise the matter with her, however difficult this seems. Try not to make it into a confrontation: 'Come into the lounge I want to talk to you. Now shut the door. Now look (dramatic flourish) at what I found in your room. I was so *ashamed* to find you with something like this. How sly can you get?' This is almost as effective a way of getting her to hide the evidence more carefully next time as flushing it down the loo. Instead, be open and low key about it: 'I was surprised to find this in your room today', and remember that when we were adolescents we most of us looked at sex magazines and wrote or received the occasional love letter (if we were lucky!). So it's part of growing up. And you've far more chance of influencing her future behaviour in the right direction if you show yourself not to be shocked but able to talk about things openly and sensibly.

Speak to your child if you're worried by what you find

Of course, if you discover drugs in her room, then the matter is altogether more serious, and you will want to take the kind of action I discuss later in the chapter.

Sometimes she carries her space around with her

Sometimes there's a rather more subtle issue involved in invading 'her' space. Parents will often notice that when they enter the lounge or one of the other shared rooms in the house, their teenager gets up after a minute or two and leaves. They're puzzled why this happens. There are no bad feelings to explain it, and when it's happened frequently enough to be beyond coincidence, they feel hurt by the idea that perhaps their teenager just doesn't like the sight of them. The reality is much less sinister. A teenager goes through this phase partly because she is discovering the pleasure of her own company and partly because, however much she loves her parents, their presence reminds her of being a child. Seeking her adult identity, there are times when she just doesn't want to be reminded of the fact that childhood is so recent and is still (in a way) with her. She doesn't really want to get away from her parents, but her need for independence is growing strongly, and she just feels more grown-up when she's on her own or with her friends than when she's with her parents.

In some cases, an additional reason is that parents don't always notice her need for silence and to be busy with her own thoughts. The entry of a parent into the room usually means that in a moment they'll start talking to her and expecting answers. If she prefers to stay with her train of thought, the only way to do so is to find another room in the house where she can be on her own.

Don't make an issue out of it   If your teenager goes through this phase of carrying her space around with her, and not wanting it invaded by you, let it pass without comment. If you start accusing her of not wanting to have you around, you only turn a minor matter into a big issue. Adolescents are never that sure about their own feelings, and love, irritation, friendliness and coolness often follow each other in quick succession in their relationships with the adults in their lives. By fastening on to her withdrawals or other signs of apparent coolness towards you and demanding she explain them, you risk making your adolescent attach far more importance to them than they really merit. You risk making her question whether she really *does* love you after all. Previously she's taken this for granted, but if you doubt it, then maybe this means she ought to doubt it too. The resultant confusion in her mind is only likely to lead to more withdrawals and more coolness. She now feels that every time you look at her you're assessing whether she loves you or not, and not surprisingly she doesn't enjoy the experience.

Leave her to grow out of this phase on her own. As she becomes more sure of herself and more confident in her adult status, so this kind of behaviour will become a thing of the past. But if you are a great talker, help things along by recognizing that she does have a right to her silences and her own thoughts, and to carry that little bit of space around with her if that's what she wants.

Getting him up in the morning

One of the big discoveries in life an adolescent makes is the pleasure of staying in bed. Up to now, particularly at weekends when you want an extra lie-in yourself, the problem has been to get him to stay in his room and keep quiet. Now, all of a sudden, come lunchtime and all you see of him is a dormant hulk under the bedclothes. This change of outlook is caused partly by the fact that the adolescent is developing quickly and needs his sleep, and partly by the fact that he now goes to bed much later. But it also seems to be due to a decline in the boundless energy, the desire to get up and meet the world, that we find in childhood. Lacking as yet the stamina of the adult, the adolescent does seem to need his weekend lie-in if he's to function properly.

Let him have his weekend lie-in

Most parents don't worry about it, but some resent the feeling that they are up and doing while able-bodied youngsters are snoozing away upstairs. But if he *has* to get up the adolescent can usually manage it as well as anyone else, and if his habits don't change of their own accord, they will when he starts work or when he's married and has young children rousting him out at the crack of dawn.

However, don't take over the responsibility for getting him up when *he* has an early appointment. As with all matters of time-keeping, from getting young children off to school to getting adolescents off to their first jobs, the law of natural consequences is a vital one. If you take all the responsibility on yourself, and protect your children from the consequences of being late, then they'll leave it all to you. 'Let Mum call a few more times. She'll see to it I get there on time.' Poor old Mum (or Dad). She's making a rod for her own back. Instead, call a child. Make sure he's heard and that he knows what the time is. If he's in bed, make sure he's properly roused and isn't going to slide back into sleep. Then let him keep to time himself. If he makes himself late, he'll soon find out how unpleasant this is.

Don't take responsibility for getting him up in time

He wants to be treated like a responsible person, so he must act like one. He can't just sit back and decide for himself what responsibilities he takes on board and what responsibilities he leaves to you. If he wants to be grown-up, that means taking a little of the rough along with the smooth. Unlike tidiness, where a little judicial clearing up after him isn't out of place (since the tidiness is your choice and not his), getting out of bed and being punctual is *his* choice if he's going to avoid unpleasant consequences. And he has to be left to take the responsibilities that go with that choice.

Getting him in at night

Another major area of conflict which parents regularly report is getting their adolescents in at a reasonable time in the evenings. Parents worry more about their daughters than their sons, which makes sense in that girls are physically more vulnerable than boys, but which can look rather unfair to the girls themselves.

Staying out late is a sign of independence to the adolescent. She likes the feeling that she is old enough now to come and go as she pleases. But whether she likes it or not, she isn't an adult yet. She still has a great deal to learn. Other people (particularly in the case of girls) may take advantage of this lack of sophistication. And when a group of teenagers get together, the behaviour of the group is often very different from the way individuals would behave on their own. There are strong pressures to keep up with everyone else, not to be left out, to show you're as daring as the next person. Of course, if things are going to go wrong, they don't only go wrong when people stay out late. But obviously parties, where drink is available and where everyone is set upon having a good time, present a particular risk.

You can't protect your teenage children from everything

The first thing I stress with parents when talking about late nights out is that you can't protect your growing youngsters from everything. They can leave home at sixteen if they wish. At eighteen they're of age, and many of them will be off to colleges and universities, where since they're legally adults the college authorities have little or no control over their private lives. If you've done the spade work in the earlier years, your teenage son or daughter will have a maturing outlook on life and a good sense of personal responsibility. He or she should behave sensibly because that's how they want to behave, and not because they have someone behind them still watching their every move and telling them what to do. They should have sound judgement, and should be able to look ahead and see the consequences of their actions.

So the time is now coming when you're going to have to start trusting your adolescent to behave intelligently. More of her life is lived outside the home. She's preparing to leave the nest. If her relationship with you is a good one, she'll still listen to you and value your advice, but your direct influence over her is decreasing, and you should be able to stand back a little and watch her begin to make her own way in the world.

The second thing I stress is that it isn't so much the staying out late that matters, it's *where she is and who she's with*. You don't want to pry into her affairs all the time, but if you've been open with her about your own life in the earlier years, she won't resent your showing an equivalent interest in her doings now. Don't submit her to an inquisition, either before she goes out or when she comes back. The chances are she'll volunteer the information you want if you allow her to do it in her own time and in her own way. But do be sure you know where she's going and who she'll be with. A question such as 'Going somewhere nice?' is more likely to get a proper answer than 'Where are you going?'. The same applies to 'Did you have fun?' as opposed to 'What did you do?'. Similarly when asking about her friends and what they're going to do it's better to say 'Will John and Susan be there?' rather than 'Who's going to be there?', 'Will you be playing records?' rather than 'What are you going to do?'. Blunt questions make people clam up. They give folk the feeling you're suspicious of them or that they've no right to be going out and enjoying themselves. Interested, more casual, questions, on the other hand, make people much more inclined to share things with you. Realistically no teenager, son or daughter, is going to tell you everything about themselves. From early childhood onwards, youngsters like having their little secrets because secrets give them a feeling of independence. They know something the grown-ups don't know. They've got a part of their lives which they can keep to themselves. In adolescence, this process continues, and the more an adolescent sees you're

What matters is who she's with and where

desperate to know all the details of her life, the more maddeningly uncommunicative she'll become.

Negotiate a time for coming home

Once you know where your adolescent is going we come to the third point, namely what time must she be home. I stress here with parents that a *negotiated* time is much more likely to be kept to than an *imposed* time. Ask your teenager what time she thinks it would be reasonable to come home, then find a compromise that's agreeable to you both. Now that you've reached it, make it clear that you trust her to keep to it. If after all this she is in late, listen to her reasons. They could be convincing. Take a reasonable view, while stressing that you really do expect her to organize herself properly and keep to an agreed time. If there are good reasons why she couldn't be home when expected, then a telephone call would have put you in the picture and stopped any anxiety.

At this point it is fair to explain to your teenager that parents do worry about their children. Maybe the youngsters feel this is unnecessary, but that's the way parents are, and the way she'll be one day herself when she has children. When she has her co-operation enlisted in this way, she'll see that letting you know she can't be back home at the agreed time is an act of thoughtfulness on her part rather than an act of duty.

Using this approach, there are unlikely to be any real problems about time-keeping. But should they arise, be firm. She's been given a chance to show she can be responsible, and isn't up to it yet. One more late homecoming, and she stays in for the next week. As with getting up on time in the morning, if an adolescent wants to take on adult responsibilities, then she must show she's ready for them. But in this and other matters, don't make the mistake of lecturing your adolescent about the *need* for responsibility without giving her the *opportunity* for this responsibility. If your adolescent sees you trust her and have confidence in her, then she's likely to live up to your trust.

The accident-prone teenager

Most teenagers are clumsy, because as mentioned earlier in the chapter they take time to adjust to the rapid growth that seems to lengthen their arms and legs almost overnight. But being accident-prone is more than just ordinary clumsiness. The accident-prone teenager (and accident-prone behaviour can start in the pre-teens) seems to be involved in an endless series of mishaps, causing damage to the environment and (often principally) to himself. Such behaviour often goes with a carelessness of attitude that maddens parents and teachers alike. The teenager appears to have scant concern for the safety of self or possessions, sometimes even deliberately disregarding the most elementary precautions.

The first thing to say about accident-proneness is that there seems to be a temperamental factor at work. Accident-prone behaviour is rarely if ever seen in individuals with anxious or rather tense natures. It's also rarely seen in those who are restrained and over-controlled in their behaviour and is less common (though by no means absent) in those with high intelligence. It occurs mainly in those who are physically active and rather haphazard by nature, and who appear less aware of the perils of the environment than others. They often also have a high pain threshold, and feel the physical bumps and bruises of everyday life less keenly than most of us.

Accident-proneness may be to do with temperament

But there's sometimes more to it than this. Some accident-prone individuals have an actual *disregard* for their own safety, which stems from an inability to care about themselves and which often goes with low self-esteem (see Chapter 7). Low self-esteem manifests itself in a number of different ways, depending upon an individual's temperament. Where the conditions are right it shows up as a couldn't-care-less attitude towards one's own well-being (a point returned to when drug-taking is discussed in due course).

Or it may stem from a lack of self-esteem

If your teenager is accident-prone, check whether this is an expression of a generally negative attitude towards himself or nothing more than a rather slap-dash approach to life. If it's the latter, your job is simply to help him be more aware of the need for safety and restraint in the way he tackles things. If it's the former, what's lacking is a respect for himself and for his body. We rarely damage the things we prize. The more he likes himself, the more care he'll take over himself. Look back at the earlier section on self-esteem and self-acceptance, and identify why he hasn't more regard for himself. Adolescence is a crucial time for the development of an adult sense of identity, and if your child has rather missed out (perhaps through a relative sense of failure at school) on the lessons of self-worth, now is a good time to remedy this. With support and encouragement, he can be helped to see himself as a valuable and valued human being, someone who deserves proper cherishing and consideration.

The risk-taker

Though the two don't necessarily go together, accident-proneness is sometimes linked with a liking for risk and excitement. More usually, though, the risk-taker has a clear grasp of the chances he's taking, and deliberately chooses them for the 'kicks' involved. Most children can be daring at times, and in young boys this is sometimes seen as a badge of manhood. But once manhood (or womanhood) is actually achieved, daring deeds are usually superseded by a more sober and realistic attitude to life, or confined to formal risk areas like sport and job hunting. Adolescence is a crucial period in this change-over from daring to responsible living. As I've said several times, much of an adolescent's behaviour is expermental, a process of trying out the adult he is now becoming. And with the freedom and the heightened emotionality of adolescence, the teenager looks for thrills and new experiences. But this is less risk-taking for its own sake than the desire to try out new interests to exercise his new-found independence and generally to taste adult life.

Risk-taking for its own sake comes from a positive liking for the flow of adrenalin and nor-adrenalin that comes from staking something you value against the possibility of gain or loss. It's seen for example in the committed gambler (more about gambling in a moment) or in the person who chooses actively dangerous pastimes like motor sport, and who confesses to positive enjoyment of the feeling of fear in the veins and the realization that fortune or life itself is being put on the line.

Risk-taking for its own sake occurs in sensation-seekers Risk-taking of this kind occurs in people whom psychologists describe as sensation-seekers. As in accident-proneness, there's a temperamental factor at work here. Sensation-seekers are usually people who have difficulty in arousing the autonomic nervous system. Without being technical about it, the autonomic nervous system is that part of us that handles the automatic processes in the body such as the rise and fall of emotions (as opposed to the central nervous system which handles our conscious processes). It's the autonomic nervous system that produces the thrill we call excitement, and the butterflies we call fear – two sensations, incidentally, which aren't that different from each other, and which both have to do with the release of the adrenalin and nor-adrenalin mentioned above. In sensation-seekers, it takes more to get the autonomic nervous system going. The result is that an experience that would be felt as frightening and unpleasant by a person with an easily aroused autonomic nervous system is felt as no more than a pleasant tingle by the sensation-seeker. So he pushes himself further and faster in his search for thrills, often only feeling fully alive when he's courting real danger of some kind.

As I've said before, you can't readily change a person's temperament, which is linked to inherited biological factors. A sensation-seeker can't easily stop being a sensation-seeker. In any case, sensation-seeking isn't necessarily bad in itself. But what you can do is help him to live with his sensation-seeking, and be more realistic over exposure to risks. It's important for a risk-taker to understand his own nature, and to see why it is that he chooses risks when others opt for safety. If he appreciates the temperamental mechanisms that are at work he's able to be more objective about himself and his behaviour, and to channel it into activities with acceptable risk levels. He's also able to appreciate that being a sensation-seeker doesn't mean one has to be dominated by sensation-seeking. There is more to life than the kicks provided by a dose of adrenalin in the veins.

Help a risk-taker to keep risks to acceptable levels

Gambling

I've already mentioned that risk-taking can show up in a liking for gambling. Not the occasional flutter, but a deep attraction that amounts virtually to an addiction. Whether it's fruit machines, cards, dogs or horses, the confirmed gambler can't resist his addiction; in adult life as much damage is done to families by gambling as by more recognized social evils like alcoholism.

Parental example is the best preventive

As with alcoholism, the best preventive in young people is parental example. One may be a sensation-seeker by nature, but gambling is very definitely a learnt piece of behaviour. Many sensation-seekers never go near it, while sometimes even those who are not sensation-seekers allow themselves to become hooked. Children who learn from an early age that in gambling the odds are almost always heavily stacked against the individual usually grow up with much better ideas on how to spend their money. They also grow up with a healthy reluctance to relieve other people of money, even when the odds work in their own favour. Reluctant to lose their own money, they sympathize sufficently with the loser not to want to take his money either.

It's true that many adolescents, even with good parental example, experiment a little with gambling (a few coins with their friends over cards, a skirmish with the fruit machine), but they usually discover they don't much enjoy it, and are happy to turn to wiser pastimes. Without this example, though, it's all too easy to become committed. Gambling is endemic in society, and the participation in it of prestige figures from pop stars to politicians seems positively to encourage the young. In adolescence, it's mostly sensation-seeking and the desire to be grown-up and emulate these idols that prompts gambling, though the belief in one's own skill and the hope of getting something for nothing (big factors in many adult gamblers) also begin to play a part. Should the adolescent get into debt over gambling, there's also the hope that one big win will put things to rights, 'And after that I'll stop'.

Never give your adolescent money to gamble

If you do find your adolescent getting the gambling habit, never give him money to feed it. Some parents say this prompts the adolescent to help himself from their purse or wallet, but this happens only in a very small minority of cases, where gambling is already a hardened habit. Most adolescents are a long way from allowing gambling to override their moral values, and for them there's no doubt that *opportunity* is needed before they can be dragged in deeper. Do away with the opportunity, and the gambling doesn't get beyond the relatively harmless experimental phase. Opportunity requires money, and if the adolescent only has enough for his more important needs, good sense usually prevails and he leaves others to do the losing. A respect for the value of money, learnt through parental teaching and the careful handling of pocket money in earlier years, is obviously of great help here, as is the possession of long-term goals and the readiness to save for the future.

For the (thankfully rare) inveterate sensation-seeker, who finds it well-nigh impossible to resist the lure of gambling, the best advice is to focus on areas which (a) depend upon skill not just on luck and (b) which allow you to place clear limits on your losses. A time-lag between the placing of money and the achievement of results plays a big part in the second of these two. The problems with gambling on cards or horses or dogs or fruit machines is that the gambler gets sucked in deeper and deeper while still in the excitement of the moment. He may promise himself he'll only stake so much money and then stop if he loses it, but once the adrenalin starts to flow this becomes harder and harder to do. A time-lag between hazarding one's money and finding out what happens to it throttles back on some of the excitement, and allows calmer decisions on how much can be risked and in what way.

Channel the inveterate gambler into the least harmful forms

Forms of gambling which allow for skill, loss limits and time-lag are football pools and the world stock markets. I'm not writing in favour of either of these. Fortunes can be lost by the unwary (or greedy) on both. But if you have an adolescent who is clearly itching to lose his money, try to channel him towards these or similar, rather than let him feed his habit with the adrenalin of more instant forms of gaming. The more the adrenalin flows, the more the gambler craves for a repetition of his excitement, whatever the cost. For some sensation-seekers, adrenalin acts very like a drug, with many of the same symptoms of addiction and many of the same pains of withdrawal. As with a drug, the answer is to take sensible avoiding action before the habit becomes fully established.

Overweight

Less dramatic than anorexia or bulimia, (discussed later) overweight is in its way almost as serious a problem. We have a tendency in the West to believe that it's natural to go on

653

gaining weight as we grow older, reaching a peak in later middle age. But studies of less affluent (and healthier) societies show that nature intended us to reach a peak in body weight around the mid-twenties, and then show a slight but steady decline as we grow older and metabolism and physical activity slow down. Studies of these societies also show us that the 'puppy fat' of many adolescents isn't natural either. We shouldn't carry any more fat in adolescence that we do in childhood. The broadening of the hips in girls and of the shoulders in boys is caused by changes in the underlying bone structure rather than in the contours of the body itself.

So adolescents should, in general, be developing the physique that they will carry through adult life. They should also be developing the respect for their own body and for their health that prompts them to keep fit and avoid unwanted inches. The sensible eating habits that you will have been teaching them from childhood are invaluable, but if your adolescent son or daughter has a tendency to overweight, now is the time to help them take effective action. Discussion of the right and wrong foods to choose in dieting lies outside the scope of this book, but the psychology behind successful dieting is very much my concern. Why is it some adolescents (and adults) diet successfully, while others find it well-nigh impossible?

Set realistic targets for weight loss Putting it all down to will-power is much too simple, because it doesn't explain what will-power *is* and how to develop it. It's much more accurate to say that the successful dieter is the person who *really wants* to be slim, the person who knows how to *play to her own strengths and avoid her own weaknesses*. Most overweight adolescents want to be slim, but need help in *really* wanting to. This help can be given in the form of setting specific slimming goals. For example, a much-coveted item of clothing can be bought for them, but one size too small and on the clear agreement that they can wear it as soon as they can get into it comfortably. If the garment is to be worn at a party a few weeks hence, or taken on holiday later in the year, this increases the sense of a definite and very desirable goal. Another example is our friend the wall-chart. Definite (and realistic) targets for weight loss can be set out on the chart, with specific rewards promised as each target is achieved. Photographs can also help, with the teenager photographed in the same clothes and in the same place at set intervals, so that she can see clearly how much better she looks now that the inches are coming off. Needless to say, all these strategies should be used with the full agreement of the teenager, and if she can think up her own strategies, so much the better.

Co-operation of this kind is even more essential when it comes to playing to one's own strengths and weaknesses. It's no good setting targets or introducing a slimming regime that's way beyond the capacity of the teenager to maintain. Targets and regime should be strict enough to show visible benefits over a reasonably short period, but lenient enough to be adhered to without too much hardship.

The word 'diet', with its negative associations, should be avoided (use a term that stresses positive things like beauty or health), leaving two enemies to be dealt with, hunger and boredom. Sensibly planned, a slimming regime should easily avoid both of these, though it does make rather more demands upon the time and ingenuity of the cook. The hungry slimmer and the bored slimmer are unlikely to remain slimmers for long, and since someone inclined to put on weight is going to have to watch their eating throughout life, now is the time to convince your teenager that slimming foods can be just as satisfying and just as much fun as fattening ones.

The slimming regime must avoid hunger and boredom

Equally important, don't tempt the slimmer by keeping a pantry full of fattening foods in the house, and don't torment her by eating mountains of wrong but appetizing meals under her nose every mealtime. If the rest of the family can eat sensibly along with her, this will both help her and do them a power of good at the same time. It also avoids the charge so dear to teenagers that 'It's all very well for *you* to talk'. And if either or both parents are overweight, the good example they set to their offspring by shedding pounds themselves is a powerful additional boost.

Smoking

There are far more deaths every year from smoking-related diseases than there are from all other forms of drug-taking put together. And smoking *is* drug-taking, whether we like it or not. If tobacco were introduced into the world for the first time today it would, like alcohol, stand no chance of being legalized. It's far too dangerous and far too addictive. Addictive both physically and psychologically, and leading to withdrawal symptoms almost as bad as those for more vilified drugs.

The best advice is not to start The best advice for smokers is not to start. Once you start, you're going to have problems breaking the habit. I'm always surprised at how unaware of this fact most young smokers are. And how unaware they are of the speed with which nicotine addiction builds up. Almost from the first few puffs the smoker begins to enjoy the habit, and a few packets later he's hooked. I'm also surprised at how light-heartedly young smokers minimize the risks to health. With great bravado they talk of 'having to die of something one day' or 'running more risk crossing the road'. The appalling suffering produced by nicotine-related illnesses is largely ignored.

Figures show that children are much less likely to smoke if they are brought up in a family of non-smokers. Parental example, as with alcohol and pill popping, seems to be the single most important factor. And research shows that if you're not a smoker by twenty, you're unlikely to start. In addition to your good example, point out to your children when they're small and impressionable and learning quickly about the world that cigarette smoking stains the lungs the same unpleasant colour as the fingers. Most children are very put off by this thought. They're in the process of discovering their bodies and getting to like and respect them, and the thought of abusing their lungs is an unattractive one. Point out as well the shortness of breath, the coughing, and the bronchitis suffered by cigarette smokers. As your children grow older, talk to them about the even more serious health hazards, such as heart disease, circulation problems so grave they can lead to limb amputations, and of course lung cancer. Don't terrify them, but don't pull any punches either. These are facts of life, and children have the right to know them. Then emphasize how much money the smoker is wasting. Help your child to work out on a piece of paper how much the average smoker is burning each year, and make a list of the sort of things he could buy with that money.

If in spite of this you find your child, either before or into adolescence, with cigarettes or in the process of having an experimental puff, it's of much more value if you can get him to destroy the things himself than if you confiscate them. After you've talked to him and reminded him of the dangers of smoking, ask him what he's now going to do with his cigarettes. If you've done your job well, he'll volunteer to throw them in the bin or in the fire. Praise him for this sensible decision. The act of destroying the cigarettes is an act of commitment on his part, and will work against his buying more in the future. You can also give him the price of the packet of cigarettes, as a token of your admiration of his good sense, but this isn't really necessary.

If you do find your child smoking

If he starts smoking when he's older and is earning his own money, and if he resists your reasoned approach, should you actually try to forbid him? Some parents insist on no smoking in the house, but this doesn't really get to the root of the problem. You're spared the sight and smell of cigarettes and the risks to your own health from inhaling his smoke, but he'll only smoke all the more when he's out, and will spend more time out of the house in order to indulge his habit. My advice is not to lay down a rigid law or turn things into a battle. Once he's hooked on smoking, it's an addiction like any other. Before long, he'll wish he hadn't started, and it's better that the habit should remain a matter for debate and discussion within the home, with you showing you want to help him break free of it. This may mean asking him to confine his smoking to one room while you and he tackle the problem.

A good start is to get him to make a list of the reasons why he smokes, and then compare it with a list of all the benefits that come from stopping. This enables him to weigh up the pros and cons of smoking, and see for himself where the advantage lies. Another valuable exercise is to list the situations that trigger off the urge to smoke. Drinking a cup of coffee, for example, meeting a particular friend, anxious feelings about something or other, the sight of a tobacconist's shop, a prestige figure with a cigarette in his mouth and so on. Once he identifies the behaviour patterns that lead to smoking he's now ready for them when they occur, and better able to resist the trigger effect. Some of the situations he can try avoiding altogether, while for the unavoidable ones he can

Get him to list the reasons why he smokes and the trigger situations

657

arm himself with alternative oral satisfiers such as packets of nuts and raisins or sunflower seeds. Another strategy is to distract himself each time he's in a trigger situation. One way shown by research studies to be effective with many people is to look for objects around you and name them to yourself ('I can see a clock, I can see a table, I can see a light bulb', etc.). By the time you've named twelve objects, the craving will usually have subsided.

Or use the financial approach Different approaches work with different people, so a certain amount of experimentation is helpful, but the smoker should always stay with one method long enough to give it a fair trial. If your adolescent isn't keen on working with trigger situations, the financial approach may be more appropriate. You agree with him that if he banks the money he saves each day by going without smoking, you'll double it when it reaches a certain sum, so that he can buy something he very much wants. This is a form of performance contract, and both parties enter a firm agreement to stick to their side of the bargain.

If he finds it hard to plan far ahead, he can watch his money grow day by day. A wall-chart is a good idea, with a target sum of money shown at the top against a picture of whatever it is he wants to buy. Each day he goes without smoking the money is put away and shown on the wall-chart. Some folk dismiss the wall-chart as kids' stuff, but even adults find it of value, particularly if they also have to mark in, for all to see, any days they gave in to their habit and failed to put money aside.

Other possible strategies Another approach is to start with the number he smokes each day, and then daily reduce by one, so that the habit is phased out over three weeks or so. A graph of progress, put up on the wall, is again a help. Useful also is the purchase of the usual packet of cigarettes each day, and its ritual incineration unopened. Each time the smoker sees his packet going up in flames he congratulates himself on his will-power, and after a few days of this decides he no longer wants to burn his money. A variant of this is to burn the money itself. If he proposes to spend £5 on cigarettes in the coming week, he burns a £5 note instead. Perhaps surprisingly this strategy quite appeals to smokers. It allows them to boast to their friends (quite legitimately) about their will-power, and once people have given up smoking using this method they have a strong vested interest in not starting again. Because if they do smoke during the week, they've 'sacrificed' their £5 in vain.

Whatever method the smoker uses to break his addiction, one major problem is that smoking is a social habit (back to trigger situations again). The smoker is offered cigarettes by his friends, and being smokers themselves most of them don't want him to succeed in giving up. His will-power in doing so reflects badly on them. There's also a calming ritual element in smoking. The smoker taps his pockets for his cigarettes and lighter, fishes them out, opens the packet, takes out a cigarette, lights it and sits back contentedly. So giving up smoking may involve avoiding friends who are smokers and finding another ritual, such as packets of nuts and raisins.

But for anyone with imagination and concern for their health a proper understanding of the medical arguments is the best method. **Stress the medical arguments** The connection between smoking and lung cancer and other respiratory diseases is too well known to need stressing. Less well known is the fact that the risk of heart attack is three times greater in smokers than non-smokers, and five times greater in heavy smokers (two or more packs a day). Smoking is increasing in young girls, and they should be helped to look ahead to the risks that occur in pregnancy. In addition to the higher foetal mortality and lower birth-weight of the babies of smokers, there is worrying evidence that childhood cancers, particularly leukemias, are more prevalent in children born to smokers. Cancer-causing chemicals present in cigarette smoke enter the mother's bloodstream and cross the placenta into the baby's blood, leading to the risk of genetic damage and future cancers. Disturbingly, the UK estimate is that one woman in three smokes regularly during pregnancy, with the risks to the unborn child increasing steadily the more she smokes. Even inhaling the smoke from other people's cigarettes in pregnancy significantly increases the risks to the unborn child.

Smokers don't necessarily have the self-destructive tendency and the low self-esteem often seen in the other drug addicts we shall be discussing, but many of them do have a disregard for themselves which isn't that dissimilar. If your child smokes, ask yourself whether he comes into this category. Or is he perhaps an extrovert character who has got in with a crowd of friends who all smoke? Or perhaps he's smoking because he's tense and anxious? (Nicotine is a depressant and does have a calming effect.) Whatever the reason, it helps if it can be identified so that you can see what you're up against.

Your daughter and sexual harassment

In addition to other concerns over sexual relationships, your teenage daughter will need guidance over dealing with unwanted attention from males. This attention can come in many different shapes and forms, but the sensible guidelines for handling it remain the same. Let's summarize them in the form in which you can present them to her.

- **Don't** encourage this attention in the first place. Many males imagine that a woman is sending them sexual invitations when in fact she's only showing normal social friendship. Be aware of how easily males can delude themselves, and how insensitive they often are to a woman's real motives and feelings.
- **Don't** use sexuality as a way of getting something you want from a man, however innocent the sexuality may be. Your sexuality will quickly be misinterpreted as one of the invitations referred to above.
- **Don't** be too easily flattered by male attention. Having attractive males dancing attendance may be good for a girl's ego, but rest assured that at least some amongst them will expect a 'return' on their investment.
- **Don't** agree to a relationship with a man just because he's persistent or you feel sorry for him. Many girls find it hard to assert themselves with men, and many find it hard to deny their natural feelings of sympathy. But relationships are much easier to start than to finish and, once embarked upon, a girl may find herself being forced or persuaded to go much further than she intended.
- **Do** appreciate how easily the male sexual urge is aroused. More immediate than that of the female (if often more superficial), even the best-intentioned of males sometimes find their sex urge difficult to cope with, and may act in ways that, when they return to their senses, they bitterly regret.

- **Do** be fully aware of the effects of alcohol upon social and sexual inhibitions. Under the influence of a few drinks, everyone is liable to act out of character, males and females.

- **Do** be prepared to complain. Sexual harassment can take many forms, from simple touching and fondling to actual sexual assault, from dirty jokes and risqué stories to outright verbal propositions. No woman should have to put up with any of this if she finds it offensive. If the males concerned don't respond to simple telling, then report them. Schools have recognized pastoral procedures for dealing with sexual harassment, and so increasingly do offices and businesses. Many males smugly kid themselves that all women really enjoy sexual overtures, even though they 'pretend' not to. Such males need to be rapidly and effectively disillusioned.

- **Do** avoid situations that may lend themselves to harassment. Being alone with a particular male for example. Or being invited to his house. A little foresight and planning can avoid all kinds of unpleasant situations. Many things which start innocently enough end up anything but.

- **Do** develop a set technique for discouraging unwanted advances. Many women confess to being taken by surprise and not knowing quite what to say when faced with unwanted sexual advances. The trick is to leave the importunate male in no doubt of your attitude right from the start. Act immediately, act with confidence and act with authority. A firm tone of voice is more important that the actual words used (these should be few in number and to the point – e.g. 'I thought you had more sense' or 'Act your age'), and a sudden physical action, like getting briskly to your feet, also disconcerts the would-be Romeo. If you feel unsure of yourself, don't show it. Speak and act as if you are used to these situations and used to being obeyed when you say no. Even if the advances come from a member of the family, make it clear that you're under no obligation to keep silent about them. Even if you like the person concerned, don't try to dissuade him with humour. Some girls are good at this, but all too often humour conveys the message that you don't really mean what you say, and that you're not averse to another advance.

You're not out to teach your daughter that there's something unpleasant about sex, or something invariably threatening about the male sexual urge. But you are trying to teach her that women are too often exploited by male sexuality, and that a woman has the right to make her own decisions about which men appeal to her and which men don't. You're also out to convince her that even men who appeal to her shouldn't always be taken at face value. Sadly, far too many girls are taken in by the unscrupulous.

One final point. Fathers have a very useful role to play in helping their daughters understand males and their motives. The stern father who forbade his daughter to speak to a young man is a thing of the past thank goodness, but fathers do know many of the strategies and wiles used by their sex in amorous adventures, and this 'insider' knowledge is invaluable.

If your adolescent child gets into real trouble

We all hope our children will avoid real trouble. But surveys show that by the time children are into their teens 60 per cent confess to having engaged in behaviour which is not only wrong but actually against the law. Usually this involves shoplifting, or stealing from classmates, or damaging property. For children brought up in inner cities, where the temptations are greater, the figure is higher than 60 per cent, and if we add in acts like taking money from parents or trespassing into neighbouring gardens and stealing apples then probably few children are completely blameless.

One of the worse nightmares any parent has is of a visit from the police intent upon interviewing their child for some offence which he's accused of committing. The usual parental response is one of disbelief. It can't possibly be my child who is to blame. He'd never do anything like that. When faced with irrefutable evidence the next response is usually a deep sense of shame, and an equivalent degree of anger against the child for letting down his parents so badly. These responses are understandable. We rightly expect better of our children. And we naturally feel, mixed in amongst our other emotions, a sense of personal guilt. We blame ourselves. Perhaps we've been too strict or not strict enough. Perhaps we've left the child too much to his own devices. Perhaps we haven't listened enough to him and taught him to discuss his life outside the home with us. Perhaps we should have explained things more fully to him. And so it goes on.

The best advice at such a worrying and distressing time is that what's done is done, and endless recriminations (and self-accusations) aren't going to help. Your child will already be aghast at the pain he's causing his parents, and he'll be frightened at what may now be going to happen to him. He'll remember this incident, clearly and in detail, for the rest of his life, and he'll remember in the same detail your reactions and the way you treated him. If you punish him severely, he'll carry the memory of that punishment. If you call him a thief or a liar, he'll carry that memory too. Maybe these bitter memories would be justified if they prevented a child from making the same mistakes in future, but there isn't much evidence they do. I know we've all heard stories of adults who confess they were given such a beating by their fathers for law-breaking in childhood that they've never transgressed again. But these stories aren't typical. More typical are those stories of adults who were treated like criminals after minor offences in their early days, and who felt excluded from decent society as a result. It takes great strength and persistence to re-establish yourself once you've been given a bad name, and many children find the task beyond them. The result is that they're often more, not less, likely to commit further offences in future. **Don't punish your adolescent too severely**

Sit down with your adolescent and find out exactly what went wrong and what needs to be done to ensure it won't happen again. As often as not you'll discover he was out with a rather irresponsible group who decided to climb into some-body's garden to steal apples, or into a builder's yard, or to do a bit of shop-lifting. Your child was teased or dared into joining them. Though he's in his teens, he still hasn't always the independence and courage to walk away from a group of friends when they're up to mischief. He joined them, and became one of the very small percentage of wrongdoers who actually get caught. **Talk to him about what's happened**

The fact that he *did* get caught is often an indication of his relative innocence. The really street-wise character is usually experienced enough to get away with it. Now he's been caught, the full stupidity of his actions has been brought home to him, and the regret and fear he's feeling as a consequence are in themselves going to teach him a valuable lesson. Go over this lesson with him and make sure it's sunk in. Whether he meant it or not, his *actions* were anti-social and dishonest, and they could get him into very serious trouble. Since he wouldn't have been so silly if he hadn't been in the company of that particular group of friends, he obviously must avoid them in future. Law-breaking has a lot to do with being 'big' and adventurous.

The way in which you handle any early instance of law-breaking will have important implications for the years that follow. If the police are involved, they'll often (provided no real damage has been done) decide to take the matter no further as long as they're sure your child comes from a responsible home and that you'll see he gets into no further trouble. And there's every chance he won't, provided he sees that you trust him and have every confidence in his future good sense. And provided you work out with him a sensible and realistic set of guidelines for avoiding trouble. These shouldn't be too draconian. If they are he'll be tempted to break them and you'll have trouble enforcing them. Far better he should agree with you that they're fair and realistic, and are a sensible way of keeping on the right side of the law rather than a long-term attempt to punish him for one small misdemeanour.

Anorexia

More a problem with adolescent girls than boys, this condition, in which the individual voluntarily starves herself down to a dangerously low weight, is on the increase (partly because of media publicity and partly because of the modern craze for stick-like figures). But it's been around for centuries. Usually it starts with extreme dissatisfaction with one's appearance. The adolescent girl starts complaining frequently about the way she looks, and constantly seeks reassurance from others, only to ignore it when it's given. Sometimes she may be noticeably overweight, perhaps after a period of inactivity (in older women it may happen after childbirth), but often there are few obvious signs of the need to slim. She starts cutting down on her food, typically not by going on a sensible diet but by skipping meals, or eating only minute portions. Should she eat a normal meal, she may often disappear into the toilet immediately afterwards in order to make herself sick. Enquiries as to why she isn't eating properly are met either with denials or with protestations that she just 'isn't hungry'. Attempts at reasoning with her are met with angry scenes or stubborn silence. Watched helplessly by anxious parents, she goes on starving herself long after the need to lose any weight is past, and reaches the point not only of dangerous (in a few sad cases even fatal) emaciation, but of revulsion at the whole idea of food and eating.

The causes of anorexia are not fully known, and may differ from one case to another. But a common feature is a deep-seated self-disgust and hatred. The sufferer punishes herself almost to death for *being who she is* (not for *looking the way she does*, though this is the excuse she makes to herself and to others). Traced back to earlier childhood, the difficulty seems to start with a lack of self-acceptance, brought on by the inability of parents and other significant adults to show they love and accept her for what she is. Or by constant unfavourable comparisons being drawn between herself and other children. Or by profound feelings of guilt and wickedness which seem to call out for self-punishment. Anorexia is seldom if ever seen amongst girls who have good feelings about themselves, and who have never doubted the fact that they are prized by those close to them.

Self-disgust is a common feature

Tendencies towards anorexia surface in adolescence rather than earlier in life not just because adolescence is a time of maximum concern with the physical appearance, but because adolescence is a time of maximum concern with personal identity and worth. The anorexic girl is telling us something tragic about her inner life. A further complicating factor is the advent of sexual maturity. If she already feels guilt and self-disgust, then the onset of menstruation, the development of primary and secondary physical sexual characteristics, and the advent of what may be seen as unwholesome sexual urges,

The anorexic girl often wishes to deny her sexuality

may all make things much worse. Through starvation, these troublesome reminders of sexuality are minimized or even removed altogether. Also minimized are the processes of digestion and excretion, processes which the girl may see as further evidence of how 'unclean' she is. This link between anorexia and a wish to deny one's sexuality and bodily excretions suggests strongly that in some cases the causes of anorexia may also lie in faulty early sex education and in rigid and punitive toilet training.

Eventually she becomes a social outcast

I mentioned earlier that anorexia has been around for centuries, but maybe in earlier times it was disguised behind retreats into nunneries and behind the fasting and self-flagellation which took place in the name of religion (which is not to say that all fasting is anorexia by another name!). One of the problems we all face these days is that society has fewer institutions and rituals through which people can work out their psychological problems without being labelled as odd or deviant or unwell. The anorexic is unable to use her fasting in a good cause so to speak, and is left isolated and exposed, misunderstood and even ridiculed by those around her. Often rejected by the opposite sex and even by friends of the same sex, she may become more and more of a social outcast, and though her energy levels may remain reasonably high for a surprisingly long time, in the end lassitude and weakness make it increasingly difficult for her to lead any semblance of a normal life.

Look out for the warning signs

Since no parent would want to see a teenager daughter reduced to this sorry state, it's important to spot the signs of anorexia early on. Don't be unduly suspicious. Many adolescents are conscious of their figures, and become faddy over their food and skip meals in order to keep up with the social whirl. It's also unusual for anorexia to occur out of the blue in a girl who is otherwise well-balanced and happy. But any unsupervised change in eating habits which leads to a rapid loss of weight, and any signs of revulsion towards food in general, need watching closely, especially if coupled with frequent emotional outbursts, withdrawal, or any other signs that all is not well. Another warning sign (though this can happen in the absence of anorexia) is a sudden preoccupation with vomiting. The girl protests that she'd like to eat, but can't do so for fear she will bring it all back up again. Sometimes this fear is specific to certain situations (for example the girl can eat at home but not when she's out), at other times it is more general. When not connected with anorexia or physical illness, this condition usually clears up on its own given a little time and sympathy and patience. But when anorexia is involved, it serves as yet another excuse for refusing food and even for refusing to sit at the table while others are eating.

If you suspect a daughter or son of becoming anorexic, get medical advice at once. Apart from brief fasts in fit people, all fasting and even serious dieting should be done under medical supervision. The body can quickly become depleted of essential vitamins and minerals, lowering resistance to illness and, in the case of the adolescent, interfering with physical and sexual development. But although your doctor can deal with the medical treatment, the psychological treatment is very much in your hands. Within the home, there should be a definite movement towards warmth, love and a non-judgemental approach. You can't force love on an anorexic girl, just as you can't force food on her, but you can give her the supportive, unpressurized, accepting environment in which she can begin to rekindle good feelings about herself. *Really* good feelings, not just the superficial pride in their slimness that some anorexics claim. Your daughter needs to feel that you understand what is going on in her life. However bizarre the notion of someone voluntarily starving themselves may seem to you, and however simple the remedy (plain common sense) may appear to be, to your daughter it's like being locked into a nightmare. Many anorexics, when they've overcome their problem, confess themselves at a loss to know how they could have behaved as they did, but say that at the time it seemed as if they had no choice. Rather like an obsessional person, they felt themselves forced by some inner power to punish and starve themselves as the only way of feeling acceptable to themselves. Physical weakness, sapping the strength to resist, usually did the rest.

At the practical level, the first rule when helping anorexics is don't fuss. You're bound to feel anxious, but as far as possible keep your anxiety to yourself. The more you fuss over the anorexic, trying to tempt her with a bit of this and a bit of that, the more stubborn she often becomes. She may also, unconsciously if not consciously, rather enjoy the attention

Try to rekindle her good feelings about herself

Keep your anxiety to yourself

667

her anorexia is attracting from you, and the power it gives her over you. With some anorexics, there are signs that their refusal to eat is an unacknowledged desire to punish parents, just as happens when a small child dramatically rejects parental offerings, so it's best not to show too obviously how hurt and puzzled you are over the whole business.

So don't fuss. On the other hand, do give the anorexic as wide a choice of food as possible. Give her responsibility wherever feasible for choosing what she wants to eat, and for preparing it too if that seems to help. If she prefers to eat on her own rather than join the family, okay. Don't keep pressing her for 'explanations'. Show that you're more than ready to listen sympathetically if she wants to talk, but that you respect her silence (or her inability to put her exact feelings into words). Don't eat in front of her if she finds this offensive. Many anorexics (like many people on fasts) claim that after a while their appetite is completely suppressed, and the sight of other people tucking in to a mammoth spread only suppresses it more. But do otherwise carry on as normally as you can; there's nothing to be gained by disrupting your own life, and if she thinks you're trying to compete with her by drawing attention to your own suffering, then you may only make things worse.

Help her feel needed and useful Since the anorexic's problems are partly bound up with an unsatisfactory body image, try to improve this image, but keep your efforts subtle and low key. If she suspects flattery or mistrusts your motives, she'll reject what you have to say. If she's withdrawing into herself, find ways of interesting her and drawing her out a little. Often this is best done through opportunities of serving others worse off than herself. Rekindling her interest in abandoned or suffering animals is one way. Helping out from time to time at an old's people's home is another. Working with small children is another. You know your daughter best and you are the best judge, but if you can help her to feel needed and useful, she'll be well on the way towards feeling more positive about herself and wanting to rebuild her energy and enthusiasm for life.

Don't push her into resuming normal life too quickly In many parts of the country, it is now possible to supplement your efforts by making use of counselling services and support groups set up specifically to work with anorexics. Sometimes a girl will resist this kind of help, protesting all the time that there is nothing wrong with her, but most anorexics genuinely want to resume a normal life and to feel better about themselves. Once they feel that you and the other people involved appreciate what they're going through, they're prepared to play their part in treatment. Progress is often slow at first, with frequent set-backs (prompted all too often by the well-meaning but thoughtless remarks of others, or by over-lavish attempts to praise each small sign of improvement), but over the weeks and months the anorexic gradually gets back to normal. Don't try to force things along too quickly though, or push her into resuming her life outside the home before she's ready. She needs to feel that she has her own full say in what's going on. And do be aware, even when she's better, of the problems that drove her into anorexia in the first place. The love, support and confidence in her that you show during her treatment are every bit as necessary to her when the treatment is over.

Bulimia

Similar to anorexia in that its causes are usually psychological, but opposite to it in effect, is the condition known as *bulimia*, or compulsive overeating. Bulimia refers not to the person who habitually overeats (the result of habit as much as anything else) but to the person who periodically indulges in a gorging binge, often secretively and often with strong feelings of guilt and self-disgust. Again the sufferer is more often a female, but unlike anorexia, which is typically a young woman's condition, bulimia is often seen in middle-aged and even elderly women. It makes its first appearance, though, in adolescence, and is usually a sign of a deep-seated need for comfort. Often the sufferer feels herself unloved and unwanted, and turns to food as a substitute for this lack of affection. Unhappily, her food binge usually leaves her feeling even less acceptable to others, and since the sufferer is often also morbidly preoccupied with her waist-line, she may end each binge by making herself vomit up her illicit feast, only to return to the kitchen and promptly binge again.

Bulimia is usually a sign of a need for comfort

Bulimia tends to occur when the individual is facing a particularly stressful period in life, and to clear up when the stress is over, only to recur if things become stressful again. Since there are rarely any physical dangers involved, it isn't easy to get professional treatment for bulimia, though if it is part of an array of stress symptoms, it can sometimes be looked at along with the rest.

The first step must be to bring it into the open

In the home, the important first step is to bring it into the open. If the sufferer has to be secretive and sly about it, then this creates a gap between her and her family and adds to her feeling of deceit and unworthiness. Half the battle with any neurotic symptom is to help the individual feel there's nothing particularly abnormal and certainly nothing intrinsically wicked in being neurotic. We are all of us anxious in one way or another – it's part of being human – and our anxiety comes out in different ways.

Once the bulimia ceases to be a guilty secret, the next step is to discuss with the sufferer the best way of handling it. One answer is to keep a supply of fruit and nuts handy, so that she can confine herself to those. Another is to provide a snack at those times during the day (usually mid-morning and evening) when she is most likely to want to indulge. Another is to arrange a performance contract, so that points are given for each day on which the urge to binge is resisted, and exchanged for a special treat (say a favourite meal) at the end of the week. The sufferer must be involved in setting the targets in any contract of this kind. Often sufferers confess to being 'weak-willed', and there is therefore a temptation to impose targets on them, in the belief that they are unable to do so for themselves. But part of the treatment must be to help them build up confidence in their own strength, and this can only be done by involving them in decision-making and in monitoring progress.

Help the sufferer feel secure in her family

Finally, since bulimia is linked to a need for comfort (a sort of reversion, if you like, to the warmth and cosiness and satisfaction that feeding times provided back in infancy), try to ensure that the sufferer is given her comfort in more mature and adult ways. Perhaps people have been too critical towards her as a person. Perhaps she feels left out of things. Perhaps she even has a sense of rejection from those to whom she wishes to be close. Examine what has been going wrong in her life, and the part that her family may have been playing in it. Show her that the comfort that comes from the security and affection of her family is readily available, and that it's more than able to meet her needs.

Serious personality problems in adolescence

Most people are surprised to learn that the early twenties are a peak age both for mental illness and for suicide, with many of the symptoms already apparent in adolescence. I don't want to overemphasize the problems, but there are certain things which indicate an adolescent is finding the transition into adult life particularly difficult.

The most serious is increasing isolation, coupled with the inability to communicate. The adolescent retreats more and more into a world of his own, becomes more and more apathetic (though sometimes given to occasional and temporary outbursts of wild enthusiasm for unlikely causes), and more and more unpredictable. His ability to concentrate declines, he becomes careless of his physical safety, appearance and hygiene, and irregular in his eating and sleeping habits. All attempts to find out what is wrong seem to fail. He doesn't know, doesn't care, or can't put it into words. His irritable retort of 'Nothing's wrong' becomes something of a theme tune, and in the end people give up asking him. What's really wrong is that he's suddenly aware that he's got no real purpose in life. He's left the world of childhood, where everything was bright with possibilities, and looking into the future he sees nothing to excite him. The things he wants look unobtainable, and he has grave misgivings about his own worth. The hormonal changes going on during adolescence bring mood changes of their own, and help him get stuck in deep depressions which make everything seem hopeless. To make matters worse, he sees his contemporaries facing the future with optimism and enjoying their new freedom to the full. Everyone seems to be having fun except him. And the fact that adults seem always on to him about how he 'ought' to behave only makes things worse. He retreats further and further into himself, reacting with outbursts of sudden rage when asked to make even the least effort, not because the demands made of him are unreasonable but because they intrude on his apathy.

Increasing isolation and apathy

Never discount a mention of suicide

Fortunately it's only in rare cases that this state of affairs becomes really serious or a suicide risk. But to avoid potential tragedies it is important to warn parents against believing the dangerous saying that people who threaten suicide never actually do it. Eighty per cent of suicides mention or threaten their intentions to others, and taking into account the reluctance of many folk to admit they've heard such intentions, the real figure is probably even higher. So never take any mention of suicide lightly, no matter how many times you hear it. Other warning signals are if the individual gives or throws away things of which he's fond, particularly if they're of sentimental value. Or if he's suffered personal disappointments like a broken love affair or unemployment. Rigid over-control, with emotions bottled up until they reach bursting point, or excessive guilt and self-accusations, are also potential danger signs.

Be sympathetic but not too intense

An adolescent going through a bad patch is best handled patiently and thoughtfully, and in an atmosphere that is warm-spirited and not too intense. The last thing he wants is someone who keeps personalizing the issue ('How do you think *I* feel seeing you around the house with a long face every day?'), or who keeps pestering him to 'tell me what's wrong'. If he's going to talk, then given the opportunity he'll do so, but in his own time and not in response to frequent questioning. Consistency and routine are also essential. Give him small tasks to perform to keep him focused on daily life. Encourage his friends to call. If you know of a sympathetic adult who's used to counselling teenagers ask him or her to come and talk. What the adolescent most needs is someone knowledgeable who can reassure him that his condition is very common in young people and will soon pass, as indeed it usually does. Most adolescents, given the right conditions, 'grow out' of their depression and come to the conclusion that life isn't so bad after all.

But with all adolescents, depressed or not, try to avoid the lonely storming off to his (or more frequently her) room to have a miserable cry behind a locked door. Frequent scenes of this kind increase his isolation. There are times certainly when the adolescent prefers to be alone, to cool off perhaps after a row. But more usually he's better off in company if he's upset. Never be afraid to make the first move if he goes off storming upstairs. Don't appear *over* concerned. Offer a cup of tea, much as you would if he'd gone upstairs to work. If there's no result, ask a little later if he'd like to talk things over. If there's still no result, let him come in his own time. The important thing is he can now do so without losing face.

ALCOHOLISM AND DRUG-TAKING

Drug-taking isn't only a problem of adolescence. It can and does make its appearance in the junior school, but I'm dealing with it now because it's in adolescence that it presents the greatest menace. These days the adolescent, even while in the lower forms of the secondary school, has access to drugs in a way that would have been unthinkable a few years back. And by drugs I mean the whole range of intoxicants, from cigarettes and alcohol through solvents to cannabis and the hard drugs such as heroin or cocaine. In discussions, adolescents admit frankly to having had drugs offered to them not only at parties but in walks through the centre of town and even at the school gates. And solvents and alcohol (to say nothing of tobacco, which I have already dealt with) are so freely available that the wonder is more adolescents don't become hooked on them.

Education helps, with campaigns against drug-taking very much under way in the schools, but drug education, like most kinds of education, begins at home. I'm not talking just about the conversations you have with your adolescent on the dangers of drugs. I'm talking about the whole atmosphere in the home and the whole nature of your relationship with your child. It would be wrong to say that adolescents from happy homes with loving, open, democratic relationships with their parents never become drug addicts. But the *chances* of an adolescent from a happy home becoming a drug addict are less than the chances of an adolescent from an unhappy background. And by 'unhappy' I mean not just hardship or violence. I mean homes which superficially appear 'good' but in which there is no real communication between parents and offspring, and in which offspring have either been left largely to their own devices or been denied the opportunity to get to know themselves and develop a true sense of responsibility.

It is mainly those from unhappy homes who turn to drugs

Drug addiction is essentially an escape from reality, and it follows that this escape appeals more to those who are unhappy with the reality of their lives than to those who feel good about themselves. Research shows that drug addiction in all age groups occurs primarily in those who feel inadequate, who have problems in communicating or in asking for help, and who find it hard to value themselves and care about the harm they're doing to themselves. Agreed there are some addicts who claim that the search for excitement rather than the conscious need to escape from anything was what motivated them in the first place. But life has plenty of excitement for healthy youngsters without turning to drugs, and those who become addicted are predominantly those who see life as unsatisfactory.

Different categories of drugs Drugs can be grouped into different categories. There are the *hallucinogenic drugs* such as LSD and psilocybin (the 'magic mushroom'), which prompt visionary states in which the world appears transformed in some way, with music for example sometimes 'seen' as colours, and with the time sense and spatial sense distorted. There are the *sedatives, depressants and hypnotics*, such as barbiturates, nicotine and alcohol, which produce temporary lowering of anxiety and changes in mood. There are the *opiate narcotics*, such as heroin, which put the individual into a state of apathy (with or without an accompanying sense of well-being). Then there are the *volatile solvents* used in glue, nail polish, lighter fuel and the like, the *stimulants* such as cocaine, caffeine and the amphetamines, the *anti-depressants* used in trade preparations such as Phenezine, and the *tranquillizers* used for example in Largactil. Some of these drugs (alcohol, nicotine, caffeine, anti-depressants, tranquillizers) are socially acceptable, others (LSD, heroin, cocaine, etc.) are not.

So the drug problem is wider than many of us imagine. Plenty of people are addicted to the socially acceptable drugs, and there's no evidence that such addiction is safe. All drugs involve the introduction of potentially harmful substances into the body, and we are only now becoming aware of the psychological and physical damage that many widely prescribed medical drugs are doing.

We most of us take drugs in one form or another every day of our lives. Thus your own example and your own attitude

towards drugs will have a major influence upon your children. **Set a good**
If drug use within the home is confined to cups of tea and **example at**
coffee and the occasional alcoholic drink, then your children **home**
will be influenced to adopt the same approach. If on the other
hand they see you misusing drugs, they may feel it's okay to
do the same. So make it clear to them that a glass of something
alcoholic is fine in moderation and can bring civilized pleasure
into life, but overdoing it is foolish and dangerous. To a lesser
extent, the same even goes for coffee. Strong coffee contains a
great deal of caffeine, and if you're drinking cup after cup
throughout the day, not only will you become addicted, there
may be a medical risk in terms of raised blood pressure,
stomach problems and heart disease.

But your own example shouldn't stop with alcohol and
caffeine. If you're in the habit of taking pills (except vitamin
pills) for anything other than a very clear medical condition,
then your children will come to see pill-popping as normal.
Whenever you feel a little low in spirits, or find trouble
sleeping, you take pills to sort yourself out instead of finding
the cause of the problem and tackling it by changing your
attitude to life. Tranquillizers, stimulants and sedatives are
very occasional first aids, and not long-term substitutes for
dealing properly with yourself. Rely on pills, and there's an
increased chance that one day your children will do the same.

Drinking

Next to smoking, alcohol causes the highest total of drug-
related death and disease in the Western world, in addition to
the appallingly violent and anti-social behaviour of many
drunkards and the devastating effects their addiction can have
on family life. When working with young people, I counsel
them strongly that if now or later in life they find themselves
in the habit of using alcohol (or even strong coffee) in a
deliberate attempt to change their mood, or because they feel
the 'need' for it, then they must recognize the dangers and
stop. I also make clear the medically 'approved' limit in adults
of twenty measures of alcohol per week for males and about
twelve for females (a measure of alcohol being a glass of wine
or sherry, half a pint of beer or a single tot of spirits), and that

should be used strictly as an inessential addition to life and never as a psychological prop.

I also point out to young people that once they develop a drink problem they've lost for good their chances of enjoying a glass or two of their favourite tipple when they fancy it. When you've a drink problem, the only effective treatment is permanent total abstinence. Foolishly you've robbed yourself of a pleasant social diversion, simply because you weren't sensible enough to keep it within the necessary limits. And I also stress that you must have a firm rule never to drink and drive. Particularly with youngsters, the intention may be simply to have a half pint and then stop, but with the first half pint the resolve is weakened. A second drink follows and then a third, and as they disappear down the throat so too disappear all the good intentions of staying sober. Here again, the right parental example is vital. It's no use preaching against drinking and driving if your children see you failing to practise what you preach. It's also important to stress that in the UK young people under eighteen are forbidden by law to buy or consume alcohol on licensed premises. To break the law is unfair to the teenager and to the licensee, since both would be in trouble if caught.

If your adolescent has been on a drinking binge

Suppose you suspect your adolescent is misusing alcohol. How can you be sure? Usually there's no difficulty. The effects of alcohol upon speech, mood and physical control are far too well known to require elaboration. The smell of alcohol on the breath is also distinctive. What's more, the effects of alcohol persist up to twenty-four hours after the last drink, so unless he's away from home your adolescent can't normally hide his binge from you. The first rule is don't tackle him while he's under the influence, even if only moderately. People react irrationally when they've had a drink too many, and may spark off an emotional scene that will do nobody any good. Instead, give him any help he may need in getting to bed and sleeping it off, though you needn't be too sympathetic towards the ensuing hangover!.

But once he's over it, have a serious talk with him. Agree that the most young people get caught out with a drink or two over the odds simply through inexperience. Show him you're confident he's too sensible to let it happen again. Tell him of a similar experience of your own when you were around his age. Then point out that the trouble with alcohol is that it really stops you having a good time. The person who drinks in moderation at a party thoroughly enjoys himself. He feels happy, takes in fully what's going on around him, doesn't do anything he'll feel ashamed of next day, and escapes the evils of a hangover. Not so the heavy drinker! Stress too that alcohol is in fact a poison. An overdose can literally kill, and the long-term damage is only too well-known. The wise guy is the one who knows when to stop.

A different problem arises if your adolescent is making a habit of drinking. He may very rarely actually be drunk, yet he seems to be relying upon alcohol for his kicks. Building up a resistance to the consequences of the drug, he's able to hide the effect it's having on him. What makes you suspect all is not well is that his general behaviour is changing. His school work suffers. He is increasingly silent and moody about the house (don't mistake this for the moroseness often seen in adolescents). The only time he seems 'happy' is when he comes in after a night out with his friends (if he's been drinking vodka you won't usually smell it on his breath), though you notice that this 'happiness' can change alarmingly quickly to anger if somebody crosses him. If the problem develops further, you may find bottles of alcohol hidden away in his room. And if you watch him closely, you may even see that he *refuses* the chance of a social drink with you, only too aware that once he has a single drink he's going to need a second and a third. When he does allow himself the single drink, you'll notice that far from raising his spirits it tends to leave him withdrawn and touchy.

If he is making a habit of drinking

If your adolescent reaches this stage before the extent of his drinking really hits you, head-on battles are of no use. Anyone who drinks too much needs help and support in overcoming his addiction, especially at this young age. Make him unhappy, and he'll only seek solace in more drinking, hiding it from you with increasing ingenuity. Anyone who gets badly into addictive drugs finds that everything is made to serve his addiction. If he sees you as standing between him and it, then in a sense he'll see you as an enemy. And since one of the unfortunate consequences of alcohol is that it can make people aggressive and hostile, a deep gulf can be created between you and your child which will make it difficult for you to give the help he needs, and for him to regain your trust and confidence.

People can slip into alcohol misuse almost by accident

Much of what I say about dealing with drug-taking in general later in the chapter applies equally to alcohol addiction. But there is a difference, in that alcohol, unlike the other drugs discussed, is not illegal. There's no law against drinking yourself under the table every night if you wish, as long as you don't drive or directly harm anyone other than yourself. And since the development of drug addiction depends upon circumstances as well as upon the drug itself and the personality of the drug-taker, it's all too easy for people to slip into alcohol misuse almost by accident. They get into a crowd of heavy drinkers, have a good time, and see no harm in it. There's also something of a macho image about heavy drinking on the one hand, and something of a romantic image about it on the other. So whether your child sees himself as a he-man or as a poet, drinking may seem not only acceptable but desirable. Since it lowers social and sexual inhibitions (by depressing one's normal responses), parties seem to go with much more of a swing if they're lubricated by alcohol, and in both boys and girls alcohol is seen as a mark of freedom and emancipation.

As a consequence, people can become heavy drinkers without necessarily having the personality problems which I discuss in connection with addiction to the other drugs described in a moment. But even with alcohol it's always right to ask why a person *needs* to get his kicks through drinking, and why he persists in his habit even when he's aware that it's gaining a hold upon him and that it may end up damaging his health. Many young adults, for example, drink quite heavily during their student days, or in connection with their involvement in team games, or when working away from home with a group of rabble-rousers, yet are perfectly happy to stop once this episode in their lives comes to an end. Others seem unable to do so. Why the difference? The answer lies in the part alcohol plays in a person's life. If this part is a pleasant but peripheral one, of secondary importance to many of the other things that bring fun – good social relationships, inner peace and a meaning to existence – then the individual can take or leave alcohol as he pleases. But if alcohol lies at the centre of life, with little else able to make the individual feel so good, then there's a real risk he will become psychologically dependent on it even before physical dependency sets in.

If your child is drinking heavily, have a look therefore both at the circumstances in which his drinking is taking place and at his personality. If he's mixing with a crowd of heavy drinkers, what can be done to help him find more suitable friends? And if he seems to need alcohol as a psychological prop, what are the things that are missing in his life? The answer to the first question is often more straightforward than the answer to the second. You can't choose your adolescent's friends for him, but you can decide who you want to encourage and who you want to discourage. Don't forbid the house to any of his friends you're unsure about (if he can't bring them home he'll meet them elsewhere, and create a divide in his mind between his friends and his family), but do agree with him beforehand about the reasonable levels of behaviour you expect from them when they're under your roof. And don't be afraid to show that these restrictions apply far more to some of his friends than to others. You may end up accused of being 'dull' or 'boring', and if that's your child's opinion he has a right to it. But remain firm. Children of this age are often easily impressed by what they see as the 'glamour' of some of their friends, and in their search for excitement may behave very foolishly in order to hang on to these friends. At times like this, the wiser counsels of parents are invaluable.

Look at the circumstances in which your child is drinking

The second question, what is it in your child's personality that makes him need drink, is more difficult. Many parents say they've thought and thought about it, without coming up with an answer. I've my doubts about this. Often the answer is clear enough, it is we who are reluctant to see it, through a fear that it may reflect back upon us. Look closely at your child. Is he lonely? Is he lacking direction in his life? Is he unhappy about himself and his relationships with others? Are his interests and outlets rather restricted, so that he's uninspired by life? Is he easily led? Is he trying to escape from something, whether a feeling of inadequacy or some discontent at home? Has he an inner conflict or feelings of depression that can only be resolved when he's been drinking? Encourage him to talk about these problems, or if he doesn't want to talk to you, see if there's another adult in whom he feels he can

What is it in his personality that makes him need to drink?

confide. Don't see difficulties where they don't exist. Remember that his drinking may only be a phase in his discovery of adult life, as it is amongst those people I mentioned a moment ago who are able to ease back on their drinking once a particular episode in their lives is over. But at the same time don't ignore difficulties when they do exist. Help from you now in seeing the trouble he may be storing up for the future is invaluable. (Other ways of helping are discussed later.)

Other drugs

Solvent abuse

The signs of solvent abuse are similar to those for drunkenness. The effects don't last long though, so if the sniffer does her sniffing away from home, she'll probably have sobered up by the time you see her. She can't rid herself of the *smell* of solvent though, so this is usually your best clue. If she indulges frequently, her eyes and nose will be red and runny, and she'll also have red marks round the mouth. Sometimes there will be recurrent stomach upsets and a crop of mouth ulcers, and she may complain of dizziness. We don't know how many youngsters sniff solvents. A large number take an experimental whiff or two, simply because they've heard so much about it. But serious solvent abuse, which involves deep sniffs with air excluded (head covered by an anorak or face buried in a plastic bag), is less common. And many children who try it once don't want to try again. So if you find your offspring with an open glue tin in the potting shed it doesn't necessarily mean the worst. Even in children who sniff regularly, solvent abuse tends to be a short-lived habit, and the user doesn't necessarily gravitate to other drugs.

Solvent abuse can be fatal *But* solvent abuse is highly dangerous. The sad deaths of teenagers, many of them experimenting for the first time, proves that. Not only can the solvents themselves cause death if inhaled in sufficient strength, there are dangers of suffocation from the plastic bag, particularly if the youngster passes out with it still over his face. Since solvent abuse is often carried out well away from adults, there's also the grave risk that if a child gets into difficulties help can't be summoned until it's too late. In the long term, it's also likely that inhaled solvents can cause respiratory, brain or heart damage, the effects of which will show up in later life.

Impress these dangers on adolescents and on children of all ages. Provided your youngster cares about herself and values her body, this is usually quite enough to prevent her from putting herself at risk. It is illegal for shopkeepers to supply solvents to anyone under eighteen if it's suspected they're going to misuse them, so if you hear the law is being broken you can take action. No reputable shopkeeper wants to put young lives at risk.

The opiate narcotics

Heroin is the best-known of these and the one most feared by parents. Like alcohol it's an addictive drug, which means that the body becomes dependent upon a regular supply. Thus although the addict may want to stop and may grow actively to dislike the drug experience (many heroin addicts admit they've never really *enjoyed* the effects of heroin at all), within hours of the last dose she's in the middle of a range of distressing symptoms. She sweats and shivers profusely. Her nose and eyes run. She feels weak, anxious and irritable. You may mistake the symptoms for the onset of flu or a heavy cold. After a few hours of troubled sleep she wakes with the onset of the much-publicized 'cold turkey' syndrome. Her skin is clammy, her pupils dilated, and there is nausea, vomiting and a loss of bowel control. Severe abdominal cramps, tremors and even convulsions occur, and these distressing effects will continue with varying ferocity up to a week or so. After that, the worst is over, though it's usually six months or so before the body is back to normal. Not surprisingly, the sufferer pleads during the worst effects of her ordeal for a dose of heroin, knowing that it will bring speedy relief, though at the cost of keeping her addicted.

Incidentally, very similar withdrawal symptoms occur if the individual is withdrawing from one of the depressants, and in both cases (but particularly with the depressants) there is the risk of fatality. So if your adolescent has been a secret addict and you cotton on only when she's suffering these symptoms, get medical help immediately. Don't hesitate while you ponder over the 'disgrace' of having your doctor find out what's been happening.

If you recognize withdrawal symptoms, get medical help immediately

Look out for the tell-tale signs Usually, though, you're going to discover your adolescent's addiction long before it gets to this crisis stage, particularly if you know what to look for. The tell-tale signs with heroin are pin-point pupils, the unsteady unco-ordinated behaviour usually associated with drunkenness, a loss of appetite except for junk food, apathy, vomiting (especially early on), pallor and sleepiness (sometimes with night-time insomnia), lack of energy, scratching, furtiveness, poor school work, withdrawal and isolation. Quite a catalogue. Since she needs money to buy her drug there may also be persistent pilfering (watch for this with all suspected drug abuse). Evidence of the drug itself usually comes from the singed tinfoil used to heat the drug, together with the straws or rolls of paper which she uses to sniff it up. The heroin itself is usually in the form of an off-white to dark brown powder, normally sold in small bags by pushers (more likely to be the addict's friends, looking to finance their own habit, than furtive characters lurking outside the school gates).

Contrary to popular belief, to be on heroin doesn't mean someone's necessarily heading for incurable addiction or for an early and painful death. Pure heroin is a dangerous substance, but the worst risks are from the poisonous adulterates with which dealers mix it to make it go further and increase their profit, and from the blood diseases – particularly AIDS and hepatitis – caused by the use of unsterile needles. Since youngsters are more likely to sniff heroin than to inject it ('main-lining'), it's likely that you'll discover the addiction before the really serious damage is done. If a youngster is 'main-lining', you'll notice needle marks on arms and thighs, and outbreaks of sores caused by blood infections. Whatever the nature and extent of her addiction, given the right help the chances of a successful end to the addiction are good.

The stimulants

The amphetamines or 'speed' Let's take the amphetamines first, since they're more likely to be a problem with adolescents than cocaine. Most amphetamines come in the form of pills or an off-white powder. Usually it's chopped up small with a razor blade and sniffed, but it can be taken orally or injected. The symptoms are a greatly speeded up lifestyle (hence the common name 'speed'). The addict acts and talks in an exhausting non-stop manner, may grind his teeth, and has no time for anything as mundane as proper meals. Usually he's thin, on a knife-edge between elation and aggression, and can't or won't concentrate on social graces or school work. There is evidence that speed is a group phenomenon, taken by young people in gangs, whether bent on mischief (as in football hooligans) or just on having a good time.

Speed is addictive, and the withdrawal symptoms usually involve great exhaustion and despair. Since the body builds up tolerance to the drug, amounts have to be increased steadily to produce the necessary 'high' (as with the opiate narcotics and the depressants), and in the medium and long term there is a serious risk of heart damage and of lowered resistance to a range of ailments.

Nevertheless, speed isn't quite as menacing as cocaine, usually available as cocaine hydrochloride or 'coke', which comes as a fine white powder. Cocaine produces symptoms much like those for speed, except that it acts as a local anaesthetic as well as a stimulant. The insensitivity to pain which it produces, though of use to the dentist, is highly dangerous in the addict since it can lead to a foolish disregard for physical risks. Worse still, coke can have a depressive effect upon the respiratory system. Since coke addiction is often linked to insomnia, the addict may take a further depressant such as alcohol or barbiturates in order to get to sleep, with the tragic result that the breathing reflex is depressed altogether, and he falls into a sleep from which there is no waking.

Cocaine or 'coke'

Cocaine is thought to produce both physical and psychological dependence, which means that the addict is sick in body and mind when he tries to break the habit. For this and other physiological reasons, cocaine is perhaps the most addictive drug on the market, and if you think your adolescent is experimenting with it, take urgent action. In some circles coke is seen (along with speed) as a 'smart' drug, associated with pop stars and a fast and exciting life. This leads people to minimize the risks associated with it and to see it simply as a slick alternative to alcohol. Alcohol is dangerous enough, but the stimulant drugs are worse. Taking them is neither smart nor clever. It is foolish and potentially tragic.

But the most menacing version of cocaine is not cocaine

683

'Crack' – the most addictive drug of all hydrochloride but alkaloid of cocaine, or 'crack'. Arriving on the drug market much more recently than coke, crack abuse is rapidly gaining popularity. A purer, more concentrated form of cocaine than coke, crack comes as fine crystals which are crushed and smoked sprinkled on a cigarette or through a hubbly-bubbly. The effect reaches the brain in under ten seconds, producing an intense, short-lived, 'high' followed by severe depression for which users take a cocktail of anti-depressants and tranquillizers (Es and Vs). Due to the rapidity with which crack reaches the brain and the intensity of the reaction, crack is terrifyingly addictive. Some experts suggest that as many as 50 per cent of users are addicted after their first high, and since the body quickly habituates to the drug ever-increasing doses are needed. Since crack is relatively simple to produce, the street price is often cheaper than coke, with the result that the drug presents a particular threat to the less well-off.

Due to the speed with which users become addicted to crack, we may have before long to change our picture of the typical drug addict. Crack presents the real risk of becoming addicted by accident. In ignorance, the individual takes crack at a party, and falls victim. However, as with any drug, the ability to break the habit and steer clear of it in future depend importantly upon the individual's psychological strength, his satisfaction with 'normal' life, and his relationship with those near to him.

The hallucinogens

LSD The best known of these, LSD, usually comes in the form of 6-millimetre (¼ in.) squares of blotting paper, known as 'tabs', or tiny pills or jelly-like blobs. It appears to be neither psychologically nor physically addicitive, and opinions vary sharply as to its harmful effects upon the body. But what is certain is that it produces mind states which, though sometimes blissful and even profoundly moving, can be terrifying or even verging on the psychotic. People have been known to kill themselves under the effects of LSD, either to escape from a 'bad trip' or because they hallucinate the power to fly or to undertake some other risk.

LSD can vary both in strength and purity, with the result that sometimes people take a much higher dose than intended. This adds to the hazards. And though many people claim that

LSD has changed their lives by opening up to them knowledge of other states of consciousness and planes of reality, the risks are far too great for the drug to be made commonly available. Besides, those who have used it to explore mystical states admit that although it may give you glimpses which motivate you to look for other safer spiritual techniques such as meditation, it's an unsatisfactory key to inner experience since it doesn't provide you with the wisdom that makes these states truly meaningful.

Psilocybin, the magic mushroom, can produce experiences similar to those of LSD. Unless the mushroom is treated in some way, it isn't illegal to possess or use it, and there's no evidence that it can become physically addictive or present a danger to physical health (though there's a very real danger that poisonous fungi may be eaten in mistake for psilocybin). As with LSD, the main problems are psychological. Psilocybin can produce weird distortions of sight, sound and touch, to say nothing of thought. Should the user already be over-imaginative or have a confused sense of personal identity, then her experiences under psilocybin could be terrifying. There's no evidence that any of the better-known hallucinogens can produce psychosis (madness) in a well-balanced person, but there is a strong suggestion that they can produce psychotic states in the less stable. These states may only be temporary, but they bring with them not only the risk of self-inflicted injury but of damaging long-term memories.

Psilocybin, or the 'magic mushroom'

In the experienced user, the effects of the hallucinogens are often difficult to detect. The pupils dilate, the blood pressure rises and there may be headaches, nausea and sleeplessness, but the experienced user can often hide these symptoms from the untrained eye. Pure LSD has no odour, and the only real give-away is discovery of the drug tabs themselves. Should you encounter someone having a 'bad trip' keep her focused on reality. One way of doing this is to make her concentrate alternatively upon her hands and her feet, switching between the two each time her concentration wavers or she experiences sensory distortions. Keep talking to her. Ask her questions so that she talks back. Reassure her that her confused state will soon pass, and keep the atmosphere calm, confident and supportive until medical help arrives.

Effects of the hallucinogens

685

Cannabis

There is some doubt amongst experts as to how cannabis should be classified, so I didn't list it earlier. The general consensus is that it's a mild hallucinogen. The drug is readily available on the black market, and can even be grown (illegally) in this country. Due to its popularity amongst the young, cannabis is the drug parents are most likely to come across, usually in the form of shredded brown or green leaves, or a brown resinous lump. It can be eaten as it is or brewed like tea, but normally it's smoked in a hubbly-bubbly or rolled cigarettes. An alternative is to let it smoulder under an upturned glass, lifting the edge of the glass from time to time to take a lungful.

The effects of cannabis vary greatly, depending upon the strength of the plant from which the leaves have been taken and the individual himself. Often the only result is a feeling of relaxation and mild euphoria, though there can be distortions of time and space rather like those produced by the stronger hallucinogens. In inexperienced users there is sometimes a loss of physical co-ordination, as after a glass or two of an alcoholic drink, but experienced users carry on much as normal. In fact cannabis users are often at a loss to say just *why* they enjoy the drug. The effects on them are mild, and there's no physical and little psychological addiction. They say simply that they just feel 'good' after using it, peaceful and benevolent and with a pleasant, slight distortion in their surroundings which shows them that the normal way of experiencing the world is only one of the many forms of consciousness of which the human mind is capable.

Should cannabis be legalized? It's apparent harmlessness and the non-violent moods which it induces leads many to argue that cannabis is a less dangerous drug than alcohol, and that it could replace the latter as the 'socially acceptable' drug with benefits all round. But the legalization of cannabis faces two obstacles. First, we don't know the long-term effects, and *any* kind of smoking is likely to damage the respiratory system. Second, the 'switched off' mood produced by cannabis may induce risk-taking in people with responsible jobs like driving and flying, and may blunt efficiency in those required to take quick or crucial decisions. The fact that alcohol already does these things is no argument in favour of legalizing cannabis.

Anti-depressants and tranquillizers

These are a mixed bag, available on doctor's prescription and the black market. At one time barbiturates used to be amongst the most commonly prescribed drugs. Classifiable along with alcohol, they produce a relaxation of normal reflexes and inhibitions. The main problems are that they are highly physically addictive and highly dangerous, especially if taken with alcohol or crushed and injected. Barbiturate overdose is the most common form of suicide, and one way and another barbiturates accounted for over 25,000 deaths between 1960 and 1975.

Because of their danger, barbiturates are now giving way to milder drugs called benzodiazepines (tranquillizers such as Valium, Librium and Ativan, and sleeping pills such as Mogadon). But the *long-term* effect of these drugs is still unknown, as are the possibilities of physical addiction. In overdose or in combination with other drugs they definitely present hazards, and in both adults and children reliance upon them as props is clearly unwise. What happens all too often is that the individual goes on sleeping pills or tranquillizers to help him over a difficult period in his life, and then stays on them when the immediate crisis is past instead of learning other ways of coping.

There are no obvious physical signs of addiction to anti-depressants or tranquillizers, so a parent may only be alerted to misuse when there's been an overdose. If this happens seek medical help *immediately*, and give artificial respiration if necessary until it arrives. Under no circumstances give alcohol or other drugs, even aspirin. *Keep the sufferer awake*, and get him to tell you how many pills he's swallowed and what kind they are. Keep the empty bottle if you can find it.

Designer drugs

These are a minor problem in the UK as yet, but could soon present a major hazard. Such is the advance of modern chemistry that unscrupulous scientists can now 'design' and make artificial drugs with the intention of producing specific physical and psychological effects. Such drugs are relatively cheap to produce, and pose a nightmare for those who try to keep the law abreast of them. The hazards presented by these drugs are incalculable. We can only guess at the devastating physical and mental damage they may do, and already some of the tragic victims are being identified by the medical profession. Since designer drugs can come in any shape or form it's impossible to tell you what to look out for. The best defence is to have a good relationship with your adolescent, to be familiar with his lifestyle and his friends, and to have confidence in his good sense. The day may not be far distant when the techniques for producing designer drugs are well enough known for a clever sixth-form chemist to have a go in the shed at the bottom of the garden, with results too frightening to contemplate.

Helping drug users

With most of the drugs mentioned here (with the exception perhaps of crack), many users experiment a time or two then stop. And there's no evidence that use of the so-called 'soft' drugs such as cannabis, which carry lower risks and lower penalties than the 'hard' or Class A drugs such as heroin and cocaine, actually *cause* people to graduate to hard drugs. True, most hard drug users begin with soft drugs, since they are more readily available, but it is less soft drugs than psychological problems which prompt drug escalation. Thus if an adolescent experiments with a soft drug this doesn't necessarily mean she's on the slippery slope (any more than it would if she enjoyed a glass or two of alcohol). And if she *is* on this slope, and if she's living at home, you should detect signs of the fact long before she becomes an addict.

Immediate action you should take

But clearly, addiction or no, immediate action is necessary if you find your adolescent on drugs. Let's look at the things you should do.

1. Your first reaction will be shock. Why should such a thing happen in *your* family? Does it mean you've gone terribly wrong somewhere? Don't waste time on such soul-searchings. You can return to them later. The first necessity is to talk to your child. Maybe you've actually caught her taking drugs, or maybe you've come across

the evidence in her room. Tell her what you've discovered, indicate you know the temptations that face young people these days, and encourage her to talk. It's no use becoming emotional. This isn't a confrontation. Anger and recriminations will make everyone's job harder. Understanding and clear-headedness will have the opposite effect.

2. Find out the actual extent of her drug-taking. When faced with the evidence of their activities, some drug-takers will try to deny it. Others will defend drug-taking and argue that it's all quite 'harmless', and that they have it under control. Others will admit to everything, own up to being foolish, but underestimate the amount they actually consume. Very few will be completely open about things from the start. The reason is usually that drug users feel ambivalent about their habit. They enjoy it, they think it's 'big' when they're with their friends, but underneath they're uncertain and afraid, and not a little guilty. Don't insist on the whole truth at this stage, simply make an estimate of what and how much your adolescent is taking. If you realize that she's been stealing money from you to finance her habit, refer to this now (bring as much into the open on both sides as you can right from the beginning) but don't dwell on it and don't insist she owns up. Say instead, 'That's something we can come back to later.'

3. Don't personalize the issue. Leave 'me' out of it. It does neither of you any good to accuse her of 'letting me down' or 'breaking my heart'. She's highly unlikely to be using drugs with the conscious intention of hurting you. The great majority of drug users drift into the habit never intending it to get a hold over them. Even many heroin addicts kid themselves they could easily give up if they wanted to, and that they aren't 'hooked' at all.

4. Decide how serious it is. If she's been taking cannabis or sniffing glue, the chances are this is only experimental behaviour, done to keep up with her friends. Explain the dangers (if she argues that cannabis isn't dangerous,

689

emphasize the legal position to her), then help her stop experimenting. You could do this by laying down the law ('Don't you ever let me catch you doing such a thing again') or you could ask for her word ('I want you to promise me you'll never . . .'). The trouble with both these approaches is that they treat her like a child. They ask her to keep off drugs as a way of obeying or pleasing *you*. And the risk is that you're daring her to assert her independence and show she can make up her own mind what to do. A better approach is to ask her, 'What are you going to do about it from now on?' This puts the onus on her. You're giving her a chance to make up her own mind, and once she does she's far more likely to stick to it than if she's simply informed (or put on her honour) to do as she's told. Time enough to try laying down the law if she *doesn't* come to a sensible decision of her own. In the future, try to have a closer relationship with her so that she'll confide more in you and give you a better idea of what she's up to.

5. Decide if outside help is needed. If her drug-taking is more established, and particularly if it involves hard drugs, you may need outside help. The dose and the time required for physical drug dependency to develop vary from individual to individual, but usually if it *has* developed you will already have seen signs of physical changes in your adolescent, and outside help will be essential. If these changes haven't taken place, things may not have gone very far, and you may prefer to point out the full extent of your anxieties to her and then say, 'We must go and talk to the doctor.' If she doesn't like the idea, this gives you a strong bargaining point. 'All right, if we don't go to the doctor, how are you going to finish with drugs?' It's now up to her to make suggestions (coming in early at night, staying away from certain friends, etc.). If you're satisfied with what she suggests, this forms the basis of a contract between you. She sticks to her word, and you agree not to call in the doctor. She breaks her word, and the doctor is called in.

You have two further strong cards in your hand. The first is that drug-taking is illegal. If you point out that you know her friends are involved, and the police should be told before the **Two further** trouble spreads further, this is a powerful deterrent. She **cards you can** doesn't want to get her friends into trouble, and will very **play** likely agree to stop in order to avoid police involvement. Remind her also that if she goes on taking drugs at home with your knowledge this makes you legally liable, and you're not prepared to allow that to happen. The law divides non-medical drugs into three categories, A, B and C, with A being the most serious, and the legal penalties vary accordingly. The better your knowledge of the law, the more forcibly you can use it as an argument to bring her off her habit.

The second card you still have to play is that drug-taking costs money. Even glues and solvents aren't cheap, while to fund a heroin habit costs tens of pounds a day. An adolescent doesn't come by that kind of money easily. If she's got a job, all the money she's earning will be going to finance her drug-taking. Alternatively, she'll be financing herself by illegal means. Show her you know what the drug habit is costing her, and that there are certain questions that have to be answered. By watching her finances more closely in future you can also monitor whether she stays off the habit.

With all drug-taking, it's important to show the user you **Show her you** have confidence in her ability to stop. If you doubt her, she'll **believe she can** be more likely to doubt herself. And belief in oneself is vital if **stop** drugs are to be resisted. It's equally important to show that you don't look upon drugs as solely 'her' problem. Once someone becomes a drug user, then the problem is shared by the whole family. It's everyone's problem, and everyone is going to help overcome it.

Always call in outside help, though, if the user shows signs of withdrawal symptoms, or if she's unable to stay off drugs or keep the agreements she's made with you. There's a great deal of specialist advice and guidance available, and your doctor will advise you on what to do and where to go.

Dealing with the longer-term problems
Now is the time to look at the factors that may have contributed to the problem and see how to put them right. One of the first things to strike you will be that communications haven't been good between you and your adolescent. You've got out of touch with his life. He's stopped confiding in you.

Maybe you've been extra busy or preoccupied. And as he's grown older so he's seemed to need you less and less. For his part, perhaps he hasn't invited communication. He's so bound up in his own pursuits that you hardly see him.

Re-open the channels of communication

Open up the channels of communication again. Don't treat him as an 'invalid', or as no longer worthy of your trust and respect. Be open and friendly. Try to develop some shared interests. If you feel you've been neglecting him say so. Show that you're aware the drug-taking is a consequence of the behaviour of the whole family, and not of his behaviour alone. If he has negative feelings towards you, let him come out with them. Don't be defensive and try to 'hit back'.

On the other hand don't be a door-mat. In any family and in any relationship there are bound to be misunderstandings and tensions that lead to negative feelings. The problem is often not so much the negative feelings but the fact that these feelings aren't brought into the open. Make up for lost time. Let him have his say, but show that you don't take anything too much to heart. You're concerned to help him, not to make yourself feel wretched. Leave your own feelings out of it.

At the same time, point out to him the areas where he's contributed to his own problems. Perhaps he's been over-secretive. Perhaps he's taken offence where none was meant. Perhaps he's alienated people by his manner. Talk more as equals than as parent and child. Remember that the problem of his drug-taking belongs equally to you both. All you're doing is clearing the decks so that the problem can be handled. If he rejects your attempts at first, don't be impatient or retreat behind the 'I've done what I can and it's no use' defence. Stick at it, diplomatically and cheerfully. Show you're not out to make life harder for him but to make life easier. You're on his side. You're in partnership with him in facing the drug-taking, not in judgement over him.

Many drug users see themselves as worthless

In addition to being poor communicators, serious drug users often have another personality problem with which they need help. This can take many forms, but what it boils down to is that they can't value themselves. Remember how strongly I've emphasized the need for a child to learn self-acceptance and self-esteem (Chapter 7). If we value ourselves, we've too much respect for our minds and bodies to abuse them through drug-taking. Many serious drug users have a poor opinion of

themselves (sometimes even a fatalistic hopelessness), however much they hide it behind bravado, even before they take
to drugs. The cause of drug abuse lies in the addict's previous
life experiences. Even though perhaps successful on the surface, he feels inadequate. At its worst, this inadequacy can
take the form of self-disgust and even self-destructiveness.
The drug user, through his drug use and the neglect of his
physical and mental welfare, is often consciously or unconsciously punishing himself. At a certain level he feels worthless, and turns his negative feelings inwards upon himself. He
becomes his own enemy, and weakened further by the effects
of the drugs themselves, he sinks all too often into an apathy
which can only be relieved by yet more drug-taking. His drug-
induced inability to make something of his life adds further to
his problems. The only escape from his meaningless life is
through yet more drug-taking. Drugs offer him an escape into
a different kind of consciousness in which nothing seems to
matter and in which he can experience a sense of release from
the reality with which he's unable to cope. Finding it difficult
to communicate with his family, he increasingly seeks the
company of other drug users. They all have problems similar
to his own. They all have the same inability to cope. With
them he finds an identity, even a fragile kind of meaning,
which binds him closer still to his habit.

Helping a drug user solve these personality problems takes **What we can do**
time and patience. Our job is to:

1. Help the drug user communicate his inner feelings and
   confusions (I've already talked about this). Sympathy
   and a non-judgemental approach are vital.

2. Help him regain his self-respect. Start at the physical
   level. Many drug users lose all interest in their personal
   appearance, and need encouragement and support in
   once more caring for how they look. A little judicious
   praise helps no end.

3. Build up his physical strength. Self-disgust, lack of concern for physical appearance, and the appetite-depress-
   ing effect of many drugs weaken the constitution of the
   addict and give him less chance of resisting his habit or

the physical infections that may go with it. Get him on to a proper diet, and give him the extra vitamins and minerals he needs.

4. Get him back into a regular lifestyle. Drug users keep odd hours, skip meals, become unreliable. The discipline of a more ordered lifestyle, with proper attention to meals and sleep, is in itself a powerful factor in rehabilitation.

5. Enlist the help of family and friends. The more he can talk to them, the less need he'll have for the companionship of other drug users. Stress to people they mustn't be patronizing towards him, or judgemental, or treat him as an invalid. What he needs are normal, sensible social contacts. Stress as well that no one should either dwell on or avoid the subject of his drug-taking. Drug users are best helped if they see that no one is ashamed of what they've been going through, or expects them to be ashamed. They've hit a problem in their lives, just as we all hit problems. And just as we all appreciate help, so we're offering help.

6. Make him feel useful and needed. Find things he can do and areas where he can help, and be patient if at first he isn't very reliable. If he should accuse you of wanting his help just as a way of building up his confidence don't deny it. He needs to feel you're being honest with him. Say, 'Sure; but I know what you can do, so I want the benefit of it. No use sitting around when you're good at . . . (whatever it is).'

7. Find a sympathetic doctor and a sympathetic support group where drug users can go and talk about themselves. Just as the addict turns to other drug users for friendship and advice when he's on his habit, so he needs the friendship and advice of ex-drug users when he's coming off it. Working with them he's able to see that it *is* possible to break the habit.

8. Help the drug user with his deeper personality problems. Low self-acceptance can come from failure to allow a child to accept his own emotions and the person he is, or to give him the interest, support and affection vital throughout childhood. But particularly in adolescence, when things are becoming more and more competitive, difficulties can arise if we constantly demand too much of a child, either in terms of school work or of behaviour in general. The adolescent is searching for a sense of identity now that he's on the brink of adult life, and if he feels he's always falling short of what is wanted of him, he can end up despairing or with a fierce resentment towards everyone for asking him to be what he's not. So have those around him failed to recognize his needs? Have they been forcing him into decisions about his life or its future direction which are unsuitable for him? Have they been showing constant disappointment in him? Have they been showing him they'd much rather he was someone else? We all need a certain outside direction in our lives, particularly when we're young, but there's a happy medium, and beyond that trouble lies.

9. Finally, give plenty of affection. Parental love should be unqualified love. The fear that his habit may be alienating his parents only makes the addict go deeper into it to escape from his fear. Those who successfully come off drugs testify time and again to the part played by the love and support of their parents. This love gives them something to hang on to. So leave him in no doubt of the existence of this love, and of the fact that it means just as much to *you* as it does to him.

No addict is ever 'cured', in the sense that his problem has gone for ever. For the rest of his life he has to be careful not to slip back, and has to avoid the opportunities and the company which will make slipping back easy. This is particularly important at times when he's feeling depressed or low, but it's also important should he become over-confident about his ability to resist further addiction. Over-confidence can lead to the feeling that 'it's okay to try it again just this once; I'm strong enough now not to get hooked again.' It isn't and he isn't.

Ex-drug users need continuing help With all drugs, including alcohol, the only way to avoid a return of addiction is to stay off for good. The mind may now be stronger, but the body can be pushed back into its craving the moment the lethal substance gets into the bloodstream again. So ex-drug users need continuing help. And here your task is difficult, because on the one hand you have to show you trust him, and on the other hand you have to be alert to any danger signs. So tact, good communication, commitment and a sense of humour are vital.

PREPARING FOR WORK

It comes as no surprise to most parents to learn that the adolescent with a clear idea about what she wants to do in life is the exception rather than the rule. Whether they go on to higher education or not, most adolescents and young adults take up their first job more on the basis of opportunity than free choice (this is less true of the second and subsequent jobs). Schools and education authorities offer careers advice, but many adolescents are too inexperienced to know what they really want to do until they've got to know themselves better and been out in the world and seen more of what's on offer. And of course for many young people there's a big gap between what they might really like to do and what they can realistically expect to achieve.

Deciding what she wants to do

It was important when making decisions lower down the school as to which subjects to study (pages 626–7) not to close off any avenues which might lead to desirable careers later on. And now that the time for choosing a career is approaching, you can help your adolescent further by helping her identify the category of job that most appeals to her. Once the category is established, you can study the range of jobs which fall within it until you find one that squares with her abilities. One way of arranging these categories, with examples of the relevant jobs, is as follows:

Medical	– doctor, nurse, speech therapist, radiographer, physiotherapist, chiropodist, ambulance crew
Caring	– social worker, probation officer, careers adviser, nursery nurse, welfare officer, care assistant
Intellectual	– university or college lecturer, teacher, librarian
Persuasive	– salesman, publicity officer, advertising agent, shop assistant
Scientific	– research scientist, pharmacist, computer programmer, laboratory technician
Managerial/ admin.	– management trainee, local government officer, secretary, storeman
Engineering	– civil, geological, chemical, mechanical, mining, electrical or electronic engineer, plumber, mechanic, electrician, factory worker
Construction	– surveyor, quantity surveyor, architect, building trades, joiner, carpenter
Aesthetic/ design	– musician, writer, designer, photographer, dress designer
Health/beauty	– hairdresser, beauty therapist, masseur, dance teacher, keep-fit teacher
Sporting	– professional sportsman or woman, swimming instructor, riding instructor, stable hand, groundsman
Media	– television and radio producer, journalist, publisher, cameraman, sound engineer, make-up artist, costume designer, wardrobe mistress, stage or floor manager, actor
Transport	– airline pilot, air traffic controller, transport manager, train driver, bus or taxi driver, travel agent
Catering	– hotel management, restaurant management, chef, air steward, waiter

Legal	– barrister, solicitor, solicitor's clerk, police officer, customs officer, traffic warden
Military	– military officer, non-commissioned military service, civilian military employee
Farming/ horticulture	– farmer, horticulturist, landscape gardener, forester, nurseryman, farm worker
Financial	– stockbroker, banker, merchant banker, economist
Insurance/ housing	– underwriter, loss adjuster, insurance agent, building society manager or clerk, estate agent

Lists of this kind can help an adolescent to see that within each of these categories something of the same interests are catered for, but at different standards of qualification. Other ways of categorizing, which can be used in conjunction with the list just given, are to group jobs into respectively those that involve work with people, with books, with animals or with things; those which involve indoor or outdoor work; those which involve regular or irregular hours; those in which one works under supervision and those in which one is one's own boss; those which involve travel and those which do not. Thus an adolescent who wants for example to work in a sporting occupation which involves animals, outdoor work, irregular hours and travel might aim at becoming a stable hand, while someone who wants to work with books, indoors and with regular hours might aim at librarianship. Where, as in the case of a stable hand, the job is difficult to come by, the individual may have to decide which of her chosen categories she can most easily drop, and what new opportunities are thereby opened up for her (e.g. if she can drop the 'sporting' category she might be drawn towards farm work or work in wild life conservation).

Finding a job

It's one thing to decide what you want to do, and quite another actually to land the job concerned. Help your adolescent to be realistic in his expectations, and set about helping him achieve them. If the job he's after is an attractive one, it's a fair bet that plenty of other people will be after it too. Assuming everyone has the right paper qualifications, how does an employer choose between applicants? In two ways. First, he looks for *personal qualities*, and second he looks for *experience*. I'm often surprised at how poorly informed many adolescents are about these two crucial issues. Let's take them one at a time.

Personal qualities

These reveal themselves from the moment the employer opens a letter of application. Many adolescents who apply for a number of jobs say they get disheartened when it comes to writing their twentieth letter or so, and just dash it off to get it out of the way. I have to remind them that to the employer it's the *first* letter he's seen from them. Since he's looking for someone who is going to be conscientious and take an interest in their work, he isn't going to be impressed by a letter that's just dashed off. Since he may also be interested in neatness, an illegible scrawl on a scruffy piece of paper isn't going to impress him much either. Nor is a letter that is clearly a copy of one sent to an earlier potential employer, and which isn't relevant to the present application.

A good letter is the first thing

Should the letter be good enough to procure an interview, personal qualities now show themselves in dress and speech (has the candidate bothered to turn himself out appropriately for the interview? Can he speak clearly and reasonably grammatically?), in manner (is he co-operative, open and confident, without being conceited and know-all?), in attitude (does he suggest honesty, reliability and conscientiousness?) and in personality (is he lively and outgoing or dull and withdrawn?). The employer is going to pay the candidate to work for him, and he wants to be sure he'll be getting value for money. The last thing he wants is to employ someone who will be untrustworthy, uninterested, unindustrious and unable to get on with colleagues and workmates.

Adolescents sometimes ask why should it matter how they dress for an interview, if once they get the job they'll have to wear overalls and spend much of their time with oily machinery. At other times I'm asked why, if an adolescent thinks he

How a job candidate dresses does matter

looks smart and fashionable, he should bother about a middle-aged employer's opinion of his clothes and hair-style. The answer to both questions is that, rightly or wrongly, many employers see the way one dresses at an interview as a symptom of one's whole attitude and personality. If someone looks clean and smart and not too outrageous it shows at least that he knows what is appropriate, and has bothered to take into account the sensitivities (however outmoded) of his future employer. He may be no better at the job than the next candidate who turns up looking like a Christmas tree, but the employer is likely to think him a much safer bet.

Rehearse your adolescent for interviews   As for good speech and the other personal qualities I've just mentioned, I'm frequently saddened at the way adolescents who have all these attributes fail to project them at interview. Half an hour, even ten minutes, spent rehearsing for interviews can lead to dramatic improvements. Many adolescents just aren't aware how poor their interview technique is. Get a friend who's used to job interviewing to run through a specimen interview with your adolescent. If you don't have such a friend, act as the interviewer yourself. Most interviews start with a few personal questions designed to put the candidate at his 'ease'. How old is he? Where does he live? How did he travel to the interview? Has he any relatives in this kind of work? Once this ice-breaking session is finished, the interviewer then goes on to ask questions which fall into four main categories:

1. Why do you want the job?
2. What are your qualifications/experience for the job?
3. What do you expect *from* the job?
4. What will you bring *to* the job?

Questions in category (1) are designed to test motivation and interest, those under (2) (which may include specific technical questions) to test knowledge, those under (3) to test expectations (and perhaps illusions), and those under (4) to test personal qualities. The questions may not be offered in this order of course. And many employers (though they mostly believe to the contrary) are relatively poor at interviewing, doing far too much of the talking themselves or showing a

strong inclination to ride their own hobby-horse. But funda-
mentally what the interviewer is looking for is someone who
can marshal his thoughts quickly and coherently, and who can
avoid on the one hand drying up after giving single word
answers, and on the other monopolizing the conversation with
rambling and often irrelevant replies. Spending time running
through typical interview questions with your adolescent, and
then discussing together the strengths and weaknesses of his
replies and the extent to which they bring out his desirable
personal qualities, is of inestimable value.

Experience

Employers understand readily enough that if an adolescent is
just out of school he won't have much in the way of specific
experience for the job. But if he's as interested in the job as he
claims, then he will have made every effort to get *some* experience, however brief. I listen to adolescents and young adults
who tell me, for example, that they want to become journalists
or work for television or become photographers or work with
the mentally handicapped, yet when I ask them if they've tried
their hand at submitting newspaper articles, or at finding out
what goes on in a television studio or in a home for the
handicapped, they look surprised and say of course not, as if
experiences of this kind only happen once you've landed the
job of your dreams. An employer interviewing a would-be
journalist won't necessarily expect you to have had anything
published, but he will expect you to have started learning your
trade (and to show your determination and interest) by studying the kind of articles that get published and then practising
writing and submitting them yourself. An employer interviewing you for your first job in television won't expect you to have
contributed to the work of a television studio, but he will be
interested to know whether you've shown the initiative to write
and ask for a visit, or whether you've tried for a weekend or
holiday job somewhere in the television building, even if only
helping out in the canteen. And an employer in the field of
mental handicap will want to know whether you've done any
voluntary work with the mentally retarded, and if not why not.

Where many people are after the one job, it's often the
person who has done just that little bit extra by way of gaining
experience who ends up successful. Help your adolescent

Any effort to get some experience will make a difference

701

appreciate this, and start trying for experience, however limited, well before the time for interviews arrives. He may not find this experience easy to come by, but his very persistence in trying for it will impress his future employer.

The unemployed teenager

As the pace of technological and industrial change (and all the factors associated with this change) hots up, more and more emphasis is placed upon qualifications for many of the best jobs. We live in a highly complex society which demands high-level skills from its workers. We also live in a society which demands geographical mobility, so that frequently the right jobs aren't readily available on the doorstep. The result is that many adolescents have to face a period of unemployment before they find something suited to their abilities and interests. This can be a worrying experience for both them and their parents, and much depends upon the attitude of mind they are both able to adopt towards it.

Show your adolescent you believe in her   Central to this attitude should be a positive and optimistic view of the future. If your adolescent is realistic about the job she's looking for, and if she has the abilities necessary to handle it, then it's vital she should go on believing in herself. Generally, she'll continue to do so as long as she sees her parents believe in her. It is sometimes said that no man is a failure until his wife thinks he is (a saying I have always made sure my wife is very familiar with) and vice versa, and it is every bit as true that no child thinks she's a failure until her parents do. As long as your adolescent is sure she has your faith and support, she stands a good chance of keeping her spirits up until she finds what she's looking for.

She needs to keep active rather than just lazing about   Since habit is another of the things that sustains a person through a period of unemployment, it's vital your adolescent should have set times in the week when she looks for jobs, and should aim at putting in a realistic minimum of applications each week. Habit extends to attending training and work experience schemes too, even if these aren't in the specific job areas she wants. The habit of keeping regular working hours, of being out of the house, of mixing with others who are working, is a powerful incentive to go on with the job-hunting.

It also impresses employers, who aren't that keen to take on people who have been idle for long periods.

Another essential is for your adolescent to develop active, creative interests. These could, for instance, be to do with sport, amateur dramatics, local history, dancing, music, or voluntary work with the under-privileged. They keep the mind and body active, encourage planning and organizing abilities, and help maintain that vital sense of self-worth and usefulness. The worst life-style to adopt is staying in bed till midday and spending the afternoon in front of the television and the evening down at the pub. However sharp the mind, a purposeless life of this kind will quickly blunt it.

If your adolescent needs a specific exercise to boost her confidence, one of the best is to encourage her to commit positive ideas about herself to paper. The act of writing these ideas down has a potentially powerful effect upon one's thinking. A good format is: **Help her feel positively about herself**

'I want a job as . . .'
'I'd be good at this job because . . .'
'I'd be good at this job because . . .'
'I'd be good at this job because . . .'
(continue with as many statements as possible)

At the same time, while giving her every support and encouragement, it's important that you don't make life financially too easy for your adolescent. It's right and proper that you should want to help her financially while she's looking for work, but it's better for her if she has the incentive of feeling hard-up and wanting to do something about it. Pay her for doing jobs at home over and above the normal line of domestic duty by all means, but prompt her as far as possible to look for income outside the home – helping neighbours, labouring for a friend, doing a part-time or temporary job.

Finally, there's no reason to give up hope, even if your adolescent is out of work for a long period. There is a fear that if she's out of work for too long she'll become unemployable, but statistics don't bear this out. As the months go by, the adolescent becomes more and more conscious of the fact that her contemporaries are all earning money and leaving her behind, and that if she goes on as she is she'll be missing out **Never give up hope** on the chance of having a home of her own one day and doing the things she wants with her life. This usually leads to increased determination to find work, even if it means initially taking the kind of job that was scorned a short while ago, or leaving home for a time. The result is that one day luck turns, and she joins the ranks of the taxpayers like the rest of us.

LETTING GO

Your adolescent still needs you. In a way, he needs you as much as he's always done. But the nature of his need for you is changing. Time passes much more quickly for parents than it does for children. You look at your adolescent and it seems only five minutes ago that he was trotting by your side on his way to infant school. You find it hard to realize how deeply the years have changed him. He's still your child, and a part of you wants the relationship with him to be the same as it's always been. But to him, those infant school days seem hidden in the remote past. To him, the world is a very different place from what it was then. His growth towards independence, steady and smooth with some children but proceeding with sudden stops and starts with others, is now reaching the point where he's ready to make his own way.

Your adolescent still needs you, but he's no longer a child

So instead of needing you as the source of authority in his life, he now needs you in more subtle ways. He needs you to approve of the adult he's becoming. He needs you as someone to swap ideas with, to debate and discuss with. Because he's still uncertain about himself and the ways of the world he needs your guidance, and he's got enough good sense to take it as long as he feels he doesn't *have* to. Heavy-handedness on the part of parents during the adolescent years will cause any spirited youngster to feel rebellious. It isn't that he minds so much your telling him what to do, it's the way you tell him that irks him. With the age of majority set at eighteen, even a fourth-former at school is only three years away from adulthood. If he thinks you're still treating him like a small child, he'll develop all kinds of subtle strategies for showing his opposition.

One of the best examples is 'dumb insolence'. He doesn't

actually *say* anything, and he does as you ask him, but by expression and demeanour he leaves you in no doubt what he thinks about it all (you included). Some parents find this goads them into anger more quickly than anything else. They feel their child doesn't respect them, yet there's nothing they can actually pin down. And the crosser they become, the more their child carries on with his act, giving them the uncomfortable feeling that he's won the battle.

The only way to handle dumb insolence is to ignore it, as if it isn't even important enough for you to notice. But better still, don't let it happen in the first place. The way to avoid it is to show that you recognize your adolescent's near-adult status, and want him as a partner. If this process of partnership has been developing from childhood, then there's no problem. It now reaches its proper conclusions, and by the time your adolescent reaches the late teens and early twenties, you've slipped almost unnoticed into a relationship of equals. If you haven't allowed for this gradual process then you're going to have to make more obvious adjustments.

Developing a relationship of equals

In adolescence, your child realizes two important things. He realizes that he is just as able as you in many areas of life (more so in some, particularly if he has a better education than you had) and he realizes that you need him as much, perhaps more, than he needs you. The balance is changing, and he knows it. Before long he's going to leave home and start his own family and present you with grandchildren. You're going to want him to keep in close touch, to visit often, to let you enjoy your grandchildren, to help you with the challenges that lie ahead in your own life. So much of this good relationship depends upon what happens *now*.

When parents find this hard to accept I ask them to think about their relationships with their own parents. If these relationships are happy, then they're essentially based upon equality, upon give and take, upon mutual respect and understanding, upon mutual *liking*, with each party relaxed in the other's company and with lots in common to talk about. Where the relationship isn't happy, people usually admit it's because their parents still treat them as children. Their parents have the unerring knack, at each and every meeting, of making them feel small and uncomfortable, guilty and inadequate.

705

Hostile even, hide it though they may. This isn't the relationship you want with your future grown-up children. You want them to come home because they enjoy seeing you, not out of duty. You want them to look forward to your company, to feel easy and relaxed when they're with you. These things don't just happen. They have to be worked for by parents who accept the changing status of their children in adolescence and who don't try to cling to a vanishing authority.

Don't insist he comes on family outings and holidays

So let me repeat that the best way to keep your children is to let them go. In adolescence, your child will be more inclined to go off with his friends than with his family. The family outings so much a feature of the earlier years are now becoming infrequent. It isn't that your teenager no longer enjoys your company. It's that he likes to be with people of his own age, people who want to do the things he likes and visit the places that appeal to him. Family holidays may also show signs of coming to an end. They've been great fun in the past, but interests are now diverging. Mum and dad want something a bit sedate, teenage son and daughter want the bright lights. By the later teens, the generations are often better going their separate ways. This is often a source of understandable sadness for parents. They want to hang on to the old days. But it's inevitable that people change with the years, and far better to leave everyone with happy memories of family holidays past than to drag these holidays out when they've ceased to serve their purpose.

Don't expect him to come to your dinner parties

It's the same when it comes to your friends. At one time, your children wanted to be counted in when you were organizing dinner parties or being invited to go visiting. Now they want to be counted out. They aren't being impolite. They're simply aware of the generation gap. Paradoxically, it's now more noticeable to them than it was when they were young children. In those days the adult world was a fascinating place, and as outsiders they enjoyed looking in and listening in. Now that they're part of that world, they're starting to make choices within it, and to choose company that appeals to them, rather than falling in with your choices. If you particularly want them to join you when you have guests coming, be frank about it and say you know it isn't very exciting for them. Make it clear that it's natural they should feel pretty unenthusiastic, and that you'd have felt exactly the same at their age. Make it clear you're asking them to come not because they 'ought' to come but to please you. Make sure they have responsible jobs to do like opening and pouring the drinks. Try to steer the conversation at table to subjects that interest them, and let them have their say like everyone else. Be subtle about it but try to show your guests that the kids are people who matter and have minds of their own. Avoid talking down to them. They're at the table because *you* want them to be there, not because they want to be there. Show that you appreciate their co-operation and are anxious they feel a full part of what's going on. If after the meal they want to go to their own rooms and listen to music then let them. They've done their part, and it's unrealistic to expect them to sit in with the adults all evening.

By loosening the reins in all areas of domestic life you ensure that your adolescent doesn't feel he has to fight to get free of them. You ensure he goes on enjoying his home and will be glad to return whenever he can once he goes off into the big wide world. And you ensure the foundations are being laid for a mutually rewarding relationship in the changed circumstances that lie ahead.

Leaving home

For those adolescents going on to universities and colleges or away to work, leaving home follows only a few weeks after leaving school. And prepare for it how we might, and rejoice in our children's success how we might, this often isn't an easy time for parents. In fact the day your son or daughter, bags packed and face (metaphorically at least) scrubbed and shining, goes off into the blue you experience what's tantamount to a bereavement. Particularly if you're at home all day, you find yourself wandering time and time again into the empty bedroom, picking up your child's things and putting them down again, reliving memories. There's a deep sense of loss. Everything seems to speak to you of your child, and the house is unbearably quiet and empty. The routine of getting her off to school and having a meal ready for her in the evening is at an end. The life she brought into the house has moved on with her to her university or her college or her new

You will experience a deep sense of loss

707

job. And it all seems to have passed so quickly. Her childhood, her first days at school, her hobbies and interests. Where, for goodness sake, have all the years *gone*? Why couldn't things stay as they were for just that little bit longer?

Some parents feel, mixed in with their loss, a sense almost of betrayal. They know it's unfair and irrational, but they have the feeling that after the care and love and attention they've lavished on their child she's now calmly walked out on them. And for all parents, there's a feeling that part of their life and their role in life has now gone, and middle age and a diminished role lie ahead.

All right, I know there are parents who say they just can't wait to get their children off their hands, and I know there are parents who look forward to the greater freedom which the future years are going to bring. But the overwhelming number, even if their relationships with their children have been fairly turbulent, find the break a painful one. Even those who claim to be looking forward to it usually discover that when it comes it's harder to handle than they ever imagined.

Coping with this mini-bereavement
The only way psychologically to ride out this mini-bereavement is to see that all living systems grow and change. Growth and change are a defining characteristic of life. Only dead things stay the same. So since we can't alter this, we must simply learn to *live* it. Notice I don't say just 'accept' it. Acceptance suggests dull resignation. Living it means realizing that we're *living change* every moment of our life. By opening ourselves to it, by welcoming it, we can find a sudden joy in the essential rightness of things. We can feel gratitude for the past, but without dwelling on it or wanting to relive it. We can chuckle over memories, without letting them become poignant or dominating or preferable to what's happening *now*. Loving life means loving it for what it is, not for what we'd like it to be. Life is change, so we must love that change and be glad of the new experiences it brings.

Leaving home matures a teenager rapidly
Console yourself as well with the thought that leaving home matures a teenager no end. So far, however much independence you've given her, she's always had you at her elbow in case of need. Now she has to do things for herself. The buck stops with her, and she can mature more in a month away from home than in a year back with you. Going away also helps her to appreciate you more. Sure she's always appreciated you

really, but since you've always been around, it's natural that she takes you somewhat for granted. You're part of the furniture of her life. Now suddenly she sees a little of what you've been doing for her over the years. You'll find as well that she becomes more assured and confident. Something of the edginess that she showed while she was asserting her independence has gone now. This independence has been confirmed for her. She's shown she can manage things on her own, and she no longer feels the need to assert herself in the same experimental way.

This new, more relaxed approach is helped greatly if you don't expect her to revert back to dependency every time she comes home. While she's away she can come and go very much as she pleases, and she'll find it irksome if you ask her to give an account of her every movement now she's back under your wing. Enjoy her company and allow her to enjoy her time at home. And give her a little space, so that she can decide for herself what she wants to tell you about her life at college. If you crowd her with questions, at best you'll get no more than brief dutiful answers. Show her the courtesy over her personal life that you would to any responsible adult, and she'll share far more of it with you. Accept, too, that she may not always want to come home for the whole of each vacation. These days there are so many opportunities for trips all over the world with student groups, and for various sponsorships and work experiences, that most young people will want to take advantage of them. The student years are an exceptionally free and happy time; all too soon the responsibilities of earning a living will start closing in.

Don't expect her to revert to dependency when she comes home

Whether your child has left home to go to university or to college or to take up a job, these same things apply. But if he's left to take up a job, there's the added factor that now he's financially independent. This will make him feel even more of an adult and even more entitled to his freedom. But if he's having problems with his new job, or worse still if he finds initially he isn't enjoying it as much as he had expected, he may need help in restoring his confidence and his belief in himself. Teenagers faced with difficulties over work adopt a number of different attitudes to handle their worries. Some adopt bravado ('I could do the job if I wanted to'). Others are defeatist ('I know I'm *never* going to be able to handle it').

Helping your child if he's having difficulties with work

Others are defiant ('It's all the fault of the boss/bad luck/the government. I'm not being given a fair chance').

Bravado, defiance and defeatism are all forms of defence

None of these attitudes is the real teenager. Bravado and defiance in particular are forms of defence, rather like the child who says it's all the fault of 'boring old school' that he isn't getting better marks. Don't expose these defences, concentrate instead on helping your child see that if he's as tough as he makes out, he must realize that ultimately *he's* the person who controls his life, not his job or the boss or luck or the government. If he wants to succeed, therefore, it's up to him rather than anyone else.

This doesn't mean that you don't sympathize with the very real difficulties that your child may be facing. Simply that you want him to look at these difficulties objectively and not emotionally. They may not be his fault, on the other hand they may be. Until it's clear where blame really lies, it isn't possible to decide what must be done about it. Prompt him to take a cool look at what's happening, and then take reasoned decisions about it, seeing himself as far as possible as an autonomous individual rather than a helpless pawn of fate.

If you child is being defeatist, this may be another form of defence, in this case a form of defence which gives him the excuse to stop trying. He's now at the age where he must accept responsibility for his own future, however. If he wants to stop trying, nobody can force him to do otherwise. But he must realize the problem he's facing now will only get worse as the years go by. Nobody else is going to make his life into a success for him. Nor can he expect always to live at home. One day he'll have to provide for himself, and perhaps a family. Re-orientate him towards more productive effort. Go over with him the things that are causing his problems. If he's been bringing them on himself, help him see how to change his own behaviour. Perhaps he hasn't been assertive enough. Or adventurous enough. Or persistent enough. Or patient enough. Perhaps he hasn't been giving a proper account of himself, perhaps he hasn't been relating properly to his employers or his workmates. Help him recognize the social skills he may be lacking, and discuss how he may acquire them. Help him think optimistically about himself and his future, and to respect and appreciate his own abilities.

For the single parent, letting a teenage son or daughter start to live their own lives is often particularly difficult. There is a tendency for the single parent to look to the child to supply the emotional support that isn't there from a partner, and this can place unfair responsibilities upon young shoulders. But youngsters have their own lives to lead, however much we miss them. And parenthood, from birth onwards, is an exercise in unselfishness, in putting the needs of your child before your own, and this is just another example of the process. One of the hardest examples perhaps, but still very much of a piece with what's gone before.

For the single parent letting go is particularly hard

Homesickness

Up to now I've been talking as if your teenager settles quite happily away from home. But this isn't true of everyone. Some young people miss their families dreadfully, and take a great deal of time coming to terms with life away from the nest. I've known students who were so unhappy they had to give up promising careers in order to go back to their parents. I don't need to say how sad this is. Young people should be able to leave home and manage happily enough, and if they can't, then the psychologist is always a little concerned about it. There are two extremes in fact that concern him. On the one hand the teenager who feels so restricted at home that she just can't wait to get away, and on the other hand the teenager who just longs every minute to get back. The first extreme we've already discussed, the second needs a little examination.

Except in very young children, extreme homesickness is nearly always a sign of insecurity. The child just doesn't feel safe unless she's with her parents. Away from them the world seems hostile and uncertain and threatening. Though she sometimes can't put it into words, she has vague fears that something terrible is going to happen. No amount of sympathy and understanding seems to help. All she wants is to get back home as fast as she can.

Homesickness is a sign of insecurity

There are various reasons for this insecurity. Perhaps the child or one or other of her parents has been ill a lot. Perhaps her parents are unhappy together, so that she's never had the security of a stable home. Or perhaps she's simply been *taught* to be insecure, by a parent or parents who are also insecure and have conveyed this insecurity and the anxieties that go with it to the child. Often the child's fears seem justified, because the other children sense her as being 'different' and take to teasing and frightening her. To a mummy's (or daddy's) boy or girl, the world is a menacing and confusing place, working to different 'rules' from those of home. Even when she's old enough and bright enough to see how silly all this is, she can't do much about it. *Emotionally* she's still in the grip of her uncertainties, even though *logically* she knows them to be groundless.

I'm not talking about the bout of homesickness many children feel when they go away on their own for the first time, and which soon passes. I'm talking about homesickness that actually gets in the way of functioning effectively away from home. Parents of homesick children often find it hard to see where they've gone wrong. They've tried to be good parents. They love their children and have always wanted what was best for them. But they have to accept that however much they have given her, they've failed to give their child the confidence to go out in the world and enjoy the feeling of being on her own two feet.

Keep your own regrets at her leaving to yourself If you think your teenager may be homesick, help her by keeping your own regrets and misgivings to yourself. Of course you don't want her to go and of course you'll miss her dreadfully. But don't let her see it. Pour out your sadness to a relative or friend, but not to her. Keep the atmosphere light and optimistic. If she says she's worried about leaving home, assure her a lot of people feel like that, but you know she'll soon settle down. She's got *far* too much sense to sit around brooding about home and missing out on all the fun around her. Don't say, 'I don't know what I'm going to do without you' or 'I'm going to miss you *dreadfully*', even if you only say such things in fun. They'll stick in her mind. Stress all the time how proud you are of her, so that she can see going away from home as a positive thing which is going to please you. And if when she is away she starts phoning up and saying she wants to come home, give her the confidence to stay on. Do this not by telling her she must stay, which just adds a feeling of hopelessness to everything else, but by encouraging her to give it just a little longer. 'Let's see how you feel next week.' 'Let's give it a few more days.' 'Let's wait until you've had a chance to start making a few friends.' Giving her a target a few days ahead each time stops her from thinking about the months and years stretching away into the distance.

Once she comes home there's the problem of going back once the break is over. That won't be easy if she still hasn't settled. If she's at university or college, try to get her to make arrangements to meet a friend and travel back together. Or if you're taking her yourself, arrive at around the same time as a friend, so that you won't have to leave her on her own. Time your arrival so that you don't get her there in the blank hours of the afternoon, with nothing much to do except mope and think of home. Arrive if you can in the early evening, when she can look forward to going out with friends to the pub or the cinema to take her mind off things.

Above all don't hang on to her homesickness. If you miss her badly, there's a temptation (as when she started school) almost to welcome the fact that she's missing you just as much, and perhaps even to encourage her in her sadness. But she has to learn to live her own life. And if she hasn't begun to learn this lesson almost from the moment she's out of the pram, then she must start to learn it now. There's no time to lose.

Don't encourage her in her homesickness

Conclusion

So we've come full circle. We started with parents-to-be, and we end up with parents whose children have left home. Now you're on your own once more, the time has come to take up many of the things that interest you but that had to be shelved when there were children to look after. Life goes in phases, and once the phase of child-rearing is over, another new and stimulating phase is ready to open up. Expenses are lower. You can go on more ambitious holidays. Evenings and weekends are freer. Life generally is less hectic. So spend more time on yourself, getting to know yourself all over again and finding out the person you are. Mothers in particular often tell me that they devote so much time to looking after their families when their children are at home that they have little opportunity to think of themselves as people in their own right. Well now that opportunity has come, and you deserve to be able to make the most of it.

From time to time, parents say that once their children have grown up and left home they feel the most significant part of their lives is over. Nonsense. The years from now on are potentially amongst the most creative of your life. It is in these years that you have the chance to widen your sphere of usefulness outside the home, to develop your awareness of the community, to reflect on the meaning life has for you personally, to stop being so frantically *busy* and take in more of what is happening around you. You'll miss your children of course, but overriding this there should be a sense of achievement. Being a parent has 'worked'. Your children are now ready and properly equipped to strike out on their own, and one day start new families in their own right.

And in any case, you haven't stopped being a parent. You and your children now have a new relationship ahead of you, one just as important in its way as anything that has gone before. A relationship of adults and of equals, in which a whole new way of being friends and of being useful to each other opens up. Before long, you'll be helping your child set up a home, and be looking forward to grandchildren and to reliving something of your child's own early years through them. Think positively and optimistically about what lies ahead in the coming years. But don't make the mistake of thinking that now grandchildren are being mentioned this makes you old. Age is very much an attitude of mind. Think young and confident and healthy, and you're half-way towards being these things. Labels are odd devices. As I hope I've made clear throughout the book, once we start applying them to people they start thinking of themselves in those terms. Don't let the label 'grandparent' define you. You are who you feel you are, and not a set of terms in other people's vocabularies.

Let me finish on a personal note. Assuming you're not a person who reads the last page of a book first, thank you for coming this far with me. Even though you won't have agreed with everything I've said, I hope you've found the book useful. But much more than that, I hope you've enjoyed raising your children, and playing your part in the magical mystery tour that is childhood. I hope you've received as much from your children as I've received from mine. In the end, I don't think even the best parents amongst us ever *quite* deserve their children. Children come as a gift, and although that gift has strings attached to it called 'hard work' and 'broken nights' and 'clash of wills' and a few other such things, the strings are as nothing when compared with the gift itself.

Appendices

Physical Growth and Development

The average birth-weight for babies born in Europe and the USA is around 3.2 kg, with boys a few ounces heavier than girls and first babies usually lighter than subsequent ones. A range from 2.5 kg to 4.5 kg is considered normal, and babies above or below these weights may need special care. During the first week of life, while they are adapting to the process of sustaining their own metabolism and still haven't started feeding normally, most babies lose weight. Thereafter they catch up quickly, regaining their birth-weight by 2 weeks and averaging about 25 g a day of weight gain during the next 3 months and a little less during the next three, with the result that they will usually have doubled their birth-weight at around 3½ months.

During the first 6 months, most babies will grow around 10 cms and throughout childhood increases in weight and height will usually follow a steady curve, steepest during the first 6 months of life then becoming progressively flatter until the adolescent growth spurt occurs during the early teens. Children whose weight or height gains do not follow the curve, or lie outside the range, must be referred immediately for medical attention. The sooner abnormalities are discovered, the better chance of effective treatment.

Growth in the first 18 months

The charts show normal weight and height gain in children from birth to 18 months. Boys and girls are presented separately, as small but significant differences between the sexes do occur. To plot your baby's weight and height on the appropriate charts first identify his or her age along the bottom axis and weight or height along the left-hand vertical axis, and then follow the upright age line and the horizontal weight line into the chart until they meet each other. Put a cross at this meeting point, and repeat the process monthly, joining the crosses up so that they form a curve.

As you can see from the charts, the steepest rate of increase of both weight and height takes place in the early months. Proportionately, a child grows more rapidly during these months than at any other time in his or her life.

Charts 1 and 2. Girls' and boys' weight charts for the first 18 months

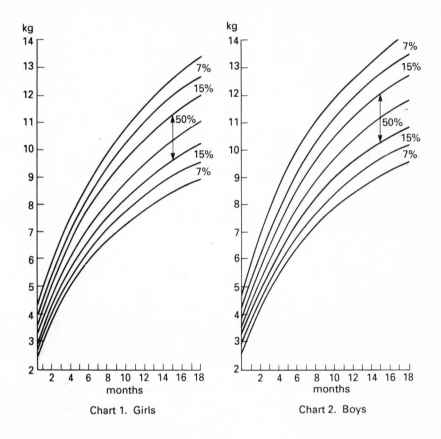

Chart 1. Girls   Chart 2. Boys

The central bands represent the range within which 50 per cent of children fall. The bands on either side of these each represent a further 15 per cent of children, while the two outer bands each represent 7 per cent. The remaining 6 per cent fall outside any of the bands, with 3 per cent heavier than the ranges shown, and 3 per cent lighter.

Charts 3 and 4. Girls' and boys' height charts for the first 18 months

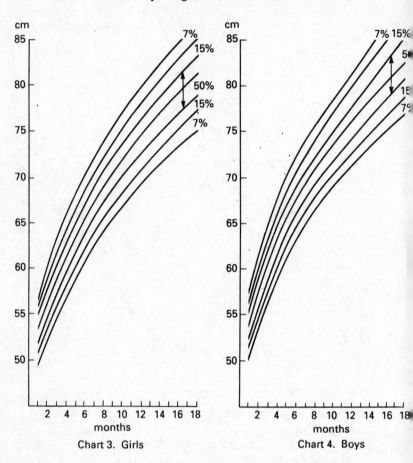

Chart 3. Girls

Chart 4. Boys

The central bands represent the range within which 50 per cent of children fall. The two bands either side of these represent a further 15 per cent of children, while the two outer bands each represent 7 per cent. The remaining 6 per cent fall outside any of the bands, with 3 per cent taller than the ranges shown and 3 per cent shorter.

Growth from 18 months to 5 years

From 18 months onwards, routine weight and height measurements are normally taken at 3-monthly rather than 1-monthly intervals. Boys tend to outpace girls slightly during the period 18 months to 5 years, but for both sexes the *rate* of gain as a proportion of overall weight and height decreases steeply after the hectic activity of the first months of life.

Tables 1 and 2. Girls and boys' weights from 21 months to 5 years

Table 1. Girls' weights

Age	Lightest 10% (less than)	Average	Heaviest 10% (more than)
1yr 9m	10.1	11.91	13.72
2yr	10.43	12.13	14.06
2yr 3m	10.87	12.7	14.63
2yr 6m	11.9	13.27	15.31
2yr 9m	12.02	13.83	15.76
3yr	12.36	14.17	16.44
3yr 3m	12.81	14.74	17.0
3yr 6m	13.15	15.2	17.58
3yr 9m	13.72	15.76	18.37
4yr	14.06	16.22	18.82
4yr 3m	14.51	16.67	19.39
4yr 6m	14.97	17.24	20.07
4yr 9m	15.42	17.8	20.75
5yr	15.54	18.37	21.43

Figures in kilos

Table 2. Boys' weights

Age	Lightest 10% (less than)	Average	Heaviest 10% (more than)
1yr 9m	10.55	11.91	13.95
2yr	10.87	12.7	14.51
2yr 3m	11.11	13.15	15.2
2yr 6m	11.79	13.72	15.76
2yr 9m	12.47	14.4	16.33
3yr	12.7	14.74	16.9
3yr 3m	13.04	15.2	17.46
3yr 6m	13.49	15.65	18.03
3yr 9m	14.06	16.1	18.48
4yr	14.29	16.56	19.05
4yr 3m	14.63	17.01	19.62
4yr 6m	14.97	17.46	20.3
4yr 9m	15.31	18.03	20.87
5yr	15.65	18.48	21.43

Figures in kilos

Tables 3 and 4. Girls' and boys' heights from 21 months to 5 years

Table 3. Girls' heights

Age	Smallest 10% (less than)	Average	Tallest 10% (more than)
1yr 9m	0.81	0.84	0.89
2yr	0.83	0.86	0.90
2yr 3m	0.84	0.87	0.92
2yr 6m	0.86	0.89	0.94
2yr 9m	0.87	0.91	0.96
3yr	0.89	0.93	0.98
3yr 3m	0.91	0.95	1.0
3yr 6m	0.92	0.97	1.02
3yr 9m	0.94	0.99	1.04
4yr	0.96	1.01	1.07
4yr 3m	0.98	1.02	1.09
4yr 6m	0.99	1.04	1.1
4yr 9m	1.01	1.06	1.13
5yr	1.02	1.07	1.14

Figures in metres and centimetres

Table 4. Boys' heights

Age	Smallest 10% (less than)	Average	Tallest 10% (more than)
1yr 9m	0.82	0.86	0.90
2yr	0.83	0.87	0.91
2yr 3m	0.85	0.89	0.93
2yr 6m	0.86	0.90	0.95
2yr 9m	0.88	0.92	0.97
3yr	0.9	0.94	0.99
3yr 3m	0.91	0.96	1.01
3yr 6m	0.93	0.98	1.02
3yr 9m	0.94	1.0	1.05
4yr	0.96	1.01	1.07
4yr 3m	0.98	1.03	1.09
4yr 6m	0.99	1.04	1.11
4yr 9m	1.0	1.06	1.13
5yr	1.01	1.08	1.14

Figures in metres and centimetres

Growth from 6 years to 18 years

Gains in both weight and height proceed steadily rather than spectacularly during the years from 6 to 10, but at age 11 most girls start the adolescent growth spurt, putting on an average of 9 centimetres in 12 months. By age 14, the spurt is over for girls, who normally grow only another 2.5 centimetres or so by age 16, at which time (or a few months later), 98 per cent have reached their final height. In boys, the growth spurt typically begins and finishes 2 years later. Gains in weight show a similar leap for both sexes in adolescence, but these are more variable and less easy to predict.

Something of the magnitude of the growth spurt can be seen from the graph, while average gains in weight and height respectively are given in the tables that follow.

Graph of approximate growth rates for girls and boys, 6–18 years

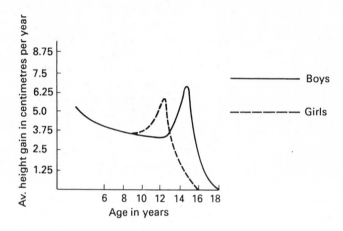

Tables 5 and 6. Girls' and boys' weights and heights from 6–18 years

Table 5. Girls' and boys' weights

Age	Girls' weights	Boys' weights
6	20.86	20.86
7	23.81	23.81
8	26.65	26.65
9	29.48	30.62
10	32.89	35.15
11	36.29	37.42
12	40.82	41.96
13	45.36	49.9
14	49.9	56.7
15	55.57	61.23
16	56.7	65.32
17	57.83	68.49
18	58.74	70.31

Age in years
Weight in kilos

725

The table shows average weights for white European and American children. Ninety per cent of girls fall within 6.5 kg and 90 per cent of boys within 7.5 kg either side of the weights shown at age eighteen. Note that *average* weights are not necessarily *optimum* weights. Some experts calculate that 20 per cent of children are overweight at 18, and since there isn't an equivalent percentage underweight, this inflates the average. Optimum weights may therefore be 4.5 kg or so less than the weights shown. Size of frame of course plays a part. The optimum weight for small-framed girls may be 5 kg less and for large-framed girls 5 kg more than the optimum average at age 18. For boys, the respective figures are approximately 3.5 kg and 6.5 kg respectively.

Children of Asian and some Afro-Caribbean ethnic groups tend to be lighter on average than white children in Europe and the USA, due to different nutritional habits and possibly inherited differences in physique. Some findings indicate the difference may be around 2 kg less for girls at maturity, and as much as 6.5 kg or more for boys.

Table 6. Girls' and boys' heights

Age	Girls' heights	Boys' heights
6	1.14	1.12
7	1.19	1.19
8	1.27	1.24
9	1.32	1.3
10	1.37	1.35
11	1.42	1.42
12	1.52	1.45
13	1.57	1.5
14	1.6	1.6
15	1.62	1.65
16	1.63	1.7
17	1.63	1.72
18	1.63	1.73

Age in years
Height in metres and centimetres

The figures are for white children, but those for non-white ethnic groups resident in Europe and the USA are not markedly different. The tendency in developed countries for average heights to increase with each generation now seems to be levelling off.

Predicting your child's height

As growth in most children follows a predictable curve, it is possible to estimate from about age 2 years onwards what height a child is likely to reach at maturity. Too much reliance should not be placed upon these estimates, particularly if they are made during the adolescent growth spurt, but they are useful if a child is planning for an eventual career in which height at maturity is a factor. If a girl is likely to be less than the average height at 16 years, for example, it might be unrealistic for her to set her heart on a career as a dancer; or as a policewoman if she is under 1.6 metres or as a nurse if she is under 1.5 metres.

At all ages, estimates based upon a girl's current height are more accurate than those for boys, but with the exception of the adolescent growth spurt (when estimates may be 5 centimetres – or occasionally more – out each way) it is a fair bet that mature height will lie no more than a few centimetres either side of the predicted figure.

To arrive at this prediction, measure your child's height, multiply by 100, and then divide by the appropriate figure in the girls' or boys' columns in Table 7. These columns show the percentage of their height at maturity that girls and boys respectively will have reached by the given age.

Table 7. Predicting a child's height

Age	Girls	Boys
2	53	50
3	57	54
4	62	58
5	66	62
6	70	65
7	74	69
8	78	72
9	81	75
10	84	78
11	88	81
12	93	84
13	97	87
14	98	92
15	99	96
16		98
17		99

Girls usually reach 100 per cent of their full height at 16 or soon after, and boys at 18 or soon after.

Norms for General Development

Careful study of young children during the first 5 years of life has established the average age at which important developmental landmarks are achieved. There is wide individual variation from these landmarks, however, and they therefore provide only a general guide. Some children who appear slow in certain areas often catch up rapidly and surpass their contemporaries as, with the exception of height and weight gains, progress in most aspects of child development tends to go in spurts rather than in a steady upwards curve. Nevertheless, any wide variation from these norms may indicate the existence of problems, and the matter should be discussed with your doctor. There could, for example, be difficulties with sight or hearing, and the sooner these are diagnosed the better the chance of correcting them or helping the child adapt to them.

In the tables that follow, the average ages (usually referred to as 'age norms') at which landmarks are reached are given. The norms are grouped under appropriate sub-headings, but clearly there is some overlap between these groupings. The tables are divided into three in conformity with the age divisions used in Chapters 3/4, 5 and 6.

Developmental norms for the first year of life

Posture and movement

1 MONTH   Lies with arms and legs bent, hands clenched.
                 Resists attempt to straighten limbs.
              Jerky movements. Moves arms more than legs.
              When lying prone turns face to one side.
              When pulled up to sitting position slumps
                 forward.
              When held in standing position makes forward
                 movement of legs (the 'walking reflex').

3 MONTHS   Limbs more pliable. Hands less tightly clenched.
              Movements less jerky. Kicks vigorously.
              When lying prone lifts head (at 6 weeks) and
                 upper chest.

When pulled up to sitting position holds upper
back straight and head briefly erect.
When held in standing position sags at knees.

6 MONTHS   Movements more co-ordinated and free. Holds
up arms to be lifted.
When lying prone extends arms and raises head
and chest.
Pulls self to sitting position when hands held.
Sits with support, head erect and upper back
straight.
When held in standing position takes weight and
bounces up and down.
Rolls over from front on to back and (usually)
from back on to front.
Turns head to look around.

9 MONTHS   Very active physically.
Sits without support. Sits upright and safely
when carried.
When held in standing position makes strong
walking movements.
Pulls self to standing position (but cannot lower
self).
Rolls, shuffles, attempts to crawl (individuals
differ).

12 MONTHS   Pulls to standing position and progresses around
furniture.
Pushes walking trolley.
May take first steps (unusual).
Rolls, shuffles or crawls actively and busily.

Manipulative skills

1 MONTH   Grasps finger when palm is touched.
Searches for nipple or teat with mouth.

3 MONTHS   Flexes and unflexes fingers spontaneously ('finger
play').
Brings hands before face and studies them.
Holds rattle briefly when placed in hand.

6 MONTHS   Stretches out both hands (occasionally one) to
grasp objects.
Shakes rattle to hear sound.
Transfers objects from one hand to the other.
Takes everything to mouth.

9 MONTHS   Stretches out one hand to grasp. Picks up large
               objects.
Pokes at small objects with index finger
               (occasionally picks up with finger and thumb).
Holds string (and hair and spectacles!).
Manipulates objects attentively.
Shakes objects vigorously and bangs them on
               table.
Holds out (but cannot effectively hand over)
               objects to others.

12 MONTHS   Picks up small objects.
Begins to show signs of preference for right or left
               hand ('hand dominance').
Repeatedly throws things on floor (!)

Feeding, dressing and toileting

1 MONTH   Cries lustily when hungry.
Watches parent intently when feeding.
Sucks vigorously and skilfully.
Generally passive acceptance of dressing and
               nappy changing.

3 MONTHS   Recognizes and welcomes breast or feeding
               bottle.
Evidence of enjoyment at bathing and toileting.
Signs of 'stilling' and 'awareness' when filling
               nappy.

6 MONTHS   Handles breast or bottle when fed.
Takes liquid from feeding cup (from 4–5 months).
Takes food from spoon and may abandon
               lunchtime bottle in favour of solids.
May eat (messily!) with fingers.
Vigorous and playful at bathing and toileting.

9 MONTHS   Puts both hands around feeding bottle.
May be on solids except for evening bottle.
Tries to grasp spoon when offered.
Holds and chews rusks or biscuits.
May show impatience and resistance at bathing
               and toileting.

12 MONTHS   May be exclusively on solids.
Takes liquid from open cup (when held by adult).
Holds (but cannot effectively use) spoon.

Holds and chews effectively at widening range of
foods.

Actively helps at bathing, dressing etc. (e.g.
holds out arm when requested).

Speech, understanding and gesture

1 MONTH
Turns head to follow near (slow) movement and
towards human face.

Depth of visual focus about 20 centimetres (8 in.).

Blinks at bright light or sudden puff of wind (4–6
weeks).

'Stilling' at sudden noises.

Stops crying ('quietens') when soothed or picked
up.

Facial expression vague (but first signs of
alertness).

3 MONTHS
Visually alert. Fixates gaze briefly on near objects.

Depth of visual focus 30 centimetres (1 ft) plus.

Turns head towards sound source.

Distressed by sudden noises or movements.

Quietens at sound of rattle or small bell.

Recognizes and smiles at familiar sights and
sounds (sometimes from 6 weeks).

Vocalizes (coos, chuckles) when spoken to or
sometimes when alone.

6 MONTHS
Visually intensely curious and purposeful. Fixates
for longer periods.

Depth of visual focus 3 metres (10 ft) plus.

Moves eyes as well as head to seek out sights and
sounds.

Turns immediately to parents' voices. Selective
response to different emotional tones of these
voices.

Signs of anxiety when parents absent or
(increasingly) in the presence of strangers.

Laughs.

Explores everything by mouth.

Vocalizes with tuneful vowel sounds (e.g. a-a,
adah, aroo, er-leh, der, goo, muh).

9 MONTHS
Visually and aurally very competent and
discriminatory.

Depth of visual focus 3.5 metres (11 ft 6 in) plus
(often much more).

Watches people and animals particularly intently.

731

Looks in direction of fallen objects.

Clings to familiar adults and hides face from strangers.

Babbles tunefully and over wide range for self-amusement and communication.

Imitates adult sounds.

Understands small number of words, especially if repeated (e.g. no-no, bye-bye).

Imitates clapping hands and plays peek-a-boo.

Searches for objects partially (sometimes wholly) hidden while he's watching.

Growing signs of independence and self-will (e.g. stiffens and throws body back in resistance)

12 MONTHS
Depth of visual focus 6 metres (20 ft) plus (often much more).

Watches wide range of stimuli very intently.

Points.

Still wary (but becoming curious) of strangers.

Babbles with great range and freedom.

Imitates adult sounds with increasing range and accuracy.

Mouth exploration ceasing (variable).

Understands several simple common words.

Imitates more complex and social adult gestures (e.g. waves bye-bye, plays pat-a-cake).

Repeats actions to produce desired effects with toys (and appreciative adults!).

Developmental norms for the second and third years of life

Posture and movement

15 MONTHS
Walks alone with feet apart and arms held out for balance.

Crawls upstairs (but not down).

Kneels.

18 MONTHS
Walks well, feet almost together, arms down.

Can carry objects when walking.

Runs (unsteadily!).

Walks upstairs one foot at a time (but not down; may come down in sitting position)

Sits himself on low chair.

Squats to pick up objects.

2 YEARS	Walks and runs nimbly and skilfully.
	Walks upstairs and down, one foot at a time.
	Pulls along wheeled toys.
	Climbs furniture.
	Squats to play.
	Sits on trike and propels with feet on floor.
	Throws ball.
2½ YEARS	Jumps with two feet together.
	Stands on tiptoe if shown.
	Kicks large ball (gently and without aim).
3 YEARS	Walks upstairs with alternating feet (downstairs one foot at a time).
	Climbs with increasing agility.
	Jumps down from low height.
	Sits with ankles crossed.
	Pedals trike.
	Catches ball with extended arms. Kicks ball forcibly.

Manipulative skills

15 MONTHS	Holds pencil in fist and scribbles (after adult demonstration).
	Puts objects in containers (after adult demonstration).
	Builds tower of two blocks (after adult demonstration).
18 MONTHS	Holds pencil in primitive finger grip and scribbles spontaneously.
	Clear signs of left or right hand dominance.
	Puts small objects in containers spontaneously.
	Builds tower of three blocks.
	Turns pages of book (usually several at a time).
2 YEARS	Holds pencil in three fingers. Scribbles circles spontaneously and copies 'straight' lines.
	Hand dominance usually established.
	Picks up and puts down accurately small objects.
	Builds six-block tower.
	Turns pages of book singly.
	Unwraps sweets.
2½ YEARS	Holds pencil like adult and with increasing control draws circles and lines and copies simple capital letters (e.g. T and V).

733

Hand dominance definitely established.
Builds seven-block tower.

3 YEARS   Draws with increasing skill and copies more
            complex shapes (e.g. X and +).
Draws man (often without body) and puts in one
  or two details.
Paints non-representationally (and messily!).
Uses scissors.
Builds nine-block tower.

Feeding, dressing and toileting

15 MONTHS   Usually exclusively on solids. Holds and brings
            spoon to mouth (though without full control).
Takes liquid from open cup (when adult hands it
  to him and takes it back).
Indicates when wet or soiled.
Helps increasingly when bathing and dressing.

18 MONTHS   Uses spoon and cup 'competently' (though may
            still need adult to take cup back).
Chews all appropriate foods.
Bowel control often achieved.
May ask (belatedly) for toilet when wetting.
Takes off (but does not put on) hat, socks and
  shoes.

2 YEARS   Uses, picks up and puts down spoon and cup.
Bowel control fully achieved.
Usually dry during day. Asks for toilet
  increasingly in good time.
Takes off and puts on hat, socks and shoes.

2½ YEARS   May use fork.
Dry by day and usually night (though may need
  lifting out).
Pulls down pants (but not up).

3 YEARS   Uses fork.
Usually dry by night without lifting out.
Pulls pants down and up (needs help with
  fastenings).
Washes (but not dries) hands.

Speech, understanding and gesture

15 MONTHS   Intense curiosity (needs careful supervision!).
Near-adult visual focus.

Watches events through window.
Points at and demands objects.
Variable response to strangers.
Babbling continues; first words may appear.
Mouth exploration virtually ceases.
Easily finds objects hidden while he's watching.

18 MONTHS Understands wide range of common words
('passive vocabulary').
Points to numerous named objects on request.
Obeys simple instructions.
Babbles to self at play.
Uses up to twenty plus recognizable words
('active' vocabulary).
Enjoys nursery rhymes and tries to sing and
participate.
Remembers where objects belong.

2 YEARS Widening passive vocabulary. Listens to
conversations.
Active vocabulary of fifty plus words. Repeats
words when asked.
Uses short (two- or three-word) sentences.
Makes verbal requests.
Sings and participates in nursery rhymes.

2½ YEARS Very wide passive vocabulary. Active vocabulary
of 200 plus words.
Frequent use of short sentences (through with
childish grammar).
Uses pronouns 'me', 'I' and 'you'.
Talks audibly and intelligently to self.
Knows full name.
May enter stuttering phase (through eagerness).
Asks 'what' and 'who' questions.
Enjoys hearing stories.
Increasing awareness of own body and body size.
Recognizes self in photos when shown once.

3 YEARS Wide and active vocabulary and sentence use
(though still some childish grammar).
Uses plurals, pronouns and simple prepositions.
Long running commentaries while at play.
Asks 'where' and (sometimes) 'why' questions.
Loves stories, rhymes and songs. Knows some by
heart.
Counts to ten (but with little real understanding
of quantity above three).

Matches and names red, yellow, blue and (sometimes) green.

General behaviour and play

15 MONTHS
Emotionally very up and down ('labile').
Response to strangers variable.
Dislikes own company. Wants adults present.
Growing self-assertion.

18 MONTHS
Emotionally labile.
More generally at ease with strangers.
Can play independently, but still wants adult present.
Clinging and resisting as the mood dictates.
Increasing self-assertion.

2 YEARS
Verbally demands attention and adult company.
Copies adult domestic tasks.
Demands immediate gratification of wishes.
Plays alongside other children ('parallel play').
Aware of (and possessive towards) own things.
Jealous of siblings and other children.
Tantrums when thwarted (though easily distracted).
Beginnings of rebellious self-assertion.

2½ YEARS
Watches other children at play and joins in briefly ('co-operative play')
Beginnings of role play (e.g. 'mummies and daddies').
Meaningful imaginative play (e.g. with dolls' house).
Tantrums when thwarted less easily distracted.
Definite independence and self-will.

3 YEARS
Likes to help with domestic tasks.
Less jealous of others and more able to share.
Begins to understand rights of others.
Begins to be able to defer satisfaction (await turn, save sweets).
Clear signs of affection for siblings.
More amenable and less tantrums.

Developmental norms for the fourth and fifth years of life

Posture and movement

4 YEARS
Walks up and down stairs with alternating feet.

Walks and runs on tiptoe if required.
Hops.
Climbs ladder.
Sits with knees crossed.
Catches, throws, bounces and kicks ball. Uses bat
and ball.

5 YEARS   Walks and runs lightly and gracefully.
Skips.
Moves rhythmically to music.
Bends to floor with knees straight.
Increasingly agile and competent.

Manipulative skills

4 YEARS   Draws and copies increasingly complex shapes.
May attempt to copy own name.
Draws man with head, body and limbs and
several features (often including fingers).
Draws outline house.
May paint representationally.
Builds ten-block tower.

5 YEARS   Copies individual letters of the alphabet and
writes some of them spontaneously.
May copy name recognizably.
Draws house with windows, door and chimney.
Draws other natural objects (e.g. trees, flowers,
dogs).
Colours in pictures with increasing skill.
Paints representationally.
Builds complex tower with several levels.

Feeding, dressing and toileting

4 YEARS   Skilful use of spoon and fork.
Washes and dries hands and sometimes
(perfunctorily) elsewhere.
Brushes teeth (with questionable effect).
Dresses and undresses (except for ties and back
buttons).

5 YEARS   Uses knife and fork.
Washes and dries hands and face and
increasingly elsewhere.
Toilets self reliably and independently.

Speech, understanding and gesture

4 YEARS   Near-adult passive and very wide active
               vocabulary.
               Good use of sentences. Few childish grammatical
               expressions.
               'Why' questions fully established.
               Gives accounts of events (often confusing fact
               and fiction).
               Makes up stories. May read a few words (often
               by heart).
               Knows own address and age.
               Enjoys jokes.
               Appreciates concepts of past and present.
               Counts to twenty plus (but with little real
               understanding of quantity above five).
               Matches and names red, yellow, blue and green.

5 YEARS   Near-adult active vocabulary for all common
               words.
               Increasingly asks meaning of abstract words.
               Knows birthday.
               Appreciates the concept of future.
               Grasps the idea of clock time and may be able to
               read clock.
               May read range of simple words.
               Matches (though cannot always name) ten or
               more colours.

General behaviour and play

4 YEARS   Very helpful in house.
               Plays co-operatively (though with frequent
               disputes!) with other children.
               Shows concern and sympathy for siblings and
               other children.
               Often understands idea of 'team' game.
               Beginnings of systematic memory for past events.
               Verbal impertinence to adults often appears.
               Growing independence of thought and action.

5 YEARS   Excellent companion. Discusses issues sensibly.
               Asks for guidance and help appropriately and
               selectively.
               Beginnings of reliable and responsible behaviour.
               Extended co-operative play. Participates in team
               play.
               Protective towards siblings, other children (and
               parents!)

Understands need for rules and fairness.

Chooses own friends.

Clear systematic memory for past. Plans for future.

Compares self with others and shows need for competence and for good opinion of others outside immediate family.

Developmental norms after age five

Once a child reaches school age, development proceeds across such a wide range of variables and is so much more linked to academic progress that it is no longer feasible to produce tables of norms like the foregoing. Much of this development is measured by schools in the form of tests which in any case are not generally available to parents. Many of these are *standardized tests*, that is they have been given to a large sample of children and figures produced which show what scores a child should be getting if he is average or above or below average for his age.

Results from these tests are often expressed in the form of a child's **Attainment** *attainment age*. If he is average for his age, then his attainment age **tests** will be the same as his chronological age, indicating that he is performing up to the average standard of the rest of his age group. Standardized tests exist for all the basic subjects in school, and are used particularly at the point of transfer from infant to junior and from junior to secondary schools. Thus a child on the basis of his scores in these tests is given, for example, a reading attainment age, a spelling attainment age and an arithmetic attainment age (usually called simply reading, spelling and arithmetic ages respectively).

Also widely used are standardized tests of *ability*. Whereas attain- **Ability tests** ment tests simply measure what a child actually knows, ability tests are claimed to measure innate ability (or potential). The best-known ability tests over the years have been intelligence tests, which produce a score known as a *mental age*. (Or sometimes as an intelligence quotient or IQ for short). A mental age does for intelligence what an attainment age does for knowledge in the basic subjects. But as the term 'intelligence' is a sensitive one (e.g. deviations below the norm can often cause anxiety in parents and children), scores in this area are usually expressed in terms of the sub-scores obtained in different sections of the intelligence tests (e.g. verbal reasoning and mathematical/spatial). Recently developed tests discard the term 'intelligence' altogether and replace it with 'ability', and contain a wide range of individual sub-tests. Many experts now believe that it is inappropriate to add up all the scores on the sub-tests to produce an overall ability (or intelligence) score, since childen may be gifted in certain areas and not in others; to add such disparate scores together is therefore unrealistic and may serve to obscure these areas of giftedness.

As indicated in the text (page 575), 'backwardness' is usually identified where a child's attainment age in a given subject falls two years or more below his chronological age, but it is often useful to talk in terms of slight backwardness (1 year behind), moderate backwardness (2 years behind) and severe backwardness (more than 2 years behind). Many schools do not, however, use terms like this when talking to parents, and this is also true of the routine tests used in British schools at ages 7, 11 and 14. Instead, they may use a 4-point (or similar) scale designed simply to describe what a child can actually *do*. Thus in reading at age 7, for example, a point 1 would indicate that the child has been introduced to books but has yet to make significant progress, point 2 that he can read up to the standard for 7-year-olds but only with help, point 3 that he can do this on his own, and point 4 that he is above the standard for 7-year-olds and can actually help others. At each age and in each subject, the child's performance is related to what can realistically be expected of someone at that stage in life.

APPENDIX 3

Your Child's Diet

Children's calorie requirements

Some experts believe that fat cells laid down by over-fed babies in the critical early months may make the individaul more prone to put on weight throughout life. Obesity renders a baby more susceptible to chest infections and less likely to take necessary exercise. In adult life it is linked with diabetes, heart disease, strokes, and other circulatory diseases. Since breast-fed babies are rarely overweight, it seems nature hasn't designed babies to be fat. So if a healthy bottle-fed baby or a baby on solids is putting on unwanted weight, this is a clear indication she's receiving too many calories. Check with your doctor. Are you making the feeds too rich, or adding superfluous sugar, or rushing to give your baby supplementary bottles when all she may need is boiled water for her thirst? Don't ignore those rolls of unnecessary fat. They could lay the foundations for a physique which will ultimately shorten your child's life expectancy.

A baby's calorie requirements depend to some extent upon how active and energetic she is. A lively baby will burn up more calories than a more placid one. But at 6 months the average healthy baby needs around 800 calories. If she's bottle-fed, each 225 ml (8 oz) bottle gives her 144 calories (493 calories per litre), so four bottles give 576 calories, leaving about 225 calories to be supplied by solids. This amounts to two tins of baby food or one tin plus one helping of cereal. If she's breast-fed, amounts are harder to calculate, but it's a fair bet she'll take around 550–600 calories from the breast, so the sums should work out rather similar.

Average calorie requirements for the rest of childhood are as follows overleaf, but again there is individual variation depending upon a child's energy expenditure and bodily metabolism (the rate at which the body burns calories during a given expenditure of energy). A child who consistently takes on more calories than she uses up will store the surplus as fat, and hence put on unwanted weight.

From age 11 onwards, there is increasing variation due to size, sex, and the age at onset of the adolescent growth spurt. Girls at 13–14 usually need 2,200–2,600 calories per day, while boys 15–16 usually need 2,600–3,200. Note that these are *peak* calorie needs.

Age	Calories per day (boys and girls)
1 year –	1,100
2 years –	1,200
3 years –	1,300
4 years –	1,400
5 years –	1,500–1,550
6 years –	1,600–1,700
7 years –	1,700–1,850
8 years –	1,800–2,000
9 years –	1,900–2,250
10 years –	2,000–2,400

Once a teenager has passed the growth spurt their needs may decline unless they are very physically active. It is difficult to define calorie needs once an individual has stopped growing, as much depends upon body build and energy output. The figure of 1,500 calories per day is sometimes suggested for the light, small-framed, sedentary adult male, twice this amount for a young, active adult male of average weight and height, and up to three times for the very strongly built, very active young man (women's equivalent needs are usually put at 1,200, 2,100 and 3,000 respectively, though in pregnancy, 2,500 calories is usually thought to be about right). Unless under a doctor's supervision, no child or adolescent should embark upon drastic dieting, as denied sufficient protein and essential vitamins and minerals there could be risks to both health and growth.

Vitamin supplements

The essential vitamins for small babies are thought to be A, B, C and D. Provided the mother is eating normally, breast-fed babies receive enough of the first three, while the bottle-fed babies get enough A and B but are usually given a supplement of C (you can't easily overdose with vitamin C, so both bottle- and breast-fed babies can be given supplements in the form of rosehip or blackcurrant or orange juice any time; *but avoid juices which contain quantities of added sugar*, and although juices must be made with boiled, cooled water, don't boil the juice itself as this destroys vitamin C).

Vitamin D is manufactured by the skin in response to sunlight, so both bottle- and breast-fed babies need supplements in northern Europe, particularly if dark-skinned (in any case, direct sunlight is harmful to a baby's skin, and she should never be left exposed to it). A supplement of 400 international units (iu) per day (usually in the form of cod liver oil drops) is recommended, but overdoses of vitamin D can be dangerous, so for bottle-fed babies check that their formula is not already suplemented by this amount, making further addition unnecessary. Some doctors recommend vitamin A supplements for premature or small babies until they're weaned, but as overdoses of vitamin A are also potentially harmful, be guided by your doctor.

As babies grow older, individual needs for vitamins may vary, and your doctor is the best guide. But the average daily requirements at 6 months for vitamins, protein and essential minerals are as follows:

Table 8. Average vitamin, essential mineral and protein requirements at 6 months

	grams (g)	milligrams (mg)	micrograms (μg)
Vitamin A	–	–	450.0
Vitamin B_1	–	0.3	–
Vitamin B_2	–	0.4	–
Vitamin B_3	–	5.0	–
Vitamin C	–	15.0	–
Vitamin D	–	–	10.0 (400 iu)
Protein	20.0	–	–
Iron	–	6.0	–
Calcium	–	600.0	–

A single pint of full-cream milk will provide the daily calcium requirements plus half the vitamin A. The juice of a single fresh orange will give the vitamin C. Two helpings of fortified cereal will give the iron (but iron is contained in all a baby eats, and a deficiency is unlikely given an adequate diet). Vitamin B occurs widely, with rice and grains especially rich in B_1, green vegetables (which together with carrots are also a source of vitamin A) in B_2, and grains, fruit and vegetables in B_3. Bottle-fed babies on suitably fortified formula may receive enough vitamin D, but once on cow's milk all babies are usually given supplements (cow's milk contains very little vitamin D or C, and only one-third the vitamin A of mother's milk).

Remember that all cooking and processing destroys some vitamins. The heat of the sun on a bottle of milk for two hours, for example, destroys half its vitamin B_2 content. Vitamin C is particulary prone to destruction in cooking, so raw fruit and vegetables are preferable to cooked (and especially over-cooked) ones – but be sure to wash and clean them thoroughly first. If you're a vegetarian, your child will thrive on a vegetarian diet after weaning, but mention the fact that you are vegetarian to your doctor, who may recommend further vitamin supplements (particulary of B_{12}, the daily requirements of which have not yet been established, but which is sometimes deficient in vegetarians).

New vitamins are still being discovered, and our daily requirements of some of those known to us (such as B_6, B_{12} and E) have not yet been established, so are not given in the tables. However, they are present in reasonable quantities in a good diet, which is why such a diet becomes increasingly important as weaning gets under way and your child comes to rely more and more upon solids for her nutritional needs.

Average daily requirements of vitamins and essential minerals for older children are as follows:

Table 9. Average vitamin, essential mineral and protein requirements 1–3 years

	grams (g)	milligrams (mg)	micrograms (μg)
Vitamin A	–	–	300
Vitamin B$_1$	–	0.5	–
Vitamin B$_2$	–	0.6	–
Vitamin B$_3$	–	7.0	–
Vitamin C	–	20.0	–
Vitamin D	–	–	10 (400 iu)
Protein	30	–	–
Iron	–	7.0	–
Calcium	–	500.0	–

Table 10. Average vitamin, essential mineral and protein requirements 3–5 years

	grams (g)	milligrams (mg)	micrograms (μg)
Vitamin A	–	–	300
Vitamin B$_1$	–	0.6	–
Vitamin B$_2$	–	0.8	–
Vitamin B$_3$	–	9.0	–
Vitamin C	–	20.0	–
Vitamin D	–	–	10 (400 iu)
Protein	40	–	–
Iron	–	8.0	–
Calcium	–	500.0	–

A healthy diet

Many illnesses are now firmly linked with undesirable eating habits. The association between a high intake of animal fats and coronary heart disease seems indisputable, as does the association between a high sugar intake and the diseases associated with obesity. A diet low in fibre seems implicated in the development of bowel disorders (and possibly heart disease), while diets high in salt may predispose towards high blood pressure, strokes and kidney disease. Finally, diets lacking in fresh fruit and vegetables also correlate with increased mortality rates, while diet lacking in essential vitamins and minerals and in adequate fluid intake are also implicated in serious health problems.

Though such things as heart disease and bowel disorders are mainly ailments of adult life, their origins may often lie in childhood. The build-up of fatty deposits in the coronary arteries, for example (one of the prime factors behind heart disease), is detectable by the late teens in one third of males, and in some cases is quite far advanced. Constipation (a predisposing factor in some bowel diseases) is also chronic in many children, while obesity has already been mentioned as apparent in 20 per cent of teenagers. Ensure your child has a healthy diet, and you'll help lay the foundations for a long and healthy life.

A healthy diet involves taking as much of the daily menu as possible in the form of fresh wholefoods, and keeping additives such as salt and sugar down to a minimum. This means wholemeal bread, plenty of fruit and vegetables (raw or steamed rather than boiled), low sugar cereals, brown rice, nuts, beans, dried fruit such as raisins, and honey rather than sugary jams and confections. It means keeping tinned or processed foods (particularly convenience foods) to a minimum, and getting into the habit of consulting labels on packaged food in order to steer clear of harmful additives (not all substances with E numbers are harmful though; buy a book which helps you separate good from bad). **Eat wholefoods, avoid additives**

A healthy diet also involves restricting animal fats. Don't give your child butter or cream, and as soon as your doctor gives the go-ahead, gradually substitute skimmed or semi-skimmed milk for full-cream. Use soft, low-fat cheeses (cottage cheese is the best of all) in place of hard cheese and plain natural yoghurt (sweetened with a little honey if necessary) in place of the sugary, flavoured variety. If you give your child meat, cut off all the fat (young children's legendary dislike of fat is now seen to have good reason behind it), or better still go for poultry and fish. If she doesn't like white fish, tinned salmon or tuna are still preferable to red meat. The oil in fish is mostly of the unsaturated variety (like most vegetable oils), not of the harmful saturated kind found in red meat. Avoid fried foods wherever possible since they greatly increase the daily intake of fat (and even unsaturated oils are converted into saturated by re-heating), and all salty and sugary nibbles and snacks. Keep nuts, raisins and sunflower seeds in the larder in place of crisps, sweets and biscuits, and natural unsweetened fruit drinks instead of fizzy colas and cordials. **Restrict animal fats**

Some parents protest their children will never take to such a wholesome menu, but the human body has been programmed by thousands of years to eat and enjoy a healthy diet, and only during the present century have we tricked our taste buds into preferring adulterated junk. Provided your child isn't allowed to develop a taste for this junk in the first place, or provided she's switched over from bad to good habits in easy stages and you explain to her the life-saving logic behind it all, you should have no real problems. Switching over is usually easiest if you use fresh fruit as your starting point. Begin with grapes, apples and oranges, then try pears, bananas and melons. Replace cordials with pure fruit juice, and make a gradual transition from hard to soft cheese, from full-cream to skimmed milk, and from butter to soft margarine. Change slowly from jam to honey, mixing the two together for a while, and ease the transition from sugary breakfast cereals to wholegrain ones by adding a little brown **Change your child's eating habits gradually** sugar at first. Gradually cut back on salt, or replace it with a salt substitute, and go from white bread to wholemeal bread via loaves that use both white and brown flour.

If you're a vegetarian or vegan family, remember that your child must have sufficient alternative sources of protein to meat (cheese, beans, pulses, etc.) and that she may need vitamin B supplements. Consult your doctor and the many good books now available on vegetarian and vegan diets.

APPENDIX 4

Immunization

Don't make the mistake of supposing that since the killer diseases against which immunization provides protection are now comparatively rare, you no longer need immunize your child. The germs responsible for these diseases are still alive and active, and would quickly gain a hold again if children were not protected. Some parents worry that immunization could trigger off a harmful reaction in their children (there is suspicion, for example, that the whooping cough vaccine could cause brain damage and developmental handicap in certain very rare cases), but doctors consider that the risk of a reaction is much less than the risk presented by the various diseases themselves. However, immunization is often not advisable if your child is currently unwell or has a history of (or comes from a family with a history of) fits, convulsions or epilepsy, and any of these conditions must be discussed fully with your doctor. After immunization, you should tell your doctor at once if your child becomes ill, and any adverse reactions should also be reported before any subsequent immunizations are carried out.

The various forms of immunization, together with the ages at which they are given, and the possible reasons for withholding immunization, are set out below.

The immunity conferred by the tetanus injection lasts only some 5 years, and boosters should be given subsequently at any time when cuts or broken skin are likely to occur in the presence of earth or dirt (as for example in some sports or in the garden). It is also wise to take your child for a booster if he ever receives a bad cut under dirty conditions. If you intend to travel abroad, particularly to developing countries or to the Far East, vaccination against such things as cholera, typhoid and yellow fever is essential. Your doctor will advise you. The only other vaccinations that are sometimes given are against influenza (if a baby suffers from some heart or lung complaint) and mumps in boys after puberty as there can be a risk of inflammation of the testes and of subsequent sterility.

Table 11. Routine immunization

Age	Disease	Possible reasons for withholding immunization	Possible side-effects
3 months	tetanus	fever or generally unwell – postpone until recovered	red swelling at site of injection
3 months	diptheria	as for tetanus	as for tetanus
3 months	whooping cough	fits, convulsions, epilepsy or a family history of such things – omit altogether. Severe reaction of any kind to previous dose – omit altogether. Fever or generally unwell – postpone until recovered	brain damage reported in very rare cases
5 months	polio	raised temperature or stomach upset – postpone at doctor's discretion	no side-effects
5 months	booster dose of all vaccines given at 3 months	as at 3 months	as at 3 months
9–12 months	booster dose of all vaccines given at 3 and 5 months	as at 3 and 5 months	as at 3 and 5 months
15–16 months	*measles (no booster needed)	as for whooping cough. Also withheld if a baby has long-standing heart or lung problems	red swelling at site of injection; slight rash 10–14 days later
5 years	booster dose of tetanus, diptheria, whooping cough and polio	as at 3 and 5 months	as at 3 and 5 months
10–13 years (girls only)	*rubella	any suspicion of pregnancy	rash 10–14 days later; slight swelling of neck glands and slight unwell feeling
13 years	TB (BCG)		
15–19 years	booster dose of tetanus and polio	as at 3 and 5 months	as at 3 and 5 months

* Due to be replaced by a triple vaccine for measles, mumps and german measles at 18 months

748

Teething

The dribbling and drooling associated with teething often begin at around 4 months, though teething proper doesn't usually begin until after six months (there's wide variation though; some babies are even born with teeth!). There isn't a great deal you can do to ease the miseries of teething. Jellies smeared on the gums sometimes help, and though teething rings don't really speed matters up, some babies seem to find them a comfort. Don't make the mistake of thinking that since a baby will one day lose his first teeth they aren't important. If a single milk tooth is lost before the right time, there's a risk the second teeth may be crowded or come through crookedly. Your baby's teeth are subject to decay the moment they come through the gums, so avoid sugar in his diet and gently brush the teeth at night (particularly after the molars come through) with a soft toothbrush.

Traditionally, teething is associated with colds and snuffles. This may just be coincidence (a breast-fed baby is losing at around 6 months the immunity to common infections given him by the antibodies in his mother's milk), or it may be that the upset of teething lowers a baby's resistance. There's no evidence that teething in itself causes colds.

The first teeth to appear are usually the front two bottom teeth (the lower central incisors), followed a week or two later by the two upper central incisors. On average, teething follows a familiar timetable:

Central incisors (bottom ones first)	6–8 months
lateral incisors (any order)	9–11 months

first molars (any order)	14–17 months
canines (eye teeth) (any order)	18–20 months
second molars (any order)	24–26 months

Report any irregularities in the appearance of your baby's teeth to your doctor. Teeth may come through crooked for example, or in the wrong place, or may fail to appear altogether. Unless treated, there's the risk that second teeth could be affected. Occasionally a baby's teeth are short of enamel, and have an almost transparent quality. This deficiency is rarely repeated in the second teeth, though it should be mentioned to your doctor.

Sleep Needs

Sleep needs vary in children just as they do in adults. Much depends upon the amount of physical energy expended, but this is only part of the picture. Some children with particularly active minds and/or bodies seem to need *less* sleep than the average, so there is probably a constitutional factor at work as well. With the advent of television many children take much less sleep these days than once was the case, even children of 7 and 8 years regularly staying up until late evening. It may be that children can adapt to less and less sleep, just as most adults can (evidence suggests that many adults who 'need' 8 hours per night can be trained to manage on 5–6 hours with no loss of daytime efficiency), and certainly there's no sign that today's curtailed sleeping habits have led to stunted growth or mental retardation – two of the dire predictions that used to be made about lack of sleep in children.

But it is a fact that growth hormones are released primarily during the hours of sleep, and an equal fact that tired children find it harder to concentrate in school or to tackle memory tasks. So the answer is to take the following table as a rough guide, and then tailor it to your child's individual needs. Make the relevant hours of sleep available to your child, but once she's in bed don't worry too much if she uses some of the time reading or playing. If she's over-excited she'll find it hard to drop off, so with young children employ calming bed-time rituals as explained in Chapter 5.

Birth to 2 years	Generally she'll take what she needs during these two years. In the first 6 months she sleeps most of the time between feeds (7 hours or so at night and four naps of 2–3 hours each during the day). At or soon after 6 months she drops one of her naps (late morning or afternoon), and by 1 year she's usually down to just two. The third daytime nap fades out between 1 year and 18 months, and the fourth usually between 2½ and 3, though many children continue with it until 4 and even school age.
2–3 years	At age 2, most children have about 12 hours sleep at night, plus a daytime nap of 1–2 hours. From 2

	onwards, their needs become more variable. Between 2 and 3 they usually drop the daytime nap, but still need around 12 hours at night.
3–5 years	If the nap hasn't already disappeared it goes during these years. Night-time needs stay around the 12 hours, though some children manage happily on 11 (less at holiday times!).
5–9 years	The average need over the years is around 11 hours, though some children vary over the 7 days, some catching up at weekends for sleep lost during the week, others sleeping less at weekends and more on weekdays.
9–12 years	Individual variations are even more marked, but the average is 10 hours, and many children find it hard to concentrate at school if they receive much less.,
12 years plus	From 12 through to 18, most children mature gradually to the point where their sleep needs are similar to those of an adult (7–8 hours). Sometimes they need extra sleep during the adolescent growth spurt, so that a child who has been taking 9 or 9½ hours before the spurt may need a full 10 hours again during it (often in the form of catch-up sleep at the weekend). From the end of the growth spurt to age 18, needs rapidly come down to those of an adult, and there is little point in trying to arbitrate on sleep needs once 18 is reached. Between 16 and 18, it's reasonable to influence an adolescent into taking her 8 hours minimum, particularly if she's in a demanding job or still studying.

The old adage that an hour's sleep before midnight is worth two after is not true, but we do seem to have a natural biological rhythm that flourishes best on early to bed and early to rise. The artificial life style imposed by modern living interferes with this, but your baby will do his best to re-educate you.

Safety In and Around the Home

Your child's safety is a vital issue throughout the childhood years. The home and its environs are highly dangerous places. It can't be emphasized too often that more people die of accidents in and around the home than are killed on the roads, with the young (and the old) particularly at risk. Parental vigilance and imagination are needed at all times, and the need increases in direct proportion to your child's increasing mobility and independence. Vigilance to spot where he is and what he's doing, and imagination to look around the house and its surroundings and realize what *could* go wrong. If it could go wrong, there's a fair chance that it might. So be prepared. Remove the threat of danger before it's allowed to happen.

The following is a list of common dangers, but in your home and in your environment there will be extra hazards which are not on the list. There are in every home and in every environment. Check them out and take immediate steps to guard against them.

Common hazards in and around the home

Baths and sinks – your child can take a nasty tumble in the bath; and hot water taps can scald terribly (set water heater thermostat to below 43°C-110°F)

Bleaches, soap powders, white spirit, other household poisons – keep well out of reach or locked away. Don't put anything poisonous in lemonade-type bottles; even typewriter correcting fluid is deadly.

Cars – children have been killed even by family cars manoeuvring in the drive, and had fingers broken by car doors slammed shut.

Cookers – never leave unattended if in use and small children are about; never leave handles of pans projecting over the side; never leave hot fat unattended, it can go up in flames.

Doors and lids on springs – in fact anything that can slam down on little fingers.

Dustbins, polybins and rubbish heaps – especially if they contain broken glass, jagged tins and bad or rotting food.

Electric blankets – shouldn't be used for small children, ever. Use special children's scald-proof hotwater bottle if necessary, and check regularly for leaks.

Enclosed hazards – anything in which or under which a small child can be wedged. Fridges and freezers, especially if out of use, are amongst the worst. So are wardrobes and cupboards with doors that can swing shut behind a small child.

Fires – guard open fires, and discard older electric fires which have bars through which little fingers and objects can be poked.

Fireworks – a much-publicized hazard, yet horrifying injuries occur every year.

Garages and their contents – power tools can cause terrible injuries if switched on by small children. Disconnect them and hang them out of reach. Wood preservers, paints, many tools (even bicycles) also cause fatal accidents every year.

Garden and park railings – sometimes with spikes on top, sometimes with inviting openings into which children can put their heads and become stuck.

Gardens and garden sheds – garden tools, ponds, weedkillers, unsafe walls and constructions are all potentially deadly, as are many leaves, seeds and berries.

Glass doors – look nice but can be lethal, whether internal or external.

Glass jars – and anything else that can shatter and cut.

Glues and solvents – the kitchen drawer isn't the place for them.

Heating appliances – each year many children die from fires caused by, or fumes inhaled from, domestic heating appliances. Have all gas boilers, fires and water heaters serviced at least once a year. Have solid fuel boilers checked and chimneys swept regularly. Have warm air central heating systems checked frequently (harmful fumes have been known to leak into the warm air and kill children in their beds). Avoid portable gas and electric heaters wherever possible; if used, make sure they're physically safe (can't be knocked over or get too hot to be touched), properly guarded, and can't leak fumes or cause electric shocks or other possible hazards.

Heavy ornaments or kitchen tools – if a child can pull them down on him, it's a fair chance he will.

Inflammable and combustible material – matches are an obvious hazard. So are clothes and bedclothes. The filling in much modern furniture produces toxic fumes that can kill in under a minute.

Ladders and step-ladders – keep them locked away, and never leave unattended when in use.

Loose-fill – and any other stuffing in furniture or elsewhere that can be sucked into the mouth and choked on.

Mats – avoid loose mats, especially on polished floors.

Nearby railway lines – children can 'escape' from their garden and wander away on to a railway line.

Nearby rivers and ponds – water has a great fascination for small children; some have been drowned within feet of their parents; others by 'escaping' from their garden and wandering away.

Needles and sewing and knitting equipment – far too often left unguarded in the lounge.

Objects that look like sweets – anything a child might mistake for a sweet and put into his mouth.

Old paintwork – if it contains lead and can be sucked or chewed.

Pets – many dogs (and some cats) just aren't safe with small children; never give an animal the benefit of the doubt.

Pills and medicines – even if they don't look like sweets or cherryade, lock them away. The bathroom cabinet isn't the place for them unless you can secure it.

Plastic and polythene bags – one placed over the head in a game can suffocate in under 2 minutes.

Playground equipment – because equipment is in public parks doesn't mean it's safe; sadly children are killed every year falling from (or being hit by) swings, roundabouts and similar attractions. Fairgrounds are potentially even worse.

Poor lighting – a child who can't see where he's going will trip and fall.

Rickety furniture – anything that can fall or be pulled down on top of a child.

Roads – early lessons in road safety are a must; no small child should be left unattended anywhere within reach of a busy street.

Rope and cord – anything that can be put around the neck or any part of the body and drawn tight; children have even strangled themselves on roller towels.

Scissors and knives – the cutlery drawer contains enough hazards to cut and maim a whole army of small children.

Small objects – anything that can be swallowed or poked into eyes and ears; even a pencil sharpened at both ends can be deadly.

Sports equipment – not just darts and airguns, but fishing tackle, camping knives and virtually anything else can prove dangerous.

Stairways – check for loose handrails and loose carpeting; *never* leave objects on stairs to be carried up next time you go, they're far too easy to trip over.

Steep front-door and back-door steps – and anything else a child can fall down.

Sweets – it's all too easy to choke on sweets, particularly if sucked while playing or running.

Tablecloths – if they hang down they can be pulled down, together with whatever is on top of them.

Teapots, coffee pots and hot drinks – a child can be literally scalded to death by pulling any one of them on top of himself.

Toys – safety standards are improving, but some toys still have sharp edges, spikes which are uncovered when heads or arms fall off, and things that can be swallowed.

Trailing electric cables – can kill, and are connected to appliances that can be pulled over.

Trees – and anything else that invites climbing and clambering, inside and outside the home.

Windows – especially upstairs ones. Make sure all windows are secured, and vulnerable ones barred.

Common Childhood Ailments and Injuries

This isn't a medical textbook, and even if it were it would be no substitute for a consultation with your doctor. Illnesses and injuries can't be diagnosed accurately from a book, only by examination by a qualified medical practitioner. If you have *any* reason for concern over your child's health, consult your doctor at once. The following details are to help you recognize important symptoms in your child and give your doctor precise information. These details can't cover all conditions though, and particularly for injuries and emergencies a valuable precaution is to take a short first aid course that teaches you what to do in potentially fatal situations such as choking, drowning, fractures, fevers and unconsciousness. Such a course provides you not only with information but with valuable opportunities to practise applying this information. Even though this practice takes place in make-believe rather than real emergencies, it gives you an opportunity to develop the right techniques and the confidence to know that you can produce them if they're ever needed.

Childhood ailments

Although these conditions vary in seriousness, with the exceptions where indicated, *all need prompt qualified medical attention*. Those marked with an asterisk are infectious or contagious.

Condition	Common symptoms
Appendicitis	See *Stomach ache*.
Asthma	Wheezing, laboured breathing, particularly on out-breath. Chest ache, coughing and sneezing, congested nose, sleep difficulties, shortness of breath.
*Bronchitis**	Usually follows chest or head cold. Wheezing, laboured breathing, fever, burning sensation in chest, hacking dry cough (changes to wet then back to dry again), streaming nose, sometimes offensive breath.

*Chicken pox**   Fever, headache, feeling fatigued and unwell. Itchy rash mainly on face and trunk; starts as red spots which turn to blisters and dries as scabs. Vomiting and swollen glands in severe cases. Infectious stage extends from 1 day before rash appears, to drying up of scabs about 2 weeks later. Incubation 11–21 days.

*Colds**   Runny nose, coughing, sore throat, mild fever. Can be serious in small children with risk of ear infections and streptococcal throat infections (report to your doctor). Vomiting in some children caused by swallowing infected catarrh. Most infectious period 3–4 days. Incubation 1–3 days.

*Conjunctivitis**   Irritated red (sometimes swollen) whites of the eyes and linings of the eyelids. Discharge and matting of eyes during sleep. Can be caused by germs or virus picked up from other children or from swimming pool or using infected towels.

Convulsions   Rigidity or uncontrolled body movements, unconsciousness, dribbling or vomiting, face and lips blue, headache, sometimes loss of bladder and bowel control. Often accompanies fever in children up to age 3 (and sometimes age 5 or 6), in which case normally over in 5 minutes or so and usually no lasting effects.

Croup   Barking cough, sudden onset (usually at night), laboured breathing on in-breath, fever, hoarseness.

Diabetes   increased and frequent urination, thirst fatigue, weight loss, irritability, rapid breathing, 'fermented' odour to breath, susceptibility to infections, coma.

Diarrhoea   Loose stools, with abdominal cramps prior and during. (Don't underestimate the dangers, especially of dehydration in babies and small children, or if there is accompanying fever in older children – see *Gastroenteritis* – and/or abdominal pains persist for more than half an hour or stools are frequent.) Infectious if caused by germs (as opposed to diet or allergies).

Dizziness   Loss of balance and co-ordination, sometimes with nausea and vomiting. Often occurs with ear, throat or sinus infections.

Earache   Pain or irritation in ear, fever, ear discharge. Common in children under 6 as complication following catarrhal infection, and in children of all ages after swimming. Dangerous if not treated promptly.

Eczema	Itchy red or pink rash that oozes when scratched and produces further intense irritation. Dry, scaly skin. Sometimes follows emotional upset, or contact with allergenic substances. May be linked to asthma or hay fever in older children. Infantile eczema usually clears up completely in time.
Fainting	Paleness, nausea, vomiting, clammy skin, dizziness, unconsciousness. Occurs spontaneously occasionally in some childen, but can be due to illness or injury. Only your doctor can decide.
Fever	A symptom of other illnesses, rather than an illness in itself. Temperature above normal (often higher at night), flushing, sweating, glazed eyes, rapid breathing. Particularly dangerous in children under 6 months, who need urgent medical attention. In older children, height of temperature not always related to seriousness of illness, but temperatures over 39°C (102°F) or that last more than 24 hours or that are linked to other symptoms must be reported immediately to your doctor.
Fits	See *Convulsions*
Gastroenteritis*	Symptoms similar to diarrhoea, only more severe and accompanied by fever and vomiting. Infectious if caused by germs, not if caused by food poisoning. Dehydration a particular hazard, especially in small children.
German measles*	Runny nose, mild fever, pain and swelling in joints, swollen glands back of neck and behind ears, rash of small, red, slightly raised spots 1–2 days after first symptoms. Not normally a serious condition for any except pregnant women, since it endangers the unborn child. All girls should be vaccinated between ages 10 and 13. Infectious for 7 days before rash and for 5 days after it disappears. Incubation 14–21 days.
Glandular fever	Symptoms very mild in young children, much more severe and long-lasting in adolescence. Fever, cold-like symptoms, tiredness, loss of appetite, sore throat, headache, swollen lymph nodes (especially sides of neck). Some possibility of cross-infection with other children while cold-like symptoms persist.

Hay fever   Cold-like symptoms, irritated eyes and headaches. Triggered by contact with any allergenic substance such as dust or cat fur, but pollen the most frequent cause, and at its worst in mid-summer.

Headache   Usually accompanies fever, but can be triggered by tiredness, crying or emotional upset. The occasional brief mild headache is rarely serious, but should be reported to your doctor in children under five. More serious or more frequent headaches or headaches accompanied by other symptoms should be reported in older children.

Hiccups   Familiar spasms of diaphram accompanied by 'hic' sounds. Very common in babies and throughout childhood, but rarely encountered after adolescence. Report to your doctor if painful or very persistent.

Hives or   An allergic skin reaction caused by bites, viruses,
nettlerash   heat, foods, etc. Red itchy bumps or weals, each one going down within 12 hours or so. Becomes serious if accompanied by fever or if weals appear in mouth. Distinguished from the less serious heat rash (prickly heat) because the latter causes smaller bumps, is less itchy, and appears more often in skin folds.

*Impetigo**   Pimples with blisters on top, usually on face, which are followed by scabs and crusts. Mild itching. Spreads rapidly if not treated, and in rare cases can lead to kidney infection. Suspect any scabs on face which do not heal quickly as impetigo

*Influenza**   Cold-like symptoms, fever, shivering, aching, headache, possible stomach upset in younger children.

Leukaemia   A group of symptoms which include anaemia, fatigue, mild fever, joint pain, heavy recurring nosebleeds, spontaneous bruising, swollen gums, blood in stools and urine. Each of these symptoms appearing singly is more likely to be caused by other, less serious complaints, but several appearing together may be associated with the condition. Only your doctor can decide. The outlook for treatment is now very much improved, particularly if diagnosis is prompt.

*Measles**   Cold-like symptoms, with fever and rash on the fourth day. Rash starts as pink spots behind ears and on neck and face, moving steadily downwards with the spots becoming darker. Eyes red, watery and sensitive to light. Possible complications are ear troubles, bronchitis and pneumonia. Infectious from beginning of cold symptoms to 10 days after appearance of rash. Incubation period 9–15 days.

Meningitis*   Occurs in viral or bacterial form, with the bacterial form particularly serious. Fever, vomiting, lethargy, stiff neck, sometimes purple spots on body. *Early treatment essential*, as otherwise the disease can kill or lead to brain damage in hours.

Mumps*   Swelling of the salivary glands in the neck and below the ears on one or both sides. Mild fever. Can affect the testes in adolescent boys, but otherwise usually a mild condition. Infectious from start of swelling until 7 days after swelling subsides. Incubation period 14–28 days. It is possible, though comparatively rare, to have mumps twice.

Nosebleed   Usually caused by injury, dry air, or vigorous blowing or cleaning. Report to doctor if frequent, or if bleeding continues for more than 30 minutes.

Pneumonia*   Not all forms are infectious. Your doctor will advise you. Cough, difficulty in breathing, fever, chest and stomach pains. Vomiting. Can follow a bad cold or measles, but more usually occurs without warning (especially in asthmatics).

Rheumatic fever   A complication of streptococcal throat infections. Fever, arthritic pain in joints, chest pains, breathlessness, rash (often) on trunk and limbs. Some tendency to run in families. Can cause heart damage. The earlier the diagnosis the better.

Scabies*   Itchy small pink bumps between fingers or in skin folds and around navel, nipples and genitals. Caused by microscopic mite and spread by direct contact with infected individual or their clothes.

Scarlet fever or scarlatina*   Streptococcal infection, which can be caught from someone who is simply suffering from a sore throat. Fever, headache, vomiting, sore throat, possibly swollen glands, followed 1–2 days later by rash of tiny red spots (which often look like a red flush) over much of body (but not around mouth). Red tongue and throat.

761

Most common betwen ages 2 and 8. Can lead to complications (including rheumatic fever) if not treated. One attack does not confer immunity. Incubation period 2–7 days. Infectious for 2 weeks from onset of symptoms.

Sore throat or pharyngitis Viral sore throats, a common cold-symptom, usually clear up without problems. Sore throats caused by streptococcal infection, however, are accompanied by fever, swollen glands around neck, difficulty in swallowing and sometimes breathing difficulties. Can develop into rheumatic fever or scarlet fever and need prompt medical attention. Common ages 5–15. (see also *Tonsillitis*)

Stomach ache Common in children. Often caused by excitement or unfamiliar or unsuitable food. Serious if very intense or frequent, if accompanied by vomiting, diarrhoea or fever, if constant and persists for more than 3 hours, if abdomen is sensitive to touch, if there is blood in stools or if child feels particularly unwell. In *appendicitis* the pain is constant. It starts around the navel before usually moving to the lower right abdomen, and is very sensitive to touch, often accompanied by fever. Can develop into highly dangerous peritonitis within as little as 24 hours, so report urgently to your doctor.

Tetanus Protect by immunization and by taking your child for a booster if she has a deep or dirty cut. Cuts from most objects outside the home carry the risk of tetanus, and immunization does not give full long-lasting protection (hence the need for a booster after injuries). Symptoms of tetanus are difficulties in breathing and swallowing, convulsions and muscle spasms, and stiffness in jaw and elsewhere. But sensible precautions should prevent this dangerous disease from ever getting to the symptom stage.

*Threadworms** Itching around the anus and vagina, particularly at night, when the worms can actually be observed as active, white thread-like creatures around these orifices.

Thrush White patches around tongue, mouth and inside of lips.

762

*Tonsillitis**	Enlarged tonsils, often flecked with white or yellow patches, sore throat, fever. Usually yet another consequence of streptococcal infection. Note that children's tonsils are normally quite large between ages 2 and 6. (See also *Sore throat*.)
Urinary infection	Frequent urination, 'dribbling' between urination, genital discharge, fever, nausea, painful or bloody or smelly urine, abdominal or back pain. More common in girls than boys.
Vomiting	A possible symptom of other conditions rather than an illness in itself. Bottle-fed babies in particular often bring back part of their feeds for no apparent reason, and older children may vomit when excited. Projectile vomiting in babies (pyloric stenosis) is caused by an over-developed muscle at the outlet of the stomach, and is cured by a small operation. Frequent vomiting attacks, vomiting accompanied by other symptoms, yellow or green vomited material, or vomiting attacks which last for more than 12 hours, should be reported to your doctor.
*Whooping cough**	Severe coughing spasms, usually with 'whooping' gasps for breath and vomiting. Mild fever usually developing before bad coughing starts. In the first week, cough is usually dry and harsh but without whooping and with few cold-like symptoms. Whooping can go on for some weeks after the worst of the condition is over. Especially serious in babies under 2 years. Infectious from onset for sometimes up to 5 weeks. Incubation period 5–14 days.

Also call a doctor if your child is off her food for 3 days; is hoarse for more than a day or two; changes her pattern (or tone) of crying, or of sleeping, or of bladder or bowel movements; swallows an object of any kind; or generally shows unusual behaviour.

Injuries

Minor clean cuts, bumps and bruises are an occupational hazard of childhood, and rarely need attention beyond normal home first-aid. All other injuries are cases for qualified medical attention. In particular:

Bites especially from unknown animals or if the wound is severe.
Bones which appear in any way deformed after injury. NB. *Do not*

move a child if you suspect she has injuries to back or neck bones; you could damage the spinal cord.

Bleeding from any body orifice, or bleeding from a wound which will not stop under direct pressure.

Bruises which are severe, or appear spontaneously, or are worse than the injury warrants, or which cause severe or lasting pain.

Bumps to head which cause unconsciousness, drowsiness, blurred vision, dizziness or any other unusual symptoms.

Burns except for mild first-degree burns (reddening of skin but without blistering) over a small area.

Cuts that become infected, especially if pus drains from them, or there are red streaks radiating from them under the skin, or the child has a fever.

Pain that is severe or persists after injury, even if there is no visible sign of damage.

Poisons that are swallowed or you think may have been swallowed, however small the amount. Also harmful substances that have got into the eyes or other bodily orifices, or on to the skin.

Splinters that cannot easily and cleanly be removed, or which you think may be infected. Also objects which are pushed into body orifices.

Stings from any insect if in mouth or nose, or which caused unwarranted pain and swelling or which produce allergic reactions.

Swellings that don't quickly subside or that are associated with numbness, coldness or blue or black discoloration.

In addition, be alert for occasions when your child doesn't quickly get back to normal after apparently minor injuries. For example, limbs that won't bear weight, discomfort that won't go away, damage to reflexes, impairment of any of the senses, mood changes, unusual sleep, eating or excreting patterns, dizziness or convulsions, uncharacteristic memory lapses, in short anything that indicates all may not be well.

Other Emergencies

Bleeding   Place a clean cloth directly on the wound, and apply direct pressure. Keep the wound higher than the heart if possible. Get medical help *immediately* if the bleeding is severe or appears uncontrollable (children cannot afford to lose as much blood as adults), or if milder bleeding does not stop after 15 minutes' direct pressure. Medical help is also necessary if the wound is dirty or deep or 2.5 centimetres (1 in.) or more long, if the edges are ragged or separated, if pain persists for more than 12 hours, or if the last tetanus injection was more than 5 years ago.

Choking   If the child is coughing, she's getting some air into her lungs, and may dislodge the object herself. Calm her if possible. Sucking in air too violently may only take the obstruction further into the windpipe. If your child can't breathe, get someone to *summon doctor or ambulance immediately* while you begin immediate emergency drill. Drape her over your thighs, with head lower than body and give four quick blows between the shoulder blades with the heel of your hand. If the object doesn't dislodge, turn her on her back with her head lower than her body and give four quick chest compressions at mid-sternum with the heel of the hand (for a baby or very young child, four quick thrusts with three fingers). Repeat back and front if necessary. If she loses consciousness and if (and only if) the obstruction is a large object, try to hook it out with your finger. If successful and breathing has stopped, begin artificial respiration as explained under *drowning* below. Do not begin artificial respiration if airway is still blocked, as this could worsen the blockage. Continue emergency drill until successful or until medical help arrives. If a child recovers from choking *without* bringing up the obstruction, tell your doctor. It could have entered her lungs and cause infection.

Sometimes when drinking liquid, or after a fit of coughing or laughing, a child's throat will go into a spasm, and she will draw in breaths with great difficulty and in shuddering gasps. If there is no solid object involved she isn't actually choking. Calm her (panic makes the spasm much worse), encourage her to breathe slowly through her nose, and reassure her that the spasm will quickly pass.

Concussion   Concussion is a blow to the head that causes temporary feelings of slight incapacity at its mildest, to complete unconsciousness at its worst. Control bleeding from head wounds by direct pressure (see *Bleeding*), and control swellings by ice pack. Get medical help *immediately* if the child loses consciousness, shows signs of amnesia or loss of co-ordination, bleeds from ears, has blurred vision or slurred speech, shows enlargement of one eye pupil, vomits, or shows general lack of alertness or other odd behaviour. Even after a mild bang on the head, watch the child closely for 6 hours or so for any warning symptoms, waking him every 2 hours if it happened at bedtime.

In the event of unconsciousness, while you're waiting for medical help check that breathing is normal. Use artificial respiration (see *Drowning*) if necessary. Keep a close watch on the child. If vomiting has occurred, turn the head on one side, wipe out the mouth, and continually monitor the breathing. If unconsciousness is due to drugs, remember that many deaths occur each year from vomiting and subsequently inhaling vomit in individuals who are left unattended.

Drowning Turn the child on to his side or hold him upside down to clear the mouth of water, then commence mouth-to-mouth resuscitation if breathing does not start immediately. Do this by turning him on to his back, tilting his head so that his chin points directly upwards, and then proceeding as follows:

For a child under 8 years, cover the mouth and nose with your mouth, and give out quick puffs, allowing the child's chest to rise and fall between each one. If breathing doesn't start, *give one puff every 4 seconds. Do not breathe out fully*; the child's lungs are much smaller than yours and can't hold your full exhalation.

For a child over 8 years, cover only the mouth with your mouth and pinch the nostrils closed. Give four quick puffs, allowing child's chest to rise and fall between each one. If breathing doesn't start, subsequently give one puff every 5 seconds. For children below full height, do not breathe out fully; their lungs are still too small to hold a full adult exhalation.

If the heart has stopped, artificial respiration should be alternated with chest compressions as explained under *choking*. *Do not abandon artificial respiration until qualified medical help has arrived.* People have been revived after hours of such respiration.

Electric shock The longer a person is in contact with live electric current, the worse the injury. If indoors, turn off the current at the switch. *Do not touch the child until the current has been turned off.* You will receive the same shock yourself. If outdoors, or anywhere where the current cannot be turned off, move the child from the current with a *dry* wooden pole or with other dry insulating material. *Do not touch him with non-insulating or wet material.* If the shock was severe, if the child was burnt or received a mouth injury, or if breathing or heart have stopped, *summon immediate medical help*. In the event of breathing or heart failure, begin immediate artificial respiration as explained under *Drowning*.

Fainting   Do not confuse with concussion. See under *Common ailments* for more details. As first aid, sit the child with head between legs and wiggle his toes. If fainting has led to unconsciousness, check the breathing (use artificial respiration if necessary), then lie the child on his side with arms outstretched, and keep warm and immobile for 10–15 minutes. If recovery is not prompt, or if fainting is frequent, consult your doctor.

Fits   See *Convulsions* under *Common Ailments* for more details. While you are waiting for medical help, the prime first-aid requirement is to prevent the child hurting himself. Lay him on his side, monitor breathing continuously, watch for risk of choking with spittle or vomit, keep teeth apart with a safe object such as a large wooden spoon if there is a risk of biting the tongue. Most fits are over in 5 minutes or so. Do not leave the child unattended during or immediately after a fit.

Gas inhalation   Turn off gas supply (if instantly accessible). Get child immediately to fresh air. If breathing or heart have stopped, begin artificial respiration and chest compressions (see *Choking* and *Drowning*). Get medical help. Remember, do not light matches or turn on electric lights in a gas-filled room (the spark could cause an explosion). Have gas appliances serviced regularly, and all gas leaks attended to by qualified gas engineers immediately.

Heart failure   Remove the child from any obvious precipitating cause (see *Drowning* and *Electric shock*). Get immediate medical help. Start first aid ABC by checking *Airways* (see *Choking* and *Drowning*), *Breathing* and *Circulation*. Re-start breathing (when airways are clear) and circulation by artifical respiration and chest compressions respectively (see *Choking* and *Drowning*).

Shock   Look for signs of injury. *Do not move child with suspected neck or spinal injury* (see *Bones* under *Injuries* for more details). Check and restore breathing and heart-beat if necessary (see *Choking* and *Drowning*). Loosen tight clothing, keep child warm, and lie him on his back with feet higher than head. Do not give him fluids. Get immediate medical help.

APPENDIX 9

Useful Addresses

Association for Speech Impaired Children
Room 11, Nuffield Centre, Swinton Street, London WC1

Association for Spina Bifida
30 Devonshire Street, London W1N 2EB

British Diabetic Association
10 Queen Anne Street, London W1

British Epilepsy Association
Crowthorne House, New Wokingham Street, Wokingham, Berks.

British Red Cross Society
9 Grosvenor Crescent, London W1

Down's Babies Association
Quinbourne Centre, Ridgacre Road, Quinton, Birmingham B32 2TW

Health Education Council
78 New Oxford Street, London WC1A 1AH

Invalid Children's Aid Association
126 Buckingham Palace Road, London SW1W 9SB

Mind (National Association for Mental Health)
22 Harley Street, London W1N 2ED

Muscular Dystrophy Group
Natrass House, 35 Macaulay Road, London SW4 0QP

National Association for Maternal and Child Welfare
1 South Audley Street, London W1

National Association for the Welfare of Children in Hospital
7 Exton Street, London SE1 8VE

National Childbirth Trust
9 Queensborough Terrace, London W2 3TB

National Children's Bureau
8 Wakley Street, London EC1V 7QE

National Council for One Parent Families
255 Kentish Town Road, London NW5 2LX

National Deaf Children's Society
31 Gloucester Place, London W1H 4EA

National Society for Mentally Handicapped Children
17 Pembridge Square, London W2 4EP

Pre-School Playgroups Association
Alford House, Aveline Street, London SE11 5DH

Royal National Institute for the Blind
224 Great Portland Street, London W1N 6AA

Royal National Institute for the Deaf
105 Gower Street, London WC1E 6AH

Spastics Society
12 Park Crescent, London WIN 4EQ

Index

Catherine Garvey

Children's Talk

This is a book about what happens to children's language after they learn their first words. It is about how children use language – in talk. Talk can be with adults, with other children, with strangers or with the family. Studying children's talk reveals their growing mastery of social situations and their developing understanding of the world.

Catherine Garvey's delightful and learned book gives a vivid picture of children's minds through the medium of their talk. But it also explains in detail how that talk can be analysed, and just what it reflects about the child's development. She shows the stages by which children overcome different aspects of talk (turn-taking in conversation, or the use of socially appropriate speech), and emphasizes the centrality of talk to children's development and socialization.

Peter Young and Colin Tyre

Teach Your Child to Read

If you have ever thought of teaching your child to read – but felt you should leave it to the professionals – this book is for you. Written by two educationalists in the forefront of reading research, it shows parents that they *can* and *should* teach their children to read, and enables them to give children a jump start in school.

Peter Young and Colin Tyre's holistic model of reading, in which reading, writing and spelling go hand in hand, is ideally suited to the warm learning environment of the home. Tried and tested with hundreds of families, it is a method which grows naturally out of the child's learning of language. Children progress from 'lap learning' with picture books to 'shared reading' and 'paired reading'. Praise and warmth are the key to success throughout. The book goes on to discuss the development of reading and study skills, reading across the curriculum, books for pleasure, and the reading of textbooks.

Alan T. Graham

Help Your Child with Maths

Here at last is a maths book which all parents will understand. It is aimed at parents with children in the 0–12 age range, and assumes no previous mathematical knowledge whatsoever. For any parent keen to help their child with maths, but not sure quite how to go about it, this book has the answers.

* It provides a clear and logical explanation of basic maths, including numbers, decimals, fractions and percentages;
* highlights the particular difficulties children have in learning maths;
* shows how the calculator, more than just an aid to calculation, encourages children to explore and discover maths for themselves;
* gives numerous examples of the sort of conversations you can have with your child in the kitchen or supermarket, or on a long journey, which will improve his or her mathematical awareness and understanding.

This book – designed to complement what goes on at school, not to replace it – comes at a time when schools are increasingly urging parents to become involved in their children's education. It is the perfect handbook which anyone can use with confidence.